SECOND EDITION

A
SOCIOLOGY
OF
AUSTRALIAN
SOCIETY

INTRODUCTORY READINGS

D1740282

SECOND EDITION

A
SOCIOLOGY
OF
AUSTRALIAN
SOCIETY

INTRODUCTORY READINGS

Edited By
Jake M. Najman and John S. Western
University of Queensland

First published 1988 (reprinted six times)
Second edition published 1993 by
MACMILLAN EDUCATION AUSTRALIA PTY LTD
107 Moray Street, South Melbourne 3205
Reprinted 1994, 1995

Associated companies and representatives
throughout the world.

National Library of Australia
cataloguing in publication data.

A Sociology of Australian society.

  2nd ed.
  Includes bibliographies and index.
  ISBN 0 7329 2004 3.
  ISBN 0 7329 2003 5 (pbk.).

1. Sociology – Australia. Australia – Social conditions. I. Najman,
  J.M. (Jakob Moses). II. Western, John S. (John Smart), 1931-   .

301.0994

Typeset in Plantin by
Typeset Gallery, Kuala Lumpur
Printed in Hong Kong

Contents

Part III: Current Issues and Concerns

Notes on Contributors

Don Anderson is Visiting Fellow in the Research School of Social Sciences at the Australian National University. His current research preoccupation is a sociological study of the public/private divide in education systems.

Michael Bittman, Senior Lecturer in the School of Sociology at the University of New South Wales, is the author of *Juggling Time: How Australian Families Use Time*. His current research interests include the family, the sexual division of labour, social change and sociological theory.

Paul Boreham is Associate Professor in the Department of Government at the University of Queensland, where he is Director of the Labour and Industry Research Unit. His research interests have focused on unemployment, labour relations and labour market conditions, and he has published six books and a large number of research papers on these issues.

John Braithwaite is a Senior Research Fellow, Department of Sociology, Research School of Social Sciences, Australian National University. He is known particularly for his research on white collar crime.

Lois Bryson is Professor of Sociology at the University of Newcastle. She has written extensively on welfare and inequality, her most recent book being *Welfare and the State: Who Benefits?*

Peter Carpenter is Dean of the Faculty of Arts and Sciences at the Australian Catholic University. He holds Honours, Master's and doctoral degrees in sociology from the University of Queensland, and did post-doctoral work in sociology at the University of Maryland, as a Fulbright Scholar. His research interests and publications concern the sociology of higher education, and the sociology of the professions. He is joint author, with J. S. Western, of *Starting a Career: The Early Attainments of Young People*.

Ian Gray is Lecturer in Sociology at Charles Sturt University. He has completed several nationally-based projects for CSU's Centre for Rural Social Research, the latest dealing with the coping strategies of farmers under stress. His book, *Politics in Place: Social Power Relations in a Country Town*, was published by Cambridge University Press in 1991.

Richard Hall is a Lecturer in the Department of Government at the University of Queensland. He has researched and published in the areas of comparative labour law, industrial relations and Australian political economy. He was previously Research Co-ordinator for the Royal Commission into Aboriginal Deaths in Custody.

Martin Hayden is Interim Director of the Academic Development Unit at Latrobe University. Over the past ten years he has contributed to several major investigations of participation by young people in higher education, including CTEC's *Learning and Earning* project and the ACER's *Youth in Transition* project.

Kayleen M. Hazlehurst worked for eight years as a Researcher and Senior Criminologist with the Australian Institute of Criminology. She is now employed as a Senior Lecturer in Cross-Cultural Studies at Queensland University of Technology. Her most recent publication is *Political Expression and Ethnicity: Statecraft and Mobilisation in the Maori World*, (1993, Praeger Press, New York).

David Ip is a Senior Lecturer in Sociology at the University of Queensland. His teaching and research interests include leisure studies, tourism, development studies and social impact assessment. He has just completed a major study on Asian migrants in multicultural Australia. His current research is on the role of Chinese Australians in the economic development of China, and the implications of this for Australia.

Ian Keen is a Senior Lecturer in Anthropology at the Australian National University. He edited *Being Black* (Aboriginal Studies Press). He has carried out fieldwork in north-east Arnhem Land and other parts of the Northern Territory.

Geoffrey Lawrence is Professor of Sociology at the University of Central Queensland. He was formerly Director of the Centre for Rural Social Research at Charles Sturt University. His books include *Capitalism and the Countryside: The Rural Crisis in Australia* (1987), *Rural Health and Welfare in Australia* (1990), and *Agriculture, Environment and Society: Contemporary Issues for Australia* (1992).

Toni Makkai is a Research Fellow in the sociology program at the Research School of Social Sciences, Australian National University. She is currently involved, with Ian McAllister, in a major study of immigrant labour markets in Australia. Her other major areas of interest are the sociology of drug use, compliance and regulation, and the sociology of the professions.

Ian McAllister is Professor of Politics at the Australian Defence Force Academy. He has written extensively on ethnicity, Australian and British politics, and drug use. He is currently involved in a major cross-national study of democratisation in the former Communist societies of Eastern Europe.

Pat Mullins is a Senior Lecturer in Sociology at the University of Queensland. He has published widely in the area of urbanisation.

Jake Najman is a Reader jointly appointed to the Departments of Anthropology and Sociology, and Social and Preventive Medicine, at the University of Queensland. He has published widely in the fields of medical sociology and research methodology.

Michael Pusey is the author of *The Dynamics of Bureaucracy* (1976), *Jurgen Habermas* (1987) and *Economic Rationalism in Canberra* (1991). He is presently Professor of Sociology at the University of New South Wales.

Julianne Schultz is an Associate Professor and Founding Director of the Australian Centre for Independent Journalism at the University of Technology, Sydney. She has worked as a print, radio and television journalist, and is actively involved in journalism education and research. She is the author of *Steel City Blues* (Penguin, 1985), co-author, with Ian Reinecke, of *The Phone Book* (Penguin, 1983) and has written librettos for two operas, *Black River* and *Going into Shadows*.

Perry Share is Lecturer in Sociology at Charles Sturt University. His main academic interests include rural ideologies and rural social structures in the advanced nations. He is currently completing a doctoral thesis at La Trobe University, Melbourne, on discourses of land settlement in Australia.

Roman Tomasic is Professor of Law and Head of the School of Law at the University of Canberra. He is also the Director of the University's Centre for National Corporate Law Research. Professor Tomasic is well known for his research into corporate law and the legal profession undertaken over the last two decades. He is the author of a number of books, including a study of insider trading, *Casino Capitalism*, and is the co-author of a company law text, *Corporation Law: Principles, Policy and Process*.

John Western is Professor of Sociology at the University of Queensland and a Fellow of the Academy of Social Sciences in Australia. He is the author or joint author of several monographs concerned with social class and social inequality in Australia, including *Social Inequality in Australian Society* and *Class Analysis and Contemporary Australia*. In addition he has worked in the social impact field, conducting a number of social impact studies both in Australia and South-east Asia.

Mark Western is a Research Fellow in Sociology in the Research School of Social Sciences, at the Australian National University, and a member of the Class Structure of Australia Project. He has a PhD from the University of Queensland, and is interested in class analysis, social stratification, and quantitative methods.

Claire Williams is an Associate Professor in Sociology at Flinders University, and is the author of *Open Cut; Blue, White and Pink Collar Workers in Australia* and (with Bill Thorpe) *Beyond Industrial Sociology*. She is an industrial sociologist whose other research interests are gender studies and methodology.

Preface

This reader introduces the basic concepts, methods and subject matter of sociology. We have taken for the major focus a structural approach to Australian society. We would argue that there are four structural bases to this society, and these we have designated as class, gender, ethnic origin and age. They are important because beliefs, behaviours and access to scarce and valued resources are, in part, derived from them.

We also stress the importance of the institutions or institutional areas that characterise society. It is commonly argued that any society comprises five major institutional areas. The first of these has been described as the polity, or the political institutions of that society — the parliament, political parties, pressure groups and the public service: indeed, the whole range of groups which adds up to the government. The second major institutional area is the economy, which is concerned with the production and distribution of goods and services. Religion is the third major area: how does it affect the social order, and are religious beliefs, values and ideas connected with other features of the society? These are questions of concern to sociologists. A celebrated account of the relationship between religion and the economy was provided by Max Weber, the nineteenth-century European social scientist. Weber argued that the Protestant ethic, which comprised a set of values and behaviours supporting hard work and achievement, was an important factor in the development of nineteenth-century capitalism.

Sociologists also see family and marriage as a central institutional area of society. To what extent is the institution of marriage changing in the latter part of the twentieth century? Is the frequency of marriage changing, or the age at which marriage takes place? Again, these are all questions which sociologists address. Finally, there is education. What is its function? Does it provide knowledge or does it equip individuals with particular beliefs which enable them to fit easily into the existing social order? In this sense does education serve to limit social change in society?

A third approach to sociology comes from an interest in the dominant social issues of a period: unemployment, health, the appropriateness of welfare services, as well as conservation, and the changing nature of political beliefs. Typically, sociologists address these latter concerns from a structural and institutionally oriented approach.

This reader, then, is loosely divided into three sections. Firstly, there are the contributions which take a structural perspective and provide a framework for understanding society in general, and Australian society in particular. Secondly, there are readings which consider the current state of some institutions in Australian society. Thirdly, the contributors discuss a number of contemporary social issues.

The book reflects, we believe, the current state of the discipline of sociology in Australia. It is notable that the contributors approach their task from different perspectives, using varying theoretical approaches and methodologies. This diversity of approach warrants some comment.

Many of the social sciences manifest such approaches to their subject matter. In this context we would suggest that each chapter reflects something of the author's personal qualities, as well as of the topic being discussed. A key tenet of science is that research is reproducible; that the personal qualities of researchers intrude only to a very limited extent into their research. Indeed, scientists rely on this reproducibility of findings to determine the level of credibility they place on a particular body of knowledge.

Does the limited agreement within sociology on theories and methods mean that it and the other social sciences are unscientific? Is sociology gradually moving to a more agreed-upon set of theories and methods? Again on this, as on other issues, there are different points of view. We would argue that sociology should become more scientific than it is; that theories and methods, as well as substantive findings, should be subjected to scientific criteria and then accepted or rejected.

Not all will share this view; even more interestingly, some sociologists would deny the possibility of *knowing* social reality. They would suggest that our understandings are largely moulded by our prior experiences and that we can only *imagine* a particular version of reality. We take the view that there is an objectively knowable reality. We suggest that it is appropriate to accept the assumption that it is, for example, a chair upon which we sit, not a construction which exists only in our minds.

Sociology, then, is concerned with understanding society and this involves understanding people's conceptions of reality, as well as the reality itself. Despite the conflicting perspectives and the

tentative nature of much sociological knowledge, sociology provides a compelling and personally involving approach to understanding not only society, but oneself. It raises important questions
about 'truths' which may previously have been taken for granted.
It provides a great deal of factual information about the social
world. A sociological approach, we suggest, enables people to make
better decisions about their lives, and be more understanding of
those with whom they come in contact.

This second edition of the reader provides an indication of the
growth of sociology in Australia. All chapters have been either
extensively revised or represent entirely new offerings. In the
previous edition we argued that much remains to be done before
we can claim to have an adequate understanding of Australian
society. This second edition contains not only a large amount of
new data, but also presents developments in theory and method.
While it is still true that much remains to be done before we can
claim a good understanding of society, it is also evident that much
has been learned since the previous edition. We invite you to join
with us in still furthering the understanding we have at the
present time.

> John S. Western
> Jake M. Najman
> University of Queensland,
> St Lucia, 1993

Part 1

Basic Structures and Concepts

Chapter One

Sociology: The Study of Social Structures and Cultural Reproduction

Jake M. Najman and John S. Western

This chapter has three goals. The first is to describe the discipline of sociology and identify some of its subject matter, its theories and methods. The second is to illustrate sociology 'in action'· that is, to give an example of how sociological research is done and identify the relevance of this research for our understanding both of society and of the relevance of sociology to social policy. The third is to introduce some of the readings which follow and identify their common thrust and purpose.

The subject matter of this chapter concerns perhaps the most fundamental of sociological questions: how does society as we understand it come to exist and cohere over time? Or, put slightly differently: what makes for social order?

The sociological response to this question begins by noting that the individual is located within a variety of sectors of the social system, at one and the same time, and is shaped by his or her position in those sectors. Elsewhere Western (1983), and Western and Turrell (1991), have argued that there are four primary sectors or structural bases that shape society, providing its form and content.

These sectors are social class, gender, ethnicity and Aboriginality. Briefly, social class can be defined in terms of the social relations of production, that is the social relationships that are established between people in the production of economic goods and services. Social class can be interpreted as the basis of the economic structure of society. It is important because it relates to a series of inequalities in education, income and occupation which, in turn, may predict one's 'life chances'.

Gender encompasses the social categories of male and female. We describe these as social because they define structural positions or statuses within the society, occupied by individuals.

Ethnicity is defined in terms of birthplace, and broadly distinguishes the Australian-born from those born elsewhere. Aboriginality distinguishes between those who are defined in the population Census as 'Aboriginal' or 'Torres Strait Islander', or those who choose to define themselves in these terms, and the remainder of the population.

These few basic aspects of an individual's social location are primary in two senses. Firstly, they are important bases for much group formation in society. Secondly, they are the bases for the patterning, maintenance and reproduction of social behaviour, attitudes, values and belief systems. These assertions do not imply the existence of simple cause/effect relationships, linking social behaviours directly with structural bases.

The complex web of society at any time is, of course, the result of the dynamic interplay of a number of forces. They do suggest, however, that underlying the complex social patterns which develop are a set of cross-cutting structures. At times directly, but at others, and perhaps more commonly, indirectly, these shape the entity we call society.

While we would want to argue that these four structural principles are at the basis of society as we understand it, it is true that of themselves they provide only the barest of outlines. The group formations that they generate, and with which they are associated, and the social consequences that follow from them, provide the flesh for the bare structural bones of society, as sociologists understand it.

What is Sociology?

We, with others, define sociology as the *scientific study of society*. There are two key words in this definition, 'scientific' and 'society'. Sociology is scientific because in the collection of data it uses methods which are based on certain principles consistent with the scientific method. Broadly, these have to do with the reproducibility of methods and the verifiability of results. The methods used by sociologists for the collection of information about society are reproducible, in the sense that the same methods can be employed by all sociologists when examining the same question. Methods are not idiosyncratic, depending on the random preferences of a particular individual. Results are verifiable in the sense that different sociologists using the same methods to address a particular problem are likely to arrive at similar conclusions, or, if they fail to do so, will be able to provide an explanation as to why different results have occurred. A careful and controlled approach to the collection of information about society is essential if we are to have confidence in the accuracy of our conclusions.

Society is the subject matter of sociology. This term includes the totality of groups within, usually, a geographically delineated nation-state. We say 'usually' because nomadic tribal groups, sometimes without a clearly defined geographical location, could be of interest to sociologists concerned with tribal societies or questions of development.

We know that individuals see society differently. Their perceptions are coloured by the groups to which they belong. Women, migrants, Aborigines and the economically disadvantaged are examples of such groups in Australian society. The members of each of these groups have experiences in common, as a consequence of their group membership. These experiences shape the group's perception of the 'real' world. The individual, from the sociological perspective, is then a product of social processes which are embedded in the groups to which he or she belongs. It is towards an understanding of these processes that this analysis is directed.

The Sociological Perspective

Perhaps one of the most difficult of all concepts to comprehend is the extent to which the world is perceived through a particular set of 'glasses'. The story of three blind people in search of what an elephant looks like, each forming different images on the basis of the varied parts they touch, is useful in an illustrative sense. Psychologists, historians, philosophers and geographers all see society through 'glasses' created by their chosen discipline. It should not be surprising, therefore, that various disciplines can inspect the same world but concentrate upon different elements of it, and come to somewhat different conclusions about it.

Where sociological explanations differ from, and possibly compete with, those of other disciplines, two interpretations should be considered. Firstly, the explanations might be seen to challenge each other, with the weaker explanation (chosen by whatever criteria) rejected. Alternatively, the explanations might be seen to be complementary. Consistent with this latter view, it is relevant to note that much social research may proceed using the best available, but nevertheless imperfect, methods, and that most quantitative explanations can claim to explain only a modest proportion of observed variations in behaviour. While sociologists may sometimes write as if they have a comprehensive explanation of a particular social concern (e.g. unemployment, poor health, urban development) they generally implicitly, but sometimes explicitly, can legitimately claim to offer only partial explanations. This is not to suggest that these partial accounts are unimportant, or that they may be disregarded, but rather that they are incomplete, and not always in conflict with similarly directed accounts from other disciplines.

A distinctive feature of sociology is that it seeks to explain social behaviour by examining social institutions and the way in which membership of social groups is structured. Social institutions are an important feature of society. They are defined in terms of complexes of groups and sets of generally agreed-upon rules or norms which prescribe how members of groups should behave, and what the functions of the groups are. Examples of social institutions would be: the family, concerned with both the physical and social reproduction of society's members; the 'polity' or political institutions, concerned with 'government' of the society; the economy, concerned with the production of goods and services; and religion, concerned with the maintenance and reinforcement of certain of society's basic beliefs and values.

Seeking to understand and explain behaviour through consideration of the significance of social institutions and membership of social groups is often described as a structural perspective. This is because it explicitly involves locating people within a social matrix. In this sense, sociology differs from disciplines which seek to explain behaviour by considering the biological characteristics or individual psychology of people.

Sociologists attend to institutions, the four we have mentioned as well as others such as the legal and educational systems. The social characteristics of individuals, their gender, class, ethnicity and Aboriginality, which reflect unique patterns of socialisation, are also of central concern. Sociologists are particularly interested in the manner and extent to which institutionally-derived beliefs, values and behaviours are learned as a consequence of an individual's location in the social order. This concern is addressed in a number of the chapters which follow, and is also discussed in greater detail later in this one.

Illustrations of the Structural Perspective

Sociologists generally argue that human behaviour is learned, and occurs in patterns associated with one's position in the social structure. Homans (1986: xxv) defines social structure as 'more or less enduring practices followed by a number of persons, whether or not these practices are made explicit. . .or defended by sanctions'. Given this definition, the term 'social structure' can apply to the society as a whole, or it can refer to the social patterning of behaviour which is found in the separate groups comprising the society — the social patterning of economic activity, for example. In the first instance, we might use the term 'societal structure', and in the second 'the structure of the economy'.

Because this sociological emphasis on structural explanations differs from that which may be both intuitively preferable and more generally familiar, the following two illustrations are taken from the chapters which follow in this book. These examples concern unemployment levels, and changes in marriage rates in Australian society.

Sociologists are frequently interested in, and wish to explain, social concerns such as unemployment. In seeking to explain such a phenomenon, the personal or individual qualities of the unemployed would generally receive less attention than would associations between structurally-derived forces and unemployment levels. A sociological approach to unemployment could begin with the observation that about 11 per cent of the Australian population (in 1992) is registered as unemployed. The unemployment rate, it could be argued, remains the same irrespective of who is unemployed at a specific time. In this sense the rate is characteristic of the society, and will vary from time to time. Bryson, in Chapter 15, shows that unemployment levels have changed over time in Australia and that some groups in society experience higher rates of unemployment.

The available data confirm the recent increase in unemployment rates. Boreham and Hall in part attribute the present high unemployment level to features of the capitalist economic system. They argue that successive Australian governments spurned intervention in manufacturing industry. As primary and manufacturing industry became more efficient and employment levels declined, the absence of prior planning and intervention meant that, except for the service sector, unemployment levels increased.

Of course, as Bryson points out, not all groups in Australian society are equally liable to experience unemployment. Those who are young, unskilled and/or Aboriginal, have the highest unemployment rates. Older males are a relatively small proportion of the total unemployed, but experience long periods of unemployment. While it is not yet possible fully to explain why the young and unskilled are unable to obtain employment, it does appear that there are increasingly fewer jobs available for unskilled people, and that increased employment opportunities are generally to be had in jobs requiring higher levels of education.

A similar structural approach is evident when we examine changes in marriage and divorce rates, as Bittman indicates in Chapter 14. Thus, over time, an increasing proportion of Australians have chosen to marry, but there has also been an increase in the proportion of those who have chosen to end their marriages (and who usually remarry). Serial marriages, where a person may change partner as his or her circumstances change, have become more common.

While in individual cases it may be possible to argue that a marriage failed because of the personal characteristics of the participants, the observation that rates of divorce have recently increased many times suggests that other explanations must be considered. Thus improved methods of contraception; legal changes which simplify divorce; the availability of child care; the decline in the extended family; the increased rate of female workforce participation; and a decline in religion, may all contribute to increases in rates of marital dissolution.

According to both these explanations, what appear to be 'individual troubles', that is, unemployment or marital breakdown, are more correctly interpreted as consequences of the structural arrangements and institutional norms which prevail within a society (e.g. the legal system, welfare and child care services, or developments in medical technology). In the above context the sociologist is less interested in why a particular marriage failed than in why the institution of marriage is no longer accepted to the extent that may have been the case previously: that is, why the institution of marriage is failing to meet the needs of many in contemporary society.

Social Research: An Illustration

To place what might be for some an abstract discussion about sociology in a relevant and meaningful context, it is helpful to consider a specific study, and the details of sociology it illustrates. We have chosen to consider a study of the impact on families of the Depression of the 1920s and 1930s. While the study is in one sense dated, in another it is timely in view of the current economic recession; also, many of its methods and findings are of contemporary relevance.

First published in 1933, Marienthal was a study of the impact of unemployment in a small Austrian town over the period 1928–30 (Jahoda, Lazarsfeld and Zeisel 1974). The authors of the resultant monograph subsequently migrated to the United States and became highly regarded for their substantive and research contributions to sociology.

The town of Marienthal grew up around a factory, which was the only major employer of labour. While serious unemployment problems first appeared in the second half of 1926, many were able to continue to work until the second half of 1929 when, in stages, the factory ceased operation. Then most of the town's population of 712 men and 774 women became unemployed. Some unemployment benefits were paid, but these were on a sliding scale which, over time, diminished, then cut out entirely.

The researchers began collecting data in 1931 and spent 120 working days in all gathering details of the consequences of the Depression. Their methods were varied and diverse. They included:

- family files: a detailed demographic record of all 478 families living in the town
- life histories: a sub-sample of 32 men and 30 women were asked to recall their life histories, with particular attention being paid to how their lives had changed since they had become unemployed
- time sheets: 80 people filled out a questionnaire describing how they spent their day
- food diary: 40 families kept detailed records of all the food they consumed, and particular interest was shown in their meals the day before and the day after they received their unemployment benefits
- statistical data: this was obtained from various agencies, including foods sold at the co-operative, books borrowed from the local library, membership lists of clubs, and migration figures

This study is distinguished not only by the breadth of information collected, but also by a strategy of comparing what is collected from different sources. In some instances such comparisons will reinforce particular assessments or interpretations. In others, the information will reflect on different concerns, while in still more, the 'facts' may be in conflict. Sociologists would generally accept that the research method one uses is, in an important sense, part of the result. That is to say, each research method predisposes to some results rather than others, and circumscribes, at least in part, the findings one may produce. It follows that sociologists need to be able to research a topic using both qualitative and quantitative methods. Students should recognise the tentative nature of much of the research which sociologists (and for that matter other disciplines) produce, particularly if it is based upon single studies using only one method.

The study of Marienthal covered a number of issues, only a few of which will be discussed here. Taking, firstly, the issue of the impact of unemployment on the standard of living, Jahoda, Lazarsfeld and Zeisel (1974: 19) note that by 1930 three-quarters of the families in Marienthal had no member employed, and were consequently dependent upon unemployment benefits.

The impact of poverty on nutrition is traced in a number of ways. Firstly, taking 38 children, they note that half of them (n = 19) had nothing but dry bread to eat the day before receiving unemployment benefit, but all except two had an 'adequate' packed lunch the day after receiving their benefit (p. 17). Secondly, they note that the local co-operative store demonstrated substantial changes in the types of food it sold over the period 1928–30, with a decline in sales of sugar and coffee and substitutions with cheaper equivalents (p. 31). Thirdly, they investigated how the families spent their unemployment benefits, finding that they were essentially reduced to buying only food — few or no new clothes, and little or no recreation or social life. In some instances they ran out of money for food days before their next benefit was available. Fourthly, they quote from the experiences of selected families, to provide the reader with an indication of what it 'means' to be unemployed. For example:

> Frau N.Z. has three children aged eight, six and three. The husband worked right up to the time when demolition started; she herself only worked until 1927, which is why her claim to relief has already expired. She finds it hard to manage on twenty-two shillings per week. Milk and bread are paid every two weeks, everything else on the spot. In this way she knows how much there is left to spend. She cannot buy anything on credit because she would not be able to pay it back. What she spends on food comes to twenty-four shillings per fortnight; another six shillings on coal, and six shillings on milk. She bakes her own bread; the few remaining shillings must be kept for shoe repairs.
>
> (Jahoda, Lazarsfeld and Zeisel 1974: 32)

Such a low income places great limits on the choices available to people. Their whole way of life becomes transformed, with a sense of misery and apathy taking over from what before unemployment was a vibrant and active community. The decline in the quality of life associated with employment is traced through changes in levels of participation in community activities. Thus in 1929, 3.23 books were borrowed per reader from the library (p. 38); in 1930, 2.30 and in 1931, 1.6 books per reader (p. 38). Despite the increase in available time, people were generally less interested in reading. There was, at the same time and with only a few exceptions, a decline in membership in the various cultural, political and sporting clubs. One hundred particularly needy families were studied and their mood assessed. Of these, 70 were categorised as resigned and apathetic (p. 56). This blunting impact of unemployment is reflected in some of the statements of respondents, e.g. 'I often used to go dancing with my wife. There was life in Marienthal then. Now the whole place is dead' (p. 37).

Describing the case of family number 467 (a husband, wife and two children), the authors note that in his first year of unemployment he wrote applications for 130 jobs, all of which were unsuccessful (p. 52):

> Now he is at the end of his tether. He told us that he spends half his day in bed now in order to save breakfast and heating. He hardly ever leaves the house. He is in utter despair.

In the above example it is clear that the families' parlous economic circumstances reflect the impact of a structural factor (unemployment) on a broad range of the families' activities. Indeed many of the families' values, beliefs and behaviours have been changed by their current economic circumstances.

Variations in Sociological Perspectives

The foregoing should not be taken, of course, to suggest that there is a single sociological view or approach to which all, or even most, sociologists subscribe. Indeed, various studies show that sociology is characterised by a diversity of theories and methods. In comparing disciplines according to the level of agreement or conflict over theories, methods and findings, Lodahl and Gordon (1972) circulated a questionnaire to staff in 80 university departments (20 each in physics, chemistry, sociology and political science. Physics was consistently ranked as having the greatest level of consensus, while sociology and political science had the least.

A similar result comes from Gareau (1985), who has compared the sociological orientations of scholars in various countries. As he points out, there is no German physics or French chemistry, but it *is* meaningful to distinguish between Russian and American sociology. Some prefer to conceive of sociology as action-oriented and concerned with redressing fundamental inequalities in society. Others perceive its mandate in more narrow terms, as concerned with understanding society. Some are interested in 'grand' theories of society, and others with understanding the day-to-day interactions which dominate people's lives. Sociology, then, is typified by a diversity of theories, methods and often conflicting conclusions. This diversity, even within a single country like Australia, is reflected in the chapters that follow.

For a student of sociology, there is a need carefully to consider the arguments presented by various authors, the quality of the evidence they bring to bear, and to determine whether the weight of proof points to one or other conclusion. In the above context, sociologists and those studying sociology have two specific tasks. The first is to examine the varieties of ideas and findings which bear upon a particular subject, and the second is to make public, in the sense that the assessments made can be explained and justified, judgements about this literature and that state of knowledge.

The acknowledged diversity of the sociological effort does not deny the existence of some common themes which bind together the various contributions to this book. This is an Australian reader, specifically concerned with national events and issues. Most contributors acknowledge a need for both historically-based and economically-derived (in a Marxist sense) analyses of the Australian condition. Most use quantitative and qualitative data to support and/or illustrate their arguments. Many refer implicitly or explicitly to policy implications of the analyses they have presented. All appear to share Homans' (1970: 27) view that the

> most interesting theoretical task will remain that of showing how structures, relative enduring relationships. . .are created and maintained by individual human choices, choices constrained by the choices of others, but still choices.

Most of the chapters manifest an interest in the social system as a whole and the extent to which this system, into which an individual is born, moulds and shapes his or her perceptions, knowledge and behaviours. The system may become, as we will observe in the pages which follow, a source of specific behavioural preferences, and a set of underlying values and beliefs which influence decision making in a range of situations not previously encountered.

The Patterning of Values, Beliefs and Behaviour

As we have argued, sociologists seek to understand and explain structurally distinguishable groups in society and their patterns of values, beliefs and behaviours. What are such patterns in Australian society? Two examples will be considered: male/female variations, and those associated with socio-economic (social class) inequalities.

Male/female differences have generated an intense and, to some extent unresolved, debate for many social scientists. Williams, in Chapter 4, goes as far as to suggest that there are male and female ways of 'knowing'. In one cross-national study involving 2,800 university students in 28 countries, comparisons of stereotypes of male and female behavioural differences were sought (Williams and Best 1982). Interestingly, males and females were generally found to agree that males were active, assertive, confident, force-ful, logical, solid and wise (this being only a partial list), while females were typically perceived as affected, charming, emotional, kind, sensitive, soft-hearted and weak (1982: 77). Similar findings emerged from a review of ethnographic reports of socialisation practices in 110 cultures. In such resports, girls were typically socialised to nurturance of others, obedience and responsibility, while males were more often socialised towards achievement and self-reliance (Barry, Bacon and Child 1973: 153). Australian studies have provided results consistent with those from other countries.

In one study in Melbourne, schoolgirls more often aspired to occupations with an altruistic component, while boys appeared more interested in 'exciting' occupations (Musgrave 1984: 205). A survey of students at a Sydney college suggested that while females were somewhat willing to assume some non-traditional domestic and work roles, males rejected these alternatives in greater numbers (Albury, Chaples and Stubbs 1977: 136). Not only are males and females believed to differ in a number of their social characteristics, but their achievement levels are also markedly different.

Thus, while approximately equal numbers of males and females enter the Australian Mathematics Competition (AMC), males gain more of the top awards. Indeed, on a 30-item paper, males score on average between one and one-and-a-half more correct answers. One interesting aspect of this difference is that females appear less willing than males to guess at an answer when they are penalised for an incorrect guess (Edwards 1984). Males, it could be suggested, are more often socialised to 'take chances': that is, to gamble, even in competitions and examinations.

Inequalities in achievement are further evident when we compare the male and female achievement levels within occupational groups. Thus in Victoria, 55 per cent of teachers but only 16 per cent of high school principals are female (Bottomley and Sampson 1977: 137). Of all full-time female university staff members, 1.3 per cent are at professorial level (males, 11.9 per cent), while 30.3 per cent are at tutor level (males, 8.9 per cent) (Sargent 1983: 110). When males enter largely segregated female occupations (nursing, secretarial, teaching), they tend to be promoted rapidly to senior positions (Currie 1982: 181–82). There is, then, general agreement that males and females differ in their values, beliefs and performance. It is, however, less clear why such differences are found so consistently.

One analysis would tend to ascribe the above inequalities to male and female biological differences. Certainly such biological differences exist and should not be dismissed. One study of 75 animal species, including crustaceans, reptiles, birds and mammals, found that, almost without exception, there was (as there is in humans), inferior male longevity (reported in Retherford 1975: 9). The human female advantage is partly attributable to biological factors: the protection from atherosclerosis provided by oestrogen hormones (Retherford 1975: 15). Further, females, as a consequence of their child bearing, may be better biologically equipped to perform integrative/expressive functions (Williams and Best 1982: 241), though the evidence for (or against) this is unconvincing.

Regardless of the specific biological differences which may arguably distinguish males from females, there is little doubt that the process of socialisation serves to exaggerate these differences and greatly to limit the alternatives available to women and, to a lesser extent, men. Thus, in a study of Euro-American children in the United States, there was clear evidence that children acquired these stereotypes with age as they were exposed to the dominant culture (see Table 1.1). One of the consequences of this process, as Edgar (1980) has shown in an Australian study, is 'that girls ...had a lower estimation of their own competence even when their measured verbal intelligence was superior to boys' (Edgar 1980: 163).

It is important here to grasp the subtle but pervasive nature of gender stereotypes. In one study children who were shown a videotape of a female doctor and a male nurse, when asked to recall the content of the tape, remembered a male doctor and a female nurse (reported in Williams and Best 1982: 24).

Another instance of socially patterned behaviour may be associated with socio-economic inequalities in society (see Western's

Table 1.1 Ages at which Children acquire Sex Stereotypes

	Stereotypes of Males	Stereotypes of Females
At 5 years of age	strong, aggressive, dominant	gentle, affectionate
By 8 years of age	disorderly, cruel, coarse, adventurous, ambitious, loud, boastful	weak, emotional, appreciative, excitable, gentle, soft-hearted, sophisticated, submissive
By 11 years of age	confident, steady, jolly	talkative, rattle-brained, complaining

Source: Williams and Best 1982: 25.

Chapter 3 for a more detailed analysis of these inequalities). Income inequalities provide unambiguous evidence of structurally determined constraints on human behaviour. The *Household Expenditure Survey Australia 1984* (1986) provides evidence of major differences in lifestyle associated with one's socio-economic position. The lowest 10 per cent of income earners spend $24 per week on housing compared with the $70 spent by the top 10 per cent. Twenty-four dollars comprises 17 per cent of the total income of the lowest income group, while $70 is only 10 per cent of the total income of the highest income group.

The wealthy spend more, both absolutely and relatively, on alcohol, clothing, transport and recreation. Lower income people spend a greater proportion of their incomes on housing, fuel, power and food — that is, essentials — and they appear to have little remaining for discretionary activities. These are not simply differences in spending power, but could be expected to influence a person's perception of the world and his or her place in it.

In the Class Study of Australia Project (Baxter *et al.* 1991: 316), the values and attitudes of people located at different levels of the class hierarchy were compared. It suggested that we live in a society in which the social class to which people belong influences their attitudes and feelings about the social world. The researchers report substantial differences in satisfaction with paid employment. In response to such cues as 'my work is important to the community', 'in general my job has lived up to my expectations' and 'my work is a major source of satisfaction in my life', individuals in what we can call the upper middle class expressed the highest levels of job satisfaction, while individuals in the working class expressed the lowest levels. Differences in political attitudes and beliefs were also observed. Opposition to government intervention in the economy was strongest among employers and weakest among the working class. Support for the free enterprise system was the strongest among employers and weakest among workers and experts. Support for trade unions was strongest among workers while opposition to unions was strongest among employers. Further details of these relationships are provided in Table 1.2.

Table 1.2   Mean Scores on Political Attitudes: Wright's Class Typology

Attitudes to:	Employers	Petit-bourgeoisie	Expert managers	Managers	Experts	Workers
Government intervention in the economy	60.4	53.1	49.6	44.0	46.9	41.0
Free enterprise system	63.1	64.1	49.9	56.2	48.6	53.1
Trade unions	68.0	66.6	59.8	58.3	51.6	54.1

Government intervention in the economy: high score indicative of opposition to intervention.
Free enterprise system: high score indicative of support for free enterprise system.
Trade union: high score indicative of opposition to trade unions.

Economic inequalities in Australian society have their starkest consequences when we compare the 'life chances' of those who are socio-economically advantaged and disadvantaged. As Taylor et al. (1983), McMichael (1985) and Siskind et al. (1987) have shown, those who are lowest on the socio-economic hierarchy have higher adult and infant mortality rates. Interestingly, these differences are evident for most causes of death. These findings suggest major variations in the structurally-determined patterning of social behaviour associated with mortality differences. The factors underlying such inequalities in health are discussed in Chapter 10.

Edgar (1980) provides some interesting Australian illustrations of the manner in which children of varying economic circumstances are reared, which partly account for the behaviour, lifestyle and health differences noted above. He notes that overseas studies have suggested that middle class parents seek to communicate particular values which the child is expected to internalise and, presumably, to apply as circumstances arise. By contrast, working class parents tend to focus on specific behaviours and to punish their children if they transgress. These findings were reinforced by his Australian research (1980: 163) which showed that:

Non-manual fathers liked their children to be interested in how and why things happen, [to be] considerate of others and self-controlled and responsible. The manual fathers ranked more highly good manners, being neat and clean, obeying parents and conforming to appropriate sex roles.

Here it is important to note that not only values, beliefs and behaviours are communicated, but a particular orientation to the culture of the society. This is likely to include perceptions of a desirable partner, expectations of future employment, and a view about the appropriateness of academic and other achievements. Indeed, while acknowledging that IQ scores (particularly verbal IQ scores) may partly reflect cultural values as well as innate ability, there is evidence to show that children born into a poverty environment but reared by adopting middle class parents manifest substantially higher IQ scores than similar children who remained in their original environment (Scarr and Weinberg 1976). Children reared in a more middle class environment appear more often to manifest personal qualities which will enable them to 'succeed' in contemporary industrial societies like Australia.

Socialisation

In describing male/female and socio-economic differences in values, beliefs and behaviours associated with one's structural location, we have noted that sociologists generally attribute these differences to the socialisation process. In this section we will consider this process in greater detail, and explore both the various ways it is believed to occur and its implications for understanding stability and change in society.

While there is general agreement that socialisation is a process which communicates societal, sub-cultural and familial knowledge and values, there are different emphases evident in writings on the subject. Denisoff and Wahrman (1975) and Baldridge (1975) take the view that infants are largely moulded by the socialisation process and made into beings who fit into the existing social order. By contrast, Douglas (1973) and Sites (1975) suggest that socialisation is an interactive process which leads to changes in all the participants, adults and children. These approaches are labelled respectively the normative and interactionist views of socialisation. They are complementary approaches to understanding the process of socialisation: that is, of the interaction of the individual and society.

According to the normative view, children in a particular sector of society are taught the culture, which includes knowledge, beliefs, morals, customs and habits of that society. The culture is successively communicated by the representatives of the society with whom the child comes into contact, the agents of socialisation. Thus, parents and close family members control initial socialisation, then peer groups, the media and school, followed by significant others — that is, people with whom there is a close relationship. Institutions like the legal system provide formal sanctions for deviation, in that they reflect the dominant ideology and are frequently communicated by the agents of socialisation. Children, it is argued, are taught a set of norms (rules of behaviour) associated with their roles (position in the social structure). Successful socialisation involves the internalisation of these norms (the belief that the rules of behaviour come from within the individual).

An important aspect of the normative view is the assumption that the child simply becomes the sum total of his or her experiences. This is argued not only on the basis that the new member of the society responds as required in order to avoid sanctions, but also because beliefs about the rights and wrongs of the values underlying decision making are also acquired during the socialisation process. A logical extension of this view of socialisation is that humans are essentially similar products of their society, their choices being constrained by their experiences.

Evidence for the validity of the normative view can be found in at least two sets of data. The first is derived from simple observation and survey research. Thus, in addition to the gender and class patterns of belief and behaviour we have noted, it is possible to observe a variety of ethnic and racial groups, and their similarities of appearance and behaviour. Indeed, as Makkai and McAllister point out in Chapter 6, migrants will frequently choose to live in parts of Australian cities with others of similar origin, retaining many of their cultural practices, presumably because they find foreign cultures less agreeable.

The second type of evidence comes from experimental research and emphasises the extent to which people appear to be willing to conform to the demands made upon them by others. In the first experiment of relevance, Asch (1955) took 7 (or sometimes 5 or 9) college students and showed them 2 large white cards. One had a vertical black line while the other had 3 lines of different length. Each of the participants was asked publicly which of the 3 lines was the same length as the single one. A test administration showed that outside the experimental situation there was less than 1 per cent of errors.

In the experimental situation, the first 6 people were, on instruction, consistently required to state an incorrect line was the same size as the single line. The subject was the seventh person and the aim of the experiment was to determine whether people would yield to group pressure to deny the reality they could unambiguously observe.

Some 37 per cent of 'errors' were made in the experimental situation, suggesting that a substantial minority of participants yielded to group pressure. One-quarter of the subjects appeared to give answers which indicated they were behaving independently of the group, while some others agreed with the group the whole time. Maximum conformity appeared to occur with 7 to 9 opponents, and after about 4 trials.

Thus the experiment by Asch suggested that some, but by no means all, yielded to group pressure. It would be simplistic to take these findings totally at face value. Some people may have agreed with others in the group to avoid conflict, and may not have been reporting what they believed they saw. This contextual behaviour (behaving in one way with one group and in another way with others) has its counterpart in many 'real life' situations. Regardless of the motives of the experimental subjects, and accepting the possibly temporary nature of the phenomena, Asch's studies raise some important questions.

Thus it is interesting to speculate about how much more conformity might have been observed had the participants been friends (a peer group), rather than strangers, and whether a high level of conformity to peer pressure characterises much human behaviour.

In the second experiment of interest, Milgram (1974) inserted an advertisement in a New Haven, Connecticut paper, inviting the public (those especially mentioned being factory workers, businessmen, construction workers, etc.) to participate in a one-hour project involving memory and learning. The participants were paid a fee on entry and told that the money was now theirs, no matter what. Two participants and an instructor were ostensibly involved in each experiment. The two participants would draw lots and one was allocated the task of teaching the other (the subject) a set of word pairs. The learner was taken to a room where he was strapped to a chair, to prevent movement. The teacher was taken to another room (a glass partition separating the two rooms in the main version of the experiment). In the latter room, there was an electric shock generator with 30 level-type switches. Under each switch (they went up in units of 15 volts, from 15 to 450 volts) was a label with the higher voltages, having the words, '*strong shock, danger: severe shock*' and, after 400 volts, just red Xs.

The reader was told that the aim of the experiment was to

assess the impact of punishment on learning. Consequently, every time the subject made an error, he was to receive a shock, with 15-volt increments for every error until he received 450 volts. In the key experiment the subject appeared to make frequent errors and, when shocked, responded loudly, yelling, screaming and, at 150 volts, refusing to continue with the experiment. The subject-learner was a stooge in the pay of the researchers, and there were no shocks. The results indicated that the members of the community were prepared to obey an instruction to harm or hurt others.

In the situation described above, 16 of 40 'teachers' administered shocks all the way to 450 volts. In another version of the experiment, where the subject could be heard but not seen, 25 'teachers' administered the maximum possible shock. When the subject could be neither seen nor heard, all 40 teachers administered 300 volts and, of these, 26 went all the way to 450 volts. In another version of the experiment where the 'teacher' was in the same room and had to arm-wrestle the victim's hand on to the electric pad, 12 of 40 participants administered the maximum shock. The final version of the experiment, of particular interest, involved a variation, where the 'teacher' read out the words and a third party pulled the lever to administer the shock, the subject becoming a small part of the task. In this latter case, 37 of 40 people continued to 450 volts. (The study was also carried out in Germany, with the finding that Germans were no more or less obedient than the Americans.)

This study raises some important questions which are relevant to the normative view of socialisation, and which warrant discussion. The 'teachers' in the above experiment appeared to be prepared to follow orders, despite the fact that these were given by strangers, and that they could leave the experiment with their money and without fear of harm to themselves. Given that we generally receive our 'orders' from people with whom we have a relationship, what is our own level of conformity?

The 'teachers' in the above experiment appeared to fear how they would be perceived if they did not obey. Presumably the fear of embarrassment was greater than the discomfort created by administering a severe electric shock to an apparently innocent and unwilling (but powerless) subject.

While there is a body of observational, survey and experimental data which suggests that much human behaviour involves a level of conformity or obedience, it is important also to consider some contrary evidence. Firstly, it is clear that behaviours of both individuals and groups change over time, sometimes over relatively short periods. Thus, in the last fifty years, the nature of work and leisure has changed greatly (see Boreham and Hall, Chapter 9 and Ip, Chapter 13), as has the structure of the family in Western industrial societies (see Bittman, Chapter 14). Such levels of change would not be possible if those who subscribe to the normative view of socialisation were completely correct. Secondly, while both Asch (1955) and Milgram (1974) identified a level of conformity or obedience, they also found experimental subjects who appeared to choose not to obey, though one might argue that these latter people may have been conforming to other influences. This raises the third reservation that, in the 'real world', as distinct from the findings of laboratory-type experiments, people are exposed to a wide variety of influences, many of which will conflict, in whole or in part. Behaviour consistent with one influence necessarily leads to disregarding another.

The second approach to understanding socialisation deals more specifically with the process itself and the manner in which the socialisation process transforms the self. This interactionist view begins by noting that socialisation is a lifelong process. As adults move either geographically or through time (i.e. as they age), they are exposed to a changing variety of factors which, to a greater or lesser extent, contribute to their personal qualities. Further, interaction is a two-way process, and even in the example of a child where the parent is largely in control, the child's behaviour can influence the parent's subsequent actions. As parents seek to control their infants, so it is possible to observe the experimentation with a variety of actions (sulking, bargaining, shows of temper) which appear to have the aim of influencing the parent.

Studies of the process of socialisation tend to focus upon communication at both the verbal and non-verbal level. Indeed, some studies now suggest that non-verbal communication conveys most information. Non-verbal communication includes physical proximity, facial expression, posture, voice tone, rate of speech and body position. Non-verbal communication has received considerable mass media attention, and been popularised using the term 'body language'.

The subtlety of this communication process is exemplified by a study of the impact of one involuntary response, the size of the pupils of the eyes (Hess 1975). In this study a group of subjects was shown two photographs of a woman. The pictures were identical except that the woman's pupils were larger in one picture than in the other. The group was then asked to report in which of the two photographs the woman appeared more sympathetic, happy, warm and attractive. There was a tendency for the group to attribute more positive qualities to the woman with the larger pupils.

These studies reinforce the early observations of Charles Horton Cooley (1964) and George Herbert Mead (1934, 1964) who suggested that we are continually 'reading' the cues of the persons with whom we interact. As a result of these real or imagined reactions of others to us, we build an image of who we are and where we fit into the total human mosaic. It is this image which then determines how we react to, and interact with others, and how they, in turn, relate to us.

This process goes some way to explaining why Edgar (1980: 162) found, in research on Australian schoolchildren, that girls had a lower view of their competence than boys. He argues that:

> If our experience...shows us to be members of a competent, respected, successful group with some status in society, then we are likely to approach life confident...if our parents are poor, of low status and exercise little control in the wider scheme of things, our horizons will be limited, our self-image will be less confident, our scope for initiatives constrained. (1980: 140)

The interactionist view of socialisation points to the importance of the continuing nature of the socialisation process, the reciprocal effects of communication and interaction, the creation of a perception of self and the subtle, often unwanted and unplanned consequences of this process.

Which view of socialisation has greater credibility? The normative view suggests that we become what those who are important to us make of us. The interactionist view, by contrast, argues that we make society in the process of being made by it. Each approach clearly adds to our understanding of society, and the utility of each will vary depending on the specific circumstances/situations we wish to explain. We are made, to some extent, in the image of an existing social structure, but in the process we have the capacity to influence and change that structure.

Further, behaviour change may result from technological changes which may physically transform human societies. As examples, the motor car increased mobility and ultimately contributed to the decline in the extended family. The contraceptive pill influenced sexual practices and ultimately contributed to altering the nature of marriage.

Accordingly, we may conclude that we are socialised by the agents of socialisation, but that this process varies somewhat from individual to individual and from one historical period to another. At the same time we react to, and influence, those around us. The society which results is, then, a product of many forces, some acting in concert, some in competition, some deliberately, some unintentionally. We become, nevertheless, the sum total of these experiences and interactions.

Conclusion

This chapter began by identifying the subject matter of sociology. Sociology, it was argued, seeks to understand how society comes to be as it is, and how it changes. Sociological explanations of behaviour begin with the axiom that human behaviours are (partly) determined by one's location within a social structural setting. One's social structural position is important primarily because it reflects both the content and the manner in which one is socialised.

Sociology should not be (some would say cannot be) an abstract and impersonal science. Sociology is intimately concerned with how we come to be as we are. In accounting for the behaviour of those in society, it provides an interpretation which we may compare with our own experiences. Ultimately it is for the student of sociology to weigh the evidence and to make an informed judgement about the validity of the explanations which sociology offers.

Sociology has the capacity to influence individuals by altering their perceptions of themselves. It has demonstrated a capacity to transform the structure of society by providing pertinent data and insightful analyses (e.g. the move for Affirmative Action comes partly from sociological research and analysis).

Above all, three qualities are required of the successful student of sociology. The first is scepticism, a willingness to question the evidence of supposed authorities and one's own senses. The second is a receptiveness to a wide variety of sometimes apparently extraordinary and diverse ideas. This means reading widely, and considering as much of the pertinent data as possible. Thirdly, an interest in the world as it is frequently perceived by the underclass in society, those who usually have no voice, is required. This is the humanistic dimension of sociology which is inextricably related to the sociologist's interest in social, political and economic inequalities, and their possible elimination.

Many relevant issues have, of course, been left undiscussed, (such as questions of the exercise of power, the extent to which the social system in which we live services the interests of some but not others, and the extent to which the institutions of society are essentially conservative and perpetuate inequalities which already exist). These will be addressed in the chapters which follow.

References

Albury, R.M., Chaples, E.A. and Stubbs, K. (1977) 'Sexism Among a Group of Sydney Tertiary Students', *ANZJS* 13 (2): 133–36.

Asch, S.E. (1955) 'Opinions and Social Pressure', *Scientific American* (November).

Baldridge, J.V. (1975) *Sociology*. New York: John Wiley and Sons.

Barry, H., Bacon, M.K. and Child, I.L. (1973) 'A Cross-Cultural Survey of Some Sex Differences in Socialization', in S. Scarr-Salapatek and P. Salapatek (eds), *Socialization*. Columbus, Ohio: Charles E. Merrill.

Baxter, J., Emmison, M., Western, J.S. and Western, M. (eds) (1991) *Class Analysis and Contemporary Australia*. Macmillan: Melbourne.

Bottomley, M. and Sampson, S. (1977) 'The Case of the Female Principal: Sex Role Attitudes and Perceptions of Sex Differences in Ability', *ANZJS* 13 (2): 137-40.

Cooley, C.H. (1964) *Human Nature and the Social Order*. New York: Schocken Books.

Currie, J. (1982) 'The Sex Factors in Occupational Choice', *ANZJS* 18 (2): 180–95.

Denisoff, R.S. and Wahrman, R. (1975) *An Introduction to Sociology*. New York: Free Press.

Douglas, J.D. (ed.) (1973) *An Introduction to Sociology*. New York: Free Press.

Edgar, D. (1980) *Introduction to Australian Society*. Sydney: Prentice Hall.

Hess, E.H. (1975) 'The Role of Pupil Size in Communication', *Scientific American* 233 (5): 110–19.

Homans, G.C. (1970) 'A Life of Synthesis' in I.C. Horowitz, *Sociological Self-Images*. Oxford: Pergamon Press.

——(1986) 'Fifty Years of Sociology', *Annual Review of Sociology* 12 (XIII-XXX), Annual Reviews Inc., Palo Alto, California.

Edwards, J. (1984) 'Raelene, Marjorie and Betty', *The Australian Mathematics Teacher* 40 (2): 11–13.

Gareau, F.H. (1986) 'The Multinational Version of Social Science', *Current Sociology* 33 (3): 169.

Household Expenditure Survey Australia 1984 (1986) Canberra: Australian Bureau of Statistics.

Jahoda, M., Lazarsfeld, P.F. and Zeisel, H. (1974) *Marienthal*. Tavistock: London.

Lodahl, J.B. and Gordon, G. (1972) 'The Structure of Scientific Fields and the Functioning of University Graduate Departments', *American Sociological Review* 37 (1): 57–72.

McMichael, A.J. (1985) 'Social Class (as estimated by Occupational Prestige) and Mortality in Australian Males in the 1970s', *Community Health Studies* 9 (3): 220–30.

Mead, G.H. (1934) *Mind, Self and Society*. Chicago: University of Chicago Press.

——(1964) *On Social Psychology*. Chicago: University of Chicago Press.

Milgram, S. (1974) *Obedience to Authority*. London: Tavistock.

Musgrave, P.W. (1984) 'The Moral Values of Some Australian Adolescents: A Report and Discussion', *ANZJS* 20 (2): 197–217.

Retherford, R.D. (1975) *The Changing Sex Differential in Mortality.* Westpoint, Connecticut: Greenwood Press.

Rosenthal, R. and Jacobson, L.F. (1968) 'Teacher Expectations for the Disadvantaged', *Scientific American*, April.

Sargent, M. (1983) *Sociology for Australians.* Melbourne: Longman Cheshire.

Scarr, S. and Weinberg, R.A. (1976) 'IQ Text Performance of Black Children Adopted by White Families', *American Psychologist* 31, October: 726–39.

Siskind, V., Najman, J.M. and Copeman, R. (1987) 'Infant Mortality in Socio-economically Advantaged and Disadvantaged Areas in Brisbane', *Community Health Studies* xi (1): 24–30.

Sites, P. (1975) *Control and Constraint.* New York: Macmillan.

Taylor, R. *et al.* (1983) *Occupation and Mortality in Australian Working Age Males, 1975–77.* Melbourne: Health Commission of Victoria and Department of Social and Preventive Medicine, Monash University.

Western, J.S. (1983) *Social Inequality in Australian Society.* Melbourne: Macmillan.

Western, J.S. and Turrell, G. (1991) 'Australian Society and the Ethnic Presence'. Paper prepared for Bureau of Immigration Research, Canberra.

Williams, J.E. and Best, D.L. (1982) *Measuring Sex Stereotypes.* Beverley Hills: Sage.

Chapter Two

Australia: State and Polity

Michael Pusey[1]

The state emerges as the true independent variable, industrialisation being only an intervening variable in countries which are all
capitalist in structure.

(Birnbaume 1980)

An intellectual sea change is under way in comparative social science
... A diverse set of scholars with wide-ranging substantive concerns has begun to place the state, viewed as an institution and
social actor, at the centre of attention.

(Evans *et al.* 1985: 347)

Australia is an English-speaking federation made up of former
British colonies, and now a nation that is firmly set within the
cultural, economic and political sphere of influence of the United
States. Given that most Australian sociologists and political
scientists were trained, if not in Australia, then almost certainly in
the United States and/or Britain, we should not be in the least
surprised that British and American intellectual traditions and
tastes have influenced, and even fixed, the priorities for research
in many areas of Australian studies.

It is for this reason, among others, that Australians have, quite
inappropriately and at some cost to our own self-understanding,
grown used to looking at the Australian polity and State from
perspectives that come to us from two nations in which the State
has, *comparatively speaking*, had a smaller historical, cultural, and

intellectual importance. The United Kingdom is a very old nation, one with a territory, a people, and a monarchical and parliamentary government which predates the modern State by some several centuries. Although the United States was the 'first new nation' (Lipset 1963)[2] it is old by comparison with Australia. The United States was founded in a political and intellectual setting that was profoundly hostile to the modern State as it is understood today in the wider community of nations, and these deeply rooted attitudes remain part of the American political and intellectual consciousness to the present day. Although Australia shares a common inheritance with the United States and Britain, the differences between these and the Australian State are at least as important as the similarities. What follows below is an outline, in a comparative and historical perspective, of the essential characteristics of the Australian State in a way that will stress the important and much neglected differences rather than the commonalities. But first some basic definitions and qualifications are necessary.

There is no definitive way of drawing the line between polity, society, economy and state: each term refers to something basic and throws the others into sharper view. Another difficulty is that usage varies according to whether the author travels on a British, American or continental European passport — and whether he or she is a political scientist or a sociologist. Yet, despite the difficulties, the concept of 'the State' is the only one that satisfactorily gathers up the military, the police, the Constitution, and more importantly, the government, the bureaucracy and the legislature, and joins them all into a single entity. The relation of the State so defined with the other categories of 'society', 'polity' and 'economy' raises absolutely basic theoretical assumptions and problems that cannot be dealt with here. A few further points of definition and perspective must suffice.

'Society' is clearly the most general and basic term. Neither 'the economy' not 'the State' fall ready made from the sky into history; nor do they obediently obey any supposedly independent laws of economic or political behaviour. As sociologists and historians must insist, State and economy are both socially constructed and situated in the history of particular nations. Since any discussion about the State raises clashes between Weberian, Marxist and pluralist assumptions, I should add that my perspective makes the basic, and I think widely shared assumptions, that in every capitalist society there is a structurally given three-cornered competition among three actors for the wealth and Gross National Product of the nation: the first, and usually the strongest, actor is capital (which is shorthand for 'business interests', 'free enterprise' or 'the private sector'); the second is labour (which for most purposes simply means wage and salary earners); and the third is 'the State'. (To avoid confusion I shall spell 'State' with a capital 'S' when the term is being used in the general sense above to refer inclusively to government, legislature and bureaucracy, and I shall use it in lower case to refer to the states of Victoria, Tasmania etc., in the Australian federation.) There is a mutually constitutive though unequal relationship between State, capital and labour. This means, among other things, that the boundaries between them are never fixed and that, for example, the State through industrial and arbitration legislation and other means, structures and defines the relationship between capital and labour.

In what follows, the State is not treated, as it is in many Marxist perspectives, as a simple extension of the power of capital: on the contrary, it is such a fascinating area for study precisely because it has some 'relative autonomy'[3] from those who own the nation's productive resources. In other words the causal arrows between economy and State run in both directions: they shape each other, and the same is true of the relationship between State and polity. The State is of course shaped by polity and politics, but so also are politics and the polity conditioned by particular features of the state. 'Polity' is the general term we use to refer to all political expression and to political norms and attitudes that are manifest in that part of society usually called 'civil society' because it lies outside the formal structures of the State (the Constitution, the government, and the bureaucracy). Many of these meanings are manifest in everyday usage. For example, when members of the business community rail against 'state intervention', they are usually referring not simply to a specific law but to a whole complex of political, legal, and economic actions and structures of the State that impinge directly and indirectly on the economy. Similarly, the distinction between civil society and the State is made in practice all the time by those people who want to protect 'civil liberties' from 'intrusions by the State'.

Birthmarks: the Legacy of Foundation

Australia, like the United States, developed in its own territory from early British colonial settlements. Like America it was geographically far removed from continental Europe and from the various struggles for emancipation from old aristocracies which so deeply marked the political constitution and temper of such continental European nations as France, Germany and Italy. The great difference is that the two settlements were separated in time by some 150 years. America was 'born liberal' in the sense that its political institutions crystallised the liberal creeds which its early settlers took from England in the second half of the seventeenth and the eighteenth centuries. The American settlers defined themselves above all as individuals who were, according to John Locke and other notable English liberals of the period, endowed by God with natural rights to 'the enjoyment of life, liberty and property'. Government was only a contrivance, almost a necessary evil, or perhaps at best 'a subordinate practical convenience' (Held *et al.* 1983: 13), but certainly not a focus of value in itself. The purpose of political life is purely to secure 'the conditions for freedom so that the private ends of individuals might be met in civil society' (Held *et al.* 1983: 13). This was the creed of a middle class, with its back turned against the despotism of an old monarchy, and bent on prosperity and individual enterprise freed from unwanted interference and restraint, 'on the enjoyment of property' (which Locke defined very broadly). This creed, and the political norms and structures which it legitimated, solidified before the Industrial Revolution, and amid a population in which as many as four-fifths of the people who worked were owners of their own means of livelihood (Mayer 1964). These people, property owners and small entrepreneurs, living in a bountiful land before the era of the factory, quickly rationalised the inequalities that they themselves would create, with a pseudo-egalitarian doctrine of equality of opportunity (Badie and Birnbaum 1964: 203–10). Some might rise like Horatio Alger, 'from rags to riches' but, no matter how extreme the differences between rich and poor, all are equal in so far as all begin with an equal chance — which they never do! One need only add the religious premiss that God chooses only those who are worthy, to find the rudiments of what Hofstader (1963) called the 'evangelical egalitarianism' of the American charter myth.

The contrasts with Australia are quite striking. Australia's early settlers were for the most part the victims of the Industrial Revolution, and of the ugliest period of militant British capitalism. They are described (McNaughtan 1955: 103) as 'the outpourings of the unions and poor houses of the United Kingdom', and it is clear, as Rosecrance (1964: 280) puts it, that they

> were largely a homogenous group of city folk of humble economic and social origins.

These people were as far estranged from the liberal American ideal of the intimate self-governing community as any English-speaking population ever could be. Whether convict or free settler, from the day of arrival their political experience was typically of a gubernatorial military government in a penal colony, and hence of a State that was, from its first moments, very much a 'strong state'.[4]

There are several features of this early formative period of Australian history, which shaped the ethos and the structures of the Australian state, dating from the full development of the penal system in the 1820s to the Depression of the 1890s:

1.   Firstly the Aborigines were quickly overwhelmed and pushed out of white Australian history and consciousness. Because they were largely nomadic hunter-gatherers who had not 'mixed their labour with the land' in a way that Europeans of the time could recognise as 'productive' they were judged to be completely un-civilised and without legal rights to their land. The continent had been declared a *terra nullius*, in effect a vacant land, and so there was no legal or cultural foundation to secure a place for the Aborigine in the political and institutional history of the white population. The point of these remarks is obvious: the foundation of the state institutionalised a basic 'structural inequality'. At the same time it estranged the white population from the cultural and historical universe of the original inhabitants, and deepened their sense of geographical isolation and general vulnerability.

2.   With the exception of South Australia, all the Australian states began as penal colonies. Just under 200,000 convicts were brought to Australia before transportation to the Eastern states was abandoned, in 1850. This would have a number of effects on the character of the colonial states:

> The indiscriminate use of the lash undermined the essential belief in the possibility of just authority. More than this, the attempt to reproduce in Australia a social hierarchy in which the legal code could achieve the more general significance it possessed in England was doomed to failure.
>
> (MacIntyre 1985: 14)

Moreover, the hopes for decent self-government of the freed con-victs, of 'the emancipists' as they were called, and of the greatly increased population of free settlers who had come with the gold rushes of the 1850s, were clearly irreconcilable with repressive laws and the military disciplines of penal colonialism. The conse-quence was that:

> legal and political disabilities were the overriding concern of the reformers, overshadowing all other complaints. . .The Australian radicals of the 1840s and 1850s were so preoccupied with political issues, so steeped in the doctrines of liberalism and constitutional

democracy, that they came to look upon the state as an instrument of popular sovereignty.

(MacIntyre 1985: 18)

In short, the brutality and human degradation of the convict system destroyed the legitimacy of the old order and made new structures of government a precondition for independence. And, perhaps most importantly, this experience focused all attention on political reform and the benefits of a reformed — but still strong — state.

3.   Just as American settlers defined themselves with political aspirations that were progressive in their own time, so the early white Australians, and certainly the rump of poor free settlers who followed the convicts from about the 1830s to the gold rushes of the 1850s, brought with them Chartist demands for political reform of the capitalist economic and social order of their time. The Chartist movement, so named after the People's Charter published in London in May 1838, embodied the resentments of the working class against the Corn Laws, the Poor Laws of 1834, the long factory working hours, and the tenuous legality of trade unions. It demanded universal male suffrage, equal electoral districts, ballot voting, and the payment and abolition of property qualifications of members of Parliament. In 1842 these demands were put in a second petition, with 3,000,000 signatures, to a Parliament which ignored it, defeated the movement, and banished many of its leaders to Australia. Nearly all the demands were soon won in Australia, only a decade later.

Although Chartism was for the most part not a revolutionary movement, it was driven by deep resentment against both the privileges of the British aristocracy and the terrible social inequalities of the Industrial Revolution. The Chartists did not succeed in making Australia a haven of popular socialism but, on the other hand, their bitter experience of *laissez-faire* capitalism and of the ugliest side of 'private enterprise' has contributed to the birth of an Australian state that was:

> born modern...in the sense that...Australians believed that the state, far from encroaching upon individual rights would be the most likely protector of rights against other agencies of social coercion. Unlike the doctrinaire liberals of Europe, Australians believed that the major constraints on individual liberty were not public, but private.[5]

The point is that, at least for these reformists, and for the working class of the time, *laissez-faire* capitalism had already lost its legitimacy. 'Economic development' was not an end in itself and would not of itself overcome bitterly resented social inequalities.

4.   Of equal importance is the intellectual and political com-
plexion of the next generation of reformists, from the 1850s to
Federation in 1901. There is no doubt that the radical voices of
the two preceding decades, from the 1830s to the gold rushes of
the 1850s, were inspired by the Chartists. But what has been
missed in the 'romantic socialist' view of this early history is that
the more radical and popular socialist demands of the time (for
social justice and for the equitable apportionment of the land)
were first mediated and then largely subsumed into the prevailing
liberalism of an increasingly influential class of successful emancipists, liberal merchants, and especially lawyers and other professional people who would take an ever-stronger role in the
articulation of popular demands, first for self-government in the
1850s and then as leaders of the movement for the creation of a
new federation.

These Australians were secular, pragmatic and utilitarian. The
traditional and religious metaphysical shroudings had disappeared
with the break with the old world. The political ideology which
found institutional expression through these reformers was
strongly coloured by the utilitarian liberalism of Jeremy Bentham
(Collins 1985). The anti-intellectualism of the Australian political
ideology originates at least in part from an ethical and intellectual
scepticism that is anti-utopian and that, in Bentham's words,
shuns

> the perplexity of ambiguous and sophistical discourse that, while it
> distracts and eludes the apprehension, stimulates and inflames the
> passions.

The more important consequence may be that this pragmatic,
utilitarian and materialist strain of liberalism cast the state more
as a neutral instrument for the efficient organisation of the
economic, political and legal-administrative structures of society.
It would easily allow the more limited ideal of fair political representation to replace the quest for social justice. Put more bluntly
it would not be unfriendly to modern capitalism in that it helped
to steer the political and institutional reforms leading to
Federation into a course that would allow labour and land to be
more easily treated as commodities.

State and Economy

Liberalism is every bit as slippery a notion as any other 'ism'.
Indeed Tim Rowse (1978: 41–42) rightly insists that liberalism is

a 'psychologically promiscuous', 'protean and flexible' doctrine that can be invoked 'to defend a wide range of political arrangements'. Liberal principles are invoked either to justify or to defend every change in the relationship between State, capital and labour.

Yet the relationship between State and capital does have an underlying pattern, and here the German political scientist Claus Offe provides a convenient way of describing the constraints and requirements which the private sector normally imposes on the State in what are commonly known today as liberal capitalist societies. According to Offe's (1975) descriptive model these constraints and requirements are summarised by four 'principles' which he identifies as: *exclusion, maintenance, dependence,* and *legitimation.* Exclusion means simply that the State has no authority to control production or to make private investment decisions, because in a 'free enterprise' = capitalist economy, production must be 'free' and this means that the State is excluded from control of private capital. The second distinguishing characteristic of the State, especially in modern, 'developed', 'late capitalist' societies, is that it has to maintain, support and protect the capital accumulation process (with State financed or provided education, transport, communications, electricity, land and labour etc.). The third principle is dependency: the State is dependent on the taxes which must be levied directly (e.g. company tax, payroll tax), and indirectly (e.g. income and sales taxes), from the capital accumulation process of a private economy that it cannot command but 'must' maintain. And, fourthly, the state 'must' legitimate itself and its relation with private interests by either hiding or justifying its role and its decisions in a way that is adequate to sustain mass popular support for both State *and capital.*

Although these 'principles'[6] describe present day realities, they can usefully be kept in the background of our following discussion as a way of clarifying some of the distinctive features of the Australian State from the 1840s to the present.

While Britain in the time of Gladstonian liberalism, in the last quarter of the nineteenth century, was coming to the peak of its industrial and commercial power, Australia was comprised of six fledgling colonies in which the institutions and role of the State were developing their own form in the very different social and political conditions of the other colonies of the period. If the British State was involved in the maintenance of capital accumulation, the involvement was largely indirect: domestically the coercive apparatus of the State — the courts and the police — were deployed both to repress the social unrest produced by the Industrial Revolution, and to discipline the labour force. Externally, its great imperial military power was used to protect British possessions, markets, sea lanes, and trading interests overseas. Within its own territory, Britain was, as the comparative literature (Nettl 1968: 574, 577, 582; Evans *et al.* 1985) insists, still the liberal 'stateless' society *par excellence* — the same was, and still is, true of the United States. Capital alone was the great engine and structuring force in society. The relationship between capital and the State, summarised in Offe's four principles, is above all a description of this British and American model of liberal capitalism.

In the colonies, everything was different. Capitalism of a particular rural/pastoral form had preceded industrialisation. In contrast to the American frontier, the Australian hinterland was suited to grazing rather than small farming. Vast holdings of grazing land were taken up by squatters and graziers who were interested only in amassing personal wealth. For the most part they cared little for the future of the colonies, with which they did not identify, because most of them intended to leave when their pockets were full (Rosecrance 1964: 289). Their monopoly over the land, together with an insatiable demand for wool from the textile mills of northern England produced a rural 'staples economy',[7] centred on the production of wool. In contrast to the American frontier, the Australian frontier produced a 'rural proletariat' of 'shepherds, boundary riders and shearers'. Although the first Australian capitalists, the squatter 'Wool Kings', would fight strongly to protect their own interests, they were successfully opposed by a working class with vivid memories of the miseries they had left behind them and by a growing reformist middle class of emancipists, merchants and professional people. These people were determined that a journey halfway around the globe must lead to something more than a leap from the frying pan to the fire. Accordingly they

> would harbour little good will for the squatter; for here, after all, were the English industrialists and the perpetrators of the Corn Laws rolled into one. If economic liberalism was not fully adequate as a social gospel, how much less tolerable would be the creation of a class which reeked of landed privilege? Indeed, many Australians qua Britons had had to fight the *ancien regime* before they arrived in Sydney; they were scarcely likely to put up with an Australian version of the old enemy.
>
> (Rosecrance 1964: 287)

Without 'state intervention' Australia would be destined to develop rather as a poor Third World *comprador* economy,[8] entirely dependent on cash crops and with a State designed only to maintain whatever measure of repression its foreign sponsors would demand.

With a form of state-led capitalism, and with state intervention on a scale that was unthinkable in Britain itself, the colonies would develop on a broader base that might accommodate the aspirations of a larger population whose voice was somehow heard in London by a relatively enlightened Colonial Office that had learned something from the errors of its own heavy-handed responses to earlier popular demands in the United States and Canada. By the 1860s, most of the Chartist demands were won and the colonies had universal male suffrage and popularly elected semi-independent governments which severely curbed the political power of large landholders.

The government was *not excluded* from the private economy, but rather joined with it in a relationship of strong partnership which, by the last decade of the nineteenth century, had secured for Australians the highest per capita incomes in the world and set a pattern of relationship between State, polity and economy that would shape the federation and its future for many decades to come. As Butlin puts it:

> Traditionally, Australian colonial government during the second half of the nineteenth century performed what was, in effect, a *general management role* in their economies. In its essence, 'colonial socialism' entailed *direct action* by governments to attract foreign (British) resources of capital and labour, through public borrowing overseas and large-scale programmes of publicly-assisted migration; the investment of British capital in publicly-owned taxed assets in Australia; the concentration of this investment in public business undertakings, primarily in transport and communications; and the delivery of marked services by these public enterprises.
>
> (Butlin *et al.* 1982: 320)

State investments in the economy were roughly equal to those of the private sector until the 1930s.

And so, clearly, in the formative period of modern Australia, up until as late as the 1930s, the pattern of relationships between State and capital defies the ordinary 'principles' of liberal capitalism proposed in the Offe model. The underlying reality is still that Australia was a relatively small, economically dependent nation, locked into the larger world economy by its still semi-colonial economic dependence upon the markets and capital resources of Britain. Yet the sheer scale of government involvement in the Australian economy contradicts liberal principles. The State could not be excluded from private investment decisions because local capital and manufacturing interests were so dependent upon it. In many vital areas, such as railways, port construction and the like, the State led and capital followed. In the United States, by contrast, it was typically the other way around. The purpose of State action was not to compete with the private economy and certainly not to build a parallel state economy on socialist or other principles. Instead, the intention was clearly to attract and support the private economy by providing the missing infrastructure for development. Yet the scale of State investment, together with the historical context in which it had developed, institutionalised a measure of State authority in economic matters that looked more like equal co-sponsorship of production, rather than the subordinate maintenance function of the normal liberal capitalist pattern.

There are four fairly constant factors which seem to explain much of what is most important in the relations between State and economy in Australia from the time of its foundation to the present day. First: Australia and its economy have always been dependent and vulnerable. This vulnerability is accentuated by a simultaneous dependence on favourable conditions for specialised pastoral/farm products and raw materials exports and, on the other hand, a need to spend large proportions of foreign earnings to pay for imported manufactured goods. To this day Australia remains a trading nation with only a small population and a correspondingly small market for its own manufacturing industries. It remains heavily dependent on the vicissitudes of commodity markets and of a world economy that is always entirely beyond its control.

Second: In its relations with both state and labour, capital in Australia has always been divided. On one side there were the large producers and collectors of raw materials for the overseas markets — mining, pastoral and shipping companies — that are generally capital rather than labour-intensive, and usually dependent on swings in demand and price in their foreign markets. On the other side of capital in Australia are the local domestic manufacturing and service industries whose interests are governed much more by wage costs and the threat of competing imported products.[9]

Third: There has always been economic rivalry among the states along with basic differences over economic policy. The form of the federation, and especially of its industrial and tariff powers were influenced by long-standing conflicts between first, Victorian interests that were, and to some extent still remain to this day, protectionist and second, New South Wales ones, which have traditionally favoured more free market/low tariff policies.

Fourth: Industrialisation in Australia was a relatively late phenomenon, occurring mainly in the early-middle decades of this century, at a time when labour had already achieved strong political representation and considerable defensive strength (Connell and Irving 1980: 279).

The interplay of these factors, set against the legacy of foundation, provides some broad historically contextualised specifications of what is distinctive about the Australian State and its relation to the economy.

Immigration
The first white Australians were brought to Port Jackson and Risdon Cove on 'assisted passages' of a very particular kind. In stark contrast with the larger established nations of Europe, immigration had, from the first white settlements of Australia, remained a centrally important function of the State. Immigration policies have reflected Australia's cultural identifications and the fears, so clearly manifested in the pre-war White Australia Policy, of a dependent nation with a vast territory. State-sponsored immigration produced the ethnic homogeneity of the white foundation population as well as the social and political cleavages that were to shape the nation and the later federation. Immigration policies have continued to shape Australians' ethnic, social, cultural and political characteristics and dispositions. They have also affected foreign policy and, although opinions differ as to whether immigration policies have on balance weakened or strengthened labour in Australia, it is clear they have always had an importance (whether in threat or action) as a potential instrument for reducing wage costs by increasing the supply of cheap labour from abroad. The wider economic importance of immigration policies is well underlined by Butlin in the following terms:

> The acquisition of foreign capital through government action was a correlative of this population aim: to combine increasing inputs of overseas capital and migrant labour with domestic natural resources in order to establish the conditions for enlarged foreign trade and domestic activity.
>
> (Butlin 1983: 83)

Tariff Protection
Australia's economically dependent situation within the world economy produced deeply engrained conflicts of interests between large, and mainly foreign owned, enterprises and the domestic manufacturing sector. 'Big' (foreign owned) capital trading and production interests have always pressed for low tariff protection

and low exchange rates. Domestic capital, on the other hand, has a common interest with labour in pressing for high tariff barriers to protect local industry from foreign competition. The State was therefore cast into the role of arbiter and broker in a triangle of conflict between these two sections of capital and labour. The complexity of these conflicts was further complicated after Federation by continued competition between the states for capital investment. The role of the State, and more especially of the new federal State, was in this respect reconstituted and vividly demonstrated in the famous Harvester Judgment of 1907, in which the Federal Arbitration Court under Mr Justice Higgins, enforced the requirement that, under the laws of the 'New Protection' policy, 'fair and reasonable wages' must be paid to the workers of the Harvester Company as a condition for tariff protection (MacIntyre 1983: 106–10).[10] This was a classical example of the way these conflicts have given the State the leeway to play the actors off against each other and thus extract concessions that would otherwise be unobtainable: in short they have given added strength to the Australian State and enhanced its relative autonomy.

Industrial Arbitration and Wage Fixation
The maritime strike of the 1890s and the armed clashes involving police and militia in 1891, 1892 and 1894 ended in the defeat of the waterside workers, miners, transport industry workers, and some 20,000 shearers, who had all joined the strike. On the face of it, the defeat was an important gain for the large early 'pre-industrial' pastoral, mining and transport capital interests which were bent on driving down wage levels by employing non-union labour at lower rates. But this was a Pyrrhic victory and, in the longer perspective, really a defeat, because it led to a consolidation of labour's political and parliamentary strength; gave impetus to the development of wage fixing and arbitration legislation in the colonial states; influenced the terms on which industrial and arbitration laws would be written into the new federation; and, perhaps most importantly, persuaded local domestic industrial interests, during the crucial formative pre-war years, that their interests lay in accepting state-determined wage levels in return for protective tariffs:

> 'New Protection' found sufficient agreement between the craft workers and their employers to outweigh the interests of capital producing for the export market and ensured industrialisation would proceed within the economic framework established by the new Commonwealth.
>
> (MacIntyre 1983: 111)

Between Federation in 1901 and World War I, the primary function of state industrial arbitration (in both the Commonwealth and the states) was to protect employed union labour by raising wage standards towards judicially declared minimum levels and to encourage the general development and re-formation of union organisations and the development of federal unions (Butlin 1983: 91). Some unions would see the arbitration system as 'the legal machinery of the capitalist class as it holds the working class sheep tight while he is being shorn by the boss' (Connell and Irving 1980: 282), while some of the more aggressive employers fought it as a violation of 'freedom of contract, upon which no self-respecting employer will ever listen to discussion'. But despite opposition, the arbitration system was in due course accepted by both sides, and cemented into the structures of the Australian State. It has to the present day institutionalised, contained, and to some extent pacified conflicts between labour and capital.

This very brief sketch captures some of the defining characteristics of the relation between State and capital in Australia from its foundation to the end of World War II. In terms of the modern debates that are 'bringing the state back in' (Evans *et al.* 1985) we see a strong state that has secured considerable authority and relative autonomy in its relations with capital; taken a nation building role; led rather than followed private enterprise in national economic development; and secured high living standards for the wage and salary earning majority of its population.

In many respects this image still holds up against present realities, and in some it is even strengthened by developments in the forty years since World War II. Yet forty years is a long time in the life of a young nation, and developments over this period raise serious questions about the durability of many of these classical features of relations between state and capital. During this period, under predominantly conservative governments led by Menzies, Holt, Gorton, McMahon and Fraser, Australian State provision in such areas as welfare and education declined to the point where they now look very meagre by comparison with other OECD nations such as France and the Scandinavian countries. During the long post-war boom, the wages and salaries proportion of Gross National Product fell slightly from 1948 to 1966 (*Yearbook Australia* 1968: 628). More significantly, the wages and salaries share of total income fell by approximately 10 per cent, from 1975–76 to 1988–89, at a time when the income share of the corporate sector had increased (Treasury, *The Economic Roundup* 1990: 43). In this period foreign and mainly American multinational capital has captured large sections of the Australian economy, while domestic manufacturing industries have fallen into rapid decline:

The total of foreign capitalists' investment in Australia rose from about 500 million [pounds sterling] in the late 1940s to about $10,000 million in the early 1970s, the American share having risen to near par with the British. By then a quarter of the fifty largest companies in the country were subsidiaries of multi-national corporations; official inquiries, when finally made, reckoned that foreign capital held between a quarter and a third of the entire corporate business of the country. Japanese investment followed American in the 1960s. From being an appendage of one, Australia had graduated economically to a field for the play of forces from several of the international centres of capitalism.

(Connell and Irving 1980: 294)

The short-lived Whitlam reformist Labor government demonstrated, among other things, that the State was not strong enough to nationalise any profitable industry, affirm national control of minerals and resource production, or control prices and incomes. In the succeeding Fraser years tax minimisation and evasion schemes were protected by the government and the High Court to permit a sizeable transfer of the total taxation burden (that is the running costs of the State) from the corporate sector to wage and salary earners.[11] As Butlin summarises

... legal support for monopolistic or oligopolistic structures offered by all governments contributed to this increase in private influence. From this development flowed the extension of monopolistic practices of almost every sort, with greater or less active assistance but almost always with legal permission given by the Federal and State governments.

(Butlin 1983: 96)

In short, the overall picture since World War II, and especially over the last decade to 1990, shows a strong assertion of capital at the expense of labour *and of the State*. This accelerating trend ever more closely resembles the free market liberal, or 'economic rationalist' pattern of relations between capital and State: the State has been increasingly excluded from the effective planning and direction of capital investments and at the same time committed, with scant regard for the longer-term national interest, to deploy declining publicly-funded resources to their maintenance and legitimation. In its more traditional form this pattern is nowhere better exemplified than in the manner in which BHP, Australia's largest company, extracted massive capital support from several governments to subsidise the Whyalla steel works. This more 'traditional' way of converting public resources into private returns to shareholders is what Szelenyi (1980) calls, with only a little exaggeration, 'the state mode of production'.

Since about 1984, and with aggressive policies of financial and labour market deregulation, privatisation of government enterprises, and cuts to public spending, the Australian pattern of development has been more strongly forced towards the liberal, 'economic rationalist' pattern of the two 'great stateless societies' of Britain and the United States.

The Federal Structure and Bureaucracy in Australia

A comparative sketch points to the distinctiveness and the complexity of State power in Australia. In one relatively 'stateless' society, the United States, power is exerted principally, on the one hand, through a political process of patronage and bargaining between central and local levels, and on the other by the courts, which dominate almost every aspect of State administration. Sovereignty in the United States is quintessentially embodied in the law, and especially in the Constitution and the Supreme Court. Together they greatly overshadow the importance of their equivalents in Australia. In the United States the law is, at least in social matters, the enabling vehicle and the focus for most significant changes, certainly those that raise explicit conflicts of interest. The law, the Constitution, and the Supreme Court are the guarantors of 'individual rights', and together they form a legal structure with an authority that towers over the other sectors of the State including, in many respects, the federal government itself, which Americans curiously perceive as a rather distant, abstract, and almost foreign entity to which newspaper articles refer with such phrases as 'the Dispute between City Hall and the United States'. In Britain, in which there is of course a monarchy, no written constitution, and a much more inward-looking legal system, it is Her Majesty's elected government which is the focus of state power. In France, traditionally the model of the 'strong' State, sovereign power is concentrated in a much more integrated apparatus, that Birnbaum (1977) describes as *la République des Fonctionnaires*: in France both the law and the elected government are perceived as emanations of a State dominated by its centralised, elaborate and highly professionalised bureaucratic apparatus — (In French *l'Etat* (the State) is significantly always written with a capital 'E'!)

Against this background we see some of the more obvious aspects of the Australian case. Like the United States, Australia is a federation. But it's a federation in which, at least since the 1930s and 40s, the central federal government and administration have had far greater importance. In as much as the law and the Constitution overshadow administration in the United States, the reverse is true in Australia. The most obvious contrast with Britain is, of course, that Australia is a federation with a Constitution. The similarity is that, under the Westminister System, in Britain as in Australia, the elected majority party is subject to a strict discipline of government and Cabinet that has marginalised the ordinary elected member of Parliament and concentrated interest group representation at the doors of ministers and senior officials. Yet in Australia the bureaucracy is more conspicuous than in Britain, and more readily accepted as a strong centre of legitimate State power: in this, as in many other respects, Australia is again closer to France and the other states of continental Europe. Certainly, one of the distinctive features of the Australian case is that it combines a federal structure with a comparatively strong State, one in which bureaucracy and administration have had a distinctive character. It is these two distinguishing aspects of the Australian State, its federal structure and its reliance on bureaucracy, that we should now examine more closely.

The Commonwealth Constitution formally allocates some exclusive powers to the federal government. In addition to the obvious responsibilities for defence and external affairs, these powers include, in Brian Head's (1983: 7) summary, 'overseas trade, immigration; customs and excise; issuing of currency; inter-state industrial arbitration; postal and other communications; corporations and aspects of banking'. Whereas the states and territories are responsible for 'the administration of most routine services as well as key areas of economic activity, they regulate or have potential power to control most aspects of industry, energy supply, prices, courts, prisons, police, mineral exploration and development, land use, environment, welfare services, consumer affairs, ports, water resources, some forms of taxation, and most aspects of criminal, civil and commercial law'.

However, despite the range of its functions in earlier periods of the nation's history, the State is now quite small by OECD standards. In 1991 the public sector as a whole accounted broadly for less than one-quarter of employment and gross product (*Budget Statements 1991–92*). However, the actual and potential predominance of the federal government is reflected in the fact that, since World War II, it has had a monopoly over income tax powers, and with this power collects over 80 per cent of all public revenues. A large proportion of this income is redistributed to the states, but in the years since the war it has become ever clearer that the federal government's hold over the purse strings and its power under the Constitution to fix the terms of its grants to the states have steadily increased its financial dominance. Indeed, in 1991, although the outlays of the federal government accounted for some 27 per cent of GNP, it employed only 6.9 per cent of the total civilian workforce. Conversely, state and local government, which in 1991 together accounted for 20.3 per cent of GNP, employed 19.8 and 2.7 per cent of the workforce respectively. This last figure eloquently represents what has always been the comparatively marginal importance of local government in Australia.

How does the federal structure of the Australian State mark the character of State power and the pattern of politics in this country? Space allows only two comments in response to this important, but very complex question. First, the powers of the federal government in relation to the states have grown steadily in the ninety-one years since Federation and this great increase in its power has acted as a kind of force field that has gradually conditioned and shaped political and economic life in Australia since Federation. Federation was created at the turn of the century, in a time when governments everywhere were very small by today's standards. In 1870, for example, the British Civil Service totalled just over 50,000 men and women, whereas by 1970 this figure had grown by a factor of 16 to number some 800,000 employees (Aberbach *et al.* 1981: 2). When the Australian federation was created, it was generally assumed that it would have only a restricted role; indeed some notables of the period, 'even anticipated that the major legislative business of the new parliament would be transacted once and for all in a fairly brief period' (MacIntyre 1983: 106). The powers of the federal government increased greatly during World War II, as attention shifted from the governments in the six states to a federal government charged both with emergency powers and the fateful responsibilities of defending a nation. It emerged from the war with a monopoly of income tax powers which it never relinquished to the states, and with its prestige and authority massively enhanced. Since then the increasing complexities of economic management and (before they were displaced in the 1980s by 'economic rationalism') the acceptance of generally Keynesian economic policies, forced the increasing centralisation of power in Canberra.

Second, the federal structure of the Australian State has *shaped the opposing positions and strategies of the major political parties*. In addressing this question it is important to note that the structure itself is by no means neutral. The idea of a federation originates not from socialist ideas, but on the contrary from Madison and other prominent liberal 'federalists' who shaped the American federal Constitution in 1787 and 1788. Accordingly, the Australian federal structure embodies most of the great normative principles of liberal political thought: in its division of powers; in the provision of constitutionally secured 'checks and balances'; in the primacy which it gives to private over public enterprise; and to the limitation of state power. Horne (1985) and others argue that the federation has an inherently conservative bias because it protects 'free trade' against competing notions of the general interest of the population and because it allows the flagrantly undemocratic practices of some of the state governments to continue behind the usually contrived excuse that the Commonwealth has no power to intervene. To this one must add a second contextual observation that, over the ninety years of the federation's existence, Labor governments have ruled for only some twenty-eight years. In these generally short and precarious terms of office, they were either blocked by hostile Senates or governing in the shadow of war.

Yet, within this context, the contrasting ways in which Labor and conservative governments have used the federal structure are fairly obvious. Labor governments have in the main been centralist. Such centralism has been:

> ...inspired by its desire to intervene actively in the economy to promote growth, foster rising living standards and full employment, equality of opportunity, and, on occasion, a more equitable distribution of income and wealth, combined with the belief that these objectives can only be effectively achieved from the centre because this eliminates the opposition which would otherwise come from conservative state governments.
>
> (Groenwegen 1983: 188)

It is hardly surprising that non-Labor governments have, on the contrary, sought to use the federal government to thwart social reforms and any redistribution of either profits or state revenues in favour of wage and salary earners. As Greenwood noted, some fifty years ago, and as Groenwegen has recently reiterated, it is therefore to be expected that conservative preferences would be legitimated by appeals to the liberal principles embodied in the federation:

> ...the defence of state rights and federalism by conservative governments, although cloaked by the ideology that federalism is essential for the preservation of individual liberty and freedom of choice, is largely designed to put a brake on...excessive government intervention and thereby safeguard what it calls the rights of free private enterprise...Continuing conservative support for the institutions of federalism is also inspired by the fact that in Australia at least, they constitute real barriers against socialism, imagined or otherwise (Groenwegen 1983: 188). As other observers

(Albinski 1985; Head 1984, 1986) have noted, these contests and related conflicts of interests surfaced again in threats to the long-term stability of the Australian federation posed by challenges from the less industrialised states of Queensland, Western Australia, the Northern Territory and Tasmania that have been willing to serve as vehicles for multi-national bids to capture Australian mineral, timber, energy and land resources. The same underlying contests drove the Hawke Labor government in the 1990s to steal the thunder of the LNP Opposition parties, firstly, by reducing federal government revenues and expenditures to the bottom of the OECD table and to the pre-Whitlam levels of 1973, and, secondly, by an electoral experimentation in 1990 with radical 'New Federalism' policies that would, if implemented, hand back most of Canberra's program and service functions to the states and territories.

Alan Davies' (1964: 1) frequently-quoted remark that 'Australians have a talent for bureaucracy' points to an essential trait of Australian society that has in various ways attracted the attention of every major study of Australian society. Encel underlines the point by listing some of the many and various functions that have at different times been performed by state enterprises: they include the acquisition and export of farm products, air transport, aluminium production, bakeries, banking, brick and pipe making, broadcasting — and, the list goes on, to home building, insurance, meat production and distribution, port administration, shipping and shipbuilding (Encel 1970: 64). We have already noted above that public capital outlays were larger than those of the private sector until as late as 1930 (Butlin 1983: 84), and that in Australia the State has at various times taken a pioneering role in opening up new areas of development. However, the true signi-ficance of bureaucracy as a feature of the Australian State lies elsewhere, beyond considerations of its relative size or even the unusual variety of its enterprises.

Its really distinctive feature is the relation and place which bureaucracy occupies in the total make-up of the State in Australia. What matters is the relative importance of bureaucracy *in relation* to the political processes of government, and to the other aspects of the State (the Constitution and the federal structure) as these interface with the polity. In Britain and America, 'allocative'[13] conflicts (over who gets what) are normally assumed to find resolution through 'the political process'. The polity, anchored as it is in civil society, must 'speak' through its elected politicians who carry the 'the voice of the people' across some invisible boundary between the polity and the State. It is these elected representatives of the people who issue directives to what is seen, in this classically liberal and prejudicial way, as the grey and mechanical world of administration and bureaucracy — a world that is either despised or, at best, grudgingly taken for granted as a neutral instrument for the implementation of *politically determined policies*, ostensibly making no distinctive and valuable contribution of its own.[14] It is this which, by contrast, points to what is distinctive in the Australian case.

Australia is distinguished by its extensive and long-standing use of semi-judicial and other statutory and administrative authorities. The examples are everywhere: fisheries and forestry commissions, water boards, the Industries Assistance Commission, the various state and Commonwealth arbitration commissions and tribunals, the former Schools Commission, the Australian Broadcasting Corporation, etc. Australians have traditionally placed greater trust in the deliberative and interest-mediation processes of these bodies (Parker 1965; Miller 1954), more so than other 'developed' English-speaking nations. The other side of the coin is that they not only mistrust politicians — that is common everywhere — but, more significantly, they mistrust the *political process itself*. For example, in the lead-up to the election of the first Whitlam government, in 1972, the Labor Party successfully insisted that a new (and very large) statutory authority, the Australian Schools Commission, would be created by a Labor government because 'the education of our children was so important that it should not become a "political football" '. This is a very Australian attitude. The underlying assumptions carry strong echoes of Australia's foundation: the State is a more reliable guardian of the common good than private interests or their political representatives. Similarly, there are other reasons for this Australian preference for bureaucracy, which also have their roots in earlier periods of our history. In Australia the polity is not, as in Britain, supported by a centuries-old middle class political tradition of debate in a well formed 'public sphere'. The vast distances and the virtual absence of local government in Australia have left their mark in as much as politics in Australia was never an intimate and familiar aspect of neighbourhood life, but rather something that is done 'out there' by self-seeking people with 'private' — which in Australia means 'vested' — interests. Traditionally, in Britain, which is still the only modern country with substantial numbers of working class Tories, large electoral majorities have proven with their votes that they have some trust in the principle of *noblesse oblige*, and some confidence still that the established upper and middle classes will govern in the common interest. Similarly, in the United States, where there has never been a Labor working class party in the normal European sense, there is still a general belief that the Congressmen, Senators and Presidents — who must all prove a strict fidelity to the sectional interests of capital and business as a precondition for political office! — will somehow govern 'for the people'. By contrast the Australian distrust of the political process and the preference instead for administrative and semi-judicial allocative structures has persisted up to the 1980s. A probable reason is that from their earliest years, Australians have never found reason to trust their business élites who are still, as Stretton argues, of generally low moral and intellectual stature (Stretton 1985). Another important factor, and one that is both cause and consequence of the Australian reliance on judicial and bureaucratic-administrative state authorities, is that despite abiding preoccupations with equity, 'social justice', and 'a fair go', Australian civil society seems to lack a 'moral vocabulary capable of connecting social realities with political institutions' (Collins 1985).

Accordingly the political process is often eclipsed, as social needs are more directly translated into bureaucratic-administrative programs.

In Australia there is also, as we have intimated, an important and paradoxical relation between the pressure for egalitarianism and social justice on the one hand, and bureaucracy on the other. It is a paradox because:

> Bureaucracy 'is the very model of the regime which acts by the rule of equality'. Herein lies the paradox of egalitarianism in Australia: the search for equality of the redistributive kind breeds bureaucracy; bureaucracy breeds authority; and authority undermines the equality which bred it.
>
> (Encel 1970: 57)

In other words, the State, the centre of institutionalised power in society gathers more power, and creates further hierarchical divisions, as its power is mobilised to redress inequalities. But is this an unavoidable consequence of state administrative action? Or are the proliferating hierarchies, of educational grades and certificates, levels and classifications of employment, of government benefits, of fee scales and residential areas, the preferred forms which business and capital interests impose on all State action as a condition for their co-operation (Connell and Irving 1980)?

Conclusion

Now as before Australians continue to face the world from their situation as a relatively small and dependent nation, an island

continent without strong economically protective regional
associations. It was Australia's dependency on the British Empire
which took battalions of its young men to fight for God, King and
Country on the other side of the globe and which also structured
its economic relations and provided a shell within which the
institutions of the Australian State would develop in their own
characteristic form. With the dissolution of the British Empire
after World War II, Australia's military, economic, political, and
cultural dependencies shifted from Britain to a radically new
empire, the United States of America. Australia was settled by a
population which emigrated from the heartland of an empire that
was ready to grant formal independence to its own British
foundation population on fairly easy terms. In the new relationship with the United States, the familial ties are absent, whereas
the means of regional and global military and economic coercion
are immeasurably stronger.

The State in present-day capitalist societies depends, as does
just about everything else, on the vagaries of economic life, and so
the future of the Australian State is likely to be shaped through its
economic dependence on a world economy that is politically controlled ever more tightly by transnational corporations and international economic organisations (such as the IMF, the World
Bank, and the OECD) that are dominated by the United States
and other major centres of world capital. This represents an
especially acute danger for Australia because, in contrast to the
member countries of the EEC, it is unprotected by regional ties
and, more importantly, because short-term multinational finance
capital continues to displace more productive domestic industrial
investment as it presses ever more relentlessly for both a larger
share and an upward redistribution of the nation's income. Under
the banners of 'economic rationalism' ('deregulation', 'privatisation'
and 'structural reform') this process goes on at the expense not
only of local manufacturing industry and of Australian wage and
salary earners, but also of the third actor, the State, which alone
has the power to protect Australian assets and to secure an equitable
distribution of the nation's wealth (Pusey 1991). By 1992
'economic rationalist' policies had reduced employment in
manufacturing industry to only 16 per cent of the workforce;
produced an unemployment rate of over 10 per cent and large
falls in real wages of employed workers; they had given Australia a
deregulated and unstable currency, the highest real interests in
the world, and a huge national debt amounting to some 43 per
cent of GDP and, by OECD standards, an underfunded and
starving public sector. Internally this had greatly reduced the
'relative autonomy' of the State and its authority over business

and investment, and left Australia more dependent on and exposed to a global economy that cares nothing for the interests of ordinary Australians.

So in this last decade of the twentieth century, the maturity of a nation and the distinctiveness of its institutions seem set for some gruelling trials. In the middle of the century Australians enjoyed very high living standards and the most equal distribution of income in the world. These great benefits were the achievements of a nation that was 'born modern' and which developed its own distinctive political and social democracy that placed great trust in the State. As a nation-society Australia has relied more than the United States and Britain on the co-ordinating work of state and bureaucracy, and comparatively less on markets and money. Indeed, it is part of the Australian legacy that the State should lead and that capital should follow.

This legacy produced a new and largely post-World War ll Canberra federal state apparatus that was never weighed down by old world aristocratic cultures and class allegiances. In the 1960s and the 70s, Canberra had what was perhaps one of the best and most highly professionalised public services in the world, less effete and introverted than the 'Yes, Minister' Whitehall Civil Service and certainly less politically compromised by big business interests than Washington. As with France, Australia's history and political culture have given bureaucracy and administration an empowering legitimacy that was, we thought, deeply engrained in the long-held belief that commissions, Royal and unroyal, tribunals, boards, and committees of inqiry, *can and should* serve and represent the general interest.[15]

As we have seen, Australia has in this respect been the exception among 'developed' English-speaking nations, and it is for just this reason that the integrity of Australia's institutional legacy will be tested in the 1990s against the pressures of an invasive free market economic 'rationalism' that came in the 1980s mainly from Britain and the United States. As always with smaller and dependent nations, the fate of the Australian pattern of development will be decided by contests among other nations. Three broad possiblilities are represented: by authoritarian business democracies of the rapidly-developing nations of south east Asia; by the social democracies of Western Europe; and, thirdly, by the free market economic 'rationalism' of the United States and Britain that Australia tried to emulate in the 1980s. Clearly the expectations of ordinary Australians for pluralist social democracy and a more equitable distribution of income point towards Western European models. The political preferences of the New Right élites that captured so much of Canberra in the 1980s led instead (probably at the moment of failure) to the American and British models. Now that Britain is finally part of the EEC, regional economic geography points Australia more strongly towards south-east Asia. How we will fare in our approach to the new millennium is entirely uncertain, and dependent on the perseverance of political and cultural norms and expectations in the face of the adverse pressures of the 'economic rationalism' that has so dominated the 1980s (Pusey 1991: 208–42). Too much optimism would be foolish.

Notes

1. I wish to express my gratitude in particular to four people, Tim Rowse, Robert van Krieken, Trevor Matthews, and Brian Head, who read the draft of this chapter and gave me some much needed and extremely constructive criticism. I would also like to thank Kees Steps and Alec Pusey. The responsibility for the flaws that remain is all mine.
2. See Chapter 5 for comparisons with Australia, and note Lipset's very American perspective that gives almost no importance to the State.
3. 'Relative autonomy' is a term originally coined by Poulantzas, and taken up in a debate with Miliband in the early 1970s. Although it is now a commonly accepted term the notion still occasions much debate — see for example the discussion between Theda Skocpol and Ralph Miliband that can be taken up through Ralph Miliband's 1983 'State Power and Class Interests', *New Left Review* 138: 57–68, and Skocpol's 1980 'Political Response to Capitalist Crisis: Neo-Marxist Theories of the State and the Case of the New Deal', *Politics and Society* 10: 155–201.
4. The important distinction between 'strong' and 'weak' States is generally attributed to Stephen Krasner. See his excellent 1984 review article, 'Approaches to the State; Alternative Conceptions and Historical Dynamics', *Comparative Politics* 16 (2), January: 223–44, and follow the connections back to its origins in the path-breaking 1968 article by J.P. Nettl, 'The State as a Conceptual Variable', *World Politics* 20, July: 557–84, and then forwards to Skocpol's work.
5. Rosecrance, p. 310.
6. The quotation marks for 'principles' here as for 'must' in the preceding paragraph are intended to indicate that there is nothing inexorably given about these 'principles'. They are, as I indicated, descriptive and not normative ones. There is no independent 'functional necessity'.
7. 'Staples economies' are those such as Canada, Argentina, and Australia which are, or were, heavily dependent on the world economy as producers of staples such as wheat, wool, meat etc. Malcolm Alexander, who explains the relevance of staples theory and its

relevance to Australia, attributes it to Canadian political economists and principally to the work of Harold Innis. See Alexander in Head.

8. Contrasts and similarities with the early development of Canada, Argentina and Brazil are available in an interesting 1983 discussion by M.L. Alexander, 'Australia in the Capitalist World Economy', in B. Head (ed.), *State and Economy in Australia*, Oxford University Press.

9. In this discussion I am heavily indebted to Stuart MacIntyre's excellent 1983 chapter, 'Labour, Capital and Arbitration 1890–1920', in Head, and also to MacIntyre's 1985 *Winners and Losers*, Allen and Unwin.

10. Although the judgment was subsequently overturned by the High Court it is of no less significance as a watershed in the linkage forged through the State between wage and tariff policies. This is discussed by MacIntyre in the Head collection, pp. 106–10, and in Chapter 3, 'A Fair Wage' in MacIntyre 1985.

11. This shift, which only caught public attention in the Fraser years, had been going on for years. Connell and Irving (p. 306) show that even in 1969, at the peak of the boom years, as many as one-third of the 150,000 registered companies in Australia recorded no profits in their annual returns.

12. It is Nettl who first treated the locus of sovereignty as an important variable among different states, and within this context dealt with these characteristics of the United States. The point has been taken up by Skocpol and Krasner, among others.

13. Politics as 'the authoritative allocation of values' (of all kinds, both material and non-material) is a widely used and largely liberal notion that comes from D. Easton, (1953) *The Political System* and it is clearly explained in the context of the State in Poggi, *The Development of the Modern State*, Chapter 1.

14. The attitude of British liberalism is nowhere more beautifully expressed than in the words of Lord Palmerston to Queen Victoria in 1837: 'Bureaucracy is a bad European system of government, created by the use of permanent public officials, a system that does not, should not, and cannot exist in England' (quoted in Encel, p. 58).

15. In French the phrase *l'intérêt général* conveys this with special authority, and is the legitimating idea *par excellence* of the French bureaucratic system. The roots of course, go back to Rousseau, the Revolution, and the consolidation of the Napoleonic bureaucratic state.

References

Aberbach, J.D., Putnam, R.D. and Rockman, B.A. (1981) *Bureaucrats and Politicians in Western Democracies*. Cambridge: Harvard University Press.

Albinski, H. (1985) 'Australia and the United States', in *Australia: The Daedalus Symposium*. Sydney: Angus and Robertson.

Badie, B. and Birnbaum, P. *The Sociology of the State*. Chicago: Chicago University Press.

Birnbaum, P. (1977) *Les Sommets de l'Etat*. Paris, Editions du Seuil, translated as *The Heights of Power*. Chicago: Chicago University Press.

────── (1980) 'States, Ideologies and Collective Action in Western Europe', *International Social Science Journal* XXXII (4): 671–86.

Butlin, N.G. (1983) 'Trends in Public/Private Relations, 1901–75', in Head, B. (ed.), Butlin, N.G., Barnard, A. Pincus, J.J. (1982) *Government and Capitalism*. Sydney: Allen and Unwin.

Collins, H. (1985) 'Political Ideology in Australia: The Distinctiveness of a Benthamite Society', *Australia: The Daedalus Symposium*. Sydney: Angus and Robertson.

Connell, R.W. and Irving, T.H. (1980) *Class Structure in Australian History*. Melbourne: Cheshire.

Crozier, M., Huntington, P., Watanuki, J. (eds) (1975) *The Crisis of Democracy*. New York: New York University Press.

Davies, A.F. (1964) *Australian Democracy*. Melbourne: Longman Cheshire.

Encel, S (1970) *Equality and Authority*. Melbourne: Cheshire.

Easton, D. (1953) *The Political System*. New York.

Evans, P., Rueschemeyer, D. and Skocpol, T. (eds) (1985) *Bringing the State Back In*. New York: Cambridge University Press.

Groenwegen, P. (1983) 'The Political Economy of Federalism, 1901–81', in Head, B. (ed.).

Head, B.W. (ed.) (1983) *State and Economy in Australia*. Melbourne: Oxford University Press.

────── (1984) 'Fragmentation, Federalism and Resources: the Australian State in the 1980s', *Australian and New Zealand Journal of Sociology*, November 1984.

────── (ed.) (1986) *Politics of Development in Australia*. Sydney: Allen and Unwin.

Held, D. et al. (eds.) (1983) *States and Societies*. Oxford: Martin Robertson.

Hofstadter, R. (1963) *Anti-Intellectualism in American Life*. New York: Alfred Knopf.

Horne, D. (1985) 'Who Rules Australia?', in *Australia: The Daedalus Symposium*. Sydney: Angus and Robertson.

Lipset, S.M. (1963) *The First New Nation*. New York: Basic Books.

MacIntyre, S. (1983) 'Labour, Capital and Arbitration, 1890–1920', in Head, B. (ed.).

MacIntyre, S. (1985) *Winners and Losers*. Sydney: Allen and Unwin.

Pusey, M. (1991) *Economic Rationalism in Canberra: A Nation-Building State Changes its Mind*, Cambridge: Cambridge University Press.

Rosecrance, R. (1964) *The Radical Culture of Australia*, in Hactz, L. (ed.) *The Founding of New Societies*. New York: Harcourt Brace.

Rowse, T. (1978) *Australian Liberalism and National Character*. Melbourne: Kibble Books.

Stretton, H. (1985) 'The Quality of Leading Australians', in Graubard,

S. (ed.), *Australia: The Daedalus Symposium*. Sydney: Angus and Robertson.

Skocpol, T. (1980) 'Political Response to Capitalist Crisis: Neo-Marxist Theories of the State and the Case of the New Deal', *Politics and Society* 10: 155–201.

Szelenyi, I. (1980) 'The Relative Autonomy of the State or State Mode of Production', in Dear, M. and Scott, M. (eds), *Urbanisation and Urban Planning in Capitalist Society*. Methuen.

Treasury Economic Roundup (1990) Canberra: Australian Government Printer.

Year Book Australia 54 (1968) Canberra: Commonwealth Bureau of Census and Statistics.

Chapter Three

Class and Stratification

Mark Western

Questions relating to class and social stratification are at the centre of sociological analysis. When we examine class and stratification we are dealing with fundamental topics relating to the basic structure of society. In this chapter we consider three sociological perspectives that address issues of class and stratification in Australia. Each of these tries to develop a framework for understanding the Australian social structure, and relates this to the social patterning of power and inequality. Common to all three approaches is the view that Australian society, like other's is neither an undifferentiated mass of people with identical interests and concerns, nor simply an aggregation of isolated and unique individuals. Rather, the key to understanding it is its group structure. Even more specifically, each of the three approaches deals with the group structure that has its origin in paid work and economic relationships.[1]

Two of the three perspectives are concerned with the analysis of classes. The common idea that unites them is that the economic dimension of the social structure is best understood as a *class structure* comprising different and somewhat distinct classes. As we shall see, the precise definition of class has been much debated in sociology, but in general a person's class membership is determined by job characteristics, such as whether she is self-employed or works for someone else. In Australian sociology there are two broad traditions of *class analysis* that we shall focus upon one influenced by Karl Marx, and another inspired by Max Weber.

The third perspective, *social stratificationism*, has its intellectual origins in the French sociology of Emile Durkheim, but in the Australian context is derived more directly from American sociology of the 1950s and 60s. Unlike the class analytic perspectives influenced by Marx and Weber, stratificationist sociology typically does not concern itself with classes. However, despite stratificationists and class analysts talking about different, albeit related, social phenomema, sociologists sometimes use the words 'class' and 'stratification' almost interchangeably, or argue that 'stratification' is an encompassing topic that includes class analysis. In this chapter I try to show that class analytic and stratificationist approaches differ broadly in the way the economic component of the social structure is conceived. For class analysts, whether Marxist or Weberian, the class structure consists of a relatively small number of fairly discrete class categories that exist in relationship to each other. These categories are defined in terms of the characteristics of people's jobs. On the other hand, social stratificationism theorises the occupational structure as a continuous hierarchy of occupations that runs from low to high on some attribute(s). There are no qualitative 'breaks' between occupations or groups of occupations, as there are between classes.

Despite this basic difference in conceptions of social structure, class analysis and social stratification share a concern with three common questions: What does the class structure or stratification hierarchy look like? What processes influence the social positions that people come to occupy as adults? What effects does social location have on people's lives? The first question asks how the class structure or stratification hierarchy is defined. The second asks why some people occupy positions of relative power and privilege while others occupy positions of relative social disadvantage. The third examines the consequences or outcomes of class membership or position in the stratification hierarchy. In particular, two general types of outcome are associated with social position. First, social location is systematically related to people's attitudes, beliefs and behaviour. Second, social location is related to social inequality, the unequal distribution of valued goods and resources, like income, wealth, leisure time and facilities, access to health care, education, and so on (Western 1983: 6).

These three questions are obviously interrelated. Different definitions of social structure suggest different ways of acquiring social positions, and different consequences of being part of a social group. Furthermore, a person's social position as an adult depends in part on her social position as a child, so the way she acquires a position in the social structure is itself a consequence of her social background.

The three sociological perspectives, Marxist and Weberian class analysis, and social stratificationism, have each given these three substantive questions varying degrees of attention. In general, recent Marxist class analysis has concentrated on the first question, and to a lesser extent, addressed the other two. Weberian class analysis has been less concerned than Marxist sociology to define class structure precisely. But Weberians have paid relatively more attention to how people come to be members of classes. Social stratificationism has tended to combine the second and third questions. In particular, social stratificationists have concentrated on what determines a person's position in the stratification hierarchy, and the further implications of social stratification for social inequality.

In practice, none of the three perspectives provides complete answers to all three questions. However, by considering the major approaches to class and stratification within sociology, I aim to provide an overview of the area, and illustrate the similarities and differences of various perspectives. The structure of the chapter is as follows: first, I present a brief exposition of (some of) Marx's and Weber's ideas about class analysis. Much of today's class analysis draws explicitly on such ideas, so being familiar with the work of Marx and Weber helps make sense of contemporary research. Unlike class analysis, social stratificationism does not draw as self-consciously upon 'classical sociology'. Consequently, I do not examine the intellectual origins of this approach. Having briefly described the work of Marx and Weber, I present some of the Australian research in class and stratification, showing how it addresses the three analytical questions already mentioned. Finally I conclude with a brief appraisal of the differing perspectives, and a description of some areas for future research.

The European Tradition: Marx and Weber on Class Analysis

Before considering Australian class analysis, we need to deal with the work of Karl Marx (1818–1883) and Max Weber (1864–1920). Their analyses represent probably the most influential legacy left to modern sociologists who concern themselves with questions of class, power and inequality. Any discussion of the emergence of class analysis necessarily starts with the work of Karl Marx, for although he was not the first person to propose a theory of class, the perspective he developed was arguably 'immensely more compelling'

(Giddens 1981: 24) than that of other writers of his time. So powerful were Marx's ideas, that they still constitute the reference point for much contemporary class analysis. Although he never provided an explicit definition of the concept, class is central to all Marx's political, economic, and historical studies (Bottomore 1965: 17; Hall 1977). Given the scope of Marx's work, the account I am providing is both simplified and abbreviated.

There is much disagreement about what 'Marx actually said' regarding class. This arises partly because he used the term in various ways with differing intentions. In general there are two senses in which Marx talks about classes (Lee and Newby 1983: 120). First is his abstract analytical usage when referring to particular kinds of economic and social relationships. Second is his more concrete, descriptive sense when referring to actual groups of people (for example, landowners, the aristocracy, even a servant class of 'men-servants, women-servants and lackeys' (Marx [1867] 1976: 574)). In this second case, Marx often uses the word 'class' quite loosely, sometimes categorising as classes groups of people who, according to his more theoretical writings, are not strictly classes at all. This confusion is further compounded because Marx's abstract theoretical writings about class comprise both a general theory of historical and social change, and a specific theoretical account of classes in capitalist society (Giddens 1981: Ch.1). Marx's general theory of the historical development of classes, historical materialism, is supposed to be relevant for all societies. It describes the economic and social organisation of societies, indicating how the economic structure fundamentally determines other aspects of social structure and social life. It outlines how social change from one type of class society to another occurs, and describes the stages of development societies pass through in the transition to an ultimately classless, communist society. The specific analysis of capitalism uses the basic ideas of historical materialism to analyse capitalist economic and social organisation. The important insights for us are the theoretical/analytical ones, particularly those that pertain to capitalist societies like Australia.

For Marx, class analysis is based upon production. Production of goods and services is one of the fundamental activities in any society. At a subsistence level, people need to produce basic require-ments like food and shelter, simply in order to survive. However, as the quantity of goods and services produced exceeds the subsistence requirements of most of the population, classes and class-based inequality become possible (Carling 1991: 13). To understand how this occurs it is necessary to recognise that human production is social, rather than individual. People produce things together. The relationships between people involved in production are the defining criteria for classes.

More specifically, Marx argued that in all capitalist societies there is a group of people who own the means of production, the technical facilities and property used in production, and a group of people (direct producers) who work using these. The means of production include things such as land, equipment, machinery, warehouses, and so on. Owners of the means of production are the *bourgeoisie* or *capitalists*. People without productive property are compelled to work in order to live. In capitalist societies, these are the *working class* or *proletariat*, employed by capitalists to use the means of production to produce goods or services for sale (Marx and Engels [1848] 1958: 34).

Marx's definition of class is an inherently relational one. Classes are defined in terms of their relationship to the means of production, and by their relationship to each other. The existence of one class (owners) presupposes the existence of the other (workers) (Giddens 1981: 28). The basic class structure of capitalist society comprises capitalists and workers, defined by their economic position within production.

A central feature of this relationship is that it is exploitative: in Marx's view, capitalists exploit workers. Although the word 'exploitation' implies a moral judgement about the relationship between capitalists and workers, for Marx, the existence of exploitation was also an objective fact about the relationship between the two classes.

To explain further, in the economic analysis of capitalism contained in two of Marx's later works, *Grundrisse* (Marx [1858] 1973) and *Capital* (Marx [1867] 1976), a key problem which Marx tried to solve was the source of the continual surplus of goods and services above subsistence levels. How is capitalism continually able to produce a surplus from which capitalists derive their profits? The answer, Marx felt, lay in the transaction between capitalists and workers. In exchange for wages, the worker sells to the capitalist *labour power*, the capacity to turn raw materials into products for sale. While the wages earned by workers must be sufficient to buy what they need to sustain and reproduce themselves and their families (food, shelter, clothing, consumer goods and the like), the value of what they produce is determined by factors such as the level of technology, the production methods used, technical organisation of work, scientific knowledge and the rhythm and pace of work. All of these aspects of production to do with methods of production Marx referred to as *forces of production*. These encompass the means of production (productive property) referred to earlier, but additionally include non-material aspects of production, such as scientific and technical knowledge. Thus while workers' wages are determined by the amount required for their reproduction, productivity is determined by the level of development of the forces of production. In general, Marx argued, workers will produce more in a day, for example, than is required for their reproduction. This *surplus value* accrues to the capitalist. If, in an eight-hour day, it takes a worker two hours to produce goods equivalent to the value of her wages, for the remaining six hours she is creating surplus value for her employer. This process, in which workers produce surplus value, and capitalists take possession of it, is what Marx means by exploitation (Edel 1981).

But Marx was not simply interested in defining class structures and identifying classes. His class analysis incorporates a theory of historical development from tribal society, through slavery (as in ancient Greece and Rome) feudalism, capitalism, socialism and communism. In this theory, the basic agents of historical change are classes.

The Manifesto of the Communist Party proposed a straightforward explanation of the role classes play in social change (Marx and Engels [1848] 1958). Nineteenth-century European society, was gradually being split 'into two hostile camps' (Marx and Engels [1848] 1958: 35), comprising the proletariat and the bourgeoisie. The middle class (tradespeople, craftworkers, shopkeepers) was being forced into the proletariat, and increased competition was driving inefficient capitalists out of business, and forcing them to become wage labourers. Eventually society would reach a stage where the two classes could no longer coexist. As industrial development continued, the antagonism and opposition of interests between capitalists and workers would become more apparent. Under these circumstances workers would become aware of their class unity, conscious of their opposition to capitalists, and politically organised. A *class-in-itself* becomes a *class-for-itself*, a class with a common consciousness and a political organisation. The result is a proletarian revolution in which private ownership of the means of production is abolished, and a new society without classes emerges (Marx and Engels [1848] 1955: 54).

Now there has never anywhere been a socialist, working class revolution of this type. The view Marx expressed in the *Manifesto* is a simplistic one, and the *Manifesto* itself is a programmatic, political text, rather than a detailed theoretical analysis of the transition from capitalism to socialism. However, Marx's argument in the *Communist Manifesto* demonstrates that Marx's own analysis is dynamic, with an internal theory of social change. Economic breakdown, class consciousness, and collective organisation or *class struggle* are the significant elements of this theory.

Politics and collective action are ultimately traced back to economic causes based upon the conflict of interests between owners of productive property and direct producers.

Marx's views on the relationship between class and social change outside the *Communist Manifesto* have been subject to a great deal of reinterpretation and debate. Even among Marxists there is disagreement, not only about how Marx's theory of historical change should be construed, but also about whether a general theory of the transformation from one kind of class society to another is tenable. These debates are well outside the scope of this chapter. Later I will, however, suggest some ways of thinking about social change. But there is no need to engage in a theoretical discussion of historical materialism to do this.

Whereas Marx never explicitly defined class, Max Weber directly addressed this question twice. This occurs in two sections of his seminal work, *Economy and Society* (Weber 1978). In contrasting Marx's and Weber's views, there are probably two kinds of important differences worth noting. First Marx and Weber disagree about the importance of economic criteria for explaining group formation and inequality. Put briefly, Weber asserts that non-economic criteria, like race or ethnicity, are as important sources of group formation and social action as economic ones. Second, there are specific definitional differences in the concepts of class that the two employed.

For Marx, the defining elements of class were given by social relationships in production. For Weber, *class situation*, the class circumstance of an individual, is based in the market. Weber does not mean an actual, physical market. Rather, the market is an abstract concept describing the arena in which buyers and sellers come together to exchange goods and services. An individual's class situation reflects the kinds of economic resources she or he has, which can be sold in the market to earn rewards, such as income, promotional opportunities and good working conditions. In other words, class situation, for Weber, reflects not how you relate to the means of production and other people in the production process (as it does for Marx), but what you have, and can bargain with for rewards in the market.

Weber called these rewards and social opportunities *life chances*. Like Marx, Weber makes a fundamental distinction between people who own productive property, and people who don't. In capitalist societies there are therefore two *property classes*: the propertied and the non-propertied (Weber 1982a). Unlike Marx, though, Weber recognised that other kinds of economic resources also generate rewards. The propertyless might have particular 'marketable skills' for which there is a demand. Privileged *commercial classes* (Weber

1982b), individuals with sought-after skills, or who provide valued services include various skilled workers and professionals, such as doctors, lawyers, engineers or computer experts. Students doing vocational and university courses to improve their chances in the job market are trying to acquire the kinds of marketable skills to which Weber refers.

Unlike Marx, Weber did not believe that people in similar class situations would necessarily develop a common awareness of class inequality, and act in an organised way. Under certain circumstances this might happen; often, however, it doesn't (Weber 1982b). Unlike Marx, then, Weber does not see any necessary relationship between common class membership, group formation, and social change. Classes have no basic priority as the fundamental agents of social change, as they do for Marx, because Weber did not believe that classes had eventually to organise into collective entities.

To illustrate how classes might become collectivities, Weber introduces the concept of *social class*. The class situation of an individual describes the particular combination of property and marketable skills she is able to bargain with in the market. There are potentially as many market situations as there are people, because each person could differ slightly regarding the kinds of property or skills possessed (Giddens 1981: 48). However, in general some market situations are very similar to one another, in the sense that there is a reasonably high probability of mobility or movement of people between them. Mobility between market situations may take place over a person's lifetime as she moves from one job to another. Mobility may also be intergenerational— encompassing parents' and children's jobs—when the son of a bank teller becomes a clerk in the Public Service for example. Weber defines a social class as the cluster of market situations characterised by high levels of such interchange or mobility (Weber 1982b).

Four social classes exist in capitalist societies like Australia: the *working class* comprising skilled, semi- and unskilled manual workers; the *petit bourgeoisie* who are 'own account' workers, self-employed but without employees; the *middle class* of 'propertyless intelligentsia and specialists' (Weber 1982b: 72), including white collar workers, technicians, and semi-professionals; and finally those 'privileged through property and education' (Weber 1982b: 72), the owners of large enterprises, managers and professionals.

In describing the social class structure of capitalist societies Weber begins to treat classes as discrete groups. Social classes are real groups of people in a way that individual market situations are not. However 'groupness', for Weber, is much more a feature of *status groups* than classes. Status groups are the second type of group in the social structure that Weber identified. Unlike classes, status groups are not economically determined. They are typically communities, groups of people with a common lifestyle, who are distinguished from others because of a specific non-economic, social characteristic (Weber 1982a).

Possible criteria for status group formation include age, race, gender, religion, ethnicity and region. Crucial to Weber's concept of status is his assumption that the status situation of people is determined by estimations of social honour or prestige. Within a status group, certain kinds of behaviour are typically regarded as being appropriate for members of the group, while others are inappropriate. When status criteria are important elements of social structure, status groups will have different levels of prestige or social honour, according to the kinds of lifestyles and behaviours their members exhibit. In a status group based around neighbourhood residence, for example, lifestyle differences may be evident in the kinds of car(s) people own, what they do in their leisure time, the clubs and organisations they belong to, whether their children attend private or state schools and so on. Furthermore, different ways of life may lead to status groups being ranked on some sort of prestige hierarchy by all members of the community, with general consensus about where groups are located. We shall see this more clearly in some of the Australian studies we consider later in the chapter.[2]

Class and status are two sources of group formation. For Weber, the group structure of any society reflects the relative importance of economic, market factors, which give rise to classes, and social status criteria like race, gender or neighbourhood, which lead to status group formation. In a community, or the wider society, class and status principles may overlap, as when people in the same social class are also in the same status group(s). Class and status may also cross-cut one another in varying ways.

The third type of group which Weber identifies, the *party*, differs from classes and status groups in that it does not represent a separate basis for group formation; rather it refers to the form or structure that a group takes. In Weber's terms, parties are *rational organisations*, collectivities organised with specific goals in mind, whose members act according to calculative or planned strategies to achieve these ends (Weber 1982a). Typically, parties have a bureaucratic structure, with written rules or a constitution, and a clear hierarchy of positions to which people are appointed according to specified criteria, such as election. Political parties are the most obvious kind of organisation that Weber has in mind, although any association which is bureaucratically organised in pursuit of established goals is a party. A football or Rotary club, and the Australian Medical Association are all parties in the Weberian sense of the term.

Note the difference between parties, on the one hand, and classes and status groups on the other. While classes and status groups are differentiated according to the attributes which are the basis for group formation, parties are distinguished in terms of their structure and goal orientation. As such, parties can be organisations which represent classes or status groups. The ACTU and the AMA can be thought of as parties representing classes or segments of classes, while a local community organisation, like a residents' association, is a party that represents some kind of status group.

This very brief treatment of Marx's and Weber's ideas illustrates some of the theoretical and conceptual issues that contemporary Australian sociologists have taken up. In the next section of the chapter, I describe some of this research, paying particular attention to the way the different perspectives approach the analytical questions with which class analysis and social stratificationism are concerned.

Class and Stratification in Australia

The three kinds of questions that motivate research into class and stratification are as follows: What does the social structure look like? How do people come to occupy socio-structural positions? What consequences follow from socio-structural location? Before addressing these questions, however, it is necessary to clarify what makes Australia a 'capitalist society'. Capitalism provides the economic context within which class and stratification research is situated. Once I have described Australian capitalism, I shall take each of the perspectives and indicate how it has dealt with the questions at issue.

Capitalism: The Australian Context

In purely abstract terms, capitalism has several elements: the economy is primarily based upon the private ownership of productive property and the employment of non-propertied wage and salary earners; goods and services are produced for sale, rather than direct use; goods and services are sold in competitive markets; continued profitability is necessary for enterprises to survive (Burawoy and Krotov 1992; Giddens 1991: 55).

These features define capitalism abstractly. But in actually existing capitalist societies the situation is obviously more complicated. In Australia, as in other capitalist countries, market activities are substantially regulated by the government. Placing tariffs and duties on imported goods, subsidising domestic producers, and regulating the wages and working conditions of employees are all examples of state activity restricting the free operation of market mechanisms. In addition, according to the 1986 Census, approximately 26 per cent of the total workforce, or 31 per cent of employees, do not work in the private sector, but for various levels of government (Australian Bureau of Statistics 1989a, Tables C29 and C33). Nonetheless, despite substantial government involvement, the economy is still distinctively capitalist. Goods and services are overwhelmingly produced in the private sector, to be sold for profit, and most people have to work, or depend on someone else who works, to maintain their livelihood.

Historically, Australia, like other British colonies, had capitalism 'imposed' upon it, from Britain. In the Australian case, capitalism emerged between white settlement in 1788, and Federation, in 1901. In this time, Australia went from being a penal colony, administered externally from Britain, to a self-governing liberal-capitalist democracy.

Several excellent accounts exist of the emergence of capitalism in colonial Australia (for example Connell and Irving 1980; McMichael 1984; Wells 1989). Although there are disagreements about specific details, the basic features are reasonably clear. From 1788 to the 1840s and 50s, capitalist property relations were introduced to the colonies, substantially encouraged by the imperial (that is British) government. Through the Governor and his representatives, the imperial state regulated the assignment of convict labour and the distribution of land. The British government also encouraged free settlers to emigrate, first by promising land grants and convict labour to British capitalists, and later by financing assisted migration. The first strategy encouraged the development of a local capitalist class, while the second provided a pool of wage labour (Wells 1989: 42–49). Between about 1860 and 1890, Australian capitalism boomed, and was integrated into an imperial economic system centred on Britain. The key to this economic expansion was agricultural and mineral production (wool, beef, gold) for export to Britain. This activity was largely financed by British capitalists, either through direct investment or loans to Australian entrepreneurs. During this time the colonial governments also helped establish capitalism, borrowing extensively on the British financial market to fund the development of essential transport and communications infrastructure (like railways, wharves and the postal system), which were too costly and unprofitable to be provided by private enterprise (Connell and Irving 1980: Ch. 3). The late 1880s and early 1890s saw the development of an organised union movement and the formation of the (then) Labour Party. During the early 1890s, several major strikes occurred, prompted by worsening economic conditions arising from falling international wool prices, and the declining availability of British capital to fund private and public investment. In the associated Depression, the labour movement was largely defeated: wages and working conditions deteriorated, union membership fell, and unemployment increased. Bankruptcies were common, and the lack of British funding caused economic and political instability among colonial governments. All of these factors contributed to widespread support for Federation. It was widely believed that a federal system would help regulate working conditions and wages, and manage immigration, borrowing and taxation at a national level (Wells 1989: Chapter 9).

The history of the development of capitalism in Australia, then, is one of *mercantile capitalism*, capitalism based around extensive primary production for trade with Britain. Economic expansion was driven by this activity. The most profitable sectors of the economy were in primary production (farming, pastoralism, mining) and activities related to primary production and trade (banking, shipping, real estate, commerce) (Wells 1989: 147–50). Moreover, capitalist economic activity was very significantly state-assisted, first by the imperial government in England, and second by the colonial governments. Finally, Australia depended upon primary production and trade right up until the 1940s, and has never substantially relied upon secondary or manufacturing industry. Some industrialisation did occur in the first half of the twentieth century (Connell and Irving 1980: Chapter 5), but the process was not as far-reaching as in older capitalist countries like Britain or the United States (see Mullins' chapter).

From World War II to the present, the Australian economy has become increasingly integrated into a world economic system. Foreign investment from the United States, and later Japan, has been especially important, particularly in mining, steel making, and the motor industry (Connell and Irving 1980: 292–97; Boreham, Clegg, Emmison, Marks and Western 1989). Trade relations have also shifted from Britain, to the United States and Japan. Along with the penetration of the Australian economy by transnational corporations have come changes in the organisation of work. Increasingly, control over production is vested with managers, rather than legal owners of productive property. Managers have many of the traditional responsibilities of property owners, such as the ability to make decisions about production methods and the use of organisational resources, but they lack formal legal ownership of corporate assets. As production processes become more complex and specialised, there has also been a growth in the number of professional and technical workers, foremen/supervisors, clerical and sales personnel (see J.S. Western 1991 for some data to this effect). Finally, there is an increasing tendency for companies to be major shareholders in other companies (Connell 1991).

This increasing complexity of the occupational structure poses a major challenge to researchers in class and stratification. With the economic context established, we can now consider how they have proceeded. We begin with Marxist class analysis.

Marxist Class Analysis
The common idea that unites Marxist research is that, as a capitalist society, Australia is subject to class domination by a capitalist ruling class. It is important to be clear about what this means. It does *not* mean that there is some kind of deliberate capitalist conspiracy to control Australian society. Rather, class domination means that the organisation of economic activity around private ownership and profits shapes other areas of social life, such as politics, industrial relations, and people's attitudes on class-related issues, and helps maintain class inequality. Because the economy depends upon private ownership of productive property, everybody has some kind of interest in continued capitalist profitability. Capitalists have a direct interest in continued profits because their incomes come directly from profits. But profits also fund future investment in new and continuing capitalist enterprises. Without investment, there is no employment, and without employment and profits, government revenues that are obtained through taxation will eventually run down (Cohen and Rogers 1983: 52–53; Przeworski 1980; Przeworski and Wallerstein 1982). Consequently, the capitalist organisation of production creates a general dependence throughout society on capitalist profitability, under which it is necessary to satisfy capitalists' interests to meet the interests of others in the system. However, satisfying the interests of capitalists involves exploiting workers and perpetuating class inequality. Capitalism therefore creates a 'systemic dependence' upon capitalist production relations, even among those who are disadvantaged under capitalism. This dependence, and the tendency it implies for capitalist inequality to be maintained over time, is what Marxists mean when they speak of class domination by a capitalist ruling class (Connell 1977: Chapter 3).

Defining the Class Structure
This notion of class domination is important for making sense of what the Australian class structure looks like. As you might expect

from the history of Australian capitalism presented above, a traditional two-class model of capitalists and workers is insufficient to address some of the specific questions with which class analysis is concerned. Dealing with the 'problem' of a 'middle class' of professional, technical and managerial workers, has been one of the key tasks of much recent Marxist and Weberian class analysis. In Marxist sociology, probably the most developed attempt to address this issue has come from the American sociologist Erik Olin Wright. Wright has actually presented two accounts of the class structure of capitalist societies (Wright 1978, 1985). The second supersedes the first, which he believes was flawed in various ways. In this chapter, I describe the second account only.

Wright begins with the basic Marxist (and Weberian) distinction between who owns productive property, and who must work for someone else for a living. However, unlike Marx, Wright does not believe all employees have the same class location. In particular, managers and supervisors—who control the technical aspects of production, make organisational decisions, and supervise other employees—should be differentiated from non-managers. Similarly, skilled professional and technical employees ('experts' in Wright's terminology) should be distinguished from employees without substantial skills.

Wright justifies these arguments by noting that productive property, skills, and managerial control all enable people to demand access to the social product, the goods and services that are produced within a society. However, through their ownership or control of productive property, skills and organisational resources, capitalists, experts and managers can claim a disproportionate share of what is produced. Under these circumstances, capitalists, managers, and experts necessarily take over part of the social product that has been produced by members of another class. In this sense they exploit the direct producers (Wright, Howe and Cho 1989). After property ownership, organisational control and skill are therefore *secondary mechanisms of exploitation* in capitalist societies.

Capitalists exploit workers by drawing income from profits. Since they do not directly produce goods and services themselves, their rights to profits necessarily imply they appropriate commodities produced by someone else (Wright 1986). Capitalist exploitation is equivalent to Marx's notion of exploitation based on surplus value (Roemer 1982).

Managers and experts exploit non-managers and non-experts, respectively, by using organisational control or skills to claim high incomes.[3] Managers are able to claim high incomes because their organisational power within a firm enables them to influence things like profit levels and operating costs. However, it is difficult for an employer to punish managers for decisions that adversely affect a firm's profitability, since, with the emergence of companies, legal ownership and organisational control are separated, as I described above. Under this organisational structure, managers rather than employers are responsible for monitoring employees' job performance. As a result, employers must try to buy managers' loyalty to the firm, by paying them high incomes. Since these benefits also derive from the sale of commodities produced by non-managerial workers, managers exploit non-managers.[4]

Among experts, high incomes occur because expert jobs frequently involve restrictions on who is eligible to undertake such work. The most obvious example is in professions like medicine and law, which limit the number of medical practitioners and lawyers, by helping regulate the numbers of students going into law and medicine, controlling the training procedures, requiring a process of registration or certification before people can practise, and so on. While these procedures are in part necessary to establish standardised levels of competence, they also severely restrict the number of doctors and lawyers. This scarcity enables professionals to demand high incomes, because they possess rare skills which employers are willing to pay for. If restrictions on expert jobs were relaxed, the supply of professionals would increase, and their incomes would fall, other things being equal (Wright 1985: Chapter 3, 1988). Like managers and capitalists, the high incomes of experts translate into a disproportionate share of what is produced in a society, and consequently, experts also exploit non-experts.[5] Treating experts and managers in this way illustrates the idea of class domination, because at least part of managers' and experts' incomes depend on employers being able to meet such costs out of profits (see also Connell 1991: 145).

Using these arguments, we can define the class structure. The fundamental distinction is between owners of productive property and non-owners. This reflects the argument that exploitation based on productive property is the key element of the class structure of capitalist societies. Among owners of productive property we can distinguish among the *petit bourgeoisie*, who own only limited property which they have to work themselves; small employers, who have enough property to be able to employ a few people to work for them; and the bourgeoisie, or capitalists proper, who have many employees.

Among non-owners of the means of production we can distinguish among people according to their organisational control and occupational skill. If we treat each secondary dimension of exploitation as having three levels, we have a class typology that has nine separate class locations for employees. The full twelve-category typology that comes from combining owners and non-owners is presented in Table 3.1. People in cells 4 to 11 of the typology are exploited themselves with respect to productive property (because they are employees), but exploiters with respect to organisational resources and/or skills. Thus, Wright describes them as occupying 'contradictory locations' within the relations of exploitation that define the class structure (Wright 1985: Chapter 3).

Wright's work extends beyond simply defining the class structure of capitalist societies. To investigate the broader questions of class analysis, he initiated and directs an international study of class structure and class consciousness. This study uses survey research methods to investigate the class structure, and its relationship to class consciousness, political behaviour, unpaid work in the home, and a variety of other factors. The study includes some fifteen or so capitalist and (once) communist countries, including the United States, Sweden, Canada, Norway, Finland, Denmark, Britain, Russia, Australia, New Zealand, Germany, South Korea, Taiwan, Spain and Japan. Other national projects are envisaged or under way in Israel, Turkey, Switzerland and Portugal. Each national project replicates questionnaire items which measure a person's class location, together with other questions pertaining to social phenomena of interest. The main Australian data collection was undertaken in 1986 by a project team based at the University of Queensland, and consisted of personal interviews with 1,195 adult women and men in paid employment.

The percentages in Table 3.1 indicate the composition of the Australian class structure, according to these data. They are estimates of percentages that would be obtained if all adult employed Australians were interviewed, within a known margin of error. From these figures we can see that about 14 per cent of the workforce is self-employed, with the majority of these being *petit bourgeois* (people like small shopkeepers, and family farmers without employees). Pure proletarians, with no skill or organisational resources, are just over 30 per cent of the workforce. If we add to this group people with minor skill or organisational assets (skilled workers and unskilled supervisors), the working class consists of about 52 per cent of the workforce. This leaves a middle class of about 34 per cent. From Wright's perspective, then, about 50 per cent of the workforce is working class, about 14 per cent is self-employed (predominantly in small business), and about 34 per cent are in middle class contradictory locations.

Considering the separate figures for men and women, we can

Table 3.1 Percentages of Women, Men and Total Workforce in Wright's Class Categories

Productive property				
Owners of productive property	Non-owners of productive property			
1. Bourgeoisie Women: less than 1 Men: less than 1 Total: 1	4. Expert Managers Women: 4 Men: 8 Total: 6	7. Skilled Managers Women: 8 Men: 12 Total: 10	10. Unskilled Managers Women: 8 Men: 6 Total: 7	Organisational resources Many
2. Small Employers Women: 3 Men: 5 Total: 4	5. Expert Supervisors Women: 2 Men: 2 Total 2	8. Skilled Supervisors Women: 5 Men: 7 Total: 6	11. Unskilled Supervisors Women: 11 Men: 6 Total: 8	Some
3. *Petit Bourgeoisie* Women: 6 Men: 12 Total: 9	6. Expert Workers Women: 3 Men: 2 Total: 3	9. Skilled Workers Women: 8 Men: 16 Total: 12	12. Proletarians Women: 42 Men: 25 Total: 32	None
	Many	Some Occupational skills	None	

Note: Percentages are based on weighted frequencies for 526 women and 670 men
Source: Class Structure of Australia Project

see that women are less likely than men to be in the three property owning classes. They are also much more concentrated in the proletariat than men, and less likely overall to be managers. There are several possible reasons for these findings. First, women, rather than men, undertake part-time work, and have careers interrupted by marriage and child rearing. Consequently, women are less likely than men to be promoted to managerial positions by their employers. In addition, women are more likely to face gender discrimination than men, since most managers and bosses are male, rather than female. Women also do not inherit productive property from their parents to the same degree as men (Western 1992). This means that one basic channel into self-employment is more restricted for women than men.

Another way into self-employment is by borrowing money to finance a business. Given their work histories, and stereotypical expectations about female roles, women probably find it harder than men to borrow funds, further restricting their opportunities to move into the bourgeois, small employer and *petit bourgeois* locations. The combined effect of these tendencies is to keep women out of self-employment and management, relative to men, and to restrict them to 'bad' proletarian jobs, to a greater extent than men.

Acquiring Class Membership
Wright has provided a powerful way of thinking about the class structure of actual capitalist societies like Australia. But class analysis also involves important questions about how class membership is acquired. In Australia, Marxist research on this topic has mainly concentrated on how the education system influences class membership from one generation to the next.

In two major studies, Connell and his colleagues examine how schools are related to the patterning of class and gender inequality in Australia (Connell, Ashenden, Kessler and Dowsett 1982; Connell 1985). The first study, *Making the Difference*, concentrates on secondary school students in Sydney and Adelaide, while the second focuses on teachers. *Making the Difference* is most relevant for this chapter since it addresses how schools shape boys' and girls' class opportunities.

Making the Difference is based on interviews with teenage students in private and state schools, their parents, teachers and principals. Connell and his colleagues try to show how working and middle class schools relate to class inequality,[6] and how the social interaction within schools is actively produced by teachers, students and parents, in light of experiences of living in a class-based society. For instance, some students in both private and state schools resist school authority by arguing and fighting with teachers, getting drunk at parties, and rejecting school and further education as pointless and boring. For a middle class student, this form of resistance is also a rejection of family class circumstances, and class privilege. For a student from a working class family, on the other hand, a similar form of resistance to school authority may reflect an identification with parents' experiences of being bossed around by employers, managers and bureaucrats (Connell *et al.* 1982: 82–89).

For middle class students, private schools typically consolidate class opportunities and experiences, reproducing class power and privilege (Connell *et al.* 1982: 149–54). Schools establish friendships, and other social networks that will be useful to students in the future, and help define middle class values and attitudes, excluding working class students and viewpoints. For working class students, on the other hand, schools may contradict family circumstances. If schools emphasise an academic curriculum around subjects like English, mathematics, physics and geography, they may marginalise practical skills and knowledge that working class parents have. The *hegemonic curriculum* that predominates in schools (Connell *et al.* 1982: 120–26) presents academic thought as valuable, 'correct' and worthwhile, and devalues other—typically working class—knowledge and experience. Accepting the hegemonic curriculum involves working class students denying their class background. But resisting an academic curriculum may worsen these students' chances in the job market (Connell *et al.* 1982: Chapter 4). In short, schools often fragment the opportunities of working class students, while reinforcing the privileges of middle class ones (Connell *et al.* 1982: 149–54, 169–73).

By perpetuating middle class privilege and working class disadvantage, schools help reproduce class inequality. Consequently, students from middle class families are likely to go on to middle class jobs, while students from working class families go on to working class jobs, and face heightened risks of unemployment.

One way of examining this process explicitly is by investigating intergenerational mobility. Studying such mobility involves asking someone about the class membership of her parents when she was a child, and her own class membership as an adult, to see if there has been a change in class circumstances from one generation to the next. By getting this information for people throughout the class structure it is possible to quantify the amount of individual 'movement' or mobility that occurs. Research into intergenerational mobility is more commonly associated with Weberian than Marxist class analysis. However the topic is important for the latter because it indicates whether class advantages and disadvantages are transmitted systematically from parents to children, so that class inequality continues from one generation to the next.

Some work that I have done takes data from the Class Structure of Australia Project to investigate intergenerational mobility (Chant and Western 1991; Western 1992). Using Wright's concept of class structure, I examined the relationship between people's class locations as adults (their *class destinations* in the jargon of mobility research) and the locations of their families when they were growing up (their *class origins*). These analyses showed that children from self-employed families (employers and the *petit bourgeoisie*) were disproportionately likely to become self-employed themselves. Children with farm backgrounds, in particular, were especially likely to become farmers. Similarly, children whose parents were in 'expert' class locations (those that exploit some kind of occupational skill) were relatively likely also to become experts. Finally, mobility between capitalists and workers was limited. The chances of capitalists' children taking working class jobs were very small, and of children of workers becoming capitalists were similarly small.

These findings make sense, given Wright's concept of class structure. Capitalists and the *petit bourgeoisie* are disproportionately likely to have had self-employed parents because their parents can will businesses to them, or use the profits from business to invest in their children's enterprises. Employee parents cannot do these things for their children. Similarly, expert parents can use their financial resources to fund their children's educations, using private, rather than state schools, supporting offspring through university, and so on. Expert parents also know the hegemonic curriculum. Consequently, they are better able to ensure that their children get the higher education that is a prerequisite for various expert jobs, particularly those in the professions. Finally, limited mobility between the capitalist and working classes occurs because children from capitalist origins are 'insulated' from working class jobs by their parents' wealth, and because most working class children come from economically disadvantaged families which cannot afford to buy the property one needs to become a capitalist.

The Consequences of Class Membership

Most Marxist research into the effects of class membership has focused on how class influences consciousness and behaviour, rather than the relationship between class and social inequality. Common to this research is a view that the experiences of living in a class-divided society provide the 'raw material' for people's beliefs about that society, and for political or industrial behaviour

of various kinds. One book that exemplifies this perspective is
Open Cut (Williams 1981).

Open Cut is a study of working class life in a central
Queensland coal mining town. It examines the experiences of
male, blue collar workers and their wives, during a period of
industrial conflict in the mid-1970s. Several features of life in the
mining town contributed to workers' industrial militancy. First,
the mining company pursued an authoritarian managerial strategy
to reorganise and intensify the work process, at the same time
punishing workers who resisted the reorganisation (Williams
1981: Chapters 3–4). The company also emphasised class differences
between workers and managers both at the mine sites, and in the
town, where the workforce lived. Workers, foremen and managers
lived in three different kinds of houses, with managers located in
the centre of town in the largest and most luxurious accommodation. Safety helmets were colour-coded to distinguish
workers from managers and supervisors (Williams 1981: 112–13).
This managerial style emphasised the differences between managers
and workers, and denied workers control over their own jobs. By
highlighting the subordinate position of non-managerial employees,
the company antagonised workers and contributed to a sense of
class solidarity, which was further heightened because workers lived
and socialised together outside their jobs. However, Williams
(1981: 95–96) notes that opposition to management was not
universal among workers and, in particular, that those in highly
paid jobs tended to be more conservative and supportive of the
company.

Open Cut demonstrates that the kinds of experiences people
have at work and in the wider community can be the basis for
political consciousness and action. *Class Consciousness in Australia*
(Chamberlain 1983) makes this idea explicit by examining three
theoretical arguments about the way people's perceptions of class
processes are created. Within Marxism are two somewhat contradictory notions about how people develop beliefs about social
processes. First is the view that day-to-day experiences of living in
a class society shape people's perceptions of that society. Marx
used this argument to explain the formation of revolutionary working class consciousness in the *Communist Manifesto*, and it is also
found in *Open Cut* and *Making the Difference*. On the other hand,
Marx and Engels ([1846] 1976: 67) also argued that 'the ideas of
the ruling class are in every epoch the ruling ideas'. By controlling
the production and distribution of knowledge, through control of
the mass media and the education system, for example, the ruling
class ensures that a dominant ideology legitimating the status quo
comes to be widely accepted.

Chamberlain examines these two arguments by considering the attitudes of a sample of Melbourne respondents to the economic system, political institutions, trade unions, strikes and the class structure. If the 'ruling ideas' argument is correct, there should be almost total consensus on these issues by people throughout the class structure. Most people should believe a dominant ideology that says that Australia is a classless society, without systematic social inequalities. Chamberlain refers to this argument as *hegemonic* theory, after the Marxist concept, *hegemony*, which refers to a system of cultural or ideological domination of one class by another. We have already seen hegemony used to describe the hegemonic curriculum. On the other hand, if people's consciousness is determined primarily by living in a class society, then ruling ideas will be interpreted in light of personal experience. Sometimes experience and the dominant ideology will coincide, and at other times they will conflict. However, there should be class differences in some beliefs, because people throughout the class structure experience class inequality differently. Chamberlain calls this *structural* theory, because it says that consciousness is the result of a person's location in the class structure. Finally, an intermediate argument suggests that consciousness is the result of both a dominant ideology, and people's direct experience. Where people lack experience on which to make a judgement, they accept the dominant ideology. However, where their experiences are relevant, these determine their beliefs. This third, intermediate position is described as *quasi-hegemonic* theory (Chamberlain 1983: Chapter 1).

On the basis of his analysis, Chamberlain concludes that hegemonic and quasi-hegemonic theories are not empirically supported. Most people's attitudes to things like strikes, class and the economic system are more consistent with their own direct experiences than with the existence of a dominant ideology, and there are systematic differences throughout the class structure in people's class consciousness. These findings support structural theory.

The strengths of Chamberlain's work lie in his attempt to theorise how consciousness should be related to class membership, and the empirical approach he takes. However, Graetz (1986), has argued that there is really more consensus about class issues than structural theory would predict. Chamberlain finds people in different classes have different attitudes, but he does not try to determine if such differences can be explained by other causal factors, apart from class. For example, factors like trade union membership, or support for a political party, are also likely to affect a person's attitudes to strikes and the economy. When Graetz

(1986) incorporates additional causal factors in his analysis, he finds that people across the social structure actually agree about class issues to a large extent. This consensus undermines structural theory and supports quasi-hegemonic theory (Graetz 1986).

Graetz (1986) is correct to argue that factors other than class membership are related to consciousness and must be included in research. Unfortunately, he does not directly address the importance of class for consciousness, because he does not measure class membership directly. Rather, he analyses a number of factors that are associated with class membership, like education level and occupation, to argue that socio-structural location has no effect on class consciousness. Against this finding, analyses from the Class Structure of Australia Project suggest there are class differences in attitudes to trade unions, government intervention in the economy, and support for private enterprise, even allowing for factors like gender, age, union membership or education (Emmison 1991a; Western, Western, Emmison and Baxter 1991). In general, capitalists, the *petit bourgeoisie* and expert managers are more strongly opposed to trade unions, and government intervention in the economy, and more in favour of big business and private enterprise, than are workers. However, the sharpness of these differences is variable, depending on the particular attitudes being investigated. On the other hand, there are few class differences with respect to two non-class issues, beliefs about appropriate gender roles for women and men and support for nuclear weapons and nuclear power (Western, Western, Emmison and Baxter 1991). These findings suggest that class-pertinent attitudes are systematically affected by class membership, as structural theory would predict. But other attitudes, whose content is not related to class processes, are themselves unrelated to class location. In examining the relationship between class and consciousness, then, we need to be aware that class membership is likely to affect specific attitudes and beliefs that are concerned with class-related issues, rather than all attitudes and beliefs in general.

Although we have focused on the relationship between class and consciousness, ultimately Marxists believe that class helps to explain social inequality: that is, who gets what in any society (Wright 1989). Surprisingly, though, there has been little empirical research on this question. However, if Wright is correct, exploitation associated with productive property, skills and organisational resources should help explain the distribution of income in capitalist societies. In particular, there should be a systematic relationship between class location and income level. In Table 3.2, I present data from the Class Structure of Australia Project, showing the 1986 average incomes of men and women through-

Table 3.2 1986 Mean Incomes for Men in Full-time and Women in Full- and Part-time Employment within Wright's Class Categories

	Productive Property			
Owners of productive property	Non-owners of productive property			Organisational Resources
1. Bourgeoisie and Small Employers Men: 28,493 Full-time Women: 12,372	4. Expert Managers Men: 42,289 Full-time Women: 34,737	7. Skilled Managers Men: 28,444 Full-time Women: 23,415 Part-time Women 9,807	10. Unskilled Managers Men: 25,450 Full-time Women: 19,646 Part-time Women: 7,060	Many
	5. Expert supervisors Men: 33,056 Full-time Women: 26,111 Part-time Women: 15,223	8. Skilled Supervisors Men: 22,465 Full-time Women: 20,505 Part-time Women: 7,874	11. Unskilled Supervisors Men: 23,085 Full-time Women: 16,090 Part-time Women: 9,432	Some
3. *Petit Bourgeoisie* Men: 28,493 Full-time Women: 21,851 Part-time Women: 6,236	6. Expert workers Men: 30,020 Full-time Women: 22,533 Part-time Women: 10,500	9. Skilled workers Men: 20,763 Full-time Women: 20,148 Part-time Women: 13,834	12. Proletarians Men: 18,190 Full-time Women: 15,554 Part-time Women: 8,475	None
	Many	Some Occupational skills	None	

Note: There are no female part-time Employers or Expert Managers

Source: Class Structure of Australia Project

out the class structure. I have combined the bourgeoisie and small employers into a single employer location, because there are very few large employers in the Australian data. The results are also presented separately for men, and women in full- and part-time employment, since women typically earn less than men, and people in part-time employment earn less than people in full-time employment. All men in the sample are in full-time employment.

Looking at results for women and men separately, the patterns are quite consistent with Wright's typology. Among employees, male and full-time female proletarians have the lowest average incomes, with earnings generally increasing as we move along either the skills or organisational dimensions of the class typology. In other words, income increases as skill or managerial control increases. Incomes of the *petit bourgeoisie* and employers are not extremely high, but the data are monetary incomes only. Self-employed people typically have a larger share of non-monetary income than employees, because they can privately consume business assets. Because their monetary incomes are more inter-mittent and fluctuating than those of wage earners, the self-employed are also less likely than employees to know how much they earn, and to under-report their incomes (Shryock, Siegel and Associates 1971: 363–64). Finally, the owners in the sample are primarily small business people, so while their assets are valuable, their incomes for any one year may be relatively low. However, among employees, for whom data on monetary income are more reliable, earnings generally increase with skill and organisation, as Wright expects.

Table 3.2 also highlights that within any class category, women earn less than men. Women's incomes are lower than men's because their labour force participation is not constant, but interrupted by marriage and child care, while men's is not. Women are also concentrated in part-time work and in occupations which historically have not been militant in pushing wage claims. This means that women lack marketable skills relative to men. They also face employer discrimination. Consequently, gender, along with class, is a major source of income inequality in Australian society (Connell 1991).

The results in Table 3.2 do not take account of factors like union membership or education, which also influence income levels. In other research, I found that men in different classes earn different amounts independently of additional factors that also determine income. Among women, class differences in income are less, once other causal factors are accounted for, although some class differences of the kind shown in Table 3.2 still persist (M. C. Western 1991).

Weberian Class Analysis
Unlike the Marxist analyses we have considered, Weberian research is not embedded within a framework of class domination. Broadly speaking, two kinds of Weberian analyses predominate in recent Australian sociology. First are studies of the relationship between class and status, typically in localised communities. Second are studies of intergenerational class mobility that use a contemporary Weberian concept of social class. The community studies primarily answer the question of what the class structure looks like, and how classes and status groups interrelate. Studies of class mobility, as we have previously seen, address the issue of how class membership is acquired from one generation to the next.

Examining Social Structures: Class and Status in Australia
An older tradition of Weberian class analysis in Australian sociology examines the interrelationships between classes and status groups. Probably the most influential work in this area is by Wild, whose first study, *Bradstow* (Wild 1974) examines class and status in a New South Wales country town, and whose second work, *Social Stratification in Australia* (Wild 1978) attempts to extend the analysis to Australian society.[7]

Bradstow is based upon participant observation and survey research. Although the research is confined to a country town, Wild's main objective is to use his findings to say something about class, status and the distribution of power in Australia. Studying a small community is simply a method of getting generalisable information about these issues (Wild 1981: 57–59).

Following Weber, Wild (1974: 2) identifies status groups, as groups distinguished by a common lifestyle, and generally accepted modes of behaviour. Status groups are differentially ranked or evaluated by members of the community, so that they can be hierarchically ordered in terms of social prestige. The kinds of behaviours and consumption patterns that identify status group members include 'conventions that relate to dress, speech, place of residence, type of house, make of car, club membership, standard and type of education, religion, occupation, and ideology' (Wild 1974: 2).

In Bradstow, Wild found six distinct status groups, ranked from high to low prestige as follows: the gentry, consisting of the oldest and most established families in the district; the 'Grangeites', newer wealthy arrivals, living in the prestigious Grange area of the town, but not working in the area; the local bosses, the most successful local business people and white collar workers; the tradesmen who are the other local small businessmen; the workers, local wage earners living primarily in the railway/

industrial area of the town; and the no-hopers who are the poorest and most 'disreputable' members of the community (Wild 1974: Chapter 3). Although these brief descriptions may suggest the status groups are distinguished objectively by economic criteria, their group identities are defined by the lifestyle and consumption factors noted in the previous paragraph. Members of each status group live in distinct areas of the town, dress and speak different-ly, drive different types of car, belong to different social clubs, and so on. As a result of these lifestyle differences, interaction between members of different status groups is limited, and the social boundaries between groups are reasonably clear-cut.

Although Wild follows Weber closely in defining status groups, he defines class in a less orthodox way. The basic distinction involves ownership of the means of production, as it does for Marx and Weber. But Wild considers not only property ownership, but whether people have to work, and whether they are employers or employees. This produces a fourfold class structure, with three property owning classes. The classes are as follows: property owners and employers who do not work, but live off their assets; working property owners with employees; working property owners without employees; and non-owners who are employees (Wild 1974: 112). The first two of these classes are equivalent to the employer classes Wright identifies. The third is the *petit bourgeoisie*. The fourth is simply all employees.

Class and status systems overlap somewhat in Bradstow, with many people in adjacent status groups belonging to the same class. Common class membership sometimes overrides status differences as people from different status groups form social ties. Wild (1974: 113) describes how one of the Grangeites joined with two local bosses to finance a new shopping arcade. In this case the status difference did not matter, because all three individuals were in the working employer class.

In *Bradstow*, Wild argues that the status system is well-defined, and reasonably accepted by members of the community. More recently, Dempsey (1990) has said there is no clear-cut status hierarchy in small communities of the sort Wild noted. Dempsey's study *Smalltown*,[8] is based on fieldwork conducted over fifteen years, from 1973 to 1987, in a Victorian farming district. He aims to document the system of age, gender and class inequality in the community, and to show how, despite the presence of such in-equalities, most people feel a sense of identification and com-munity solidarity (Dempsey 1990: 2–4).

Unlike Wild, Dempsey (1990: Chapter 7) does not find a number of discrete status groups in Smalltown. Instead he says beliefs about status and class are diverse, and that people typically downplay class and status as causes of social interaction and inequality. The disagreement between Wild and Dempsey hinges partly on a disagreement about the definition of status group, and partly on a difference in method. Weber's definition of status groups has two components: a behavioural one incorporating lifestyles and consumption patterns, and a symbolic one involving evaluations of social honour and prestige. Wild emphasises the behavioural aspects of status group formation more than Dempsey does, and he draws inferences about status groups indirectly from discussions with several informants, and participant observation of everyday social interaction (Wild 1974: 209–10). Dempsey, on the other hand, emphasises the symbolic manifestation of the status system. There should be very widespread consensus about the causes of social prestige and the ranking of groups within the status system, so that even subordinate groups should accept their position in the status hierarchy (Dempsey 1990: 131). Unlike Wild, Dempsey also relies more heavily upon direct methods to investigate status group formation, asking people explicitly whether Smalltown has a prestige hierarchy, and if so what it looks like. Because people cannot consistently identify status groups, or rank groups or voluntary organisations, Dempsey (1990: Chapter 7) argues that Smalltown does not have the kind of unitary status system Wild described.

It may be that Bradstow has a status system and Smalltown does not. However, in part, I think Dempsey and Wild disagree because each emphasises different aspects of social status. For Wild, observed differences in lifestyles, consumption patterns and association, imply status differentiation, and it does not matter if people express disagreements about the system, so that prestige evaluations are not identical across groups (Wild 1974: 35). For Dempsey, the most important requirement is a consensual perception of the hierarchy. If people cannot describe the status system, we cannot say it exists (Dempsey 1990: 136), regardless of objective differences that might exist in lifestyles, consumption or social interaction.[9] Because Wild and Dempsey define and measure status group formation differently, it is hard to say whether Bradstow and Smalltown actually differ in regard to status group formation, or whether the disagreement occurs because they are talking about different social phenomena.

Smalltown and *Bradstow* represent the older Australian tradition in Weberian research into class and status. More recently, Weberian analysis has turned from looking at the relationship between class and status to our second question, namely: How is class membership acquired? The answer has been framed in terms of intergenerational mobility. The Australian research, like overseas research on this topic, uses a Weberian conception of class structure developed by a British sociologist, John Goldthorpe (Goldthorpe 1980; Goldthorpe and Payne 1986).

Following Weber, Goldthorpe argues that class situation depends upon market situation, particularly source of income and level of reward. However, in addition, class situation depends upon relationships of authority and autonomy in the workplace, such as whether people can make decisions about how they do their own work, whether they supervise others, are supervised themselves, and so on. The class structure is defined by groups of occupations with comparable market and work situations (Goldthorpe 1980: 39). As with Wright, the actual number of class categories is somewhat flexible, and, within limits, can be scaled up or down, depending on the research question and the data available.

In its basic form Goldthorpe's class scheme identifies eight occupationally-based classes. Classes I and II consist of individuals in upper and lower level professsional occupations, administrators, managers and large proprietors. Together they make up the service class. Classes IIIa and IIIb are white collar or non-manual employees in routinised occupations. Class IIIa consists of clerical workers, and Class IIIb comprises employees in personal service (for example, hairdressers or flight attendants) and sales occupations. Class IV is small employers and the traditional *petit bourgeoisie*. Class V is lower technicians and foremen. Class VI is skilled workers, and Class VII is made up of semi- and unskilled workers. Classes IIIb and V through VII represent blue collar or manual workers (Goldthorpe and Payne 1986).

The service class is so called because it is distinguished by an ethos of service or moral commitment to the employing organisation. Goldthorpe's argument here is almost identical to Wright's, regarding managers. Bureaucrats, administrators and professionals have considerable autonomy in their jobs, and as a result organisations have to trust these people to carry out their work competently. Organisations try to buy trust from the service class by guaranteeing economic rewards, a career structure, security of tenure and the like (Goldthorpe 1982). One difference between Wright and Goldthorpe is that Goldthorpe does not think that the economic rewards of the service class represent exploitation of people outside the service class, while Wright believes that managers exploit non-managers.

Using Class Structure of Australia Project data once more, we can see what the class structure looks like, from Goldthorpe's perspective.[10]

As can be seen, the service class makes up about 35 per cent of the workforce, routine white collar workers are about 22 per cent,

Table 3.3 Percentage of Women, Men and Total Workforce in Goldthorpe's Categories

Class		Women	Men	Total Workforce
I	Upper Service	5	15	10
II	Lower Service	27	21	24
IIIa	Routine non-manual: Clerical	18	4	10
IIIb	Routine non-manual: Sales and Personal Service	22	4	12
IV	Small Proprietors and *petit bourgeoisie*	9	13	11
V	Technicians and Supervisors	6	9	8
VI	Skilled Manual	3	18	12
VII	Semi- and Unskilled Manual	10	17	14

Note: Percentages are based on weighted frequencies for 526 women and 670 men
Source: Class Structure of Australia Project

and small business people and the *petit bourgeoisie* are about 10 per cent. Technical, non-manual supervisory and manual workers make up the remaining 33 per cent. Men are more likely to be found in the upper service class and in manual work, than are women. Women are much more likely than men to be found in routine white collar work, and overall are concentrated in Classes II, IIIa and IIIb. Men, on the other hand are spread more evenly throughout the class structure. Because Goldthorpe's class scheme draws so closely on occupation, gender differences in the class structure reflect gender differences in the occupational structure, and in particular women's concentration in semi-professional, clerical and sales jobs.[11]

If lower white collar workers (IIIb) are treated as part of the working class along with manual workers, the working class in Australia is about 36 per cent of the workforce, the service class is about 35 per cent, and the intermediate 'middle class' is about 30 per cent. However, although this is a familiar way of thinking about the class structure, it is a simplification. Goldthorpe, like Wright, does not believe that classes can be hierarchically ranked from top to bottom.

Intergenerational Mobility and the Acquisition of Class Membership
In common with Marxist analysis, Weberian analysis is not merely about mapping the class structure. Instead, the real object of class analysis, in Goldthorpe's (1982, 1983) view is to assess the extent to which the classes described above exist as real empirical groupings, differentiated in terms of lifestyle socio-political atti-

tudes and behaviour and forms of collective organisation. This process assumes that classes exhibit some stability of membership over time. People's class membership must endure over their lives, because it takes time for membership to affect consciousness, behaviour and social inequality. It makes little sense to say that these are determined by class membership if a person's class is constantly changing, or can be changed at will.

As a result, Goldthorpe sees social mobility as an important element of class analysis. If the class structure is very 'rigid', so that most people cannot move between classes, it seems more likely that people will develop a common identity and consciousness with others in their class, than if the class structure is 'open' to mobility between classes. Similarly, if class membership shapes access to social rewards, then it will probably be a more important determinant of life chances when mobility is limited, than when it is relatively common.

Goldthorpe has analysed men's intergenerational mobility in Britain, Europe, the United States and Japan (Goldthorpe 1987; Erikson, Goldthorpe and Portocarero 1979, 1982, 1983; Erikson and Goldthorpe 1985, 1987a, 1987b; Ishida, Goldthorpe and Erikson 1991). Most Australian research using Goldthorpe's class scheme has concentrated on men's mobility (Jones and Davis 1986, 1988a, 1988b), although more recent work also examines women's mobility (Emmison 1991b; Hayes 1990). In studying intergenerational mobility, two processes shape the patterns we observe. First, changes in the occupational and industrial structure over time mean that children may have different job opportunities from their parents. For example, as the number of professional and technical occupations has increased, there has been a corresponding increase in available service class, and technical positions, in the class structure. The changing composition of the occupational structure provides an avenue into the service class for people whose parents did not belong to the service class.

Second, mobility also results because children from different classes have specific advantages and disadvantages with respect to particular class destinations, regardless of changes in the class structure. For example, children of farmers have a better chance of becoming farmers, than children from non-farm origins, irrespective of how the class structure is changing. Farmers' children can inherit farms, and also typically work on family farms while they are growing up, learning necessary skills. Neither of these things applies to people from non-farming families. The processes associated with family farming mean that farmers' children are more likely to become farmers than children who don't have a farming background.

When we simply ask people about their class destinations, and their class origins, count up the numbers of people who have moved or have stayed in the same class, and describe the patterns, we are studying *absolute mobility patterns*, or *absolute mobility rates*. These are just observed patterns of mobility and immobility apparent from inspecting the data. Absolute mobility patterns reflect both changes in the class structure over time, and the fact that children from particular class origins are more likely to move to some classes than others, when compared with children from other class origins.

Sometimes, however, we want to ignore changes in the class structure and ask questions like the following: Are children from farming backgrounds more likely to become farmers than children from working class backgrounds? When we examine the relative chances that farmers' children become farmers, compared with the corresponding chances that working class children become farmers, we are studying *relative mobility patterns* or *relative mobility rates*. Relative mobility patterns are important, because they indicate how opportunities for moving into the class structure are different for people from different class backgrounds, irrespective of how the class structure is changing. Relative mobility patterns are not immediately obvious from absolute mobility patterns. Instead they have to be isolated with more complex statistical methods. The mobility research I described previously, using Wright's typology, investigated relative mobility patterns.

Australian research using Goldthorpe's scheme looks at both absolute and relative mobility. In a study of men's absolute mobility patterns, Jones and Davis (1986: Chpter 2, 1988a) found that about half of men in the working class had working class fathers, and between another 20 and 30 per cent had fathers who were farmers. This suggests that working class men come from a fairly homogeneous class background. However, farmers themselves have the most restricted class origins, with three-quarters of male farmers having fathers who were also farmers. Among farmers and workers, then, are many people whose class membership has been stable over their lives. The service class is less heavily self-recruited than the working class or farmers. Only about one-third of service class men have service class fathers. In part, this finding reflects growth in the service class due to the increase in professional and managerial occupations noted above. As the service class gets larger it draws men from throughout the class structure to meet the increasing demand for service class jobs.

The patterns Jones and Davis report for men are somewhat similar to those found by Emmison (1991b), using Australian

Class Project data. Again, about half the men in Classes V, VI and VII come from working class origins, and about one-third of lower service class men have service class origins. But Emmison finds two-thirds of upper service class men come from service class families, rather than just over one-third, as reported by Jones and Davis. Although Jones and Davis' data are confined to men aged between 30 and 69 (Jones and Davis 1986: 14), and men in the Class Project data set are at least 18, restricting the Class Project sample to 30 to 69-year-olds still suggests that almost two-thirds (64 per cent) of upper service class men are self-recruited. Without further investigation I cannot tell if the different findings actually represent a trend of increasing self-recruitment among the service class — Jones and Davis' data were collected in 1973–74, while Class Project data were collected in 1986 — or if they are due to other sources of non-comparability of the two studies.

The most interesting part of Emmison's (1991b) analysis concerns differences in men's and women's mobility patterns. In general women are more concentrated in Classes II, IIIa and IIIb than are men, and regardless of class origins, tend to move into these classes. As a result, women throughout the class structure experience 'marginal downward and upward mobility' (Emmison 1991b: 45) into the lower service class and routine white collar work. Consequently, women's absolute mobility patterns seem less dependent on their class origins than men's patterns, and instead reflect their location in semi-professional, sales and clerical occupations.

In their analysis of men's relative mobility patterns, Jones and Davis (1986: Chapter 3, 1988b) find a high level of mobility overall, along with very limited mobility between specific classes. In particular, there is very little mobility between farming and non-farm classes, and between the working class and the upper service class. There is also a very strong tendency for the sons of farmers to inherit their father's class membership, and a slightly weaker tendency for sons from upper service class families to enter upper service class jobs.

Hayes (1990) also uses a modified version of Goldthorpe's class scheme to investigate mother-daughter mobility. Like Jones and Davis (1986, 1988a), Hayes finds substantial mobility throughout the class structure, coupled with limited mobility between the service class and semi- and unskilled manual workers. In addition, there is strong class inheritance among the *petit bourgeoisie*, technical workers and skilled manual workers, and weaker class inheritance within the service class and among semi- and unskilled manual workers.

The Consequences of Class Membership

Although most Weberian sociologists who are influenced by Goldthorpe accept his argument that class analysis should ultimately address consciousness, political behaviour and social inequality, very little Australian empirical work exists on these issues. Analyses from the Australian Class Project show that there is a systematic relationship between class membership and attitudes to trade union and business activity (Emmison 1991a). In particular, members of the service class, clerical workers, technicians, small proprietors and the *petit bourgeoisie* are all more 'pro-capitalist' with respect to the activities of trade unions and business than semi- and unskilled manual workers are. Pro-capitalist, in this context, means being opposed to trade union and strike activity, and being in favour of the rights of business and management. Skilled manual workers (VI), and sales and personal service workers (IIIb) are not more pro-capitalist on these issues than semi- and unskilled manual workers. The findings persist, even allowing for gender, education level, union membership and age.

The effect of class on social inequality can again be approached by examining the relationship between class and income inequality, as we did with Wright's typology, earlier in the chapter. Table 3.4 presents Class Project data on this issue for men and full-time and part-time women. As we saw with Wright's typology, in each class, women earn less than men, and part-time women earn less than full-time ones. The class patterning of incomes agrees gene-

Table 3.4   1986 Mean Incomes for Men in Full-time and Women in Full- and Part-time Employment within Goldthorpe's Class Categories

Class		Men	Women, full-time	Women part-time
I	Upper Service	37,505	31,831	13,341
II	Lower Service	28,737	22,208	9,527
IIIa	Routine non-manual: Clerical	20,451	16,890	8,118
IIIb	Routine non-manual: Sales and Personal Service	16,306	16,069	8,594
IV	Small Proprietors and *petit bourgeoisie*	25,766	16,885	5,778
V	Technicians and Supervisors	23,011	17,202	9,828
VI	Skilled Manual	19,707	15,466	7,500
VII	Semi- and unskilled Manual	17,753	12,722	8,519

Source: Class Structure of Australia Project

rally with Goldthorpe's class scheme. Individuals in the service class have the highest incomes, and manual workers and sales and personal service workers tend to have the lowest incomes. The average income of the upper service class is greater than the average income of the lower service class. These findings suggest that class differences in income are sharpest between workers and members of the service class.

Although we would want to incorporate other factors in a complete analysis of the relationship between class and income, overall, class and earnings are related in a manner that largely agrees with Goldthorpe's arguments. Since a person's standard of living in capitalist societies is largely determined by the amount of money she earns, the findings in Table 3.4 imply class membership is likely to be strongly related to other aspects of social inequality, like access to health care, the legal and education systems and leisure activities.

Social Stratificationism

Social Structure as an Occupational Hierarchy
Class analysis defines the class structure as a number of distinct, relationally-based, classes. The definitions are 'relational' because they emphasise relationships in production (Marx and Wright), or that occur in the market and/or workplace (Weber and Goldthorpe). Furthermore, because Marxists and Weberians define classes in relation to one another, often using several criteria (like property ownership and skills), classes cannot be ranked straightforwardly from top to bottom on any underlying characteristic. Although we often use words like 'upper', 'middle' and 'lower' to name classes in everyday language—and I have used them myself for convenience in this chapter—the class structure cannot be ordered along a single dimension, if one accepts either Weberian or Marxist definitions of class. With Wright's concept, for instance, we cannot say if experts are 'higher' or above 'managers' in any overall sense. The comparison is meaningless because managerial authority and skills are separate, and incommensurable, elements of class. Similarly, Goldthorpe's classification says nothing about whether self-employed small business owners are above or below routine clerical workers in any objective way. Property ownership and white collar work are distinct aspects of market and work situations, and cannot be compared.

Within class analysis, then, someone's class membership is determined by relationships associated with factors like property ownership, and managerial position. Within social stratificationism, on the other hand, the occupational structure is thought of as a hierarchy, running from low to high. A person's position in the *stratification hierarchy* is determined by her occupation, which is assigned a score or value, indicating the relative standing of the occupation against others. Different stratification scales have different ranges, running between zero and one hundred, say, and individual occupations take values along this range.

Two kinds of stratification scales are common in sociology. In the first, a researcher asks people to rate individual occupations on a scale of 'social standing', or 'prestige'. Such a scale might have seven points, for example, with a score of one indicating highest social standing, and a score of seven indicating lowest. Individuals give each occupation in the list a rating between one and seven. Ratings are then compiled to rank order the list of occupations from low to high social standing. These scales are called *occupational prestige scales*. In Australian sociology, occupational prestige scales have been developed by Congalton (1953, 1962, 1963a and 1963b) and more recently Daniel (1983), building upon Congalton's work. Daniel developed her prestige scale in the manner described above, asking different groups of respondents to rate a list of occupations on a seven-point scale, and then aggregating the information to give each occupation a score indicating its overall placement in the prestige hierarchy (Daniel 1983: Chapter 3).

In the second strategy, the researcher combines prestige evaluations with other information about occupations, such as the average education and income levels of people in these jobs. These data are used in a statistical analysis to create a new measure of *occupational* or *socio-economic status*, which allocates each occupation a score on a status scale. One advantage that occupational status scales have over occupational prestige ones is that we can give any occupation a status score, even if it is not included in the list of occupations that was initially evaluated. All we have to know about the occupation is how it fares on the other characteristics that were used to construct the status scale (education, income, and so forth). This information is usually available in official statistics like Census data. On the other hand, if an occupation is not included in the list of occupations given to respondents, it is difficult to assign it a score on a prestige scale. In Australia, occupational status scales have been developed by sociologists at the Australian National University in Canberra (Broom, Duncan-Jones, Jones and McDonnell 1977; Jones 1989), building on work pioneered in the United States in the 1960s (Duncan 1961; Reiss 1961).[12] The most recent Australian occupational status scale, called ANU3, uses prestige evaluations, along with additional information pertaining to factors like the age, sex, income and educational qualifications of people in the different occupations (Jones 1989).[13]

Table 3.5 presents a subset of occupations from Daniel's (1983) scale, together with their prestige scores, and a subset of occupations from Jones's (1989) scale, together with their ANU3 scores. The lists do not exhaust the occupations covered by the scales, but are intended to illustrate what stratification scales look like. Daniel's (1983) prestige measure runs from 1 to 7, with a low score indicating high prestige. Jones's (1989) index runs between 0 and 100, with a high score indicating high socio-economic status. On both scales, professional and administrative occupations tend to score highly, followed by skilled white collar jobs, and skilled and semi- or unskilled manual work. Specific individual occupations may deviate from this general pattern.

What aspect of occupations do these scales measure? Despite being called scales of occupational prestige and status, they do *not* measure prestige or status in the classical Weberian sense. For Weber, social prestige was associated with status groups of the kind Wild (1974) described in *Bradstow*. Status groups are defined symbolically and behaviourally by lifestyles, forms of speech, prestige evaluations, consumption behaviour and patterns of social interaction, as we have seen. Stratification scales do not measure prestige or status in the strong Weberian sense of these terms (Goldthorpe and Hope 1972), and you should not confuse the words 'status' or 'prestige' in the stratification literature with concepts in Weberian sociology. In social stratificationism, 'status' means position in the stratification hierarchy, and prestige does not have all the symbolic and behavioural implications of a Weberian analysis of prestige and status group formation.

Table 3.5 Occupational Prestige and Socio-economic Status Scores for Selected Australian Occupations

Occupation	Status Score	Prestige Score	Occupation	Status Score	Prestige Score
Judge	1.2	96.1	Primary School-teacher	3.8	62.5
General Practitioner	1.8	91.9	Publican	4.0	42.2
Architect	2.2	67.5	Stenographer	4.5	32.6
Veterinary Surgeon	2.5	85.4	Undertaker	4.8	33.1
Geologist	2.7	79.2	Nurse's Aide	5.5	30.7
Physiologist	3.2	67.9	Debt Collector	6.2	26.9
Systems Analyst	3.4	60.5	Wharf Labourer	6.5	15.3
Personnel Officer	3.7	56.1	Road Sweeper	6.7	6.3

Source: Adapted from Daniel (1983: 196–206) and Jones (1989)

Instead, prestige and socio-economic status scales measure the 'general desirability' of occupations to people, with perceptions of general desirability being largely determined by socio-economic characteristics of the occupations in question (Daniel 1983: Chapter 2; Featherman, Jones and Hauser 1975; Jones 1988; Reiss 1961: 37–42). In particular, occupations are seen as desirable according to the socio-economic power and privileges associated with them. Socio-economic power and privilege depend upon the skills and qualifications occupations require, the authority over people and resources that occupations involve, and the rewards that they command (Daniel 1983: 29; Featherman, Jones and Hauser 1975). The score that an occupation gets on a prestige or status scale is a single value giving a rough indication of how desirable a job is thought to be, in light of its presumed socio-economic power and privileges.

Although prestige and status scales differ in the way they are constructed, for research purposes they are almost indistinguishable. When researchers have compared the ANU status measures with Daniel's prestige scale, they find a very strong association between the scales (Jones 1989; Quine 1986). A person whose occupation is high status according to ANU3 will also have a Daniel score that indicates high prestige, while a low status occupation on ANU3 will get a Daniel score indicating low prestige. The close relationship between prestige and status measures holds throughout the stratification hierarchy. The fact that prestige and status measures are so strongly related, and produce virtually identical results in empirical analysis, justifies the argument that they both measure the socio-economic power inherent in occupations.

I have emphasised that class analysts have a relational understanding of the class structure, while stratificationists have a hierarchical conception of the occupational structure. A further difference that this produces between class analysis and social stratificationism is that there are no inherent conflicts of interest between occupations as far as stratificationists are concerned. But class analysts do believe that classes are inherently conflictual, because of their relational nature. For Marxists like Wright (1989), the fact that relations between property owners and non-owners, experts and non-experts, and managers and non-managers involve exploitation, means that there is an intrinsic tendency for economic and political conflicts of interest to occur between these groups. Williams documented some of these in *Open Cut*. For Weberians, relations between classes do not involve exploitation. Nonetheless, because classes are defined in terms of possession of marketable resources, and relations of authority and autonomy at work, conflicts of interest around resources and workplace relations are potentially likely (Goldthorpe 1983, 1984).

For stratificationists, on the other hand, the score that an occupation receives on a stratification scale simply indicates the amount of prestige, or socio-economic status that occupation has. This places the occupation in the stratification hierarchy relative to others, but the stratification score is not defined in relationship to the scores of other occupations in the way that classes are defined in relation to others. If we know the average education and income levels of people in an occupation, for example, and we know how these factors influence socio-economic status, we can give the occupation a status score, without taking into account anything about the relationship between this occupation and others. Because stratification measures do not intrinsically incorporate relations between people or occupations, but only the amounts of socio-economic power and privilege that occupations have, there is no inherent linkage between the stratification hierarchy and social conflict. Conflicts of interest occur between actors, whether individuals or organisations, that are in some kind of relationship with one another. Where social structure is not defined by such relationships, there is no intrinsic link between social structure and social conflict.

Social Attainment and Effects on Social Inequality: The Status Attainment Model

Unlike class analysis, much social stratificationism integrates the investigation of our last two analytical questions into a single package, called the *status attainment model* of socio-economic achievement. Typically, the status attainment model combines an investigation of how people acquire social positions, with an examination of the consequences of social position for social inequality, particularly income inequality. For this reason, I shall not separate stratificationists' analyses of the second and third questions, as I did for class analysis.

Status attainment research originated in the United States in the 1960s in the work of Blau and Duncan (1967), and has been represented in Australia primarily by researchers at the ANU (for example, Broom and Jones 1976; Broom, Jones, McDonnell and Williams 1980; Jones and Davis 1986, 1988b). Additional studies have been undertaken at the Australian Council for Educational Research in Melbourne (Williams 1987; Williams and Carpenter 1991; Williams, Long, Carpenter and Hayden 1992), and at the University of Queensland (Carpenter and Western 1989). The status attainment model describes the causes and consequences of socio-economic position over a person's life. Status attainment research views an individual's position in the stratification hierarchy as the result of different causal factors which combine to determine her socio-economic status. This status, and its determinants, then causally effect a person's access to socially valued rewards. In particular, status attainment researchers have concentrated on the relationship between occupational status and earnings. The status attainment approach therefore embeds the analysis of our last two questions in a causal framework which first explains how people acquire positions in the stratification hierarchy, and then considers how position in the hierarchy influences earnings (cf. Broom *et al.* 1980: 9).

In explaining how people acquire occupational positions, status attainment research focuses on two kinds of personal attributes. First, socio-economic attainment reflects the advantages and disadvantages of social origins. We have already encountered this argument in social mobility research. However, status attainment models explicitly incorporate many aspects of social origins that are likely to influence occupational attainment. Factors like family size, parental income, education and occupation, are all relevant. Sociologists call such features of a person's social background *ascribed characteristics*, because they result solely from growing up in a particular family of origin, rather than being subject to individual choice. Social background characteristics are ascribed or assigned to individuals, rather than being selected by them. Second, social attainment also reflects factors which, to some extent, are individually chosen. A person's own education is an important determinant of the job she gets, and within limits, educational attainment is open to choice. Similarly, the job a person ultimately has is partially determined by jobs she has had in the past. These previous jobs reflect individual career decisions and actions. The determinants of socio-economic attainment that are not ascribed, but accessible to choice and action, are called *achieved characteristics*. A large part of status attainment research is about determining whether socio-economic attainment is due more to ascription or achievement. If ascription predominates, then people's socio-economic statuses are principally determined by their social background. Parental circumstances are inherited by children. If achievement is more important than ascription, status attainment is less influenced by social background and is more responsive to individual endeavours. By imposing a detailed causal model on the attainment process, and using statistical techniques that quantify the effects of various causal factors on attainment and inequality, status attainment research tries to assess both the determinants and outcomes of position in the stratification hierarchy (Broom *et al.* 1980: Chapter 1).

The explicit focus on how individuals acquire positions in the stratification hierarchy differentiates status attainment research from intergenerational mobility research. Like status attainment research, mobility research investigates individual movement throughout the social structure from one generation to the next. However, by documenting mobility patterns, mobility analysis tells us something about the class structure of a society. We know whether mobility is common or rare, and whether some movements between specific classes are more likely than others. The overall pattern of mobility that is the object of mobility analysis is a feature of the class structure of a society. On the other hand, status attainment research inquires into the processes shaping individual socio-economic attainment, and the relative importance of ascribed and achieved characteristics to these processes. In this respect, status attainment research is more individualistic than social mobility research.

Most early status attainment research is confined to men (for example Broom and Jones 1976; Broom *et al.* 1980). However, Jones and Davis (1986) supplement their Weberian analysis of men's intergenerational mobility with a stratificationist model of women's and men's attainment (Jones and Davis 1986: Chapter 6). I shall illustrate status attainment research with this example.

Jones and Davis (1986: Chapter 6) propose a status attainment model which lays out the causes and effects of occupational status in sequence as they occur over a person's lifetime. In this sequence, occupational attainment is determined by social background factors and intervening processes of education and entry into paid work. Occupational status and the other ascribed and achieved characteristics then explain how much people earn. The model uses survey data collected in 1973–74. Formally, the model presents status attainment in the following stages: first, the level of education a person obtains before entering the workforce is shaped by social background factors like family size, wealth and parental education; second, social background and educational attainment determine the occupational status of the respondent's first job; third, all these factors influence how much further education a person obtains after beginning paid work; fourth, additional education, plus the other ascribed and achieved characteristics determine a person's occupational status at the time of being surveyed; finally, all the previously mentioned factors (social background, initial education, first job status, additional education and current occupational status) influence how much someone earns (Jones and Davis 1986: 131).

After saying the attainment process follows this causal structure, Jones and Davis (1986) apply statistical techniques which estimate the effects of ascribed and achieved factors at each stage. This analysis suggests that status attainment is largely similar for men and women, with some minor differences. Women's educational attainment is more strongly influenced by their mothers' education than men's education is, and basic education does not influence occupational status as strongly for women as for men. On average, increased schooling produces bigger increases in occupational status for men than women. For both men and women, the main determinant of earnings is current occupational status. However, increases in occupational status result in smaller increases in earnings for women, than men. This is probably because women are more concentrated in particular occupations than men are, so their full-time earnings vary less than men's. In addition, for women, education is a major determinant of earnings, while for men the second strongest cause of earnings is family wealth (Jones and Davis 1986: 129–35). Overall, Jones and Davis' results suggest that social background factors have important effects on educational attainment and first job status, and weaker effects on current job status and earnings. Ascribed social background characteristics therefore affect position in the stratification hierarchy and income level, indirectly, by shaping educational achievement and first job status. A person's educational attainment and first job then determines later occupation and earnings.

The gender differences in attainment are consistent with findings noted several times in the chapter. Jones and Davis' results (1986: Chapter 6) imply women occupy a more limited range of positions in the occupational structure than do men, and that income differences among women throughout the stratification hierarchy are smaller than corresponding income differences among men.

Conclusions

Where do we stand after this long treatment? Most sociologists think Australian society is marked by real divisions of class and occupational position. The evidence from all three perspectives suggests that position in the class or stratification structure has a major impact on people's lives. All approaches agree that the significance of social location arises from differences in power and privilege across the social structure.

Choosing which perspective is 'best' is not easy. My own view is that Marxist analysis is the most powerful way of addressing the questions with which class and stratification research is concerned. Defining class in terms of property, skills and managerial control comes to grips with the empirical complexity of classes in advanced capitalist societies, yet preserves necessary distinctions among the different elements of class structure. Furthermore, Marxists have emphasised causal explanations of how class affects social inequality, mobility, consciousness, and collective action. Social stratificationists and Weberians have also stressed causal processes to varying degrees, but I believe their analyses are compromised by weaknesses in the underlying models of social structure that they use.

Status attainment research has an explicit theory about the causes and effects of occupational status. But stratification scales are conceptually imprecise. An occupation's position in the stratification hierarchy reflects its socio-economic power — a composite of the skills and qualifications the occupation requires, and the rewards and authority it involves. By reducing diverse aspects of socio-economic power to a single score, stratificationists lose the ability to say precisely why position in the social structure is significant for the questions we are interested in. A similar problem faces Weberian class analysis. Goldthorpe, who has the most developed Weberian account of class structure, argues that the service class consists of large business owners, self-employed and salaried professionals, and managers and administrators, all of whom are loyal to the organisation that employs them. This loyalty justifies treating them as a single class. But organisational commitment clearly has a different source for different people within the service class. Business owners and professionals in private practice are committed to organisations that they own, because they own them. Employee managers and professionals are committed to the organisations that employ them because these organisations pay high rewards. These forms of commitment are not the same. To see this, we have only to ask if service class owners and employees would react in the same way to proposals to increase the incomes of service class employees. Other things being equal, employees would likely favour the proposal, while employers would oppose it. The service ethos of managerial and professional employees also seems to differ. Both groups are rewarded for service because their work is difficult to monitor, according to Goldthorpe. But managers and professionals have job autonomy for separate reasons. Managers are not closely supervised by employers, because under corporate capitalism, employers have delegated supervisory responsibilities to managers. Professionals are not tightly supervised because they allegedly have special skills which they must be free to exercise. There is a different basis to the loyalty shown by managerial and professional employees, as there is to that of employers in the service class and employees belonging to the service class. Since the notion of service is internally incoherent, it seems difficult to interpret research findings based on Goldthorpe's scheme.

However, Weberian class analysis and social stratificationism have obviously made very important contributions to class and stratification research. Weberians correctly emphasise that the relationship between class and collective action is less straight-forward than Marxists have commonly assumed, and draw attention to intergenerational mobility to inform this question. Status attainment researchers present an integrated framework for studying the causes and effects of position in the social structure, which class analysis could emulate to clarify further how class shapes the lives of people in class societies.

Common problems also face the three perspectives. One of the most basic involves women's position in the social structure. I have assumed that a women's position in the class or stratification system is determined by her own paid work. This is the strategy adopted by the research in this chapter. In most early research, however, women's paid work was ignored. This view was justified by saying that women's participation in the workforce was so limited that it had no effect on any of the questions in which class analysis and stratificationism was interested. Instead, women's social opportunities were shaped by the social location of a household 'head', like a father or husband. An adequate understanding of how class and stratification affected both men's and women's lives could be derived by focusing solely upon male breadwinners (Goldthorpe 1983, 1984).

Whatever merit this argument might have once had, it carries little weight in a society in which over half of all married women are now in the workforce (McDonald 1988, cited in Baxter 1991: 204), and in which labour force participation rates among all women, especially married ones, are increasing (Australian Bureau of Statistics 1988: 43). An alternative strategy for defining a woman's social location is the one adopted in this chapter. A woman's position in the class or stratification system reflects her own paid work. However this, too, is probably inadequate for some questions. Women still make up about 80 per cent of part-time workers, with married women comprising over half of part-time employees (Women's Bureau 1989). Women, rather than men, interrupt jobs for housework and child rearing. Therefore, many women, for at least part of their lives, depend partially or totally upon the class or stratification circumstances of men. Baxter (1991) found, for example, that when married women in part-time employment are asked to say which class they belong to, they are more strongly influenced by their husbands' jobs than their own.

In considering specific questions of social inequality, consciousness and political behaviour among married and cohabiting women, then, it is sometimes necessary to consider the social circumstances of both spouses.

Furthermore, in defining women's social locations, it is especially important to track work histories over the lifetime. All research in this chapter defines a social location using a 'snapshot' of job characteristics at one time. Non-employed people are 'outside' the class or stratification structure, or are located indirectly by the paid work of another person such as a husband or parent. This strategy presupposes a predominantly male pattern of continuous paid employment. People are only in the class or stratification system directly when they have paying jobs. However, if movement between paid and unpaid work is a common feature of women's employment histories, definitions of social structure should reflect this reality. Future research needs to trace women's and men's work histories, to see if movements in and out of paid work, and from one job to another, follow regular patterns. Then social locations can be redefined to take account of the many ways men and women relate to paid work, rather than basing concepts solely on a male model of labour force attachment. As we move from a snapshot understanding of social structure, to a more realistic approach based upon experiences over the lifetime, we should be able to develop more powerful answers to the other analytic questions in which class and stratification research is interested.

Finally, we need to address the question of social change. Class analysis, in particular, is concerned with this issue, but the research described in this chapter has had little to say on the topic. At the societal level, investigating social change involves studying class and stratification comparatively, either by observing a society over time, or by comparing different societies. Comparative analysis is necessary to understand social change since it permits us to examine similarities and differences in class and stratification processes over historical and national contexts. There is a substantial body of comparative class and stratification research, but rather than referring to this literature, I shall briefly indicate some of the relevant issues. There are two ways (at least) to investigate social change. One is to study the extent to which economic activity is capitalist, since capitalism underpins the class and stratification processes we have been considering. The key elements of capitalism are private ownership of productive property, and production and distribution according to market forces. If societies deviate substantially from these conditions we might argue they are non-capitalist, or 'less capitalist' than societies in which the economy is heavily privatised and market-oriented. The once communist countries of Eastern Europe were distinguished by extremely limited private ownership and centrally organised command economies, and were non-capitalist for these reasons. But capitalist societies also vary in the extent to which market principles guide economic activity. Scandinavian countries like Sweden and Norway have actively pursued government policies which undermine capitalist production and distribution of goods and services. These policies attempted to provide facilities like health care, housing and education to all citizens, regardless of their ability to pay, equalise incomes across the social structure, give employees a say in national economic planning, and generally ensure that a person's standard of living did not depend primarily on how she was located in the class and stratification structures. In contrast, countries like the United States are much more capitalist in economic organisation and public policy. Comparative analysis can tell us what causes these kinds of differences, and how class-based organisations like trade unions or business groups are involved in the process.

In addition, variations in capitalism, over time and between countries, affect how class structures and stratification hierarchies work. We can investigate these processes by examining class and stratification in different national and historical contexts. Given Scandinavian social policy, for example, we might expect smaller income differences between classes in Sweden than in the United States, as well as a weaker overall relationship between class and inequality in Sweden. If we also found major Swedish/American differences in consciousness and behaviour, mobility patterns and so on, we might want to conclude that these were different kinds of societies, since key class and stratification structures operate so differently in each country.

Social change can therefore be examined by looking at the forms of economic organisation societies exhibit, as well as by considering national and historical differences in class structures and stratification hierarchies. Such comparative analyses extend our understanding of class and stratification beyond a single society, or point in time. They also deepen our knowledge, because they show how class and stratification systems are reproduced, and that they are capable of being transformed.

Notes

1. Social groupings that are determined by economic relationships are fundamental because they affect most people's lives in very significant ways, as we shall see. But they are not the only kind of

fundamental group or 'social category' to which people belong. In Australia, as elsewhere, gender, race and ethnicity are all integral dimensions of the social structure which also shape people's lives in various ways (see Williams, Makkai, McAllister and Keen, this volume for discussions of these other dimensions of social structure).

2. Weber's notion of a status hierarchy is superficially similar to the stratificationists' idea of an occupational hierarchy, because both assume that social positions are ranked or ordered from high to low. However, Weber's ideas of status group formation depend heavily upon the lifestyle and consumption factors noted above. The stratificationist concept of social structure does not. Furthermore, Weber, like Marx, does not think that classes can be ranked simply from high to low, on any single characteristic. Thus, in their class analyses, Weberians and Marxists are more similar to each other than to social stratificationists.

3. I use the word 'income' to refer both to monetary (wages and salaries) and non-monetary benefits ('perks').

4. Connell (1991: 145) provides an example of managerial incomes, citing a 1987 assessment by *Business Review Weekly*. This includes a base salary of $60,000, and with additional non-cash benefits, like a car, medical insurance, superannuation, and a housing loan, is worth over $140,000.

5. In some later work, Wright (1989) says that the high incomes of experts need not always be exploitative. However, the technical details of this argument are outside the scope of this chapter.

6. *Making the Difference* refers to private school students as ruling class, and state school students as working class. Since not all the private school students are from capitalist families, I call them middle class, rather than ruling class.

7. Wild's book title, *Social Stratification in Australia*, illustrates the fact that some sociologists use the term social strafication to describe all social differences in power and privilege. From this viewpoint, 'class' is one basis of stratification, along with others such as gender or race. However, I specifically reserve the term 'stratification' for conceptions of social structure that assume that occupations can be hierarchically ranked. On the other hand, 'class' designates relationally defined groupings, that cannot be ranked from high to low.

8. 'Smalltown', like 'Bradstow', is a pseudonym.

9. In fact Dempsey also finds some disparities between Smalltown and Bradstow, with respect to behavioural aspects of status. Unlike in Bradstow, there are few differences in lifestyles and consumption patterns (Dempsey 1990: 178–85) across the community, and friendship patterns are open rather than closed (Dempsey 1990, Ch. 11). However, Dempsey's (1990: 131-141) disagreement with Wild is over the lack of any symbolic prestige hierarchy.

10. Although the Australian Class Project is based around Wright's work, the questionnaire is flexible enough to investigate alternative class conceptions.

11. In 1989, for example, 32 per cent of women were employed in clerical occupations, a further 18 per cent were employed in the

professions and semi-professions, and 23 per cent were in sales and personal service (Australian Bureau of Statistics 1989b, cited in Jamrozik 1991, Table 5.6).

12. Jones is also identified with Weberian class analysis through his mobility research. As we shall see in the next section, Jones' focus on occupational status allows him to approach the question of how people acquire social positions in a slightly different way than mobility research permits. In this case, different perspectives enable complementary research strategies.

13. Often sociologists use the terms occupational prestige scale and occupational status scale synonymously. I distinguish between them to highlight differences in the way they are constructed.

References

Australian Bureau of Statistics (1988) *Census 86 — Australia in Profile*. Canberra: Commonwealth of Australia.

———(1989a) *Census 86 — Summary Characteristics of Persons and Dwellings, Australia*. Canberra: Commonwealth of Australia.

———(1989b) *The Labour Force, Australia, August 1989*. Canberra: Commonwealth of Australia.

Baxter, J.H. (1991) 'The Class Location of Women: Direct or Derived?', in Baxter, J.H., Emmison, J.M., Western, J.S., and Western, M.C. (eds), *Class Analysis and Contemporary Australia*. South Melbourne: Macmillan.

Boreham, P., Clegg, S.R, Emmison, J.M., Marks, G.N. and Western, J.S. (1989) 'Semi-peripheries or Particular Pathways? The Case of Australia, Canada and New Zealand as Class Formations', *International Sociology* 4: 67–90.

Bottomore, T. (1965) *Classes in Modern Society*. London: Allen and Unwin.

Broom, L., Duncan-Jones, P., Jones, F.L. and McDonnell, P. (1977) *Investigating Social Mobility*. Canberra: Department of Sociology, The Research School of Social Sciences, The Australian National University.

———and Jones, F.L. (1976). *Opportunity and Attainment in Australia*. Canberra: Australian National University Press.

———McDonnell, P., and Williams, T. (1980). *The Inheritance of Inequality*. London: Routledge and Kegan Paul.

Burawoy, M. and Krotov, P. (1992) 'The Soviet Transition from Socialism to Capitalism', *American Sociological Review* 57: 16–38.

Carling, A. (1991) *Social Division*. London: Verso.

Carpenter, P.G. and, Western, J.S. (1989) *Starting A Career: The Early Attainments of Young People*. Hawthorn: The Australian Council for Educational Research.

Chamberlain, C. (1983) *Class Consciousness in Australia*. Sydney: Allen and Unwin.

Chant, D.C. and Western, M.C. (1991) 'The Analysis of Mobility Regimes: Implementation using SAS Procedures and an Australian Case Study', *Sociological Methods and Research* 20: 256–86.

Cohen, J. and Rogers, J. (1983) *On Democracy: Toward a Transformation of American Society*. Harmondsworth: Penguin.

Congalton, A.A. (1953) 'Social Grading of Occupations in New Zealand', *British Journal of Sociology* 4: 45–59.

——(1962) *Social Standing of Occupations in Sydney*. Sydney: School of Sociology, University of New South Wales.

——(1963a) *Occupational Status in Australia*. Sydney: University of New South Wales.

——(1963b) *Nurses' Evaluation of Occupational Status and Other Studies*. Research Reports in Nursing, No. 3. Sydney: New South Wales College of Nursing.

Connell, R.W. (1977) *Ruling Class Ruling Culture*. Melbourne: Cambridge University Press.

——(1985) *Teacher's Work*. Sydney: Allen and Unwin.

——(1991) 'The Money Measure', in O'Leary, J. and Sharp, R. (eds) *Inequality in Australia: Slicing the Cake*. Port Melbourne: William Heinemann.

——Ashenden, D., Kessler, S. and Dowsett, G. (1982). *Making the Difference: Schools, Families and Social Division*. Sydney: Allen and Unwin.

——and Irving, T.H. (1980). *Class Structure in Australian History*. Melbourne: Longman Cheshire.

Daniel, A. (1983) *Power, Privilege and Prestige: Occupations in Australia*. Melbourne: Longman Cheshire.

Dempsey, K. (1990) *Smalltown: A Study of Social Inequality, Cohesion and Belonging*. Melbourne: Oxford University Press.

Duncan, O.D. (1961) 'A Socio-economic Index for All Occupations', in Reiss, A.J. *Occupations and Social Status*. New York: Free Press.

Edel, M. (1981) 'Capitalism, Accumulation and the Explanation of Urban Phenomena', in Dear, M. and Scott, A. (eds), *Urbanisation and Urban Planning in Capitalist Society*. New York: Methuen.

Emmison, J.M. (1991a) 'Conceptualising Class Consciousness', in Baxter, J., Emmison, J.M., Western, J.S. and Western, M.C. (eds), *Class Analysis and Contemporary Australia*. South Melbourne: Macmillan.

——(1991b) 'Wright and Goldthorpe: Constructing the Agenda of Class Analysis', in J. Baxter, J.M. Emmison, J.S. Western and M.C. Western (eds), *Class Analysis and Contemporary Australia*. South Melbourne: Macmillan.

Erikson, R. and Goldthorpe, J.H. (1985) 'Are American Rates of Social Mobility Exceptionally High?' New Evidence on an Old Issue', *European Sociologial Review* 1: 1–22.

——and Goldthorpe, J.H. (1987a). 'Commonality and Social Fluidity in Industrial Nations. Part I: A Model for evaluating the "FJH Hypothesis" ', *European Sociological Review* 3: 54–77.

——and Goldthorpe, J.H. (1987b) 'Commonality and Variation in Social Fluidity in Industrial Nations. Part II: The Model of Core Social Fluidity Applied', *European Sociological Review* 3: 145–66.

——and Portocarero, L. (1979), 'Intergenerational Class Mobility in

Three Western European Societies: England, France and Sweden, *British Journal of Sociology* 30: 415–41.

———(1982) 'Social Fluidity in Industrial Nations: England, France and Sweden', *British Journal of Sociology* 33: 1–34.

———(1983) 'Intergenerational Class Mobility and the Convergence Thesis: England, France and Sweden', *British Journal of Sociology* 34: 303–43.

Featherman, D.L., Jones, F.L. and Hauser, R.M. (1975) 'Assumptions of Social Mobility Research in the US: The Case of Occupational Status', *Social Science Research* 4: 329–60.

Giddens, A. 1981 *The Class Structure of the Advanced Societies*. London: Hutchinson.

———(1991) *The Consequences of Modernity*. Stanford, CA: Stanford University Press.

Goldthorpe, J.H. (1982) 'On the Service Class, Its Formation and Future', in Giddens, A. and Mackenzie, G. (eds), *Social Class and the Division of Labour: Essays in Honour of Ilya Neustadt*. Cambridge: Cambridge University Press.

———(1983) 'Women and Class Analysis: In Defence of the Conventional View', *Sociology* 17: 465–88.

———(1984) 'Women and Class Analysis: A Reply to the Replies', *Sociology* 18: 491–99.

—— (with C. Llewellyn and C. Payne) (1987) *Social Mobility and Class Structure in Modern Britain*. Oxford: Clarendon Press.

———and Hope, K. (1972) 'Occupational Grading and Occupational Prestige', in Goldthorpe, J.H. and Hope, K. (eds), *The Analysis of Social Mobility: Methods and Approaches*. Oxford: Clarendon Press.

———and Payne, C. (1986) 'On the Class Mobility of Women: Results from Different Approaches to the Analysis of Recent British Data', *Sociology* 20: 531–55.

Graetz, B. (1986) 'Social Structure and Class Consciousness: Facts, Fictions and Fantasies', *The Australian and New Zealand Journal of Sociology* 22: 46–64.

Hall, S. (1977) 'The "Political" and the "Economic" in Marx's Theory of Classes', in Hunt, A. (ed.), *Class and Class Structure*. London: Lawrence and Wishart.

Hayes, B.C. (1990) 'Intergenerational Occupational Mobility Among Employed and Non-employed Women: The Australian Case', *The Australian and New Zealand Journal of Sociology* 26: 368–88.

Ishida, H., Goldthorpe, J.H. and Erikson, R. (1991) 'Intergenerational Class Mobility in Postwar Japan', *American Journal of Sociology* 96: 954–92.

Jamrozik, A. (1991) *Class, Inequality and the State: Social Change, Social Policy and the New Middle Class*. South Melbourne: Macmillan.

Jones, F.L. (1988) 'Stratification Approaches to Class Measurement', *The Australian and New Zealand Journal of Sociology* 24: 279–84.

———(1989) 'Occupational Prestige in Australia: A New Scale', *The Australian and New Zealand Journal of Sociology*. 25: 187–99.

————and (1986) *Models of Society: Class, Gender and Stratification in Australia and New Zealand*. Sydney: Croom Helm.

————and Davis, P. (1988a) 'Class Structuration and Patterns of Social Closure in Australia and New Zealand', *Sociology* 22: 271–91.

————(1988b) 'Closure and Fluidity in the Class Structure', *The Australian and New Zealand Journal of Sociology*.

Lee, D. and Newby, H. (1983) *The Problem of Sociology*. Hutchinson: London.

Marx, K. (1976) *Capital*, Vol I. Harmondsworth, Middlesex: Penguin.

————(1983) *Grundrisse*. Harmondsworth, Middlesex: Penguin.

————and Engels, F. (1958) *The Manifesto of the Communist Party*. Moscow: Progress Publishers.

McDonald, P. (1988) 'Families in the Future: The Pursuit of Personal Autonomy', *Family Matters* 22: 40–47.

McMichael, P. (1984) *Settlers and the Agrarian Question: Foundations of Capitalism in Colonial Australia*. Cambridge: Cambridge University Press.

Przeworski, A. (1980) 'Material Bases of Consent: Economics and Politics in a Hegemonic System', *Political Power and Social Theory* 1: 21–66.

————and Wallerstein, M. (1982) 'The Structure of Class Conflict in Democratic Capitalist Societies', *The American Political Science Review* 76: 215–38.

Quine, S. (1986) 'Comparison of Australian Occupational Prestige Scales', *The Australian and New Zealand Journal of Sociology* 22: 399–410.

Reiss, A.J. (1961) *Occupations and Social Status*. New York: Free Press.

Roemer, J. (1982) 'New Directions in the Marxian Theory of Exploitation and Class', *Politics and Society* 11: 253–87.

Shryock, H.S, Siegel, J.S. and Associates (1971) *The Methods and Materials of Demography*. Washington: US Bureau of the Census.

Weber, M. (1982a) 'Status Groups and Classes', in Giddens, A. and Held, D. (eds). *Classes, Power and Conflict: Classical and Contemporary Debates*. London: Macmillan.

————(1982b) 'The Distribution of Power: Class, Status, Party', in Giddens, A. and Held, D. (eds) *Classes, Power and Conflict: Classical and Contemporary Debates*. London: Macmillan.

Wells, A. (1991) *Constructing Capitalism: An Economic History of Eastern Australia, 1788–1901*. Sydney: Allen and Unwin.

Western, J.S. (1983) *Social Inequality in Australian Society*. South Melbourne: Macmillan.

Western, J.S. (1991) 'Class in Australia: The Historical Context', in Baxter, J.H., Emmison, J.M., Western, J.S., and Western, M.C. (eds), *Class Analysis and Contemporary Australia*. South Melbourne: Macmillan.

————Western, M.C., Emmison, J.M., and Baxter, J.H. (1991) 'Class Analysis and Politics' In Baxter, J.H., Emmison, J.M., Western, J.S., and Western, M.C. (eds), *Class Analysis and Contemporary Australia*. South Melbourne: Macmillan.

Western, M. C. (1991) 'The Process of Income Determination', in Baxter, J.H., Emmison, J.M., Western, J.S., and Western, M.C. (eds), *Class Analysis and Contemporary Australia*. South Melbourne: Macmillan.

————(1992) 'Class Structure and Intergenerational Class Mobility: A Comparative Analysis of Nation and Gender', Paper presented to the Annual Meeting of the American Sociological Association, Pittsburgh, Pennsylvania.

Wild, R. A. (1974) *Bradstow: A Study of Status, Class and Power in a Small Australian Town*. Sydney: Angus and Robertson.

————(1978) *Social Stratification in Australia*. Sydney: Allen and Unwin.

————(1981) *Australian Community Studies and Beyond*. Sydney: Allen and Unwin.

Williams, C. (1981) *Open Cut: The Working Class in an Australian Mining Town*. Sydney: Allen and Unwin.

Williams, T. (1987) *Participation in Education*, Hawthorn, Victoria: Australian Council for Educational Research.

————and Carpenter, P.G. (1991) 'Private Schooling and Public Achievement in Australia', *International Journal of Educational Research* 15: 411–31.

————, Long, M., Carpenter, P., and Hayden, M. (1980) *Year 12 in the 1980s*. Canberra, AGPS.

Women's Bureau (1989) *Women at Work — Facts and Figures, July 1989*. Canberra: Department of Employment, Education and Training.

Wright, E. O. (1978) *Class Crisis and the State*. London: Verso.

————(1985) *Classes*. London: Verso.

————(1986) 'What is Middle about the Middle Class?', in Roemer, J. (ed.), *Analytical Marxism*. Cambridge and Paris: Cambridge University Press and Editions de la Maison des Sciences de l'Homme.

————(1988) 'Exploitation, Identity and Class Structure: A Reply to My Critics. *Critical Sociology* 15: 91–110.

————(1989) 'Rethinking, Once Again, the Concept of Class Structure', in Wright, E.O., Becker, U., Brenner, J., Burawoy, M., Burris, V., Carchedi, G., Marshall, G., Meiksins, P., Rose, D., Stinchcombe, A., van Parijs, P., *The Debate on Classes*. London: Verso.

————, Howe, C., and Cho, D. (1989) 'Class Structure and Class Formation: A Comparative Analysis of the United States and Sweden', in Kohn, M.L. (ed.), *Cross-national Research in Sociology*. Newbury Park: Sage.

Chapter Four

Patriarchy and Gender: Theory and Methods

Claire Williams

Feminist theories are located within political agendas about appropriate social change strategies. The most enduring political agenda has been the equality project, where feminist politics and theory has been oriented to the issues of women obtaining parity with men in such areas as pay and employment. One problem with it has been that the issue of equality does not address all questions satisfactorily: for example, abortion as an issue has no male counterpart. A further related area where the question of equality does not assist us is in the way women's daily location across spheres such as paid and unpaid work (or, to put it another way, across work and the family) has to be addressed. It is the lack of fit between men's continuous work histories and women's often interrupted ones, through child rearing, which leads to women having inferior access to income, including margins for skill, promotional opportunities, superannuation, employment related social security benefits and workers' compensation.

A quite different strategy from the equality project has come from the influence of French post-structuralist thinkers, such as Foucault, Derrida and Irigaray, which draws attention to the way the world is ordered or conceptualised rather than the losses and gains caused by inequality, and 'strikes at the basic categories that enable sexism to exist' (Ferguson 1991: 337). This focus on categories of thought has been called the deconstruction project. It seeks to deconstruct gender in order to reject the very dualism of men/women, public/private which has resulted in a hierarchy in which one group (men) was declared primary and the other (women) subordinate. Deconstruction tries to transcend the binary differences that govern how all codes work. Some people are excluded because of the categories of thought commonly used. In acknowledging this, we can recognise the political claims of those marginalised by these prevailing categories of thought; this acknowledgment is often referred to as the politics of difference. The deconstruction project also encourages us to conceptualise people as subjects with bodies rather than as disembodied brains. Much of what has passed for rational thought is increasingly regarded as the product of masculinity. It contains an unsatisfactory notion of a rational, cognitive male subject, always disembodied. Bringing the body centrally into feminist theory marks an advance on previous conceptualisations because so much of what women do is related to the body.

Ferguson argues that while the deconstruction project seems at times to oppose other projects such as the equality project, we should seek to strengthen the connections between them. The equality project remains an important cornerstone of much feminist theorising. The charismatic appeal of the call for equality with men has provided much of the impetus for the gains of the women's movement in countries like Australia.

This chapter provides an overview of the major feminist theories and research findings relating to gender issues which are relevant for an understanding of Australian society. Following an introduction to the equality project and the deconstruction project, a discussion of the dimensions of gender inequality in Australian society is provided. These findings are then considered in the context of feminist theories. Feminist methodologies which have been developed to overcome the inadequacies of traditional positivist research methods are then outlined and finally examples of Australian studies informed by feminist consciousness are presented.

Dimensions of Inequality

In the 1970s, a number of researchers (Power 1975; Moir and Selby-Smith 1979) pointed out the marked degree of sex segregation of occupations in Australia, where 80 per cent of women are concentrated in occupations which are disproportionately female, such as clerical, service and sales. Moir and Selby-Smith also found segregation by industry, with women concentrated in particular industries. One reason for the preoccupation with the process of sex segregation by occupation and industry is that, without its recognition and substantial modification, women workers are unlikely to obtain economic equality with men. The industries where women predominate, such as retail, textile, clothing and footwear, finance and business services, have the lowest average weekly earnings. By contrast, certain male-dominated sectors such as mining, basic metal products, electricity, gas and water, transport and storage, have average weekly earnings above the mean (National Women's Consultative Council 1990: 24). Power was pessimistic about the possibilities of this situation changing because of the way in which male-dominated occupations became women's occupations once a large number of women entered them; men no longer entered the occupation (Power 1975: 31).

Nearly two decades later, women still tend to be clustered in positions which pay less than men's jobs, usually in less powerful industries (Table 4.1). At one level Australian women under the centralised wage fixing system have fared better in terms of the gender gap than their sisters in decentralised systems in Japan, Canada and the United States which have the highest wages

Table 4.1   Occupational Segregation, Full-time and Part-time Employment by Occupation, February 1991

| Major occupational group | % of Women | Females | | Males | |
		Full-time '000	Part-time '000	Full-time '000	Part-time '000
Managers and administrators	24.8	14.4	6.0	60.2	1.6*
Professionals	42.1	19.7	11.4	39.6	3.1
Para-professionals	46.3	12.6	6.6	21.7	0.7*
Tradespersons	12.6	8.6	4.5	88.1	3.4
Clerks	78.4	49.5	28.8	20.7	0.8*
Salespersons and personal service workers	61.9	22.8	35.8	29.4	6.6
Plant and machine operators and drivers	17.4	6.2	1.9*	36.6	1.8*
Labourers and related workers	40.3	18.3	29.6	56.3	14.8
Total		152.0	124.6	352.4	32.8

*Subject to sampling variability too high for most reasonable uses
Source: ABS, Labour Force Survey, unpublished data; south Australia Women's Adviser's Office, Department of the Premier and Cabinet and the Australian Bureau of Statistics, Adelaide, *Women's Work*

gender gaps. It is likely that this gap will now widen in Australia as the centralised wage fixing system is dismantled and replaced by 'enterprise bargaining'. In 1989, women earned 83 per cent of the average ordinary time earnings of their male counterparts, but this ratio drops to 65 per cent when part-time and overtime earnings are included. Women on average work only one-quarter of the overtime than do men, but even more significant is the fact that women receive fewer over-award payments than men — with the exception of managers and administrators. Women professionals and clerks in the private sector earn only 80 per cent of the over-award payments of men in the same categories, and women in sales and trades earn a mere 31.7 per cent and 29.2 per cent respectively of the over-award payments of their male counterparts (National Women's Consultative Council 1990: 25, 40). In the professions, women predominate in those with lower status and salaries, such as teaching, social work, the therapies, and in what is called the semi-professions, such as nursing (Mumford 1989: 20).

In many areas of employment-related conditions and benefits, considerable changes will have to ensue before women workers have access to benefits on a par with male workers. Before the recent changes to superannuation, only 25 per cent of women workers were members of a superannuation scheme, compared with 49 per cent of male workers. Only 4 per cent of part-time workers, who are mainly women, were members of a super-annuation scheme (Sharp and Broomhill 1988). The reforms to superannuation have improved this situation, but women have consistently lower scheme membership yet live longer than men, so their need for retirement income is on the average greater. Women's interrupted job histories, through primary responsibility for the couple's parenting, reduces women's capacity to accu-mulate significant superannuation benefit (Tiddy 1992), and for full-time homemakers there is no independent income to accumulate.

Women's subordination clearly persists and the next section will consider feminist theories which have the power to amplify our understanding of why this occurs, and to suggest directions not only in terms of thinking about these issues but in framing the directions of political activity to remove this subordination.

Feminist Theories

Over the last two decades of feminist writings, quite varied feminisms have emerged. When the second wave of feminism to follow the suffragette movement emerged in the 1960s, two of the most influential theoretical perspectives were radical feminism which has manifested itself more recently in cultural feminism, and socialist feminism influenced by Marxism. Both of these will be outlined briefly before other kinds of feminisms, influenced by the deconstruction project, are discussed.

The radical feminist, Adrienne Rich, first coined the term 'patriarchy' to refer to the universal oppression of women. Patriarchy is the power of the fathers: a familial-social, ideological, political system in which men, by force, direct pressure, or through ritual, tradition, law and language, customs, etiquette, education and the division of labor, determine what part women shall or shall not play, and in which the female is everywhere subsumed under the male. Under patriarchy, I live in purdah or drive a truck (Eisenstein 1984: 5).

Shulamith Firestone, in *The Dialectic of Sex* (1972) is perhaps the best known exemplar of radical feminist thinking. Firestone and other radical feminists hold that gender oppression (the oppression of women by men) is the oldest and most profound form of social inequality, predating and underlying all other forms, including race and class. Firestone argues that the Marxist analysis of the class division in society is not radical enough, because it does not relate the structure of the economic class system to its origins in the sexual class system (Firestone 1972: 43). She believes that Freud grasped the crucial problem of modern life: sexuality. Freud, when referring to the Oedipal complex, describes power in a patriarchal family where women and children are dependent on the father (Firestone 1972: 48). She makes a somewhat crude cultural dichotomy between men and women, seeing men as essentially intellectual and creative, whereas women are preoccupied with love: 'Women live for love and men' (p. 1). She sees two basic cultural divisions: the male technological mode and the female aesthetic mode (p. 165).

Firestone analyses romanticism and the part it plays in re-inforcing sex class. Eroticism is part of romanticism. The distinguishing characteristic of women's exploitation as a class is sexual. For each woman, her sexuality becomes synonymous with her individuality. Men characterise women physically, as walking embodiments of breasts, legs or bottoms, singly or in combination. As a result, women come to value themselves in this way. This sex privatisation causes women to become preoccupied with their worthiness as sex objects, while blinding them to their sexploitation as a class (1972: 142). If such characteristics are the only things valued, why trouble to develop real character? As

Firestone put it, it is therefore far easier to light up the room with a smile until that day when the 'chick' graduates to 'old bag' and finds that her smile is no longer 'inimitable' (p. 143). The kind of face that is typified as the sex object ideal does not allow for growth, flux and decay. Firestone wonders whether such a face expresses negative as well as positive emotions or 'does it falsely imitate the very different beauty of an inanimate object, like wood trying to be metal? (p. 147).

Radical feminists locate gender as a main form of oppression in its own right, a subordination whose dynamic lies in sexuality, reproduction and culture. Because they tend to regard the oppression of women as universal, crossing race and cultural boundaries, as well as those of race, class, age and physical ability, they have been accused of an unjustified assumption of female commonality. In countering this charge, they argue that everywhere women still have to fight to control their own bodies and that the basic right to divorce has still to be won in many countries. From the beginning, the crucial value of their approach has been in directing attention to women's control of their bodies, and the analysis of the body as a primary site of women's oppression. Their critique of the male control of medicine and the influence of the Women's Health Movement have formed one of the main catalysts for a revision of how women's health is regarded and managed (Rowland and Klein 1990: 285). In addition, radical feminists have been unafraid to look at the violence done to women by men and this focus has led to an extensive body of work on rape, pornography, incest and sexual slavery (Rowland and Klein 1990: 287).

Socialist feminism aims to focus on the system of subordination of women, which increasingly and loosely has come to be referred to as 'patriarchy', and the relationship of this subordination to the capitalist mode of production. As Eisenstein points out (1979: 16), the study of women's oppression must deal with both sexual and economic material conditions if we are to understand oppression rather than merely economic exploitation. At the same time, patriarchy should not be understood as merely biological. She argues that capitalism and patriarchy are neither autonomous nor identical systems. They are, in their present form, mutually dependent (1979: 21). This assumes that the patriarchal structure will change its form in response to the essential nature of capitalism. An example of this would be the way the family changed under capitalism. Production was no longer based on the family, as it had been in the non-capitalist period, but men still retained their dominance. At the same time, capitalism incorporated patriarchal forms into its structure. For example, labour recruitment reflected aspects of the gender division of labour.

Within a similar frame of reference, Hartmann (1981) developed a socialist feminist analysis through a concept of patriarchal capitalism (p. 18). Her concept of patriarchy rests upon two notions, one of hierarchy and the other of male dominance. She defines patriarchy as a set of social relations between men which has a material base, which depends on men owning and organising the economy. Even though class society is hierarchical, there is sufficient interdependence and solidarity among men to enable them to dominate women (p. 14). In the hierarchy of patriarchy all men, whatever their rank, are bought off or rendered less oppositional by being able to control at least some women (p. 15).

While Hartmann does at times discuss interdependence, her analysis is firmly subsumed under what rapidly came to be termed 'dual systems' theory. There is an assumption here that there are two separate systems of subordination with separate central determinants, a class system and a patriarchal or gender system. However, dual systems theory has been criticised on a number of grounds. Hartmann's definition of patriarchy tends to conceive of women's subordination in terms of individual men and collectivities of men dominating women. However, the way the system is structured, with women primarily responsible for child rearing, is more important than the wilful actions of individual men. Hartmann's most important contribution lies in her critique of Marxist categories such as class, which she describes as 'sex blind', since a concept like 'class' does not explain why particular people fill particular places, and why women are concentrated in working class positions. It gives no clues as to why women are subordinate to men inside and outside the family, not the other way round (p. 10).

While socialist feminist analysis has the strength of allowing us to consider the inter-relation of two sets of hierarchies, those based on gender and those based on class, partly under the influence of the deconstruction project, class increasingly came to be regarded as a limited concept which foregrounds other bases of subordination such as those based on sexuality or disability. Not only is the old industrial proletariat declining and being replaced by service workers, but newer forms of cultural experience are demanding attention. In addition, challenges to feminists from women of colour, lesbians and disabled women have led to a growing awareness of the important differences among and between women, and prompted attention towards the existence of a number of distinct projects of equality as well as those based on gender and class. These include race, sexuality, disability and age. In this schema, Cockburn (1990: 172) describes power as not one but rather a set of mutually reinforcing dominance relations. The upper reaches of the hierarchies of this class power are held not only by white men but by those who are primarily heterosexual and non-disabled.

The deconstruction project mentioned at the beginning of this chapter, and Foucault's work in particular, allows an earlier recognition of the importance of the body and the way it does not merely exist but is actively and historically produced through power. Foucault's conception of the body as an historical and culturally specific entity rather than a biological one, and his insight that sexuality (rather than a pre-given state) is produced in the body in order to structure social relations, breaks with one of the most important and implicit Cartesian dualisms of Western thought: that the mind is separate from the body. These insights about the body have provided the impetus for recent work on femininity and masculinity (McNay 1991). Unfortunately Foucault's analysis does not pay enough attention to the gendered nature of disciplinary techniques on the body. A number of feminist writers (Harding 1986; Smith 1987; Pateman 1988) have explored the specific cultural and historical embodiment of men and women in particular societies, regarding this as fundamental to the way inequality is perpetuated. In Smith's analysis, in the public world of work and organisations, professionals and managers proceed in an abstracted conceptual mode which is based on other people performing their bodily maintenance. It is a condition of anyone's being able to enter, become and remain absorbed in the conceptual mode of action that they do not need to focus their attention on their labours or on their bodily existence (Smith 1987: 81). Pateman similarly argues that the notion of the citizen is based on the disembodied notion of a universal individual who is a man (Pateman 1988: 223; Acker 1990: 149). For this citizen to go out to work, women must specialise his embodiment and that of their children: she must attend to his body, feed him, clean up after him and look after their children. This hidden embodiment of men through the specialisation in embodiment by women, produces the false construct of the rational actor going out to work. As a result, women are conceptualised as the repositories of embodiment, and can be regarded as bringing embodied, and thus illegitimate, qualities such as emotions and different needs for working hours to the 'rational', 'public' workplace. Smith regards the sanitised non-emotional public world of men as the product of a bifurcated consciousness:

At almost every point women mediate for men the relation between the conceptual mode of action and the actual concrete forms on which it depends. Women's work is interposed between the abstracted modes and the local and particular actualities in which they are necessarily anchored. Also women's work conceals from men acting in the abstract mode just this anchorage.

(Smith 1987: 83–4)

In addition to Foucault, other post-structuralist writers such as Derrida, Lyotard and Lacan have had effects on the direction feminist theories have taken, and as a result post-modern feminists have emerged. In a deliberately schematic way, a range of positions will be set out distinguishing these thinkers from those such as Marx. With these thinkers we return in sociology to the pre-eminent importance of language. For social interaction, language is regarded as an active medium rather than a transparent one. Foucault takes the position that language is at the heart of critique. A central tenet of Western metaphysical thought, the innocence of reason, is destabilised by focusing on language or, in Foucault's terminology, discourse. According to Poster (1989: 109), French post-structuralists ground their critiques in forms of linguistic experience, as opposed to forms of consciousness or action. Language is the place where our sense of ourselves, our subjectivity, is constructed (Weedon 1987: 21). For example, the meaning of woman is not fixed by the natural world, but is socially produced within language and discourse, the latter becoming sites of political struggle.

In his work, Derrida undertakes a critique of Western metaphysics with an aim to destabilise confidence in it. He particularly attacks the assumption that we can grasp the essence of a thing in itself, its integrity. For him there is no possibility of grasping the essence of an object, a concept or person in an unmediated way, because we must always pass through language; for him, there is no reality outside the discourse. Because of this assumption of essence, Western thought is based on a set of binary oppositions. Being is always contrasted to absence so we apprehend the world through dualisms like man/woman, culture/nature, good/evil, speech/writing, raw/cooked. Each of these pairs has the first term valued at the expense of the second. Derrida's concept, *differance* refers to the inevitable gap between the object and our perception of it, through language.

Derrida developed a technique called deconstruction of texts designed not to 'prove wrong' what is written in any text, but rather to show how the primacy of one meaning in the text is created by the suppression of others (Duchen 1986: 75, 153). The reversal of binary pairs, however, is merely to remain within logocentrism or the dominant form of Western thought. Sometimes he creates a third term beyond the binary pair such as *differance* which is poised over both binary categories, sameness and difference (Grosz, 1989: 30–31).

Feminists saw potential in Derrida's critique of binary oppositions because, for example, it left open the way for the feminine not to be bound to the masculine, and recognised that other forms of thought could exist. French Feminists philosophers such as Kristeva, Irigaray and Cixous used the concepts and ideas of Derrida and Lacan as frameworks to locate their own reflections, and later to challenge them.

It is helpful to be aware of the concept of 'other' in French philosophy which provides a conceptual context for some of these ideas. 'Otherness' in French philosophy has two connected meanings: first the other in relation to the speaking subject (French radical feminists said that women have been defined as 'other' by men in the sense of 'inferior'). Second, 'otherness' refers to that which is outside a dominant conceptual scheme. This meaning of 'otherness' does not subscribe to an identifiable set of norms, values and practices that the Western Judeo-Christian world can assimilate and understand. For feminist thinkers such as Cixous and Irigaray, 'otherness' is the feminine, to be understood as a new way of thought beyond the dominant patriarchal ways of thinking (Duchen 1986: 70–71).

French feminists took advantage of these developments in, and critiques of, the French philosophical tradition to reorientate the destabilisation of meaning and identity in a way that was favourable to women, and to try to bring the 'feminine' into existence. Patriarchy inhabits the individual through language and in binary methaphysical thinking. For Irigaray, language, though presented as universal and neutral, is in fact patriarchal and masculine; she seeks to uncover its seemingly neutral stance. For Irigaray and Cixous, if the basic drive of the masculine is to unify, stabilise and rationalise, then the feminine must resist, and remain multiple and diffuse. Irigaray re-examines women's sexuality as the possible location of the feminine and proposes that women engage in homosexual and auto-erotic practice, because female sexuality is self-sufficient and not dependent on the penis for pleasure (Duchen 1986: 90). Another defiant strategy against the Symbolic Order is women's writing, and here feminine texts are regarded as dislodging the masculine and inscribing the feminine libidinal economy on the culture. 'Irigaray's strategy consists in disentangling the human (and the divine) from the masculine order to make women's self-representations (of the human and the divine) possible. This is not simply the placing of female and male viewpoints side by side but the transformations of the "universal", neutral human. Her subversion involves calling the masculine by its name, refusing it the status of the universal' (Grosz 1989: 232). On a political level, this means resistance to organisation and hierarchy of structure, and commitment to a plurality of voice, style and structure (Duchen 1986: 97).

While Duchen recognises the value of the concept of sexual difference, in terms of the basis of women's cultural and material oppression, she regards the feminism based upon this framework as élitist and anti-women in its practice, fearing it will lead to a theoretical and political impasse. In her view, the reliance on sexual pleasure ignores the person, and the other baggage brought to such pleasure. The new feminine identities are heavily reliant on the body rather than incorporating other elements with it. In her view the concept of feminine is still located in binary oppositions, in this case between masculine and feminine, because only the masculine sexual pleasure can be described in the masculine-derived language currently available.

Duchen's outline of French feminism locates each school of thought within specific politics of women's liberation in France itself. In terms of those concerned with the concept of the feminine, their political expression tends to be a group called Psych et Po which grew out of a women's study group at the University of Paris at Vincennes (Duchen 1986: 32). It aims to undermine masculinity and to bring the feminine into existence. It is at odds with feminist groups who stress the material conditions of working class women's lives. Other French feminists, particularly materialist ones, regard the concept of the feminine as based on an ahistorical essence, which in their view is essentialist. Duchen goes as far as to say that to posit a real feminine implies a stage prior to social existence, an undistorted female sexuality libidinal economy, waiting for the right time to emerge, like a butterfly. In her view, this is simply a romantic notion, like the idea of the noble savage. In this sense it is profoundly unsociological. Duchen ultimately regards feminine thought as élitist because other feminist approaches are denied any value. It works against having any respect for what other women are trying to do.

Grosz, an Australian advocate of the deconstruction project, in asserting the importance of the work of Kristeva, Irigaray and others, is at pains to acknowledge the importance of 'other forms of struggle in which feminists are engaged', such as the equality project. In her view, however, without the critical feminist awareness of the ways patriarchal knowledges informs everyday language and life, provided by the deconstruction project, and without alternative frameworks of knowledge and representation, women will remain tied to a series of oppressive concepts and values (Grosz 1989: 234).

Advocates of the equality project and the deconstruction project often write as if they were in total opposition to each other and had nothing in common. Ferguson has pointed out ways that the two projects are interrelated and both could benefit from what she calls a 'conversation' with one another. In the end, the deconstruction project is a dependent one relying on other writings 'in order to have something to deconstruct' (Ferguson 1991: 337). Its single-minded pursuit avoids the problem of political action. The equality project, on the other hand, has been over-confident about the goals we should pursue, and offers us a simplistic solution of a better, alternative society. As a result of seeking unity between women, it has flattened out important differences between women. The goals of the deconstruction project have been to 'unsettle the settled contours of knowledge and power in order to make way for disunities and misfits, to let difference be' (Ferguson 1991: 333). Both projects present dangers. For the deconstruction project, the danger is paralysis: that nothing can be done because no final truth can be found. The equality project poses the danger of presenting a false authoritarian certainty: that there is only one way to do things. This will be oppressive for certain people excluded by the 'truth', which has been found. To borrow an idea from Ferguson, the various projects need to listen to one another: deconstruction keeps the equality project honest, and the equality project gives deconstruction direction (Ferguson 1991: 337). One of the lasting legacies of the deconstruction project is the observation that we should exercise caution in wanting a simple transcendent position toward a higher unity. We have to learn to live with a lack of completion.

The next section will take up some of these themes, not in relation to theories of feminism, but to the methodological writings which have appeared in the last decade addressing questions of how we should go about the complex process of studying gender, and women in particular. Writings about methods are based on questions of both ontology and epistemology: questions about how we know what we know, and questions about how we represent complex social reality in the rather crude ways that are available to us. Do we reproduce these complex processes with numbers, as the men who studied sociology until 1960 preferred to do? Do we use the qualitative methods developed by other men? Are the existing methods available in sociology merely further examples of logocentrism (dominant forms of masculine thought), and should we be trying to transcend these methods to develop entirely new ones?

Feminist Methods

One of the main ways that sociologists have hitherto studied people is to use a scientific frame of reference and techniques such as surveys, interviews and statistical analysis. Such research is based on a number of scientific values: the verification principle or the search for evidence, and a belief in objectivity (facts and values can, it is argued, be separated). In scientific sociology, values are only permitted expression at the stage of choosing the subject to research; otherwise they are regarded as contaminating.

Many feminists have opposed this view of what constitutes a scientific (positivist) approach, because the separation of facts and values in mainstream sociology and social science has produced 'facts' which are male-biased and which have helped perpetuate the invisibility of women in 'legitimate' intellectual discourse and pursuits. These so-called 'facts' are based, it is argued, on assumptions which remain unquestioned. A different set of assumptions — in effect, values — is required to point out that the facts are biased.

Male-centred or androcentric 'objective' methods, without the challenge of feminism, were unable to detect or eliminate what have now come to be regarded as blatant gender biases (Harding 1990: 94). But the situation is more complex than just remedying the bias and doing 'better', 'more objective' science by including women, for the reasons suggested by the deconstruction project. As Dorothy Smith has pointed out, male social scientists have constructed the abstract, conceptual world of objective research methods out of their partial consciousness, based on the camouflage of their own embodiment. Harding (1990: 93) dubs this false objectivity the disembodied mind. By contrast, because most women in cultures such as our own specialise in embodi-ment and the world of emotions and subjectivity, their lives are much more centred within the very experiences that are regarded as the epitome of contamination of the 'objective'. So for a strand of feminist methodology, it is frequently this private, subjective, interiorised, intimate world that their scholarship and research seeks to validate (Cook and Fonow 1986: 5).

In addition, Harding (1986: 249) maintains that what she calls coercive values — those based on racism, classism and sexism — distort and colonise objectivity, the result being not objectivity, but rather 'objectivism'. It is not the spurious doctrine of value freedom, but rather the explicit participatory values of anti-racism, anti-classism and anti-sexism which reduce the distortions and have positive effects on the growth of knowledge (Harding 1986: 249, 1990: 92).

It is possible to characterise the writings on feminist epistemology and methods in terms of two waves. The first included Bowles and Duelli Klein's (1983) collection of essays, *Theories of Women's Studies*, Stanley and Wise's (1983) *Breaking Out: Feminist Consciousness and Feminist Research* and Roberts' (1981) collection of essays, *Doing Feminist Research*, including Oakley's (1981) chapter on interviewing. Oakley's critique of the sanitised textbook mode of interviewing, and her feminist re-formulation of it (plus the debate it engendered with McRobbie and others), raised many of the issues which have remained hallmarks of debates about feminist methods. Oakley was one of the first feminist inquirers to raise the issue of research for women as subjects, not objects, and to underscore that research should gesture towards emancipatory social change for women. She also brought the emotional dimension of the conduct of inquiry to centre stage: she regarded her emotional involvement with the mothers in her study as a strength of her research. Other pre-occupations of writers of the first wave included a critique of objectivity. The answer at the time to this problem was to be explicit about bias by including an account of the research process as central part of the final research report (Stanley and Wise 1983a: 196), and the development of epistemology influenced by the sociology of knowledge (Eisenstein 1982). This emphasis was extended and deepened by second wave thinkers such as Harding.

An article by Acker, Barry and Essenveld (1983: 431) raised three influential themes. They located their research as being at odds with the positivist aim of prediction, and instead described their activity in terms of an adequate reconstruction or faithful depiction of the social world, in line with phenomenological sociology. They were concerned with issues of reciprocity towards the women being studied, and their solution to this was to take back transcripts of analysis to a selection of the women they studied. But at the same time, while they adopt an experiential perspective, they pose their research questions and conduct their analysis using *a priori* theory from feminism and Marxism. There is a possible clash in these two perspectives, in that while they take care to remain close to the women's accounts of social reality, the data is analysed using externally derived theories which may be threatening to them and the patterns of life on which they rely. There has been a strong strand of writing on feminist methods

which recommends that theory should be grounded in the subjects' categories of thought and action, and that samples should
be small, with the principal investigator fully participating in
interviewing, taping interviews, transcribing and gathering up what
is already 'there' (Reinharz 1983: 178). In the second wave of
writing, this emphasis has continued through researchers such as
Billson (1991), who combined it with the reciprocity principle to
develop the 'progressive verification method' in her study of nine
distinct cultural communities in Canada. In this study, there does
not seem to be an obvious conflict between *a priori* feminist theories
and the people's commonsense accounts of reality, because the
latter have predominance. As will be discussed later, Lather (1988)
discusses these conflicts more overtly, where she is retaining a
stronger commitment to *a priori* theory than Billson (in her case,
feminist and post-modernist theory), and the relationship of the
research to social change which benefits women.

The present stage of development is in many ways an exciting
one. Moves in many positive directions in feminist methods and
epistemology are possible. Because of the present turmoil in the
human sciences created by the challenges of post-modernism, the
collapse of old certainties (whether science or Marxism) and the
challenge of anti-sexist, anti-racist, gay and disability movements,
we are more free than ever before to construct new designs based
on alternative tenets and epistemological commitments (Lather
1988: 272). In this sense, alternative feminist epistemologies and
sets of methods are in the process of articulation, and Cook and
Fonow (1986) warn against premature closure 'by stipulating a
"correct" set of techniques without adequate opportunity to
examine a wide variety of other approaches for their feminist
relevance' (1986: 3). Harding (1990: 101) regards us as needing
both enlightenment and post-modernist agendas.

There is no doubt that post-modernist writings have been
influential catalysts for the direction the second wave of feminist
writings on methods and epistemology have taken. A number of
commentators regarded feminism as ultimately located on the
terrain of the Enlightenment. If Enlightenment assumptions were
removed, feminist leanings would no longer be there. In Harding's
view, some post-modernist feminists have gone too far in re-
nouncing the science-based goal of telling 'one true story about
reality'. They have, unfortunately, also given up trying to tell less
false stories (Harding 1990: 100). Lather suggests ways of proceeding which include the post-modern critique. Instead of
presenting one's work as the true discourse, under the influence
of Foucault, she suggests we must view feminism as 'permanently
partial' but less false than androcentric male-centred knowledge.

This framework draws us toward the complexity, contingency and fragility of historical forms and events. So we collect data on changeable, marginal, deviant aspects, anything not integrated, which might suggest fermentation, resistance, protest and alternatives (Lather 1988: 576).

Issues which were embryonically developing in the first wave of writing about feminist methods, the reflexivity of the feminist researcher and the general issue of the politics of research, have gained central prominence under the influence of post-modernism. In mainstream British sociology, there has been a post-modern-inspired debate about the politics of research, the location of the researcher and his/her reflexivity. Reflexivity refers to the location of the researcher and a critical awareness on her or his part of the ways they create the research, affect the participants, and are part of a power relationship with those being researched. The images of the window and the mirror are deployed to capture a continuum of positions about reflexivity. The window characterises the näive view of the empiricist, who looks out the window and tries to reproduce social reality without themselves being included in the picture that is created. The position of ultimate reflexivity, with its nihilist and self-indulgent overtones, would be that of inquirers studying themselves in mirrors. Turner, one of the contributors to this debate, takes what could be regarded as an archetypal post-modernist position. He is influenced by both Gadamer's notion that the researcher is necessarily affected by what he is studying, and Foucault's that the researcher is produced by it. He rejects the näive Enlightenment perspective that the inquirer could go to the field as an agent of knowledge, certainty and control, with the aim of reforming and revising the lifeworld on behalf of his/her fellow men/women (Turner 1989: 19). Instead he takes the view that the researcher shares the moral world which inquirer and subject jointly inhabit, and that part of his task is to clarify the life that the inquirer herself/himself represents. He coins the term 'the connected critic' to describe the necessary reflexive activity.

Gubrium and Silverman use a Foucauldian analysis to show how research itself is deeply implicated in disciplinary regimes. Questionnaires and interviews are new forms of the confessional (telling what is most difficult to tell), and are frequently used as part of establishing what is normal and what is pathological. Researchers, therefore, are part of subjecting people to science's normalising gaze, but often do not question their role in supplying concepts and information to the state (Gubrium and Silverman 1989: 7). While Silverman does not regard sociology as tied into the prevailing cultural apparatus, it always has such potential.

Because he regards knowledge as always implicated in power, his own analysis is quite nihilistic and determinist. He asks whether the researcher can do anything other than survey populations, while embedded in circuits of professional and practitioner power (Silverman 1989: 43). Because he shares Foucault's concept of the subject whose subjectivity is grounded in discourses like those of the professionals, he regards feminist experiential and pheno-menological research such as that described earlier by Billson, as both romantic and essentialist. He dubs them romantic because they assume personal narratives (collected in interviews) are based on some notion of an authentic subjectivity, rather than a self, itself created through disciplinary technologies. He regards such accounts as essentialist because they assume an underlying authentic reality, independent of language and context. Knowledge is always implicated in power (Silverman 1989: 39, 42).

The issue of reflexivity preoccupies Silverman and Turner in terms of less näive epistemology. Despite token gestures, in the end Silverman's 1989 work can be read in terms of his repulsion, like Foucault's, from research which seeks social change. This is where post-modernist methodologists part company with femini-nist researchers, who have always been fundamentally concerned with social change: this is where their notions of reflexivity are often located. Cook and Fonow (1986) write that women researchers like themselves feel a sense of separateness from their research subjects, and that the challenge is to create new and different types of relationships. They admire research on Peruvian women by Barndt, regarding it as work which maintains the dignity of the researcher and those being researched: it is col-laborative because it is aimed at social change: 'The study's focus on women's lives, the importance of consciousness-raising [in this case Barndt talks about the raising of her own consciousness as well as that of the women in her study], the feedback of ideas and world views between the feminist researcher and her Third World women subjects, and an emphasis on the empowerment of women to address their problems and seek changes in their villages' (1986: 15).

Lather, too, regards reflexivity as integrally related to the social change outcome of the research process, which she calls praxis-oriented inquiry. Here her feet are planted well and truly in the Enlightenment, in that while she is clearly influenced by Foucault in her aims to collect data which focuses on fermentation and resistance, in her 1988 work at least, she discusses what feminist and post-modern ways of knowing have to offer towards the development of a less patriarchal, dogmatic Marxism. She goes as far as to say that the type of praxis-oriented inquiry is a reciprocally educative process for the researcher and the researched, and this process is more important than the product because empowering methods contribute toward consciousness-raising and transformative social action. She is very aware of this issue of reflexivity, and sees it partly in relation to the heavy-handedness in the way feminist researchers have used *a priori* theory. On this she says 'reflexivity which will keep us from becoming impositional and reifiers ourselves' (Lather 1988: 576); in her view such work has yet to be done.

Australian Research

Australian feminist research tends to be eclectic, reflecting a range of theoretical concerns raised by radical and socialist feminisms, post-modern feminism, and the feminism of difference. Some interesting recent research is making a significant contribution to transcending the binary divide between the public and private by deconstructing the concept of work. Two such pieces of work will be reviewed. They are Baldock's study of volunteer work and Meekosha's studies of repetition strain injury among women workers. Each in its own way is doing what Smith has urged us to do, since these studies bring into the open the hidden world of both unpaid labour, and embodiment on which the abstract conceptual mode of the world of work and organisations is based. Both studies are influenced by the equality project in the form of socialist feminism, and also by the deconstruction project. Both researchers also have a commitment to putting into practice the principles of treating subjects reciprocally and both have a reflexive research practice.

Baldock's Western Australian study of volunteers in welfare organisations was carried out from 1984 to 1987. It consisted of four phases, an initial interview with 61 representatives of welfare organisations, an initial and a follow-up questionnaire administered to paid and unpaid workers in these organisations, and in-depth interviews with 61 of these workers. Before the study, Baldock also carried out a participant observation study by attending a training course with volunteers. The study is within the tradition of socialist feminism in making the connection between the central use of volunteers (largely women) and the state's response to fiscal crisis.

Baldock argues that the government has rolled back welfare provisions by passing responsibility but not full funding on to non-government organisations and the community. With insufficient funds to cover administrative costs, the latter have responded by using volunteers. By selectively funding acceptable social causes in this minimalist manner, the government maintains social harmony.

Baldock demonstrates that Australian welfare is much more predicated on the unpaid workforce of women than in the United States or Scandinavia. In the former, volunteers tend to be restricted to fund raising and in Scandinavia, there is an absence of volunteers in welfare. Baldock attributes this to the lack of equivalent dependence in Scandinavia created by poverty and inequality, and the much more validated right to paid employment, where women's employment is not marginalised but instead is supported by extensive child care, parental leave and part-time work provisions. Borrowing Hartsock's formulation (1983), Baldock suggests that women's work in most known societies brings them into close contact with 'concrete material life', from which men distance themselves. In addition women deal with human relationships through their continuing responsibilities for the care of kin (1990: 119). In Australia, women's work is much more rigidly separated from men's work, trivialised, regarded as unskilled, transitory and of low value. This marginal attachment of Australian women to the paid labour force has made available a pool of unpaid female volunteers who combine and intersperse volunteer labour with other unpaid work, or with paid work (Baldock 1990: 8). In addition, the Australian community does not provide an adequate level of income security to the poor and other groups, creating a magnified demand for caring labour, which increases people's dependency.

The strength of Baldock's analysis is the connections she makes between unpaid and paid work, the embodied nature of women's work in Australia, the sexual division of labour, and the maintenance of the public sphere in its present form. 'Given the economic climate in which welfare agencies operate in Australia, they can only maintain their assigned role in delivering welfare services if they have access to a pool of workers willing and able to dedicate their time and skills without remuneration'(Baldock 1990: 8).

Using the data from questionnaires and interviews about the background of voluntary workers and their accounts of why they volunteered, Baldock explodes a series of myths about why women do so, especially in relation to the stereotype of altruism. While most are women and in older age groups, a substantial minority are not married, most are white and Australian-born, but 25 per cent also carry out paid work, and a substantial number were defined as working class. However, in relation to motives for joining, she regards the expected motive of altruism as a doubtful one. When it was given as a motive, it was in conjunction with others related to personal development and a desire for social interaction. Baldock regarded altruism as part of an accepted vocabulary of motives for volunteering, but she cautions against regarding it as a mere extension of the compulsory altruism women display in their caring labour for their immediate family. Many women, in fact, engaged in it as a break from the traditional role of wife and mother, and did so against the expressed wishes of their spouses. Some women talked about the respect and recognition volunteering gave them, which they felt they lacked in their roles as housewives or paid workers (p. 95). In addition, it was not uncommon for volunteering to represent a re-entry into the public world, and a way of moving into paid work. Finally, Baldock calls for demystification of the notion of altruism, which she regards as making volunteers hesitant to demand basic rights such as legal protection, specified hours including leave periods, Equal Opportunity, training, promotion and a job description. These provisions would encourage paid staff to treat volunteers as equals, rather than as unreliable amateurs requiring special treatment. The presence of the ideology of altruism has a particularly negative impact on paid workers in community organisations, who were already likely to suffer burn-out, but also then came under added pressure to work excessive amounts of unpaid overtime (Baldock 1990: 115, 135).

But Baldock's analysis is subject to similar criticism levelled by feminists with disabilities at the narrow focus of the caring literature, which has been almost entirely from the point of view of those identified as carers — namely non-disabled women (Morris 1991-92: 22, 38). While Baldock's work importantly argues for the extension of basic employment right to volunteers, a rights-based discourse needs to be extended also to those subject to their labour, who are a fundamental part of the process being described. From the point of view of the latter, more analysis is warranted on the relationship of volunteer labour to the charity discourse which can perpetuate a system denying them their civil rights (Nothdurft and Astor 1986).

However, despite this caveat, I regard this study as valuable in validating the work and concerns of a category of labour rendered invisible by the binary oppositions of private/public and unpaid/paid work. In addition, Baldock's study conforms to some of the canons of feminist research, as summed up in her final methodological statement: 'In fact, as a feminist researcher, I was throughout the study concerned more with quality of interaction and communication than with "representativeness" in conventional survey terms' (1990: 152).

Meekosha's research is particularly innovative, because she is one of the few Australian feminists addressing the question of women and disability (1990), especially in relation to work and occupational health and safety. Her initial research was based on informal discussions with RSI sufferers from many different ethnic backgrounds, working in many industries, and with health professionals, in 1984 and 1985. Its strength lies in the entirely fresh interpretation she brings to RSI research, locating it in a gendered world of work and social reproduction. In doing this, she seeks to transcend the dichotomies of production/social re-production, work/home, body/mind. She began to write this up in a seminal 1985 paper, and since then she and Jakubowicz have co-authored a series of related articles. In the 1985 paper, she argued that the social relations of work are not limited to factory or office, but are indivisibly wound throughout society, and such social relations are not static or gender free. In addition, Meekosha and Jakubowicz (1991) examined the set of professional discourses which successfully delegitimised RSI as an injury throughout the 1980s. They regard RSI as an important example of the way in which technology, class, gender and ethnicity/race are interwoven. Repetition strain injuries were widespread amongst blue collar immigrant workers, particularly women process workers, mainly from Europe and Asia, by the mid-1970s. Recognition as an industrial issue only occurred, however, when the injuries appear-ed in the early 1980s in English-speaking women working with new information processing technologies (1991: 21).

The dichotomies of work/home and public/private are un-fortunately particularly damaging to women RSI sufferers, because the separation between domestic labour and paid work is embedded in the workers' compensation legislation. This means that women are placed in an impossible situation. They have a second unpaid job in the home which means they cannot rest their injured necks, arms and hands, and they rarely have anyone to care for them there as most injured male workers do. They have to pretend they do not have their unpaid job of work in the home because they will be photographed and accused of malin-gering if they are seen to be carrying children or hanging clothes out on the line or washing up, mandatory tasks which they usually continue to perform in a context of pain, because they are not usually in a position to abandon them as responsibilities. This second set of work obligations in the home means that women's experience of RSI is a particular gendered one. Women sufferers receive 23 per cent less money compensation than men, and cases have taken 13 per cent longer to settle (Meekosha and Jakubowicz 1986: 399). Married women have no right to sickness benefit — a situation which applies to married men but is far less likely to affect them. There are no strong norms that husbands should nurse wives and take over their domestic work when they become incapacitated. The compensation system is insensitive to the rehabilitation needs of injured women, and their needs for child care and bus fares to attend relaxation classes.

The majority of sufferers face poverty, isolation, depression, relationship problems, harassment, victimisation and a no-work future (Meekosha and Jakubowicz 1991: 398). These problems have been compounded by public ridicule resulting from both the success of overt media campaigns, and the labelling of sufferers as 'hysterical', following the successful pursuit of key prosecutions by the federal government and insurance interests, with the assistance of professionals (pp. 19, 23). The income loss can be catastrophic to the point of loss of house and car, and being forced back into the home with no real change in the domestic division of labour. Meekosha analyses the way medical practice in relation to the handling of RSI plays a role in constituting and controlling women. The medical literature resorts to stereotypes: that women are physically feeble, unable to survive without male protection, frivolous and irrational. RSI also confounds the simplistic orthodox view that medicine is a science, and that scientific medicine provides the only viable means for mediating between people and disease. Clearly RSI cannot be accommodated within this model and so a common reaction in the medical fraternity is to reject its existence. The sufferer is not in control of the definition of what constitutes disability and how it can be managed (Meekosha and Jakubowicz 1986: 399).

With her socialist feminist emphasis coming to the fore, Meekosha says that the most damaging aspect of the way RSI is managed is the way insurance companies do more than any other institution to ensure it is a permanently disabling condition. This point is particularly significant, because Meekosha is making a connection between disability and the management of occupational health and safety, a point that is rarely made. In their later research into the way medical and social science professionals contributed to the delegitimisation of RSI as a compensatable injury, Meekosha and Jakubowicz's (1991) discourse analysis is influenced by the deconstruction project. In addition, their view of industrial injury as a site of power, through which broader social struggles are given physical form in the body of the injured worker, is redolent of the work of the Foucauldian social historian, Figlio (1982). Meekosha and Jukubowicz identify two major discourses in the Australian medical press which tend to reflect the simplistic popular press debate: Is there a physical injury, or is it all being faked and therefore 'all in the mind'? (Meekosha and Jakubowicz 1990: 399). Similarly, the medical debate has focused on physical causation. While it has been a minor strand within the relevant medical discourse, nevertheless, a number of medical researchers have described a basic biomechanical process of physiological causation which does not deny organic causation and suggests that sufferers exhibit several chemical and structural changes. Other research on causation proffers the view that RSI is caused by a virus striking anyone predisposed to muscle strain (1990: 24). However, the focus on organic pathology has been overtaken by the major preoccupation of influential psychiatrists such as Lucire, Russell and Black, with explanations reverting to the realm of the psyche. The latter are sceptical of physiological evidence, and 'opt for mass hysteria/conversion disorder hypothesis' (Meekosha and Jakubowicz 1991: 24). Thus the medical debate is caught in a mind/body dualism that it is either in the mind (hysteria) or in the body. It cannot encompass an interaction between occupational demands, psychological well-being and physical symptoms. Meekosha and Jakubowicz extend their analysis to scrutinise the discourses of social scientists themselves, which have not been neutral, and have the potential to contribute to undermining the legitimacy of the physical existence of the disease category, RSI. 'Those arguing that RSI is generated socially slip dangerously between arguing that it is caused by trade unions and feminists and that trade unions and feminists responded to the increase of RSI in the workplace' (Meekosha and Jakubowicz 1991: 24).

This account of the social processes surrounding RSI from a feminist viewpoint is important because we know that women under-report, to a marked degree, the extent of their occupational injury and disease (Williams with Thorpe 1992: 153–54). RSI represents the only major claim women workers have made on the workers' compensation system. The 'ferocious' and 'malevolent' resistance of employers, governments, insurance interests and certain professionals to this claim, marks an important episode in the history of women's work in Australia.

Both Baldock, and Meekosha and Jakubowicz, in their modest ways, have completed studies which implicitly challenge one of the main sets of binary oppositions in the way we conceptualise employment. Both studies transcend the separation of the public and the private, welfare and work, the paid and unpaid spheres, but there is also strong political engagement in both studies.

The final study under review is a recent one of Australian men, whose gendered nature has hitherto remained invisible. Connell (1990) is engaged in an Australian study of contemporary masculinity. He is a foremost theorist on masculinity, writing with Carrigan and Lee (1985) one of the germinal articles containing a key concept, hegemonic masculinity. In this recent empirical work, he has chosen several groups of men among whom contradiction in gender relations open up the possibility of historical change. For example, one of the groups studied is young men with fragmentary experiences of the labour market. This chapter will review his study of six life histories of men who, as a result of engagement in Green politics, came under pressure from feminists in the movement, and subsequently engaged in a reconstruction of their masculinity. Connell concludes from this study that the environmental movement is a midwife in terms of gender politics, with the feminist presence providing the social leverage on conventional masculinities (Cannell 1990: 477). In terms of the theories reviewed earlier, this study draws specifically on Connell's own theory of gender as a structure of social practice as set out in his book, *Gender and Power* (1987), and in this is influenced directly by Freud, Sartre and the writings of Foucault on the body, with other writers such as Smith, and transformative goals from the equality project ever-present.

Connell's methodological approach is set out clearly from the start. He adapts the life history approach of Plummer, Dollard and Sartre to incorporate what he calls the 'theorised life history', which allows the studying of personal experience and subjective experience but within a framework of theory about the social process: in this case, masculinity and gender. The life history or autobiographical narrative is derived from descriptions of practices of boy and father interactions; institutional transitions such as entry to the workforce; accounts of interactions in institutions such as families, schools and workplaces. He seeks the emotional dynamics in accounts of early memories, family constellations and relationship crises. As essential starting points for the study of masculinity, he makes use of Freud's concept of the Oedipal crisis, and the dynamic unconscious.

Connell (1990: 454) defines masculinity as 'socially constructed'. It 'has a material existence at several levels: in culture and institutions, in personality and in the social definition and use of the body. It is constructed within a gender order that defined masculinity in opposition to femininity and in so doing sustains a power relation between men and women as groups.'

With each of the six unfolding life histories, he describes a moment at which each boy took up the project of hegemonic masculinity as his own. Danny actively appropriated the world of football as a way of 'being in the world' separate from his father and brother. All six were more or less on track in terms of the reproduction of patriarchy, showing the familiar features of competitiveness, career orientation, a suppression of emotions and homophobia. This is not just a matter of attitudes and style, but the development of a particular experience of the body and physical sensibility.

Within the environmental movement, they embraced a set of values such as a sharp critique of hierarchy and authoritarianism, which even without feminism, provide a challenge to hegemonic masculinity at the level of ideology. The drive to dominate is challenged by the Green movement's emphasis on the democratic process, and the emphasis on personal growth is a challenge to the closed and defensive posture of hegemonic masculinity. Their image of feminism was positive in contrast with the other groups of men in Connell's study, who responded negatively to it. Often they had renounced a career, and were thus separated from the masculine emphasis of workplaces. In Connell's view the moment of separation from hegemonic masculinity involved choosing passivity. 'Since all these men were initially engaged with a masculinity defined by dominance and assertiveness, this choice is likely to be difficult.' In Connell's view, there is something inherently problematic about an active choice to be passive, but renunciation and denial provide the space for new personal qualities to grow. The qualities they admired and wanted to develop most were the capacity to tell the truth, especially about feelings, and to have 'the capacity to have feelings worth expressing: to be sensitive and to have some depth in emotion, to care for people and for nature' (1990: 468). In sexual and domestic relationships they expressed a need to be careful not to act oppressively, not to dominate conversation, or use sexist language. Throughout the record of evidence from this study, there is a great deal of discussion of feelings, and language but not much talk about men doing domestic tasks, which for the present author should have a higher priority as a counter-hegemonic outcome. The men had a great deal of difficulty establishing better relationships with other men, which they desired but could not achieve. Even though, politically, they expressed pro-gay views, Connell found a touch of homophobia in several cases. The body is not perceived as being embodied socially by masculinity as a construct. Instead it was regarded as naturally constituted and harmonious with other parts of nature.

According to Connell's Freudian-influenced analysis, the commitment to a politics of personality in adulthood involved considerable risks because it challenged emotions 'at archaic levels in personality'. To support this analysis Connell highlights one man who described his relationship with a feminist woman like this: 'I felt like I was losing my centre.' Connell's commitment to Freud's notion of Oedipal crisis causes him to liken the men's relationships with strong women to their early relations with their mothers, and leads him to comment: 'To undo masculinity is to court a loss of personality structure that may be quite terrifying: a kind of gender vertigo'(1990: 471). While Connell's use of a personality theory is increasingly necessary to acknowledge the context on which sociological forces operate, Freudianism does not exhaust the possibilities of relevant theories (including non-psychoanalytic ones) which could be used to describe the complex interplay through which identities are constructed and reconstructed.

In his conclusion, Connell suggests that while the men engaged individually with challenging practices, a shift to the level of collective practice is required to reconstruct gender any further than these men have experienced under the influence of feminist politics. In this case, the Green movement's gender politics was limited to the individualised pursuit of the 'true self', emphasising the individual man become more considerate towards women, more emotionally open and sexually passive. In Connell's view, however, the absence of a collective gender project runs the risks of merely reforming and modernising patriarchy, not abolishing it. While a couple of men were involved in tentative small-scale projects (Bill was trying to combine a role in men's counter- sexist groups with environmental activism, and mobilising other men in projects using photography), the logic of such activities contesting the patriarchal order, the individualised outcome for the six men overall suggested only a slight capacity to change social institutions. In the end, degendering was occurring in a still patriarchal society, leaving key issues evaded: the outcome was not transformative. For Connell, this requires the recomposition of the social elements of patriarchy; such a strategy would seek to diversify, rather than homogenise, its social base. Transformation requires a gendered counter-sexist politics for men who reject hegemonic masculinity, based not only on interpersonal but also collective practice working through the contradictions of the oppositions hetero and homo, masculine and feminine, and linked to other solidarities such as those based on racial oppression.

Although I acknowledge the need for a processual theory which provides a link between the personality, emotions and social structure embedded in individual bodies, I have some difficulty accepting the simple Freudian Oedipal crisis theory base of this study. In other respects, the study is innovative and valuable. There is depth and care in the way the data is collected and reproduced. This is one of the first studies to explore the many dimensions of hegemonic masculinity and the processes involved in men coming to terms with challenges from feminism. This study raises issues in relation to dilemmas canvassed in the methods section of this chapter about the relationship of *a priori* theory to phenomenologically-based methods such as life histories. In the best traditions of grounded theory and depth interviewing, Connell's life history method is very careful to remain close to the men's recreation of their own experiences, with them controlling how they reproduce that experience to remain authentic to the way they see their lives unfolding. The small sample size allows a richness of detail to be collected and reproduced. However, it is also clear from the analysis of the research that *a priori* theory has a strong priority in this study. This is really theory-driven research, with care taken to recreate complexity and richness of experience and to explore process. The researcher, however, is firmly in control of the processes chosen to be explored. This contrasts with other uses of similar methods, such as Billson's study of Canadian women, where the theory is subordinated to the research subjects' control of the data. In my view, feminist-influenced researchers have to face this dilemma and make a decision about the use of *a priori* theory, as Connell has done. Billson's study faces the danger that she has merely reproduced the commonsense understandings of her research subjects, and not subjected them to sufficient scrutiny. The dilemmas of feminist research have to be faced openly. Because there are now so many different feminist approaches, it is unlikely that we would want a single solution. Each feminist-influenced researcher will seek a different relationship between theory and the recreation of subjects' meanings, depending on their feminist standpoint.

Conclusion

This chapter began by setting out influential feminist theories, from the earliest radical feminist and socialist feminist approaches to more recent feminisms influenced by the work of Foucault on the body and the deconstruction project of French feminists and their reading of Derrida. What was called the equality project was compared with the deconstruction project. The equality project seeks to analyse women's situation by pointing out commonalities between the lives of women which cause them to be subordinated to men. The political goals are clear: to give women access to the public world hitherto monopolised by men. The deconstruction project has pointed out that the very concepts by which we analyse society derive from male constructs. Smith and other feminists urge that we use as a starting point for theory and research the world of women, which is often focused on the messy realm of the body: caring for it, feeding it, handling it. The objective, so-called 'rational', public intellectual world is a false construct, the product of masculinity based on the hidden body work of women.

The methodologies which have been developed to examine gender and the world of women who were rendered invisible in past research strategies are in a process of development. No firm guidelines exist as yet — nor, possibly, should they. A range of methodologies has been tried, from a preference for experiential methods such as depth interviewing, life histories to triangulation, where quantitative methods are combined with qualitative methods. The latter is chosen partly to expose the past claims of androcentric research to 'objectivity'. The chapter canvassed various dilemmas which concern feminist researchers, including the conflict between *a priori* feminist theory and women's own accounts of their lives. Another dilemma is the issue of the feminist research act which, of itself, causes social change in the lives of those involved in the research. Some handle these issues by developing a collaborative research strategy; others give precedence to their subjects' own accounts over *a priori* theory. One principle which is emerging in answer to the issues of the false objectivity of past research excluding women, is that of reflexivity, which attempts to locate the researcher as an active participant in the research, and an official part of it rather than pretending to be a neutral observer.

Finally, the chapter reviewed three pieces of Australian research which in various ways address the theoretical and research issues developed earlier in the chapter. Baldock's study *Volunteers in Welfare* and Meekosha's analysis of RSI were both presented as examples of research and theoretical assumptions which began from the standpoint of the women themselves, and addressed intractable binary oppositions between paid/unpaid work, and public/private, seeking to transcend them. They represent eclectic approaches influenced by the socialist feminist impetus of the equality project, but both also grapple with issues of deconstruction. Meekosha's work is influenced by Foucault's insights about the body, in this case the body which is rapidly becoming disabled because of the practice of social institutions upon it. Both are trying to put into practice feminist principles about reflexive research practices. Baldock chose to use triangulation or the mixing of a simple quantitative survey with depth interviews.

The third example of Australian research is the third part of Connell's masculinity study, where changes to masculinity, engendered by encounters with the gender politics of the Green movement, are examined through life history studies of six men. These histories provide the opportunity for contextually complex studies of the masculinity process, through recounting memories of their fathers, and encounters in the environmental movement in relationships with feminist women. In the study under review, Connell does not explicitly address issues of researcher reflexivity. However, the study does implicitly take a strong position on the salience of *a priori* theory and social change. The theory used does not involve vulgar categories, and is concerned to interrelate structure and process. But Connell is clear in using the term 'theory life history' that the *a priori* gender theory will make sense of the life histories, rather than a phenomenological assumption that he is merely providing a vehicle for the men's authentic meanings to emerge. One of the goals of the study is well within the parameters of the equality project, uncovering the conditions under which changes to masculinity will transform gender relations, rather than just modernising them. Thus all three pieces of work engage in varying degrees with the main theoretical and methodological issues outlined in this chapter.

References

Acker, J., Barry, K. and Esseveld, J. (1983) 'Objectivity and Truth: Problems in doing Feminist Research', *Women's Studies International Forum* 6 (4): 423–35.

Baldock (Vellekoop), C. (1990) *Volunteers in Welfare*. Sydney: Allen and Unwin.

Bernard, J. (1973) 'My Four Revolutions: An Autobiographical History of the ASA', in J. Huber (ed.), *Changing Women in a Changing Society*. Chicago: University of Chicago Press.

Billson, J.M. (1991) 'The Progressive Verification Method: Toward a Feminist Methodology for Studying Women Cross-Culturally', *Women's Studies Int. Forum* 14 (3): 201–15.

Bowles, B. and Klein, R.D. (eds) (1983) *Theories of Women's Studies*. London: Routledge and Kegan Paul.

Bryman, A. (1984) 'The Debate about Quantitative and Qualitative Research: A Question of Method or Epistemology?', *British Journal of Sociology* XXXV (1), March: 75–92.

Carrigan, T., Connell, B. and Lee, J. 'Toward a New Sociology of Masculinity' (1985) *Theory and Society* 5 (14).

Connell, R.W. (1987) *Gender and Power: Society, the Person and Sexual Politics*. Allen and Unwin, Sydney.

———(1990) 'A Whole New World: Remaking Masculinity in the Context of the Environment Movement', *Gender and Society* 4 (4), December: 452–78.

Cook, J.A. and Fonow, M.M. (1986) 'Knowledge and Women's Interests:

Issues of Epistemology and Methodology in Feminist Sociological Research', *Sociological Inquiry* 56: 2–29.

De Vault, M.L. 'Women Write Sociology: Rhetorical Strategies' in A. Hunter (ed.), *The Rhetoric of Social Research: Understood and Believed.* New Brunswick: Rutgers University Press.

Duchen, C. (1986) *Feminism in France, From May '68 to Mitterrand.* London: Routledge and Kegan Paul.

Eisenstein, Z. (ed.) (1979) *Capitalist Patriarchy and the Case for Socialist Feminism.* New York: Monthly Review Press.

——(1981) *The Radical Future of Liberal Feminism.* New York and London: Longman.

Ferguson, K. E. (1991) 'Interpretation and Genealogy in Feminism', *Signs: Journal of Women in Culture and Society* 16 (2): 322–39.

Fonow, M.M. and Cook, J.A. (eds) (1991) *Beyond Methodology: Feminist Scholarship as Lived Research.* Indiana University Press: Bloomington.

Figlio, K. (1982) 'How Does Illness Mediate Social Relations? Work-men's Compensation and Medico-legal Practices, 1890–1940', in P. Wright and A. Treacher (eds), *The Problem of Medical Knowledge, Examining the Social Construction of Medicine.* Edinburgh: Edinburgh University Press.

Firestone, S. (1972) *The Dialectic of Sex.* London: Paladin.

Foucault, M. (1980) *The History of Sexuality Vol 1: An Introduction.* sqqNew York: Random House.

Gientziotis, J. (1992) 'Pay Equity for Women in Australia', Gender and Work, A Multidisciplinary Conference, University of Sydney: Australian Centre for Industrial Relations Research and Training.

Graham, H. (1983) 'Do Her Answers Fit His Questions? Women and the Survey Method', in E. Gamarnikow *et al.* (eds), *The Public and the Private.* London: Heinemann.

Grosz, E. (1986) 'Philosophy, Subjectivity and the Body: Kristeva and Irigaray', and 'Conclusion: What is Feminist Theory?' in C. Pateman and E. Gross, *Feminist Challenges: Social and Political Theory.* Sydney: Allen and Unwin.

Grosz, E. (1989) *Sexual Subversions, Three French Feminists.* Sydney: Allen and Unwin.

Haraway, D. (1988) 'Situated Knowledges: the Science Question in Feminism and the Privilege of Partial Perspective', *Feminist Studies* 14 (3), Fall: 575–99.

Harding, S. (1986) *The Science Question in Feminism.* Ithaca and London: Cornell University Press.

——(1990) 'Feminism, Science, and the Anti-Enlightenment Critiques' in L.J. Nicholson (ed.), *Feminism/Postmodernism.* New York: Routledge and Kegan Paul.

Hartmann, H. (1981) 'The Unhappy Marriage of Marxism and Feminism: Towards a More Progressive Union', in L. Sargent (ed.) *The Unhappy Marriage of Marxism and Feminism.* London: Pluto.

Hartsock, N.C.M. (1984) 'The Feminist Standpoint, Developing the Ground for a Specifically Feminist Historical Materialism', in S.

Harding (ed.) (1987) *Feminism and Methodology*. Bloomington: Indiana University Press.

Jayaratne, T.E. (1983) 'The Value of Quantitative Methodology for Feminist Research', in G. Bowles and R.D. Klein (eds), *Theories of Women's Studies*. London: Routledge and Kegan Paul.

Lather, P. (1986) 'Research as Praxis', *Harvard Educational Review* 56 (3): August: 257–77.

———(1988), 'Feminist Perspectives on Empowering Research methodologies', *Women's Studies Int. Forum* 11 (6): 569–81.

———(1991) *Getting Smart, Feminist Research and Pedagogy Within the Postmodern*. New York and London: Routledge.

McNay, L. (1991) 'The Foucauldian Body and the Exclusion of Experience', *Hypatia* 6 (3), Fall: 125–39.

Meekosha, H. (1985) 'Gender, the Labour Process and Medicine: Women and RSI', *Conference Proceedings, Vol. 3, Women's Health in a Changing Society*.

———(1986) 'Eggshell Personalities Strike Back — A Response to the Bosses' Doctors on RSI', *Refractory Girl* 29, May: 2–6.

———(1990) 'Is Feminism Able Bodied? Reflections from Between the Trenches' *Refractory Girl* 36. August: 34–42.

———and Jakubowicz, A. (1986) 'Women Suffering RSI: The Hidden Relations of Gender, the Labour Process and Medicine', *The Journal of Occupational Health and Safety — Australia and New Zealand* 2 (5): 390–401.

———(1991) 'Repetition Strain Injury: The Rise and Fall of an "Australian" Disease', *Critical Social Policy* 31, Summer: 18–37.

———(1986) 'Some Social Implications of the Medical Effects of the Introduction of New Technology: RSI — A Case Study', in J.L. Sheppard (ed.), *Advances in Behavioural Medicine*, Vol. 3. Sydney: Cumberland College of Health Sciences: 111–40.

Moir, Hazel and Selby-Smith, Joy (1979), 'Industrial Segregation in the Australian Labour Market', *Journal of Industrial Relations* 21, September: 281–91.

Morris, J. (1991–92) '"Us" and "Them"? Feminist Research, Community Care and Disability', *Critical Social Policy* 33, Winter: 22–39.

Mumford, K. (1989) *Women Working, Economics and Reality*. Sydney: Allen and Unwin.

National Women's Consultative Council (1990) *Pay Equity for Women in Australia*. Canberra: Australian Government Publishing Service.

Nothdurft, J. and Astor, H. (1986) 'Laughing in the Dark — Anti-discrimination Law and Physical Disability in New South Wales', *Journal of Industrial Relations* 28 (3): 336–52.

Oakley, A. (1974) 'The Invisible Woman: Sexism in Sociology' in A. Oakley, *The Sociology of Housework*. Oxford: Martin Robertson.

———(1981) 'Interviewing Women: A Contradiction in Terms' in H. Roberts (ed.), *Doing Feminist Research*. London: Routledge and Kegan Paul.

Plummer, K. (1983) *Documents of Life: An Introduction to the Problems and Literature of a Humanistic Method*. London: Allen and Unwin.

Power, M. (1975) 'The Making of a Woman's Occupation', *Hecate* 1 (3), July: 25-34.

Reinharz, S. (1983) 'Experiential Analysis: A Contribution to Feminist Research', in G. Bowles and R.D. Klein, *Theories of Women's Studies*. London: Routledge and Kegan Paul.

Roberts, H. (ed.) (1981) *Doing Feminist Research*. London: Routledge and Kegan Paul.

Rowland, R. and Klein, R.D. (1990) 'Radical Feminism: Critique and Construct', in Sneja Gunew (ed.), *Feminist Knowledge: Critique & Construct*, London: Routledge.

Sharp, R. and Broomhill, R. (1988) *Short Changed: Women and Economic Policies*. Sydney: Allen and Unwin.

Silverman, D. (1985) *Qualitative Methodology and Sociology, Describing the Social World*. Aldershot: Gower.

———(1989) 'The Impossible Dreams of Reformism and Romanticism', in J.F. Gubrium and D. Silverman (eds), *The Politics of Field Research: Sociology Beyond Enlightenment*. London: Sage.

———and Gubrium, J.F. (eds) (1989) 'Introduction', *The Politics of Field Research: Sociology Beyond Enlightenment*. London: Sage.

Smith, D.E. (1979) 'A Sociology for Women' in J.A. Sherman and E.T. Beck (eds), *The Prism of Sex. Essays in the Sociology of Knowledge*. Wisconsin: University of Wisconsin Press.

———(1987) *The Everyday World as Problematic. A Feminist Sociology*. Toronto: University of Toronto Press.

Stacey, J. (1988) 'Can there be a Feminist Ethnography?', *Women's Studies Int. Forum* 11 (1): 21–27.

Stanley, L. and Wise, S. (1983a) 'Back into the Personal or Our Attempt to Construct Feminist Research' in G. Bowles and R.D. Klein, *Theories of Women's Studies*. London: Routledge and Kegan Paul.

Still, L.V. (1985) 'Women Managers in the Advertising Industry: An Exploratory Study', Women in Management Series, Paper No. 3, Kingswood, NSW: School of Business, Nepean College of Advanced Education.

———(1986) 'Women in Management: The Case of Australian Business', *Human Resource Management Australia*, February: 32–37.

Strong, P. and Dingwall, R. (1989) 'Romantics and Stoics', in J.F. Gubrium and D. Silverman (eds), *The Politics of Field Research: Sociology Beyond Enlightenment*. London: Sage.

Tiddy, J.M. (1992) 'Superannuation, Gender and Work', A Multi-disciplinary Conference, University of Sydney, Australian Centre for Industrial Relations Research and Training

Turner, R. (1989) 'Deconstructing the Field', in J.F. Gubrium and D. Silverman, *The Politics of Field Research: Sociology Beyond Enlightenment*. London: Sage.

Weedon, C. (1987) *Feminist Practice and Poststructuralist Theory*. Oxford: Basil Blackwell.

Weinsheimer, J.C. (1985) 'Introduction: Hermeneutics and the Natural Sciences', *Gadamer's Hermeneutics: A Reading of Truth and Method*. New Haven: Yale University Press.

Williams, C.R. (1981) *Open Cut. The Working Class in an Australian Mining Town*. Sydney: Allen and Unwin.
———'Domestic Flight Attendants in Australia: A Quasi-occupational Community?', *Journal of Industrial Relations*, September: 237–51.
———(1988) *Blue, White and Pink Collar Workers in Australia. Telecom Technicians, Flight Attendants and Bank Employees*. Sydney: Allen and Unwin.
———with Thorpe, B. (1992) *Beyond Industrial Sociology, The Work of Men and Women*. Sydney: Allen and Unwin.
Young, I. (1981) 'Beyond the Unhappy Marriage: A Critique of the Dual Systems Theory', in L. Sargent (ed.) '*The Unhappy Marriage of Marxism and Feminism. A Debate on Class and Patriarchy*. London: Pluto.

Chapter Five

Ideology and Coherence in the Australian Legal Order

Roman Tomasic

The legal system and legal order were of considerable interest to classical sociologists such as Max Weber and Emile Durkheim, among others. While sociologists have tended in more recent years to turn to other aspects of social life, the legal order remains a central aspect of any overall study of society. Indeed, over the last two decades there has been an international revival of interest in the sociology of law, in view of the renewed recognition of the place occupied by law and legal institutions in society (see further Ferrari 1990; Podgorecki 1991; Tomasic 1985). It is evident that the sociological study of law can contribute greatly to the enrichment of sociology itself (Hopkins 1978). This is especially true in Australia, a society which has relied heavily on law and legal institutions in dealing with complex socio-economic problems and the allocation of rights and benefits. This is part of a broader process of the legalisation of various social processes, and is in turn attributable to the authority or ideological utility of the processes of law as instruments of the modern state, and the decline of alternative mechanisms such as religion and traditional authority as bases for social organisation.

The appeal of law and legal institutions as bases for public and private power lies in broad acceptance of what might be regarded as a sociologically naïve stereotype of law. Thus, for example, law is frequently perceived to be a rational, coherent and efficient instrument or mechanism for social action. This is quite misleading, especially when social behaviour in legal institutions is scrutinised. Close observation of these structures quickly reveals that legal institutions such as courts, administrative and regulatory agencies, the legal professions and the legislatures are extremely diverse and fragmented entities, despite their appearance of coherence or composure. This raises a central theme of this chapter, namely, the manner in which the legal system and the legal order are able to maintain the appearance of unity despite the abundant evidence of their decay, fragmentation and disintegration. This is of course a central concern of all sociology: the problem of order or the manner in which society is able to maintain and reproduce its organic appearance of coherence, what sociologists used to call the question of social control (Ross 1901).

The appearance of a coherent and authoritative set of legal institutions is also based upon popular misconceptions concerning the nature of law itself, as well as of the nature of the power and impact of legal institutions. Thus, for example, law and legal doctrine are frequently perceived to compromise a 'gapless' or complete set of rational and consistent principles which can be applied to deal with social problems as they arise. While lawyers and judges have sought to foster this perception with a view to preserving the authority and legitimacy of law, it should be realised that this picture is highly misleading. Law and legal institutions actually comprise a complex array of competing and often inconsistent principles and practices. In fact, it would be sociologically unrealistic to expect anything else than this in practice, but the positivistic view of law as a set of hard and fast principles and practices has considerable ideological force. Nevertheless, as we shall see, negotiation and bargaining rather than strict adherence to legal rules or procedures are at the core of the legal system, constituting the lubricating mechanisms which help to sustain or mobilise the otherwise rigid formalities of the legal order.

The power and impact of legal institutions are particularly apparent in some respects if they are seen to comprise streamlined systems of authority in which ultimate legal control rests, respectively, with appeal courts in the case of the judicial system; with Parliament in the case of all law making authorities and with the heads of administrative and regulatory agencies in the case of administrative or enforcement structures. This highly formalised view certainly makes the authority of these processes of adjudication, law making and enforcement easier for the community to accept, although it is far from being the complete picture of the nature of the legal process. For example, the formalistic view of the court system in Australia would see the High Court as the most important court. However, this is true in only a very narrow sense, namely that it can lay down principles which seem to bind courts below it in the court structure.

On the other hand, in terms of its impact upon the community, the High Court may be quite marginal to the lives of the vast majority of individuals and groups. It handles only several hundred cases in any one year, while courts at the so-called bottom of the judicial hierarchy, such as Magistrates' or local courts, and intermediate courts such as District or County courts actually process hundreds of thousands of cases in any one year, usually without any reference to principles laid down by the High Court. This seems to suggest that the legal pyramid, which places the High Court at the apex and local Magistrates' courts near the base, needs to be inverted to emphasise the sociological significance of these lower courts.

As a matter of practice, we have a two-tiered system of courts in which the higher ones serve mainly to preserve the myth of adversary justice according to which parties are represented by opposing legal counsel and in which considerable legal procedural formality exists. In contrast, the lower courts are much less obviously concerned with reproducing the adversary myth or ideology. As the British sociologist of law, McBarnet (1981), has shown, the social function of the lower courts is simply to convict offenders and not in each case to provide opportunity for extensive argument and procedural niceties. McBarnet and many others have shown that contrary to the adversarial myth of the rule of law whereby court proceedings constitute an equal fight between two opposing sides, very few defendants in lower courts are actually found to be innocent by the courts. Such high conviction rates are incompatible with the expectation of an equally balanced fight, in which one might anticipate much lower conviction rates. Thus for example, as Table 5.1 shows, less than 5 per cent of people appearing before New South Wales lower courts are found to be not guilty, with, in 1982, over 75 per cent being sentenced in some way.

The lack of a real adversary system in the judicial process is also evident to some degree in the higher criminal courts. In New South Wales higher criminal courts in 1982, for example, only 7.4 per cent of offenders were acquitted as such, and 71.2 per cent did not even bother to contest the case against them, simply pleading guilty (New South Wales Bureau of Crime Statistics and Research 1983: 55-56). The high conviction rates in Australian Magistrates' courts are by no means a recent phenomenon, as Table 5.2 illustrates.

Lest it be thought that these kinds of trends are only to be found in criminal cases, it should be noted that the lower courts

Table 5.1 Penalties handed down by New South Wales
Magistrates' Courts, 1978–82 (Column %)

Penalty	1978	1979	1980	1981	1982
Not guilty	3.8	4.3	4.8	4.6	4.9
Withdrawn/dismissed	15.3	15.5	14.6	13.6	12.4
Recognisance with/without fine/probation	10.0	10.5	12.2	12.3	11.8
Fine	52.4	50.7	53.4	55.9	56.5
Community service	—	—	0.1	0.7	1.3
Periodic detention	0.3	0.5	0.6	0.6	0.8
Imprisonment	5.6	5.1	5.1	5.1	5.0
Other	12.5	13.4	9.2	7.1	7.3

Source: New South Wales Bureau of Crime Statistics and Research (1983) *Court Statistics, 1982* Sydney, New South Wales Government Printer

also process vast numbers of non-criminal or civil cases, and once again the pattern emerges of decisions being found in favour of those bringing the proceedings. Thus, for example, in debt collection cases, very few of the summonses issued actually lead to a trial. For example, the Poverty Commission found that in 1974, of the 93,210 debt recovery summonses issued in South Australia, only 1,316 (or 1.4 per cent) led to a trial, while 36,895 (or 38.5 per cent) were decided in favour of the plaintiff in view of the failure of the defendant to appear in court. In the remaining cases

Table 5.2 Convictions for Offences charged before Australian
Magistrates' Courts per 100,000 Population, Aged 10
years and Over, 1900–76

	All offences charged	Offences against the person	Offences against property	Offences against good order	All petty offences	Total Convictions
1900	5,728	165	302	2,232	1,797	4,496
1910	5,535	104	243	2,545	1,372	4,164
1920	4,529	85	293	1,445	1,709	3,532
1930	4,869	68	368	1,337	2,184	3,956
1940	5,343	52	388	1,361	2,836	4,638
1950	6,571	77	343	2,304	2,956	5,680
1960	10,010	89	694	2,111	6,139	9,083
1970	10,756	130	965	1,397	6,592	9,084
1976	11,474	150	934	1,315	7,192	9,591

Source: Mukherjee 1981: 164–72 (figures have been rounded off to nearest whole number)

the debt was acknowledged by the defendant (Kelly 1977: 35). In New South Wales in 1977, over 210,000 civil actions were commenced in courts of Petty Sessions with a view to recovering payments of debt or making monetary claims. Some 95 per cent proceeded simply without going to trial (Collins 1979: Foreword). This emphasises the conclusion to which numerous studies have come, namely, that the lower civil courts are to a large extent merely debt collection agencies, rather than places where the full paraphernalia of the ideology of adversarial justice is revealed or applied (see further Caplovitz 1983; Jacob 1969; Rock 1973; Willis 1980).

In addition to the above patterns of the 'law in action', one should point to the fact that the legal process is tending to become increasingly routinised in its handling of legal problems. Wherever possible, the courts, administrative agencies and law-makers have sought to divert complex and contentious matters to other, often less formal agencies, so as not to upset the smooth flow in the handling of legal matters. Thus, for example, courts have increasingly sought to divert disputes to less formalised mechanisms such as mediation centres, arbitration, conciliation and counselling. Similarly, law-makers have tended to refer more complex issues to Committees of Inquiry, Royal Commissions and Law Reform bodies, often with a view to defusing potentially explosive socio-legal issues.

Finally, administrative disputes have increasingly been referred to the array of new administrative tribunals and new institutions, such as the Ombudsman, which have emerged over the last few decades. All of these actions are examples of the routinisation of legal decision making which has taken place in this century. This in part reflects the considerable increase in the workloads of judicial, administrative and legislative agencies, and the need in some way to control their caseloads. As our state and society relies increasingly upon these kinds of legal institutions to perform basic social tasks, it will be inevitable that there will be occasions when these legal institutions will be unable to provide solutions to the problems brought to them — without entirely disrupting these institutions, so that alternative avenues need to be found into which more complex matters can be channelled. This is in part also attributable to the fact that our society cannot afford to deliver the rights and procedural guarantees which the ideal of the rule of law evokes. Thus, we sometimes hear of calls for the introduction of less expensive and time-consuming legal machinery to deal with disputes and the allocation of rights and benefits. Similarly, we often hear that the availability of legal mechanisms to ensure that legal rights are provided to all who need them —

such as through legal aid — should be curtailed in some way, because of the damage which such wider access to the legal process is causing to the justice system itself, through greater delays and longer cases and trials (see e.g. Yeldham 1984).

It is not only the poor who are thus being diverted from the judicial process, since business itself has been calling for less costly and time-consuming mechanisms for dealing with commercial disputes, such as by resort to arbitration. It is interesting to note that business entities have long been reluctant to resort to the formal legal process in dealing with disputes with other businesses. As a number of studies have shown since Macaulay's (1963) landmark research into this area, businessmen and corporations tend to prefer to resort to less formal mechanisms such as blacklisting and the termination of business relationships as a means of achieving social control and order in the marketplace (see further Macaulay 1977; Kurczewski and Frieske 1977). Moreover, other research into litigants has shown that it is rare for large corporations or organisations to seek to deal with their disputes through court action. They tend mainly to initiate litigation against individuals or small entities, using courts largely as collection agencies.

Corporations, however, have tended to resort to litigation against other corporations when their existence is threatened, as frequently occurred during the 1980s, in the area of corporate takeovers (see further, Tomasic and Pentony 1989a, 1989b, 1991a). Moreover, it is the 'repeat player', or that type of litigant who is frequently involved in court action (and these are largely organisations), which is most successful in litigation and so able to structure the judicial process to suit the needs of 'repeat players' as opposed to the 'one-shotter'. This is achieved by being able to gain strategic advantages through the making of critical decisions such as the informal settlement (rather than the adjudication) of a case which might otherwise produce a ruling which may have adverse consequences to the 'repeat player'. On the other hand, 'repeat players' are in a much better position to select cases to pursue to the judgment stage with a view to producing new principles conducive to their organisational interests (see further Galanter 1974, 1975). Although there has been a large increase in the number of court cases involving individuals, in areas such as family law and industrial and motor vehicle accidents, there has not been an increase in the number of business disputes handled by the courts, despite the considerable degree of economic growth this century. This is an intriguing phenomenon in some ways. The American legal historian, Lawrence Friedman, has sought to explain this as follows:

For whatever reasons, courts in Western industrial societies do not seem well suited to resolving certain kinds of disputes. They thus fall far short of the ideal of 'justice for all', if by justice we mean a cheap, fair, effective tribunal close at hand ... Note that we are talking here mainly about private disputes. We are not talking about great constitutional cases, environmental disputes or major labour cases. We are talking about ordinary bread-and-butter cases, disputes between neighbours, family squabbles, small personal injury cases ... We are talking about most business disputes ... The courts are stiff, formal and expensive. Ordinary people do not like to use them, or they find them too costly or too remote. There are good reasons, too for business to avoid litigation.

(Friedman 1983: 21)

Although both law and sociology seek to be applicable to all aspects of society, the formalistic model of law falls far short of being so widely applicable. Formal legal institutions are severely limited in being able to meet the ideological claims made by their proponents. This stresses the need to distinguish between the form and content of law and legal institutions, as their actual meaning and impact will often be quite different from what the rhetoric of the rule of law might suggest.

Ideology and Legal Process

The above discussion suggests a basic contradiction or conflict of purposes or rationales within the legal system. Another way to put this is to see the legal system as operating at a number of different levels, each of which are at first sight incompatible, even though on closer scrutiny they are mutually sustaining. Thus, at one level the legal system can be seen as a powerful repository of symbols and ideological mechanisms — such as the rule of law and the notion of adversary justice — which sustain the legitimacy and authority of the modern state. At this more formal level, law and legal institutions seek to set parameters for legitimate social, political or economic action. The Australian federal Constitution is one of the best illustrations of the attempt to structure social change by the imposition of an inflexible legal form, as Encel (1979), a sociologist, has shown. The same point has been made by Sawer (1967: 208), a lawyer, when he observed that 'constitutionally speaking, Australia is a frozen continent'. In other words, laws such as the federal Constitution serve to define the parameters of social change. This is not to say that law is a sufficiently powerful mechanism to prevent change taking place at all, for it is far from being this. Frequently, however, it has sufficient legitimate authority to structure the nature of change and to direct it along some often quite convoluted or even irrational pathways.

A good illustration of this is to be found in the 1990 Corporations Case in which the High Court struck down as unconstitutional the efforts of the Commonwealth Parliament to enact a comprehensive and nationally applicable Corporations Law in conjunction with a single system of national corporate regulation. This court decision was only avoided by resort to a political and financial compromise between the Commonwealth and state governments under which the states allowed a national system of corporate regulation to emerge (see further, Tomasic *et al.* 1992: 23–53). Thus the Constitution could only be avoided by resort to a rare political compromise. However, laws such as the Constitution do not have this influence merely because of their formal content, but because they have reflected broader structural features of the social fabric, even though these may be less evident today than when the laws were enacted.

It should be said that while law is often perceived to be a tradition-bound and conservative social institution, it is not always a static one, despite the frequent claims of law reformers to this effect. To some extent law and legal institutions do reflect changes taking place in the broader social and economic base of society, although there may not always be a directly evident causal link. As law and legal institutions have developed their own values and culture, it frequently appears that the legal system seems to be acting autonomously from the dominant social, economic and political structures in society. This in part serves to enhance the authority of the legal system and is consistent with the ideological claims made for it, in relation to the rule of law, for example. As there is in fact considerable diversity and even fragmentation in the Australian legal system, partly due to the existence of a federal system of government, ideological factors play a very important part in maintaining the appearance of unity and coherence in the legal system.

We need therefore to ask how the system actually achieves order and coherence within the wider social context, as well as to look at the ideological and other means by which the legal system gives the impression of coherence. These two questions are actually merely two sides of the same one, since it would be quite misleading to give the impression that the law and legal institutions are in some way isolated from, or independent of, the society in which they exist. Those who assume that the law is separate from society often expect that the law and legal institutions will be used as instruments to change society or for purposes of social engineering. This strategy is highly problematic, and has been described as the instrumentalist fallacy, since law is in fact deeply embedded in social structures in which change is sought (see further Gusfield 1963; Massell 1968; Burman and Harrell-Bond 1979). It has even been suggested that if the measure of law's importance in society is its effectiveness as an instrument, then clearly law is not very important (Griffith 1979). However, law is important for many other reasons including its symbolic, ideological, legitimating and social ordering functions.

One way of exploring the apparent conflict between the pretensions of law and legal institutions and their actual significance, is to focus upon a series of legal processes which are at the heart of what the legal system actually constitutes. The process metaphor is valuable since it serves to focus our attention upon the manner in which legal rhetoric and discourse are a product of social interaction, of negotiation and bargaining and the transformations which take place in the course of the processing of matters within legal institutions. The process metaphor has often been relied upon in ethnographic and similar approaches to legal institutions to provide a more realistic understanding of these than is available from formal legal statements as to their roles or purposes. However, this is not to suggest that the latter, more doctrinal view be abandoned entirely — only that it be assessed critically, since traditional or formal legal rhetoric often serves as the legitimating ideology which holds these disparate legal processes together. Moreover, legal ideology, perhaps like all ideology (see Carlton 1977: 20–21), is more than a mere veneer upon a somewhat chaotic legal order or process: it actually influences that process to some extent. This is illustrated by the fact that at various times courts and legal institutions feel genuinely constrained by their own rhetoric — we might even say they become captives of that ideology — and so may act in ways which seem to run contrary to what one might predict, given the close relationship between the state and legal processes.

In other words, ideologies such as the rule of law and the doctrine of precedent have even been used in such a way as to induce the courts to reach decisions which seem to be ones which judges themselves might not prefer. Ideological artefacts such as the rule of law can therefore serve to give the legal process a relative degree of autonomy from other state institutions. This reflects a broader contradiction which the executive arm of government has increasingly sought to neutralise by removing disputes out of the realm of traditional judicial processes and diverting them into tribunals and informal forums which are more readily controllable by governmental agencies. What is also notable about legal ideologies is that these tend to be reified in the legal process by legal functionaries such as lawyers, police officers and judges. It is this concretisation of legal ideologies (at least in the minds of their proponents) which gives them their potency. Thus, far from our moving into a period when ideology will be at end, it seems that, if anything, law has become an increasingly powerful ideological system which is relied upon both to impose discipline in society and to distribute symbolic and substantive goods (see further Hunt 1985; Hirst 1979; Sugarman 1983; Sumner 1979).

Finally, it can be noted that a common stereotype of the legal process gives the impression that its principal purposes are related directly to the maintenance of coercive social control in society. While to some extent it is true to say that some aspects of the legal process are so directed, it would not be correct to conclude that social control is as important a function as many believe. Only a very small part of the infrastructure of the legal process is directed to purposes of this kind. The vast bulk of the personnel, structures and rules which comprise the process are concerned with a diversity of other goals, including the legitimation of resource allocation and decision making structures, the maintenance and protection of property relations, and the production and reproduction of ideological mechanisms such as the rule of law. It should also be realised that much of the legal process is also directed to sustaining itself and its structures and therefore seeking to avoid their collapse or fragmentation. To this extent it is therefore locked in, in a somewhat inward-looking way, to its own myths and rhetoric, and as such, is ill-equipped to be an effective instrument of social control.

Specific social control activities, therefore, do not figure largely in the overall concerns of the legal system. These concerns might be described as being of a 'civil law' kind, covering such things as legal problems relating to contractual disputes and arrangements, compensation claims, the protection of property, commercial law, revenue law and so on. Areas of public law such as constitutional and administrative law are also far removed from the narrow social control model. All this suggests that the study of the legal process needs to take issue with long-cherished stereotypes of it. One means of doing this is to emphasise the manner in which ideologies and legal processes interrelate.

Legal Processes and the Legal System

It is perhaps appropriate that we now turn to look more closely at some of the legal processes which constitute the legal system. As has been suggested above, the legal system is only part of a wider social system. Like society, it is far from being an organic whole or totality, for as Touraine has argued:

> ... it is divided against itself; each of its orientations is the object of opposing attempts at appropriation ... [despite] ... illusions of social integration.
>
> (Touraine 1977: 10)

Luhmann has likewise pointed to the problem of integration or homogeneity which confronts society in general and the legal system in particular. Discussing the legal profession in the Federal Republic of Germany, for example, Luhmann observed:

> ... the profession as a whole is composed of heterogeneous elements, as far as values, interests, and attitudes are concerned, and is only differentiated within itself with regard to typical roles. These conditions are not very favourable for the internal coherence of the profession, let alone its efficiency as a political factor in society.
>
> (Luhmann 1976: 103)

These kinds of observations have now been empirically supported by research on the legal professions in a number of countries, including Australia, as we will see later. For the moment, however, it is sufficient to note that diversity in the legal profession is a reflection of both diversity in the processes of the legal system itself as well as in the client base which lawyers serve. Broadly speaking, it could be argued that there are at least three main sets of processes within the Australian legal system, namely, law making, the implementation of law, and its interpretation.

The Law-making Process
Firstly, there is what might be called the law-making processes, those which involve the legislature, the courts and administrative officials engaged in formulating regulations or delegated legislation. While many, more conservative judges, reject the view that they are engaged in law-making when they decide a case, it would be fair to say that this apparent judicial reticence is a reflection of the ideology of the separation of powers (between judicial, legislative and executive authority) as well as of the traditional common law view that judges merely find the law rather than making it for the first time. This narrow view of law-making is far from being an accurate reflection of what is widely recognised by judges as a reality of law-making in the court process. It might also be argued that law-making takes place at a less formal level in the form of the customs and rules formulated or evolved by

private groups or associations, such as business associations, cultural and sporting groups. Often the laws or norms developed by these less formal mechanisms have much greater significance for the lives of individuals than do the formal rules made by state agencies like the courts and Parliament. However, it would divert us too much from our primary concerns to look more closely at these informal law-making mechanisms in society. If for no other reason than their restricted authority or legitimacy in comparison with the rules produced by more formal structures, we can for the time being leave aside further consideration of these less formal, but nevertheless important structures.

In many respects, judicial law-making can be more difficult to overturn than legislative law-making. For example, to overturn a new ruling of the High Court, it could require at least seven Acts of Parliament, one from each state and one from the federal Parliament. Having said this, however, it should be stressed that the vast bulk of official law-making activity takes place at the parliamentary rather than the judicial level. Moreover, few judicial opinions actually constitute a real innovation, in the sense of laying down a new code of conduct, since most decisions are written to apply only to the very narrow set of factual circumstances in that case. One reason for this is the reluctance of judges to lay down new broad general principles which may well constrain their future decision making and so prevent them, in later cases, from reaching the decision which they might see as being the most just (see further Aubert 1983: 77–97).

Sometimes, however, parliaments may be deadlocked or unable to act unilaterally or with sufficient authority in proposing a new law and so may turn to the courts for assistance. The so-called Tasmanian Dams Case of 1983 was an instance of this situation. Here, the federal government went to the High Court in an effort to clarify its powers in relation to the preservation of a world heritage area in south-west Tasmania which would have been threatened by the proposed damming of the Franklin River by the Tasmanian government's Hydro-Electricity Authority. The High Court's decision in this case, although close, can be seen as a law-making one, because in addition to upholding federal government regulations regarding work on the Franklin Dam site, the court established new principles regarding the relative powers of state and federal parliaments. However, constitutional cases such as this comprise only a tiny proportion of the High Court's workload, and by no means provide the only illustration of its law-making activity.

Parliaments, however, make the vast bulk of our laws, since courts are poorly equipped to formulate broad sets of rules seek-

Table 5.3   Average Yearly Number of Statutes passed by various Australian Parliaments, 1901–79

Years	Commonwealth statutes per year	New South Wales statutes per year	Victorian statutes per year
1901–09	21.2	52.5	58.5
1910–19	38.6	48.6	80.0
1920–29	44.3	48.8	81.0
1930–39	73.0	52.8	86.6
1940–49	74.4	47.9	72.9
1950–59	92.4	51.5	115.5
1960–69	118.2	66.9	132.5
1970–79	168.4	94.8*	143.75**

*Average figure for years 1970–75
**Average figure for years 1970–79
Source: Tomasic 1979: 11

ing to cover the whole of a particular area of law. The twentieth century in particular has seen a great increase in legislative law-making, with the rise of what might be called the bureaucratic state and the consequent extension of law into many more sectors of society. The law-making activity of all Australian legislatures seems to have increased greatly over this century, as Table 5.3 illustrates. The volume of delegated legislation or regulation made by statutory authorities and government departments has also increased over recent decades, as Table 5.4 illustrates.

Table 5.4   Comparison of the Volume of Regulations made in Australia during the 1960s and 70s

Number of Regulations Made

Period	Federal	NSW	Vic.	Qld	SA	WA	Tas.	NT	Total
10 years to 1969	1,963	1,557	2,190	3,179	924	184	2,433	—	12,420
10 years to 1979 increase	3,017	3,511	4,072	4,494	1,697	274	3,030	36	20,131
second period on first	+54%	125%	+86%	+41%	+84%	+49%	+25%	—	+62%

Source: Confederation of Australian Industry (1980) *Government Regulation in Australia*, p. 51

While a variety of reform conclusions can be drawn from figures such as those in Tables 5.3 and 5.4, it is apparent that the cumulative effect of this growth is to emphasise the extent to which society has come to rely upon legislatures and their attendant bureaucratic regulation-making structures.

Whilst some have argued that the bulk of this kind of law-making activity constitutes a 'mountain of minutiae', rather than being major turning points (Chambliss 1979: 149), it can nevertheless be argued that its sheer bulk does more to characterise the nature of the legal order in Australia than do occasional attempts to strike out in a new direction with a 'significant' legislative innovation. To put it another way, the legal order seems to be structured more by what Hurst has called a process of 'drift' than by a conscious 'direction' in law-making activity. The unwieldy growth of corporate social welfare and taxing legislation seems to provide some of the best illustrations of the extent to which law-making seems to have become the creature of the bureaucratic state. Attempts to rationalise it by resort to law reform commissions seem only to further entrench this bureaucratisation of law-making, since only those proposed law reforms which seem either to serve the broad interests of bureaucracy, or at least do not threaten these, ever seem to be implemented (see further Tomasic and Bottomley 1984).

We have noted that bureaucratic concerns play an important part in shaping the legislative product. However, this is far from being the only source of input into the law-making process. Economic interests and considerations also frequently play an important part. This, of course, was long ago recognised by Weber when he observed that '... economic interests are among the strongest factors influencing the creation of law' (1954: 32). This has been most clearly the case in respect to the making of the Australian federal Constitution, as Encel (1979) has illustrated so well. Seeing the Constitution as a social document, Encel argued that its framers sought to preserve the array of local economic interests which were dominant in the latter decades of the nineteenth century in the Australian colonies, rather than allowing the new national government to gain economic hegemony. The dominance of economic considerations is also evident in the evolution of Australian land legislation from the selection Acts of the 1850s, aimed at breaking the economic dominance of the squatters (Baker 1979) to the introduction of strata title legislation in New South Wales in the early 1960s, aimed at facilitating the greatest use of capital by developers concerned about the economic insecurities inherent in the pre-existing system of ownership of home units (Kondos 1979). The continuing debate over formulating appropriate land rights legislation is also largely based upon economic considerations arising out of the conflicting claims of the mining industry and other lobbies (see e.g. Keon-Cohen 1979). It has been well documented that laws regarding such fields as broadcasting, trade practices and companies and securities regulation have been heavily influenced by the interests of economic forces (see e.g. Armstrong 1979; Hopkins 1979; Sutton and Wild 1979; Hart 1979).

However, this is not to suggest that economic interests have always had their way. One obvious reason for this is of course that they are far from being monolithic, so that government may be swayed by pressures from small rather than big business, as Hopkins (1979: 207) has shown in respect to the 1977 amendments to the Trade Practices Act regarding price discrimination rules. On the other hand, as Hopkins has also shown, at times other pressures, such as those coming from the electorate or from consumers, may entirely outweigh those emanating from business groups. In seeking to explain the intricacies of law-making processes one therefore needs to be wary of single cause or structural explanations, as O'Malley (1979) has argued, and to realise that different explanatory theories may be required to deal with different periods of time or types of law-making.

The Implementation Process
A second set of legal processes found in the Australian legal system deal with the implementation of legal rules which have been produced by law-making institutions. The impact and effectiveness of law does of course depend upon the processes of implementation which have been established both in the legal system and, more importantly, in society at large. This is not, however, to suggest that law and legal institutions are quite separate from society, for as we have seen, legal processes are embedded within broader social processes, so that there is considerable interaction and interdependence between them. This has frequently been overlooked by enthusiastic social reformers who have seen law as a powerful instrument for the purposes of social engineering. Such reformers have frequently been disappointed when seeking to use law in this way, especially where the proposed change runs counter to deeply entrenched social values, such as in relation to addiction (Gusfield 1963), religious belief (Massell 1968) and drink driving behaviour (Ross 1981).

It is no wonder, therefore, that implementation can be the most agonising and frustrating feature of the legal process. This is because it is usually a far more complex process than that of creating the law in the first place. However, the simplicity of the latter process should not be taken for granted, because many of the difficulties which may be experienced in seeking to implement a new law may be traced back to problems which were insufficiently thought out or resolved during the law-making stage. Frequently, therefore, the implementation process tends to involve a variety of games or strategies of opposition by those who were unsuccessful in having their views taken into account during the law-making stage. It is not surprising, therefore, that Bardach (1977) has characterised the post-law-making process as 'the implementation game'. Another aspect of the implementation process worth noting is that sometimes a law is not intended to be carried out at all, and that its passage or enactment merely represents a symbolic victory, while the real gains are received by those who are able to avoid or undermine its implementation. Edelman (1964, 1977) has characterised this situation as one of the symbolic uses of politics, involving 'words that succeed and policies that fail'.

An illustration of the symbolic aspects of law-making as seen from the implementation process is provided by some advice given by the then-Prime Minister R.J. Hawke to the then-Queensland Premier Joh Bjelke-Petersen, as to how the latter could save face in dealing with some crippling anti-union legislation passed in Queensland in 1985. The Prime Minister reportedly observed:

> ... I mean you can have legislation on the statute book which is not implemented ... so the matter is capable of resolution without the actual repeal of the legislation ...
> (*Sydney Morning Herald*, 18 April 1985, p. 1)

In other words, this leading law-maker was suggesting that this particular piece of legislation might be retained on the statute books as a symbolic statement of the Queensland government's desired position, but for practical purposes, it should simply not be implemented. Such a situation is probably quite common, although few politicians are likely to be prepared to be so frank about it.

It is not unusual for an administrative or regulatory agency to be set up to enforce or apply a policy, but it may be given very few resources to fulfil its function. Alternatively, the agency may be subject to ministerial discretion to intervene and prevent it from major actions, such as commencing protracted and expensive court proceedings. Bardach's (1977) study of the implementation process is a catalogue of such strategies. So, the mere passage of a piece of legislation, such as that dealing with Affirmative Action, privacy, environmental control or corporate regulation may merely constitute a symbolic reassurance to some elements in the community that these issues are important. In practice, the legislation may be so vague and difficult to implement that it does little to control the areas of social life to which it may be directed. It has become commonplace in the sociology of law, therefore, to point to the so-called 'gap' between the 'law in the books' and the 'law in action'. What is perhaps more interesting is to explain why this gap exists and what purpose it serves (see further Nelken 1981).

Despite the fact that a vast bulk of legal sociological research has been directed to documenting the impact, effectiveness or implementation of law, the theoretical understanding of this process is far from being satisfactory. We tend to have limited sets of hypotheses about segments of this process, but very few broader attempts have been made to theorise the relationship between law and social change (see, however, Friedman 1975; Chambliss 1979; Ross 1982; Evan 1965; Podgorecki 1974, 1991). Much of this literature has focused attention upon the limits of law as an instrument of social change (e.g. Allott 1980; Packer 1968). In Australia, for example, we have seen a series of studies on the limits of drink driving legislation, of drug laws, of juvenile delinquency legislation and of family law (see e.g. Robinson 1979; Hiller and Hancock 1979; Ozdowski 1979; Tomasic 1977a, 1977b). In a study of the Australian Family Law Act, for example, Ziegert (1984) argued that the implementation of some of the more radical objectives of this legislation, such as seeking to escape from the fault concept in dealing with marital breakdown, has been severely limited by the somewhat legalistic constraints which the involvement of lawyers and their legal culture brings with it, such as the appropriate role of the judge. This stresses the fact that implementation takes place in a sub-cultural context and that the impact or effectiveness of a law will depend upon the support and enthusiasm for it by those whose task it is to implement it, such as lawyers and law enforcement officers.

This raises a theoretical issue which has been described as that of the mobilisation of law. Unless a law can be effectively used it will lie dormant, or at best it will be of only symbolic significance. Mobilisation can take place in two broad kinds of ways. Firstly, we can have what has been described as the 'reactive' mobilisation of law, merely responding to a complaint about the breach of a law. This is by far the most common manner in which a law is implemented. This is particularly evident in the actions of regulatory and law enforcement agencies. Secondly, we can have what is known as the 'proactive' mobilisation of law, or the deliberate and premeditated attempt to seek out those who have breached a rule.

Since proactive mobilisation is a far more labour-intensive and time-consuming method of seeking to implement law, it tends to be resorted to much less frequently than is the reactive kind. A good illustration of proactive mobilisation is a police blitz campaign against drink driving based upon random breath testing, or an audit of a selected group of taxpayers by the Australian Taxation Office.

This can be contrasted with a reactive approach to the same problem, which sees law being mobilised only once a suspicion of drink driving behaviour has been raised, such as through erratic driving conduct or as a result of blood tests following an accident. Police morale tends to sag as a result of proactive policing, since this is both more time-consuming and less likely to produce results. Thus in the proactive area of random breath testing, for example, a New South Wales Parliamentary Committee of Inquiry was told by a highway patrol officer that police morale here was low because of the 'soul-destroying nature of random breath-testing — it's a very repetitive job ... saying the same lines to motorists hundreds of times a week ... And out of the thousands of tests, well under 1 per cent of motorists are charged' (*Sydney Morning Herald*, 30 January 1985, p. 3). Moreover, as the deterrent effect of proactive policing of this kind is often doubtful (see e.g. Ross 1981), it is difficult to sustain this kind of policing without incurring significant economic and psychological costs. It is for this reason that bodies like the Australian Taxation Office seek to build what is sometimes described as a 'partnership' with tax advisers so as to seek to create an atmosphere of compliance and minimise the need for proactive tax law enforcement actions.

By contrast, reactive policing does at least allow enforcement authorities to satisfy bureaucratic performance criteria by more easily producing a reasonable number of breaches. Unfortunately, reactive policing tends to lead to a focus upon trivial offences while proactive policing finds it much more difficult to meet simple performance criteria due to the fact that it tends to focus upon much more complex offences, or scrutinise vast numbers of cases to reveal the existence of an offence. Thus, there is a tendency to resort to the reactive prosecution of drug users, rather than a proactive prosecution of the more difficult-to-discover drug traffickers. Some of the best illustrations of the complexities of the proactive mobilisation of law have arisen in recent years in Australia from the areas of corporate crime and tax avoidance and evasion. These kinds of offences are extremely difficult to detect and prosecute, even though there is little debate as to their seriousness. Nevertheless, the number of successful prosecutions of such offences have been relatively few, as the work of the

Costigan Commission and that of the various special prosecutors appointed to deal with tax avoidance, illustrates. For example, in his 1984 Annual Report, Special Prosecutor R.V. Gyles QC reported to the federal government that he had initiated twenty-eight court actions against promoters of tax avoidance schemes, but completed only one matter despite a staff of over 160 officers (Gyles 1984 : 11-13). Special Prosecutor Gyles provided an insight into why proactive enforcement is so difficult when he observed that:

> Up to 30 June more than 500 search warrants had been executed by members of this office. In the year under review other documents have been forthcoming from sources such as the Australian Taxation Office, the Costigan Royal Commission, and the various Corporate Affairs Commissions. Approximately 1,000 persons have been interviewed, and over 4,000 statements and records of interview have been obtained. A number of other persons have been contacted but declined to be interviewed at all. In the main, those declining to be interviewed at all were principals who were or are likely to be charged. The task of analysing the documents obtained and the information obtained from interviews, and then carrying out the necessary follow-up enquiries, has been extremely time consuming, even with the assistance of the computer system . . . I indicated in my last Report that I had chosen in the first place to concentrate investigations on some identified large scale promoters, even though this necessarily involved a substantial commitment of resources to a small number of targets and a relatively long lead time before a brief could be prepared to deal adequately with the target.
>
> (Gyles 1984: 3)

He went on to argue that it was necessary to abandon the procedural niceties usually followed when a decision to prosecute such offences was made, if the whole effort was not to be a waste of time. Gyles noted therefore that in complex fraud cases:

> A prima-facie case may be established upon materials falling short of strictly admissible evidence long before compilation of the final brief of evidence to be presented at the committal proceedings. Indeed further evidence may be produced during the course of the committal proceedings, or between committal and trial. If the compilation of a full brief is awaited before the decision to charge is taken, the risk of the suspect absconding is greatly increased, and the inevitable delays in the court process lead to stale cases being brought, with all the attendant injustice to both prosecution and defence. While the decision to charge should never be made lightly, in my view there is a strong public interest in laying charges, where otherwise appropriate, as soon as the prosecution is in possession

of material of appropriate credibility which establishes a prima-
facie case.

(Gyles 1984: 4)

As evident from this quote, one of the problems often seen with proactive enforcement is that it undermines the usual procedural guarantees and leads to criticisms of the emergence of a police state. It is interesting to note that Gyles' successor as Director of Public Prosecutions, Ian Temby QC, quite predictably called for greater powers and increased staffing. There are clearly major limits, therefore, to the proactive mobilisation of law arising out of available resources and the degree of public tolerance of official interference in private lives. This suggests that the proactive mobilisation of law will remain far less common as a technique for implementing law than the reactive method, despite the fact that the latter is really only effective against minor offences. All of this does not bode well for the implementation of those laws which encounter any real resistance in society, especially where such resistance comes from more powerful and established sectors. Moreover, it also highlights the fact that despite the rhetoric of equal treatment under the law for all, the problems of implementing or mobilising law against some individuals and groups will be such that the impact of law will vary considerably across society.

For example, it is much more difficult to investigate and prove complex commercial fraud than it is to deal with minor and more visible public order type offences, such as assault and disorderly conduct, so that it is inevitable that enforcement activity will be directed against the latter. Similarly, it is much more difficult to deal with complex and sophisticated tax avoidance schemes than it is to deal with minor breaches of taxing statutes, such as the failure to furnish a tax return on time, so that the latter type of conduct will bear the brunt of enforcement practice, despite its relatively lesser significance.

The Interpretation Process

A third set of legal processes which we need to consider involves the interpretation of rules produced by law-making authorities. As the sociologist Talcott Parsons (1980) has pointed out, the interpretation function is probably the most important one the legal system performs (1980: 65). This is because the very effectiveness and impact of rules is dependent upon the meanings attributed to them. Interpretation takes place at several levels. Firstly, and most obviously, there is the judicial level, especially in appellate courts. Interpretations which are made of rules at this level are a critical factor in their legitimation and authority, so that one could argue that appeal courts such as the High Court largely serve to legitimate laws made by the federal Parliament, even though there may be some time lag between the making of these rules and their interpretation, so that the High Court may actually be out of step with the government of the day. However, the interpretation of rules also serves an important political function at this level, as has long been recognised in the role of the United States Supreme Court (see e.g. Dahl 1978; Casper 1978; Adamany 1978; Choper 1980; Hodder-Williams 1980; Shapiro 1967; also see Griffith 1977).

At a second level, interpretation is much more pervasive, since it is an activity undertaken by a whole range of legal functionaries, including the police officer on patrol, the regulatory inspector investigating compliance with environmental or health and safety regulations, and lawyers giving advice to their clients, as well as by citizens faced with the problem of determining whether rules, such as those regarding the availability of social security benefits, apply to them. Although we tend to emphasise the first or 'top down' view of interpretation, the second, or 'bottom up' approach is really of much greater significance for the day-to-day operation of legal processes. The fact that so many rules are actually negotiated, and so either avoided in part or even wholly, does not negate the significance of interpretation, since negotiation needs to be broadly seen as part of the process of giving meaning to rules.

The 'top-down' and 'bottom-up' nature of interpretations given to rules will vary considerably, therefore, depending on the position of the interpreter. This suggests that the meaning attributed to the same rules may well vary depending on the object or purpose of the interpreter. Judges, as we have seen, often seek to interpret general principles as narrowly as possible, to give themselves the greatest degree of freedom of movement in subsequent cases. In the bureaucratic context, rules will often receive quite different interpretations depending on both the position of the interpreter within the bureaucracy and also on that of the bureaucracy or agency in relation to the degree of support received from outside. Thus, rules may be interpreted far more formally at the head office of an agency than at the local or regional one. Similarly, the policeman on patrol, the regulatory inspector or the official at the front desk of the agency will usually interpret rules much more informally or resort to their discretion as to whether to apply a rule or not, than would the official higher up in each respective agency (see e.g. Lipsky 1980; Kaufman 1960). These variations in the interpretation of rules appear throughout the legal process and have their most publicised illustrations in the discrepancies which frequently appear in the decisions handed down by different judges under the same piece of legislation.

Sentencing disparities have long been of concern to law reformers but these seem to be an inevitable aspect of the problems of interpretation, and disparities in interpretation arise in all contexts where laws are applied in society by individuals. All this variability in meaning also derives from what might be called the open-textured or porous nature of rules, which illustrates the fact that meanings are made in a process of application, rather than being fixed or predetermined. This once again emphasises the problem of coherence facing the legal system and its processes. Thus, for example, the official at the peak of an agency will tend to interpret rules fairly strictly in terms of structuring and controlling the discretionary behaviour of lower level officials. In contrast, as one descends the bureaucratic ladder, the interpretation of rules is seen as a production process with considerable room for the use of discretion and choice. The work of the mythical policeman on the beat, for example, would be impossible if every apparent breach of a rule led to an inevitable apprehension of the suspected offender. In practice, a decision has to be made as to which rules to enforce, and hence which to give legal meaning and effect to, since it is simply impossible to act meaningfully in response to all rule violations, due to limits upon enforcement resources. This is also a consequence of the fact that there is always an element of ambiguity as to whether the particular constellation of facts observed in a case fall precisely within the ambit of a rule (see further e.g. Weaver 1977; Black 1980).

The meanings attributed to a rule will also be influenced by the level of insecurity which the interpreter of that rule may experience within a bureaucratic agency. Thus agencies which are new and which enjoy considerable support from outside constituencies (such as consumer groups in the case of a consumer protection agency) will be likely to interpret rules far more strictly than would an agency which is isolated or which is being attacked from all sides. Thus the old Australian Broadcasting Control Board was very reluctant to adopt a strong legalistic approach with broadcasters, since it was constantly afraid of ministerial interference as a result of lobbying from broadcasters who might be threatened by the agency. Eventually, the Board had to be replaced, as it became an embarrassment in that it seems to have become 'captured' by the industry (Armstrong 1979). It was replaced by a body far more ready to interpret its powers broadly in view of the fact that its active constituency was perceived to be wider than that of the industry alone. A good illustration of this forthright interpretative style is to be found in the 1989 decision of the Australian Broadcasting Tribunal to find that Mr Alan Bond was not a fit and proper person to hold a broadcasting licence. In other words, pressures from consumer groups have provided the Tribunal with a wider social base of support and hence greater freedom in its interpretation of broadcasting legislation.

The actual social context in which the process of interpretation takes place is therefore likely to be extremely important in determining the meanings to be given to rules. It goes without saying that this is in marked contrast to the popular conception of rules as being fixed and inflexible. They are only such if the context requires that this be so. Thus, for example, where the context of the interpretation of a rule is such that there is considerable time and legal talent brought to bear to elucidate its meaning, it is remarkable how an otherwise straightforward rule gains added complexity. Magistrates may, for example, assume that the meaning of a rule may be quite simple, especially where the case is not contested. However, when there is an opportunity for greater legal argument, as occurs in higher courts, or when senior barristers descend into lower courts to argue cases, the interpretation of rules becomes far more problematic, since their ambiguities are exposed, and as the complexities of the facts to which the rules are to be applied are revealed.

While the existence of the High Court of Australia as the ultimate court of appeal in many matters, as well as the highest single authority on the interpretation of law, is often said to facilitate greater uniformity, this claim is more ideological than completely accurate. This is so for a variety of reasons. Firstly, the High Court has not sought to provide definitive interpretations in more than a relatively few areas, and even where it has clearly sought to do so, this will not be communicated to all interpreters of the law. There is also the problem of determining which, if any, principle has been established in a High Court case, since up to seven judgments may be given: that is, one by each judge. Furthermore, even where a High Court principle is well established, an interpreter may seek to avoid it by some legalistic means, or to distinguish that decision as being based upon quite different circumstances or, even to ignore the High Court decision entirely in the knowledge that interpretation is unlikely to be challenged.

The processes of interpretation, therefore, seem to be characterised by considerable diversity and conflicting approaches, in spite of the legal theory that certainty in the meaning of law is a basic principle. Once again, then, we see that the legal process is an extremely loose array of practices which seem to be tolerated in view of the overarching ideologies which proclaim the existence of fixed, certain and uniform patterns of interpretation. Yet, despite the critical importance of the interpretation process, sociologists have devoted very little attention to it, certainly in comparison with the processes of law-making and implementation. This is unfortunate, since it is clear that all three are closely related in that together they comprise much of what we might call the legal process. Moreover, each can only be adequately understood by reference to the other, as none stands alone. Together they do, however, emphasise the problems of integration and coherence which underlie the entire legal system.

Structure and Organisation in the Legal System

So far, we have emphasised the importance of ideological concerns within the legal system as well as some of the key processes through which these ideologies are generated and through which the tasks of the system are performed in Australia. Taking a somewhat different approach to these issues, it is useful to focus upon some of the principal actors who constitute the social structure and organisation of the legal system. These include such groups as lawyers; third party dispute-handlers such as judges and magistrates; administrators and regulators who may seek to apply rules; as well as consumers of legal services from the wider community, such as litigants and clients. The roles which each of these sets of actors performs tell us a great deal about the operations of the legal system, as may already be evident from our discussion of legal processes. It is therefore useful to look briefly at some of these.

Lawyers and Lawyering
One of the principal misconceptions about the legal profession is that it is a unified and coherent group. Although professional associations, legal education and judicial rhetoric often seem to foster this myth or misconception for their own quite different reasons, it is quite clear that many lawyers often have very little in common with other lawyers, particularly in terms of the legal work which they do and the client interests which they serve. It is thus evident that there are wide gulfs between different groups of lawyers and that there is relatively little mobility between these. These gulfs are relatively enduring features of the social organisation of the profession, which are sustained by rigid status differences between practitioners doing different types of legal work, as well as by the types of clients served by different lawyers. These two factors, type of legal work and type of clientele, probably do

more to differentiate and distance lawyers from each other than any other factors, as a number of empirical studies in Australia (Tomasic 1983; Hetherton 1981) and in the United States (Heinz and Laumann 1982) have amply attested.

In a study of New South Wales lawyers it was found, for example, that the prestige attached to various types of legal work varied greatly, with areas such as taxation, equity, superior court civil litigation, commercial and constitutional law work, ranking the highest in prestige, while the least prestigious work included fields like general legal aid work, family law, tenancy law, petty sessions litigation and acting for unions and applicants in workers' compensation cases (Tomasic and Bullard 1978: 38). These differences were obviously related to the social status of the respective clients served in relation to each type of legal work. Work undertaken for corporate organisational clients clearly had the greatest prestige, while that undertaken for individuals, particularly poorer clients who rarely sought the use of legal services, tended to have the least prestige. Based upon various measures of the kinds of legal work performed by lawyers, it has been possible to isolate a number of discrete types of lawyer. Four distinct types emerged from the New South Wales study referred to above.

These were respectively, property lawyers, commercial lawyers, litigation lawyers and generalist lawyers (Tomasic 1983: 456). There were significant client-related differences between each of these four main types. For example, commercial lawyers devoted between five and nine times more time to serving major corporate clients than did the other lawyer types, but other lawyers devoted three to six times more to small business clients than did commercial lawyers. Also, while commercial lawyers reported seeing an average of only one individual client per week, other lawyers saw between nine and seventeen such clients during the same period (Tomasic 1982: 460; see also Tomasic 1981a) .

These differences seem to have the effect of fragmenting the profession quite considerably. The question arises, therefore, as to how exactly the legal profession is able to preserve the impression of coherence and purpose. One answer is to be found in the ideological mechanisms developed within it, or what might otherwise be described as the legal culture of lawyers. Although there are a number of subcultural values or orientations found within different sectors of the profession, it seems evident that there is at least an overarching set of values and predispositions amongst lawyers which serves to set them apart from the wider community, and in fact to paper over the gulfs between them arising out of work and client-related differences (see further Tomasic and Bullard 1978). Attitudinal data from lawyers suggests that it is the value of 'cynical realism', which is shared by the vast bulk of lawyers. This is to be contrasted with the often-espoused ideal of service, suggesting instead that lawyers are primarily concerned with advancing their own, or their firms', narrow economic interests, rather than broader social justice concerns. What is doubly remarkable about the widespread nature of this predisposition within the profession is that the larger community seems to be all too well aware of this lawyer orientation (Tomasic 1983: 464–70).

At a different level, it could be argued that another mechanism bonds together an otherwise fragmented profession. This is the broader role which Cain (1983: 12) has pointed to in a small-scale study of London solicitors. Cain argued that lawyers can be seen, in Gramscian terms, as 'conceptive ideologists', in that they are concerned to constitute the form of legal relations in capitalist society. With this in mind, they serve a critical function of translating client problems into acceptable legal categories, then retranslating these for clients once an outcome has been achieved. Cain concluded (1983: 129):

> . . . it has been argued that lawyers' characteristic and specific practice is translation into a discourse which they both use and create. It was shown that translation work is undertaken even for impecunious clients. However . . . research has shown that lawyers do this work most and best for the *haute bourgeoisie* and the state which represents it. It is also appropriate, therefore, to theorise lawyers as organic intellectuals of the bourgeois class.

It is this overarching ideological role, therefore, which further counteracts the divisions in the social base of the profession and gives it the appearance of coherence. However, it should be realised that there are limits on the extent to which lawyers can go in pursuit of ideological goals in the interests of their clients, such as the rule of law. For example, although the rule of law ideology is to be implemented through the ideal of adversary proceedings, the profession has placed severe constraints upon overly-zealous advocacy in defence of a client, particularly where this might threaten the legitimacy or integrity of the judicial process. This was highlighted, for example, in a 1984 decision of the New South Wales Court of Appeal against a barrister who had over a long period provided an extremely vigorous defence of his clients, but who in so doing had been overly zealous in his abuse of magistrates whom he saw as likely to decide against his clients. The court ordered that the barrister was guilty of professional misconduct. (*The Prothonotary vs Costello*, 13 December 1984, unreported). This kind of decision seems to suggest that the role of lawyers as 'conceptive ideologists' is not free of constraints imposed by the need to preserve the broader ideological framework within which they work.

In another study, Cain (1976) argued that the legal ideology of English judges and barristers is clear-cut. She suggested that this has four components, which she described as the reification of law, reverence regarding objects constituted by reification, righteousness and rectitude. She suggested that the effect of this ideology was that these lawyers necessarily remained out of touch with the wider concerns of the population, or as she put it: 'Maintenance of the unity of legal thought is contingent upon their being impervious to the day to day rationalities of other sections of the population . . .' (1976: 246). As Sexton and Maher (1982) have also put it in relation to Australian lawyers, techniques such as these are essential to the preservation of the mystique of lawyers. Moreover, they serve to neutralise the tendencies toward disintegration which are so much a part of the social organisation of the legal profession in Australian society. These tendencies are only slightly less pronounced in that other arm of the legal profession, the judiciary, to which we can now turn.

Judicial and Other Third Party Dispute-Processors

It is clear from the above discussion that the legal system has evolved an ideology of legalism which is maintained and reproduced by a rigid hierarchy of centres of legitimate authority in relation to rule making and dispute resolution activity. McBarnet has referred to this as the two tiers of justice (1981: 123). Put another way, we might say that on the one hand there is the more formal 'top-down' approach (as illustrated by judicial decision making in the higher courts) and, on the other hand, there is the more informal 'bottom-up' approach (as illustrated by tribunals, lower courts and non-judicial dispute processes, such as mediators, conciliators and arbitrators). In other words, looking at the dispute handling process, it could be argued that it tends to become increasingly formal and legalistic as one ascends the legal hierarchy. This is not to suggest that no informalities are allowed to creep in at this level, but that these would be quite uncharacteristic. By contrast, from the 'bottom-up' point of view, dispute handling seems to be embedded in a sea of informality and the further one moves from the peaks of the judicial system, the less formality is evident.

Once again, this is not to suggest that non-judicial dispute processing cannot be quite formal, for in some circumstances, such as in respect to sporting disputes involving substantial sums, formalism does seem to have a habit of creeping in. However, this is again far from being characteristic of non-judicial dispute handling. What is clear, however, as Galanter (1983: 132) observed, is that the legal system and law exist in the shadow of informal decision making and bargaining, so that far from formality being the most characteristic type of dispute processing, informality tends to prevail. This would again suggest that the traditional lawyer's pyramid, which sets the superior courts at the apex of the system and the informal or less formal dispute handlers at the base, should be inverted. As argued earlier, the apex receives the priority it does for ideological, not substantive reasons, as the impact of the base-level dispute handlers upon the processing of disputes in society at large tends to be of greatest social significance, even though lawyers have tended largely to ignore this 'bottom-up' perspective. One reason for this has been suggested by Black and Baumgartner, who argue (1983: 87) that settlement roles can be distinguished by reference to their degree of authoritative intervention. Thus, these students of the dispute process point out that the least authoritative type of settlement role is that of the friendly peacemaker. This is followed, respectively, in terms of increasing authoritativeness, by the mediator, arbitrator, judge and repressive peacemaker.

No doubt we could include further types along this continuum. Black and Baumgartner also point out that the dispute process draws upon supporters for the principal disputants. They suggest that these support roles can be found in a continuum of the degree of partisan intervention in support of a disputant. Thus, these support roles range from informers, at the least partisan end, through advisers, advocates and allies, to surrogates, at the most partisan end (1983: 87). How it is that particular settlement and support roles are drawn upon by disputants would depend greatly upon the local legal culture, the social proximity of disputants (or what Black has elsewhere called their 'relational distance'), their respective resources, and the technological complexity of the society in which the dispute takes place (see further Felstiner 1974).

Despite the vast range of variables at play in the resort to dispute processing mechanisms (see further Fitzgerald 1983), prevailing ideologies have had a considerable bearing upon the manner in which disputes are channelled in society. For example, the prevailing ideology of legalism in Australian society has had a major influence upon reformers, who have argued that one of the most effective means of redressing inequities in bargaining endowments is to make available lawyers and legal services. Thus, 'legal needs' have tended to be seen in terms of the need for the services of lawyers so as to enable disputants to contest claims in the usual judicialised forums. Almost a decade was to pass in Australia before the limitation of this strategy, and its roots in the ideology of legalistic advocacy were to become apparent (see e.g. Sackville 1978). It is interesting to note that in more recent years the revolt against judicial formalism has been largely led by the judiciary itself, as judges and court administrators have advocated greater resort to mediation and formalised bargaining as illustrated in the emergence of Community Justice Centres (see further Tomasic 1982), and in the use of pre-trial or pre-hearing conferences. This has been motivated by the hope of reducing court caseloads and delays, and has to a large extent been a product of the over-selling of the ideology of legalism. This is further illustrated by the frequent attacks by judges upon the recent greater availability of legal aid, which has apparently led many more disputes to be legalised and litigated than would previously have been the case (Yeldham 1984).

Associated with this kind of criticism is the fact that the ideology of legalism can become a destabilising element in society if it is made available too widely by the state. It is for this reason that many of the more aggressive legal aid strategies, such as test cases and class actions, have tended to be frowned upon by governments and other power centres in society, such as by business leaders threatened by the spectre of class action on behalf of disgruntled consumers. Whatever the real explanation for these ideological shifts in the official rhetoric associated with various dispute processes and alternatives, it seems to be true that the judicial process is, as Weber pointed out, an amalgam of formally and substantively rational approaches. It is for this reason, as Pound (1922) has observed, that over a number of decades we seem to have witnessed periodic lurchings from formalistic to informal approaches to dispute processing. This instability seems to be embedded in the uneasy balance which legal ideology seems to comprise, for by themselves, neither formalism nor informalism are very satisfactory bases for legitimate and authoritative dispute-processing. This is because a too-formalistic legal system may be seen as inflexible and rigid, whilst a too-informal system may be seen as erratic and arbitrary.

Individual Litigants and Consumers of Legal Services

The roles of litigants and consumers of legal services within the legal system are very much influenced, if not entirely determined, by the bargaining endowments enjoyed by them. Such endowments range from the availability of legal information and legal professional assistance, the familiarity which a litigant may have with the particular legal problem area, and the resources, whether financial, psychological or social, which might be available to citizens to pursue legal action to their best advantage. Information in itself is insufficient to allow individual litigants and consumers of legal services to redress the strategic disadvantages or inequalities in power which they tend to encounter in the legal process. One of the assumptions of the legal services movement has been that inequalities in access to legal services can be redressed by providing information about the availability of such services, and to enable such services to be evaluated. On the face of it, this is a deceptively simple solution to the problem of solving legal needs. However, on closer scrutiny, it has become apparent that legal information is in itself insufficient to redress inequalities, since it is the manner in which such information is organised and applied which is critical. Thus, for example, it has been shown by Mayhew and Reiss (1969) that property ownership is an important channel by virtue of which information is conveyed. Consequently, those who have frequent occasion to be involved in property transactions tend to be much more likely to seek the services of lawyers and so to become familiar with how best to use such services. So, legal contacts, and the availability of legal information, are heavily influenced by property ownership. As wealthier sectors of society are more likely to have recurrent property transactions, they are more likely than poorer sectors to obtain and maintain access to legal services (see further, Tomasic 1978: 59–65).

Related to the property ownership dimension of the social organisation of legal contacts is the fact that 'repeat players' or recurrent users of legal services enjoy further advantages over those who only intermittently seek to use legal services or gain access to the legal system. Repeat players, as we have seen, are far more likely to be able to structure the legal process to their advantage and so to succeed than are the so-called 'one shotters' (Galanter 1974). Since organisations are much more likely to be 'repeat players', they enjoy further resource advantages over the 'one shotter', who is most likely to be an individual. Repeat player organisations are therefore usually far more likely to be effective mobilisers of law, whether reactively or proactively, than are individual consumers of legal services, unless the latter either have the economic resources to engage the services of a repeat player such as a lawyer, or else access to networks which are powerful enough to create an alternative organisational structure, such as a consumer group.

It is evident that it is quite rare for large organisations to take legal action in the courts against each other, since in cases such as this the costs of such litigation may be seen as excessive. Disputes between large organisations tend, therefore, to be dealt with informally rather than formally, although there will always be the occasional exception. In view of this somewhat stark picture, it is not surprising that many researchers have concluded that there is little or no access to law available to the vast majority of consumers with comparatively minor grievances, even though collectively these might constitute a major problem (Nader 1980). It is clear, therefore, that we need to look closely at ideologies which sponsor such notions as 'justice for all' or 'due process', since these notions can only be taken as far as existing structural barriers to access allow, and as far as available bargaining endowments permit.

Conclusions: Legal Change and the Problem of Order

The legal system, like society itself, is in a continuous process of change, despite its appearance of being tradition-bound or even stagnating. Although legal reasoning rests upon the static doctrine of precedent which assumes that contemporary cases can be matched to earlier ones, this matching is invariably rough, because the extent to which change is occurring in society is such that one can never find exact parallels between earlier and current cases. Having said this, we need to ask why it is that law reform receives the governmental support that it does in the form of extensive funding for law reform agencies. There is a paradox here, since it is apparent that law reform often has little to do with legal change in any serious sense. Although law reform commissions sometimes bring about change, this is in fact rarely the case. It can be argued that law reform agencies are more accurately seen as ideological mechanisms which serve to legitimise the law by creating the impression that legal power is being updated and made more responsive to the needs of the population at large. Put simply, law reform is frequently more symbolic than real, and this can be better appreciated if it is realised that law reform agencies are often largely extensions of governmental bureaucracies, despite the occasional forays which they may make into what has been called community law reform, which is based upon reform proposals received from the wider community. In fact, more often than not, the vast bulk of law reform activity seems to be generated by problems of a political or bureaucratic nature which are simply too hard or too complex for politicians or bureaucrats to handle.

The law reform agency, like many a Royal Commission of

Inquiry (See Tomasic 1981b), serves the function of providing community reassurance that problems are being dealt with. In other words, in the vast majority of cases, when controversial matters are referred to law reform agencies, we could argue that there is strong evidence to suggest that the impact of the agency is symbolic rather than substantive. This is not to say that sometimes 'rather technical' or 'lawyer's law' matters referred to such reform agencies do not lead to changes, but these are far removed from the popular conception of the nature of law reform activity. Ironically, some of the most significant law reform initiatives have not come from the work of the law reform commissions, but from the enthusiasm of a particular minister or bureaucracy determined to see their ideas enacted. This suggests that the kinds of matters sent to law reform commissions often tend to be those about which there is no consensus or clear-cut position, although they might be seen to require some action. All of this explains why some sociologists have come to see law reform as a problematic activity (see further Tomasic and Bottomley 1984; Arthurs 1984).

This chapter has sought to cover a considerable amount of ground, since the legal system impacts on all sectors of society and on all aspects of social life. Having such broad and wide-ranging applications, it should not be surprising if we come across discontinuities or conflicting rationales at the margins of the legal system. What is significant, however, is that the problem of coherence does not strike only at the margins or peripheries, but is also to be found at the core of legal institutions, and is reflected, too, in the processes and structures which constitute the legal system as we know it. This, as we saw, raises serious problems, since it threatens the legitimacy of the system because its authority is based on its adoption of a rational and consistent approach to the tasks which are required of it. However, the legal process is far from being as consistent and formally rational as many might expect. Inevitably, inconsistencies, gaps and formally irrational tendencies appear. This is because it is simply not possible for the system to deliver the kind of mechanistic uniformity in approach which might otherwise be expected, due to the vast array of problems brought to it.

Where attempts are made to streamline the legal system through law reform, these strategies need to be seen as part of a broader attempt to preserve the integrity and legitimacy of legal structures. They do little more than repair the damage to the legal system by failures of different legal ideologies to be able to fulfil the claims which their proponents make for them. In any event, it is clear that sociologists need to direct their attention to the interaction between diverse legal behaviours and legal ideology, for both serve to make the legal system work. Legal behaviours and legal processes inevitably reflect diversity and inconsistency, since this flexibility is essential if the processes of law are to be able to operate. However, because this incoherence may cause immense damage to the authority of law and legal institutions, an array of legal ideologies has been developed with a view to preserving the appearance of coherence. The strength of law as an institution is very much based on this capacity to integrate under this ideological appearance much that is diverse and often contradictory. Legal ideology, therefore, must be seen as that vital social glue which keeps the legal order intact, so that threats to dominant ideologies become threats to the very existence of the legal order itself.

References

Adamany, D. (1978) 'Legitimacy, Realigning Elections, and the Supreme Court', in S. Goldman and A. Sarat (1978) *American Court Systems; Readings in Judicial Process and Behaviour*. San Francisco: W.H. Freeman and Co.

Allott, A. (1980) *The Limits of Law*. London: Butterworth.

Armstrong, M. (1979) 'The Broadcasting and Television Act, 1948-1976: A Case Study of the Australian Control Board', in R. Tomasic (ed.), *Legislation and Society in Australia*. Sydney: Allen and Unwin.

Arthurs, H. (Chairman) (1984) *Law and Learning*. Ottowa: Social Sciences and Humanities Research Council of Canada.

Aubert, V. (1983) *In Search of Law: Sociological Approaches to Law*. Oxford: Martin Robertson.

Baker, D.W.A. (1979) 'The Origins of Robertson's Land Acts', in R. Tomasic (ed.), *Legislation and Society in Australia*. Sydney: Allen and Unwin.

Bardach, E. (1977) *The Implementation Game: What Happens After a Bill Becomes Law*. Cambridge: MIT Press.

Black, D. (1980) *The Manners and Customs of the Police*. New York: Academic Press.

————and Baumgartner, M.P. (1983) 'Toward a Theory of the Third Party', in K.O. Boyum and L. Mather (eds), *Empirical Theories About Courts*. New York: Longman.

Bottoms, A.E. and McClean, J.D. (1976) *Defendants in the Criminal Process*. London: Routledge and Kegan Paul.

Boyum, K.O. and Mather, L. (eds) (1983) *Empirical Theories About Courts*. New York: Longman.

Buckle, S.R. and Buckle, L.G. (1977) *Bargaining for Justice: Case Disposition and Reform in the Criminal Courts*. New York: Praeger.

Burman, S.B. and Harrell-Bond, B.E. (eds) (1979) *The Imposition of Law*. New York: Academic Press.

Cain, M. (1976) 'Necessarily Out of Touch: Thoughts on the Social

Organisation of the Bar', in P. Carlen (ed.), *The Sociology of Law*, the Sociological Review Monograph 23. Keele: University of Keele. Keele: University of Keele, Sociological Review Monograph 23.

————(1983) 'The General Practice Lawyer and the Client: Towards a Radical Conception', in R. Dingwall and P. Lewis (eds) *The Sociology of the Professions*. London: Macmillan.

Caplovitz, D. (1983) *Consumers in Trouble: A Study of Debtors in Default*. New York: Free Press.

Carlen, P. (1976) *Magistrates' Justice*. London: Martin Robertson.

Carlton, E. (1977) *Ideology and Social Order*. London: Routledge and Kegan Paul.

Casper, J.D. (1978) 'The Supreme Court and National Policy Making', in S. Goldman and A. Sarat (1978) *American Court Systems: Readings in Judicial Process and Behaviour*. San Francisco: W.H. Freeman and Co.

Chambliss, W.J. (1979) 'On Law-making', *British Journal of Law and Society* 6 (2): 149–71.

Choper, J.H. (1980) *Judicial Review and the National Political Process: A Functional Reconsideration of the Role of the Supreme Court*. Chicago: Chicago University Press.

Church, T.D. *et al.* (1978) *Justice Delayed: The Pace of Litigation in Urban Trial Courts*. Williamsburg: National Centre for State Courts.

Collins, D.A. (1979) *Guidebook to Civil Claims' Practice in New South Wales*. Sydney: CCH Publishers.

Dahl, R.A. (1978). 'The Supreme Court's Role in National Policy Making', in Goldman and Sarat (1978).

Edelman, M. (1964) *The Symbolic Uses of Politics*. Urbana: University of Illinois Press.

————(1977) *Political Language: Words that Succeed and Policies That Fail*. New York: Academic Press.

Einsenstein, J. and Jacob, H. (1977) *Felony Justice: An Organizational Analysis of Criminal Courts*. Boston: Little, Brown and Co.

Encel, S. (1979) 'The Social Impact of the Australian Constitution' in R. Tomasic (ed.), *Legislation and Society in Australia*. Sydney: Allen and Unwin.

Evan, W. (1965) 'Law as an Instrument of Social Change', in A. Gouldner and S.M. Miller (eds), *Applied Sociology*. New York: Free Press.

Feeley, M.M. (1979) *The Process is the Punishment*. New York: Russell Sage Foundation.

Felstiner, W.L.F. (1974) 'Influences of Social Organization on Dispute Processing, *Law and Society Review* 9: 63–94.

Ferrari,V.(Ed) (1990) *Developing Sociology of Law: A World-Wide Documentary Enquiry*. Milan: Dott A. Giuffre Editore.

Fine, B. (1984) *Democracy and the Rule of Law: Liberal Ideals and Marxist Critiques*. London: Pluto Press.

Fitzgerald, J. (1983) 'Grievances, Disputes and Outcomes: A Comparison of Australia and the United States', *Law in Context* 1: 15–45.

Fleming, R.B. (1982) *Punishment Before Trial: An Organization Perspective of Felony Bail Processes.* New York: Longman.

Friedman, L.M. (1975) *The Legal System: A Social Science Perspective.* New York: Russell Sage Foundation.

——(1983) 'Courts Over Time: A Survey of Theories and Research' in K.O. Boyum and L. Mather (eds), *Empirical Theories About Courts.* New York: Longman.

——and R.V. Percival (1976) 'A Tale of Two Courts: Litigation in Alameda and San Benito Counties', *Law and Society Review* 10 (1): 267–301.

Friedman, L.M. and Percival, R.V. (1981) *The Roots of Justice: Crime and Punishment in Alameda County, California, 1870–1910.* Chapel Hill: University of North Carolina Press.

Galanter, M. (1974) 'Why the Haves Come Out Ahead: Speculations on the Limits of Legal Change', *Law and Society Review* 9: 95–160.

——(1975) 'Afterword: Explaining Litigation', *Law and Society Review* 9: 347–68.

——(1983) 'The Radiating Effects of Courts' in K.O. Boyum and L. Mather (eds), *Empirical Theories About Courts.* New York: Longman.

Goldman, S. and Sarat, A. (eds) (1978) *American Court Systems: Readings in Judicial Process and Behaviour.* San Francisco: W.H. Freeman and Co.

Grabosky, P. (1977) *Sydney in Ferment: Crime, Dissent and Official Reaction 1788 to 1973.* Canberra: ANU Press.

Griffith, J. (1979) 'Is Law Important?' *New York University Law Review* 54: 339-74.

Griffith, J.A.G. (1977) *The Politics of the Judiciary.* Manchester: Manchester University Press.

Grossman, J.B. *et al.* (1981) 'Measuring the Pace of Civil Litigation in Federal and State Trial Courts', *Judicature* 65 (2): 86–113.

Gusfield, J.R. (1963) *Symbolic Crusade: Status Politics and the American Temperance Movement.* Urbana: University of Illinois Press.

Gyles, R.V. (1984) *Report to the Attorney General for the Year Ended 30 June 1984 by R.V. Gyles QC, Special Prosecutor.* Canberra: AGPS.

Hart, G. (1979) 'Some Aspects of Government Regulation of the Capital Markets: An Assessment of the Securities Industry Acts' in R. Tomasic (ed.), *Legislation and Society in Australia.* Sydney: Allen and Unwin.

Heinz, J.P. and Laumann, E.O. (1982) *Chicago Lawyers: The Social Structure of the Bar.* New York: Russell Sage Foundation and American Bar Foundation.

Hetherton, M. (1981) *Victoria's Lawyers: The Second Report of a Research Project on Lawyers in the Community.* Melbourne: Victoria Law Foundation.

Heumann, M. (1977) *Plea Bargaining: The Experiences of Prosecutors, Judges and Defense Attorneys.* Chicago: Chicago University Press.

Hiller, A.E. and Hancock, L. (1979) 'Juvenile Delinquency Legislation and the Processing of Juveniles in Victoria' in R. Tomasic (ed.), *Legislation and Society in Australia.* Sydney: Allen and Unwin.

Hirst, P. (1979) *On Law and Ideology.* Atlantic Highlands. NJ: Humanities Press.

Hodder-Williams, R. (1980) *The Politics of the US Supreme Court*. London: Allen and Unwin.

Hopkins, A. (1978) 'The Uses of Law to Sociology', *Australian and New Zealand Journal of Sociology* 14 (3): 266–73.

———(1979) 'The Evolution of Trade Practices Legislation in Australia' in R. Tomasic (ed.), *Legislation and Society in Australia*. Sydney: Allen and Unwin.

Hunt, A. (1985) 'The Ideology of Law: Advances and Problems in Recent Applications of the Concept of Ideology to the Analysis of Law', *Law and Society Review* 19–37.

Jacob, H. (1969) *Debtors in Court*. Chicago: Rand McNally.

Kagan, R.A. Cartwright, B. Friedman, L.M. and Wheeler, S. (1978) 'The Business of State Supreme Courts', *Michigan Law Review* 76 (6): 961–1,005.

Kaufman, H. (1960) *The Forest Ranger: A Study in Administrative Behaviour*. Baltimore: Johns Hopkins Press.

Kelly, D. St L. (1977) *Debt Recovery in Australia*. Canberra: AGPS.

Keon-Cohen, B. (1979) 'Aboriginal Land Rights in Australia: Beyond the Legislative Limits?', in R. Tomasic (ed.), *Legislation and Society in Australia*. Sydney: Allen and Unwin.

Kondos, A. (1979) 'The Hidden Faces of Power: A Sociological Analysis of Housing Legislation in Australia', in R. Tomasic (ed.), *Legislation and Society in Australia*. Sydney: Allen and Unwin.

Kurczewski, J. and Frieske, K. (1977) 'Some Problems in the Legal Regulation of the Activities of Economic Institutions', *Law and Society Review* 11 (3): 489–505.

La Trobe University (1980) *Guilty, Your Worship: A Study of Victoria's Magistrates' Courts*. Melbourne: Department of Legal Studies, La Trobe University.

Lipsky, M. (1980) *Street-Level Bureaucracy: Dilemmas of the Individual in Public Services*. New York: Russell Sage Foundation.

Luhmann, N. (1976) 'The Legal Profession: Comments on the Situation in the Federal Republic of Germany' in D.N. MacCormick (ed.), *Lawyers in Their Social Setting*. Edinburgh: W. Green and Son.

Macaulay, S. (1963) 'Non-Contractual Relations in Business', *American Sociological Review* 28: 55–60.

———(1977) 'Elegant Models, Empirical Pictures and the Complexities of Contract', *Law and Society Review* 11 (3): 507–28.

Mather, L.M. (1979) *Plea Bargaining or Trial?: The Process of Criminal Case Disposition*. Lexington, Mass.: Lexington Books.

Massell, G.J. (1968) 'Law as an Instrument of Revolutionary Change in a Traditional Milieu: The Case of Soviet Central Asia', *Law and Society Review* 2 (2): 179–228.

Mayhew, L. and Reiss, A.J. (1969) 'The Social Organization of Legal Contacts', *American Sociological Review* 34 (3): 309–13.

McBarnet, D.J. (1981) *Conviction: Law, the State and the Construction of Justice*. London: Macmillan.

Mukherjee, S.K. (1981) *Crime Trends in Twentieth-Century Australia*. Sydney: Allen and Unwin.

Nader, L. (1980) *No Access to Law; Alternatives to the American Judicial System*. New York: Academic Press.

Nelken, D. (1981) 'The Gap Problem in the Sociology of Law: A Theoretical Review', *Windsor Yearbook of Access to Justice* 1: 35–61.

New South Wales Bureau of Crime Statistics and Research (1983) *Court Statistics 1982*. Sydney: New South Wales Bureau of Crime Statistics and Research.

O'Malley, P. (1979) 'Theories of Structure Versus Causal Determination: Accounting for Legislative Change in Capitalist Societies' in R Tomasic (ed.), *Legislation and Society in Australia*. Sydney: Allen and Unwin.

Ozdowski, S.A. (1979) 'The Family Law Act 1975 and The Family: A Study in Knowledge and Attitudes' in R. Tomasic (ed.), *Legislation and Society in Australia*. Sydney: Allen and Unwin.

Packer, H.L. (1968) *The Limits of the Criminal Sanction*. Stanford: Stanford University Press.

Parsons, T. (1980) 'The Law and Social Control' in W.M. Evans (ed.), *The Sociology of Law: A Socio-Structural Perspective*. New York: Free Press.

Podgorecki, A. (1974) *Law and Society*. London: Routledge and Kegan Paul.

Podgorcki, A. (1991) *A Sociological Theory of Law*. Milan: Dott A. Giuffre Editore.

Pound, R. (1922) *An Introduction to the Philosophy of Law*. New Haven: Yale University Press.

Robinson, C. (1979) 'Drink-Driving: Social and Legal Considerations' in R. Tomasic (ed.), *Legislation and Society in Australia*. Sydney: Allen and Unwin.

Rock, P. (1973) *Making People Pay*. London: Routledge and Kegan Paul.

Ross, E.A. (1901–70) *Social Control*. New York: Johnson Reprint Corporation.

Ross, H.L. (1981) *Deterring the Drinking Driver: Legal Policy and Social Control*. Lexington, Mass.: Lexington Books.

Ross, S.D. (1982) *Politics of Law Reform*. Melbourne: Penguin Books.

Sackville, R. (1978) 'Lawyers, Law Reform and Legal Institutions — Some Reflections' in R. Tomasic (ed.), *Understanding Lawyers*. Sydney: Allen and Unwin.

Sawer, G. (1967) *Australian Federalism in the Courts*. Melbourne: Melbourne University Press.

Sexton, M. and Maher, L. (1982) *The Legal Mystique: The Role of Lawyers in Australian Society*. Sydney: Angus and Robertson.

Shapiro, M. (1964) *Law and Politics in the Supreme Court*. London: Free Press of Glencoe.

Simon, W.H. (1978) 'The Ideology of Advocacy: Procedural Justice and Professional Ethics', *Wisconsin Law Review* 1978 (1): 29–144.

Sugarman, D. (ed.) (1983) *Legality, Ideology and the State*. London: Academic Press.

Sumner, C. (1979) *Reading Ideologies*. London: Academic Press.

Sutton, A. and Wild, R. (1979) 'Companies, the Law and the

Professions: A Sociological View of Australian Companies Legislation', in R. Tomasic (ed.), *Legislation and Society in Australia*. Sydney: Allen and Unwin.

Tomasic, R. (1977a) *Deterrence and the Drinking Driver*. Sydney: Law Foundation of New South Wales.

———(1977b) *Drugs, Alcohol and Community Control*. Sydney: Law Foundation of New South Wales.

———(1978) *Lawyers and the Community*. Sydney: Allen and Unwin.

———(ed.) (1979) *Legislation and Society in Australia*. Sydney: Allen and Unwin.

———(1981a) 'Criminal Lawyers and their Clients', *ANZJ Criminology* 14: 147–55.

———(1981b) 'The Politics of Implementing Drug Law Reform in Australia', *Australian Crime Prevention Council Forum* 4(1): 69–80.

———(1982) 'Mediation as an Alternative to Adjudication: Rhetoric and Reality in the Neighbourhood Justice Movement' in R. Tomasic and M.M. Feeley (eds), *Neighbourhood Justice*. New York: Longman.

———(1983) 'Social Organization Amongst Australian Lawyers', *ANZJ Sociology* 19(3): 447–75.

———(1985) *The Sociology of Law*. London: Sage.

———and S. Bottomley (1984) 'Editorial: Law Reform and Social Change', *Legal Service Bulletin* 9(6): 251–52.

———and C. Bullard (1978) *Lawyers and their Work in New South Wales*. Sydney: Law Foundation of New South Wales.

———and C. Bullard (1979) 'Lawyers and Legal Culture in Australia', *International Journal of the Sociology of Law* 7: 417–32.

———J. Jackson and R Woellner (1992) *Corporation Law: Principles, Policy and Practice*, Sydney: Butterworths.

———and B. Pentony (1989a) 'Fast Tracking Takeover Litigation and Alternatives to the Courts, in Company Takeover Disputes', *Australian Business Law Review* 17: 336–55.

———(1989b) 'Judicial Technique in Takeover Litigation in Australia, *University of New South Wales Law Journal* 12: 240–61.

———(1990) 'Litigation in Takeovers — The Decision Making Process', *Australian Bar Review* 6: 67–80.

———(1991a) 'Resisting to the Last Shareholders' Dollar: Takeover Litigation — A Tactical Device', *Australian Journal of Corporate Law* 1: 154–64.

———(1991b) 'Tax Compliance and the Rule of Law: From Legalism to Administrative Procedure', *Australian Tax Forum* 8: 85–116.

———(1991c) 'Taxation Law Compliance and the Role of Professional Tax Advisers', *Australian and New Zealand Journal of Criminology* 24: 241–57.

Touraine, A. (1977) *The Self-Production of Society*. Chicago: University of Chicago Press.

Weaver, S. (1977) *Decision to Prosecute: Organization and Public Policy in the Antitrust Division*. Cambridge: MIT Press.

Weber, M. (1954) *On Law in Economy and Society*. Cambridge: Harvard University Press.

Willis, J. (1980) 'The Regulation of Debt Collection Practices' in A.J. Duggan and L.W. Darvall (eds), *Consumer Protection: Law and Theory*.

Yeldham, D.A. (1984) 'Delays in Criminal Trials', Paper presented to Criminal Law Committee, Sydney University Law Graduates Association, 13 March 1984, Sydney Law School.

Ziegert, K.A. (1984) 'The Limits of Family Law: A Socio-Legal Assessment', *Legal Service Bulletin* 9(6): 257–63.

Chapter Six

Immigrants in Australian Society: Backgrounds, Attainment and Politics

Toni Makkai and
Ian McAllister*

Australia is a nation built on immigration. In 1991, almost one in four of the population had been born overseas, with the majority coming from non-English-speaking countries. In total, around one in every three Australians is either an immigrant or the child of an immigrant. The level of immigration to Australia is matched in the Western world only by Canada and the United States, which both maintained large-scale immigration programs in the late nineteenth and early twentieth centuries. In the post-war years, the only country to sustain a level of immigration comparable to Australia is Israel, which is also a country that has been created by large-scale, recent population movement.

In contrast to the United States or Canada, where immigrants have been highly visible members of the society for more than a century, it is only in the last two decades that the migrant presence in Australia has had any significant impact on the country's culture, socio-economic structure or politics. In part, this change has been brought about by the different ethnic composition of the migrant intake, the rise of ethnic lobby groups and by the government's policy response to this change. But in part, too, the higher profile of immigrants has followed a worldwide trend in which ethnicity has become an increasingly salient characteristic for group loyalty and political mobilisation. Ethnic conflict in the

* We would like to thank Jeannie Martin and the editors for their comments on an earlier version of the chapter.

former Soviet Union, the ex-Communist states of Eastern Europe, or in the liberal democracies of Western Europe, are all indicative of this trend.

Rather than disappearing, then, as traditional sociological theories once predicted, ethnicity has become more important in many societies, regardless of their stage of socio-economic development. The resurgence of ethnicity represents the failure of three major theories about change in industrial societies: functionalism, developmental or modernisation theory, and Marxism. All of these theories viewed ethnicity as a 'premodern phenomenon, a residue of particularism and ascription incompatible with the trend toward achievement, universalism and nationality supposedly exhibited by industrial societies' (van den Berghe 1981: 17). As society developed, these theories predicted that ethnic differences would simply cease to be important. But contradicting these predictions, ethnicity has re-emerged as an important factor in many societies in the late twentieth century.

Multiracial and ethnically plural societies are generally a consequence of one of two types of immigration or, very occasionally, a combination of the two. The first type of immigration occurred when some societies experienced population movements many thousands of years ago, at which time indigenous ethnic minorities were settled. The second type of immigration has taken place in modern times, either by legal or illegal means, producing an ethnically distinct minority or group of minorities. In Australia, both of these processes have occurred: Aborigines are thought to have arrived on the continent many thousands of years ago, while white settlement began in 1788 and the large-scale migration of non-English-speakers did not begin until 1947.

This chapter examines the background to immigration in Australia, focusing particularly on the post-1947 period, and the emergence of multiculturalism in the mid-1970s. We also analyse the socio-economic backgrounds and attainments of immigrants, their role in the labour market and the social mobility that they are likely to experience. Finally, the chapter examines immigrant political behaviour in Australia and traces the emergence of the elusive 'ethnic vote'. The data rely mainly on a survey conducted in 1988–89 on behalf of the Office of Multicultural Affairs, details of which are provided in the Appendix.

An Immigrant Society

Immigration to Australia has progressed through four major phases, each drawing migrants from a different part of the world,

Table 6.1 Stages and Policies in Australian Immigration

Time period	Immigrant groups	Government policy
Pre-1901	Anglo-Celtic, European, Asian	None
		Ban on Asians (after 1860)
1901–47	Anglo-Celtic	Assimilation
1947–1972	Anglo-Celtic, European	Assimilation (to 1964)
		Integration (to 1972)
1972–	Broadly-based	Multiculturalism

and each relying on a different set of policies and priorities. As Table 6.1 indicates, the Anglo-Celtics were the major focus of immigration policies until the 1970s, with gradual supplementation by continental Europeans after 1947. Prior to 1901, immigration was largely uncontrolled. With federation, assimilation became the prevailing policy for the first half of the twentieth century, with a change to integration during the late 1960s. Set against patterns of pre-1972 immigration, the situation in the 1970s and 80s represents a radical departure: not only have the regional origins of migrants changed dramatically — from Europe to Asia — but government policy has moved through three phases, from assimilation to integration and most recently, to accepting migrants' languages and culture through multiculturalism.

Pre-1947 Immigration
Since Governor Phillip arrived in Sydney Harbour with eleven British ships in 1788, over 6 million people have emigrated to Australia (Armit *et al.* 1988: 1). The history of immigration has been an interaction between demand and supply. The initial immigrants were mainly convicts, for whom Australia provided a secure prison, as well as maintaining the country as a British colony. The first significant numbers of free immigrants did not arrive until the late 1820s, attracted by the expansion of the wool industry. Many saw little future in remaining in Britain as the population was dispersed from rural to urban areas by the Industrial Revolution. During the late 1840s the number of settlers was swelled by Irish immigrants escaping the potato famine.

The largest influx of migrants per head of population in the history of white settlement occurred during the 1851–61 goldrush period, when the white Australian population of just under half a million was swollen by 700,000 immigrants (Armit *et al.* 1988: 13). The goldrush immigrants included a substantial minority of Chinese workers, the first non-white immigrants to arrive in Australia. These workers were viewed by white immigrants as dirty, drug-addicted and as a threat to the Australian way of life, particularly because of their willingness to work long hours for little reward in poor and often dangerous conditions. The anti-Chinese feelings that developed on the goldfields culminated in Victoria and New South Wales passing immigration laws to restrict the entry of Chinese into their jurisdictions.

The decline in gold mining coincided with the industrial expansion of Sydney and Melbourne. The gold miners of the 1850s became the industrial workforce of the 1860s and one of their prime concerns was to protect their jobs and livelihoods from other immigrants (Armit *et al.* 1988). As a consequence, New South Wales and Victoria opposed further immigration, but Queensland and South Australia continued to encourage immigrants in order to develop their own economies. There was a continuing problem in recruiting labour for the Queensland canefields which resulted in farmers importing Pacific Islanders (referred to as Kanakas), many of whom were kidnapped or duped into working in Australia.

Federation in 1901 provided the two southern states with the opportunity to further restrict non-white immigration, a view that was endorsed by the trade union movement, since it was feared that 'Asian' or 'coloured' people would take the jobs of white workers by accepting a lower standard of living and hence lower wages. These two issues — jobs and quality of life — were to simmer quietly in debates about immigration until they were resurrected in the 1980s during the economic recession. The trade unions also opposed assisted passages from the United Kingdom, and by the 1880s they had been virtually abandoned, although they were reintroduced in the early 1900s. Despite the anti-immigration lobby, around 1.3 million people immigrated to the colonies between 1851 and 1891. Nevertheless, Table 6.2 shows that by the turn of the century, more than three in four of the population had been born in Australia, a proportion almost exactly the same as that for the present day.

One of the first acts of the federal Parliament was to implement the Immigration Restriction Act 1901 or the 'White Australia policy' (Sherington 1990; Hawkins 1989). A steady stream of British immigrants continued to arrive until World War I, although there was also some migration from outside the British Isles, mainly from Germany and Scandinavia, who as northern Europeans were regarded as acceptable entrants. After World War I, the pre-war immigration program was re-introduced, but consistent with the White Australia policy, two-thirds of the immigrants who arrived during the 1920s had assisted passages and were predominantly British (Armit *et al.* 1988: 25).

Table 6.2 The Birthplace of the Australian Population, 1990–91

(%)

Country of birth	1901	1947	1961	1971	1981	1991[a]	Change, 1901–91
Australia	77.1	90.2	83.1	79.8	78.2	77.2	+0.1
New Zealand	0.7	0.6	0.5	0.6	1.2	1.7	+1.0
British Isles	18.0	7.1	7.2	8.5	7.8	7.0	−11.0
Rest of Europe	2.0	1.5	8.0	8.7	7.5	6.9	+4.9
Asia	1.2	0.3	0.1	1.3	2.5	5.2	+4.0
Other	1.0	0.7	1.1	1.1	2.8	2.0	+1.0
(N, thousands)	(3,773)	(7,579)	(10,508)	(12,755)	(14,576)	(17,336)	

[a] Estimated figures

Source: McAllister *et al*. 1990: 216; ABS, Cat. No. 3221.0

1947–72: Assimilation to Integration

After World War II the second major influx of immigrants began. The threat of invasion by the Japanese had brought home to the government the indefensibility of Australia in the absence of a large population (Western 1983; Jupp 1988). The government's response was to adopt a policy of 'populate or perish' and the mechanism to achieve this was a vigorous immigration program. Under the direction of Arthur Calwell, the first Minister for Immigration, the government aimed to increase the population through immigration by 1 per cent annually. It was clear that the British Isles could not provide the level of immigration required for this ambitious target, and as a replacement, the government targeted the enormous number of displaced persons generated by World War II. From 1948 to 1952, the assisted passage scheme was extended to a wide range of continental European countries, whose people were seen as being easily assimilated into Australian society.[1]

Until the 1970s, British migrants were given special status, and privileges denied to other immigrant groups. In the early post-war migration, European refugees with assisted passage were required to perform two years' labour for the government, while their British counterparts were exempt. In 1958 the Migration Act was revised so that British citizens were eligible for social security but non-British migrants were required to become citizens before becoming eligible. British immigrants were not required to obtain visas for either visitor or permanent residency status and they had the right to vote in Australian elections regardless of their citizenship. These more favourable conditions offered to British migrants were gradually removed after 1975.[2]

During the 1950s and 60s, prohibitive restrictions on the immigration of non-Europeans were gradually removed. In 1958, the controversial dictation test, whereby potential immigrants were required to pass a written examination in any language specified by the Department of Immigration, was abolished. At the same time, the 1901 Immigration Restriction Act was replaced by the Migration Act (Hawkins 1989). It was this particular reform that has often been seen as the first step in the policy shift away from assimilation (Martin 1978). In 1966, immigration policy towards non-Europeans was reviewed and applications were considered from anyone who was well-qualified and prepared to integrate into Australian society.

Prior to the mid-1960s, the government did little to assist migrants other than to place them in their first job, a policy which was effectively assimilationist: to find work, migrants had to conform to the norms and values of Australian society (Collins 1988). Nowhere was the goal of social conformism more evident than in the Good Neighbour movement established in the 1950s, which was intended to help migrants adjust to the Australian way of life through widening their contacts with the English-speaking population (Jupp 1966: 9). The problem, however, was that it became increasingly obvious that migrants were not assimilating into Australian society. First, significant numbers were returning to their country of origin: it was estimated that over 15 per cent of immigrants who arrived between 1959 and 1965 returned home (Western 1983: 255). Second, many immigrants did not acquire English language skills, largely because the English requirements were minimal in most unskilled occupations.

The 1960s heralded a subtle change in government policy, away from assimilation and towards integration. The first indication of this change was the renaming in 1964 of the Assimilation Section within the Department of Immigration as the Integration Section (Collins 1988). In 1968, intensive English training courses for immigrants were started for the first time, and in 1969 the Committee on Overseas Professional Qualifications was established to seek ways of utilising more effectively the qualifications gained by immigrants in non-English-speaking countries. In June 1969, the Labor Party modified its immigration policy, stating that race, colour or nationality should not be considered as criteria for immigration to Australia.

Post-1972: Multiculturalism

With the election of the Whitlam Labor government in 1972, the White Australia policy was finally laid to rest. While integration acknowledged that immigrants would have early adjustment difficulties and therefore would need to retain their culture and language, the new policy of multiculturalism accepted that the retention of culture and language should not only be allowed but actively encouraged. In 1973, A. J. Grassby outlined the government's new policy towards immigrants in a booklet called *A Multicultural Society for the Future*. The adoption of the term 'multiculturalism' had much to do with the Canadian experience. The idea of encouraging cultural pluralism had emerged in Canada in the 1930s, becoming associated with the catchword 'mosaic'.[3] However, it was not until the early 1970s that the term multiculturalism entered everyday use (Bullivant 1980). Canadian experience and terminology was the model adopted by Australian observers.

When the Liberal Party was elected in 1975 they confirmed their commitment to multiculturalism and provided the resources to establish ethnic councils. These have emerged as powerful pressure groups, exerting considerable influence on government policy (Jupp 1991). The *Galbally Report* on the post-arrival programs and services available to migrants, published in 1978, listed 57 policy objectives, to which the government responded with five major policy initiatives (Collins 1988; Jupp 1991; Betts 1988; Hawkins 1989). These initiatives included reversing the previous government's policy and increasing the number of immigrants, introducing programs in schools to promote migrant languages and cultures, and establishing the National Ethnic Broadcasting Advisory Council and the Special Broadcasting Service (SBS).

One notable change in the migrant intake in the post-1972 period has been the increasing numbers of refugees. In the immediate post-war period, refugees came mainly from Poland, the Baltic states and other Eastern European countries that had fallen under Communist rule (Collins 1988: 55). In the most recent period, the major source has been Indochina, with refugees fleeing the consequences of the Communist takeover of South Vietnam (Viviani 1984). Throughout the 1980s, Indochinese refugees accounted for more than half of all refugee arrivals in Australia under the Special Humanitarian Program established in 1981. As Figure 6.1 demonstrates, among developed nations, Australia has taken the largest proportion of Indochinese refugees relative to population size.

In terms of party politics, the period since 1975 has been marked by a bipartisan policy favouring a high level of immigration and support for the concept of multiculturalism. However, there has been considerable questioning of the political and economic advisability of current immigration policies. In 1984, a

Figure 6.1 Indochinese Refugees accepted by Four Western Countries, 1975–85

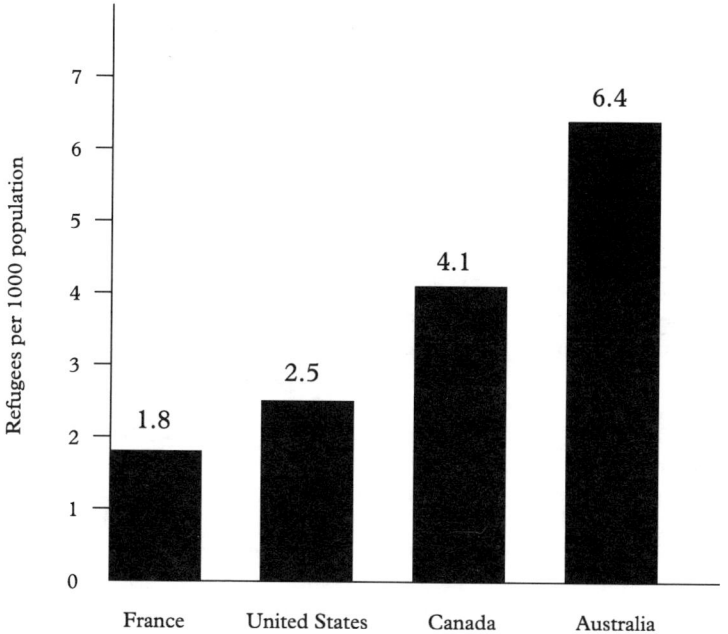

Note: Figures are refugees per thousand population.
Sources: Hawkins 1989: Table 8; Bair 1988: 122–29

Melbourne University academic, Professor Geoffrey Blainey, delivered a speech criticising the high levels of Asian immigration and the difficulties in assimilation. As Table 6.2 indicates, just over 5 per cent of the population in 1991 had been born in Asia, about half of them in Southeast Asia.[4] It is estimated that by 2010, the Asian component of the population will be no more than 7 per cent. Moreover, a large proportion of Asian immigrants are from former British colonies. As Jupp (1991: 90) argues, many of these immigrants are better educated than the average Australian, are fluent in English, and 'are culturally closer to the Australian norm than most of the Europeans who arrived in the 1950s and 1960s'.

The government policy of multiculturalism has removed many of the obligations previously placed on immigrants by the policies of assimilation and integration. This debate resurfaced with the publication of the *FitzGerald Report* in 1988, which reviewed

Australia's immigration policies. It recommended that immigration should be increased, but with a greater emphasis being placed on economic migrants, and those demonstrating a stronger commitment to Australian values and institutions. The report was opposed by the major ethnic groups, who saw it as an attack on the family reunion program, and the government rejected its major recommendations. In 1989, government policy on multiculturalism was further refined with the publication of a *National Agenda for a Multicultural Australia*. This represents a new phase in Australia's treatment of migrants, heralded some years before, in which barriers towards access and equity for migrants are removed, mainly in the areas of government services and programs (Jakubowicz 1987).

Given the high levels of immigration, it is perhaps surprising that Australia has not experienced race riots or popular support for neo-facist organisations, as has occurred in countries like Britain, France, Germany or the United States. Both Collins (1988) and Jupp (1991) argue that the diversity of the migrant intake has played an important role by creating a plural society. In addition, despite the recent emphasis on Asian immigration, two-thirds of the population have either been born in the British Isles or have one or more parents who are descended from British settlers. Three other factors have also been important in maintaining ethnic and racial stability. First, the social structure is relatively open compared with most other countries, permitting social mobility (National Population Council 1991). Second, there has been relative prosperity during periods of high immigration, reducing potential native-settler conflict. Finally, Australia has traditionally granted full social and political rights to all immigrants, thereby ensuring their support for the prevailing political system (Collins 1988; Population Issues Committee 1991; Jupp 1991).

Public Opinion on Immigration and Multiculturalism

Since bipartisanship on immigration and multiculturalism became the norm in the early 1970s, immigration or multiculturalism have rarely surfaced as political issues in party political debate. The reasons behind the lack of an informed political debate include the parties' desire to preserve their own positions by restricting electoral competition along a single economic dimension; the fear that a debate over such fundamental social issues could threaten regime stability and the political 'rules of the game'; and the importance of multiculturalism as a means of extending fundamental citizen rights (McAllister 1992a). In the absence of a public debate between political élites, public opinion, therefore, does not possess the necessary information with which to reach an informed decision; the net effect has been that such opinion on these issues lacks consistency and coherence over any extended period of time.

Although the debate over immigration has been eschewed by the political parties, periodic conflict over the issue between a variety of interest groups and individuals has served to make public opinion aware of at least some of the arguments. In the 1980s, the debate was concerned mainly with Asian immigration, but in the early 1990s it focused on whether any immigration at all — regardless of immigrants' geographical origins — was desirable. This view has been supported by environmentalists, with writers such as Birrell and Birrell (1981) arguing that continuing immigration results not only in a decline in Australia's standard of living, but also in irreparable environmental damage. The government responded to this debate by commissioning the National Population Council to examine all aspects of immigration and associated population growth (Population Issues Committee 1991).

Although public opinion on immigration is unstable, and the differences in identifying trends are further compounded by changes in question wordings in the opinion polls, Figure 6.2 suggests two patterns. First, the post-war years show that while popular opinion has fluctuated considerably, there have been two periods in which immigration has been especially unpopular. These periods — in the early 1970s and early 1980s, respectively — correspond roughly to peaks in the immigrant intake, suggesting a popular reaction against high levels of immigration. Second, public opinion on Asian immigration is closely linked with opinion on immigration as a whole, and is not seen as a separate issue. As a result, popular views on Asian immigration tend to reflect shifts in opinion on the question of immigration as a whole.

Identifying trends in public opinion on multiculturalism presents greater difficulties. The major problem is that considerable ambiguity surrounds the use of the term 'multiculturalism'. Some use it as a simple description of a society that contains a variety of ethnic and racial groups; others see it more positively, as a policy for securing equal ethnic and racial representation in the community. The former definition has few, if any, policy implications; the latter definition has distinct implications for government policies across a wide range of areas. Given the confusion

Figure 6.2   Public Opinion on Immigration, 1952–90

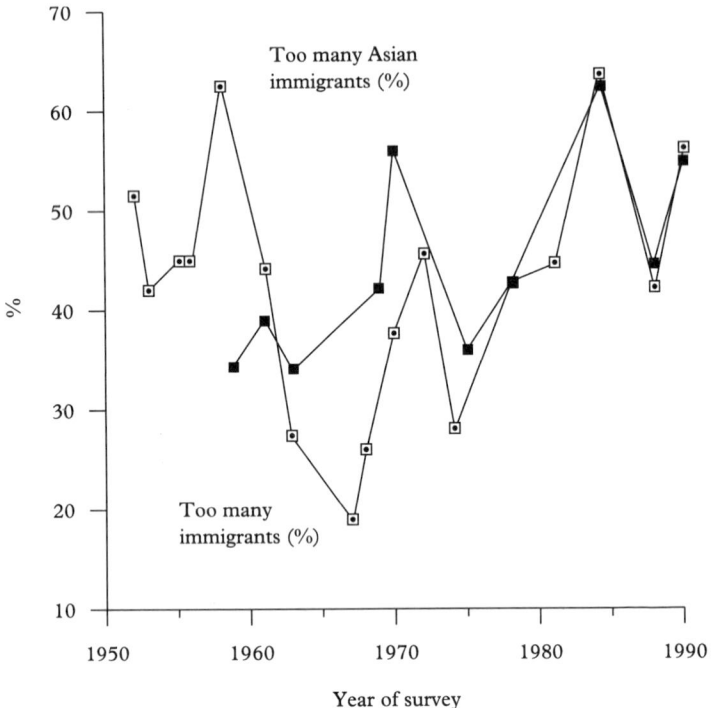

Note: Question wordings change between surveys, but most refer to 'too many
        immigrants' or to 'restrict immigration'
Sources: Extracted from Goot 1984, 1991

over its meaning even within political élites, it is not surprising
that there is even more confusion within public opinion.

At a theoretical level, however, the term has a clearer meaning.
A society can respond to cultural diversity in a variety of ways.
One approach is to ensure that minority cultural groups assimilate
into the culture of the majority, and this was the policy of
successive Australian governments towards immigrants until the
1960s. Perhaps the best known version of the assimilationist
approach is the 'straight line' theory of Gans (1968; see also
Gordon 1975), whereby ethnic groups are systematically absorbed
into the host society with the passage of time. An alternative
approach to cultural diversity is to see it as an asset and to
encourage it, so that minorities retain their own cultures so long
as an overall loyalty is maintained to the society as a whole. This

has been the approach adopted by Australian governments since the early 1970s.

Given that multiculturalism only became government policy in relatively recent times, we would expect some residual popular support for assimilation to remain, and Table 6.3 shows that this is indeed the case. Around one-third of the Australians in the 1988 survey agreed 'very much' with the three assimilationist statements. English-speaking-born (ESB) and non-English-speaking-born (NESB) migrants are actually more supportive of assimilation, with the exception that NESB immigrants are less likely to support the statement that 'different cultural groups in Australia causes lots of problems'. There is, however, very considerable support for the three statements reflecting multiculturalism. A large majority of Australians support all three, and the level of support increases among ESB and NESB immigrants.

Table 6.3 Public Opinion on Assimilation and Multiculturalism, 1988[a]

| | 'Agree very much' (%) | | |
	Australia	ESB	NESB
Assimilation			
1. People who come to Australia should change their behaviour to be more like other Australians	33	40	40
2. If members of ethnic groups want to keep their own culture, they should keep it to themselves	28	30	41
3. Having lots of different cultural groups in Australia causes lots of problems	38	40	25
Multiculturalism			
4. It's important that we make use of the skills and education of all immigrants	69	79	85
5. No matter whether Australians were born here or come from overseas they should all be given equal opportunities	78	87	92
6. So long as a person is committed to Australia it doesn't matter what ethnic background they have	59	71	80
(N)	(1,020)	(156)	(883)

[a] The question was: 'Please tell me if you agree very much, agree a little, disagree a little, or disagree very much with the following statements'

Source: *1988–89 Issues in Multicultural Australia Survey*, general population (N=1,552) and NESB (N=986) samples

It is this strong popular support which provides a base for the policy of multiculturalism. In this sense, multiculturalism conforms to the notion of a valence issue, which is defined as an opinion which records a vast majority in support of it, and produces unity rather than division (Stokes 1966: 170–71). For example, posing an undeniable social good — such as asking voters if the government should try and eliminate poverty or spend more on health — constitutes a valence issue. Multiculturalism has become such an issue because there has been a party political consensus to support it, and considerable steps have been taken to ensure that it has not become politically divisive. The divisions within public opinion over the level of immigration have more serious consequences for government, for although immigration policy is not driven by public opinion, nor can such strong popular opinions be ignored.

A major assumption underlying multiculturalism, as already noted, is that ethnic groups will develop a loyalty to their new country, while retaining cultural and social links with the country in which they were born. Of the major ethnic groups, however, Table 6.4 shows that all but one have lower levels of identification with Australia than the Australian-born, some of them registering

Table 6.4 Australian and Ethnic Identification, Major Birthplace Groups, 1988[a]

	Say Australian 'very important' (%)	With ethnic identification (%)	(N)
Greece	72	59	(82)
Australia	62	—	(1,021)
Yugoslavia	61	51	(75)
Netherlands	60	5	(38)
India	55	35	(32)
Italy	53	46	(164)
Vietnam	44	61	(59)
Lebanon	44	38	(34)
Germany	41	18	(57)
British	34	12	(126)

[a] The questions were: 'How important is Australian in describing who you are?'; 'People often talk about the many ethnic or cultural groups making up Australian society today. Do you think of yourself as belonging to any ethnic or cultural group?'

Source: *1988–89 Issues in Multicultural Australia Survey*, general population (N=1,552) and NESB (N=986) samples

significantly lower levels. The exception is Greek immigrants, 72 per cent of whom reported that they regarded the term 'Australian' as being very important to them. However, at the other end of the scale, only 34 per cent of British immigrants regarded it as very important. The data also show that some immigrant groups retain high levels of ethnic identification, most notably the Vietnamese (61 per cent) and, again, the Greeks (59 per cent).

These comparatively low levels of identification can be explained by several factors. First, Australia has traditionally harboured lower levels of nationalist feelings than many other countries, notably Britain and the United States, and this has been reinforced by the absence of a strong indigenous military tradition and a relatively secure sea frontier. Second, most countries use citizenship as a means of increasing regime support, but in Australia most immigrants lack any incentive to become citizens — a situation which the 1988 *FitzGerald Report* sought to change.[5] Finally, as we argue in the context of political behaviour, the major incentives for immigrants to come to Australia are social (such as family reunion), necessity (refugees) or economic (seeking material success). In this context, developing an affective attachment to the nation they have joined is likely to have a low priority.

Family and Acquired Capital

Immigrants bring to Australia a wide variety of skills, qualifications and experiences, and these differ considerably between the birthplace groups. The major theory that accounts for differences in socio-economic attainments assumes that individuals receive economic rewards that are commensurate with their skills, qualifications and experience — the individual's *human capital* (Jencks 1972, 1979). The human capital acquired by an individual is reflected not only in his or her own socio-economic attainments, but in the capital that they inherit from their family, which has a direct bearing on the attainments that they themselves will achieve later in their life. For example, a wealthy family will have more money to spend on a child's education than a poor family and this will, in turn, be converted into a higher status occupation and larger income. In the case of migrants, the concept of human capital can be expanded to include English language proficiency and length of residence in the adopted country, both of which are attributes that are valued by potential employers and which attract economic rewards in the marketplace (Evans and Kelley 1986).

There are clear differences in the family capital that immigrants bring to Australia (Table 6.5). With the exception of Asian immigrants, all the other immigrant groups come from families in which the father's mean occupational status was lower than that of these born in Australia. For example, among Australians, the average father worked as an electrician or a technician when the child was aged 16 years (both occupations scoring approximately 43 points on the zero to 100 status scale). By contrast, the average occupation of a Southern European migrant's father is 5 points lower, representing an occupation such as a salesperson or an inspector. The pattern is similar for father's education, although Northern European fathers have about nine months more education than their Australian-born counterparts.

Although family inheritance and social origins are important factors in determining subsequent social status, individual achieve-

Table 6.5 Family and Acquired Capital

	Australia	Northern Europe	Southern Europe	Eastern Europe	Asia	Middle East
Family capital						
Father's occupational status (0 to 100)[a]	43	39	38	41	50	38
Father's education (years)	10.7	11.5	7.7	9.3	11.4	7.7
Acquired capital						
Education (years)[b]	12.3	12.3	9.9	12.0	14.2	12.2
No formal qualifications (%)	36	36	68	42	11	24
University education (%)	12	10	3	9	25	3
Acquired capital, migrants						
Length of residence (years)	—	23.2	26.5	25.5	9.6	13.7
Speaks English at home	—	—	35	45	41	23
English proficiency (zero to 10)	—	—	6.0	7.3	7.5	6.8
(N)	(1,021)	(167)	(299)	(151)	(227)	(58)

[a] According to the ANU-III scale
[b] Primary and secondary schoooling

Source: 1988–89 Issues in Multicultural Australia Survey, general population (N=1,552) and NESB (N=986) samples

ments are also an important determinant of where an individual ends up within the occupational hierarchy. There are a variety of ways in which acquired capital can be measured, but the major indicator is education. Table 6.5 shows that only the Southern Europeans and the Asians differ markedly in the years of primary and secondary education that they possess, the former having just under 8 years of education (representing a school leaving age of about 13 years), while Asians have just over 14 years. In keeping with their commitment to education, one-quarter of Asians have a university education, compared to only 3 per cent of Southern Europeans.

In the acquired capital that migrants possess, Asians would appear to be at a considerable disadvantage by their relatively short period of residence in Australia — just under 10 years, on average. However, their levels of self-reported English language proficiency are the highest of the five groups, and they rank second in the proportion who speak English in the home, just behind the Eastern Europeans, who are a much longer established group. At the other end of the scale, despite their average of 26 years' residence in Australia, only 35 per cent of Southern Europeans speak English at home and they rank lowest in self-reported English proficiency.

The backgrounds that migrants come from have a significant bearing on the economic rewards that they receive in Australian society. The patterns apparent in Table 6.5 suggest that Southern Europeans and Asians represent different ends of a continuum, with other migrants and the Australian-born occupying an inter-mediate position. Southern Europeans come from less privileged backgrounds and, at least partly as a consequence of this, acquire lower levels of educational attainment. The net result is that they find themselves at a particular disadvantage within the labour market. By contrast, Asians have considerable family and acquired capital, and despite their relatively recent arrival, have high levels of English proficiency.

These results illustrate a pattern that is similar to that found in the United States, where Asian immigrants, many of them Indochinese political refugees, have made considerable economic gains despite the less-than-favourable circumstances surrounding their arrival (Caplan, Whitmore and Choy 1989). This is in contrast to longer-established groups such as Puerto Ricans or, indeed, blacks. The children of Asian immigrants are dispro-portionately more likely to go to major universities compared with American-born, and to study in high status professions such as law and medicine (Bell 1985; Hsia 1987). Based on the American experience and the evidence on family and acquired human capital presented here, we would expect the economic position of Asian immigrants in Australia to improve at a faster rate than that of other immigrants.

Occupational and the Labour Market Characteristics

Viewed as a group, immigrants do less well in socio-economic terms compared with their counterparts who have been born in the country, and this finding holds for almost all societies which have experienced large-scale immigration. Two theories have been advanced to explain this disparity within the labour market. The first, which is based on neo-classical economics, argues that immigrants fare less well because they have fewer of the skills that are valued by employers, such as education, English proficiency, or labour force experience — the human capital examined in the previous section. Since it is in the economic interests of employers to use the skills and experience of workers within a competitive labour market, immigrants are placed at a disadvantage. It is therefore the lack of appropriate skills among them which accounts for their lower socio-economic position.

The second theory argues that there is overt and conscious discrimination against immigrants within the labour market; for a variety of reasons, employers prefer Australian-born workers. There is, however, considerable disagreement about the social and economic processes by which this discrimination takes place. One view is that discrimination stems directly from racial or ethnic prejudice, so that the labour market is only one of many areas in which immigrants are disadvantaged. In turn, prejudice is a consequence of certain personality characteristics in the society as a whole (Feagin 1978). This explanation has its roots in psychological studies in the immediate post-war years which sought to explain the Nazi persecution of the Jews through the interaction between prejudice and authoritarianism (Adorno *et al.* 1950; Allport 1987).[6]

Two other explanations have been put forward to account for discrimination. The first is that discrimination is caused by a segmented labour market, whereby immigrants are forced into a sector of the labour market which is characterised by poor working conditions, reduced social mobility and recurrent un-employment (Bonacich and Modell 1980; Kringas 1984). The economic disadvantages faced by immigrants therefore stem from the nature of the labour market within which they are employed. The second explanation is that immigrants constitute a 'reserve army of labour' who are imported in times of economic boom to fill menial manual jobs; when the boom collapses and the capitalist economy is depressed, they join a large pool of unemployed who must wait until the next boom arrives (Collins 1988; Lever-Tracy and Quinlan 1988). As Wooden (1990: 3) puts it, 'simply stated, ethnic divisions are seen as a capitalist strategy of control of the labour market'.

There is little disagreement about the socio-economic disadvantages that immigrants face within the labour market. Figure 6.3 shows the unemployment rate for Italian immigrants (representing longer-established groups), Vietnamese (more recent arrivals), and for all NESB immigrants and the Australian-born. The trends show that Vietnamese fare particularly badly, and are

Figure 6.3 Unemployment Rates among Italians, Vietnamese, NESB and Australians, 1978–92

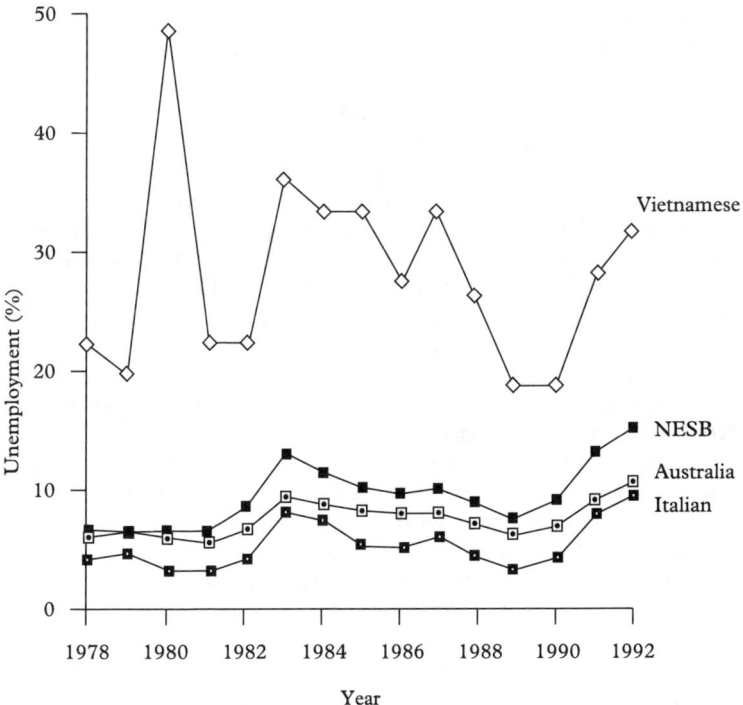

Note: Estimates for 1992 are for January–March only
Sources: Jones and McAllister 1991; ABS

likely to experience an unemployment rate which is about three times higher than that of Italians, longer-established immigrants. Indeed, Italians do considerably better, even when compared to the Australian-born (Jones and McAllister 1991: 11–12). It is notable that the NESB rate of unemployment, while always higher than the Australian-born figure, is now almost 5 percentage points higher.

A variety of explanations have been advanced to explain these patterns, and they have focused on three major factors. First, poor English proficiency is an important predictor of who is or is not unemployed, and as we saw in Table 6.5, immigrants from Southern Europe and the Middle East are particularly disadvantaged in this regard (Jones and McAllister 1991; Wooden and Robertson 1989). Better English proficiency, other things being equal, can significantly improve a migrant's chance of securing a job. With longer residence comes a greater familiarity with the customs and procedures of the society, including those of the labour market. Finally, longer-established groups have less chance of unemployment, and this is particularly important for NESB groups (Beggs and Chapman 1988). Third, while educational qualifications reduce the probability of unemployment, the economic returns from qualifications gained overseas are significantly less than those gained from qualifications attained in Australia. Wooden (1990) suggests that this is attributable to differences in the quality of education and to problems in gaining recognition for overseas qualifications, particularly in the professions.

Once in employment, immigrants continue to experience disadvantages. As Table 6.6 demonstrates, they do less well than the Australian born on a wide range of occupational indicators. In terms of occupational status, Southern European immigrants lag 11 status points behind their Australian-born counterparts, while only 26 per cent of them are employed in white collar occupations, compared to 54 per cent of Australians. Australians and Northern Europeans also predominate in supervisory positions, where immigrants from the Middle East appear to be particularly disadvantaged: only 5 per cent in the 1988 survey reported that they supervised others at work, compared to almost one-third of Australian and Northern European workers.

One notable exception to this general pattern is the high level of self-employment among Southern Europeans. Small business activity is particularly prevalent among Italians and has been advanced as one explanation for their low levels of unemployment, particularly among the young, where unemployment is traditionally high during economic recessions (McAllister 1986). Small business has also been a mainstay of Asians in the United

Table 6.6   Occupational Character[a]

	Australia	Birthplace: Northern Europe	Southern Europe	Eastern Europe	Asia	Middle East
Occupational status						
(0 to 100)	42	44	31	34	42	28
Non-manual						
(per cent)	54	53	26	35	54	34
Supervisor (per cent)	32	31	15	25	19	5
(1–4 workers)	(17)	(20)	(8)	(12)	(12)	(5)
(5+ workers)	(15)	(11)	(7)	(13)	(7)	(0)
Self-employed (per cent)	13	12	18	14	8	6
(no workers)	(7)	(4)	(8)	(6)	(3)	(3)
(one worker or more)	(6)	(8)	(10)	(8)	(5)	(3)
Government employee						
(per cent)	23	23	13	20	23	10
Income ($100s per week)	432	431	396	425	443	318
(N)	(1,021)	(167)	(299)	(151)	(227)	(58)

[a]   Estimates are for those in the labour force only

Source: *1988–89 Issues in Multicultural Australia Survey*, general population (N=1,552) and NESB (N=986) samples

States and is one explanation for their rapid economic success. Comparatively lower levels of government regulation, large concentrations of racial and ethnic groups within inner city areas lacking normal consumer outlets, and a reluctance among established white business people to trade in these areas, have all combined to provide an incentive to establish small shops and businesses run and frequented by ethnic groups (Bell 1985).

Overall, however, the last line of Table 6.6 shows that Southern Europeans and Middle Eastern immigrants receive considerably less weekly income than Australians. Since Australia's central wage fixing system provides a rigid structure for wage levels, most of the disparities arise from differences in family and acquired capital. For example, while the average Australian income is $432 (at 1988 prices), the same figure for Southern Europeans is $396, and $318 for immigrants from the Middle East. By contrast, Asians gain, on average, an extra $11 per week when compared to the Australian-born.

One final piece of evidence bearing on the labour market success of immigrants is the industries in which they work. Different industries require particular skills and experience, and provide different economic rewards, levels of job security and opportunities for promotion. Particular industries also experience high levels of risk when faced with an economic recession. Table 6.7 shows that the overseas-born are disproportionately concentrated in the manufacturing industry, where periodic downturns in the economy are reflected in high unemployment, particularly in the unskilled and semi-skilled grades where migrants predominate. Immigrants are under-represented in the agricultural sector, but have similar levels of representation to the Australian-born in most other industries.

There are, then, considerable differences in terms of the qualifications, skills and experience that migrants bring with them to Australia, in the types of jobs they get, their industrial location, and in the economic rewards that they receive for their work. To what extent do the disparities endorse one or other of the two theories, the competitive labour market theory or the discrimination theory? While the evidence is mixed, it is clear that many of the differences between immigrants and the Australian-born can be explained by family and acquired capital, and by variations in length of residence and in English proficiency (Broom *et al.* 1980; Graetz and McAllister 1988: 88–89; Jones and Davis 1986). Nevertheless, even taking these factors into account, it is evident that Southern Europeans encounter more fundamental economic problems than do other immigrants (Kelley and

Table 6.7   Industrial Location, 1991

	Birthplace	
	Australia	Overseas
Agriculture, forestry, fishing	6.3	2.3
Mining	1,3	1.2
Manufacturing	12.4	20.5
Electricity, gas and water	1.4	1.1
Construction	6.6	6.9
Wholesale and retail	21.1	19.5
Transport and storage	5.2	5.1
Communication	1.7	1.9
Finance, property, business	11.8	11.4
Public administration, defence	5.0	3.9
Community services	19.4	18.1
Recreation, personal services	7.8	8.1
Total	100.0	100.0
(N, thousands)	(5,743)	(1,926)

Source: ABS Labour Force Surveys

McAllister 1984). While explanations are necessarily speculative, factors such as the quality of education they have to offer, their industrial location and consequent levels of unionisation, may all play a role in accounting for this disadvantage.

Social Mobility

Within modern, liberal democracies, equality of opportunity is seen as the core value which differentiates them from other societies. In Australia, equality of opportunity is the main motivation behind the government's access and equity program, which is designed to ensure that all programs and services are equally available to those who may require them. In turn, the ability to shift one's occupational position on the basis of individual achievement and merit is a crucial element in sustaining widespread popular support for the prevailing social and economic order. The absence of opportunities for social mobility risks the formation of an 'underclass' which is distinguishable only by poverty, race and ethnicity. This has occurred among many black and Puerto Rican groups in the United States, where long-term structural unemployment is merely one component among a host of social, economic, and psychological problems that have closed most normal opportunities for upward social mobility (Trenda and Lii 1987).

Social mobility researchers examine two types of occupational change. The first is *intergenerational* mobility, or the degree to which sons inherit the class position and occupational status of their fathers.[7] If a system of social stratification were based solely on intergenerational inheritance individuals would simply recreate the social stratification of their parents. The second form of social mobility is *career* mobility, which indicates the amount of mobility within an individual's working career, usually from first to current job. However, for immigrants, the act of moving from one country to another creates an additional form of mobility, resulting from a comparison of the last job prior to migration and the first job in the host society; this form of mobility is referred to as *migratory* mobility (McAllister 1992b). These three types of mobility are defined in Table 6.8.

Research on social mobility in Australia has tended to confirm the prevailing view that there is extensive mobility. In their major study of social mobility, Broom, Jones *et al.* (1980; see also Baxter, Emmison, Western and Western 1991) found that there was more upward mobility among individuals coming from

Table 6.8   Types and Consequences of Social Mobility

Type of mobility	Comparison	Change in status points[a]			
		Australian	Maltese	Lebanese	Vietnamese
1. Inter- generational	Father's occupation/son's occupation[b]	+1	+1	−12	−19
2. Career	First occupation/[c] current occupation	+9	+7	+4	+2
3. Migratory	Last occupation prior to migration/first occupation in Australia	—	−5	−12	−9
(N)		(509)	(272)	(254)	(402)

[a] Based on the ANU-III status scale; estimates are for men only
[b] Defined as current occupation
[c] First occupation in Australia for immigrants

Source: 1988–89 Issues in Multicultural Australia Survey, general population (N=1,552) and birthplace group (Maltese N=506, Lebanese N=679, Vietnamese, N=554) samples

families where the father was a semi-skilled or an unskilled worker, compared with families where the father was a professional worker. Among migrants, Broom, Jones *et al.* (see also Zagorski 1984) found that NESB immigrants did less well than either ESB immigrants or the Australian-born, although they concluded that the processes of status attainment were much the same for the various groups once differences in social background had been taken into account. Their overall conclusion was that Australia was very similar to other societies, and that migrants were as likely to experience either upward or downward social mobility as their counterparts who had been born in the country.

In practice, both intergenerational and career mobility result in either little change in social status or in upward social mobility for all groups except the Lebanese and Vietnamese (Table 6.8).[8] Although intergenerational mobility results in a slight decline for the Australians and Maltese — one status point on a scale running from zero to 100 — both groups gain more substantially in career mobility. For the Lebanese and Vietnamese, however, intergenerational mobility results in substantial drops of 14.1 and 20.0 points, respectively. This represents a Vietnamese whose father was a civil engineer in Vietnam working as a metal fitter or tool maker in Australia. All groups gain in status as a result of career mobility, ranging from 2.4 points for the Lebanese to 8.8 points for the NESB group as a whole. For all three immigrant groups, the act of migration results in a drop in status ranging from 1.9 to 18.2 status points.

Given that information is available not only on the occupational status of respondents at various points in their lives, but also on the age at which they worked in particular occupations, it is possible to analyse changes in occupational status across the lifecycle. This is shown in Figure 6.4 for the three immigrant groups, the combined NESB group and for the Australian-born. The most striking observation is the extent of the disruption caused by the act of migration. For each of the three immigrant groups, the act of migration results in a substantial drop in status when the last job prior to migration is compared with the first job in Australia. The disruption caused by migratory mobility is, then, a major one, and would appear to reduce all migrants to a uniform level of occupational status within Australia, at least in the initial years of settlement. This levelling process occurs regardless of family capital or whether migration took place at age 18 years (the mean for the Maltese) or at age 28 years (the mean for the Vietnamese).

A second observation from Figure 6.4 is that the processes of intergenerational and career mobility appear to operate similarly for the immigrant groups and for the Australian-born. There is a decline in status comparing the father's status with that of his son's first job. In comparing first job in Australia with current job, all groups show a gradual improvement in their status. In each case, the slopes are remarkably similar, suggesting that once immigrants are established in the country, their career mobility follows a substantially similar pattern. This provides evidence to endorse the competitive labour market theory, which was outlined in the previous section: once established in Australia, immigrants are likely to do as well or as badly economically as Australians with similar skills and experience to offer potential employers. What economic disadvantages immigrants face are very substantially caused by the movement from the donor to the host society, which depresses their occupational status in a uniform way.

Political Behaviour

Migration has had a major impact on the social, economic and cultural character of Australia, particularly in the past two

Figure 6.4   Social Mobility across the Lifecycle among Maltese, Lebanese and Vietnamese Immigrants and the Australian-born, among Men Only

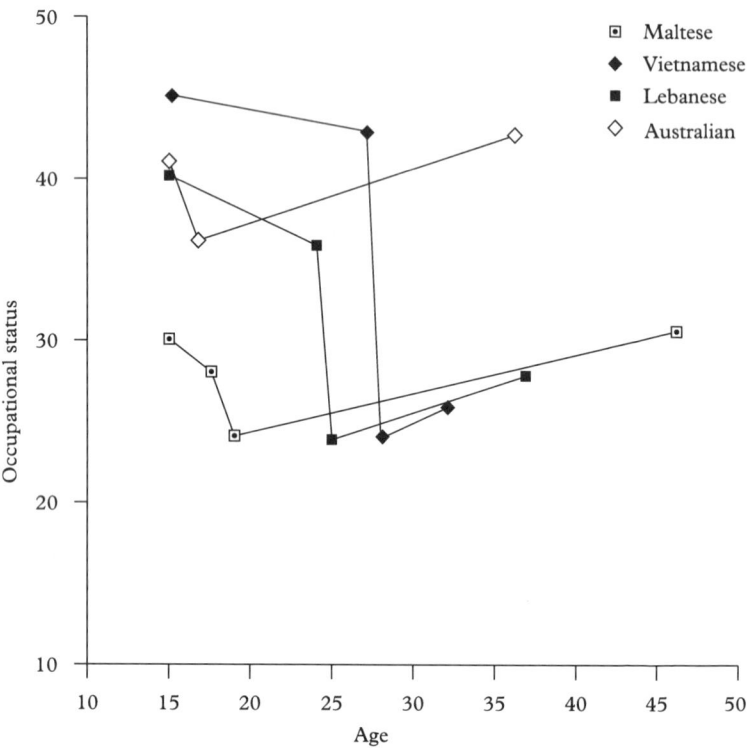

Note: Occupational status is estimated at the mean age when the occupation was recorded with the exception of father's occupational status, which is 15 years for *all* groups. For the immigrant groups, the first plot is father's occupation at age 15 years, the second plot last occupation prior to immigration, the third plot first occupation in Australia, and the fourth plot current occupation in Australia. The plots for the Australians are father's occupation, first occupation, and current occupation, respectively.

Sources: Hawkins 1989: Table 8; Bair 1988: 122–29

decades. By contrast, migration has had relatively little influence on Australian politics. Until the 1970s, there were few ethnic pressure or interest groups actively canvassing migrant causes and the major political parties made little effort to attract migrant votes or party members. Perhaps most striking of all, there were few non-English-speaking migrants within the ranks of federal and state elected representatives. The political invisibility of migrants began to change in the early 1970s, largely as a consequence of changes in the pattern of migration to Australia, but also as a result of changes in government policies towards migrants.

Despite the fact that many migrants come from politically volatile countries, immigrants are often seen as lacking interest in politics in the Australian context. Many have, however, come from countries which do not have democratic traditions, and therefore lack the political socialisation, the knowledge or the information to immediately participate effectively in the democratic process. The incentive for many migrants to leave their home countries has been economic, and to engage in political activity would be to detract from their goal in migrating to Australia in the first place (McAllister and Makkai 1991, 1992). An additional factor in migrants' lack of political interest is that not all become citizens and therefore have the right (and, because of compulsory voting, the obligation) to vote. The predominant influence on who decides to take out citizenship is length of residence, not political or national commitment: the longer migrants remain in Australia, the more remote the possibility of a return to their homeland becomes and the greater the probability is that they will become Australian citizens (Kelley and McAllister 1982).

Survey results confirm that non-English-speaking immigrants demonstrate lower levels of political interest than their Australian-born counterparts. This is particularly true among Southern European and Middle Eastern immigrants (Table 6.9).[9] There are also considerable differences in levels of political participation. Southern Europeans and Asians are significantly less likely to talk to others about politics, although Eastern European and Middle Eastern immigrants report higher levels. All immigrants are less likely to have contacted a federal official on a community problem,[10] but there are few differences on their level of contact regarding a family problem — perhaps a reflection of the need to contact officials about problems related to their own migration or that of their family.

The political values that individuals hold have their roots in pre-adult socialisation. These values are important influences on subsequent political behaviour, and from the perspective of the political system, positive political values act as 'a reservoir upon which the [political] system typically draws in times of crises, such as depressions, wars, and internecine conflicts' (Easton and Dennis 1967: 63). This should have particular consequences for migrants, since most will have experienced little or no socialisation in Australia. Compared to the Australian-born, however,

Table 6.9 Levels of Political Participation and Political Values[a]

	Australia	Birthplace Northern Europe	Southern Europe	Eastern Europe	Asia	Middle East
Political interest						
High political interest	41	47	20	35	37	17
Political participation						
Talks about politics during elections	21	22	14	25	17	25
Worked with others on community problem	29	23	12	14	10	
Contacted federal official on community problem	12	9	2	4	4	10
Contacted federal official on personal or family problem	6	6	6	5	6	1
Political efficacy						
Definitely treated as well by MP	35	41	28	39	38	7
Political trust						
Government can be trusted	29	21	28	26	37	35
(N)	(1,021)	(167)	(241)	(132)	(155)	(4629)

[a] The exact questions were: 'How much interest do you usually have in what's going on in politics?'; 'During elections, do you ever talk to people and try to show them why they should vote for one of the parties or candidates?'; 'Have you ever worked with others in Australia to try and solve some of the community's problems?'; 'Have you (or anyone in your family living here) ever contacted an elected representative or a government employee about some need or problem concerning the local community?'; 'Have you (or anyone in your family living here) ever contacted an elected representative or a government employee to seek help with a personal problem you or your family had?'; 'Suppose you had a problem which needed the help of your Member of Parliament. Do you think that you would be treated as well as everyone else or do you think that others would be given more attention?'; 'In general, do you feel that the people in government are too often interested in looking after themselves, or do you feel that they can be trusted to do the right thing most of the time?'

Source: As for Table 6.3

the results in Table 6.9 show that immigrants generally have the same or higher levels of political efficacy and trust. For example, Asian immigrants are 3 percentage points more likely to consider that they would be 'definitely treated as well as anyone else' by their MP, and 8 points more likely to agree that the government can be trusted. In this sense, migrants have more positive political values than their counterparts who have grown up in the society.

These apparently anomalous patterns of lower political interest and participation but higher levels of political efficacy and trust have several explanations. First, although immigrants have not been socialised into the Australian political system and are therefore less interested and familiar with its operation, the act of migration provides them with a positive political commitment, which is in turn reflected in their political values. Second, even though many immigrants come from countries which lack democratic traditions, research has shown that they are nevertheless more likely to exhibit a stronger democratic commitment (McAllister and Makkai 1992). This is particularly the case for Asian immigrants, who are influenced very strongly in their behaviour by traditional cultural values.

In recent years, the idea of an ethnic vote has gained widespread currency, with the major political parties going to considerable lengths to attract immigrant support and consult ethnic interest groups before embarking on new policy directions. Placing the voting patterns of the major ethnic groups in a longitudinal perspective confirms that the ethnic vote is a relatively recent phenomenon (Figure 6.5). In 1967, only 6 percentage points separated the Southern Europeans from the Australian-born, and there was little to distinguish the vote of Northern and Eastern Europeans from other Australians. By 1979, the situation had changed dramatically, and while Labor voting among Southern Europeans had almost doubled, it had almost halved among Eastern Europeans (McAllister and Kelley 1983). For example, in 1987, 63 per cent of Southern Europeans voted Labor, compared to 22 per cent of their Eastern European counterparts.[11]

There was, then, a major shift in the voting patterns of these ethnic communities in the early 1970s. While explanations for this change are necessarily speculative, it seems likely that two factors were important. First, the concerted efforts made to attract the ethnic vote — particularly the votes of Greeks, Italians and Yugoslavs — by the 1972-75 Whitlam Labor government were successful, and established a pattern of ethnic voting that has remained in place ever since. Second, the Whitlam government's recognition of the incorporation of the Baltic states into the Soviet Union served to drive Eastern European voters away from Labor and towards the Liberal-Nationals.

The net effect of these factors has been to establish a pattern of ethnic voting which produces a considerable electoral advantage

Figure 6.5   The Increasing Influence of Ethnicity on the Vote, 1967–87

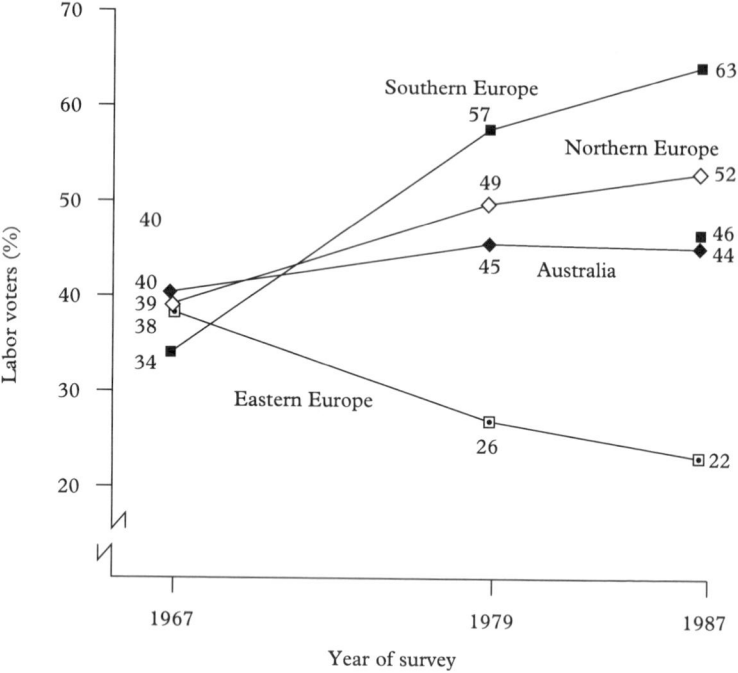

Note: Figures show the percentage of Labor voters among five birthplace groups
Source: McAllister 1992c: Figure 6.8

for Labor; indeed, without the support of the ethnic vote in the 1987 federal election, it is possible that Labor would not have been re-elected (McAllister 1988). While the collapse of Communism in Eastern Europe and the bipartisan consensus towards ethnic and immigration-related issues may moderate these trends during the 1990s, strong Asian support for Labor seems likely to provide the party with a significant electoral advantage for many years to come. Meanwhile, the ethnic voting that has emerged in the past two decades has given ethnic groups more political visibility and influence on the policy making process, particularly in regard to immigration and multiculturalism.

Conclusion

Judged in relation to the large numbers of immigrants who have come to Australia during the course of the twentieth century, until comparatively recently immigration had little impact on Australian society. Even now, ethnic diversity has few implications for the functioning of the nation-state and Australia remains a liberal democracy which is based on institutions and principles established a century ago. In this sense, Australia is not, like the United Kingdom, a multi-national state where competing ethnic minorities articulate political claims for territorial autonomy. Australia is more properly viewed as an ethnically plural nation-state, within which different ethnic groups are bound together by a common loyalty to the territorial integrity of the state.

The growing political and economic importance of the Pacific Rim is likely to guarantee continued immigration to Australia in the twenty-first century, making it the last liberal democracy, with the exception of Israel, to maintain a large-scale immigration program. Similarly, Australia's international obligations, particularly towards refugees but also to the principle of family reunion, are likely to ensure that there will be significant numbers of immigrants coming to Australia, even if the migration program were to be progressively reduced over a period of time.

Some of the reasons explaining why large-scale immigration has been so easily accommodated have already been mentioned: the desire of immigrants to improve their material standard of living; the bipartisan political consensus on immigration and multiculturalism; widespread commitment to democratic values in the political culture; the responsiveness of political élites to specific immigrant demands; and the granting of fundamental citizen rights to all new immigrants. So far, there is little indication that any of these factors which have facilitated immigration and the absorption of immigrants in the past will change in the future.

Appendix

The 1988–89 Issues in Multicultural Australia Survey was designed by Roger Jones and Ian McAllister and funded by the Office of Multicultural Affairs. The fieldwork was carried out by AGB: McNair and Reark Research. The data are available from the Social Science Data Archives at the Australian National University. Neither the original collectors of the data, the funding agency, nor the SSDA are responsible for the analyses or interpretations presented herein.

The survey was conducted in two parts, each of which contain two separate subsamples. The first part, conducted in 1988, contains four samples: a sample of the general population (N=1,552); a sample of non-English speakers (N=986); a sample of second generation Australians (N=823); and a sample of immigrants who had arrived in Australia since 1981 (N=1,141). Full details of the sampling methods can be found in Social Science Data Archives (1989). The second part contains samples drawn from three birthplace groups, Maltese, Lebanese and Vietnamese, which, when combined with respondents from those birthplace groups already interviewed in the first part of the survey, produced Ns of 506 (476), 679 (341) and 554 (491), respectively, where the figure in parentheses is the N of respondents in the second part of the survey.

The five overseas born groups analysed here are made up as follows:

1. *Northern Europe*, including the United Kingdom, Ireland, Belgium, Denmark, Finland, France, Germany (GDR and GFR), Netherlands, Norway, Sweden, and Switzerland;
2. *Southern Europe*, including Albania, Greece, Italy, Malta, Portugal, and Spain;
3. *Eastern Europe*, including Austria, Bulgaria, Czechoslovakia, Hungary, Poland, Romania, USSR and Yugoslavia;
4. *Asia*, including China, Hong Kong and Macau, Japan, Korea (Democratic Republic and Republic of), Taiwan, Burma, Indonesia, Kampuchea, Laos, Malaysia and Brunei, Philippines, Singapore, Thailand, Timor, and Vietnam;
5. *Middle East*, including the Gulf states, Cyprus, Iraq, Iran, Israel, Lebanon, Turkey, Syria.

Notes

1. In March 1948, persons from Italy, Romania, Bulgaria and Hungary were permitted to apply for immigration. In May 1948 the assisted passage was extended to cover Malta, and in September to Ireland. In 1951 the assisted passage program was extended to the Netherlands and Italy, and in 1952 to Austria, Belgium, Greece, Spain and Germany (Armit *et al.* 1990).
2. In 1975, all entrants to Australia were required to obtain appropriate visas, and in 1981 voting was restricted to Australian citizens and British citizens who were already registered on the Australian electoral rolls.
3. One of the most famous works on cultural pluralism of the 1960s and 70s used this word and was written by a Canadian: see John Porter (1965) *The Vertical Mosaic*.

4. The 5.2 per cent includes the Middle East and North Africa, which represents 1.1 per cent of the total.

5. The *FitzGerald Report* recommended that a wide range of welfare and other government services should be available only to immigrants who had become Australian citizens. Following opposition from the ethnic communities, the government rejected this recommendation. In recent times, however, refugees have been faced with substantial restrictions on their access to welfare and other government services.

6. For an examination of levels of prejudice in Australian society, see McAllister and Moore (1991).

7. The only major study of mother to daughter intergenerational mobility is by Hayes (1990).

8. For clarity of presentation, these results are based on individual birthplace groups rather than on groups from broader geographical regions, as in other analyses. The three NESB groups — Maltese, Lebanese and Vietnamese — are intended to represent longer-established migrants, migrants with medium-term residence, and new arrivals, respectively.

9. We have used a single item measure here; it might be the case that a series of more focused questions could elicit a different picture.

10. Lack of contact with officialdom may also be a result of (a) language difficulties and (b) class position.

11. The 1990 Survey asked birthplace in a closed format, thereby restricting the range of birthplaces that could be included. The questions in the previous surveys were open-ended. As a result, ethnicity in the 1990 survey could not be made comparable with previous surveys, and is excluded.

References

Adorno, T.W. *et al.* (1950), *The Authoritarian Personality*. New York: Harper.

Allport, Gordon W. (1987 [1954]) *The Nature of Prejudice*. Reading, MA: Addison-Wesley.

Armit, Michael, John Larkins, Dennis Godfrey and Gordon Benjamin (1988) *Australia and Immigration 1788 to 1988*. Canberra: AGPS.

Bair, Frank E. (ed.) (1988) *Countries of the World and their Leaders, Yearbook, 1988*. Michigan: Gale Research Company.

Baxter, Janeen, Michael Emmison, John Western and Mark Western (1991) *Class Analysis and Contemporary Australia*. Melbourne: Macmillan.

Beggs, John J. and Chapman, Bruce J. (1988) 'The International Transferability of Human Capital: Immigrant Labour Market Outcomes in Australia', in Lyle Baker and Paul Miller (eds), *The Economics of Immigration*. Canberra: Department of Immigration and Ethnic Affairs.

Bell, D.A. (1985) 'The Triumph of Asian Americans', *New Republic* 193: 24–31.

Betts, Katherine (1988) *Ideology and Immigration.* Melbourne: University of Melbourne Press.

Birrell, Robert and T. Birrell (1981) *An Issue of People: Population and Australian Society.* Melbourne: Longman Cheshire.

Bonacich, Edna and Modell John (1990) *The Economic Basis of Ethnic Solidarity,* Berkeley, California: University of California Press.

Broom, Leonard, *et al.* (1980) *The Inheritance of Inequality.* London: Routledge and Kegan Paul.

Bullivant, Brian (1980) 'Searching for an Ideology of Pluralism: Some Results of a Cross-National Survey', *Ethnic and Racial Studies* 5: 53–70.

Caplan, Nathan, Whitmore, John K. and Choy, Marcella H. (1989) *The Boat People: Employment and Achievement among Southeast Asian Refugees.* Ann Arbor, MI: University of Michigan Press.

Collins, Jock (1988) *Migrant Hands in a Distant Lands.* Sydney: Pluto Press.

Easton, David and Dennis, Jack (1967) 'The Child's Acquisition of Regime Norms: Political Efficacy', *American Political Science Review* 61: 25–38.

Evans, M.D.R. and Kelley, Jonathan (1986) 'Immigrants' Work: Equality and Discrimination in the Australian Labour Market', *Australia and New Zealand Journal of Sociology* 22: 187–207.

Feagin, Joe R. (1978) *Racial and Ethnic Relations.* Englewood Cliffs, NJ: Prentice-Hall.

Gans, Herbert J. (1968) *More Equality.* New York: Random House.

Goot, Murray (1984) *The 1984 Immigration Debate: The Myths and the Facts.* Sydney: Ethnic Affairs Commission of NSW.

———(1991) 'Public Opinion as Paradox: Australian Attitudes to the Rate of Immigration and the Rate of Asian Immigration, 1984–1990', *International Journal of Public Opinion Research* 3: 277–94.

Gordon, M.M. (1975) 'Towards a General Theory of Race and Ethnic Relations', in Nathan Glazer and Daniel Moynihan (eds), *Ethnicity: Theory and Experience.* Cambridge, Mass: Harvard University Press.

Graetz, Brian and McAllister, Ian (1988) *Dimensions of Australian Society.* Melbourne: Macmillan.

Hawkins, Freda (1989) *Critical Years in Immigration: Canada and Australia Compared.* Canada: McGill University Press.

Hayes, Bernadette (1990) 'Intergenerational Occupational Mobility Among Employed and Non-employed Women: The Australian Case', *Australian and New Zealand Journal of Sociology* 26: 368–89.

Hsia, J. (1987) *Asian Americans in Higher Education and Work.* Hillsdale, NJ: Erlbaum.

Jakubowicz, Andrew (1987) 'The State and the Welfare of Immigrants in Australia', *Ethnic and Racial Studies* 10: 1–35.

Jencks, Christopher *et al.* (1972) *Inequality: A Reassessment of the Effects of Family and Schooling in America.* New York: Basic Books.

———*et al.* (1979) *Who Gets Ahead? The Determinants of Economic Success in America.* New York: Basic Books.

Jones, Frank L. and Davis, Peter (1986) *Models of Society: Class*

Stratification and Gender in Australia and New Zealand. Sydney: Croom Helm.

Jones, Roger and McAllister, Ian (1991) *Immigrants, Unemployment and Labour Markets Programs in Australia*. Canberra: AGPS.

Jupp, James (1966) *Arrivals and Departures*. Melbourne: Cheshire-Landsdowne.

———(1988) 'The Defused Issues: Ethnic and Aboriginal Affairs', in Ian McAllister and John Warhurst (eds), *Australia Votes*. Melbourne: Longman Cheshire.

Jupp, James (1991) *Immigration*. Sydney: University of Sydney Press.

Kelley, Jonathan and Ian McAllister (1982) 'Class, Ethnicity and Voting Behaviour in Australia', *Politics* 17: 96–107.

———and———(1983) 'Contextual Characteristics of Australian Federal Electorates', *Australia and New Zealand Journal of Sociology* 19: 113–35.

———and———(1984) 'Immigrants, Socioeconomic Attainments, and Politics in Australia', *British Journal of Sociology* 35: 387–405.

Kringas, Paul (1984), 'Really Educating Migrant Children', in James Jupp (ed.), *Ethnic Politics in Australia*. Sydney: Allen and Unwin.

Lever-Tracy, Constance and Quinlan, M. (1988) *A Divided Working Class: Ethnic Segmentation and Industrial Conflict in Australia*. London: Routledge and Kegan Paul.

Martin, Jean I. (1978) *The Migrant Presence*. Sydney: Allen and Unwin.

McAllister, Ian (1986) 'Explaining Unemployment Experience: Social Structural and Birthplace Variations in Australia', in Australian Institute of Multicultural Affairs (ed.), *Migrants, Labour Markets, and Training Programs*. Melbourne: Australian Institute of Multicultural Affairs.

———(1988) 'Ethnic Issues and Voting in the 1987 Australian Federal Election', *Politics* 23: 11–15.

———(1992a) 'Public Opinion, Multiculturalism, and Political Behaviour in Australia', in Chandran Kukathas (ed.), *Multiculturalism*. Sydney: Centre for Independent Studies.

———(1992b) *Immigrant Social Mobility: The Determinants of Economic Success Among Lebanese, Maltese and Vietnamese in Australia*. Canberra: Office of Multicultural Affairs.

———(1992c) *Political Behaviour: Citizens, Parties and Elites in Australia*. Melbourne: Longman Cheshire.

———and Makkai, Toni (1991) 'The Formation and Development of Party Loyalties: Patterns Among Australian Immigrants', *Australian and New Zealand Journal of Sociology* 27: 195–217.

———and———(1992) 'Resource and Social Learning Theories of Political Participation: Ethnic Patterns in Australia', *Canadian Journal of Political Science* 25: 269–93.

———and Moore, Rhonda (1991) The Development of Ethnic Prejudice: An Analysis of Australian Immigrants', *Ethnic and Racial Studies* 14: 127–51.

———*et al.* (1990) *Australian Political Facts*. Melbourne: Longman Cheshire.

Population Issues Committee (1991) *Population Issues and Australia's Future: Environment, Economy and Society*. Canberra: AGPS.

Porter, John (1965) *The Vertical Mosaic*. Toronto: University of Toronto Press.

Sherington, Geoffrey (1990) *Australia's Immigrants*. Sydney: Allen and Unwin.

Social Science Data Archives (1989) *Issues in Multicultural Australia Survey 1988: User's Guide for the Machine-Readable Data File*. Canberra: Social Science Data Archives, Australian National University.

Stokes, Donald (1966) 'Spatial Models of Party Competition', in Angus Campbell *et al.*, *Elections and the Political Order*. New York: Wiley.

Trenda, Marta and Lii, Ding-Tzann (1987) 'Minority Concentration and Earnings Inequality: Blacks, Hispanics and Asians Compared', *American Journal of Sociology* 93: 141–65.

van den Berghe, Peter (1981) *The Ethnic Phenomenon*. New York: Elsevier.

Viviani, Nancy (1984) *The Long Journey: Vietnamese Migration and Settlement in Australia*. Melbourne: Melbourne University Press.

Western, John S. (1983) *Social Inequality in Australian Society*. Melbourne: Macmillan.

Wooden, Mark (1990) *Migrant Labour Market Status*. Canberra: AGPS.

——and Frances Robertson (1989) *The Factors Associated with Migrant Labour Market Status*. Canberra: AGPS.

Zagorski, Krzystof (1984) *Social Mobility into Post-Industrial Society: Socioeconomic Structure and Fluidity of the Australian Workforce*. Canberra: ANU Sociology RSSS Monographs No 5.

Chapter Seven

Aborigines and Islanders in Australian Society

Ian Keen*

This chapter examines the position of Aborigines and Torres Strait Islanders in Australian society in the context of the historical development of their relationship. Key factors in this history have been the evolution of the British industrial economy in relation to the British colonies, the related development of Australian economy and society, and the nature of indigenous economic and social life.

The Aboriginal and Torres Strait Islander population forms about 1.5 per cent of the Australian one. The 1991 Census puts the Aboriginal population at about 260,0000, compared with a total Australian population of nearly 17 million. But just who counts as an 'Aborigine' is not a simple matter (Beckett 1988; Keen 1988; Smith 1980; Thiele 1992). The category 'Aborigine' (or 'Aboriginal') arose through interaction with colonising peoples, mainly from Europe (Crick 1981). In pre-colonial Australia, the population was divided by many different kinds of ethnic categories, on the basis of language, locality, descent and totemic ancestry (Merlan 1981). Originally 'aborigine' was a term applied by colonisers to the people they found living in the continent. In time

*I would like to thank Pat Mullins, Jake Najman, David Trigger and John Western for advice and comments on the manuscript. Steven Thiele's (1992) timely critique on treatments of the issue of identity in this and related writings led to what I hope are improvements in this revised version of the chapter.

this category, together with related ones, came to be adopted by these people themselves and at least some of their descendants, contrasting their identity with that of 'white' or other kinds of people.

For the purposes of this chapter, 'Aborigines', 'Aboriginal' and 'Islander' are used in two main ways. First, Aborigines or Torres Strait Islanders are people who identify as such, and who are identified in this way by other Aboriginal and Islander people. These are not clearly demarcated categories; in periods when legislation removed from Aboriginal people many of the freedoms enjoyed by the majority, lighter-skinned people were classified by the authorities in racial terms such as 'half-caste' or 'quadroon'. People may now choose to identify themselves as 'Aboriginal' on the grounds of descent from Aboriginal people, or they may choose not to take this identity. For reasons such as these, the Aboriginal population revealed in the Census has grown in recent decades partly due to more people identifying as Aboriginal, and partly through natural increase.

Another way in which the terms 'Aboriginal' and 'Islander' are used in this chapter, is to refer to the indigenous inhabitants of Australia and the Torres Strait Islands and their ways of life, before these became social identities for the people themselves. It is in this sense that I write of pre-colonial 'Aboriginal economy'. Torres Strait Islanders are treated here as a somewhat distinct category because many regard themselves as different from mainland Aborigines. Moreover, their pre- and post-colonial cultures were and are very different from Aboriginal cultures of the mainland and Tasmania.

It is important to stress the heterogeneity of Aboriginal and Islander lifestyles, beliefs, and degrees of integration with the wider society. It is important also to emphasise the great difference between Aboriginal and non-Aboriginal cultures. Many people whom non-Aborigines do not recognise as Aborigines, but label 'half-castes' as against 'real' 'full-blood' Aborigines, maintain a strong sense of cultural distinctiveness, and identify as Aboriginal or by means of a more local identity such as Koori, Murri or Nyungar. Recent anthropological accounts of the ways of life of Aboriginal people of southern Australia (i.e. those areas most densely settled by Europeans) show that they have distinctively Aboriginal cultures, demonstrated for example in modes of speech, kin relationships and family organisation, socialisation of the young, and general values (Keen 1988).

The chapter begins with a discussion of the development of Australian capitalism and its impact on Aboriginal social life.

The Development of Australian Capitalism

The industrial capitalist economy began to develop in late eighteenth century Britain (Wolf 1982; Hobsbawm 1969). Following a broadly Marxist analysis, the capitalist economy can be understood to involve a division of society into socio-economic classes, the most fundamental of which are the working class which sells its labour in return for the necessities of life, and the class of those who own and control the means of production — machines and other capital equipment, land, factories etc. This simple model, which fits early capitalism well enough, is complicated by the emergence of managerial and executive classes, the existence of independent small-holders and the ownership of shares by working people.

These features of the social organisation of capitalist societies (some shared with other types of industrial society) contrast strongly with Aboriginal social organisation, but there are many other important contrasting features. For example, the 'organisation' is typical of industrial society; it is a clearly defined body with a specialised function (e.g. government, mining, education, religion, health care, sport), and with an internal structure of control, usually hierarchical in form, and sometimes involving a bureaucracy. The nation-state could be regarded as the most inclusive of these organisations. Another characteristic is the existence of highly specialised governmental, judicial, military, police and educational structures. Certain conditions led to the industrialisation of producting and the emergence of capitalism in Britain (Hobsbawm 1969). England had no land holding peasantry; rather there was a system of large landowners, tenant farmers, and landless agricultural labourers. Technology was sufficiently developed for it to be relatively cheap to adapt to the mechanisation of production. Entrepreneurs were induced to industrialise the production because of the existence of a large and growing domestic market, especially for food and textiles, so that flour milling, brewing and cotton production were at the forefront of industrialisation.

The export market was expanded by means of war and colonisation, through which England captured the former export markets of other European nations, and created new ones, making it profitable for its entrepreneurs to industrialise. Crucially, the British government was willing to subordinate foreign policy to economic ends, gaining a virtual monopoly of sea power. Thus certain colonies were established as markets for British goods, as well as sources of raw materials to feed industry. As the British capitalist economy developed, however, Britain's capacity to feed its people through its own agricultural production decreased, so that the colonies supplied this need to an increasing extent. As well, it became more profitable to invest labour in the colonies than at home. As Britain became less able to compete effectively with other industrial nations, especially Germany and the United States, it relied on colonial expansion to supply an export market.

Settler Capitalism
The Australian economy and society developed in a way that was to radically affect the lives of Aborigines and Islanders. Australian economy and society had some features in common with certain other colonies of Europe — Argentina, Uruguay, Chile, and New Zealand — and has been labelled 'settler capitalism' by Denoon (1983). In common with several of these colonies, Australia began as a military garrison outpost of a European empire. The hunting and gathering mode of subsistence of the indigenous peoples was such that they could not be exploited in order to support a population of conquering settlers. Rather, the new population was introduced as an enclave, absorbing some of the indigenous people, but destroying and replacing the indigenous economic system. (In some of these colonies, but not Australia, the colonisers did encounter agricultural communities, after a period of consolidation.) As the colonisers fanned out into the hinterland of the garrison outpost, they found plenty of land, but little labour, and pastoralism dominated production. The administration centred at the entrepôt registered titles and protected the property of the new landowners within the frontier, who consolidated control over land, labour and income from herds. On the frontier, with the support of police and the military, individuals fought to appropriate land, defeat the indigenous people, and survive.

The colony of New South Wales, established in 1788 primarily as a gaol, was at first dependent on England for supplies, but as Drakakis-Smith (1981) points out, a major goal of the early colonial administration in Australia was self-sufficiency in agriculture, put into practice by encouraging small-scale ex-convict (emancipist) farming. At the same time the military/bureaucratic élite obtained large grants of land to which they constantly added by buying out indebted farmers, so creating a class of wage labourers. The principal source of labour during this period, however, was assigned convict labour; indigenous labour was rarely used except in the earliest years for harvesting, and 'bush work' such as tracking, and searching for water (Drakakis-Smith 1981: 38).

From the 1820s, the colony became a supplier of primary products to feed British industry and the home market, with a strong emphasis at first on wool production and, later, meat and wheat. Between 1821 and 1833 more than 22,000 convicts were transported to Australia, with a further 27,000 between 1833 and 1841; unemployment in Britain accelerated the pace of voluntary migration (Drakakis-Smith 1981: 39). From the 1820s to the 1920s there was an associated increase in production for local consumption, accompanied by a high level of prosperity and expansion, both demographic and territorial.

In Australia and similar colonies, hunter-gatherer peoples suffered a very different fate from agricultural communities: they were displaced and destroyed, whereas agricultural communities often entered into cash crop production, converting part of their agricultural production to crops suitable for sale through the colonising power, and subject to taxation by it. They became peasants, at least for a generation or two, then migrant labourers, agricultural labourers, or plantation workers (see Wolf 1982). Aboriginal economies, however, were not converted to the requirements of capitalism. In large areas of Australia, where European settlement was most dense or land-intensive, they were largely destroyed. There were no products of value to the colonisers, nor could Aboriginal production systems be converted to cash crops.

It was not possible to sustain the indigenous economy in order to provide a pool of migrant labour, as occurred, for example, in central and southern Africa. A hunting and gathering mode of subsistence requires large tracts of land with a varied ecology, in order to provide an adequate diet all the year round, and to give groups access to alternative areas in case of food shortage. Furthermore, hunter-gatherers and agriculturalists tended to compete for water as well as land, and introduced animals changed the ecology, and often displaced the indigenous fauna.

Thus the course of development of Aboriginal-white relations was partly conditioned by the fact that Australia was a continent of hunting-gathering-fishing economies in temperate to subtropical environments. As van den Berghe (1981) points out, Europeans, with their deep plough agriculture, were better adapted to such regions as North America, the southern tip of South America, southern Africa and temperate and sub-tropical Australia, than to the tropics. In these regions the colonisers could adapt their agricultural practices to local conditions, and they did not face problems with tropical diseases. Conversely, the indigenous populations were prey to introduced diseases — even the common cold had devastating effects. The relatively sparse distribution of the Aboriginal population allowed the colonisers to swamp them, and the relatively egalitarian and small scale organisation, together with the less effective military technology, made it difficult for Aborigines to put up an effective resistance to invasion in the long term, although local resistance was often fierce and protracted (Reynolds 1987). However, accounts which tell of the total destruction of Aboriginal culture and social life are distorted. Even where many groups were destroyed or decimated, and a population of mixed descent grew, these people have maintained a distinctive, and separate, culture and identity. The degree of cultural continuity is greatest among Aborigines living in regions more remote from European settlement.

The next section outlines some aspects of Aboriginal culture and social life as they were in the eighteenth century, and as they continue to varying degrees.

Aboriginal and Islander Economy and Social Life

A sketch of patterns of Aboriginal social life as they were presumably lived before European colonisation will help to understand the way in which the position of Aborigines in Australian society has developed. Necessarily this sketch is based on ethnographic descriptions made after substantial colonisation. It is phrased here in the past tense, but the modes of life of many Aboriginal people display a high degree of continuity with the pre-colonial past, more or less modified with the adoption of items of European technology, and institutions (such as community councils and Christianity), as well as participation in the money economy.

Australia was populated by peoples with an intricate mode of life, bound through a dense network of inter-relations throughout the continent, and linking to the island of New Guinea, as well as to the Celebes, via Macassan traders. Moreover, anthropological studies of Aboriginal social life increasingly reveal a great variation in social arrangements, due not simply to differences in relations with non-Aborigines, but to the persistence of past variability.

Aboriginal Population and Subsistence
The conventional estimate of the size of the Aboriginal population at the end of the eighteenth century, made by the anthropologist Radcliffe-Brown (1930), is about 300,000. Some demographers and archaeologists now think this estimate to be conservative, and that a figure of 500,000 or even higher is more reasonable (Smith 1980; Mulvaney 1989: 97). The population would have fluctuated due to disease, climatic variation, and changes in the size of the land mass with the rise and fall of sea level, as well as other factors. Recent archaeological evidence suggests that Australia has had a human population for at least 55,000 years (White and O'Connell 1982; Roberts, Jones and Smith 1990), although there is no direct

evidence that the first people were ancestral to the present Aboriginal population. The population was distributed most densely along the coasts and islands, with densities of the order of one person per square kilometre. In the very arid regions, densities were probably as low as one person per hundred square kilometres. This pattern was correlated in part with the rainfall (Birdsell 1953).

The Aborigines were hunters, gatherers and fishers, using a technology of stone, wood, fibre, bone and skin. There was a marked division of labour, with women predominantly gathering vegetable foods and shellfish, hunting small game, and in some areas fishing; while men mainly hunted larger game and fished. The sexes co-operated in large-scale game and fish drives. Food processing was often elaborate, and involved leaching out toxins (e.g. from cycad palm nuts); drying and storing meat; winnowing and grinding seeds; and cooking in earth ovens. The stereotype of the poor hunter/gatherer scratching a bare existence from the desert is largely false. Sahlins replaced this stereotype with what has become another stereotype: that of 'the original affluent society' in which foragers had limited wants, and people only needed to work for an average of four to five hours per day to obtain a very adequate diet (Sahlins 1974; McCarthy and McArthur 1960; Lee 1968). However, Altman (1987) concludes that this very low level of labour has only been possible, at least in Arnhem Land, in post-colonial conditions, where a bush diet is supplemented by store-bought foods purchased with cash obtained primarily from welfare entitlements.

Archaeologists and anthropologists now tend to stress the land management aspects of hunting and gathering, through selective burning off to stimulate regrowth and attract game, by replanting yam tops to ensure the next year's supply, and by the prohibition of hunting certain species during certain seasons to ensure reproduction. From this perspective the distinction between foraging and horticulture is less clear-cut. Nevertheless, the development of horticulture which occurred in the New Guinea highlands 10,000 years ago (White and O'Connell 1982: 173) did not diffuse into Australia, although the Torres Strait Islanders practised both kinds of subsistence economy, as do the people of the trans-Fly region of Papua New Guinea. Perhaps the concentration of the rather low rainfall in the tropical north into the summer months inhibited the adoption of horticulture, or perhaps people were making a good enough living without the use of more labour-intensive methods.

Settlement
Another common stereotype is of Aborigines as nomads, wandering

over the landscape. In fact the degree of sedentism varied. Some coastal communities were and are quite sedentary, moving only a few kilometres between seasons (Meehan 1982). In more arid regions the search for water necessitated movement over much larger areas, but within known and owned land (Gould 1969; Tonkinson 1978; Myers 1986).

People lived in groups of relatives. The modal community was the 'band' of between 14 and 50 people (Peterson 1986), but where the seasons necessitated movement the band would split up into smaller units, or aggregate into groups of several hundreds to exploit localised resources and hold major ceremonies. Recent studies show that Arnhem Land people live in 'hearth-holds' consisting of a nuclear family, or a single adult, or a group of bachelors. The members of a hearth-hold had a common shelter (wet season house, windbreak etc.) and hearth. Hearth-holds grouped to form clusters within which food was distributed, although work teams often crosscut hearth-hold clusters (Altman 1984). People tended to choose to live near or with close siblings, a brother-in-law or sister-in-law, a parent, or a son- or daughter-in-law. It was common for a son-in-law to live with his wife's parents in the early years of marriage to provide hunting services and gifts.

A Universe of Kin

Kin relations were not confined to the band. Aboriginal people traced kin relationships to a far wider network than people of European cultures, and extended fictive kin relations to strangers, in order to incorporate them into the social universe. (The use of the term 'aunt' for a parent's friend is an example of fictive kinship). Some kin relationships entailed specific rights and obligations; for example it was very general for a brother and sister to have to avoid all social interaction after early childhood and at least until old age and a man had to avoid contact with the woman who was, or would be, his wife's mother. Brothers-in-law commonly had the duty to help each other with gifts, or support each other in disputes.

In many regions marriages were arranged through a system of 'promise' marriage: that is by contracts, sometimes arranged even before the birth of the potential wife, in which rights in a woman as a wife and in her children were transferred in return for gifts and services over a long period. In such systems spouses had to be in a particular kin relation, usually some kind of cousin, although some groups prohibited marriage with a close cousin. The degree of polygyny varied. (Polygyny is the marriage of one man to more than one woman at the same time.) In some regions an older man might acquire twenty wives or more (e.g. the Tiwi of Melville and

Bathurst Islands; see Hart and Pilling 1960), whereas in others, such as Western Desert groups, polygyny was rare.

Age and gender were other important bases of social organisation. In general, older people were accorded authority and respect as holders of knowledge, especially religious and magical knowledge, although this does not mean that all older people were revered or regarded as wise. Economic production, child rearing and the organisation of religious practices were organised along gender lines. But the degree to which men as a category were politically dominant seems to have varied: in some areas men had sole access to secret religious knowledge and were highly polygynous; in others women, too, had their secret religious life and polygyny was less common, reflecting a greater degree of autonomy (Hamilton 1981a).

Social Units

I have discussed variation between Aboriginal 'regions' rather than 'societies', for there were probably few, if any, clearly bounded Aboriginal societies. Older or more general sources describe the structure of Aboriginal society in terms of a hierarchy of more inclusive units: families, clans, bands or hordes and tribes. This model is misleading. The 'tribe' notion implies the existence of discrete territorial groups, each having a common language and an internal political organisation under the control of 'elders'. Recent discussions of this topic suggest that the model is by no means universally valid (Peterson 1976; Sutton 1978; Merlan 1981; Keen 1989), implicitly based as it is on the concept of the nation-state. Rather, Aboriginal social life was (and is) organised in terms of intersecting and overlapping social categories and networks. These are too complex to discuss in any detail here, but some features can be described.

Bands were somewhat open in composition, with a core of more of less permanent members and a periphery of more transient ones. In many areas the most inclusive social category was based on a language or dialect, and it is this category that has become known as the 'tribe'. Language was commonly mapped on to territory, so that in being affiliated to a language through one or both parents, a person was also related to land. (A person could be affiliated to a language even if he or she did not speak it; it was a matter of identity.) But in many regions, such as north-east Arnhem Land or Cape York Peninsula, speakers of one language or dialect were dispersed, and several discrete areas were associated with the same language or dialect. Furthermore many people were bi- or polylingual, some identifying with more that one language or dialect. Finally, the language group was probably nowhere a distinct political unit, although in some areas it was a land holding unit (see Merlan 1981).

Land was held or 'owned' in many regions by a group based on filiation (i.e. the relationship of a parent to a child), often through the male line (patri-filiation), but with people also having strong rights in the country of their mother (through matri-filiation) and other close relatives. In some regions, especially the Western Desert, claims to country were made on a variety of grounds, such as place of conception and birth, knowledge of the country and associated ceremonies, as well as patri- and matri-filiation (Myers 1986). These groups of people, some of which are referred to as clans by anthropologists, held areas of land focused on clusters of sacred sites associated with ancestral beings, and had rights in related ceremonies and sacred objects. Land holding groups were not autonomous, for members were often dispersed by marriage and other ties among several bands, and groups were linked through ties to the same ancestral being and rituals. Moreover, close relatives of members of a land holding group often had a say in its affairs, such as religious ceremonies, land management and the settlement of disputes.

For the purposes of the organisation of marriage and religious practices a local population was often divided into categories of other kinds. These included moieties, in which the population was divided into two named categories on the basis either of descent or generation; as well as more complex systems of phratries, sections, subsections and semi-moieties (see Elkin 1954; Shapiro 1979; R.M. and C.H. Berndt 1981; Maddock 1982). Variants of these and other modes of organisation were put together in different configurations, so that Aboriginal social organisation varied greatly. The general picture is not one of discrete, localised societies, but of a continuous but ever-changing network with, as it were, localised clusterings and overlapping patterns.

Religion and Government

It is appropriate to place Aboriginal religion and government together, for the government of Aboriginal social life was, in many regions, organised through religious belief and practice. There were probably no specialised governmental structures — no legislatures, judiciaries, or bureaucracies with general powers to control aspects of most social activities of people living within a defined territory, although some older sources do describe 'councils' and 'courts' of elders in several regions (R.M. and C.H. Berndt 1981: 348). Aboriginal government, by which I mean the control of social activities, was diffuse (Keen 1989). One could generalise by saying that those people with an interest in the matter at hand had a measure of control, and who had an interest depended above all on kin relations. Hence each different activity and occasion — a hunt, a ceremony, a dispute, a fight, a marriage etc., involved a somewhat different network of people. But certain individuals within any network had more authority than others by virtue of their age, religious status, and gender. Certain individuals managed to build a high level of status through fighting ability or by marrying well, or the acquisition of religious knowledge, placing themselves at the focus of a network of support and influence. Such people, predominantly men, had more influence and power than others, but they did not hold chiefly office, and nor were their positions hereditary.

Social activities were subject to rules or laws founded on religious belief. Laws and conventions governing marriage, kin relations, exchange of goods and ceremonies, land tenure, and religious practice itself, were legitimised through the belief that ancestral beings laid them down long ago. Present practice 'followed' these activities. Because such laws were not regarded as having been instituted by people, nor as changeable, they were enforced by members of the community at large, especially those with a particular interest and rights in the matter as well as those with authority, rather than by a specialised body of law enforcement agents. Thus those who dealt with a breach of the religious law were those with rights in, and control of, religious practice; those who dealt with an offence against the person were that person (if still alive) and his or her close relatives.

Religious beliefs were part and parcel of cosmologies in which the powers and other attributes of the natural world were thought of as having the attributes and powers of people. In Aboriginal belief, the land and waters consisted in part of the substance of ancestors, and were inhabited by them; so that natural forces were explained as the actions of these beings. Belief in a creative period, usually referred to in English as the Dreamtime, was pervasive. In this period ancestral beings, conceived of as having the attributes at once of humans and other species and phenomena (such as Shark, Kangaroo, Water, Sores, Hollow Log, Rock), lived and travelled, leaving traces of their activities in the land and waters; instituting ceremonies and sacred objects, customs, laws and languages; and creating the forerunners of present groups as well as the powers to ensure their reproduction. Religious practice was believed to re-enact ancestral events, and to make available to living people the powers of the ancestral and other spirit beings. Rituals achieved a number of purposes, including disposal of the dead, the initiation of the young, the subduing of rebellious youth, revelation of religious secrets, peace making, and exchange.

Thus religious belief, law and ceremony brought together many disparate activities and united them under a coherent system of religious law, subject to the authority of those knowledgeable in the law. Politics took the form of competition for the control of sacred objects and ceremony, and hence for authority; the control of land; and, indirectly, for the control of marriage-bestowals in some regions.

A corollary of this world view is the belief that human beings can avail themselves of these powers, and control natural processes to some extent through ritual action. In this way, beliefs in sorcery, love magic, healing powers, rain making and foretelling the future were within one general conceptual framework. Belief in sorcery is widely reported to have been an element in interpersonal relationships. Other people were commonly blamed for causing sickness and death through ritual action on faeces or other bodily products, by singing over an image, pointing the bone etc. Belief in access to the power of ancestral spirit beings is the obverse of this: recreating the image and actions of the being gave access to the being's powers, to be utilised in sexual relations, reproduction, or fighting, or counteracting the effects of sorcery. (For accounts of Aboriginal religion and belief see R.M. and C.H. Berndt 1981; Maddock 1982; Charlesworth *et al.* 1984; for Yolngu beliefs in sorcery and healing, see Reid 1983.)

Co-operation in religious practices such as major revelatory ceremonies often brought hundreds of people together from a wide region, and thus forged and reinforced wide ranging social links. Such occasions were often linked to the exploitation of a major seasonal resource such as cycad palm nuts or bogong moths (Flood 1980). 'Trade' relations also created wide networks. Interpersonal relations between kin were marked by obligations to make and receive gifts of food and objects such as tools, weapons, sacred objects and clothing. Through these hand-to-hand exchanges goods travelled many hundreds or even thousands of miles along sometimes quite well marked 'trade routes' (McCarthy 1939; McBryde 1978). Some items of exchange, such as *pituru*, native tobacco, involved groups of people travelling many hundreds of miles to acquire the substance, then distributing it through exchange and barter in markets (Watson 1983).

Torres Strait Islanders
The ways of life of the Torres Strait Islanders were rather different from those of the people of the mainland and Tasmania (Beckett 1972, 1987; Moore 1978). The Islanders lived in a variety of island environments, including small volcanic islands with dense vegetation, low sandbanks, large low-lying swampy islands, and large

high rocky islands with good water and vegetation on the lower parts. There were in the eighteenth century perhaps 3-4,000 Islanders living in thirteen or fourteen communities.

The Islander economy emphasised hunting, gathering, fishing and horticulture to varying degrees. In the eastern islands the emphasis was on gardening, in which the main crops were coconuts and yams. In the western islands, some of which were rather infertile, people depended more on hunting, gathering and fishing, and obtaining vegetable foods through trade.

The Islander communities were up to one thousand strong, often much smaller, and the larger ones were composed of several smaller settlements. There were no formal leaders; rather, the leader of the religious cult associated with head hunting had the greatest authority. As with Aboriginal communities, disputes were settled by the interested parties, with leaders playing a mediating role. Named groups held defined tracts of land, but garden land and some other key resources were individually owned, or owned by a groups of relatives, and daughters were given land as dowry. Some communities, such as the people of Badu and Mabuiag, were nomadic between islands, whereas others, such as the Saibai people, were sedentary.

The Islander communities were related to one another, to Cape York Peninsula Aborigines, and to people of Papua New Guinea, through trade and warfare carried out by means of large, double outrigger canoes, among defined trading partners. People exchanged canoe hulls, bows and arrows, drums, feathers and pigments from New Guinea; wood, pigments, spears and spear throwers from the Australian mainland; and vegetable foods, marine products, harpoons, shells and human heads from and among the islands.

The language of the western Torres Strait was closely related to Aboriginal languages, whereas the eastern languages were New Guinean. The religion was centred on the increase of resources through ritual, head hunting and war. People believed that they could obtain power through ritual, and from sacred objects which represented the head hunting Hero, and also from the head of an ancestor or war victim.

The European Colonisation of Australia

Features of Aboriginal and Islander social and economic life summarised in the previous section go some way to explain the nature and results of the European colonisation of Australia.

Some of the major effects on Aborigines of European colonisation of Australia are simply stated: the population was decimated by disease and homicide, totally destroyed in some regions, and displaced in many others. Aborigines were swamped by the sheer size of the invading groups, overcome by superior military technology and organisation, and were prey to introduced infectious diseases. In the regions of Australia most densely settled by whites and others, the Aboriginal population was transformed through miscegenation. The Aboriginal population as a whole declined from some half a million in 1788 to about 67,000 in the mid-1930s. It has now recovered, as mentioned, to nearly 260,000 (1991 Census: see Table 7.1).

Historians now stress the degree of resistance which the Aborigines mounted against invasion of their lands, often characterising the conflict as guerilla warfare. Conflict arose basically over access to land, exacerbated by differences in property laws, patterns of obligations and other cultural differences. Colonisers appropriated lands and key water sources; their stock transformed the ecology. Some historians point to the 'brutalisation' of the convicts as contributing to conflict, and to the imbalance of the sex ratio of the colony as leading to conflict over women, with thirty-eight males to every female among the settlers in the 1840s. In conflict with European concepts of private property, Aborigines treated stock as they treated wild species, as common resources. Initial conflicts escalated into patterns of killing and retributive massacres (Broome 1982: 38; Reynolds 1987; Lippmann 1991: 8).

In the early decades of the colonies, Aborigines were able to mount a more effective resistance against the settlers armed with muzzle-loading weapons, than they could when breech loading weapons were introduced in the 1870s. However, the small scale of Aboriginal social organisation, the absence of hierarchically organised groups, and the absence of specialised armies, limited the degree to which Aborigines could combine effectively for military action. Furthermore, Aborigines were commonly divided into numerous local networks, divided by enduring enmities. The formation in the 1850s of the Native Police Force in New South Wales and Queensland, which exploited enmities among Aboriginal groups, as well as the introduction of the faster breech loading rifle, turned the tables decisively in favour of Europeans.

The most drastic example of the destruction of Aboriginal people and their social life was that of Tasmania (Ryan 1981), where the majority of the population was killed by force of arms and disease, the remnants rounded up by 1831, finally to die without issue on Flinders Island. The present Aboriginal population of the island is descended from Aboriginal women and the white sealers of Cape Barren Islands, as well as people from the mainland. Within 'settled' Australia Aborigines were forced into a dependent role, living on the fringes of white society.

Economic Relations

We have seen that Aboriginal and Islander economies were not incorporated into capitalism in the form of cash cropping and large-scale migrant labour. However, recent studies show that Aborigines and Islanders often played a crucial role in the development of the Australian economy, and that continuity to some degree of a hunting-gathering-fishing economic base was important in the pattern of exploitation of Aboriginal and Islander labour.

In the south-east, Aborigines were employed as trackers, timber cutters, drovers, domestics, shepherds, station hands, shearers, as sickle reapers, and in such industries as whaling (Jenkin 1979; Christie 1979). In Victoria, men on Aboriginal reserves worked as part-time labourers or seasonal workers on pastoral properties. About one-quarter of Victoria's Aboriginal population lived on reserves by the 1860s, with the remainder living as fringe-dwellers or rural labourers (Broome 1982: 85). On the whole, Aboriginal people worked to fulfil short-term economic goals (Broome 1982: 66).

As long as convict labour was available, Aboriginal participation in the capitalist economy was limited. Morris (1983, 1989), however, criticises images of Aborigines as wholly unprepared culturally to come to terms with Western society, as well as beliefs that Aboriginal culture simply collapsed passively under the impact of British colonisation (1983: 500). The Dhan-gadi of the MacLeay River initially resisted pastoral incursions by systematically spearing cattle, but were defeated during 1856-58 after the introduction of the Native Police; their population was reduced to about one-sixth of its former size (1983: 504). The dominance in the 1850s and 60s, of beef production, which was not labour-intensive, and for which employers preferred white labour, meant that little Aboriginal labour was required until the economy diversified towards the end of the century. The Dhan-gadi men living in strategically located camps worked on pastoral properties clearing land and in stock work. Some of those who lived on Bellbrook Reserve successfully grew maize. However, the Aboriginal population gradually consolidated on to the reserve, with men employed seasonally by larger property owners in bush work, fencing and corn pulling, and women employed as domestics. Possum, rabbit and dingo hunting provided an alternative source of income. Morris stresses that the Dhan-gadi 'did not have the same expectations or priorities in relation to the local economy' as whites did (p. 510). Men preferred contract employment in which, for example, a certain area was cleared for a certain sum of money. This gave them a degree of independence and fitted in with relatively short-term economic goals (i.e. gaining employment for a period of time in order to earn money for a specific limited purpose). The rural sector, with its seasonal demand for labour, was able to accommodate this task-oriented approach (p. 513).

With the specialisation, capitalisation and consolidation of the rural economy since the 1950s, the demand for labour has fallen, with Europeans occupying most of the jobs that are available. Aborigines have thus become displaced from the rural economy.

Cheap Aboriginal labour was also an essential component of the cattle industry for a hundred years or more (Stevens 1974; McGrath 1987). Station owners in more remote areas who encountered difficulties of labour supply employed Aborigines as station hands, domestic servants and sexual partners, initially for payment in kind. The relationship between station owners and Aborigines in the cattle industry had some of the features of internal colonialism (Wolpe 1975; Hartwig 1978; Beckett 1977, cf. 1987). In such a regime the indigenous population meets part of the costs of its own reproduction through its own economy: foraging, fishing and horticulture in the case of Aborigines and Islanders. However, the indigenous people are not provided with sufficient (or sufficiently good) land to maintain themselves, and so are forced into participation in the capitalist economy, e.g. as migrant mine workers. Workers were often laid off in the off-season without sufficient remuneration to tide them over, and so fell back on hunting and gathering. In this way the costs of labour were drastically reduced. Costs were reduced also through the provision of only basic shelter, the non-provision of education, health and other services and, of course, very low or non-existent money wages. Aborigines in the cattle industry were often paid in kind. A minimum wage for Aboriginal pastoral workers was introduced first in Queensland early this century. Brutality and sexual exploitation were commonplace, and master-servant relations were enforced by punitive legislation in, for example, Western Australia and Queensland (Stevens 1974; Trigger 1991). McGrath (1987) shows, however, that many Aboriginal people of the Northern Territory have a positive view of their involvement in the industry; it was no 'shame job' to help white men look after cattle, or white women in the homestead (McGrath 1987: 14).

In Queensland, the majority of squatters supported a policy of exclusion. Aboriginal settlements established after the 1897 Aboriginals' Protection and Restriction of the Sale of Opium Act were formed to protect Aborigines from abuses in employment, such as in the pearling industry, in part to remove Aborigines from stations, and in part to provide pools of cheap Aboriginal labour. In Western Australia the rapid pastoral expansion (sheep and cattle) led to a great demand for Aboriginal labour, which provided the main source of shepherds, shearers, as well as stock-riders and fencers in the districts north of the Murchison River. Remuneration took the form of rations, clothing and tobacco. Aboriginal workers in Western Australia were virtually enslaved by legislation of the 1880s, which provided for the imprisonment of employees who absconded, for up to three months' hard labour, and for flogging (Rowley 1970).

In the post-World War II period of consolidation and capitalisation, beef prices rose, money wages for Aborigines became more equitable, and capital equipment increased. In 1968, Aborigines were included in the Cattle Station Industry award of the Northern Territory, the Federal Pastoral award, and the Queensland award. However, the resultant increase in the cost of Aboriginal labour, together with increased capitalisation and lower demand for labour in general, led employers to lay off Aboriginal workers in favour of whites.

In some industries, albeit marginal ones, Aborigines formed more equitable and mutually beneficial relations with entrepreneurs. Two examples are: the Kuku-Nyungkul people of the Annan River, north of Cairns, with the tin-miners (Anderson 1983); and groups of Aborigines in the Alligator River region of the Northern Territory with white buffalo hunter 'bosses', in which labour was exchanged for resources such as tobacco and food (Levitus 1982; Keen 1982).

Although there are some early examples of Aboriginal communities succeeding in independent economic enterprises recorded in the literature (Broome 1982:72-73, 78ff), these seem invariably to have been under the direction of a white organiser, a mission superintendent in the case of the Coranderrk community (Barwick 1972), or an independent such as Don McLeod (Biskup 1973). These enterprises seem to have been opposed and undermined both by landowners and the authorities (see Mulvaney 1989: 146). Numbers of individuals or small family units, however, have operated as independent farmers, prospectors, hunters etc., as well as contract workers (Broome 1982), and Torres Strait Islanders purchased luggers to become independent pearlers (Beckett 1977, 1987). More recently, Aborigines have formed pop music groups, such as No Fixed Address and Yothuyindi, have acquired and run cattle stations (Thiele 1982), and have formed contracting companies servicing mining towns.

The lives of Aborigines were least affected in regions least subject to intensive European economic exploitation, such as Arnhem

Land and parts of Cape York Peninsula. In these regions, missions and government settlements were the means of controlling the Aboriginal people, and Aboriginal modes of economic and social life continued with varying degrees of disruption and interference. Many settlements were established specifically as sources of cheap labour, in effect subsidised by mission and government funding, as well as subsistence products of settlement farms (Rowley 1971; Morris 1983). Most set out to inculcate the work ethic, and teach Aborigines skills associated with agricultural production, and related technologies, as well as Christianity (see Swain and Rose 1988).

The Development of Policy

European interpretations of the vast differences between nascent industrial society and hunter-gatherer social life gave rise to particular attitudes and policies in relation to Aborigines. The seventeenth and eighteenth century philosophers and legal theorists did not regard hunters and gatherers as fully human — but as 'savage' (which meant 'wild') people, close to animals. Philosophers interested in the origin of private property assumed that fully developed property rights were individual rather than communal, and were necessarily related to the development of agriculture; hence they attributed no property rights in land to the hunting and gathering 'stage of development'. Furthermore, fully developed property rights were believed to be necessary for the existence of government. For example, Hobbes wrote that the 'savage' peoples of America had no government except that of small families:

> It is a consequent to this condition that there be no Proprietary, no Dominion, no *Mine* and *Thine* distinct; but only that to every man that he can get; and for so long as he can keep it.
> (Hobbes 1968 [1651]: 188)

Locke argued that rights in land follow from cultivating the soil; hunters and gatherers let the land lie 'waste' and so had no property, and hence no government.

The rights of colonising nations in international law were related to these notions (Bennett 1978). For example, in his *Commentaries on the Laws of England*, Blackstone (1765) distinguished two types of colony: conquered or ceded territory, and settled or occupied territory. The lands of peoples recognised as having systems of law and government were deemed to be colonised by conquest or cession, but lands inhabited by peoples who did not cultivate the land, and who were not recognised as having systems of law and government, were deemed to be colonised by settlement or occupation. In the first type of colony the indigenous systems of law were taken to be binding on the indigenous inhabitants until revoked by the Crown; in the second case, indigenous peoples came immediately under English Law (in the case of English colonies), and indigenous law went unrecognised.

The British recognised Native American property rights and made treaties with the Native Americans, despite the fact that many were hunters and gatherers, probably in order to form alliances with them against other colonial powers, as well as for other reasons (Bennett 1978). In New Zealand, the British negotiated the Treaty of Waitangi with the agricultural Maoris. In Australia, however, until the recent High Court decision in the Mabo case (1992), it gradually became established in law that Australia was a 'settled' colony, and not a conquered or ceded territory, and that Australia had been *terra nullius*, 'no-one's land'. In 1770, Cook had claimed possession of the east coast of Australia, and reported that the Aborigines 'move about like Wild Beasts in search of food', and do not cultivate. His 'discovery', together with the fact of British settlement, established sovereignty in international law.

It was for reasons such as these that the British did not recognise the existence of any Aboriginal or Islander states or nations with which to make treaties, and did not recognise Aboriginal or Islander modes of law, property or land rights. One of the duties of a colonising power was seen to be to protect indigenous peoples, who were accorded the legal status of children — as 'wards' of the colonising 'guardians'. So it was that colonial governments, prompted by humanitarian pressure groups, also sought to segregate and protect Aborigines, regarded by many as a 'child race', from the effects of colonisation, and to 'civilise' them. But there was little in the way of coherent government policy in relation to Aborigines in the late eighteenth century and the first half of the nineteenth century.

After early attempts at 'protection', the first comprehensive legislation in relation to Aborigines did not appear until the end of the nineteenth century. Aboriginal people were treated similarly to the destitute. Those in absolute want were given rations, and labour colonies and farms were set up to provide training for the urban unemployed. Similarly, reserves were set aside for Aborigines, and missions encouraged to Christianise them and to inculcate the work ethic.

Legislation in relation to Aborigines was both protective and restrictive: it tended to segregate Aborigines from non-Aborigines, set up protective structures, and restrict Aboriginal rights and freedoms. For example the Queensland Aboriginals' Protection and the Restriction of the Sale of Opium Act of 1897, which became a model for legislation in other states, empowered the Government to force Aborigines on to reserves and keep them there. For the next fifty years, Aboriginal people were steadily removed to reserves. The Act empowered the Minister, through police Protectors and reserve superintendents, to control movement on to and out of reserves, enter employment contracts on behalf of Aborigines, hold their funds, control their spending, and have legal custody of their children. Regulations prohibited alcohol and certain customary practices, and provided penalties for breaches of discipline and insubordination. 'Half-castes' could seek exemption from the Act. Queensland Acts in relation to Aborigines and Torres Strait Islanders Acts remained restrictive, although with periodic amendments, to a decreasing degree, until their replacement in 1985 with the community services legislation.

People of mixed descent were picked out for special treatment from the late nineteenth century onwards. For example, legislation in Victoria in 1886 removed 'half-castes' under thirty-four years of age from reserves, on the grounds that they should earn a living and merge into the general community. However, many of these people became fringe-dwellers, and the legislation was revoked. Later legislation (1915) provided for 'half-caste' youths to be taken into homes. In the Northern Territory, many children with non-Aboriginal fathers were removed from their mothers to be raised in homes in Darwin and southern cities. In this way the normal processes of cultural transmission through the socialisation of the young was interrupted (see Broome 1982: 82–84).

After World War II, the Australian economy rapidly expanded to become more complex structurally, providing a rising standard of living. Welfare policies, increasingly centralised in the federal sphere, changed direction. The concern became to provide support for a variety of 'disadvantaged' categories, such as Aborigines. 'Cradle to the grave' social security included old age pensions, invalid pensions, maternity allowances, and veterans' pensions, financed by universal taxation (Butlin *et al.* 1982). Access to such benefits, and to education, became universal.

From the 1940s, Aboriginal and Islander people were increasingly incorporated into Australian society through the extension to them of such benefits, and through a policy of assimilation, adopted by a Native Welfare Conference of all the states, called by the Minister, Hasluck, in 1951 (see Altman and Sanders 1991a). When fully articulated, the policy extended the same rights and privileges to Aborigines that other Australians enjoyed, but at the same time expected that they would eventually 'attain the same manner of living as other Australians and. . .live as members of a single Australian community'. This policy paralleled a similar one in relation to migrants; indeed, large numbers of non-British migrants had arrived in Australia since 1947, and in 1966 the Government lifted restrictions on Asian immigration. The federal government took over specific needs of Aborigines as a disadvantaged minority after the 1967 referendum, which extended the Census to include Aborigines, and gave the federal government the power to legislate in respect of Aborigines. A Department of Aboriginal Affairs was established and an advisory committee, including the anthropologist W.E.H. Stanner, and H.C. Coombs, a leading economist, set up.

It was not until the early 1970s that Aboriginal cultural distinctiveness was given official recognition, along with a general policy change towards 'multiculturalism'. This was in a changing international context, in which former British colonies had become politically independent, and were exerting pressure on the white nations over the treatment of their indigenous minorities. It was in a period of political radicalism, partly sparked off by the Vietnam War, that can now be seen as transient.

The Labor Party, under Whitlam's leadership, introduced a policy of 'self-determination' in 1972. This policy was manifested in the Aboriginal Land (Northern Territory) Bill (enacted in a revised form by the Fraser government in 1976), which followed a decade of strikes and protests on the part of Aborigines and their non-Aboriginal supporters. Other legislation and policies encouraged a degree of local autonomy on the part of Aboriginal communities, particularly in the Northern Territory, such as the formation and incorporation of Aboriginal Community Councils (with the concomitant phasing out of the supervisory role of missionaries), and the provision of grants for the purchase of land for Aboriginal groups by the Aboriginal Land Fund Commission, and for the setting up of 'outstations'.

The last two decades have seen a burgeoning of independent Aboriginal organisations. Support organisations for Aborigines and Torres Strait Islanders have a long history, and include the Federal Council for the Advancement of Aborigines and Torres Strait Islanders, founded in 1958, mainly by Europeans, and the One People for Australia League. More recently, Aboriginal and Islander people have formed many independent schools, Aboriginal legal services and Aboriginal health services, as well as independent Land Councils, particularly in Queensland and Western Australia. Governments have established advisory committees with Aboriginal membership in fields such as education, and at the national Level the National Aboriginal Conference (formerly Consultative Committee), whose solely advisory role was a source of contention (Tatz 1979), and which the Hawke government disbanded.

The fundamental issue is that of separateness and autonomy. A frequently-expressed non-Aboriginal view is that all Australians should have the same rights and opportunities — Aboriginal people should have no more and no fewer rights than other Australians. Such a view does not acknowledge Aboriginal cultural and social distinctiveness, or the validity of separate rights. Indeed many non-Aborigines fear such distinctiveness, labelling it as akin to 'apartheid'. Many Aborigines, on the other hand, express a strong desire to have control of their own affairs, both at the local and the federal level, and to maintain their own particular lifestyles, while at the same time participating in the Australian community as a whole.

The replacement in 1990 of the federal Department of Aboriginal Affairs (DAA) by the Aboriginal and Torres Strait Islander Commission (ATSIC) has gone some way towards meeting such demands. ATSIC brought together the DAA and the Aboriginal Development Commission (ADC), with Aboriginal Hostels Ltd. and the Australian Institute of Aboriginal and Torres Strait Islander Studies, as autonomous subsidiaries. The re-organisation had the broad aim of amalgamating all agencies delivering special services to Aboriginal and Islander people, while decentralising decision making about how money was to be allocated. The structures attempted to combine Aboriginal political aspirations to determine government policies that affect them, with the broad government aim of improving Aboriginal socio-economic status. As Rowse (1992) points out, Aboriginal people seek self-determination and management that is primarily local in form and purposes. It is doubtful whether there is any national issue that mobilises Aboriginal people nation-wide.

Subject to the powers of the Minister, ATSIC's role is to determine the overall direction of policies and strategies for Aboriginal and Islander advancement. Sixty elected Regional Councils draw up local policy, and determine the spending of funds on local programs, administered by thirty regional offices. The twenty Commissioners, seventeen elected by the members of Regional Councils and three appointed by the Minister, determine overall policy, drawing on the advice of various policy development branches of the bureaucracy (Australia 1991a).

ATSIC was one major initiative of the Hawke government in Aboriginal affairs; the move towards an instrument of reconciliation between white and black Australians was another. A Treaty of Commitment or Makarrata was suggested by the National Aboriginal Conference in 1979. In the same year, a non-Aboriginal

Treaty Committee chaired by H.C. Coombs formed as a lobby group, and the Fraser government expressed an interest in the helping the NAC develop the idea of a Makarrata. In 1983 a Senate Standing Committee recommended that a provision be inserted into the Constitution giving the Commonwealth broad powers to enter into a 'compact' with representatives of the Aboriginal people. In 1988 the Prime Minister declared at the Barunga Festival that 'there shall be a Treaty or Compact negotiated between Aboriginal people and the people of Australia'. In part because of legal difficulties with the notion of a 'treaty' between a sovereign state and some of its own citizens, this promise was transformed into a proposed 'instrument of reconciliation', a document whose contents are to be worked out by the year 2001. Towards this end the government established in 1991 a Council for Aboriginal Reconciliation. This initiative appears primarily to be an exercise in public relations and education rather than entailing a real change in legal and political status (see Lippmann 1991: 79–80; Brennan 1991).

The issue of land rights, touched on at the beginning of this section, warrants a separate discussion.

Land Rights

Since the Gove land rights case (1971), the general view has been that in law the Australian colonies were colonies of settlement rather than conquest, and that for legal purposes Australia was *terra nullius*, 'no-one's land', for all intents and purposes uninhabited. Reynolds' (1987) has shown, however, that there was by no means a uniform view about the existence of Aboriginal proprietary rights in land during the nineteenth century. However, in the landmark Gove land rights case (*Milirrpum vs. Nabalco Pty Ltd and the Commonwealth of Australia* 1971), heard in the Supreme Court of the Northern Territory, Judge Blackburn found that New South Wales had been established as a 'settled' colony by a Privy Council decision, that native title had never been recognised in Australia, and that north-east Arnhem Land clans did not own land in any sense recognisable in Australian law.

As a consequence of the Gove case, the Whitlam government established the Land Rights Commission, with Judge Woodward as Commissioner, to investigate possible ways of granting land rights to Aboriginal people. The resulting 1976 Aboriginal Land Rights (Northern Territory) Act, passed by the Fraser government, gave Northern Territory Aborigines freehold title over reserve lands, and the right to claim title to vacant Crown land, and lands held by, or on behalf of, Aborigines.

Land rights Acts have also been passed by state governments in

New South Wales, South Australia and Queensland. The Queensland Bjelke-Petersen government vested reserves in Aboriginal Councils not on the basis of freehold title, but as deeds of grant in trust, a weaker form of tenure. The Labor government in that state has since provided for freehold ownership of former reserves by Aboriginal groups, and some limited ability to claim land. Land rights legislation proposed in Victoria and Tasmania has been blocked by the upper houses, and vigorously opposed, particularly by mining interests in Western Australia (Maddock 1983; Peterson and Langton 1983; Reynolds 1987). Uniform national land rights legislation was part of Labor Party policy in 1982, but pressure from mining interests led to compromises which Aboriginal communities found unacceptable, especially the absence of any provision for rights to control mining exploration and extraction. By 1987, the Labor government had abandoned this proposal. Bennett (1989: 151) comments that the national scheme 'grossly underestimated the political power of the states and the immense difficulties in achieving any sort of meaningful uniformity in governmental arrangements'.

The court's findings in the Gove case were based on legal fictions and contestable interpretations, as the recent High Court findings in the Mabo case show. In June 1992, the High Court of Australia brought down its findings on the claim of the Meriam people of the Torres Strait to title over the Murray Islands which they inhabited and with which they had a long historical association. The court affirmed the right of the Crown to sovereignty by virtue of settlement of Australia, but overturned the legal status of Australia as *terra nullius* 'no-one's land', at the time of British settlement. Aboriginal and Islander people might retain native title to particular areas of land where the Crown had not extinguished that title. The Murray Islanders had established a long historical association with the land on which they resided, their title had not been extinguished by the Crown, and the land was not Crown land. A minority of the Court found that Aboriginal people whose title to land had been extinguished could claim compensation, but only within a short period from the date of extinguishment. The wider implications of the High Court findings in the Mabo case for Aboriginal land rights are not yet clear, but may well be profound.

A Heterogeneous Category

The varying conditions and distinct histories of different parts of Australia have given rise to an extremely varied range of Aboriginal styles of life.

Table 7.1 Aboriginal and Islander Population

Aboriginal and Islander Population								
NSW	Vic.	Qld	SA	WA	Tas	NT	ACT	Australia.
68,941	16,570	67,012	16,020	40,002	8,683	38,337	1,768	257,333
Aboriginal and Islander Population (% of total)								
NSW	VIC	QLD	SA	WA	TAS	NT	ACT	AUST.
1.2	0.4	2.2	1.1	2.5	1.9	21.9	0.6	1.5

The size of the Aboriginal population, as well as the proportion of the Aboriginal to non-Aboriginal people, varies greatly from state to state. Table 7.1 shows preliminary figures from the 1991 Census (Australian Bureau of Statistics). The ennumerated population grew by 2.4 per cent per annum between the 1986 and 1991 Censuses, but between 1981 and 1986, the growth was a massive 13 per cent. This is thought to be due to a variety of factors, including a greater willingness to identify as Aboriginal, as well as an awareness campaign before the 1986 Census. The enumerated Aboriginal/Islander population had declined between 1976 and 1981, probably as a result of Census error (Tesfaghioghis and Gray 1991; Gaminiratne 1992).

Aboriginal and Islander people live in a wide variety of social conditions: in townships (former missions and government settlements) with Aboriginal councils, outstations on Aboriginal land and reserves, cattle station communities, town camps and town reserves, fringe camps on the margins of towns and cities, households and communities in country towns and cities, and in hostels. There is space here to describe only some of the variety. The following contrasts township with urban life.

Aboriginal Townships

Many Aboriginal people live on townships of several hundred to over a thousand people, located on former Aboriginal reserves, lands held by land trusts, or Aboriginal land. Such communities were established, mostly after 1900, as missions or government settlements, with the purpose of protecting Aborigines from the worst effects of contact with whites, Chinese and others, to instil Christianity and the value of 'work', and to train people in agriculture and other activities associated with 'civilised' social life. Some Aboriginal people established independent settlements, including the very large number of small outstations in remote areas.

The inhabitants of such townships in the Northern Territory are typically affiliated to land surrounding, or fairly close to, the township. In Queensland, however, it was government policy to remove Aboriginal people from their own areas to distant settlements, with the consequent separation of people from the territorial basis of their systems of religious law, and mixing of people with distinct cultures. The authorities removed people to certain settlements such as Palm Island as punishment for infringements of regulations, and other offences.

Townships were formerly administered mainly by mission authorities, backed by the state in the form of small subsidies, by access to police power, and support from the courts. In effect, where Aborigines were not forced on to reserves and settlements, they were induced there by the provision of rations of flour, tea, sugar and tobacco, in return for work in gardens or workshops . The degree to which the missionaries intervened in Aboriginal religious life, marriage systems, and socialisation of children varied greatly. In some cases dormitory systems were introduced, removing children from the care of their parents and other relatives, and communal feeding was instituted; in others the dormitory system and communal feeding were short-lived. In some communities, Aboriginal religious ceremonies were vigorously discouraged (Trigger 1991), in others tolerated (McKenzie 1976), or continued clandestinely (Tonkinson 1974). During the last two decades, Aboriginal councils have taken over the administration of townships, working with white advisers and community workers, or in Queensland under a white manager.

Life in such communities was routinised, dominated by a daily round of work in gardens, on housing and town maintenance and servicing, and weekend church attendance. Adults in some communities, such as Doomadgee (Trigger 1991), have been employed in the cattle industry and as domestics; in others employment has been wholly internal. The passing of community control to Aboriginal councils has resulted in an increased emphasis on traditional activities.

Since the granting of a 'training allowance' of less than the normal wage, then award wages on settlements, and the extension of access to transfer payments (widow's pension, supporting mother's benefit, old age pension, disablity pension, unemployment benefit), wages and social security payments have formed the main sources of income. People supplement these sources with income from such activities as the sale of art and craft work and subsistence activities. Transfer payments have the advantage of regularity and reliability, while other sources are more sporadic and uncertain. Governments have made attempts to increase Aboriginal employment with measures such as the Community Development Employment Projects scheme (CDEP) under which unemployment benefits are consolidated to be used as wages for part-time employment within communities (Australia 1985).

A notable recent feature of settlement in the Northern Territory and to some extent in Queensland has been the 'outstation' or 'homeland centre' movement. Increasing access to cars, four-wheel drive vehicles and boats, has enabled people to move out of large townships to establish centres on their traditional lands where they can re-establish or reinforce traditional modes of social control and religious practices. Hunting, gathering and fishing become significant in the economy of these communities, and religious life more vigorous (Altman 1987; Blanchard 1987; Coombs *et al.* 1980).

On many Aboriginal townships, as well as among cattle station and other communities, the religious law continues (Morphy 1984), albeit adapted to changing conditions to varying degrees (Kolig 1982), and incorporating Christian beliefs to varying extents (Swain and Rose 1988). Where they are maintained, indigenous forms of religious practice continue to establish relations of power and authority within the Aboriginal communities.

Cities

Australia ranks as one of the most urbanised societies in the world. Until recent decades, the Aboriginal population was predominantly rural, with only 15 per cent living in major urban areas in 1971. However, a high rate of migration out of rural areas and into the cities during the 1960s has changed the balance; they moved to find employment, visit relatives, and obtain education, and to escape race prejudice (Gale 1972; Gale and Wundersitz 1982; Eckerman 1977; Smith and Biddle 1975). About one-third of Aboriginal and Islander people now live in rural areas; this is still twice as high a proportion by comparison with the non-Aboriginal population (Tesfaghiorgis and Gray 1991). Many Aboriginal people in 'settled' Australia live as small minorities in towns and capital cities. Aboriginal households in cities have a characteristic extended and matrifocal structure (Smith and Biddle 1975). The economic status of Aborigines in both cities and rural areas is depressed.

Aboriginal Cultural Continuity and Identity

Recent anthropological and socio-linguistic research (see Keen 1988), as well as the writings of Aboriginal people (e.g. Gilbert 1977; Morgan 1987), show that Aboriginal people living in the south-east and south-west of the continent, maintain cultures which are distinct from that of white Australians, not only because of their relative poverty. These are not uniform patterns among all who identify as Aboriginal, for styles of life and culture are very varied; some Aboriginal people live in a manner little different from the white middle class.

The dimensions of cultural continuity and distinctiveness include: a more extensive network of kin relations than among white Australians, with people recognising and remembering relationships at a degree of remove far beyond that of white Australian kinship, and incorporating non-kin as fictive kin. Moreover, obligations to support relatives tend to be stronger in Aboriginal social life, and take precedence where there is a conflict with other obligations or interests, such as work or education. These obligations are evidenced in patterns of visiting and living in extended 'concertina' family households of variable size and composition (Sansom 1982).

Socialisation practices among Ipswich Aboriginal people (Eckerman 1977) have some similarities with those described for a remote North Australian community (Hamilton 1981b), with an emphasis on the freedom of children, especially males, from adult control, until puberty. People maintain indigenous languages to a greater degree than formerly realised, using them in specific contexts such as where privacy is desired. Furthermore, Aboriginal English has a rather distinctive pattern of use; for example, the Aboriginal people of southern Queensland tend to avoid the use of direct questions, and etiquette does not demand that a person answer a question put to them, as white etiquette does (Eades 1981, 1988). Baines (1988) documents continuities in belief and social practices among Nyungar people of Perth. And both Langton (1988) and Macdonald (1988) show that modes of public swearing and fighting are socially sanctioned and formalised modes of dispute resolution, not mere mayhem.

Some writers, notably Morris (1988) and Cowlishaw (1988) attribute the cultural distinctiveness of Aboriginal people of the south-east to a 'culture of resistance' rather than continuities from a pre-colonial past. According to this view, Aboriginal people deliberately instituted some practices and maintained others in order to resist attempts on the part of the authorities to control them, or in order to assert distinctive values.

I said at the beginning of the chapter that the social identities 'Aborigine' and 'Islander' are not clearly demarcated. As Thiele points out, groupings such as 'white' and 'black' are the product of social processes that are never final. 'They are not seamless entities, fully-formed groups, or unitary social actors with parts in a single moral or political drama' (1992: 192). A few examples must suffice to illustrate this openness of identity.

The official definition includes three criteria: an 'Aboriginal' is a person of Aboriginal or Torres Strait Islander descent, who identifies as an Aboriginal person, and who is accepted as such by his or her local Aboriginal or Islander community. But the purpose of this definition is only to provide guidelines. Jordan (1985: 31) has shown that government authorities are inconsistent in the way they apply ethnic categories, in one case classifying the same person in official transactions as 'white' and 'half-caste' on the same day.

As mentioned, people may identify themselves as 'Aboriginal' in one context and not in another, or having discovered that they are of Aboriginal descent, then decide to maintain that identity. During the assimilation period, it was often in a person's interests to forego Aboriginal identity in order to shake off restrictions on personal freedom. But one outcome of the policies of the Whitlam government was that it was in people's interests to identify as Aboriginal.

Some people, however, identify as 'coloured' or 'dark' rather than 'Aboriginal' (Lynne Hume, personal communication, and see the film *Sister if You Only Knew*), as 'part-Aboriginal' (Gilbert 1977: 175), or as 'descendants' of Aborigines (Hayden 1977). Aboriginal people of the south-east and south-west are increasingly choosing to use an indigenous term such as Koori or Murri in preference to 'Aborigine', contrasting these with indigenous terms for 'white' people such as Gubba.

A person identifying as an Aborigine includes descent as one criterion of identity, but membership of a continuing community is just as important (see Schwab 1988). Many Aboriginal people conceive of the essence of Aboriginality as inner and spiritual, transmitted from one generation to the next (Schwab 1991), a concept of identity that can accommodate variation in skin colour. Identity as an Aboriginal person, then, is a social construct (Beckett 1988; Thiele 1992).

Dimensions of Disadvantage
Aborigines and Islanders are economically and socially disadvantaged in terms of normative standards applied within the community in general. We can measure the degree of disadvantage along several dimensions, such as health status, educational, economic and legal status (for more detailed studies, see Altman and Niewenhuysen 1979; Western 1983; Altman 1991).

Economic Status
To generalise, because of the young age structure of the Aboriginal population, Aboriginal people make up only about 1 per cent of the labour force (less than 60,000 in 1986), workforce participation rates are low, and earned income is a less important source of total income than for the rest of the population, with at least 50

per cent of total income coming from government benefits and pensions, as against 28 per cent for the population as a whole (Jones 1991: 28-29). Unemployment is over four times as high (34-36 per cent compared with 8 per cent for Australians of Anglo-Celtic origin) (Jones 1991: 32). The average status of jobs that Aborigines do is low compared with white Australians, especially for men. Aboriginal men are most likely to have a job in unskilled work, and women in clerical employment. Few Aboriginal people find their way into administrative, professional or para-professional positions. Hourly earnings are relatively low, with men earning only 76 per cent of the average for white males in 1986. The figure for women is 87 per cent. Most work for wages or salary, and few are currently married, reflecting the relative youth of the Aboriginal workforce (Jones 1991: 33).

Altman and Sanders (1991b: 9) identify four aspects 'of the deep-rooted nature of low Aboriginal employment and income status'. First is the historical exclusion of Aboriginal peoples from many mainstream institutions of Australian society and the welfare state, such as award wages, the social security system and the education system; this exclusion has left a long legacy. A second aspect is the demographic structure of the Aboriginal population, which, in comparision with the population as a whole has a very young age structure. There are two consequences: one is a very high dependency ratio, and the other is that the number of Aboriginal people just entering the workforce is very large, and will increase more rapidly than planners have anticipated. A third aspect is locational disadvantage, with perhaps half the Aboriginal population living in more remote areas where labour markets are limited or nonexistent; there are few opportunities for market-oriented activities to develop. Fourth, where Aboriginal people are living a tradition-oriented lifestyle in remote areas, formal employment may not be culturally appropriate. For these reason, Altman and Sanders (1991b: 10) believe that the low employment and income status of Aborigines is highly intractable.

Governments have recently instituted a variety of schemes to boost Aboriginal employment. These include the various enterprise loans and grants made by the Aboriginal Development Commission (now replaced by ATSIC), as well as land and property acquisition by that body; the Aboriginal Employment Development Policy launched by the Hawke government in 1987 in response to the *Miller Report*, which articulated as its long-term objectives the achievement of employment and income equality for Aboriginal people, and a shift away from a 'welfare dependency approach'. Under this policy programs were renamed and redefined, and include the Community Economic Advancement Projects Scheme, the Community Employment and Enterprise Development Scheme and the Aboriginal Employment Action program (Altman and Sanders 1991b: 7).

Health

Aboriginal health is very much worse than that of the non-Aboriginal population of Australia, though improving. A broad trend can be identified, from a high infant mortality rate and high death rate, towards a lower infant mortality rate combined with a high death rate due to 'lifestyle' diseases. We have seen how introduced diseases have had a profound effect. Changes in environmental conditions and new habits of diet have been just as significant. Practices of hygiene and waste disposal suitable for a semi-nomadic life are not well adapted to life on permanent settlements, but the provision of services such as water supply generally has not been adequate. The poor conditions of the physical environment account for a high incidence of intestinal infections such as gastroenteritis, intestinal parasites such as hookworm, and skin diseases such as scabies. The adoption of a diet of white flour, sugar, tea and, often, alcohol, in place of a varied and nutritious diet of wild foods, has led to malnutrition, diabetes, dental caries and alcoholism, and resultant low resistance to infection (Hetzel 1980). Widespread heavy smoking has also had deleterious effects on health.

Infant mortality rate (IMR) is a good indicator of the general health of mothers as well as infants. The IMR of the Aboriginal population of full descent in the Northern Territory for 1965–67 was 143 per 1,000 live births, compared with a figure of 21 for Australia as a whole (Hetzel 1980). By 1981, the rate for Aboriginal people as a whole had fallen to about 30.3 per thousand, as against 10.2 for the whole of Australia (Thomson 1983), and to 9.3 for the 1983-86 triennium (Gray 1990). In spite of improvements in the Aboriginal IMR and a steady decrease in mortality generally, life expectancy for Aboriginal men and women is still about fifteen years less than for Australians as a whole (Divakaran-Brown and Honari 1990; Yard *et al.* 1990; Hogg 1990). For Aboriginal males, disease of the circulatory system, injury and violence, and respiratory system disease account in that order for a high proportion of excess mortality, and among women, circulatory system disease is especially important (Honari 1990: 142–43).

Social factors also influence health. For example, there is a greater incidence of infectious disease in Queensland townships to which people were moved from many different areas (Trigger *et al.* 1983), and such communities are riven by alcoholism and violence (Wilson 1983).

Education
Although Aboriginal involvement in schooling and higher education
has increased markedly since the early 1970s, it still indicates a
disadvantaged position. The 1986 Census shows that most Aborigines (61 per cent), like other Australians, stayed at school
until the legal minimum of 15-16 years. However, fewer obtained
formal School Certificates as a result of remaining at school. This
performance is reflected in employment: Jones (1991: 37) shows
that Aboriginal people end up in low status jobs regardless of how
long they stayed at school, unless they gained a post-school qualification.

Over four times as many Aborigines as white Australians (9 per
cent) either did not go to school or left before they were 14 years
old. Aboriginal people are much less likely to have tertiary qualifications: only about 5 Aborigines per 1,000 as against 70 to 80
per 1,000 among Australians of Anglo-Celtic origin. Even trade and
other certificates are rare (Jones 1991: 30–38). Participation in
higher education is increasing, fostered by the institution of support
programs such as Aboriginal 'enclaves', liaison offices, and study
skills programs.

Government spending on Aboriginal education has been high
since the 1960s, with the institution of special programs such as
bilingual programs, provision for Aboriginal teacher aides, ap-
pointment of advisory committees, and funding of research into
Aboriginal education. Among the many recent programs and
initiatives that target Aboriginal and Islander education under the
National Aboriginal and Torres Strait Islander Education Policy
are the Aboriginal Education Strategic Inititatives Program and
the Aboriginal Student Assistance Scheme (ABSTUDY). In 1989-
90, funding was provided under the Higher Education Equity
Program and the Aboriginal Participation Initiative to assist institutions to provided greater equality of access to higher education
for disadvantaged groups, including Aboriginal and Islander people
(Australia 1990).

Several Aboriginal communities have recently instituted independent Aboriginal and Islander schools and pre-schools
(Lippmann 1991:149).

Aborigines and the Law
The legal disabilities imposed by protective and restrictive
legislation in the first half of this century were gradually removed
through the era of assimilationist policy which came into effect
after World War II, and increasingly so after the 1967 referendum.
However, Aboriginal people are severely disadvantaged in relation

to the legal system, manifested primarily in the very high proportion of the Aboriginal population who are imprisoned. The number of Aboriginal people in custody came to public attention as a result of the findings of the Royal Commission into Aboriginal Deaths in Custody established in 1987. Research for the Commission has shown that Aboriginal deaths in custody, including suicides, are not unusually high as a proportion of the Aboriginal prison population, but because of the over-representation of Aboriginal people in prisons and lock-ups, in 1989 about twenty times the rate for non-Aborigines (Biles 1989).

The explanation of Aboriginal over-representation in prisons is a contentious issue, but it probably reflects poverty and alienation as well as bias at various points in the legal process (Walker 1987). Courts have adopted measures to ameliorate some aspects of bias, including procedures to be followed by police when interviewing Aboriginal witnesses (Ligertwood 1984). The Royal Commission into Aboriginal Deaths in Custody has also recommended a number of measures to reduce Aboriginal imprisonment and to improve their treatment while in custody (Australia 1991b). Aboriginal and Islander people have taken action themselves by the creation of legal services under their control (Lyons 1984). These help to ensure adequate representation of Aboriginal defendants, press for the reform of the legal system, and operate as political pressure groups.

Conclusions

The last two centuries have seen great changes not only in the structure of Australian society as a whole, but also in the position of Aborigines and Torres Strait Islanders in relation to that structure.

During the last two decades Aborigines and Islanders have become more vocal in Australian political life, and more effective in developing political organisations, using organisations established by legislation such as land rights Acts, and establishing their own community services and support groups. At the same time the wave of public support apparent during the late 1960s and early 70s has retreated, as the opposition to land rights expressed in the press during the 1980s suggests. It is clear that Aborigines and Islanders have values, interests and enduring cultures generally very different from those of the white majority. The fact is that Australia is a plural society, and the differences, as well as the resulting conflicts, will endure.

References

Altman, J.C. (1984) 'Hunter-gatherer Subsistence Production in Arnhem Land: the Original Affluence Hypothesis Re-examined', *Mankind* 14 (3): 179–90.

——(1987) *Hunter-Gatherers Today: An Aboriginal Economy in North Australia*. Canberra: Australian Institute of Aboriginal Studies.

——(1991) (ed.) *Aboriginal Employment Equity by the Year 2000*. Canberra: Centre for Aboriginal Economic Policy Research, Australian National University.

Altman, J.C. and Nieuwenhuysen, J. (1979) *The Economic Status of Australian Aborigines*. Cambridge: Cambridge University Press.

Altman, J.C. and Sanders, W.G. (1991a) 'From Exclusion to Dependence: Aborigines and the Welfare State in Australia', *CAEPR Discussion Paper 1*. Canberra: Centre for Aboriginal Economic Policy Research, Australian National University.

——(1991b) 'Government Initiatives for Aboriginal Employment: Equity, Equality and Policy Realism', in J.C. Altman (ed.), *Aboriginal Employment Equity by the Year 2000*. Canberra: Centre for Aboriginal Economic Policy Research, Australian National University.

Anderson, J.C. (1983) 'Aborigines and Tin Mining in North Queensland: A Case Study in the Anthropology of Contact History,' *Mankind* 13 (6): 473–498.

Australia (1985) *Government Expenditure on Aboriginal Programs 1985–86*. Canberra: Department of Aboriginal Affairs.

——(1990) *Department of Employment, Education and Training: Annual Report*. Canberra: Australian Government Publishing Service.

——(1991a) *ATSIC Annual Report 5 March 1990-30 June 1991*. Canberra: Australian Government Publishing Service.

——(1991b) *Final Report of the Royal Commission into Aboriginal Deaths in Custody*. Canberra: Australian Government Publishing Service.

Baines, P. (1988) 'A Litany for Land', in I. Keen (ed.) *Being Black: Aboriginal Cultures in 'Settled' Australia*. Canberra: Aboriginal Studies Press.

Barwick, D. (1972) 'Coranderrk and Cumeroogunga: Pioneers and Policy', in T.S. Epstein and D.H. Penny (eds), *Opportunity and Response*. London: C. Hurst and Company.

Beckett, J. (1972) 'The Torres Strait Islanders', in D. Walker (ed.), *Bridge and Barrier*. Canberra: Australian National University Press.

——(1977) 'The Torres Strait Islanders and the Pearling Industry: A Case of Internal Colonialism', *Aboriginal History* 1: 77–104.

——(1987) *Torres Strait Islanders: Custom and Colonialism*. Cambridge: Cambridge University Press.

——(1988) 'Introduction', in J. Beckett (ed.), *Past and Present: the Construction of Aboriginality*. Canberra: Aboriginal Studies Press.

Bennett, G. (1978) *Aboriginal Rights in International Law*, Occasional Paper No. 37 of the Royal Anthropological Institute of Great Britain and Ireland.

Bennett, S. (1989) *Aborigines and Political Power*. Sydney: Allen and Unwin.

Berndt, R.M. and Berndt, C.H. (1981) *The World of the First Australians* Sydney: Lansdowne Press.

Biles, D. (1989) 'Aboriginal Imprisonment: A Statistical Analysis', Research Paper No. 6, Royal Commission into Aboriginal Deaths in Custody, Parkes.

Birdsell, J. (1953) 'Some Environmental and Cultural Factors Influencing the Structuring of Australian Aboriginal Populations', *American Naturalist* 87: 171–207.

Biskup, P. (1973) *Not Slaves, not Citizens: the Aboriginal Problem in Western Australia 1898 - 1954*, St Lucia: University of Queensland Press.

Blackstone, J. (1765) *Commentaries on the Laws of England.* Oxford: Clarendon Press.

Blanchard, C.A. (1987) *Return to Country: The Aboriginal Homelands Movement in Australia.* Report of the House of Representative Standing Committee on Aboriginal Affairs, March. Canberra: Australian Government Publishing Service.

Brennan, F. (1991) *Sharing the Country: The Case for an Agreement Between Black and White Australians.* Ringwood, Victoria: Penguin Books.

Broome, R. (1982) *Aboriginal Australians: Black Response to White Dominance 1788-1980.* Sydney: Allen and Unwin.

Butlin, N.G., Barnard, A. and Pincus, J.J. (1982) *Government and Capitalism.* Sydney: Allen and Unwin.

Charlesworth, M. *et al.* (1984) *Religion in Aboriginal Australia: An Anthology.* St Lucia: Queensland University Press.

Christie, M.F. (1979) *Aborigines in Colonial Victoria 1835-86.* Sydney: Sydney University Press.

Coombs, H.C, Hiatt, L.R. and Dexter, B. (1980) 'The Outstation Movement in Aboriginal Australia,' *Australian Institute of Aboriginal Studies Newsletter* 14 n.s.:16-23.

Cowlishaw, G. (1988) *Black, White or Brindle: Race in Rural Australia.* Sydney: Cambridge University Press.

Crick, M. (1981) 'Aboriginal Self-management Organisations, Cultural Identity and the Modification of Exchange', *Canberra Anthropology* 4 (1): 52–81.

Denoon, D. (1983) *Settler Capitalism: the Dynamics of Dependent Development in the Southern Hemisphere.* Oxford: Clarendon Press.

Divakaran-Brown, C. and M. Honari (1990) 'Aboriginal Mortality in South Australia,' in Alan Gray (ed.), *A Matter of Life and Death: Contemporary Aboriginal Mortality.* Canberra: Aboriginal Studies Press..

Drakakis-Smith, D. (1981) 'Aboriginal Underdevelopment in Australia', *Antipode: A Radical Journal of Geography* 13 (1): 35–44.

Eades, D. (1981) "That's our way of talking ": Aborigines in southeast Queensland,' *Social Alternatives* 2 (2): 11–15.

———(1988) 'They don't speak an Aboriginal language, or do they?', in I. Keen (ed.), *Being Black: Aboriginal Cultures in 'Settled' Australia.* Canberra: Australian Institute of Aboriginal Studies.

Eckermann, A.K. (1977) 'Group Organisation and Identity Within an Urban Aboriginal Community', in R.M. Berndt (ed.), *Aborigines and*

Change: Australia in the 70s. Canberra: Australian Institute of Aboriginal Studies.

Elkin, A.P. (1954) *The Australian Aborigines: How to Understand Them.* Sydney: Angus and Robertson.

Flood, J. (1980) *The Moth Hunters: Aboriginal Prehistory of the Australian Alps.* Canberra: Australian Institute of Aboriginal Studies.

Gale, F. (1972) *Urban Aborigines.* Canberra: Australian National University Press.

Gale, F. and J. Wundersitz (1982) *Adelaide Aborigines: A Case Study of Urban Life 1966–1981.* Canberra: Development Studies Centre, Australian National University Press.

Gaminiratne, K.H.W. (1992) 'First Counts, 1991 Census: A Comment on Aboriginal and Torres Strait Islander Population Growth', CAEPR Discussion Paper 24. Canberra: Centre for Aboriginal Economic Policy Research, Australian National University.

Gilbert, K. (1977) *Living Black: Blacks Talk to Kevin Gilbert.* Ringwood, Victoria: Penguin Books.

Gould, R. (1969) *Yiwara: Foragers of the Australian Desert.* New York: Charles Scribner and Sons.

Gray, A. (1990) 'National Estimates of Aboriginal Mortality', in Alan Gray (ed.), *A Matter of Life and Death: Contemporary Aboriginal Mortality.* Canberra: Aboriginal Studies Press.

Hamilton, A. (1981a) 'A Complex Strategical Situation: Gender and Power in Aboriginal Australia,' in N. Grieve and P. Grimshaw (eds), *Australian Women: Feminist Perspectives.* Melbourne: Oxford University Press.

———(1981b) *Nature and Nurture: Aboriginal Child-rearing in North-Central Arnhem Land.* Canberra: Australian Institute of Aboriginal Studies.

Hart, C.W.M. and A. R. Pilling (1960) *The Tiwi of North Australia.* New York: Henry Holt and Company.

Hartwig, M.C. (1978) 'The Theory of Internal Colonialism—The Australian Case', in E.L. Wheelwright and K. Buckley (eds), *Essays in the Political Economy of Australian Capitalism.* Sydney: Australian and New Zealand Book Co.

Hayden, T. (1977) *The Last Tasmanian* (feature film). Directed by Tom Hayden. Tasmania: Artis Film Productions.

Hetzel, B.S. (1980) *Health and Australian Society.* Ringwood, Victoria: Penguin Books.

Hobbes, T. (1968 [1651]) *Leviathan.* Harmondsworth: Penguin Books.

Hobsbawm, E. (1969) *Industry and Empire,* Pelican Economic History of Britain, Volume 3. Harmondsworth: Penguin Books.

Hogg, R. (1990) 'Insights into Aboriginal Mortality in Western New South Wales', in Alan Gray (ed.), *A Matter of Life and Death: Contemporary Aboriginal Mortality.* Canberra: Aboriginal Studies Press.

Honari, M. (1990) 'Causes of Aboriginal Mortality', in Alan Gray (ed.), *A Matter of Life and Death:* Contemporary Aboriginal Mortality. Canberra: Aboriginal Studies Press.

Jenkin, G. (1979) *Conquest of the Ngarrindjeri: The Story of the Lower Murray Lakes Tribes.* Adelaide: Rigby.

Jordan, D.F. (1985) 'Census Categories — Enumeration of Aboriginal People, or Construction of Identity' *Australian Aboriginal Studies* 1: 28-36.

Jones, F. (1991) 'Economic Status of Aboriginal and Other Australians: A Comparison', in J.C. Altman (ed.), *Aboriginal Employment Equity by the Year 2000*. Canberra: Centre for Aboriginal Economic Policy Research, Australian National University.

Jordan, D.F. (1985) 'Census Categories — Enumeration of Aboriginal People, or Construction of Identity', *Australian Aboriginal Studies* 1: 28-36.

Keen, I. (1982) 'The Alligator Rivers Aborigines: Retrospect and Prospect', in R. Jones (ed.), *Northern Australia: Options and Implications*. Canberra: Research School of Pacific Studies, the Australian National University.

———(ed.) (1988) *Being Black: Aboriginal Cultures in 'Settled' Australia*. Canberra: Aboriginal Studies Press.

———(1989) 'Aboriginal Governance', in J.C. Altman (ed.), *Emergent Inequalities in Aboriginal Australia* (Oceania Monograph 38). Sydney: University of Sydney.

Kolig, E. (1982) *The Silent Revolution: The Effects of Modernisation on Australian Aboriginal Religion*. Philadelphia: Institute for the Study of Human Issues, Inc.

Langton, M. (1988) 'Medicine Square', in I. Keen (ed.), *Being Black: Aboriginal Cultures in 'Settled' Australia*. Canberra: Aboriginal Studies Press.

Lee, R.B. (1968) 'What Hunters Do For a Living, or, How to Make Out on Scarce Resources', in R.B. Lee and I. DeVore (eds), *Man the Hunter*. Chicago: Aldine.

Levitus, R. (1982) 'Everybody Bin All Day Work', Unpublished manuscript.

Ligertwood, A. (1984) 'Aborigines in the Criminal Courts', in Peter Hanks and Bryan Keon-Cohen (eds), *Aborigines and the Law: Essays in Memory of Elizabeth Eggleston*. Sydney: Allen and Unwin.

Lippmann, L. (1991) *Generations of Resistance: Aborigines Demand Justice*. Melbourne: Longman Cheshire.

Lyons, Gregory (1984) 'Aboriginal Legal Services ', in Peter Hanks and Bryan Keon-Cohen (eds), *Aborigines and the Law: Essays in Memory of Elizabeth Eggleston*. Sydney: Allen and Unwin.

McBryde, I. (1978) '*Wil-im-ee Moor-ing*: or, where do axes come from?' *Mankind* 11: 354–82.

McCarthy, F.D. (1939) '"Trade"' in Aboriginal Australia and Trade Relationships with Torres Strait, New Guinea and Malaya', *Oceania* 9: 405, 10: 80.

McCarthy, F.D. and MacArthur M. (1960) 'The Food Quest and the Time Factor in Aboriginal Economic Life,' in C.P. Mountford (ed.), *Records of the Australian-American Scientific Expedition to Arnhem Land*, Vol 2: *Anthropology and Nutrition*. Melbourne: Melbourne University Press.

Macdonald, G. (1988) 'A Wiradjuri Fight Story', in I. Keen (ed.) *Being*

Black: Aboriginal Cultures in 'Settled' Australia. Canberra: Australian Institute of Aboriginal Studies.

McGrath, A. (1987) *'Born in the Cattle': Aborigines in Cattle Country.* Sydney: Allen and Unwin.

McKenzie, M. (1976) *Mission to Arnhem Land.* Adelaide: Rigby.

Maddock, K. (1982) *The Australian Aborigines: A Portrait of their Society* Ringwood, Victoria: Penguin Books.

———(1983) *Your Land is Our Land: Aboriginal Land Rights.* Ringwood, Victoria: Penguin Books.

Meehan, B. (1982) *Shell Bed to Shell Midden.* Canberra: Australian Institute of Aboriginal Studies.

Merlan, F. (1981) 'Land, Language and Social Identity in Aboriginal Australia', *Mankind* 13 (2).

Moore, D. (1978) *Islanders and Aborigines at Cape York: An Ethnographic Reconstruction Based on the 1848-50 Rattlesnake Journals of O.W. Brierly and Information he Obtained from Barbara Thomson.* Canberra: Australian Institute of Aboriginal Studies.

Morgan, Sally (1987) *My Place.* Fremantle: Fremantle Arts Centre Press.

Morphy, H. (1984) *Journey to the Crocodile's Nest.* Canberra: Australian Institute of Aboriginal Studies.

Morris, B. (1983) 'From Underemployment to Unemployment: The Changing Role of Aborigines in a Rural Economy', *Mankind* 13 (6): 499–516.

Morris, B. (1988) 'Dhan-gadi Resistance to Assimilation,' in I. Keen (ed.) *Being Black: Aboriginal Cultures in 'Settled' Australia.* Canberra: Australian Institute of Aboriginal Studies.

———(1989) *Domesticating Resistance: The Dhan-gadi Aborigines and the Australian State.* Oxford: Berg.

Mulvaney, J. (1989) *Encounters in Place: Outsiders and Aboriginal Australians 1606-1985.* St Lucia: University of Queensland Press.

Myers, F. (1986) *Pintubi Country, Pintubi Self: Sentiment, Place and Politics among Western Desert Aborigines.* Canberra: Australian Institute of Aboriginal Studies.

Peterson, N. (1976) 'Introduction,' in N. Peterson (ed.), *Tribes and Boundaries in Australia.* Canberra: Australian Institute of Aboriginal Studies.

———(in collaboration with Jeremy Long) (1986) *Australian Territorial Organisation: A Band Perspective.* (Oceania Monographs 30) Sydney: University of Sydney.

Peterson, N. and M. Langton (eds) (1983) *Aborigines, Land and Land Rights.* Canberra: Australian Institute of Aboriginal Studies.

Radcliffe-Brown, A.R. (1930) 'Former Numbers and Distribution of the Australian Aborigines', *Australian Yearbook* 23: 687–96.

Reid, J. (1983) *Sorcerers and Healing Spirits.* Canberra: Australian National University Press.

Reynolds, H. (1987) *Frontier: Aborigines, Settlers and Land.* Sydney: Allen and Unwin.

Roberts, R.G., Jones, R. and Smith, M.A. (1990) 'Thermoluminescence dating of a 50,000-year-old human occupation site in northern Australia', *Nature* 345: 153-56.

Rowley, C.D. (1970) *The Destruction of Aboriginal Society*. Canberra: Australian National University Press.

———(1971) *Outcasts in White Australia: Aboriginal Policy and Practice — Volume II*. Canberra: Australian National University Press.

Rowse, T. (1992) *Remote Possibilities: The Aboriginal Domain and the Administrative Imagination*. Darwin: North Australia Research Unit, Australian National University.

Ryan, L. (1981) *The Aboriginal Tasmanians*. St Lucia: Queensland University Press.

Sahlins, M. (1974) *Stone Age Economics*. London: Tavistock.

Sansom, B. (1982) 'The Aboriginal Commonality', in R.M. Berndt (ed.), *Sites, Rights and Resource Development*. Canberra: Academy of the Social Sciences in Australia.

Schwab, R.G. (1988) 'Ambiguity, Style and Kinship in Adelaide Aboriginal Identity', in I. Keen (ed.), *Being Black: Aboriginal Cultures in 'Settled' Australia*. Canberra: Australian Institute of Aboriginal Studies.

———(1991) 'The "Blackfella Way": Ideology and Practice in an Urban Aboriginal Community', Unpublished PhD thesis, the Australian National University.

Shapiro, W. (1979) *Social Organisation in Aboriginal Australia*. Canberra: Australian National University Press.

Smith, L.R. (1980) *The Aboriginal Population of Australia*. Canberra: Australian National University Press.

Smith, H.M. and Biddle E.H. (1975) *Look Forward not Back: Aborigines in Metropolitan Brisbane 1965–1966*. Canberra: Australian National University Press.

Stevens, F. (1974) *Aborigines in the Northern Territory Cattle Industry*. Canberra: Australian National University Press.

Sutton, P. (1978) 'Wik: Aboriginal Society, Territory and Language at Cape Keerweer, Cape York Peninsula, Australia', Unpublished PhD. dissertation, University of Queensland.

Swain, T. and Rose, D.B. (eds) (1988) *Aboriginal Australians and Christian Missions*. Bedford Park: the Australian Association for the Study of Religions.

Tatz, C. (1979) *Race Politics in Australia*. Armidale: University of New England Press.

Tesfaghiorghis, H. and Gray, A. (1991) 'The Demographic Structure and Location of the Aboriginal Population: Employment Implications', in J.C. Altman (ed.), *Aboriginal Employment Equity by the Year 2000*. Canberra: Centre for Aboriginal Economic Policy Research, Australian National University.

Thiele, S. (1982) *Yugul: An Arnhem Land Cattle Station*. Darwin: North Australia Research Unit, Australian National University.

———(1992) 'Taking a Sociological Approach to Europeanness (Whiteness) and Aboriginality (Blackness)', *Reconsidering Aboriginality* (The Australian Journal of Anthropology Special Issue 2). Sydney: Anthropological Society of New South Wales.

Thomson, N. (1983) 'Aboriginal Infant Mortality', *Australian Aboriginal Studies* 1: 10–15.

Tonkinson, R. (1974) *The Jigalong Mob: Victors of the Desert Crusade*. Benlo Park: Benjamin Cummings.

———(1978) *The Mardudjara Aborigines: Living the Dream in Australia's Desert*. New York: Holt, Rinehart and Winston.

Trigger, D. (1992) *Whitefella Comin': Aboriginal Responses to Colonialism in North Australia*. Cambridge: Cambridge University Press.

Trigger, D., Anderson, C., Lincoln, R.A. and Maitlis, C.E. (1983) 'Mortality Rates in 14 Queensland Aboriginal Reserve Communities: Association with 10 Socioeconomic Variables', *Medical Journal of Australia* 1: 361–65.

van den Berghe, P. (1981) *The Ethnic Phenomenon*. New York: Elsevier.

Walker, John (1987) 'Prison Cells with Revolving Doors: A Judicial or Societal Problem, in Kayleen M. Hazlehurst (ed.), *Ivory Scales: Black Australia and the Law*. Kensington: New South Wales University Press.

Watson, P. (1983) *This Precious Foliage* (Oceania Monograph No. 26).

Western, J. (1983) *Social Inequality in Australian Society*. Melbourne: Macmillan.

White, J.P. and O'Connell, J.F. (1982) *A prehistory of Australia, New Guinea and Sahul*. Sydney: Academic Press.

Wilson, P. (1983) *Black Death, White Hands*. St Lucia: University of Queensland Press.

Wolf, E. (1982) *Europe and the People Without History*. Berkeley: University of California Press.

Wolpe, H. (1975) 'The Theory of Internal Colonialism: The South African Case', in I. Oxaal *et al.* (eds) *Beyond the Sociology of Development*. London: Routledge and Kegan Paul.

Yard, M., B. Moody, Divakaran-Brown, C. and Butler, E. (1990) 'Review of Data Quality for Aboriginal Death Records in South Australia', in Alan Gray (ed.), *A Matter of Life and Death*: Contemporary Aboriginal Mortality. Canberra: Aboriginal Studies Press.

Part II
Socially Patterned Behaviours

Chapter Eight

Education and the Social Order: The Effect of the Private Sector

Don S. Anderson

Ever since the dawn of civilisation, class inequality has existed . . .
Where education is concerned . . . an attempt is made to make the
children of the poor to think themselves inferior to the children of
the rich.

Bertrand Russell, *Education and the Social Order*

Of the 17 million people inhabiting Australia, almost one-fifth are
children enrolled in pre-school, primary school and secondary
school. Another 1.2 million are students enrolled in courses of post-
secondary education. Within these two main sectors of formal
education, schools and post-school, there are structural divisions
which provide a convenient vantage point for the study of education and society. In this chapter we shall use one of these, the
public-private division of schools, to explore three issues:

The extent to which the divisions among different types of school parallel
the main class and cultural contours of Australian society;

Whether schools which serve particular sub-groups in the broader
community are agents for the role socialisation of their students,
inculcating beliefs and dispositions which will make them good
functioning members of particular subcultures;

The effectiveness of private schools, and the impact of the division
between public and private on pupils' scholastic attainment overall.
Before we consider these questions it will be helpful to review the
broad structure of Australian schooling, how it differs from that in
other countries, and how it got that way.

Australia Compared

There are divisions between political regions associated with Australia's federal system, there being separate systems of public schooling in each of the eight states or territories. But such is the homogeneity of Australian society and political systems that there is little variation in structures, practices or outcomes across state borders. There are, however, divisions of considerable social significance within school systems. There is age-related segregation of students into grades and primary and secondary schools; there is some streaming between certain schools according to academic promise; and there is some separation of the sexes. But, as we have intimated, the division which is of greatest sociological interest is that between public and private schools. Almost three-quarters of all school students are in public schools which are the responsibility of the various state education departments; about one-fifth are in Roman Catholic schools (mostly in so-called systemic schools which are organised and generally co-ordinated by state Catholic education offices); and the remaining 7 or 8 per cent of students are in other non-government schools, most of which are associated with religious denominations.

These last are subject to no overall co-ordination except the somewhat light requirements of financial accountability now required because of the extent to which their costs are subsidised from the public purse. Most receive more than half of their recurrent expenditure needs from federal and state governments. Australia, with so many of its children in private schools, is fairly high on the list of educational privatisation at school level, especially among developed countries. Furthermore, the private sector's share increased by about one-quarter during the 1980s.

Of the 350 million children in countries where private education has been permitted, some 50 million are in private schools. At the primary level, just under 12 per cent in both developing and developed countries are in the private sector. But at secondary level there is a large difference, with 28 per cent of children in developing countries in private schools compared with 14 per cent in developed countries. During the 1980s, there were increases in the private share of enrolments in Africa, Europe and Oceania; and a decline in Asia (UNESCO 1989).

Of all Western industrialised countries, only Spain has a private sector as large as Australia's or as influential in the political realm. Furthermore, while the private sector has been growing in Australia, in most other such countries it has generally been static or declining. The most informative comparisons that we can make are those among countries which are not dissimilar, economically or politically. In the present case useful comparisons may be made with other Anglo-American countries: the United Kingdom, the United States, Canada and New Zealand, which share language and other cultural inheritances; and with the three Scandinavian countries, where standards of living and levels of industrial development are not unlike Australia's. Compared with any one of these seven countries, Australia has more than double the proportion of children in private education.

There are four social and educational conditions that make Australia unique, and which together contribute to this level of privatisation. First, unlike the Scandinavian countries, Australia is a highly pluralist country with large religious and ethnic sub-cultures, the Catholic community being the largest. The success of the Catholic authorities in maintaining a separate school system, and in obtaining public subsidies, has become an incentive for other religious and ethnic groups to press for separate schools as a means of transmitting their cultures to successive generations. Secondly, the politics of state aid for education have taken different courses in Australia and the United States. An almost identical provision concerning support for religions in the constitutions of both countries has been interpreted quite differently in each. In Australia the direct funding of religious schools is legal; in the United States it is not. It has been shown by Williams (1984) that the growth of the Australian private sector has closely followed the amount of public subsidies and the consequent fall in the real cost to parents of private schooling.

Thirdly, unlike the United Kingdom, there has been little provision within the Australian public sector for academically selective schools. As we shall see, this has contributed in Australia to a flight of middle class parents from the public to the private sector. And finally, unlike the other Anglo-American countries, historical and geographical circumstances in Australia led to highly centralised and bureaucratically controlled public school systems, causing a sense of powerlessness among public school parents and providing a further excuse, for those who could afford it, to send their children to private schools.

Historical Origins

Australia's public-private school systems have their roots in the beginning of European colonisation of the continent, two hundred years ago. The First Fleet brought not only British civil and military authority, but also spiritual authority in the form of representatives of the Church of England. The latter were inclined to regard themselves as the custodians of the morals and manners, as well as of the religious welfare, of the first white residents and, among other things, soon took initiatives in schooling the young. This monopoly over faith and morals was, before long, challenged by representatives of the Churches of Rome and Scotland, who claimed responsibility for the not-inconsiderable numbers of Scots and Irish whose transgressions had earned them a trip to New South Wales. Because large sections of the population were not being educated even to minimal standards, and because of denominational squabbling over the teaching of religion, the state intervened, exercising its secular authority to ensure that education became more readily accessible. The dual system of Australian education emerged from a conflict between church and state.

It took almost a hundred years after the first settlement for the pattern with which we are now familiar to become established. By that time, social class as well as religion had become a factor associated with division between different sets of schools. In the period 1870-1900, the six colonial administrations, strung out along the southern and eastern coastline, had become exasperated with acrimonious inter-denominational bickering. Emboldened by post-Darwinian religious scepticism and, inspired by newly-emerging democratic sentiments they enacted legislation which, in one form or another required that the government should ensure that there was compulsory, free and secular education. State aid to church schooling ended, for the time being.

Allocation of children to schools according to their religion followed an historic directive of the Roman Catholic bishops in 1879 that Catholic parents should send their children to Catholic schools. This placed on parishes the burden of providing a comprehensive and separate system of education for all Catholic children. Until the 1960s, the costs of Catholic schooling were met from the contribution of religious teachers, fees paid by parents and parish contributions. By the mid-twentieth century around half the children of Catholic parents were attending Catholic schools which, as Encel (1970) points out, was a much higher proportion than in other countries, where the average was more likely to be around 20 per cent.

By the late 1950s, denominational rivalry had diminished and this, together with political upheavals in the Labor Party, contributed to the reintroduction of state aid to private schools. Of special concern at the time was the overcrowding and desperately poor level of education in many Catholic parochial schools. Conservative Prime Minister Menzies, himself the product of an élite private school, was not unsympathetic towards assisting religious schools; more importantly he saw an opportunity to reap political advantage. Financial support for Catholic schools would help capture some of the traditional Catholic Labor vote whose allegiance had been weakened following the 1954 split in the Australian Labor Party.

Following the end of state aid, the Protestant churches also continued to sponsor schools, but their funding came almost entirely from fees, and herein lay the beginning of élite Anglican and non-conformist church schools which, as we shall see, are now noted more for their social distinctiveness than their Christian ethos.

Countries differ in their responses to contemporary pressures on what has been for many an historic balance between the public and private sectors. Among the pressures are tight budgetary constraints. In some countries a strong private sector is a response to excess demand, since governments are unable or unwilling to find the resources to build schools and staff them with trained teachers.

Pressures from minorities are a second reason for renewed interest in private schools, as organised religious and ethnic sub-cultures come to regard public education as an ineffective means of transmitting group identity to the rising generation. Ideological preferences of governments are a third reason for the expansion of the private sector. Following the global economic downturn starting in the mid-1970s, belief in the efficacy of market forces as superior to regulation and planning led a number of countries to favour privatising public institutions, including education.

Private schools may also be regarded as 'lighthouse' institutions, adding diversity to a country's stock of schools, and as a 'safety valve' easing the pressure from those who are disaffected with their state schools. During the 1980s, the terms 'vouchers', 'choice of schools', 'devolution' and 'privatisation' entered the vocabulary of school reformers, especially in Anglo-American countries. In April 1991, in the United States, President Bush made a major policy speech devoted solely to education. He stressed that parents should be free to choose the sort of schooling they wanted for their children, and that public schools should be freed from bureaucratic control. In the United Kingdom, the government of Mrs Thatcher encouraged state schools to 'opt out' of the publicly managed system, becoming in effect unregulated and self-managing, but with their resources still being supplied by government. Following the election of the Major administration, this move is accelerating in the United Kingdom.

Other European countries are devolving authority from central government to regions and individual schools. Sweden, for example, has transferred control of its schools to municipalities with few restrictions on the sorts of schools that will qualify for funding. The small number of private schools in Sweden will be supported. They educate fewer than one per cent of all children at the present time but, under the new dispensation, many more are likely to be established, for example Waldorf (Rudolph Steiner) and Christian community schools.

Privatisation

In the following discussion the terms 'public', 'Catholic' and 'other private' will be used to distinguish the three main classes of school in Australia. The terms originate from administrative practice, and refer to the categories into which the government places schools for the purposes of subsidies. For sociological purposes, a more useful classification would distinguish academically selective schools, whether public or private. Furthermore, schools which serve the aspiring socially élite sector of society would be distinguished from schools whose chief purpose is religious or ethnic cultural maintenance. This classification will be elaborated in the next section; the data are, however, generally not available for these categories, and the administrative classifications must serve our analytic purposes.

In the sense that privatisation means rolling back the power of the state, recent changes in Australia and elsewhere imply that the management of schooling is being privatised. A stronger meaning of privatisation of 'fee for service' applies in some, but not all, of the proposed reforms. One application of 'fee for service' is represented in the idea of educational vouchers. Parents would have entitlement to a set amount of educational services which could be 'cashed' at the school of their choice. The idea has been talked about a great deal since it was first suggested by Milton Friedman (1962), but there are not many places where it has been tried in practice. One version of the voucher idea would allow schools to charge tuition fees in addition to the entitlements. Fee charging private schools that also receive per capita government subsidies represent this form of voucher funding, each additional child entitling the school to a grant. As we have noted, in Australia, where 'freedom to choose' receives strong political support, 28 per cent of all children (the majority of them Catholic) are in schools which are outside the state-managed systems. These schools receive substantial government subsidies. (In both the United States and the United Kingdom, where there have been no direct government subsidies for private schools, the private sector is much smaller, in each case educating approximately 10 per cent of all children.)

Establishment of more private schools is sometimes advocated, notably in some Third World countries, as a means of expanding educational provision without government funding. For example, the World Bank has recommended privately-funded schools as a solution for excess demand, especially for secondary education. In Russia, where until recently there was no private sector, although there were élite public schools, the impact of the financial crisis on education is leading to the rapid development of private schools, some of them subsidised.

In several other countries of the former Eastern bloc, interest in private education is growing as a reaction against state directed schools. Impetus is added to the move as churches try to recover former school properties, as ethnic groups seek to re-establish their traditions among the young, and as impoverished governments seek alternative sources of funding. The benefits expected by reformers from the introduction of market principles include greater effectiveness, greater efficiency and enhancement of parents' freedom to choose. Critics are sceptical, pointing out that there is little evidence to justify the changes, and that they would cause even greater social polarisation of schooling and inequality of educational opportunity.

Whereas effectiveness and efficiency are capable of being evaluated empirically, freedom to choose is ultimately a matter of value preference. Nevertheless, it is regarded as of central importance, particularly in countries where there is a pluralism of religious and ethnic communities. Freedom of choice is also seen by advocates of a market solution not so much as an end in itself but as a means of causing schools to become more efficient.

Types of Public and Private Schools

The most common definition of a private school is that used by UNESCO and the OECD in their statistical surveys of education. Private schools are those not managed by or within the government sector. Government aided schools are classified with the private sector if they are privately managed. This leaves open the question of the proportion of funding from public sources. A few countries like Denmark and Australia grant substantial subsidies to religious and other schools outside the publicly managed sector; elsewhere, as in New Zealand and the United Kingdom, approved religious schools are fully funded within the public sector, but are free to retain their special character. The definition also leaves aside the question of autonomy: whether a private school is one that stands alone or whether it may be part of a system managed by some non-state authority. Catholic schools and Seventh Day Adventist schools often belong to managed systems, sometimes involving bureaucratic control similar to that likely to be found in public school ones. It is misleading to talk of the public and private sectors, since if there is a similarity of sorts of school within each, there can be as much variation within the sectors as there is between them. For the purposes of a social analysis it is helpful to consider the social functions of schooling and to distinguish the following 'ideal types', most of which are represented to a greater or lesser extent in both the public and private sectors:

- Academically selective schools for pupils of high ability;
- Socially selective schools which, because of their location, high fees or selection practices, recruit children of greater-than-average social status, and serve an élite function in the sociological sense of the term;
- Schools of commitment which cater for the children of particular religious or ethnic subsectors of a society;
- Community schools which are open to all children in a particular neighbourhood;
- 'Free' or alternative schools which espouse some particular educational or social philosophy;
- Market schools run by their owners as a business enterprise;
- Charity schools sponsored by philanthropic organisations for children who are handicapped, physically, socially or intellectually.

Many schools exhibit more than one of these functions but there is usually a dominating characteristic. Academically selective schools are to be found in both the public and private sectors of some countries. In public school systems there is often contention over whether all schools should be comprehensive, whether schools should be specialised or whether there should be a few schools for pupils of outstanding ability. Sometimes the euphemisms 'technical' or 'general' are used for schools or streams intended for children of lesser ability. Socially selective schools are usually found in the private sector, high fees helping to deter enrolments from poorer families. Some public schools acquire an élite character because of residential segregation. Because many socially selective private schools also aim to prepare their pupils for university entrance, there tends to be an overlap between social and academic élites. As will be seen later, it is the élite categories of schools which can cause particular difficulties for educational planning. Schools of commitment function to protect and reproduce a particular religious or other subculture within the wider society. Most such schools are religious but, with the recent resurgence of ethnic minorities in many countries, there is renewed interest in using education as a means of promoting ethnic identity. Public schools are not necessarily precluded from teaching religion or giving recognition in the curriculum to other subcultures. They find it difficult, however, when their children represent diverse backgrounds.

Community schools are open to all children from a neighbourhood and are held to represent values such as tolerance, understanding of others and social cohesion. Nearly all such schools are in the public sector. Free or alternative schools are similar to schools of commitment except that they attract parents who subscribe to a particular educational philosophy rather than those from a coherent subculture. They are more likely to be in the private sector, but in recent years have developed in some public sectors where central control has been relaxed.

Market or free enterprise schools run by their owners to make money (as well as to provide an educational service) are not found as frequently today as they were in the nineteenth and early twentieth century. These days the most common examples tend to be specialist or vocational schools teaching, for example, computing or accountancy. Some cater for pupils who have been unable to gain entry to the academic programs of regular schools or university entrance.

Charity schools are also less frequently found today in developed countries, but they were once common. They offered education to children who were poor or otherwise handicapped. In many countries the service once provided by charity schools has been taken over by free public schools, and by special schools for the handicapped which are most frequently found in the public sector. In thinking about education and social order it is useful to have in mind the various functions served by schools and the educational or social objectives that are at issue.

Social and Cultural Influences

The shift from public to private in Australia has by no means been an even movement across the social landscape. For 150 years, élite private schools have been patronised by the wealthier and more influential. In the last couple of decades, they have attracted upwardly mobile families at a rate which has caused them to double their share of the market.

The sociologists' holy trinity of social class indicators, occupational status, level of education and income, is linked with parents' choices of the sort of school they want for their children. For example, the 1976 Census reveals that whereas family incomes over $20,000 were 'enjoyed' by only around 9 per cent of public school children, and 15 per cent of Catholic school children, some 50 per cent of private school families were in this bracket. The association would be sharper if the Census had asked about family wealth rather than just income.

Comparisons of the Censuses of 1976 and 1986 show that the new clients are concentrated in the gentrified suburbs of the capital cities. In some regions the proportion of resident children attending non-government schools has trebled. A map of Sydney and Melbourne, shaded according to the intensity of residents' participation in private schools, would coincide closely with another showing the social standing of the suburbs, based on averages of household income, educational levels and property values. For example, a child living in Woollahra or Kew is about six times more likely to attend a private school than a child living in Sunshine or Bankstown.

Advocates of a fully-deregulated school system assume that parents will assess schools on their educational merits and that competition will be a spur for schools to become more efficient; otherwise they will go to the wall. But in a society which is both pluralist and socially stratified, parents will be inclined towards schools which they see as congruent with their position in the community, to a large extent irrespective of educational judgements. This observation leads us to a more sociological answer to the question of school choice. It does not need a sophisticated study to reveal that the overwhelming majority of students in the subsidised sector are there because they belong to Catholic families.

From a Catholic perspective, their schools are community schools, providing for a Catholic neighbourhood. They are also, of course, schools of subcultural maintenance in a society where a large minority (27 per cent) of the population is Catholic, and where for over 100 years the church has placed great pressure on Catholic families to use Catholic schools. Inglis, writing of the late nineteenth century, said that it was becoming normal for Catholic and non-Catholic children to be strangers. In 1890, possibly half the children of Catholics were attending state schools. The proportion dropped to one-third by 1933, and by 1950 to about one-fifth, of whom almost half were in country areas (quoted in Mol 1985). More recent information from

Censuses and surveys indicates that the sources used by Inglis over estimated the proportions of children from Catholic families who were in Catholic schools, at least since the 1950s.

While the social profile of Catholic schools approximates much more closely that of public schools than to other private, there are élite schools within the Catholic sector. If these are put aside the remaining, mainly parochial, Catholic schools would still exhibit a social profile closer to, but still 'above', that of public schools. The Catholic sector has increased by about 17 per cent since 1975, and constitutes the second large growth area in the non-public sector. This contrasts with the trend in the United States, where the proportion of children in Catholic schools has declined.

Most of the newcomers to Catholic schooling in Australia are recruited from the children of Catholic families who are in public schools, although there is also some demand from non-Catholic children. Since 1976, the Census has only asked whether schooling was government or non-government, not whether it was Catholic, so is not possible to be precise about denominational dimensions of the 'shift to private'. The Censuses do show, however, that the suburban regions where growth of participation in Catholic schooling is taking place are of intermediate social standing. This suggests that Catholic school authorities are having difficulty keeping up in the newer Western suburbs of Sydney and Melbourne, and maybe that even their modest tuition fees are something of a deterrent in working class suburbs.

Not all the clients of non-Catholic private schools are well off. Some of the poorest schools in Australia have been set up by parents following alternative lifestyles in northern New South Wales communes and elsewhere. And the schools recently set up by groups with a strong commitment to ethnic or sect-type cultures cater in the main for families of average or below-average means.

In both Australia and the United States, schools sponsored by fundamentalist Christian religions comprise the fastest-growing private group. They are relative newcomers to the private sector and include some evangelicals whose predecessors supported public schooling as an expression of common citizenship. Seventh Day Adventists who, along with the Catholic Church, have been the most successful in getting members to send their children to their own schools, are also expanding in Australia. We may also find, when the data are analysed, that migrants, or rather the children of migrants, are prominent in the shift from public to private. A small proportion of these will be found in ethnic schools; by far the greater number are likely, as their economic circumstances change, to shift from public to élite private schools.

Some idea of the extent of the shift from public to private from one generation to the next is revealed in a national longitudinal study of individuals who commenced full-time university studies in the mid-1960s (Anderson *et al.* 1982). (This study will be used several times in the next two sections.) Fifteen years after they graduated, the former students in the study, now mainly professionals in engineering, law, medicine and teaching, were asked about the type of school they had in mind for their own children. There is some continuity of school type between one generation and the next, but more striking is the shift from both public and Catholic to non-Catholic private. The percentages of respondents who themselves had attended non-Catholic private schools and who sent, or intend to send, their children to a similar type of school are: medicine 37 and 73, law 36 and 57, engineering 17 and 41, teaching 17 and 32. Teaching is the only profession in which a majority of the sample both attended public school and intended sending their children to public school.

The evidence reviewed in this section cannot resolve the question of whether schools serve to reproduce the existing social order or whether they provide a vehicle for social mobility. As we have seen, élite private schools on balance recruit from the materially better-positioned sections of society and their graduates are more likely than others to enter high prestige professions. We shall see in the next section that they also impart some distinctive values. Furthermore, the longitudinal study showed that 'privilege' continues across generations. All of this is not inconsistent with the productionist interpretation of schooling.

When the focus is on the individual rather than the group, it is clear that mobility is not entirely absent. For example about half the students in the national longitudinal study had been to public schools, and 12 per cent came from families where the father was an unskilled manual worker: engineering 6 per cent, law 5 per cent, medicine 8 per cent and teaching 19 per cent. Evidence of social mobility is not inconsistent with a stable class structure which persists across generations. Those who are well positioned in the hierarchy make sure their children get a flying start, but this does not completely prevent able students from poor families advancing their life chances through good academic performance at school.

Socialisation

The concepts of socialisation and role theory are closely connected. Here we shall use 'role' in the sense defined by Biddle (1979): 'those behaviours characteristic of one or more persons in context', and socialisation to mean those environmentally-induced beliefs, preferences, skills, norms and dispositions which are characteristic of a particular social system, the possession of which facilitates an individual's participation in that system. In the case of occupations, socialisation is like Procrustes with his bed, lopping off superfluous members and stretching others, until the recruit fits the role.

As we have seen, private schools in Australia are generally used by parents wishing to maintain or advance their children's position in the social order, or who regard public schools as not providing the particular religious, educational or cultural emphases they desire for their children. Only the latter objectives appear in official or formal statements of objectives of private schools. These may be expressed in terms of transmitting the Christian faith, or, in the case of élite non-Catholic private schools, educating students in a Christian ethos. Scholastic excellence and character development also feature prominently in their statements of objectives. Many recently established private schools are also concerned with the cultural maintenance of particular religious sects or ethnic groups.

But all social institutions also serve unofficial or unstated purposes, and schools are no exception. As has been noted, the so-called hidden agenda of a significant set of private schools may be inferred from the social profile of the families which use them. Partridge (1968), in analysing the social functions of non-Catholic private schools, concluded that 'motives connected with social exclusiveness are amongst the strongest forces that have sustained them'. He went on to observe that it is a little odd that it should be the churches that maintain institutions which gratify ambitions of social pride and exclusiveness. Similar conclusions concerning the functioning of non-Catholic private schools have been reached by Martin (1957), who saw them performing 'the task of preparing the child to take his place among the highest status members of the society by teaching him their customs, imbuing him with their values, and providing him with friends and contacts within this section of society'. Encel (1970) makes similar observations after an analysis in which he concludes that the most distinctive contribution of the education system to inequality is 'through the medium of private schools which help to create and perpetuate class, religious and economic divisions'.

The socialisation outcomes which might be expected from such analyses of the social functions of private schools would include conservative political values, career ambitions in the more prestigious occupations and, in accord with official objectives, religious beliefs and behaviour.

Evidence from numerous surveys shows that people who have

attended non-Catholic private schools are, on average, disposed to conservative political preferences, while former Catholic school and public school students are likely to be more social democratic. For example, the ANU's National Social Science Survey (NSSS) study reported over 40 per cent of former non-Catholic school respondents identifying themselves as Right of centre compared with under 30 per cent of former Catholic and public school students (Anderson 1988). Studies of political party preference made in the late 1970s reached similar conclusions. For example, the Aitkin (1982) data set shows that identification with the political Right was even slightly higher than it is now for non-Catholic school students (44 per cent), identical for public school (28 per cent), but higher than now for Catholic school (41 per cent). Voting preferences were similar: support for the ALP was public, 38 per cent; Catholic, 40 per cent; and other private, 19 per cent.

The longitudinal study of university students who were in Australian universities in the mid-1960s reported associations between type of school and voting preference which were not dissimilar to the above figures. In 1984, a follow-up revealed that relative political positions of the three school types remained much the same, although the graduates generally were less conservative than when they were students.

The longitudinal study also showed that students who had attended non-Catholic private schools were more likely to choose a career in law or medicine than in the less prestigious professions, that they expected to earn higher incomes and, consistent with this, that they were more likely to have rated financial rewards as having been important when they made their career decisions. These results are probably best interpreted as 'knowing the ropes' rather than being due to any differences of altruistic disposition between the school types. Survey evidence generally shows only slight differences between types of school with respect to such motives. The NSSS shows, for instance, that on the question of paying more taxes so as to improve the quality of social services, agreement was expressed by 78 per cent from public schools, 85 per cent from Catholic schools, and 75 per cent from non-Catholic private schools.

Not unexpectedly, people who have attended Catholic schools report more frequent church attendance and greater strength of belief in God than students who have attended public schools. It may be of surprise to some, however, to learn that there is not much difference between public school students and non-Catholic private school students in these respects.

In a major study of religion in Australia, Mol (1985) concluded that Catholic schools make a significant contribution to the religious development of their students. The problem with this conclusion, as with all the associations which have been presented so far in this section, is that there is no effective control for other possible influences. The inference that Catholic school, or any other type of school, is somehow the cause of particular attitudes may be flawed because of unknown conditions which are the source of both choice of a particular school and of certain beliefs. The obvious possibility in the case of religion is that the underlying influence is family, and that religious families both send their children to church schools and inculcate religious beliefs. The evidence is conflicting. Mol, for instance, found that 80 per cent of his respondents who had attended parochial schools and who had parents who were regular church attenders, had no doubts about the existence of God. The proportions were lower, around 60-70 per cent, among Catholics, who had either no parochial education or non-church-attending parents. Unfortunately the numbers involved in Mol's study are so few that differences of this magnitude could simply be due to chance fluctuation.

In the matter of church attendance, Aitkin's surveys reveal that Catholics are considerably more frequent attenders than non-Catholics, whether or not they had attended Catholic schools. Those who had attended Catholic schools were somewhat more frequent than Catholics who had attended public schools. This certainly points to a family effect, but leaves open the question of the possibility of an additional contribution from school.

Further evidence is provided by re-analysis of an interesting survey of school students in Victoria which was conducted by Poole (1983). In connection with students choosing a job, she asked about the importance of a variety of motives such as usefulness to the community, status, wages, security, interest and independence. Among these considerations was 'serving God'. Assuming that those students who gave this item a high rating would have some religious commitment, 'serving God' can be used as an indication of religious purpose.

Many students at Catholic schools rated 'serving God' as important in connection with choosing a job: 59 per cent of the 14-year-olds and 44 per cent of the 17-year-olds. Next, however, were not the students from other private schools, despite their avowedly religious objectives, but students from public technical schools (which recruit from a lower SES population than high schools), where 41 per cent of the 14-year-olds and 40 percent of the 17-year-olds averred that 'serving God' was an important consideration when it came to choosing a career. In this respect other private schools were much more like public high schools, both having substantially fewer students with this particular religious motivation (30 per cent and 12 per cent in high schools, 23 per cent and 24 per cent in other private schools).

Thus we have the odd result that the officially Christian Catholic schools and the officially secular public technical schools are the ones where students appear to be most religious; officially Christian other private schools and officially secular public high schools are the least religious. The evidence points to family rather than school as the source of the career motive 'serving God', but it does not, of course, rule out school influence.

The national longitudinal study of university students is one of the few which attempts a rigorous statistical control of variables which might explain the connection between type of school and the socialisation outcomes which we have been considering — political, career and religious. Using regression methods to control for family, social and religious background, it was concluded that, once account is taken of family background, especially father's and mother's denomination and attendance, the statistically significant connection of school with religious feeling vanishes.

This conclusion is in line with the findings of Greeley (1960) and his associates in the United States, and with the data of Mol in Australia. Of course, we cannot conclude that school has no effect, but simply that this study and others like it have been unable to find evidence of one. At different times, with different measures, or with different samples, it is possible that connections between school and religious behaviour will be found and will remain even when allowance is made for family religion. (That of course would not prove that schools were having an effect since it always remains possible that there is some other influence at work not represented in the analysis, such an influence being responsible for both school type and apparent school effects.)

Whereas it is difficult to find evidence that religious schools influence their students over and above family influence, the longitudinal study suggests that the non-Catholic private schools may influence political and career attitudes net of background effects. Thus, private school remains related to political conservatism after allowance is made for effects from the father's occupation and income. Similarly, private school seems to enhance inclination to choose medicine rather than teaching, to have regard for financial rewards in making a career choice, to expect a high income in ten years' time, and to regard having been to a private school as important for career advancement (Anderson 1988b).

In these respects experience at non-Catholic private schools appears to be producing and reinforcing in students values and beliefs which are not inconsistent with the position in the social order which they will attain by virtue of their family. To the extent that it is possible to generalise from the evidence from this one study, it appears that school not only advances students who possess what Bourdieu (1977) has termed 'cultural capital', it also influences them.

Effectiveness

It is rarely easy to determine how well the official objectives of a school or set of schools are attained, because purposes vary a great deal, and because precise statements of objectives tend to be elusive. In trying to settle the argument over the relative merits of public and private schools, researchers have focused mostly on scholastic attainment.

Research findings are still being contested in the scholarly literature but, for practical purposes, the answers are pretty clear: there is no reliable evidence which justifies the conclusion that either public or private management consistently leads to more effective pedagogy. Often there is a slight statistical margin in favour of private. But critics point out that it is not justified to attribute this to superior teaching because 'all other things' are not equal — there almost always being critical differences in the family backgrounds and abilities of pupils recruited to public and private. There can never be certainty that all such factors have been identified and allowed for in the statistical equations. An example often cited is the freedom that private schools generally have to maximise their outcomes by selecting those pupils who are most likely to succeed and by discarding pupils whose performance or behaviour is not up to scratch. These practices are most likely to be found among élite private schools.

In any event the average statistical differences between sectors are so small that they do not provide any practical basis for planners to favour one sector over the other. Furthermore the variation of scholastic attainment between the public and private sectors is far less than the variation within public or private. It follows from this that parents seeking a school which will maximise their children's scholastic chances should be advised to forget about whether a school is public or private and evaluate those schools that are available on their merits.

A connection between sociological processes and educational outcome is demonstrated in studies which relate the social mix of a school to students' performance. Children of relatively poor scholastic promise are liable to have their performance lifted when they are in a class with a critical core of able and well-motivated pupils, as Murnane (1986) showed in a re-analysis of Coleman's study, *High School and Beyond*, in the United States. But if this core is lost, the average of the remainder is likely to decline. The connection is not a linear one: the loss of two or three high fliers makes little difference, but there comes a point when the group's learning dynamics change and average performance plunges. Continued privatisation of Australian schooling, with the consequent loss to public schools of pupils well endowed with 'cultural capital', may lead to public education being left with the residual role of educating those children who are not catered for by the private sector. These would be largely children from poor families, children who live in areas remote from private schools, and children who are handicapped. Should this occur, public schooling would approximate to the 'charity schools' of our ideal typology.

Evidence suggesting that the process may be approaching a critical point comes from a series of longitudinal studies carried out by the Australian Council for Educational Research (1991). During the 1980s, when retention of secondary students to Year 12 doubled, and the university system grew by 50 per cent, nearly all the indicators of participation in higher education by under-represented groups such as country residents, women, migrants, Aborigines and those with handicaps, showed an increase. The one category where transition from Year 12 to university declined was 'public school'.

The likely explanation is that, due to middle class flight, many public schools are losing their critical mass of able and motivated students, with a consequent drop in the scholastic attainment of many who remain to a point below the level necessary for university admission.

There is a policy dilemma here, because the option to choose private education means that individual interests and collective interests diverge. Parents who take their children from the community public school and put them in an élite school may well be acting rationally if their aim is to gain a competitive edge in the race for university entry. But the effect of a large number of such decisions impoverishes public schools to the point where overall quality drops as the critical mass of able and well motivated pupils in many schools is lost. In other words, the aggregate of a host of individual decisions, each made in the interests of advancing a particular child's life chances, does not lead to the most effective system. In education it is the back of Adam Smith's invisible hand that is at work.

References

Aitkin, Don (1982) *Stability and Change in Australian Politics*. Canberra: Australian National University Press.

Anderson, D.S. (1988) 'The Influence of Public and Private Schools on Religious and Social Attitudes', in Jonathan Kelley and Clive Bean (eds), *Australian Attitudes: Social and Political Analyses from the National Social Science Survey*. Sydney: Allen and Unwin.

———(1988b) 'Values, Religion, Social Class and Choice of Private School in Australia', *International Journal of Educational Research* 12 (4): 351–73.

Anderson, D.S., Carpenter, P.G., Western, J.S. and Williams, T.H. (1982) 'Professional Socialisation in Training and Work', Canberra: Working Papers in Sociology, Department of Sociology, RSSS, Australian National University.

Australian Council for Educational Research (1991) 'Higher Education in the 80s', mimeo.

Biddle, B.J. (1979) *Role Theory: Expectations, Identities, and Behaviours*. New York: Academic Press.

Bourdieu, P. (1977) 'Cultural Reproduction and Social Reproduction', in J. Karabel and A.H. Halsey (eds), *Power and Ideology in Education*. New York: Oxford University Press.

Encel, S. (1970) 'Education and Society' in A.F. Davies and S. Encel (eds), *Australian Society: A Sociological Introduction*. Melbourne: Cheshire.

Friedman, Milton (1962) *Capitalism and Freedom*. Chicago: University of Chicago Press.

Greeley, Andrew M. and Rossi, Peter H. (1966) *The Education of Catholic Americans*. Chicago: Aldine.

Martin, Jean I. (1957) 'Marriage, the Family and Class' in A.P. Elkin (ed.), *Marriage and the Family in Australia*. Sydney: Angus and Robertson.

Mol, Hans (1985) *The Faith of Australians*. Sydney: Allen and Unwin.

Murnane, Richard J. (1986) 'Comparisons of Private and Public Schools: What Can We Learn?', in Daniel C. Levy (ed.), *Private Education*. Oxford: Oxford University Press.

Partridge, P.H. (1968) *Society, Schools and Progress in Australia*. London: Pergamon.

Poole, Millicent E. (1983) *Youth: Expectations and Transition*. London: Routledge and Kegan Paul.

Radford, W.C. and Wilkes, R.E. (1975) *School Leavers in Australia 1971–1972*. Melbourne: ACER.

UNESCO (1989) *Development of Private Enrolment First and Second Level Education 1975-1985*. Paris: UNESCO.

Williams, R. (1984) 'The Economic Determinants of Private Schooling in Australia,' Discussion Paper 94, Centre for Economic Policy Research, Australian National University, April.

Chapter Nine

Work, Employment and Labour in Australian Society

Paul Boreham and Richard Hall

Since the early decades of this century the leading capitalist industrial societies have witnessed a transformation in the organisation of work, in patterns of participation in the labour market, and in relationships between employers and employees in the processes of production. In the 1990s, the world of work continues to be characterised by change: calls for increasingly flexible production techniques have been made in the context of a reduction in government regulation in many areas of the economy and in labour markets and industrial relations in particular. One of the consequences of these changes that is now becoming apparent is that enterprises have become more exposed to product market fluctuations, and workers have been increasingly exposed to hostile labour market conditions characterised by widespread unemployment and underemployment. In this changed context of employment there is little doubt that work remains of crucial significance in the explanation of contemporary social life (Therborn 1986a: 123–24). In most of the advanced capitalist countries, labour force participation has been greater at some point in the 1980s than in any previous decade. Workers continue to organise in unions and unions continue to engage in struggles with employers in both industrial and political arenas. Issues directly related to work, of which unemployment is the most prominent example, continue to be a central preoccupation of the political system and the policy process.

Labour, Capital and the State

The pre-eminent classical account of work and its place in society is that provided by Marx. He argued that humans were distinguished by their capacity to produce the means of their own subsistence, and that productive activity constituted the definitive expression of humanity. This essential quality of work as self-realisation was, however, seen to be distorted in industrial society because work in capitalism, *wage labour*, was both alienating and exploitative. Marx (1867) argued that work was inherently *exploitative* because in the capitalist labour process workers, through their labour, add a value to the product as a commodity that is greater than the value of their compensation in the form of the wage. The extra or *surplus value* produced is appropriated by the owner of the means of production, the capitalist, as profit when the commodity is sold. Thus the exploitative character of the wage labour relation generates conflict not only between workers and capitalists at the point of production but also, given the dependence of workers on wage labour as the source of the means for securing their subsistence generally, across society as a whole.

The character of capitalism has been transformed in three senses from the 'classical' version studied by Marx: first, markets and production units have been altered through the emergence of large-scale corporations and corporate ownership networks that (very often) span numerous state economies; second, the role of the state in the economy and in the regulation of the labour-capital relation has expanded; third, the social circumstances of the working class have altered, through changing employment patterns and different forms of access to significant resources, such as education. Any assessment of change and continuity in Australian society must accept the potential impact of these broad developments. Nevertheless, the continuing antagonism between capital and labour in contemporary capitalism is manifested in the manner in which work is organised and controlled, or what is termed the labour process, in labour markets and across the economy more generally.

Recent theories have attempted to relate these areas of conflict with one another and to significant social outcomes. 'Labour' and 'capital' have been used to describe the conflicting tendencies or forces in capitalist political economy, and used to explain the particular social structures and social outcomes that characterise different societies (Korpi 1985). This research has suggested that, among other things, capital and labour are engaged in a continuous process of struggle over the degree of control and autonomy enjoyed by workers (in the labour process), over the wages and conditions and security of jobs (in labour markets), and over the economic policies that determine the extent to which welfare services and resources are provided as a right of citizenship by the state or, alternatively, the extent to which these goods must be purchased in markets with the income and wealth that accrues to individuals. Labour-capital relations in any given society are understood as the expression of these continuing struggles, and the relative power of capital and labour has been used to explain the different economic and social outcomes which characterise different societies.

The power of organised groups and individuals to influence prices and conditions in markets, and to use their resources to dominate these markets, is an outcome of these processes of conflict and accommodation. Moreover, the pattern of outcomes may be significantly reinforced if it is supported by the state through law and regulation (Crouch 1977). On the other hand, an important aspect of the extension of political democracy in capitalist societies has been that individuals who may be disadvantaged in the market may be collectively empowered through the political process. For individual workers, trade unions and labour parties are the vehicles of such empowerment. In short, democratic capitalist societies provide the basis for a greater degree of *political* equality than they do for equalities in power based on market status. State intervention may thus be viewed as a countervailing force to that of the market. It is for this reason that the state and its institutions have been an arena of negotiation and struggle over the regulation of employment. Contemporary labour movements in Western societies have therefore pursued a blend of *industrial* strategies which have sought to improve the material conditions for workers at work, and *political* strategies which have aimed to introduce social policies favourable to wage earners, their dependants and those needing state welfare.

Extensive empirical research undertaken throughout the 1970s and 1980s indicates that various dimensions of labour movement strength, indicated by high rates of unionisation or union movement centralisation, have been important factors in the achievement of national economic and social policy performance and, in particular, low levels of unemployment (Cameron 1984; Paloheimo 1990; Boreham and Compston 1992). Other studies have indicated the importance of broader economic planning institutions sometimes referred to as 'neo-corporatist' in providing a formal role for labour in the formulation of national economic policies (Korpi 1983; Esping-Andersen 1985, 1990; Clegg *et al.* 1986). In sum, these studies have served to underline the importance of the participation of the major actors representing labour and capital in the institutions of state policy making for the achievement of national economic outcomes.

Alongside the research into comparative political economy, other studies have pointed to various changes in the economic and industrial conditions of contemporary capitalism that mediate the links between, on the one hand, the power of labour and, on the other, economic and social outcomes. A broad range of transformations, particularly since 1945, has been identified as altering the character of industrialism: the relative decline of the production of goods and the relative increase in the provision of services; the impact of technological innovation and the introduction of new methods of production that have changed if not reduced the role of labour in production; and (closely associated with these developments) the proliferation of non-manual 'white collar' occupations at the expense of manual 'blue collar' jobs (Badham 1986: 72). Again, while the extent and implications of these changes is disputed, some particular theories regarding the nature of contemporary industrialism can provide a focus for the subsequent analysis of patterns of work, employment and labour in Australia.

The Labour Process and Contemporary Work Organisation

During the 1960s, a growing concern with the processes through which work was organised and controlled manifested itself in a wave of industrial conflict. The key issues at the centre of this were also broader in focus than simply concerns with the economic rewards from work. It was the nature of the job itself that was at stake in these often bitter disputes: questions concerning the organisation of production (the extreme division of labour through which work activities were broken up into their most trivial components); the relations of authority at the workplace (the existence of elaborate hierarchies which eliminated most of the discretion available to individual workers); and the control of work processes (the speed of production lines and other technologies which determined the flow and pace of work).

The seminal contribution to the analysis of these issues was the work of Braverman, who in *Labor and Monopoly Capital* (1974) combined a renewed analysis of Marx's account of changes in the mode of production with an explanation of what he called the degradation of modern labour. Labour process theory is concerned with the organisational and management processes through which the capacity to work (labour power) is converted into actual work effort. In essence, Braverman argued that the practice of management was focused on the division of the work process into the greatest number of constituent parts so that broader knowledge and skills were removed from workers who would become deskilled operatives. Through this process, the major tasks of conception and control of production would become the sole prerogative of management. These arrangements would be facilitated by the application of new technologies in the workplace and the refinement of organisational structures across both industrial blue collar and white collar occupations.

The processes described by Braverman and others as *deskilling* (Clawson 1980; Zimbalist 1979) have been subject to further critique and analysis on a number of dimensions. First, studies by Friedman (1977), Edwards (1979) and Burawoy (1979) have indicated that control over the labour process has impacted on the labour force in a much more uneven fashion than the unidirectional process of deskilling emphasised by Braverman. The general argument is that managerial practices will range from direct personal control to strategies described by Friedman as 'responsible autonomy', in which workers central to the firm's operations are allowed a degree of discretion in return for adopting a responsible attitude towards their work. Edwards points out that control is thus embedded in the social and organisational structure of the workplace and that forms of control reflect changes in the industrial and political power of particular groups of workers and employers. Whatever the cogency of these critiques, recent reviews of the labour process literature (Thompson 1989; Bray and Littler 1988; Knights and Willmott 1990) have concluded that the deskilling thesis is supported by the evidence from the majority of studies undertaken during the period characterised by the modern factory and assembly line production which has been labelled 'Fordism', and which extends well into the 1970s.

In the 1980s, the work of Piore and Sabel (1984) initiated a change of emphasis. These authors and others argued that, where modern production technologies have been used to substantially lower the skill and quality of labour, this has resulted in a lack of flexibility, since workers do not have sufficient skills either to contribute to the decision making process affecting their work, or to react quickly to modify or repair production processes. It is said to be precisely these skills which are important in a changed climate of production in which new materials, technologies and production methods allow a more immediate reaction to consumer demands for new specialised products. The term *flexible specialisation* is used by Piore and Sabel to describe an alternative *post-Fordist* perspective which allows workers a greater degree of control over the immediate labour process and provides for multiskilling.

Theories of post-Fordism have argued that production systems in advanced capitalist countries have shifted from an emphasis on the mass production of single product types based on an extreme division of labour to an emphasis on small batch production of more specialised and 'customised' products, based on a decentralised, more flexibly skilled workforce. Such theories of flexible specialisation have considerable implications for the analysis of labour processes and labour markets. With respect to the former, it is argued that workers are becoming more *functionally flexible*, acquiring and developing a diversity of skills appropriate to constant changes in the production priorities of 'flexible firms' (Atkinson 1985). With respect to the latter, it has been argued that employers require greater flexibility in their capacity to engage, dismiss and deploy labour. These trends have been related to the cultivation of labour markets that are internal to particular firms in which a *core* of privileged workers are employed, and other labour markets that are external to the firm and constituted by a *periphery* of less skilled, marginalised workers who can be drawn on for temporary requirements.

The universality and significance of these alleged developments has received a great deal of critical attention in the literature (see e.g. Pollert 1991; Bramble 1988; Lever-Tracy 1988). Some of the benefits derived from these changes also need to be considered alongside the increasing participation of women in the labour force and the proliferation of 'atypical' forms of part-time and casual employment (Dawson and Turner 1989). It appears to be the case that the feminisation of certain occupations is closely associated with the cultivation of peripheral labour markets and the proliferation of relatively insecure, low skill, low trust employment.

Labour Markets and Employment Conditions

The labour market is one of the first structural elements of modern society that is personally encountered by all people who seek employment. Discussion of labour markets in the literature of sociology and economics has portrayed them as structures of constraint and choice. Studies from economics draw on a set of assumptions concerning a system of free and equal exchange, based on informed rational choices matching individual interests and skills with wages and conditions. These exchanges occur in markets conceptually abstracted from any context of social relations which might structure them. An important variant of these studies stresses the importance of *human capital* in the sense that occupational status and earnings are represented as a return on investment by individuals in education, vocational credentials and skill.

Much of the sociological literature, on the other hand, is critical of such an individualistic approach to the social, cultural and political divisions which empirically structure inequalities of access and reward in labour markets. A number of contributions have therefore sought to clarify a theoretical perspective on these social dimensions of labour market organisation. First, an institutionalist perspective associated with the work of Kerr (1954) proposes separate and competing labour markets in which boundaries of access are established by the formal rules and informal conventions of companies and trade unions, by collective agreements and by the actions of governments.

A second perspective builds on the notion of a dual labour market in which the structured inequalities are not only horizontal, as in the institutionalist model, but also vertical. Importantly, these processes are viewed as outcomes of the structural effects of jobs rather than individual attributes, as in the human capital model. Dualist perspectives offer a model of the labour market divided into two major segments. The *primary sector* is characterised by stability, relatively good wages and working conditions, and career paths often based on skills acquired on the job. Firms in this sector are usually larger organisations, often in the public sector, and highly unionised. *Secondary sector* jobs have only limited promotion opportunities, wages and conditions are relatively poor, and there is likely to be a high degree of turnover. The secondary sector largely consists of small, labour-intensive firms operating in highly competitive conditions with low rates of unionisation. They provide the majority of jobs requiring low qualifications and little opportunity for the development of skills through on-the-job training or through participation in decisions about product or organisational design. These are jobs whose incumbents are readily and easily fired and rehired as a result of fluctuations in the business cycle. Employees working under these conditions are placed in situations of considerable economic vulnerability, from which opportunities for escape are limited.

Significant changes have taken place in the way work is organised in modern societies, which reflect the utility of evolving labour market structures for management flexibility. A great deal of white collar work which formerly enjoyed primary sector status is now subject to restructuring in internal labour markets where wages and conditions of secondary workers reflect the peripheral status of such work. It is important to maintain a clear distinction between the propensities of these jobs and the characteristics of those who hold them. The unattractive features of such jobs are not a product of their incumbency by workers who are regarded as marginal, but because they are jobs characterised by conditions which only marginalised workers are forced to accept. These processes are portrayed in a model of labour market segmentation which demonstrates the manner in which social divisions overlap with labour market structure.

The structural inequality revealed in segmented labour markets derives from social and political processes in the wider society. As a result of these, certain categories of people acquire labour market status while other categories are generally excluded from positions of authority and status at work. It is important to focus here on the relationship between the manner in which the labour process is organised and forms of social stratification in spheres outside work. It is in this way that specific relations of status and power at work are constructed as part of the normal reality of life for a large proportion of working people. In Australia, the most frequently observed pattern of discrimination in labour markets surrounds the employment of ethnic and women workers in unskilled, manual production work. Young workers and women also constitute an important source of secondary labour market employment in retailing, and in the services sector.

Women tend to occupy positions which are typically regarded as being less skilled as well as being largely excluded from channels of promotion in internal labour markets, and which hence tend to be less well paid (O'Donnell and Hall 1988). The determinants of these circumstances may be discovered in the social organisation of gender relationships. This is because the requirements that workers must satisfy if they are to qualify for, and remain in, unexposed segments of the labour market include long-term uninterrupted employment, full-time work, a commitment to career development, and geographic mobility. However, these are conditions which are unable to be met by many women, because of the expectations placed on them in their family relationships. These cultural and ideological perceptions are produced and reinforced by structural factors, manifested in the lack of adequate provision of child care facilities, for example, which work against the development of institutional means for breaking down barriers to more privileged labour market segments.

In the following section, we turn to some of the empirical evidence concerning the recent history of the social experience of work, employment and labour in Australia and review it in the light of the theoretical debates, arguments and themes to which we have referred. First, significant changes in the patterns of employment and unemployment in Australia since the 1970s are considered. Second, the general conditions of work in Australia are analysed, and patterns of training and education of workers are assessed. Third, we turn to the labour market predicament of disadvantaged social groups. Fourth, the extent of trade union organisation and mobilisation is considered. This material will show that these changes have not impacted uniformly, but have created new patterns of social inequality with effects that have important consequences for Australian society. This, in turn, demonstrates changing strategies for the collective organisation of work and representation of employment issues, and changing approaches to the regulation of employment by the state.

Employment Patterns

We have argued that the organisation of work and the quantity and quality of employment are central issues in the political life of the nation and the everyday lives of almost all of the population. In 1992, the Australian labour force comprised 75 per cent of the male civilian population aged 15 and over, and 52 per cent of the female population. The unemployment rate stood at 11 per cent, higher than at any time since the 1930s. In this climate there is a tendency for analysis and policy to concentrate on the quantity of employment, but it is important to retain a focus on the quality of employment in areas such as the security of employment, discriminatory practices, and wages and conditions. The following section considers these issues against significant changes in the labour market that have occurred over the past two decades.

An important aspect of these changes since the 1960s is illustrated in Figure 9.1. During the 25-year period from 1966 until 1991, participation rates of particular groups have altered quite markedly. The participation rate for males has dropped from 83.5 per cent to 74.8 per cent, while that for females has increased, from 37.2 to 52.2 per cent. Underlying these figures are a number of significant developments in the way work is performed. For example, while the proportion of males employed part-time increased from 4 per cent in 1967 to 9.2 per cent in 1991, the proportion of females in part-time work increased, from 24.5 to 40.9 per cent during the same period. Currently, 59.3 per cent of female employees compared with 90.8 per cent of male employees are engaged in full-time work, while women make up 76.1 per cent of the part-time workforce. Some significant relationships may also be discerned in these data between age and gender. Younger workers aged 15–19 years are much more likely to be employed part-time. However, whereas over 90 per cent of male employees (under 60 years of age) work full-time, female employees tend to remain in part-time employment, especially in the age categories over 35 years.

Employment patterns are also contingent upon longer-term changes in the pattern of Australian industry. Figure 9.2 is an

Figure 9.1 Trends in Male and Female Labour Force Participation, 1966–91

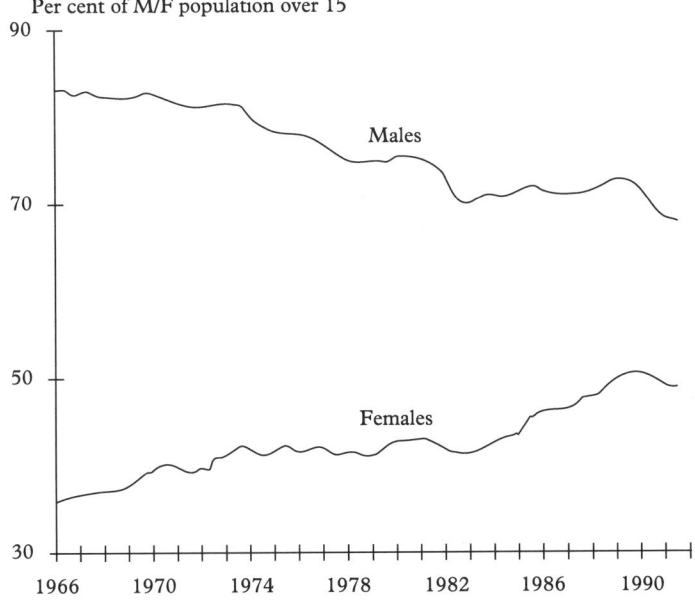

Per cent of M/F population over 15

Source: ABS 1992, Cat. No. 6203.0

index which graphically illustrates the relative growth and decline of employment in the various industry sectors. Reflected in the figure is the fact that manufacturing has undergone a continuing decline as a source of employment, from 23.7 per cent of all jobs in 1972, to 16 per cent in 1989. At the same time, the proportion of employment in community services has increased, from 11.8 to 17.6 per cent. Figure 9.3 portrays the effects on both 'blue collar' industrial jobs and other 'white collar' clerical and non-manual jobs. Clearly a major restructuring is taking place in the Australian economy as the decline in the manufacturing sector, abetted by the government's non-interventionist policy approach to manufacturing industry and the reduction in tariff protection, severely constricts the major area of male full-time employment. At the same time, there is a large increase in (often part-time) service sector jobs, in which the growing number of women being drawn into the workforce have found employment. Figure 9.4 illustrates the gendered pattern of full and part-time employment that

Figure 9.2   Index of Employment in Industry Sectors, 1973–89

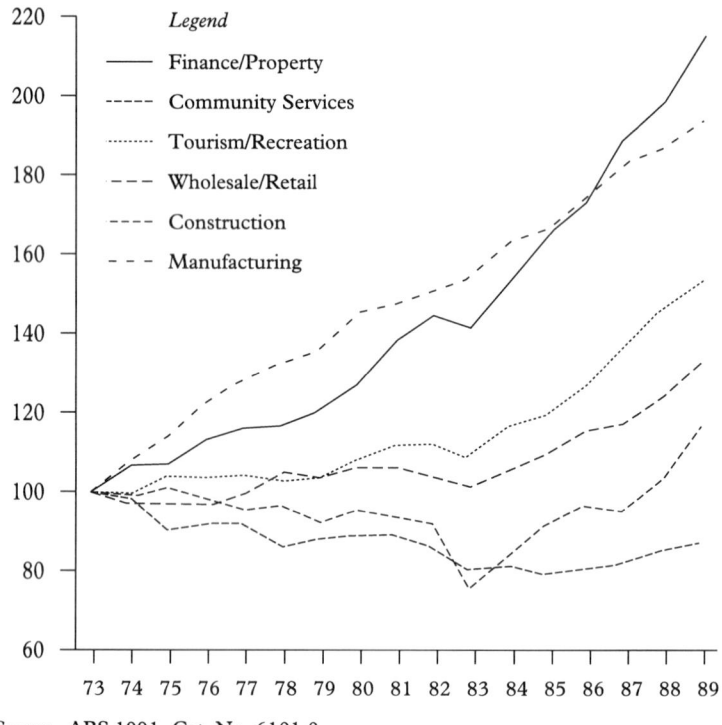

Source: ABS 1991, Cat. No. 6101.0

Figure 9.3   Persons Employed by Occupational Category, 1966–91

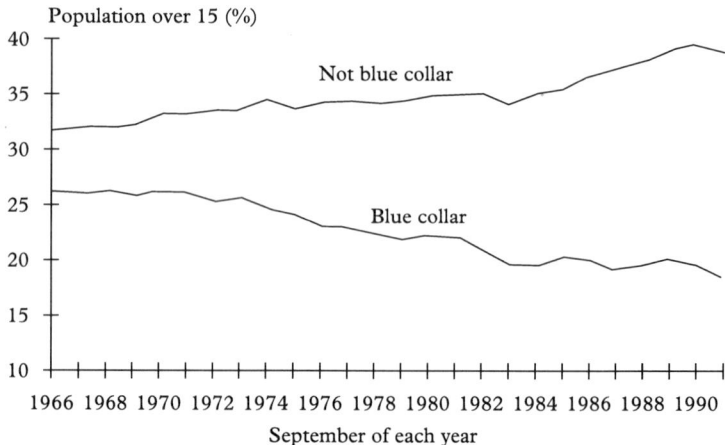

Source: EPAC 1992, from ABS Cat. No. 6203.0

Figure 9.4 Full-time and Part-time Employment by Industry Sector, August 1989

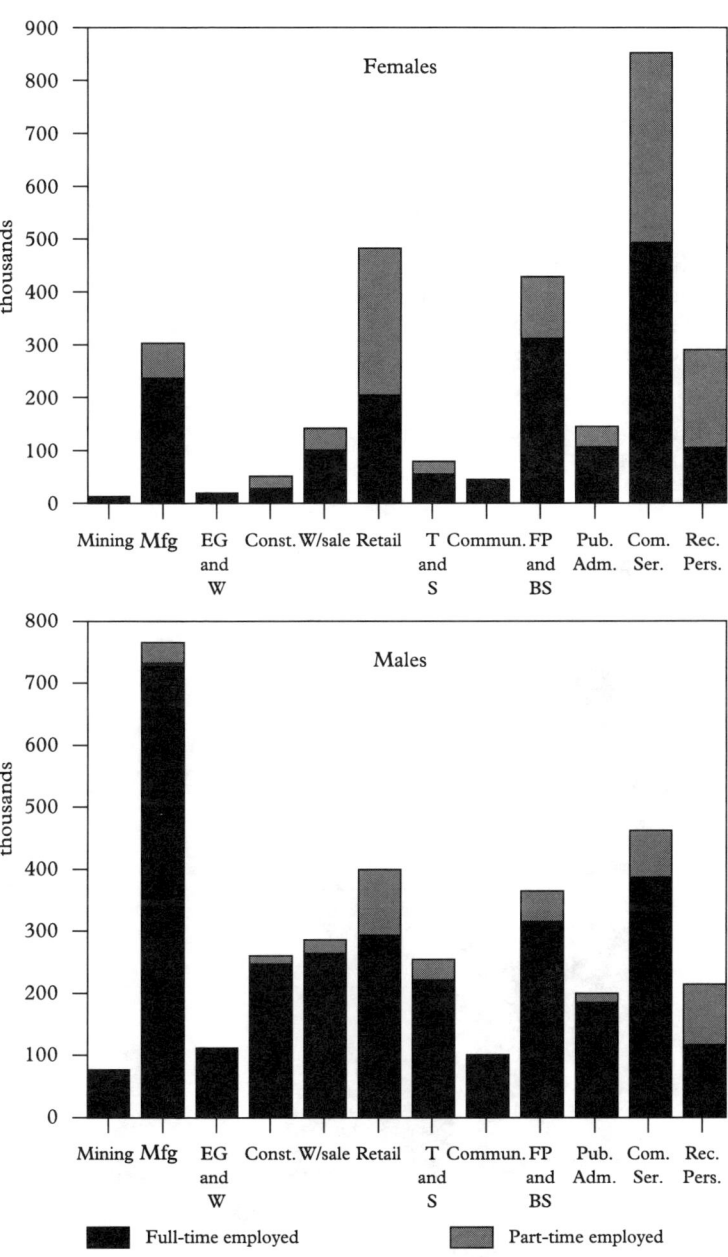

Source: DEET 1990

characterises the Australian workforce at the commencement of the 1990s.

While the data described above are indicative of processes of labour market segmentation linking industrial sectors and gender, a much more striking pattern is evident in the gender segmentation of occupations. There is a high concentration of female workers in clerical, sales and personal service occupations, while they are relatively excluded from managerial ranks and trades. The data also point to the inability of human capital theory to explain the variation, and especially the conclusion drawn by Baxter *et al.* (1990: 75) that where men and women hold similar educational qualifications, men are markedly more likely to be in primary labour market positions. The manner in which these statistical aggregates manifest themselves at the organisational level is demonstrated in Figure 9.5, which shows how the Queensland

Figure 9.5 Queensland Government Female Employment by Income, 1985–86

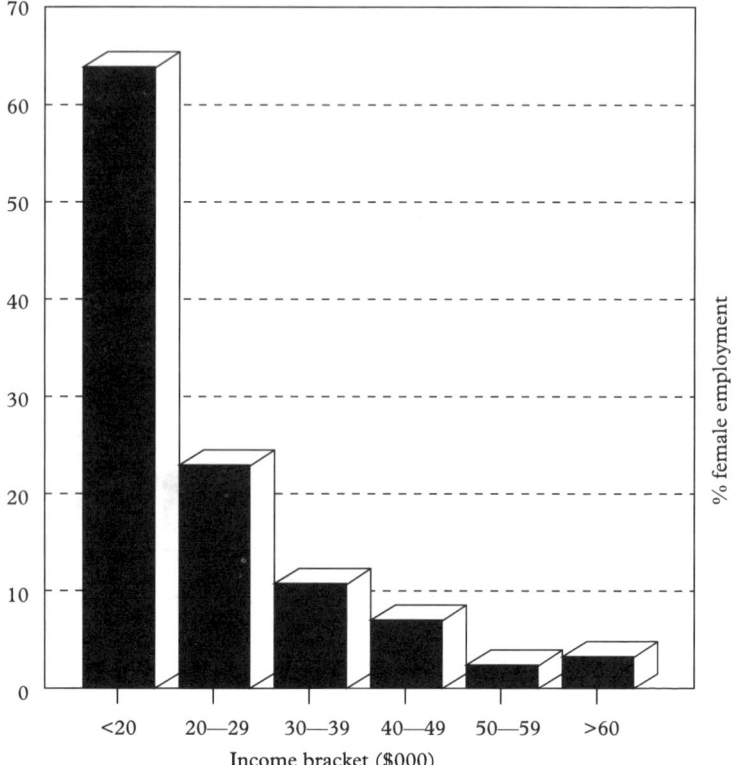

Income bracket ($000)

Source: Public Service Board, Queensland, *Annual Report 1986*

public sector concentrates female employment in the lower paid clerical grades but leaves women largely excluded from managerial and professional jobs in the upper income brackets (Boreham *et al.* 1988).

In summary, these trends suggest significant long-term changes in the way work is organised. There has been a decline in full-time career opportunities which has been only partly compensated for by an increase in part-time work. There has also been a 'feminisation' of the workforce, with the rate of increase of female employment being more than four times that of male employment. As the next section shows, these changes have allowed for a much greater degree of flexibility in the manner in which work is deployed. Part-time and casual employment at lower rates of pay, and lacking the costs of training normally associated with full-time career development, has provided employment for a large number of young and female workers, but at considerable cost to the quality of employment available more generally in the economy.

Unemployment

Australia's unemployment rate generally fell within the 1.5 to 2.5 per cent range throughout the 1950s and 60s. During the early 1970s, in common with virtually all of the advanced capitalist economies, the first signs of recession began to be felt. This trend was exacerbated by the 1974 OPEC oil price increases, which were to see unemployment maintained at levels of around 6 to 7 per cent for the six years through to 1983. Further recessionary impacts in 1983 and 1991 have seen the unemployment rate range up to the current levels of 11 per cent. The average duration of unemployment was 44.5 weeks in 1989, an increase of 50 per cent from 1979 levels. These quite dramatic changes in the economy have combined with forces for the transformation of the labour process and patterns of change in manufacturing and service sector labour markets, illustrated in the previous section, to bring about wide-ranging consequences affecting the entire society. The most significant effects may be observed in the differential impact of unemployment on gender and age groups, the development of a pattern of long-term unemployment, and the real costs of unemployment in terms of social inequality, crime and mental and physical illness. These issues will be briefly addressed in the material which follows.

As Figure 9.6 shows, the historical pattern has been for female unemployment to significantly exceed that of males. However, in 1991, major downturns in the male dominated industries of

Figure 9.6   Unemployment Rate by Gender, 1971–91

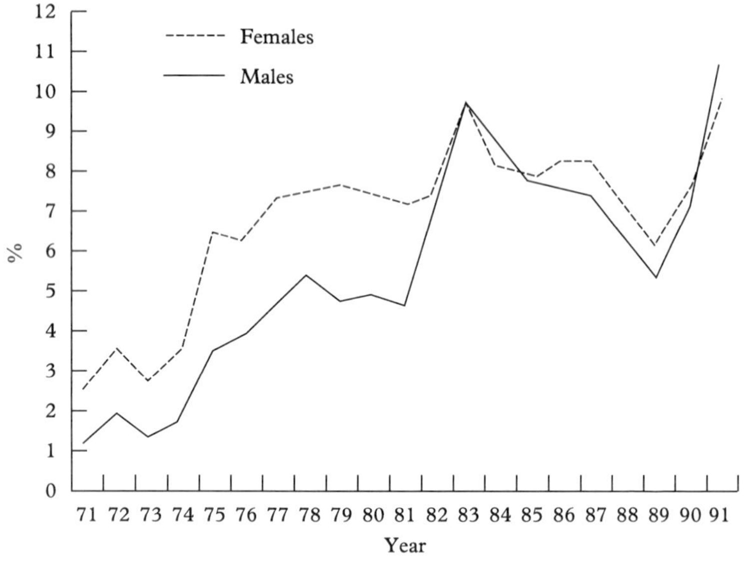

Source: Howard 1992, from ABS, Cat. No. 6202.0

mining, manufacturing and construction saw the unemployment rates for males increasing at a significantly faster rate than for females, whose employment is concentrated in financial and community services, personal services, recreation, and retailing — all sectors still exhibiting some growth.

There are several additional considerations which underlie these figures. First, among those with marginal attachments to the labour force, there is a strong gender-based profile. Table 9.1 indicates that women predominate among what are termed 'the hidden unemployed' — those persons who currently want work and are available for it, together with those people who are actively seeking work but are not available to start within the next four weeks. Within this category, women also make up the great majority of 'discouraged job seekers' who want work but do not actively seek employment because they believe that they lack necessary training, skills or experience, or because jobs are not available in their locality or type of work.

Further evidence concerning the different employment status of men and women is reported by Baxter *et al.* (1990). They show that, for more than twice as many women as men, domestic responsibilities and associated constraints are incompatible with

Table 9.1 Marginally Attached and Discouraged Job Seekers by Gender, September 1990

	Female	Male	Female as % of total
Persons not in the labour force	2,451.3	1,098.8	69.0
With marginal attachment	557.1	195.4	74.0
Wanted to work and were actively looking for work	31.3	26.3	54.3
Wanted to work but were not actively looking for work and were available to start work within four weeks[a]	525.8	169.2	75.7
Discouraged jobseekers[b]	76.6	24.2	75.9
Others	449.2	144.9	75.6
Without marginal attachment	1,894.2	903.4	67.7

[a]179,000 of persons in this category (25.8 per cent) cited 'child care' as the main reason for not participating

[b]14,100 persons considered they had insufficient schooling/training/skills/experience, and 38,900 considered the main reason to be no jobs in locality, or line of work, or at all

Source: DEET 1991a

the requirements of many primary sector jobs, such as the need to work overtime, to develop a long-term commitment to a career, to socialise with colleagues or customers after hours, or to be able to move to another town. These factors often combine so as to prevent women from applying for such positions (Young 1989).

Young people have always experienced significantly higher levels of unemployment than the general population, as indicated in Figure 9.7. This is particularly evident during the 1991–92 period, when the rate of unemployment among 15–19-year-olds rose to 34 per cent, in seasonally adjusted terms. These data also need to be interpreted in the light of increases in the school retention rate, from 33 per cent in 1974 to 60 per cent in 1989 (DEET 1991b: 54). The absolute numbers of unemployed in this age category have, in fact, declined. Finally, it should be noted that the figures tend to obscure very high levels of localised unemployment in particular country towns and regions where youth unemployment rates of up to 60 per cent have been recorded.

Costs associated with the rates of unemployment prevailing in Australia in the 1990s may be measured in a number of ways. The first measure captures the cost to the nation and therefore the entire community of production forgone. One recent study

Figure 9.7   Youth Unemployment Rate, 1978–92

Note: Defined as full time unemployment among 15–19-year-olds, seasonally
adjusted
Source: EPAC 1992, from ABS, Cat. No. 6203.0

estimated the loss associated with one percentage point of unemployment to be between $3 and $6 billion per year. This needs
to be combined with the loss of revenue to governments, and the
additional spending required to meet various forms of welfare
assistance, estimated at around $2 billion per year (Junankar and
Kapuscinski 1992).

The second measure concerns the direct financial cost to
individuals. The most direct measure indicates that the unemployment benefit rate in 1991 was about 34 per cent of average weekly
earnings (net of tax) for females, and 28 per cent for males. In
only exceptional instances (fewer than 1 per cent of cases) could
the unemployed earn more from unemployment benefits than
from full-time wages (EPAC 1992). On the contrary, as Saunders
(1990a: 41) concluded from a study of employment and poverty
in Australia in the 1980s, the rise in unemployment 'left its mark
in terms of a "new poor" comprising working age families, many
with children, whose unemployment condemned them to a situation
of joblessness and poverty'. Similar results were reported by Cass
(1988), who showed that the unemployed fell within the poorest

10 per cent of income units. These social and economic costs impact very heavily on the long-term unemployed.

The final dimension through which unemployment creates a major cost to individuals and the community is the strong correlation between employment status and physical and mental illness and crime. Much of the literature concentrates on the effect of the lack of security associated with regular employment in increasing the potential for criminal behaviour (Hensen 1990). The unemployed are significantly over-represented among people who appear before the courts, and a recent study reported by Devery (1991) demonstrated a strong association between high crime rates and socio-economic disadvantage. Unemployment has also been strongly linked to high suicide rates for males, with one study finding that the attempted suicide rate for unemployed persons was twelve times the average rate (Krudinski 1977). In general, unemployment severs an important set of social relationships without which many people have little support or security in dealing with often profound economic hardship. Self-esteem, stress and dietary inadequacy have been shown to be significantly associated with mental and physical illness (Windschuttle 1980).

Disadvantaged Groups: Migrants and Aboriginal People

Aboriginal people and migrants constitute two very different groups subject to structural disadvantage in the Australian labour market. Deteriorating labour market conditions since the early 1970s have disproportionately affected both groups. The material which follows provides a comparison of the labour market status of the Australian-born population with the overseas-born one, and the predicament of Aboriginal people is set against that of non-Aborigines.

In 1990, approximately 26 per cent of the Australian labour force was born overseas. The most striking feature of the labour market profile of this extremely diverse group is their higher rate of unemployment. However, much of this is attributable to length of residence in Australia and degree of English language proficiency, rather than being attributable to birthplace as such (DEET 1991b: 92). The probability of unemployment is higher where the migrant is from a non-English-speaking background (NESB), where they are a relatively recent arrival and where they have refugee status. For example, the difference in unemployment rates between the Australian-born and migrants from English-speaking backgrounds is negligible. In 1987 the unemployment rate for Australian-born males was 7.9 per cent, compared with 7.6 per cent for English-speaking background (ESB) male migrants, and 10.7 per cent for NESB male migrants. Analyses controlling for English language proficiency indicate that the only birthplace group to emerge as significantly more prone to unemployment are Asian migrants, and the higher rate of refugee status amongst them is likely to be associated with their relative disadvantage (Wooden 1990: 30). While educational attainment appears to be associated with the likelihood of employment, NESB migrants and those who have been educated overseas do not receive the same return on their education as ESB migrants, the Australian-born or those who were educated in Australia (Evans and Kelley 1986). Finally, length of residence is a very important variable for all migrant groups (especially NESB migrants), with the probability of unemployment falling dramatically in the first five years of residence, and declining steadily thereafter (Wooden 1990: 31–32).

According to Census data, Aboriginal unemployment rates compare extremely unfavourably with those of the nation as a whole. A comparison of the labour force status of the Aboriginal population with all Australians shows not only dramatically higher unemployment levels, but also a much greater proportion of the population outside the labour market altogether. Table 9.2 demonstrates that, in 1986, almost half the Aboriginal population was labelled 'not in the labour force', compared with 37.9 per cent of the Australian population as a whole. When it is taken into account that, of those categorised as not in the labour force, a

Table 9.2 Labour Force Status of Aboriginal and Torres Strait Islander Population and Total Australian Population by Gender, 1986

Labour force status	Aboriginal and TSI population			All Australians		
	Male	Female	Total	Male	Female	Total
Employed	40.4	22.7	31.3	66.9	42.3	54.4
Unemployed	22.7	11.8	17.1	6.6	4.5	5.5
Not in the labour force	32.2	60.0	46.6	24.4	51.1	37.9
Total N('000) (=100%)	66.4	70.7	137.1	5,904.3	6,061.0	11,965.3

Note: Percentages are based on the total population 15 years and over; totals include those in the 'not stated' category and so columns do not add up to 100%. The discrepancy is greater for the Aboriginal and TSI population, more of whom fall into the 'not stated' category

Source: ABS, 1986 Census of Population and Housing

much greater proportion of the total Australian population compared with the Aboriginal population is located in the educational system, it becomes clear that the extent of disadvantage is even greater. The table also shows that far fewer Aboriginal women than Aboriginal men are in the labour force, indicating that their lower unemployment rate is rather misleading. These figures indicate that the problem of hidden unemployment is particularly relevant to Aboriginal people, given their frequent geographic and cultural isolation.

A further facet of Aboriginal unemployment which distinguishes it from the broader picture of unemployment in Australia is its disproportionate concentration among younger people. The Aboriginal population is young in comparison with Australians as a whole. In 1986, for example, 40 per cent of the Aboriginal population was under 15 years of age, compared with 23 per cent in this age group in the total population. Table 9.3 shows that, in 1986, the unemployment rate for male Aborigines aged 15–24 years was 45.9 per cent compared with 16.4 per cent for the total male population in that age group. Unemployment for female Aborigines aged 15–24 years was 45.2 per cent, compared with 16.1 per cent for the corresponding section of the total population. Of total recorded Aboriginal unemployment, 15–24-year-olds accounted for 52.5 per cent.

High levels of Aboriginal unemployment tend to be associated with a concentration of employment in vulnerable rural labour markets, coupled with low levels of education and marketable skills. The relatively large proportion of Aboriginal people who

Table 9.3 Unemployment Rate of Aboriginal and Torres Strait Islander Population and Total Australian Population, by Gender and Age, 1986

Age group (years)	Aboriginal and TSI Population			Total population		
	Males	Females	Persons	Males	Females	Persons
15–24	45.9	45.2	45.6	16.4	16.1	16.3
25–34	33.3	28.0	31.5	8.5	9.0	8.7
35–44	27.1	22.1	25.3	5.8	6.6	6.1
45–54	25.4	21.7	24.2	5.8	5.6	5.7
55–64	25.2	20.8	24.0	8.1	4.4	7.1
65 and over	36.2	49.5	40.4	4.1	6.2	4.8
Total	36.0	34.1	35.3	9.0	9.6	9.2

Source: ABS, 1986 Census of Population and Housing

leave school earlier than non-Aboriginal people, who are less likely to have post-secondary school qualifications, are placed at a significant disadvantage on entry to the labour market. For Aboriginal people who do gain employment, segregation into lower occupational ranks and low incomes is common. In 1966, for example, 98 per cent of Aborigines were employed in the lowest skill levels of their occupations, compared with 65 per cent of all Australians (Beaumont 1974). More recent data from the 1986 Census show that this is still the predominant tendency, and regional studies such as Zwang's (1984) of rural South Australia show that rural employment conditions are typically worse than those in urban areas.

The income status of Aboriginal employees is what might be expected in the light of the labour market patterns so far identified. Data from the 1976 Census indicated that the per capita income of Aboriginals was about half that of the Australian population as a whole (Treadgold 1980, 1988). Fisk (1985) argued that the situation deteriorated between the 1976 and 1981 Censuses. In general terms, the situation described in this section is one in which, on all criteria (labour force status, occupation and income), Aborigines have nowhere near the access to productive labour market participation that is available to other Australians. Moreover, what regional studies are available (Boreham *et al.* 1992) emphasise that conditions in rural areas are worse than those in urban regions.

The Experience of Work in Australia: Pay and Conditions

The majority of Australians rely on wages and salaries for their main form of economic support. This support is supplemented through the 'social wage', the benefits received through welfare spending in areas of social security, health, education and housing. Together these sources of support have profound implications for the living conditions of Australians. Comparatively and historically the income strategy pursued in Australia can be understood as 'wage earner security' characterised by the protection of the living standards of those in employment and by the acceptance of the distribution of income achieved through the labour market (Castles 1985, 1988). As a consequence, Australia has endured a partial and limited form of welfarism, which can be contrasted with more generous and universal welfare systems in other advanced capitalist societies. Thus, welfare provision in Australia has traditionally been limited to old age pensions, sickness benefits and unemployment benefits (Ewer *et al.* 1991: 4).

Examination of the evidence relating to personal wages and the social wage since the early 1970s indicates that the traditional pattern of real wage protection and modest social wage expenditure has altered, on balance, to the disadvantage of wage earners, their families and those dependent on welfare. Figure 9.8 shows the annual changes in real wages and the social wage since 1976. Following a substantial decline in both real wages and the social wage between 1976 and 1980, both forms of income increased until 1984. Since then, real wages have declined dramatically. This trend has been only marginally offset by the slight increase in the level of the social wage between 1985 and 1990.

Figure 9.8   Real Wage and Social Wage, 1976–90

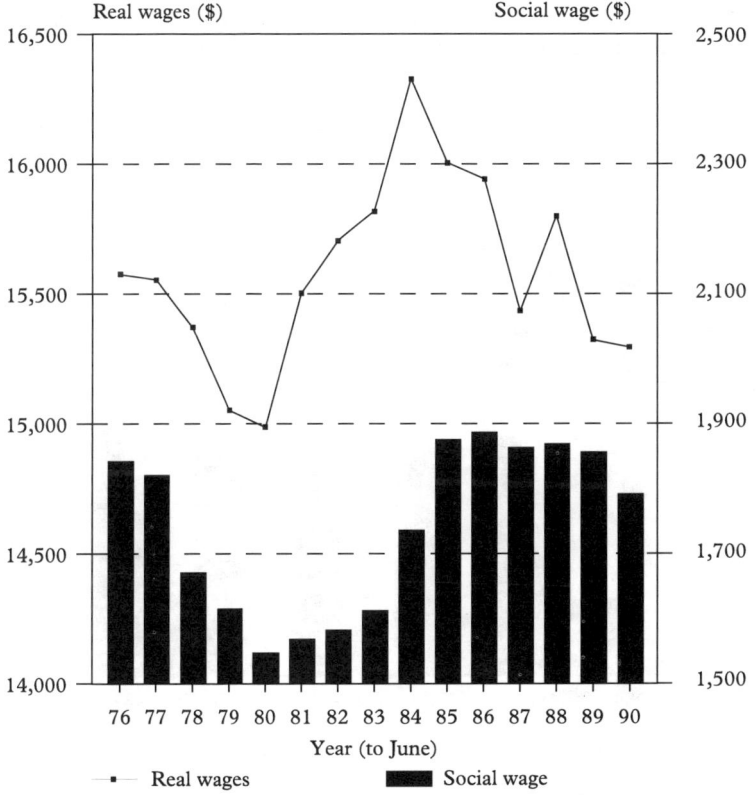

Source: Ewer *et al.* 1991: 35, from ABS, Budget Papers

The contemporary experience of the wages system in Australia indicates the relatively worsening position of low income earners. In Australia, awards determine minimum rates of pay for the vast majority of workers, and tend to reflect the actual earnings of the lowest income earners, while other workers, owing to their labour market position, are able to negotiate various over-award payments. Figure 9.9 demonstrates that for each year since 1985 the Consumer Price Index has been increasing at a greater rate than both award rates and average weekly earnings. These data also show that since 1986 lower income earners reliant on award adjustments have been faring much worse relative to inflation than those able to secure over-award payments, as reflected in increases to average weekly earnings.

There is little doubt that since the early 1970s, the share from Australian production going to capital and labour has shifted from the advantage of labour, between 1974 and 1983, to the advantage of capital. Since 1984, the wages share has slipped from 69 to 65.6 per cent, while the share to profits has gone from 31 to 34.4 per cent (Ewer *et al.* 1991: 30). Alongside the inequali-

Figure 9.9   Annual Change in Award Rates of Pay, Average Weekly Earnings and Consumer Price Index, 1984–89

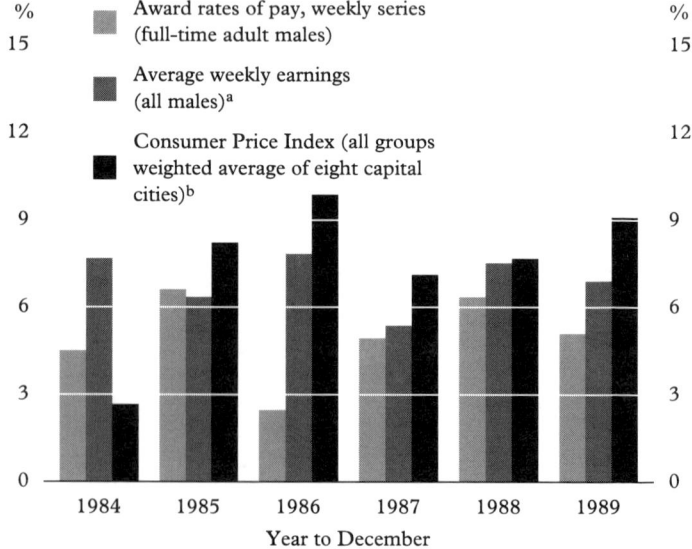

Source: ABS 1991a: 88
[a] Year to November
[b] Year to December quarter

ties between those who live from the profits of capital and those who rely on wage labour, Australia continues to demonstrate a high degree of inequality within the full-time employed labour force. Thus, for example, in the 1985–86 financial year, the lowest 10 per cent of full-time income earners earned 3 per cent of all income, while the highest 10 per cent earned 21 per cent (ABS 1988: 14).

Although, as noted above, awards provide effective minimum wages and conditions for the vast majority of Australian employees, there is evidence that this form of coverage is becoming less common and that the adherence by employers to award conditions and rates of pay is less than complete. While it was estimated that in 1985, 85 per cent of employees were covered by an award (or similar determination or collective agreement), by 1990 it was estimated that only 80 per cent of workers were protected by such agreements. All this reduction in award coverage occurred in the private sector. Second, evidence from a recent random survey of employers conducted by one state department of industrial relations revealed that over one-third of employers failed to provide to their employees the level of wages and/or conditions stipulated by the relevant award (DEVETIR 1991: 20).

The equal pay decisions taken by the then-Conciliation and Arbitration Commission in 1969, 1972 and 1974, and the enactment of Equal Employment Opportunity and Sex Discrimination legislation have seen a significant improvement in gender-based earning differentials (Whitehouse 1990). In 1970, female average weekly earnings for full-time adult non-managerial employees in the private sector were approximately 59 per cent of male earnings. By 1991, this ratio had reached 85 per cent. This ratio is based on full-time employees only, and does not therefore reflect the relatively high representation of women in part-time employment. When part-time and junior employees are included, the ratio falls to 67 per cent of that of men (DIR 1990b: 7). This persistent differential, although greater in the private sector than in the public, exists in differing degrees across all major occupational groupings and industry sectors.

The Labour Process, Skills and Training

Central to the labour process debate referred to above is the argument that in the course of contemporary capitalism, many workers have been deskilled through the Taylorist design of work, under which most work tasks in both blue and white collar occupations involve little more than the repetition of single procedures (Willis 1988). It has also been argued that alongside the 'degradation of work' in some areas, other workers have benefited through reskilling or through the promotion of the skill status of their occupations. Theories of dual and segmented labour markets have identified peripheral labour markets characterised by limited access to training opportunities, traditionally low valuations of skill, and highly restricted (or non-existent) career opportunities. The incidence and trends of deskilling and re-skilling, and patterns of access to training in Australia, can be considered in terms of the provision of education and training provided within both the public and private sectors.

Generally, the Australian labour force is becoming increasingly educated. While, in 1979, 36.2 per cent of the labour force possessed some post-school qualification, by 1988 that proportion had reached 45.5 per cent. However, despite the evidence of increasing levels of educational attainment in Australian society, there is widespread recognition of the deficiencies of the system of vocational training provided at the workplace, where employers tend to view training as a cost rather than as an investment (Boreham *et al.* 1988). The data show that prior to the recent introduction of the training levy, Australia had a very poor record of developing labour force skills (ASTEC 1987). According to a survey of Australian employers conducted from July to September 1989, only 22 per cent of employers reported training expenditure during the period. Expenditure on training by different categories of employers also varied considerably. Expenditure (as a proportion of gross wages and salaries) was higher in the public sector (3.3 per cent) than the private (1.7 per cent), higher in large enterprises than in small, and higher in some industries (electricity, gas and water and the communications industry) than others (ABS 1991b).

There are also considerable differences between the categories of employees who actually receive training. In a 12-month period in 1988–89, a survey undertaken by the Australian Bureau of Statistics revealed that 71 per cent of all Australian employees were provided with some form of on-the-job training (ABS 1990). A detailed analysis of the findings of that survey (Baker and Wooden 1990: 34–39) revealed that the incidence of training was much lower amongst casual and part-time employees than permanent full-time employees; the probability of receiving training increases with educational attainment; migrants with a non-English-speaking background are less likely to receive training; financial support from employers for training is highest for 'white collar' occupations, and less likely for casual and female employees.

Evidence relating to employer support for study towards educational qualifications also indicates a significant pattern of discrimination against migrants and female employees, of whom only about one-half as many are studying compared with males (Baker and Wooden 1990: 29).

An increasing concern with the depth and flexibility of labour force skills to enable employees at all levels of design, management and production to move from one task to another within the workplace complements an important shift from conventional processes of co-ordination and control over the labour process to what has been termed a post-Fordist form of flexible work organisation. It is proposed that these changes should involve 'a co-operative strategy where the employer concedes issues previously held to be "managerial prerogatives"...a form of democratisation involving full participation of workers in organised structures and through collective associations' (Mathews 1989: 158–59). Empirical data on these issues are somewhat limited; however, data from one recent study (Boreham 1991) shown in Table 9.4, indicates that skilled and unskilled workers, both white and blue collar, are largely excluded from decisions about almost all aspects of their employment conditions, or the products and services they produce. Women are also significantly more likely to be excluded from such decisions at virtually every occupational level, while a similar pattern of discrimination exists for trade union members. In general, there is little evidence in these data to suggest that participative organisational practices of the kind predicted by post-Fordist theory have made any significant incursion into traditional managerial prerogatives in Australia.

Table 9.4 Participation in Decision-making by Occupation and Gender (% of Employees with any Significant Participation)

Occupation	Production decisions		Financial decisions	
	Male	Female	Male	Female
Managers	75.0	77.8	58.3	44.4
Professionals	49.2	44.8	26.6	18.9
Clerks	19.8	11.7	12.9	3.5
Skilled workers	13.8	20.3	6.3	2.5
Semi and unskilled workers	6.3	5.0	1.4	0.0
Total	561	473	562	471

Source: Boreham 1991

Unions and Industrial Conflict

Trade unions are key social institutions in Australian society. In 1991, almost 3.4 million employees were members of Australia's 275 unions. Unions are important social actors both in their capacity to provide material benefits and a sense of collective identity for individual workers, to promote the collective social interests of wage earners and, less auspiciously in Australian history, those of the unemployed and persons dependent on welfare. Many suggest that the reasons for employees joining unions cannot be satisfactorily isolated (Plowman and Ford 1983: 2), and that any examination of the diversity of union strategies defies the identification of any single rationale (Deery 1983: 60). Others have emphasised the over-riding logic of unions in capitalism in terms of their opposition to markets (in labour itself, as well as in goods and services) as the means of allocating important resources, and the replacement of them with allocations according to political criteria, which respect the moral and human needs of people and recognise their different capacities to participate in markets (Ewer *et al.* 1991: 2). The apparent logic and strategy of Australian unionism has evidently shifted in the course of the past twenty years, from a narrow emphasis on the wages and conditions of their members to the promotion of the broader economic interests of all employees through placing pressure on governments for the provision of equitable incomes policies, active labour market interventions and public welfare services (Dow *et al.* 1984).

Australian union membership has been in relative decline since the mid-1970s. While in 1976 approximately 51 per cent of all employees were union members, by 1990 that figure had fallen to just over 40 per cent. Figure 9.10 illustrates the decline in female, male and total membership density.

While it can be argued that this decline is indicative of the shift in employment from the (traditionally highly unionised) manufacturing sector to the (traditionally lowly unionised) services sector, there has been a relative decline in all industry sectors except mining since 1976. Nevertheless, the decline has been especially severe in a number of the high growth services sectors that the union movement sees as most difficult to organise (Berry and Kitchener 1989): recreational, personal and other services from 41 to 26 per cent; finance, property and business services from 42 to 28 per cent. The relative shift in employment from the public to the private sector, the growth in female employment and the relative growth of part-time and casual employment, all contribute to an explanation of the fall in union membership (Peetz

Figure 9.10   Union Membership Rate by Gender, 1976–90

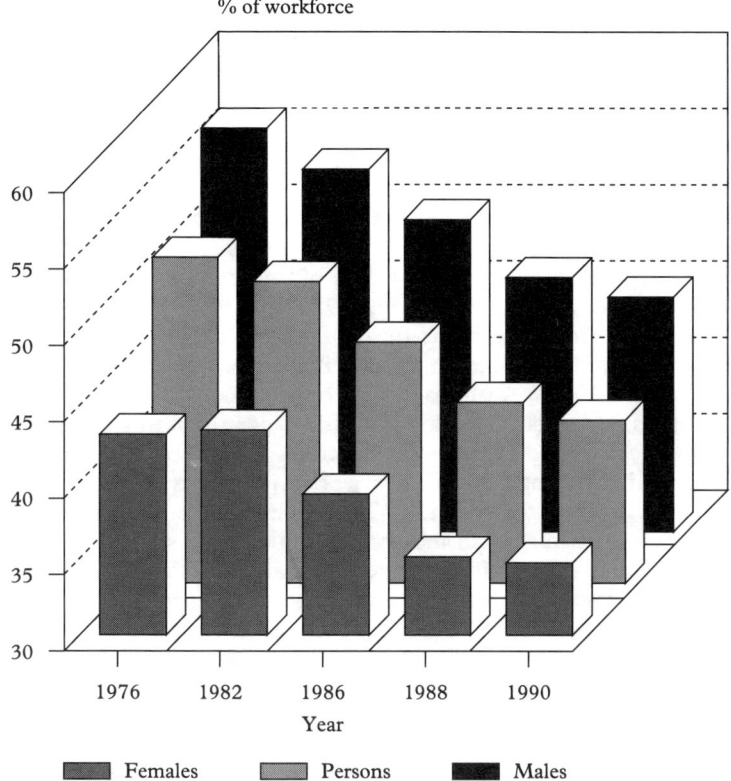

% of workforce

Females   Persons   Males

Source: Ewer *et al.* 1991: 94 from ABS, Trade Union Members, Australia

1990: 210). In summary, these changes in the pattern of trade unionism have witnessed a concentration of relatively good employment conditions, protected by union intervention in the public sector with 74 per cent union density, compared with 44 per cent in the private sector and in larger workplaces (over 200 employees), with 71 per cent density, compared with only 20 per cent density in smaller workplaces (5–19 employees) (Callus *et al.* 1991: 246).

The significant decline in union membership in Australia can be explained only in part by changes to the industrial structure of employment. A detailed analysis of the Australian union density data over the period 1976 to 1988 concluded that one-half of the reduction in density is attributable to a declining propensity to join or remain in unions, in turn explicable in terms of unfavourable legislative reforms in some states (most notably Queensland) and the impact of new management strategies designed, in part, to weaken employees' identification with unions (Peetz 1990). In any event, if unions are to arrest declines in membership, improved recruitment will need to focus on women (Davis and Pratt 1991), young workers, part-time and casual employees, and those employed in the service sector.

In all industrialised countries, industrial conflict is endemic to labour-capital relations. However, in the 1980s, Australia witnessed a significant decline in the number, size and average duration of industrial disputes. Over the course of the 1970s, each Australian worker spent an average two-thirds of one day per year involved in industrial disputation. From 1980 to 1990 that figure had fallen to approximately one-third of a day. Table 9.5 shows the magnitude of the reduction since 1980.

Over the 1980s, Australia ranked eighth amongst twenty OECD countries in terms of working days lost per thousand employees (Dabscheck 1992: 74). Australian strikes tend to be short and are often ended through a return to work without explicit settlement of the cause of the dispute. These characteristics reflect two dimensions of Australian industrial conflict: first, short strikes are regularly used by unions to demonstrate the significance of a particular issue prior to its consideration before an industrial tribunal or commission. Second, Australia has a relatively poorly-

Table 9.5 Industrial Disputes, 1980–90

Year	Number of disputes	Workers involved directly and indirectly ('000)	Working days lost ('000)	Working days lost per employee
1980	2,429	1,172.6	3,319.7	0.649
1981	2,915	1,247.2	4,189.3	0.797
1982	2,060	706.1	1,980.4	0.358
1983	1,787	470.2	1,641.4	0.249
1984	1,965	560.3	1,370.4	0.248
1985	1,895	570.5	1,256.2	0.228
1986	1,754	691.7	1,390.7	0.242
1987	1,517	608.8	1,311.9	0.223
1988	1,508	894.4	1,641.4	0.269
1989	1,402	709.8	1,202.4	0.190
1990	1,177	726.2	1,366.9	0.216

Source: Dabscheck 1992: 68, from ABS, Industrial Disputes, Australia

developed level of collective organisation at the shop floor level and some have argued that short strikes characterise rank-and-file worker protest in the absence of effective grievance handling mechanisms at the workplace (Dabscheck 1992: 78–79).

The reduction in Australian strikes, particularly pronounced since 1983, can be explained in terms of various political and institutional factors. The Accord, signed between the Australian Labor Party and the Australian Council of Trade Unions in 1983, and subsequently renegotiated, has involved a partial shift in the emphasis of union action away from industrial disputation and favouring political negotiation (Clegg *et al.* 1986). Second, settlements struck between unions and employers since the 1981 agreements between the Metal Trades Industry Association and the relevant unions have regularly included 'no extra claims' undertakings, according to which unions have generally been precluded from making claims beyond the scope of wage increases awarded centrally by the federal Commission (Dabscheck 1992). It cannot be concluded that there has been any decline in the nature or extent of the conflict between labour and capital in Australia since the Accord. Rather it is likely that the inherent antagonism between unions and employers has become increasingly mediated by state institutions.

The Future of Work

We have argued that patterns of employment and social outcomes associated with work and employment in contemporary societies have been affected both by changes in the organisation of the labour process and labour markets as well as by the relative strength of labour organisation and mobilisation. We noted that while some theories suggest that changes characterised by greater flexibility (of both production and labour) are advantageous to workers (as well as owners of enterprises), other theories suggest that such changes tend to have adverse effects which impact disproportionately on particular social groups. Union mobilisation and state intervention and regulation were identified as providing opportunities for resisting these trends and promoting labour's interests.

The overview of the data relating to work, employment and labour in Australia presented here suggests that changes in both labour markets and the organisation of labour processes since the early 1970s have had adverse consequences for Australian employees, their dependants, and those reliant on state welfare. This adversity has affected different social groups in different ways: declining employment opportunities and declining wages have affected male full-time employees with devastating consequences for families dependent on a male 'breadwinner'. Increasing feminisation, casualisation and the proliferation of part-time (in place of full-time) employment have provided women with some labour market opportunities, but they remain disproportionately locked into jobs characterised by low pay, poor conditions, limited career opportunities and low levels of job security. Tight labour market conditions, inadequate training and low returns on education have compounded the predicament of disadvantaged social groups, particularly Aboriginal people, youth and migrants. Present trends suggest a deterioration rather than an amelioration of these conditions. The union movement faces the challenge of declining membership, especially in growth areas of the economy. Despite the presence of a Labor federal government since 1983, personal wages have been declining since 1984, while small increases in the social wage have not adequately compensated for these losses.

The available evidence suggests that Australian workers do relatively poorly in comparison with the employees of other advanced capitalist countries. The wages/profits share of national income has seen a smaller proportion accruing to labour since at least 1960 than in most of the OECD countries, including the United Kingdom, the United States, Canada, Sweden and Germany. The magnitude of the decline in Australia since 1983 has also been greater than in all of these countries (Dowrick 1991: 136). Table 9.6 shows that of ten selected OECD nations, Australia had the second lowest rate of relative wages and benefits for production workers, although it ranked sixth in terms of the average salary levels of managers. Australia's social wage in the 1980s was also comparatively low. In 1985, out of nineteen industrialised countries, Australia ranked thirteenth in education expenditure, fifteenth in health, and nineteenth in social security expenditure (Saunders 1990b). Australia is one of a small group of OECD countries which has consistently performed badly with respect to unemployment (Therborn 1986b), and current trends are indicative of a worsening in Australia's relative position. Finally, future prospects are not helped by the fact that Australia spends a lower proportion of Gross Domestic Product on training than many other industrialised countries (Baker and Wooden 1991: 25).

More ominously, current government policies aimed at microeconomic reform and labour market deregulation suggest further deterioration. Modern capitalist societies such as Australia, faced with longer-term high levels of unemployment, have severe strains

Table 9.6 Relative Wages and Earnings by OECD Country, 1989

Country	Hourly compensation of production workers[a] US$	Salary levels of managers[b] US$000
Germany	17.50	37.6
Switzerland	16.70	45.2
Netherlands	15.30	23.6
Canada	14.70	30.0
USA	14.30	40.3
Austria	13.50	25.5
Italy	13.20	18.2
France	12.70	52.7
Australia	*12.10*	*28.2*
United Kingdom	10.50	26.1

[a]Total hourly compensation for production workers (wage plus supplementary benefits, including leave).
[b]Average net earnings of department managers in major cities

Source: EPAC 1991: 32, from IMD (1990) *The World Competitiveness Report,* US Department of Labor, Bureau of Labor Statistics, 1990

placed upon the social fabric. Apart from the economic, social and psychological damage inflicted on the community, there are also significant stresses placed upon the political decision making process. The balance of political power is tilted away from the collective actors such as trade unions representing labour interests, and they tend to be forced into a defensive position as employment conditions are eroded. Despite the rhetoric of a search for solutions to unemployment, there are already extensively tested policy interventions considered in the social science literature.

These strategies tend to take two distinct forms. The economics literature focuses on the ability of the labour market, if unfettered by government regulation, to clear the surplus of labour. The aim is to reduce unit labour costs. The policy vocabulary is one of flexibility, so that management can redeploy labour outside the constraints of custom or legal convention. Micro-economic reform also concentrates on intervening in the social and historical structures which have determined how work is done and the social relations through which it is collectively organised. Both of these developments are fostered by a deregulation of employment and labour market conditions and an accompanying shift from more centralised regulatory structures for the control of wages and industrial relations to unregulated bargaining at the workplace level.

The outcomes of these policies lead inevitably to a deterioration of employment conditions. Labour movement achievements through the political process and enshrined in legislation or regulation are whittled away. The ability of the organised labour movement to contest these changes is significantly reduced through enterprise-level negotiations where employers are more likely to hold sway, particularly in times of high unemployment. Governments under pressure to create jobs at any cost and who pursue these policies will need to pay very serious attention to questions about the nature of the new jobs that have been created, the extent to which they fulfil the aspirations of current and potential employees, and the ability of the national economy to sustain a restructuring of industry and employment favouring sectors in which skill formation, innovation and the development of secure careers have scarcely been emphasised.

The alternative approach favours political intervention and regulation not only to create employment but to ensure that it is created in ways that meet socially desirable goals and values. In this context, the political economy and sociology literature focuses on a number of factors. The most important is the commitment by governments to policies directed towards maintaining low levels of unemployment and the development of permanent political institutions to implement these (Therborn 1986b). A second issue is the need to allow labour movements to have a broader institutional participation in economic policy in order to introduce a longer-term perspective on industry development and employment on to the policy agenda (Clegg *et al.* 1986). The final set of measures, in part an outcome of the former, for which there is considerable empirical support (Boreham and Compston 1992) concerns the implementation of policies concerned with public infrastructural development, industry policy, and active labour market policies. Under these circumstances there is a high probability that developments in the organisation of employment will move beyond a narrow focus on short-term enterprise profitability to accord with broader national goals and the interests of working people.

References

ABS (1988) *1986 Income Distribution Survey, Persons with Earned Income, Australia*, Cat. No. 6546.0. Canberra, ABS.

——*How Workers Get Their Training, Australia, 1989*, Cat. No. 6278.0. Canberra: ABS.

———(1991a) *Labour Statistics, Australia, 1989*, Cat. No. 6101.0. Canberra: ABS.

———(1991b) *Employer Training Expenditure, Australia, July to September 1990*, Cat. No. 6353.0. Canberra, ABS.

ASTEC (1987) *Wealth From Skills — Measures to Raise the Skills of the Workforce*. Canberra: Australian Science and Technology Council, AGPS.

Atkinson, J. (1985) *Emerging UK Work Patterns*. Brighton: Institute of Manpower Studies.

Badham, R.J. (1986) *Theories of Industrial Society*. New York, St Martin's Press.

Baker, M. and Wooden, M. (1992) 'Training in the Australian Labour Market: Evidence from the How Workers Get Their Training Survey', *Australian Bulletin of Labour* 18 (1): 25–45.

Baxter, J. and Gibson, D. with Lynch-Blosse, M. (1990) *Double Take: The Links between Paid and Unpaid Work*. Canberra: AGPS.

Beaumont, P. (1974) 'The Disadvantaged Labour Market Position of Australian Aborigines', *Pacific Viewpoint* 15 (2): 165–70.

Berry, P. and Kitchener, G. (1989) *Can Unions Survive?* Canberra: Building Workers Industrial Union.

Boreham, P. (1991) 'Class and Control: The Labour Process and the Politics of Production', in J. Baxter, M. Emmison and J. Western (eds), *Class Analysis and Contemporary Australia*. Melbourne: Macmillan.

———and Compston, H. (1992) 'Labour Movement Organization and Political Intervention', *European Journal of Political Research* 20: 1–28.

———Dow, G., Littler, C. and Stewart, R. (1988) *Society and Economy in Queensland: The Strategic Role of the Public Sector*. Brisbane: Labour and Industry Research Unit.

Bramble, T. (1988) 'The Flexibility Debate: Industrial Relations and New Management Production Practices', *Labour and Industry* 1 (2): 187–209.

Braverman, H. (1974) *Labor and Monopoly Capital*. New York: Monthly Review Press.

Bray, M. and Littler, C.R. (1988) 'The Labour Process and Industrial Relations: Review of the Literature', *Labour and Industry* 1 (3): 551–87.

Burawoy, M. (1979) *Manufacturing Consent: Changes in the Labor Process Under Monopoly Capitalism*. Chicago: University of Chicago Press.

Callus, R., Morehead, A., Cully, M. and Buchanan, J. (1991) *Industrial Relations at Work: The Australian Workplace Industrial Relations Survey*. Canberra: Department of Industrial Relations, AGPS.

Cameron, D. (1984) 'Social Democracy, Corporatism, Labour Quiescence, and the Representation of Economic Interest in Advanced Capitalist Society', in J.H. Goldthorpe (ed.), *Order and Conflict in Contemporary Capitalism*, Oxford: Clarendon Press.

Cass, B. (1988) *Income Support for the Unemployed in Australia: Towards a More Active System*, Social Security Review, Issues Paper No. 4. Canberra: AGPS.

Castles, F.G. (1985) *The Working Class and Welfare: Reflections on the*

Political Development of the Welfare State in Australia and New Zealand, 1890–1980. Wellington: Allen and Unwin.

——(1988) *Australian Public Policy and Economic Vulnerability.* Sydney: Allen and Unwin.

Clawson, D. (1980) *Bureaucracy and the Labor Process.* New York: Monthly Review Press.

Clegg, S., Boreham, P. and Dow, G. (1986) *Class, Politics and the Economy.* London: Routledge and Kegan Paul.

Crouch, C. (1977) *Class Conflict and the Industrial Relations Crisis.* London: Heinemann Educational Books.

Dabscheck, B. (1992) 'A Decade of Striking Figures', in B. Dabscheck *et al.* (eds), *Contemporary Australian Industrial Relations.* Melbourne: Longman Cheshire.

Davis, E.M. and Pratt, V. (eds) (1991) *Making the Link: Affirmative Action and Industrial Relations.* Sydney: Affirmative Action Agency and Graduate School of Management, Macquarie University.

Dawson, W. and Turner, J. (1989) *When She Goes to Work She Stays at Home: Women, New Technology and Home-Based Work,* Women's Research and Employment Initiatives Program, DEET. Canberra: AGPS.

Deery, S. (1983) 'Union Aims and Methods', in B. Ford and D. Plowman (eds), *Australian Unions, An Industrial Relations Perspective.* Melbourne: Macmillan

DEET (1990) *Women in the Labour Market: A Statistical Profile.* Canberra: Women's Bureau, Department of Employment, Education and Training.

——(1991a) *Women and Work* 13(3).

——(1991b) *Australia's Workforce in the Year 2001.* Canberra: Department of Employment, Education and Training, AGPS.

Devery, C. (1991) *Disadvantage and Crime in New South Wales.* Sydney: NSW Bureau of Crime Statistics and Research.

DEVETIR, Department of Employment, Vocational Education, Training and Industrial Relations, Queensland, (1991) *Annual Report, Industrial Relations, 1990–1991,* Brisbane.

DIR Department of Industrial Relations (1990a) *Annual Report 1989–1990.* Canberra: AGPS.

——(1990b) *Equal Pay, A Background Paper.* Canberra: AGPS.

——(1991) *Annual Report 1990–1991.* Canberra: AGPS.

Dow, G., Clegg, S. and Boreham, P. (1984) 'From the Politics of Production to the Production of Politics', *Thesis Eleven* 9: 16–32.

Dowrick, S. (1991) 'Has the Pattern of Australian Wage Growth Been Unique?', in F.G. Castles (ed.), *Australia Compared: People, Policies and Politics.* Sydney: Allen and Unwin.

Edwards, P.K. (1990) 'Understanding Conflict in the Labour Process: The Logic and Autonomy of Struggle', in D. Knights and H. Willmott (eds), *Labour Process Theory.* London: Macmillan.

Edwards, R. (1979) *Contested Terrain: the Transformation of the Workplace in the Twentieth Century.* New York: Basic Books.

EPAC (1991) *Competitiveness: The Policy Environment,* Economic Planning Advisory Council Paper No. 47. Canberra: AGPS.

———(1992) *Unemployment in Australia,* Economic Planning Advisory Council Paper No. 51. Canberra: AGPS.

Esping-Andersen, G. (1985) *Politics Against Markets: The Social Democratic Road to Power.* Princeton, NJ: Princeton.

———(1990) *The Three Worlds of Welfare Capitalism,* Cambridge, Polity Press.

Evans, M.D.R. and Kelley, J. (1986) 'Immigrants' Work: Equality and Discrimination in the Australian Labour Market', *Australia and New Zealand Journal of Sociology* 22: 187–207.

Ewer, P., Hampson, I., Lloyd, C., Rainford, J., Rix, S. and Smith, M. (1991) *Politics and the Accord.* Sydney: Pluto Press.

Fisk, E. (1985) *The Aboriginal Economy in Town and Country.* Sydney: Allen and Unwin.

Friedman, A.L. (1977) *Industry and Labour: Class Struggle at Work and Monopoly Capitalism.* London: Macmillan.

Hensen, P. (1990) 'Employment — The Key to Keeping People Out of Prison', Paper to Australian Institute of Criminology Conference, Hobart.

Howard, R. (1992) *Unemployment in Australia: The Problem, Its Causes, Policy Responses.* Melbourne: VCTA.

Junankar, P.N. and Kapuscinski, C.A. (1992) *The Costs of Unemployment in Australia,* Forthcoming, Office of EPAC Background Paper, Canberra: AGPS.

Kerr, C. (1954) 'The Balkanisation of Labour Markets', in E. Wright Bakke *et al.* (eds), *Labor Mobility and Economic Opportunity.* Cambridge, Mass.: MIT Press.

Korpi, W. (1983) *The Democratic Class Struggle.* London: Routledge and Kegan Paul.

———(1985) 'Power Resources Approach vs Action and Conflict: On Causal and Intentional Explanation in the Study of Power', *Sociological Theory* 3: 31–45.

Krudinski, J. (1977) *Attempted Suicide: Report to the Victorian Minister for Health.* Melbourne: Victorian Mental Health Authority.

Lever-Tracy, C. (1988) 'The Flexibility Debate: Part Time Work', *Labour and Industry* 1 (2): 210–41.

Marx, K. (1867) *Capital. Volume 1* (1970) London: Lawrence and Wishart.

Mathews, J. (1989) *Tools of Change: New Technology and the Democratisation of Work.* Sydney: Pluto Press.

Minister for Employment, Education and Training (1989) *Employment, Education and Training: Key Trends and Government Initiatives,* Submission to the Economic Planning Advisory Council. Canberra: AGPS.

O'Donnell, C. and Hall, P. (1988) *Getting Equal, Labour Market Regulation and Women's Work.* Sydney: Allen and Unwin.

Paloheimo H. (1990) 'Between Liberalism and Corporatism: The Effect of Trade Unions and Governments on Economic Performance in Eighteen OECD Countries', in R. Brunetta and C. Dell'Aringa (eds), *Labour Relations and Economic Performance.* New York: New York University Press.

Peetz, D. (1990) 'Declining Union Density', *Journal of Industrial Relations* 32 (2): 197–223.

Piore, M. and Sabel, C. (1984) *The Second Industrial Divide*, New York: Basic Books.

Plowman, D. and Ford, B. (1983) 'Australian Unions: An Introduction', in B. Ford and D. Plowman (eds), *Australian Unions, An Industrial Relations Perspective*. Melbourne: Macmillan.

Pollert, A. (1991) (ed.) *Farewell to Flexibility?* Oxford: Basil Blackwell.

Saunders, P. (1990) *Employment Growth and Poverty: An Analysis of Australian Experience, 1983–1990*. Discussion Paper No. 25. Kensington, NSW: Social Policy Research Centre.

Saunders, P. (1990) *Efficiency and Effectiveness in Social Policies: An International Perspective*, Discussion Paper No. 28. Kensington, NSW; Social Policy Research Centre.

Therborn, G. (1986a) 'Class Analysis: History and Defence', in U. Himmelstrand (ed.), *The Sociology of Structure and Action*. London: Sage.

Therborn, G. (1986b) *Why Some Peoples are More Unemployed than Others — the Strange Paradox of Growth and Unemployment*. London: Verso.

Thompson, P. (1989) *The Nature of Work: An Introduction to Debates on the Labour Process*. London: Macmillan.

Treadgold, M. (1980) 'Aboriginal Incomes: An Aggregative Analysis of the 1976 Census Results', *Australian Bulletin of Labour* 7 (1).

———(1988) 'Intercensal Change in Aboriginal Incomes, 1976–1986', *Australian Bulletin of Labour* 14(4).

Whitehouse, G. (1990) 'Unequal Pay: A Comparative Study of Australia, Canada, Sweden and the UK', *Labour and Industry* 3 (2–3): 354–71.

Willis, E. (ed.) (1988) *Technology and the Labour Process: Australian Case Studies*. Sydney: Allen and Unwin.

Windschuttle, K. (1980) *Unemployment: A Social and Political Analysis of the Economic Crisis in Australia*. Ringwood, Penguin Books Australia.

Wooden, M. (1990) *Migrant Labour Market Status*, Bureau of Immigration Research. Canberra: AGPS.

Young, C. (1989) *Balancing Families and Work: A Demographic Study of Women's Labour Force Participation*, Women's Research and Employment Initiatives Program, DEET. Canberra: AGPS.

Zimbalist, A. (ed.) (1979) *Case Studies On the Labor Process*, New York: Monthly Review Press.

Zwang, S. (1984) *Aboriginal Employment in South Australia*. Adelaide: Aboriginal Employment and Training Section, Department of Employment and Industrial Relations.

Chapter Ten

Health and the Australian Population

Jake M. Najman

The observation that the health of people is intimately connected with the way they think, feel and their related values and beliefs, is not new. Such an observation strikes a responsive chord in many, not least because many people have directly experienced instances when their own health, or the health of their family or friends has been influenced in this way.

However, such personal experiences and observations may fail to identify the 'common lot' of particular groups in the social structure: that is, of people who share patterns of lifestyle and the health consequences which flow from them. The individual who experiences a heart attack is not likely to note that he or she shares common beliefs and behaviours with others who may be disproportionately at risk of a heart attack. It is these shared experiences of social groups in society that provide the subject matter of sociology.

These shared experiences, to the extent that they are observed, are of interest primarily for two reasons. Firstly, they may be an important guide to the causes of illness and death. Thus the observation that, for example, divorced/widowed persons have higher suicide rates, is of etiological (i.e. of causal) significance. This type of finding directs attention to those aspects of the lives of divorced or widowed persons that may cause their suicide. Secondly, such observations may have great significance for the treatment (and prevention) of the matter in question. If, as we argue, a group's location in the social structure causes many health problems, then it would seem important to attend to the relevant aspects of the structure. Otherwise, treatments are likely to be only of temporary and palliative significance. These issues are further explored in this chapter.

It begins with a short review of the development of medical sociology to the present time. It considers the contributions of sociologists who have studied health and illness both in Australia and overseas. Following this, it continues with a social epidemiological analysis of the health of Australians. This analysis comprises an overview of patterns of illness and death, and an assessment of the association between these disease outcomes and the characteristics of groups who differ in their gender, racial composition, socio-economic and marital status.

Early Developments

Sociology has, from its beginning, demonstrated a concern for those factors which threaten the health of groups living in various societies. Engels (1845), in describing Manchester in 'The Condition of the Working Class in England', focused upon the filth, squalor and thus, implicitly, the impact of industrialisation and urban living on the health of the people.

When the American Social Science Association was created in 1865, it included reference in its aims to the health consequences of poverty (Lazarsfeld and Reitz 1975: 1). While much has been written in the intervening years (see for example, Durkheim's 1912 *Suicide*), the beginning of the mid-1950s is when major developments in the field of medical sociology occurred.

In 1954, Simmons, a sociologist, and Wolff, a neurologist, published the first introductory medical sociology text. It pointed to those aspects of society and social interaction which were of relevance to health and health care delivery. The text suggested that much illness was stress-induced. This orientation underlines a body of current research. Koos (1954) at the same time described class differences in health and health-related behaviour in Regionville, and his work stimulated two major continuing debates in the literature. The first concerns the impact of social and economic inequality on health. The second involves the identification of the social factors which influence those who have symptoms to seek medical and other help for them.

In 1957, Merton and his group (Merton, Reeder and Kendall 1957) published a series of reports of medical student socialisation. These continue to guide current thinking on the education and training of medical practitioners, nurses, dentists and other health workers.

Two papers reviewing the field of medical sociology appeared in 1957, both predicting rapid growth (Freeman and Reeder 1957; Strauss 1957). In his review, Strauss was able to find 110 Americans who worked primarily in the field of medical sociology, the majority of whom were employed by universities in teaching medical and nursing students, or who were working in government health departments or hospitals.

By the early 1960s a number of medical sociology texts had appeared (Jaco 1958; Apple 1960; Freeman, Levine and Reeder 1963), as had major studies on such topics as patients' perceptions of their doctor and the doctor-patient relationship (Freidson 1961), medical student culture (Becker *et al.* 1961) and life in a hospital ward (Coser 1962). At about the same time, Goffman described the perceptions and experiences of both staff and patients in psychiatric institutions (Goffman 1961). Research into the social basis and definition of mental illness has a long history in sociology (see e.g. Faris and Dunham 1939; Hollingshead and Redlich 1958) and, allied to the contributions of some medical psychiatrists (Laing 1961; Szasz 1970; Cooper 1970), has transformed psychiatric institutions and psychiatric care. Since the early 1960s, there has been a rapid growth in the field of medical sociology. The relevant section of the American Sociological Association subsequently grew to become (and remains) its largest section (in 1986 it had 961 members, an increase of 15 per cent over the previous year — ASA Footnotes, March 1986: 20).

This review of early developments is provided to emphasise two points. Firstly, it suggests that sociologists have had, and continue to have, a significant impact on developments in the health care field, though they are rarely directly involved in the delivery of health services.

Secondly, the subject matter with which sociologists deal in their studies of health and illness is extraordinarily varied. In this report of (predominantly) the Australian literature, it is not possible to discuss the full range of topics, and only some are included. This chapter emphasises one of the key areas of medical sociological research, namely the environments and behaviours which produce health and illness.

The Most Common Illness

One might begin a sociological analysis of the health of society by asking whether health care is provided, as one might presume, to those who are ill. This question raises three issues of interest to medical sociologists. Firstly, it would seem important to know if some groups in Australian society (say the poor or aged) fail to obtain medical or other care when they are ill. Secondly, it may be the case that some groups receiving health care may not require such care. These persons might be using medical care services in circumstances where previously a priest or family member would have been consulted. Thirdly, it may be that some health care fails to benefit the patient or the benefit is less than alternative (non-medical) care could have provided. These issues are (somewhat indirectly) addressed in Table 10.1.

The data in Table 10.1 are taken from the 1989–90 ABS National Health Survey. They suggest that, in a randomly chosen two-week period, the most common illnesses were headaches, the common cold, hypertension and injuries. For most of the eight most common conditions, women report higher illness rates than men.

The earlier Australian Health Survey (1986) sampled 18,000 private dwellings between February 1983 and January 1984. Of the 1983 Australian population of 15,166,900, it was estimated that 10,767,000 persons (71 per cent) took some action related to their health and that 9,446,200 persons (62 per cent) experienced an 'illness condition' *in the two weeks prior to interview.* Some 18 per cent of the population consulted a doctor in this two-week period though a smaller proportion sought help from (in order of frequency) a chemist, chiropractor, physiotherapist, optician and district nurse. In this same two weeks, 33 per cent of the population used pain relievers, 25 per cent used vitamins and minerals and 12 per cent used skin ointments and creams.

A similar type of survey undertaken in 1975 in Gosford-Wyong

Table 10.1   Recent Illness (last 2 Weeks) by Sex, 1989–1990: Eight Most Reported Conditions

	Males (%)	Females (%)
Headache	9.7	14.7
Common cold	9.7	9.4
Hypertension	6.5	9.4
Injuries	8.0	6.3
Eczema, dermatitis	4.8	6.3
Dental problems	5.0	5.6
Arthritis	3.4	6.1
Asthma	4.5	4.1

Source: Australian Institute of Health and Welfare 1992: 46

and Illawarra found that 53 per cent of the former population and 35 per cent of the latter had a chronic illness (Shiraev and Armstrong 1978). Sample surveys in Canberra (Hennessy, Bruen and Cullen 1973), and Melbourne (Krupinski and Stoller 1971) have suggested that about 20 per cent of the Australian population has some symptoms of mental illness at any chosen time, principally feelings of anxiety and/or depression.

These findings would seem to suggest that illness or the experience of symptoms is not only common, but in a statistical sense, normal in society. Further, the majority of people who report that they have symptoms also report attending to these symptoms either by taking medications for them, discussing them with friends and relatives and, less frequently, seeking the help of a doctor or other health care provider. It is important to note that many of these illnesses are not curable (e.g. colds, emotional problems), and nor may the condition benefit from the care provided. But such care nevertheless demands substantial medical resources. It is also pertinent to observe that for most illness conditions the majority of those experiencing the relevant symptoms do not appear to suffer serious consequences, despite their failure to obtain medical care.

The Most Common Causes of Hospital Admission

Hospital admission and length of stay data provide another approach to measuring the health of people in the community. Such data are available only on a state-by-state basis. According to them, the major reasons for hospital admission are, for males: accidents, poisoning and violence, then diseases of the digestive system, principally chronic liver diseases and ulcers, and diseases of the circulatory system, principally heart disease and strokes. For females the most common causes of hospital admission are pregnancy and childbirth, followed by diseases of the genito-urinary system (*Social Indicators* 1984, 1987). However, if we consider the length of hospital stay as a relevant factor in determining the importance of a particular condition, then mental disorders (male average stay 91.8 days, females 100 days) must also be added to the conditions which are a major source of morbidity in Australian society (with accidents, poisonings and violence, males average a stay of 7.1 days, and females 13.7 days). Perhaps a better estimate of the importance of a condition could be derived by multiplying the number of people admitted for a condition by their length of stay, but such data are not generally available.

As we will note in the sections which follow, the illnesses which lead to death or hospital admission are (partly) a consequence of lifestyle and of the interaction of people with their environments.

Changing Patterns of Mortality

While Australian morbidity data has only recently become available, mortality data has long been used as an indicator of national health. Such analyses of mortality data can be divided into three important and distinct historical phases: that period prior to the availability of modern (antiobiotic) medicines, say to 1940; the period from 1941 to about 1970; and the period 1971–85.

In the late nineteenth century and until the 1940s, the major causes of death in Britain (Powles 1973; McKeown 1976), the United States (McKinlay and McKinlay 1977) and Australia (Gordon 1976), were the infectious diseases, principally respiratory conditions like pneumonia and influenza. Gastric infections, tuberculosis and diptheria were also major causes of death. The first effective treatments for these conditions became available in the mid-1940s and early 1950s. Figure 10.1 illustrates this point

Figure 10.1   Male Deaths from 'Gastro' in First Year of Life, per 1,000 Live Births

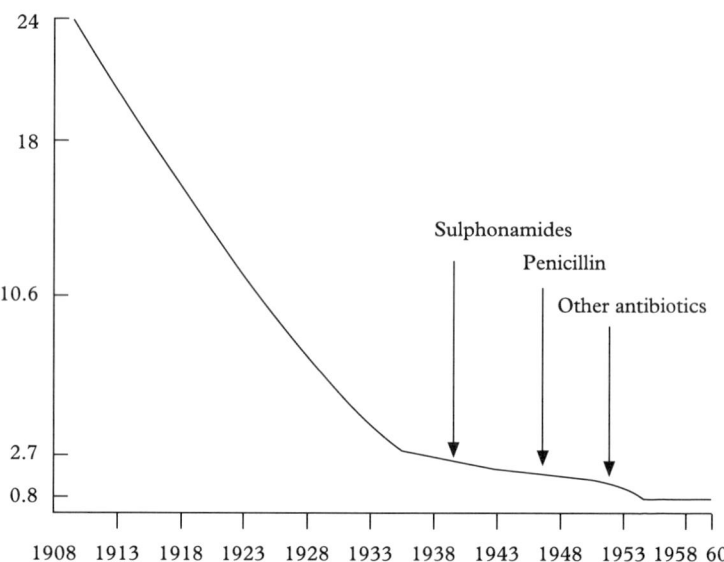

for gastric infections in males (in 1908–10 the major cause of death) in their first year of life, but similar figures could be produced for adults and children, and respiratory conditions, diphtheria, whooping cough and many other causes of death (see Gordon 1976; McKinlay and Mckinlay 1977). Note that the decline in mortality began well before effective remedies became available and appeared to continue apparently unaltered by medications, which subsequently appeared. However, as both Gordon, and McKinlay and McKinlay point out, other conditions such as tuberculosis and whooping cough had an acceleration in their mortality decline once the new therapies became available. These patterns may have implications for health care planning at the present time. Since the major decline in mortality occurred prior to the availability of effective medical treatments, it probably occurred as a result of improved sanitation, hygiene and the nutritional status of the population. Thus changes in personal lifestyle (diet) and in the physical environment had the major impact of reducing death rates. Once remedies became available, then the decline in mortality for some of the infectious diseases accelerated. Thus, largely as a result of the improved nutritional status and hygiene experienced by the population, and partly as a result of the new medications, infectious diseases were reduced to a minor factor in Australia's death rates (with the notable exception of Aboriginal mortality rates).

The second period (1941–71) was associated with the development of a wide range of treatments for infectious diseases, and the introduction of numerous medications which could be used to alter mood (the psychotropic drugs) and which led to the technological transformation of medical care, with the widespread introduction of body scanning, foetal monitoring and organ replacement surgery. In this period the major causes of death were heart disease, cancer, strokes and accidents: that is, conditions which were, in the main, chronic and incurable. During this period a variety of secular trends (e.g. changes in the extended family, increased mobility) and the availability of seemingly effective mood-modifying medications led to medical practitioners supplementing (and sometimes supplanting) the family as a source of emotional support — that is to say, the kind of help doctors were expected to provide changed. Further, as Powles (1973) points out, this was a period (1960–70) of increasing health care costs at a time when Australian adult mortality rates remained at similar levels.

While it is true that the 1960s was a period of relatively unchanged mortality despite an increased input in health resources, it may be the case that some of the new therapies and procedures significantly improved the quality of life of many whose life expectancy remained unaltered. However, such a benefit is not self-evident in all instances (see Najman and Levine 1981), and one consequence of this dissonance between increasing health costs and unchanged mortality rates was the increasing demand for evaluation, for new treatments and procedures to be scientifically assessed and their benefits judged against their costs. Assessment of effectiveness remains a consideration in the delivery of health care services at the present time. While the precise figure remains a matter of speculation, it is not yet possible to refute the suggestion that the majority of medical care services delivered lack demonstrable benefit.

In Australia from 1921 to 1945, the male age-standardised mortality rate declined from 1,689 to 1,388 deaths (22 per cent) per 100,000 population. To 1970 the male rate remained more or less stable at 1,417 deaths per 100,000 population. However, since 1970 the male mortality rate has declined by about 50 per cent to 941 deaths per 100,000 population in 1988 (see d'Espaignet 1991: 5). Whereas the mortality decline over the period 1921–45 primarily benefited the young, the mortality decline since 1970 has provided an increased life expectancy for the middle aged.

A similar overall mortality decline has been noted in the United States (*Health United States* 1985: 11) and Britain, where the decline appears to have selectively benefited non-manual workers more than those in manual occupations (Marmot and McDowall 1986: 274). The decline in mortality since 1970 is particularly evident for coronary heart disease and strokes. It appears to comprise a reduction in the incidence of these diseases rather than improved survival following hospital admission, suggesting that the decline is a result of changed lifestyle and better control of high blood pressure (Siskind *et al.* 1987; Holman 1986: 14). While both these explanations go some way to explaining the mortality decline, it is not clear whether other factors should also be considered, or what the relative contribution of lifestyle and medical care is to the mortality decline. In any event, major fluctuations in mortality rates suggest that the way people live has, and continues to have, a major impact on their 'life chances'.

In sum, many of the health workers practising at the present time and many features of our health care system originated in circumstances where there was a major decline in mortality, which some have erroneously attributed to the 'magic bullet' of antibiotics. This was followed by a period during which mortality rates altered little, while the cost of health care increased. More recently, the major causes of death have, with the exception of cancer, become less important.

In the context of contemporary industrial society and a chronic disease pattern of mortality, some question the appropriateness of the 'magic bullet' way of thinking, which appears to dominate health care delivery. This approach places an inappropriate emphasis on the treatment of existing conditions, rather than on their prevention.

Gender and Health

Differences in the health and health needs of men and women provide an excellent illustration of the extent to which biology, behaviour and socio-structural location interact and impinge on an individual's life chances. It has been noted that for almost every species of known insect or animal the female outlives the male (Retherford 1975). Thus it is not surprising to find that women outlive men in Australia.

Such a consistent pattern does suggest that females have a biologically determined survival advantage. Table 10.2 indicates that, in 1921, male death rates were 24 per cent higher than female death rates. By 1960, male death rates were 53 per cent higher than female, and since 1975 have remained at about 70 per cent higher. Such a change over a relatively short period of time cannot be attributed to biological factors, but must reflect other aspects of the way men and women live in society.

Table 10.2   Changes over Time in Male as Compared to Female Age Standardised Mortality Rates

	Ratio of Male to Female
1921	1.24
1925	1.26
1930	1.24
1935	1.27
1940	1.33
1945	1.30
1950	1.40
1955	1.49
1960	1.53
1965	1.60
1970	1.63
1975	1.69
1980	1.74
1985	1.68
1988	1.69

Source: d'Espangnet *et al.* 1991: 5

The disease which makes the single greatest contribution to overall mortality is coronary heart disease. While there remains some debate about its causes, being overweight, inactive, smoking cigarettes, drinking alcohol to excess and hypertension (high blood pressure) are all generally agreed to be factors associated with an elevated risk of heart disease. As Table 10.3 indicates males are more often overweight and inactive; they more frequently smoke cigarettes, drink alcohol to excess and manifest high blood pressure. This evidence suggests that at least part of the difference between the mortality rates of men and women is attributable to behavioural differences, which in turn reflect underlying patterns of values and beliefs. Thus, for example, women are less likely to take risks — and their lower death rates from motor vehicle accidents appear to partly reflect this pattern of female socialisation. Women also appear to be more concerned about health issues and their appearance than are men. Consequently, women seem to be more willing to seek help for medical conditions before they become serious, and also appear to consume a healthier diet.

Race

Prior to European colonisation, the bulk of Aborigines lived a semi-nomadic existence stopping at different temporary campsites

Table 10.3   Male/Female Differences in Health Related Behaviours in Australia: Adults 25–64+

	Female (%)	Male (%)	Rate ratio
Overweight	32.8	48.6	1.48**
Inactivity	32.9	37.6	1.05*
Smoking	25.6	33.8	1.32**
Alcohol risk	7.6	15.7	2.06**
Hypertension	11.2	17.2	1.54**

Overweight:	self-reported, BMI 25.0 kg/m^2+
Inactivity	self-reported, based upon per cent reporting no physical exercise for recreation in last two weeks
Smoking	self-reported current smokers
Alcohol risk	self-reported, with level based upon NHMRC recommendations
Hypertension	per cent diastolic 95 mmhg+ or systolic 160mmhg, or on tablets
**P<.001	*P<.05

Source: National Health Strategy 1992: 11 (Supplement)

in a defined geographic area.[1] Aborigines were tied to their land and dependent upon it for survival. Generally, social organisation comprised relatively small clans or bands (estimates vary but are generally between 10 and 200 persons) who shared a language and customs. Population estimates of Aborigines in 1788 are the subject of some debate. Original estimates were of about 300,000 Aborigines in about 500-600 tribes, with distinct dialects or language but Butlin (1983) argues that there were up to five times that number.

Laws and mores were largely administered by the older men who enforced a code of rigid rules. Of particular relevance was a belief in the supernatural and a fear of events beyond the familiar. Thus disease might be interpreted as a consequence of sorcery, as a result of an offence one might have given to another person. European notions of infectious agents and of hygiene and sanitation were (and in some cases still are) foreign (see Reid 1982 for a discussion of various Aboriginal conceptions of health).

Aboriginal laws prescribed and proscribed the content and nature of relationships between relatives and placed an obligation on individuals to share their resources. There was an emphasis on formalised reciprocity, of sharing with others according to set rules. It could be argued that this emphasis on reciprocity was a consequence of living in a subsistence economy where the survival of individuals and groups was dependent upon receiving 'gifts' at times when food was in short supply.

Keen (1993) and others (Reynolds 1972; Rowley 1978; Stevens 1981) have traced the history of early contact between the white European settlers and Aborigines in Australia. Determining features of this contact were massive numbers of deaths attributable to contact with common European infectious agents; an imperialist/ capitalist ideology which demanded the exploitation of land for economic reasons; and a popular stereotype of Aborigines as a debased and primitive people. This was a time when undiluted ethnocentrism ruled popular thinking. British values and culture were held to be necessary, and others, particularly those of persons of non-European origin (e.g. Chinese, Australian Aborigines) were treated with derision, and disparaged. Consistent with this approach there were claims that :

> Moral laws they [Aborigines] have none; their festive dances and corroborees are of the most lewd and disgusting character, their songs, rites and ceremonies utterly revolting and fiendish ... [if we] ask the question as to the possibility of chastity among their women the idea becomes preposterous.
> (Comment of a pastoralist, quoted in Stevens 1980)

while the Bulletin of 1897 suggested that:

> Christianity was never intended for Black-Fellows. Its higher doctrines they are incapable of understanding ... [they are] spineless creatures with all the savagery taken out of them.
>
> (Quoted in Stevens 1980)

In the above context is not surprising that those Aborigines who survived the infectious diseases which were perhaps deliberately introduced (Butlin 1983), were systematically exterminated, either by being shot or by consuming poisoned food which might have been left for them. There are many recorded instances of atrocities, including the almost total destruction of the Aboriginal population of Tasmania and the murder of infants (see Stevens 1980; Keen 1993).

Of particular relevance to the present circumstances of Aborigines were laws passed which denied normal rights and freedoms to black Australians. Most states passed Aboriginal Protection Acts, purportedly to protect 'the natives'. These had a two-edged intent, to protect, but also to control, the Aboriginal people. In Queensland, for example, Aboriginal settlements were established in 1897, and Aborigines were required to live on these. They were often located away from traditional lands, in places where familiar foods might not be available. Superintendents of these reserves had great control of movement and behaviour. They could, for example, beat young children (and even adults) for trying to escape. In Western Australia, Aborigines who absconded from work (i.e. quit their jobs) could be flogged and gaoled. They were rarely paid in money for their work. A major employer in the Northern Territory stated he was 'opposed to the payment of wages to natives ... money seems to be the root of all evil'.

The more recent period of White-Aboriginal contact is perhaps best charactertised as a series of attempts to redress and undo the past, at least by some groups and movements. Many of these efforts have been a consequence of studies showing extraordinarily high rates of Aboriginal morbidity and mortality. Thus blindness among Aborigines has been of epidemic proportions (Taylor 1980), while the rate of ear infections is one of the highest recorded for any group in the world (Moran 1979). Not only do Aborigines manifest high rates of diseases which are more generally common in a developing country, but they also appear to have developed high rates of heart disease, hypertension and diabetes (Bastian 1979), diseases usually associated with affluent, developed societies.

Recent data show that Aboriginal infant death rates are between two and five times white Australian rates, that the life expectancy of male Aborigines at birth is about 50 years in rural New South Wales and 56 years in Western Australia (compared with 74 years for all male West Australians). Comparable data for females is 55 years, 63 years and 79 years (Hicks 1985). Thomson (1985) in a review of Aboriginal mortality rates, suggests they are between 2 and 4 times those of non-Aborigines 'and up to 7 times those for post-neonatal deaths' (p. 547). Of perhaps greater concern, however, was his suggestion of a 'marked worsening of Aboriginal adult mortality, in country regions of New South Wales at least' (p. 48).

Kunitz (1990) has compared the life expectancies and infant mortality rates of various indigenous peoples from North America, New Zealand and Australia (see Table 10.4). The data clearly indicate that American Indians, Canadian Indians and New Zealand Maoris have a substantially longer life expectancy than Aboriginal Australians. In America, Canada and New Zealand, health and social policies have reduced inequalities in life expectancy between the indigenous and non-indigenous people to a few years. In Australia the gap in life expectancy remains only a little below twenty years. Part of the reason for this is the higher rate of diseases of the circulatory system (e.g. heart disease)

Table 10.4   Life Expectancy and Infant Mortality of Segregated Indigenous and Non-indigenous Populations (around 1980s)

	Life expectancy		Infant mortality (per 1,000 live births)
	Male	Female	
United States			
Indigenous*	67.1	75.1	9.7
Non-indigenous	70.7	78.1	
Canada			
Indigenous	64.0	72.8	21.8
Non-indigenous	72.4	80.1	
New Zealand			
Indigenous	65.2	68.3	18.0
Non-indigenous	70.8	77.0	
Australian			
Indigenous	54.0	61.6	20–34**
Non-indegenous	72.8	79.1	

* Includes Indian and Alaskan natives
** Various estimates from different states
Source: Kunitz 1990: 650–51

experienced by Aboriginal Australians (compared to other native groups). Many Aboriginal groups have reacted to their physical, cultural and social dislocation by adopting unhealthy 'white' patterns of behaviour, often without the limits and controls that European culture provides.

Are the high morbidity and mortality rates experienced by Aborigines a consequence of inadequacies in health care delivery? Without discussing this possibility in detail, it seems unlikely that more health services of the type provided to other Australians will significantly improve Aboriginal adult health.

In one interesting study of the impact of modern medical care on the health of an Aboriginal group, Navajo Indians living in poverty were provided with sophisticated medical services, including doctors, drugs, vaccines, diagnostic equipment and surgery. Their morbidity and mortality levels were then monitored over a five-year period. There was no evidence that this medical care had a significant impact on infection levels or upon the mortality rate (McDermott *et al.* 1972: 25). Another experiment in three villages in rural Guatemala produced similar results. One village was monitored (the control village), a second received dietary supplements but no additional medical care, while a third received comprehensive medical care, immunisation and some help with sanitary services. While there was some evidence of reduced morbidity in both the treatment and nutritional supplement villages, the improved diet seemed to have the greater impact. On some measures, the health of those in the treatment village remained very poor (Scrimshaw *et al.* 1969). Thompson (1985)[2] has suggested that the improvement in diet and the social and physical environment represent minimal prerequisites to better Aboriginal health, and that more medical care is perhaps best conceptualised as fine tuning, once major improvements have occurred.

The cumulative impact of these studies is to question the likely reduction of Aboriginal health problems by providing more of the types of medical services already available to the white community. These studies re-emphasise the point we have already noted, that health is dependent upon a variety of social and environmental factors. A New Zealand study (Smith *et al.* 1985) has reinforced this point, by noting that New Zealand Maoris who had converted to the Mormon religion and adopted a set of behaviours and circumstances which differed from their non-Mormon Maori counterparts, had substantially lower(ed) mortality rates.

In the context of Australian Aborigines, the key social and environmental factors include:

- a history of cultural and ideological dislocation which limits Aborigines adopting either traditional or white lifestyles;
- a history of political oppression, working against Aboriginal participation in the dominant political processes;
- a consequent high level of cigarette use, alcohol consumption, poor diet and other adverse lifestyle characteristics;
- health services which are generally limited to treating acute illnesses, with little attention to the circumstances which generate such conditions.

The health of Australia's Aborigines remains a national disgrace. The evidence from other countries clearly suggests that more effective ways of addressing their health problems are available.

Social Class

While the existence of social and economic inequalities has fuelled intense debates and, on occasion, rapid change, it is the consequences of such inequalities which are of major concern in this section. Koos, in a 1954 study of 514 families living in a small town in New York state, described class differences in morbidity. This study was extensively quoted in subsequent writing, and its importance is evidenced by its re-publication thirteen years after it originally appeared. Koos divided his sample into three groups, Class 1, comprising business and professional persons; Class 2, skilled and semi-skilled workers; and Class 3, labourers and itinerant workers. Koos' major findings were that Class 3 persons:

- were less 'sensitive' to symptoms and, compared with Class 1, reported they would be less likely to seek medical care for the same symptoms;
- were found to have a higher rate of disabling illnesses;
- were less likely to have received medical care for their reported illnesses;
- more often sought non-medical (e.g. chiropractor) help for their illnesses;
- were much less likely to report having a family doctor;
- were more likely to be dissatisfied with the medical care they had received;
- more frequently consulted a pharmacist for their health problems;
- generally did not have family dentists and when they went to a dentist were likely to go for an extraction, while Class 1 persons more often went for preventive care and dental repairs.

Studies in a number of countries have confirmed some of Koos' findings, but not others. It appears clear that there are substantial class inequalities in mortality in adults (Antonovsky 1967) and infants (Antonovsky and Bernstein 1977), with lower class groups having higher mortality rates. Some have raised methodological objections to these findings and argued that they fail to address the possibility that persons who are ill are downwardly mobile — that is they become lower class following an illness which limits their capacity to work. However, research on people who were healthy at the beginning of the study, has noted class differences in subsequent mortality, confirming that lower class groups manifest higher mortality rates (Goldblatt 1990).

The question of whether Australia is a more or less equal society than others has been addressed in other papers (see Western 1993). Using the Henderson poverty levels,[3] it is estimated that over 9 per cent of Australians are living in poverty, this being concentrated in such groups as the unemployed and sole parents (*Report on Poverty Measurement* 1981). What, then, is the impact of social class on morbidity and mortality in Australia? This question needs to be answered separately for children and adults.

Australian data for child morbidity are few. Data derived from the 1989-90 ABS Health Survey (National Health Strategy 1992: 135) indicate that children from low income families have higher rates of serious chronic illness. Data from the Mater — University of Queensland Study of Pregnancy (MUSP) and its outcomes, show that children born to parents of lower socio-economic status have higher rates of developmental delay (Najman *et al.* 1992). Similar findings are observed for children manifesting what is generally described as psychiatric morbidity (behaviour, thought and personality problems). Children living in poverty manifest substantially higher rates of 'problem' behaviour (Najman *et al.* 1993).

Australian findings of child mortality confirm the existence of an inverse association with social class (Siskind *et al.* 1987a). Data recently published by the Australian Institute of Health and Welfare (National Health Strategy Supplement 1992: 1) indicate that children living in the most socio-economically disadvantaged areas have mortality rates about 50 per cent above those of children living in the most advantaged areas.

There have been relatively few Australian studies of adult morbidity (illness) and social class. Data from three of these, the Australian Health Survey (Broadhead 1985), Brisbane (Najman *et al.* 1979) and Gosford-Wyong/Illawarra (Shiraev and Armstrong 1978), show that there are few consistent or strong associations when occupation type is the relevant criterion of social class.

However, when income differences are used, and these arranged to reflect those below, at, or above the Henderson poverty line, then both males and females below it experience higher rates of recent illness, more chronic conditions and higher rates of mental and emotional problems (Broadhead 1985: 95).

Australian occupational mortality data have only recently become available, but they have been consistent in confirming the inverse association between social class and mortality, whether Census-based occupational criteria are used (Taylor *et al.* 1983) or occupational status (McMichael 1985), or whether the analysis is based on individual or area data (Siskind *et al.* 1987). Thus Brisbane data (Siskind *et al.* 1987) show that those living in the lowest status areas have, overall, mortality rates which are about 35 per cent higher than those experienced by persons living in the highest status areas. The trend appears consistent for the major causes of death, except for lung cancer rates for women, which do not follow the general pattern. This inconsistency may change as more lower class women become smokers. Similarly, breast cancer rates, accident rates (females only) and suicide rates did not manifest the general trend in the Brisbane study.

There is, then, general consensus that those living in poverty, whether child or adult, and irrespective of whether one considers morbidity or mortality, have worse health. It is, however, less clear why such differences exist. Certainly the lifestyle of those living in poverty places them at higher risk of poor health (see Table 10.5). Those in the lowest income groups are more often overweight, inactive and smoke cigarettes. There is also some evidence of class differences in diet and nutrition (Calnan 1990). One plausible explanation of these differences is that living in poverty places certain limits on particular behaviours and predisposes the individual to certain other behaviours. It would be a mistake to, for example, 'blame' the victim (the smoker), if — as the data suggest — poverty itself may lead some people to smoke, or forego exercise, or eat less healthy foods.

Marital Status

Marital status represents another social structural characteristic with health implications. Durkheim (1912) found that single people had higher suicide rates, and he interpreted this as demonstrating the importance of an individual's social networks and ties to the broader social system. More recent research has suggested that many other disease conditions are influenced by marital status.

Table 10.5 Income Inequalities in Health Related Behaviours in Australia, Adults 25–64+ (Ratio of Unhealthy Characteristics in Medium and Low Income Groups compared with High Income Groups)

		Income Category	
	High	Medium	Low
Overweight			
Males	1.00	1.02	1.05
Females	1.00	1.28★	1.47★
Inactivity			
Males	1.00	1.40★	1.42★
Females	1.00	1.19★	1.28★
Smoking			
Males	1.00	1.21★	1.40★
Females	1.00	1.22★	1.39★

★ Asterisk here and in Tables 10.6 and 10.7 indicates that there is less than 1 chance in 20 that the association is due to chance: that is, there are 19 chances out of 20 that there is a relationship between the variables indicated (★P<0.05)

Overweight: self--reported BMI 25.0 KG/M^2 +

Inactivity: self-reported, based upon per cent reporting no physical exercise for recreation in last two weeks

Smoking: self-reported current smokers

Source: National Health Strategy 1992: 2 (Supplement)

Table 10.6 illustrates some of the typical findings of this research. It shows that for all the causes of death listed, married males and females have lower age-adjusted mortality rates. For example, for males the never-married and divorced/widowed groups have death ratios some 50 per cent higher than married males. Thus, whether one is considering the infectious diseases, cancer of the lung or digestive organs, stroke or heart disease or the violent causes of death, widowed and divorced persons die at higher rates. Further, in some instances the magnitude of advantage of married persons is such that they have a death rate half that or less of those who are not married.

While the data appear relatively clear (see Kobrin and Hendershot 1977 for an American example), they are susceptible to various interpretations. Some would suggest that unhealthy single persons are less likely to marry. According to this view, those who are married are healthier because of a selection process. Another interpretation is that social bonds and strong social ties serve to protect or buffer the impact of stress on health. Yet another view is that much health-related behaviour (e.g. smoking

Table 10.6 Marital Status and Age Standardised Mortality
Ratios From Selected Causes, Persons 25–64,
Australia 1985–87

	Married	Never Married	Divorced/Widowed
Lung cancer			
Males	1.00	1.52	1.53*
Females	1.00	1.13*	1.39*
Ischaemic heart disease			
Males	1.00	1.94*	1.78*
Females	1.00	1.64*	1.54*
Cerebrovascular disease			
Males	1.00	2.73*	2.34*
Females	1.00	1.88*	1.54*
Motor vehicle accidents			
Males	1.00	2.11*	2.42*
Females	1.00	1.94*	1.83*
Suicide			
Males	1.00	2.84*	3.37*
Females	1.00	2.76*	3.33*

Source: National Health Strategy 1992: 2 (Supplement)

or excessive alcohol consumption) occurs in a family context and
that single people behave in a less healthy way because they are
less subject to the moderating influence of family members. As
Table 10.7, indicates, the marital status groups differ in some
lifestyle characteristics but not others. The data never indicate
that married and divorced/widowed groups smoke and drink
alcohol to excess more frequently.

At the present time we are unable completely to account for
the marital status differences in mortality. Selection factors
undoubtedly contribute to observed differences in health, but they
appear unlikely to account for the poor health of widowed persons
(what type of selection could produce these differences?). Strong
social networks appear to offer some health benefits, particularly
in respect to emotional and psychological problems, but it is not
apparent that they protect individuals from the range of causes of
death identified in Table 10.6. Finally, it does appear that married
persons behave in a healthier manner (Wilsnack *et al.* 1984;
Layne and Whitehead 1985). These behavioural differences undoubtedly contribute to the poorer life expectancy of those not
presently married.

Table 10.7 Marital Status Differences in Health-related
Behaviours in Australia, Adults 25–64

	Married	Never Married	Divorced/Widowed
Overweight			
Males	1.00	0.86**	0.90
Females	1.00	0.91	0.97
Inactivity			
Males	1.00	0.91***	0.95
Females	1.00	0.83*	0.92
Smoking			
Males	1.00	1.20**	1.53**
Females	1.00	1.23**	1.90***
Alcohol risk			
Males	1.00	1.22*	1.73***
Females	1.00	1.67***	1.58***

Overweight: self-–reported BMI 25.0 KG/M^2 +
Inactivity: self-reported, based upon per cent reporting no physical exercise
                for recreation in last two weeks
Smoking: self-reported current smokers
Alcohol risk: self-reported, with level based on NHMRC recommendations
Source: National Health Strategy 1992: 6 (Supplement)

Discussion

There have been a number of major changes in patterns of morbidity and mortality since the beginning of the twentieth century. These serve to emphasise the impact of the social and physical environment on health.

Much of what constitutes 'illness' in contemporary Australian society comprises either minor and self-limiting infections (respiratory and digestive system conditions), or 'problems of living' (headaches, nervous and mental disorders), both of which are unlikely materially to benefit from medical care. Hospital admissions also appear to be a consequence of some social and environmental processes (e.g. pregnancy and childbirth, accidents, mental illness), though in some instances the factors involved are poorly understood.

However, the most compelling illustration of the impact of Australian social organisation on health is provided by changes to, and contemporary patterns of, mortality. Thus the major decline in mortality in the twentieth century is, as we have noted, largely a consequence of the manipulation and engineering of the human environment. It has led to a pattern of mortality largely involving the chronic diseases. These appear to have their causes in the lifestyle of individuals and the social structures which generate them. While male and female death rates have decreased since the beginning of the century, it would appear that the decrease in female death rates has been proportionately greater — leading to an increase in the difference between male and female death rates. In a similar vein, the high mortality rates, by both Australian and overseas standards, of Australian Aborigines, points to environmental and lifestyle causes. Both social class and marital status variations in morbidity and mortality raise similar concerns.

In each of the above instances we observe major health differentials which need to be understood. The factors leading to such health inequalities have been introduced, but these may now be reconsidered in a broader context.

The sociological perspective is distinguished, in part, by an emphasis on the extent to which human behaviour is interpreted from the perspective of a person's membership of a social group within the social structure. Structural location is perceived as important for a number of reasons. At its simplest level, people in the same position in the social structure are exposed to a similar socialisation process. While not denying that there are many similarities in the socialisation of different social groups (for example, most groups have access to similar mass media, and mass media are one of the main agents of socialisation), social groups tend to differ in important respects. From a health perspective, these differences include attitudes to risk taking, to what constitutes a health problem, to their willingness to use medical services, and to key aspects of lifestyle (see Figure 10.2 for a schematic description of this point).

Figure 10.2   Model of the Likely Sequence of Events Associating Social Structures and its Health Consequences

Social structure	Attitudes, beliefs, values	Behaviour	Physiological changes or pathology	Illness or death
Gender	Risk taking	Exercise	Changes in	Lung cancer
Race	Health beliefs	Diet	cell structure	Heart disease
Class	Use of health	Smoking	Changes in	Suicide
Marital status	services	Alcohol	immune	Accidents
Age	Lifestyle	Preventive	response	Quality of life
	preference	checks	Changes in	
		Sex practices	physiology	

These attitudes, beliefs and values in turn influence key health-related behaviours (sometimes labelled 'lifestyle'), which in turn have a marked impact on human physiology and pathology — and consequently on morbidity and mortality.

Policy Implications

If health and illness are, as this chapter argues, substantially influenced by the social and physical environment, then presumably health care delivery systems may be assessed in terms of the extent to which they deal both with the immediate manifestations of, and the factors that produce, illness. While this chapter is not specifically concerned with the effectiveness or appropriateness of medical treatment, such care appears to be the main activity of the current Australian health care system.

If, as we suggest, types of social structure produce identifiable health consequences, then these should also be the focus of therapeutic efforts. Jenkins (1977) has pointed out that those areas experiencing natural disasters are frequently the subject of emergency aid, yet in situations where large numbers of persons become ill or die as a consequence of their social and environmental circumstances, little is done. Presumably in situations which are chronically 'disastrous', the status quo is accepted. Such appears to be the situation with respect to the lower life expectancy of Australian Aborigines, men, those living in poverty, and those not married.

Others have already noted that the solution to these distressing states of poor health may be outside what has traditionally been defined as the health care sector (see Gray 1982: 369; Egbuono and Starfield 1982: 555). It was this perception of health as dependent upon political and structural changes which motivated Virchow to join the 1948 Berlin working class revolt (Navarro 1976). Similarly, one of the fathers of the discipline of sociology, Georg Simmel, noted in 1897 that structural solutions were needed to solve problems created by the social structure (see Casparis and Higgins 1968–69). If, for example, people smoke as a response to the impoverishment of their lives, then it is the impoverishment that must be addressed. Blaming the victim not only serves no constructive purpose, but distracts from the primary task of finding an effective response.

Of course it is somewhat easier to call for change than to identify specific changes, and their intended and possibly unintended consequences. Unfortunately, when one deals with the details of possible structural changes, they frequently represent 'a shot in the dark' (Scrivens and Holland 1983: 104). There appears to be a need for more innovative social experiments to test the impact of proposed structural changes. If poverty, unemployment and racial injustice lead to unhealthy lifestyles, then programs which diminish such inequalities should be expanded on a trial basis, possibly through the income redistributive mechanisms of the taxation system.

Conclusion

Health and illness are fundamentally a consequence of the way societies are organised and function. Health is substantially influenced by the political, economic and cultural processes which prevail in any society. It follows from these observations that continued attention must be paid to racial, economic and other inequalities and their reduction as a necessary step in the improvement of health of minority groups in Australia. At the same time it is clearly appropriate that a redirection of health effort take place, with a greater emphasis on specific health promotion and disease prevention programs.

The cost of delivering health care services remains considerable, accounting for over 8 per cent of the GDP. Approximately half of all health care expenditures are incurred in hospitals, where the cost of a bed involves greater expense than in a luxury international standard hotel. While such a comparison (between hospital beds and luxury hotels) is somewhat beside the point, it serves to emphasise that unhealthy social structures generate substantial health care costs. It is perhaps unfortunate that health statistics do not generally count these costs, and thus enable policy makers to argue more strongly for the need for structural solutions to health problems.

Notes

1. Many discussions of traditional Aboriginal society and its early contact with European culture are available: see, for instance, Rowley 1972.
2. Personal communication.
3. Using criteria which emphasise the minimum needs of people for food, housing and clothing.

References

Alderson, M.R. (1972) 'Some Sources of Error in British Occupational Mortality Data', *British Journal of Industrial Medicine* 29: 245–54.

Antonovsky, A. (1967) 'Social Class, Life Expectancy and Overall Mortality', *Milbank Memorial Fund Quarterly* 45: 31–75.

———and Bernstein, J. (1977) 'Social Class and Infant Mortality', *Soc. Sci. Med.* 11: 453–70.

Apple, D. (ed.) (1960) *Sociological Studies of Health and Sickness.* New York: McGraw-Hill.

Australian Bureau of Statistics (1986) Australian Health Survey 1983, No. 4311.0. AGPS: Canberra.

Australian Institute of Health and Welfare (1992) *Australia's Health 1992: The Third Biennial Report of the Australian Institute of Health and Welfare.* Canberra: AGPS.

———(1986) Household Expenditure Survey, Australia No. 6530.0. AGPS: Canberra.

Bastian, P. (1979) 'Coronary Heart Disease in Tribal Aborigines — the West Kimberley Survey', *ANZJ Med.* 9: 284–92.

Becker, H.S. *et al.* (1961) *Boys in White.* Chicago: University of Chicago Press.

Broadhead, P. (1985) 'Social Status and Morbidity in Australia', *Community Health Studies* 9 (2): 87–98.

Butlin, N.G. (1983) *Our Original Aggression.* Sydney: Allen and Unwin.

Calnan, M. (1990) 'Food and Health: A Comparison of Beliefs and Practices in Middle-Class and Working-Class Households', in S. Cunningham-Burley and N.P. McKeganey (eds), *Readings in Medical Sociology.* London: Tavistock.

Casparis, J. and Higgins, A.C. (1968–69) 'Georg Simmel on Social Medicine', *Social Forces* 47: 330–34.

Cooper, D. (1970) *Psychiatry and Antipsychaitry.* St Albans, Merts.: Paladin.

Coser, R.L. (1962) *Life in the Ward.* East Lansing: Michigan State University.

d'Espaignet, E. *et al.* (1991) *Trends in Australian Mortality 1921–1988.* Canberra: AGPS.

Durkheim, E. (1912) *Le Suicide,* originally published in Paris, various translations available, including that by J.A. Spaulding, and G. Simpson (1952). London: Routledge and Kegan Paul.

Egbuono, L. and Starfield, B. (1982) 'Child Health and Social Status', *Pediatrics* 69 (5): 550–57.

Engels, F. (1845) 'The Condition of the Working-Class in England' reprinted in *Karl Marx and Frederick Engels, Collected Works,* Vol. 4. London: Lawrence and Wishart.

Faris, R.E.L. and Dunham, H.W. (1939) *Mental Disorders in Urban Areas.* London: Phoenix Books.

Fox, A.J. and Goldblatt, P.O. (1982) *Longitudinal Study,* Series LN No. 1. London: HMSO.

Freeman, H.E. and Reeder, L.G. (1957) 'Medical Sociology: A Review of the Literature', *American Sociological Review* 22 (1): 73–81

————, Levine, S. and Reeder, L.G. (eds) (1963) *Handbook of Medical Sociology*. Englewood Cliffs: Prentice-Hall.

Freidson, E. (1961) *Patients' Views of Medical Practice*. New York: Sage.

Goffman, E. (1961) *Asylums*. Harmondsworth: Penguin.

Goldblatt, P. (ed.) (1990) *Longitudinal Study: Mortality and Social Organisation*. London: Office of Population Census and Surveys, Series LS No. 6.

Gordon, D. (1976) *Health, Sickness and Society*. St Lucia: University of Queensland Press.

Gray, A.M. (1982) 'Inequalities in Health. The Black Report: A Summary and Comment', *International Journal of Health Services* 12 (3): 349–80.

(US Department of) Health and Human Services (1985) *Health United States*, Hyattsville DHHS Pub. No. (PHS): 86–1,232.

Hennessy, B.L., Bruen, W.J. and Cullen, J. (1973) 'The Canberra Mental Health Surveys: Preliminary Results', *MJA* 1: 721–28.

Hicks, D.G. (1985) *Aboriginal Mortality Rates in Western Australia 1983*. Perth: Health Department of Western Australia.

Hollingshead, A.B. and Redlich, F.C. (1958) *Social Class and Mental Illness*. New York: Wiley.

Holman, C.D.J. *et al.* (ed.) (1986) *Our State of Health. An Overview of Health and Illness in Western Australia in the 1980s*. Perth: Health Department of Western Australia.

Jaco, E.G. (ed.) (1958) *Patients, Physicians and Illness*. New York: Free Press.

Jenkins, C.D. *et al.* (1977) 'Zones of Excess Mortality in Massachusetts', *NEJM* 296 (23): 1,354–56.

Keen, I. (1993) 'Aborigines and Islanders in Australian Society', in J.S. Western and J.M.Najman (eds), this volume.

Kobrin, F.E. and Hendershot, G.E. (1977) 'Do Family Ties reduce Mortality? Evidence from the United States, 1966–1968', *Journal of Marriage and the Family*, November: 737–45.

Koos, E.L. (1954) *The Health of Regionville*. New York: Columbia University Press.

Kunitz, S.J. (1990) 'Public Policy and Mortality among Indigenous Populations of Northern America and Australasia', *Population and Development Review* 16 (4): 647–72.

Laing, R.D. (1961) *The Self and Others*. London: Tavistock.

Layne, N. and Whitehead, P.C. (1985) 'Employment, Marital Status and Alcohol Consumption in Young Canadian Men', *Journal Studies in Alcohol* 46 (6): 538–40.

Lazarsfeld, P.F. and Reitz, J.G. (1975) *An Introduction to Applied Sociology*. New York: Elsevier.

McDermott, W., Deuschle, K.W. and Bornett, C.R. (1972) 'Health Care Experiment at Many Farms', *Science* 175: 23–31.

McKinlay, J.B. and McKinlay, S. (1977) 'The Questionable Contribution of Medical Measures to the Decline of Mortality in the United States in the Twentieth Century', *Milbank Memorial Fund Quarterly*, Summer: 405–28.

McMichael, A. (1985) 'Social Class (as estimated by Occupational

Prestige) and Mortality in Australian Males in the 1970s', *Community Health Studies* 9 (3) 220–30.

Marmot, M.G. and McDowall, M.E. (1986) 'Mortality Decline and Widening Social Inequalities', *Lancet* 2 August: 274–76.

Merton, R.K., Reader, G.G. and Kendall, P.L. (eds) (1957) *The Student Physician*. Cambridge Mass.: Harvard University Press.

Moran, D.J. *et al.* (1979) 'Ear Disease in Rural Australia', *MJA* 2: 210–12.

Najman, J.M. *et al.* (1979) 'Patterns of Morbidity, Health Care Utilisation and Socio-economic Status in Brisbane', *ANZJS* 15 (3): 55–63.

——(1992) 'Child Developmental Delay and Socio-economic Disadvantage in Australia: A Longitudinal Study', *Social Science and Medicine* 34 (8): 829–35.

Najman, J. and Levine, S. (1981) 'Evaluating the Impact of Medical Care and Technologies on the Quality of Life: A Review and Critique', *Soc. Sci. Med.* 15F: 107–15.

National Health Strategy (1992) *Enough to Make You Sick: Home Income and Environment Affect Health*. Canberra: Australian Institute of Health.

Navarro, V. (1976) 'The Underdevelopment of Health of Working America: Causes, Consequences and Possible Solutions' *AJPH* 66: 538–47.

Powles, J. (1973) 'On the Limitations of Modern Medicine', *Science, Medicine and Man* 1: 1–30.

Registrar General (1971) *Decennial Supplement England and Wales 1961: Occupational Mortality Tables*. London: HMSO.

Report of the Director General of Health 1983–84 (1984) Canberra: AGPS.

Reid, E. (1982) *Body, Land and Spirit*. St Lucia, University of Queensland Press.

Retherford, R.D. (1975) *The Changing Sex Differential in Mortality*. Westport, Conn.: Greenwood Press.

Reynolds, H. (ed.) (1972) *Aborigines and Settlers*. Melbourne: Cassell.

Richard, J.J. (1985) 'The Epidemiology of Coronary Heart Disease: A Review', *Effective Health Care* 2 (5): 197–209.

Rowley, C.D. (1972) *The Destruction of Aboriginal Society*. Melbourne: Pelican.

——(1978) *A Matter of Justice*. Canberra: ANU Press.

Scrimshaw, N.S. *et al.* (1969) 'Nutrition and Infection Field Study in Guatamalan Villages, 1959–64'. *Arch. Environ. Health* 18: 51–62.

Scrivens, E. and Holland, W.W. (1983) 'Inequalities in Health in Britain. A Critique of the Report of a Research Working Party', *Effective Health Care* 1 (2): 97–109.

Shiraev, N. and Armstrong, M. (eds) (1978) *Health Care Survey of Gosford-Wyong and Illawarra 1975*. Sydney: Health Commission of New South Wales.

Simmons, L.W. and Wolff, H.G. (1954) *Social Science in Medicine*. New York: Sage.

Siskind, V. *et al.* (1987) 'Socio-economic Status and Mortality: A Brisbane Area Analysis', forthcoming in *Community Health Studies*.

Smith, A.H. *et al.* (1985) 'Mortality among New Zealand Maori and non-Maori Mormons', *Int. J. Epid.* 14 (2): 265–71.

Social Indicators (1984) Canberra: Australian Bureau of Statistics.

Social Welfare Policy Secretariat, Report on Poverty Measurement (1981). Canberra: AGPS.

Statistics on the Distribution of Income and Wealth in Australia (1981) Canberra: Department of Social Security, Research Paper No. 14.

Stevens, F. (1980) *The Politics of Prejudice*. Sydney: Alternative Publishing Co-op.

———(1981) *Black Australia*. Sydney: Alternative Publishing Co-op.

Strauss, R. (1957) 'The Nature and Status of Medical Sociology', *American Sociological Review* 22 (2): 200–04.

Szasz, T.S. (1979) *The Manufacture of Madness*. New York: Harper and Row.

Taylor, H.R. (1980) 'Prevalence and Causes of Blindness in Australian Aborigines', *MJA* 1: 71–76.

Taylor, R. *et al.* (1983) *Occupation and Mortality in Australian Working Age Males, 1975–77*. Melbourne: Health Commission of Victoria and Department of Social and Preventive Medicine, Monash University.

Thomson, N. (1985) 'Review of Available Aboriginal Mortality Data, 1980–82', *MJA* 143, 28 October, Special Supplement: 546–49.

Webster, I.W. and Rawson, G.K. (1979) 'Health Status of Seventh-Day Adventists', *MJA* 1: 417–20.

Western, M. (1993) 'Class and Stratification', Chapter 3, this reader.

Wilsnack, R.W. *et al.* (1984) 'Women's Drinking and Drinking Problems: Patterns from a 1981 National Survey', *AJPH* 74 (11): 1,231–38.

Wise, P.H. et al. (1985) 'Racial and Socio-economic Disparities in Childhood Mortality in Boston', *NEJM* 313: 360–66.

Chapter Eleven

Political Behaviour: Explaining Australian Political Stability*

Ian McAllister

In approaching the study of Australian politics, the problem that requires explanation is simple: compared with other advanced industrial societies, Australian politics has demonstrated great stability during the course of the twentieth century.[1] Evidence of this is the stability of popular voting patterns and the consistency of the votes that the major parties receive from election to election. To explain this stability, the chapter shows how levels of popular political participation are finely balanced between activism and apathy, with the vast majority of voters eschewing support for extra-constitutional political protest. In addition, although the social bases of the major political parties have changed over the past century, the parties have altered their appeals to adapt to these changes. The net result is a degree of political stability which is found in few other liberal democracies.[2] The analyses are based on the respondents to four opinion surveys, conducted in 1967,

* The 1967 and 1979 Australian National Political Attitudes Surveys were collected by Don Aitkin; the 1987 Australian Election Study by Ian McAllister, Anthony Mughan and Roger Jones; the 1990 Australian Election Study by Ian McAllister, Roger Jones and David Gow; and the 1988 Issues in Multicultural Australia Survey was designed by Roger Jones and Ian McAllister and collected by AGB-McNair. All the data are publicly available from the Social Science Data Archive at the Australian National University. Neither the original collectors of the data nor the data archive are responsible for the analyses or interpretations presented here.

1979, 1987 and 1990; these responses are treated as representative of the Australian electorate as a whole in the four years in question.

Political Participation

The notion of democracy assumes that all citizens participate equally in political affairs and that their decisions carry equal weight. Without active citizen involvement in politics, democracy would cease to be meaningful, both in a literal and a practical sense. Yet there is general agreement that democracy fails if there is too much citizen participation in politics; indeed, it is often argued that democracy is most likely to prosper when there is a balance between widespread political apathy and involvement.

Survey-based studies of political participation have identified three forms of participation in addition to voting: *campaign activity*, involving active participation in election campaigns; *communal activity*, which is concerned with organisational involvement within the local community; and *personal contacts* with government officials on matters of personal or family concern (Verba and Nie 1972; Verba, Nie and Kim 1971, 1978). Aside from voting — which involves 95 per cent of Australian citizens because of the system of compulsory voting — communal activity is the most frequently used form of political participation. In total, just under half of all citizens have, at some point in their lives, been concerned enough about a community problem to become involved with others, to form a group, or to contact government officials (Table 11.1). Fewer citizens have become involved in campaign activity, with the most common form of activity being persuading others how to vote. Finally, 22 per cent report contacting government officials about a personal or a family problem.[3]

The overlap between the various forms of conventional political activity is small. Rather than using all the means at their disposal, citizens tend to specialise in one or other form of political participation. The proportion of political activists in Australia — those who use a variety of forms of participation — is therefore no more than a small proportion of the total population; estimated from Table 11.1, only 6 per cent of the population can be considered to be complete political activists, in the sense that they have participated in all three dimensions of participation — campaign, communal and personal contact. A much larger proportion — 23 per cent — have engaged in two of the three activities, and are therefore partial political activists, while 33 per cent have participated in one of the activities. At the other end of the spectrum,

Table 11.1   Conventional Political Participation, 1988*

	Per cent
Campaign activity	
Persuade others how to vote	22
Attend meetings or rallies	7
Work for party or candidate	10
(Used at least one)	(29)
Communal activity	
Worked with others	29
Formed group	13
Contacted officials	31
(Used at least one)	(45)
Personal contact	
Contacted official	22
(N)	(1,152)

*The questions were: 'During elections, do you ever talk to people and try to show them why they should vote for one of the parties or candidates?'; 'Do you go to any political meetings or rallies or things like that?'; 'Have you helped a political party or candidate, for example, at a polling booth or working in a candidate's office?'; 'Have you ever worked with others in Australia to try and solve some of the community's problems?'; 'Have you ever taken part in forming a new group or a new organization in Australia to try and solve some community problem?'; 'Have you (or anyone in your family living here) ever contacted an elected representative or government employee about some need or problem concerning the local community?'; 'Have you (or anyone in your family living here) ever contacted an elected representative or a government employee to seek help with a personal problem you or your family ever had?'
Source: Issues in Multicultural Australia Survey 1988

the largest single group (38 per cent of the electorate) are completely inactive politically.

Political protest represents another form of political participation. It is generally agreed that such protest covers political activities that depart from orthodox forms of participation and which involve direct as opposed to indirect methods of exerting political pressure (Barnes, Kaase *et al.* 1979; Bean 1991). To differentiate it from conventional forms of participation, protest is sometimes called 'unorthodox political participation' or 'direct political action'. As with conventional political activity, the methods used can vary greatly, ranging from signing petitions or participating in legal demonstrations, to the use of violence against individuals or property. Protest activities can therefore be arranged on a continuum, starting with those that are most acceptable and widely used by citizens, and ending with those which use violence

Table 11.2 Support for Political Protest, 1987*

	Have done	Might do	Would never do	% Total	(N)
Legal protest					
Signing a petition	72	22	6	100	(1,792)
Joining in boycotts	9	47	44	100	(1,744)
Attending lawful demonstrations	13	44	43	100	(1,759)
Semi-legal protest					
Joining unofficial strikes	3	22	75	100	(1,752)
Occupying building and factories	1	10	89	100	(1,754)
Radical protest					
Damaging things, like breaking windows, removing road signs	1	2	97	100	(1,762)
Using personal violence, like fighting with other demonstrators or the police	1	4	95	100	(1,763)

*The question was: 'There are various forms of political action that people can take. Please say, for each one, whether you have actually done any of these things, whether you would do it, or would never, under any circumstances, do any of them?'

Source: 1987 Australian Election Study

and are endorsed by only a small minority. The 1987 Australian Election Survey asked respondents whether they had done, might do, or would never do, six separate acts of political protest (Table 11.2). Signing a petition, joining a boycott or attending a lawful demonstration are the activities which are most acceptable to citizens. Slightly less than half the electorate say that they would never engage in boycotts or demonstrations. Semi-legal activities, such as participating in unofficial strikes or occupying buildings or factories are supported by only 25 per cent and 11 per cent of citizens, respectively, while the two radical activities which involve the use of violence gain minimal support.

The distribution of these types of protest across the electorate shows that the largest single group, 41 per cent, consists of those who have used, or would use, legal forms of protest only. Given the proportion who are completely inactive in terms of conventional political participation, it is hardly surprising that a substantial proportion (32 per cent) have not and would not use any of these three forms of protest. Semi-legal protesters represent 22 per cent of the electorate, the bulk of them saying that they had the potential to carry out one of the two acts in question, rather than that they had actually done it. Finally, and perhaps most importantly for the future of Australian democracy, only 5 per cent report that they would use some form of violence as a political protest. This distribution corresponds very closely to the proportions of protesters in other advanced industrial societies (Barnes, Kaase *et al.* 1979).

Since the French Revolution ushered in the era of popular participation in politics, there has been general disagreement about the contribution of political participation to democratic stability. To some extent, the dynamics of political participation have managed to resolve this dilemma. Citizens who are politically uninterested or misinformed are also those least likely to participate. In that sense, they are excluded from active involvement in politics, other than through the most basic — and in many respects, the least influential — act of voting. The majority of citizens are involved in political activity in a variety of ways, thereby at least partially meeting the requirement for popular involvement in politics. Political protest provides further scope for citizens to convey their views to political authority. Democracies have therefore managed to strike a balance between activity and apathy which, in Australia as elsewhere, has helped to ensure long-term political stability.

Parties and the Party System

Without political parties, modern liberal democracy would cease to be practical. It is the modern political party that structures the range of beliefs, opinions and expectations that exist within the electorate. As the British political scientist, Bryce, argued more than half a century ago, 'political parties bring order out of the chaos of a multitude of voters' (Bryce 1921). The focal point for this activity is elections, which are the means by which citizens in a liberal democracy express a collective opinion about which party they want to place in government. As a result, parties orient most of their activities and commit most of their resources to the electoral process.

While party political debates reflect contemporary issues and concerns, the organisation of the party system is a consequence of the historical circumstances that prevailed a century or more ago. In Australia, the emphasis on socio-economic debate between the Labor and Liberal parties stems from the divisions that dominated Australian society when the party system was formed at the turn of the century. Writing a quarter of a century ago, Lipset and Rokkan (1967) argued that Western party systems had been 'frozen' by the circumstances surrounding their formation. They identified two processes. First, a *National Revolution* took place which involved conflict over the territorial boundaries of state. This was reflected in a centre-periphery cleavage, placing regional groups in opposition to the dominant culture, as well as in a religious cleavage, as the Catholic Church sought to protect its influence from secular groups. Second, an *Industrial Revolution* created divisions based on conflict between rural groups and newly industrialised entrepreneurs, and between industrial owners and workers — the genesis of the modern class cleavage.

The colonisation and settlement of Australia after 1788 meant that it avoided most of the conflicts stemming from the National Revolution, although it has suffered from some regional and religious conflict (Figure 11.1). The nineteenth century witnessed regional rivalry between the colonies, although in the latter part of the century, colonial governments were preoccupied with security and trade issues. The patterns of religious support evident in Europe during the nineteenth century were also imported into Australian party politics, and religion has surfaced periodically as an issue within the Labor Party, the 1915 conscription debate and the 1950s opposition to Communist influence in the trade unions being the best examples. Apart from the last vestiges of religious influence on party support, the National Revolution has had little long-term impact on the Australian party system.

By contrast, the Industrial Revolution had a decisive impact. In the 1880s and 1890s, rural-urban divisions dominated political conflict, with the rural areas opposing the economic policies of the rapidly industrialising cities. This regional conflict was gradually overtaken in the early years of federation by conflicts between industrial owners and workers. In the first decade of the twentieth century, three parties dominated federal politics: the Labor Party, which was formed in 1901 from the various colonial Labor parties, and the Protectionists and Free Traders (Loveday 1977). In 1909, the Protectionists and the Free Traders settled their differences and combined to form the Liberal Party (later the United Australia Party, and later again re-adopting the Liberal Party title), thereby establishing the pattern of two-party competition that has been the basis of the Australian party system ever since.

Despite the dominance of the owner-worker cleavage, reflected in Labor-Liberal party competition, the rural-urban division has remained politically salient through the Country (later National) Party. Between 1914 and 1919, a sustained period of low prices for agricultural produce stimulated the rise of country parties

Figure 11.1   Development and Institutionalisation of Social Divisions within the Australian Party System

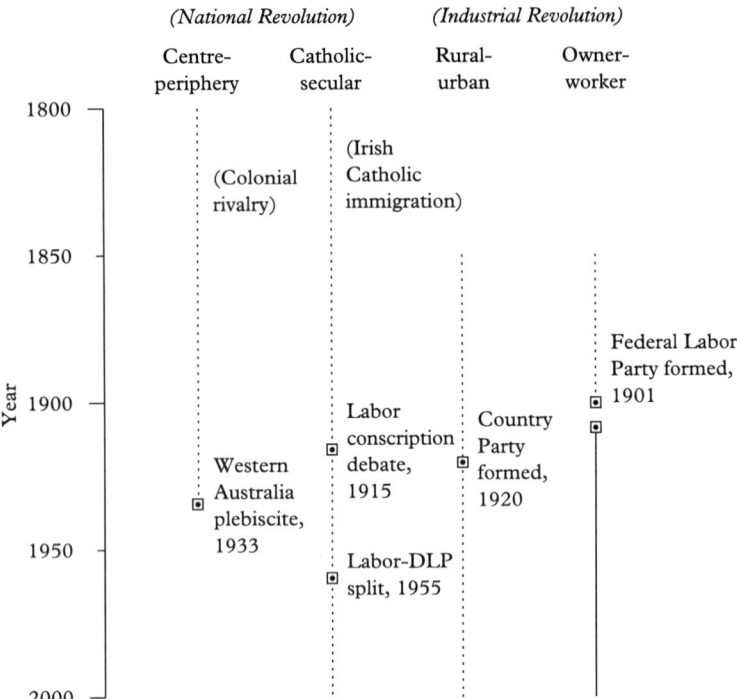

Type of social division

Note: A dotted line represents a minor cleavage, a solid line a major cleavage
Sources: McAllister (1992)

dedicated to defending agricultural interests, and they combined to form a single party in 1920, shortly after entering into a Coalition with the Liberal Party. The Coalition has remained in existence since then, except for two short periods in 1973–74 and 1987.

The long-term stability of the Australian party system over the course of the twentieth century sets it apart from other such systems. The parties that vie for electoral support at the close of the twentieth century are very much the descendants of the parties that existed at the beginning. Moreover, with the exception of some comparatively minor splits and fissures, parties outside the major Labor-Liberal and National division have gained little electoral success. Of the 36 federal elections between 1901 and 1990, only 4 have produced a non-major party vote that has exceeded 10 per cent of the first preference vote[4] and in only one federal election — 1990 — has a single minor party gained more than 10 per cent of the vote.[5]

Such long-term electoral stability is regarded as one of the fundamental preconditions for a liberal democracy. Taking into account the widespread social, economic, political, cultural and technological changes that have taken place during the course of the twentieth century, how have so many political parties in Western democracies managed to survive intact, in line with the Lipset and Rokkan 'freezing' hypothesis? First, the inheritance and transmission of party loyalties from generation to generation has helped maintain the stability of the party system. Second, parties are highly adaptable organisations, ensuring their own survival by moulding their outlook and appeals to new popular issues, demands and circumstances (Mair 1983). The net result, in Australia as well as elsewhere, has been a high level of party and electoral stability.

Party Identification and Voting

Prior to the widespread use of political opinion surveys in the late 1940s, it was assumed that citizens based their voting decision on issues, in a 'consumer choice' model of voting, choosing the party or candidate that offered them most. This view accorded with the conduct of election campaigns, which consisted of debates between candidates over issues and policies. However, the first two major survey-based voting studies conducted in the United States, *The People's Choice* (Lazarsfeld, Berelson and Gaudet 1944) and *Voting* (Berelson, Lazarsfeld and McPhee 1954), uncovered two problems with this explanation for voting behaviour. First, they found that many voters had made up their minds which party to vote for well before the election campaign had commenced, so the campaign could not be a major cause of their vote. Second, few voters had an accurate perception of where individual candidates stood on particular issues.

Later it appeared that the membership of social groups explained voting behaviour, with group loyalties fostering particular views towards parties. This still provided, however, only a partial explanation. For one thing, citizens' group loyalties were shown to change frequently over the lifecycle, while party loyalties remained stable; other influences were clearly at work in shaping the vote. The authors of *The American Voter*, Campbell *et al.* 1960, argued that the missing element was a sense of party identification among citizens. They argued that just as individuals identified with particular social, religious or ethnic groups during their lives, they also identified with political parties. It was a sense of party attachment that accounted for how people voted, not election issues or loyalties towards particular social groups.

The concept of party identification (or partisanship) rests on three main assumptions. First, partisanship is conceptually and theoretically distinct from the vote. Even if a partisan of one party were to vote for another party, he or she would later return to vote for the original party (often called 'the homing tendency'). Second, partisanship is stable over time. Since political parties, like other social groups, do not change the fundamental premises on which they appeal to voters for support, partisanship represents a long-term influence on political behaviour. Finally, the influence of partisanship extends beyond voting, providing a filter through which individuals evaluate and interpret the political world around them.

In Australia, party identification is often viewed as the basis for party stability. As Aitkin (1982: 1) argues, 'the causes of ... stability are to be found in the adoption, by millions of Australians then and since, of relatively unchanging feelings of loyalty to one or other of the Australian parties'. Trends in the direction of party identification in Australia demonstrate that, with the exception of 1967, a period of Labor decline, no more than 3 percentage points separated the proportions identifying with the two major parties (Figure 11.2). In 1990, the increase in identification with non-major parties (mainly the Australian Democrats and environmental candidates) increased to 12 per cent, but reduced identification with both major parties by about the same amount. The period since 1979 has therefore been one in which the direction of party identification has remained remarkably stable.

There has, however, been a decline in the strength of party identification, as the second part of Figure 11.2 demonstrates. Those who see themselves as very strong identifiers have declined by almost half, from 34 per cent in 1979 to 18 per cent in 1990. The net increase resulting from this weakening in partisanship has taken place among those who are 'not very strong' partisans, who now make up just over one-third of all voters. This declining strength in partisanship is a trend that has been apparent in Britain and the United States, where it was first evident in the 1960s, somewhat earlier than in Australia.

An additional evaluation of the importance of party identification is the proportion of partisans who vote for their preferred party — what is called the 'normal vote'. While overall levels of

Figure 11.2 Direction and Strength of Party Identification, 1967–90

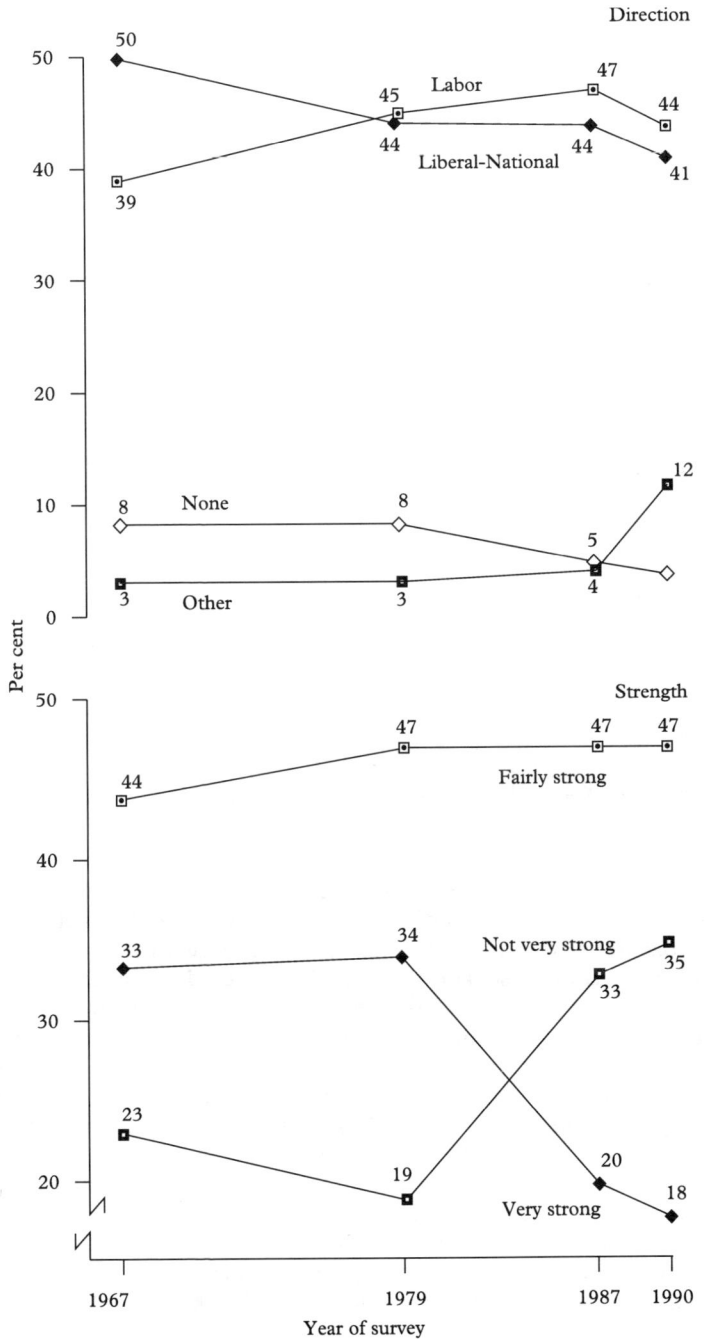

Sources: 1967 and 1979 Australian National Political Attitudes Surveys; 1987 and 1990 Australian Election Studies

Figure 11.3   Proportion of Major Party Identifiers who vote for their Party, 1967–90

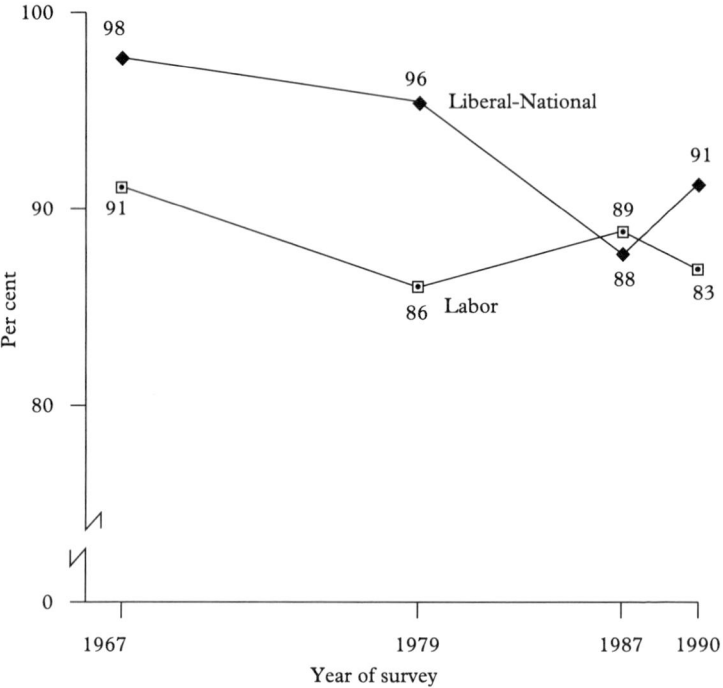

Source: As for Figure 11.2

identification remain high in Australia, the decline that has taken place in the strength of partisanship should increase the likelihood that partisans will vote for other parties. Figure 11.3 shows that this is indeed the case, and there has been a gradual decline in the proportions of partisans who vote for their party. In 1967, no less than 98 per cent of Liberal-National partisans also chose to vote Liberal-National, compared with 91 per cent in 1990. There is a similar decline among Labor identifiers, from 91 per cent in 1967 to 83 per cent in 1990. Nevertheless, despite this long-term decline, the congruence of party identification and the vote in Australia still remains impressive, at least by the patterns observable in the rest of the Anglo-American world.

Party identification remains high in Australia, and it is un-doubtedly one of the major factors contributing to political stability. Why has Australia not followed other countries and registered a decline in the direction of partisanship? The main explanation is probably Australia's system of compulsory voting,[6] which ensures that all voters are forced to make a frequent choice between competing political parties. Nevertheless, the decline in the strength of partisanship may presage the long-term erosion of party identification, as has occurred elsewhere. There is little doubt, for example, that it was a major factor underlying the unprecedented support for minor parties in the 1990 federal election.

The Social Bases of Parties

Until recently, much of the research on the social bases of the parties in Australia focused on the role of class in shaping political behaviour. Some studies have argued that it is a major influence, albeit one of several, which structure citizens' votes (Alford 1963; Aitkin 1982), while other studies have questioned its importance (Kemp 1978). A third view has argued that class remained important until the 1960s, but its subsequent decline was less dramatic than others have suggested (Jones and McAllister 1989). More recently, debates about Australian voting behaviour have moved beyond class to examine such factors as gender, religion, ethnicity and more sophisticated conceptions of socio-economic status (for an overview, see McAllister 1992). The range of social influences on the vote can be grouped under three headings: parental political socialisation; ascribed characteristics (measured by gender, religion, ethnicity and urban-rural residence); and socio-economic status (measured by social class and trade union membership).

Parental Political Socialisation

For an adolescent, the party orientation of his or her parents provides a ready-made cue for party support — a view that may well remain unchanged throughout the course of their lifetime. Table 11.3 shows that more than two-thirds of voters come from families in which their parents' party loyalties are known and in which their parents agreed politically; Labor has a slight advantage, with 38 per cent of voters coming from Labor families, compared to 31 per cent who come from Liberal-National families. By contrast, only 31 per cent of voters come from families in which the party loyalties of parents are not known, or are divided. Among voters who come from divided families or from families that had no clear party preferences, party identification is evenly divided between the Labor and Liberal-National parties. How-

Table 11.3 Parents' Partisanship and Vote, 1990*

	Both Labor	Both Liberal-National	Both none/don't know	Divided
Labor	58	17	45	41
Liberal-National	26	67	40	44
Other	16	16	15	15
Total	100	100	100	100
(N)	(730)	(584)	(314)	(282)
(Row per cent)	(38)	(31)	(16)	(15)

*The question was: 'Did your father/mother have any particular preference for one of the political parties when you were young, say about 16 years old?'
Source: 1990 Australian Election Study

ever, for voters coming from families in which there is political agreement, no such ambiguity exists; among voters coming from Labor families, 58 per cent inherit their parents' party identification, compared to 67 per cent of voters coming from Liberal-National families.

There is international evidence that the transmission of partisanship from parents to children has declined since the 1960s (Rose and McAllister 1990: 175), and this decline also appears to have taken place in Australia, although not to the same extent as elsewhere. Figure 11.4 shows that in 1967, no less than 87 per cent of those who came from Liberal-National families followed their parents' choice; by 1990, this had declined to 67 per cent — still a significant level of party inheritance, but nevertheless a decline of almost one-fifth in little over two decades. The pattern for Labor is different though it, too, declined between 1979 and 1990, albeit less dramatically, and Labor inheritance actually experienced an increase between 1967 and 1987. In summary, 6 per cent fewer respondents who came from Labor families supported Labor in 1990 than supported the party in 1967.

Ascriptive Characteristics
This refers to the characteristics that individuals possess and with which they are born, such as their gender or race. Also included in this broad category is religion, since it is largely inherited,[7] as well as place of residence. It is these characteristics which often form the basis for political conflict in pre-industrial societies, where the division of labour is not sufficiently advanced to produce a complex class system. Even in advanced industrial societies, vestiges of these older social divisions often remain politically salient, as in today's Eastern Europe.

Figure 11.4   Transmission of Partisanship, 1967–90 (Proportions of Labor and Liberal-National Voters coming from Families in which Both Parents agreed Politically)

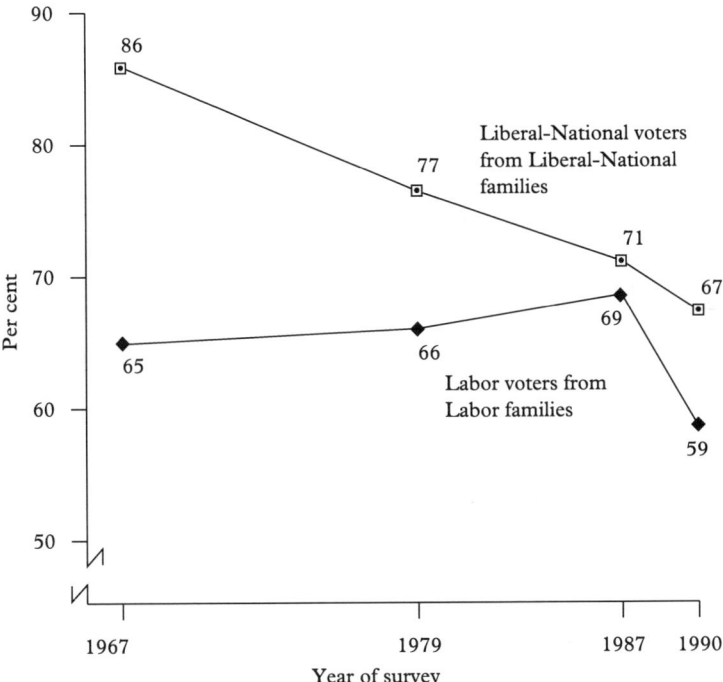

Sources: As for Figure 11.2

In most Western societies, gender differences in politics were considered sufficiently important for women not to be granted the vote until early in the twentieth century. Women voted in the Australian federal election of 1902.[8] However, in other countries, this right was not granted until much later: Belgium, for example, did not grant women the vote until 1948, with Switzerland being the last European country to do so, in 1977. Based on their traditional biological and cultural role of child care and family support, women have been shown to be more likely to support conservative political parties when compared with men (for a review, see Goot and Reid 1975). But in the last two decades, the political gender gap has all but disappeared.

In the 1990 election, there are minimal differences between men and women in their party support — three percentage points

Figure 11.5   Declining Influence Gender on Voting 1967–90

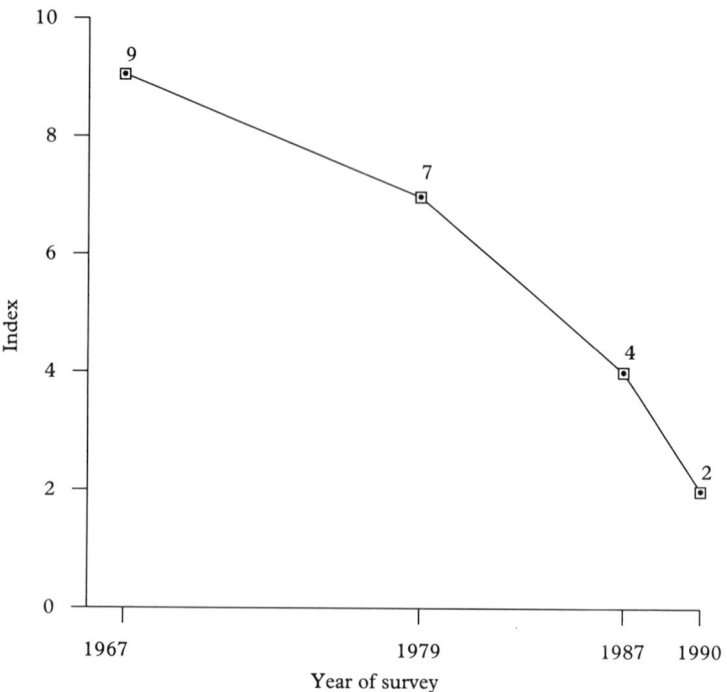

Note: The index is estimated as the percentage of male respondents voting
Labor, minus the percentage of female respondents voting Labor
Source: as for Figure 11.2

at most (McAllister 1992: 136). As Figure 11.5 demonstrates, the
political gender gap has declined significantly since the 1960s. In
1967, 9 per cent more men supported Labor than did women, a
gap which declined to 7 per cent in 1979, and 4 per cent in 1987.
This decline has been attributed to the increasing proportion of
women in the paid labour force, and to the declining significance
of religion; both are major influences on the political behaviour of
women (De Vaus and McAllister 1989).

Historically, religion has been a major influence on political
behaviour. Although Australia was colonised after religion had
ceased to hold centre stage in European politics, the country inherited many of the religious divisions of the early European
settlers. At the turn of the century, when the party system was

being formed, class often reinforced religion, and religion was the source of periodic political conflict. But in the past two decades, religion has declined dramatically as a political influence. This is reflected in the large increase in the proportion of individuals who disavow any religious affiliation, which now stands at about one in seven of the population (McAllister 1988; Hogan 1979). Despite its declining significance, religious denomination still exerts a significant influence on the vote (Table 11.4), with Catholics tending towards Labor support, Anglicans and other Protestants towards the Liberal-Nationals. In 1990, 6 per cent more Catholics than Anglicans voted Labor, while secularists were more likely to support either Labor or the Australian Democrats.

Church attendance often has a greater influence than religious domination on voting behaviour since it reflects social patterns of behaviour which mould outlooks, beliefs and values. These, in turn, have consequences for political outlooks. Table 11.4 shows that while 60 per cent of weekly church attenders voted Liberal-National, the same figure for those who reported never attending church was only 38 per cent. Although the division is not as great among Labor voters, 49 per cent of those who never attended church voted Labor, compared with 33 per cent of the most frequent attenders.[9] In addition to influencing party choice, church attendance also shapes opinions on a wide range of social issues on which the churches hold strong views, such as abortion, permissiveness and the role of the family.

Table 11.4 Religion and Voting, 1990*

	Labor	Liberal-National	Democrat	Total	(N)	(Column %)
Religious denomination						
Anglican	42	48	10	100	(598)	(31)
Other Protestant	33	53	14	100	(319)	(17)
Catholic	48	41	11	100	(525)	(27)
Other religion	39	48	13	100	(195)	(10)
None	44	34	22	100	(281)	(15)
Church attendance						
Weekly	33	60	7	100	(298)	(16)
Occasionally	38	48	14	100	(388)	(21)
Hardly ever	42	43	15	100	(551)	(29)
Never	49	38	13	100	(652)	(34)

*The question were: 'What is your religion or faith?'; 'Apart from weddings, funerals and baptisms, about how often do you attend religious services?'
Source: 1990 Australian Election Study

Table 11.5   Urban-Rural Residence and Vote, 1987*

	Large city	Medium city	Town	Rural area
Labor	47	55	44	31
Liberal	44	28	30	31
National	3	10	20	34
Democrat	6	7	6	4
Total	100	100	100	100
(N)	(714)	(420)	(376)	(185)
(Row %)	(42)	(25)	(22)	(11)

*The question was: 'Would you say you live in a: rural area (under 1,000 people); country town (1,000 to 20,000 people); a medium-sized city (20,000 to 100,000 people); a large city(over 100,000 people)?'
Source: 1987 Australian Election Study.

The urban-rural cleavage in voting behaviour stems from the Industrial Revolution, when the political authority of rural groups was threatened by new urban entrepreneurs within the rapidly growing cities (Leithner 1991). Although this conflict was resolved in favour of the urban majority, remnants of the cleavage remain. In Australia it is represented by electoral support for the National Party. Table 11.5 shows that the urban-rural cleavage remains alive and well in Australian voting behaviour. Among voters living in large cities — who account for 42 per cent of the total electorate — the two major parties attract more than 9 out of every 10 voters, with the Nationals attracting a mere 3 per cent of the vote.[10] At the other extreme, in rural areas consisting of under 1,000 residents, the vote is divided 3 ways, with the Nationals gaining a small advantage over the 2 major parties. Indeed, even in country towns, the Nationals gain about one-fifth of the vote.

The explanation for the continuing salience of the urban-rural division in Australian politics is the presence of the National Party and the political power it exercises through the Coalition with the Liberals. In the absence of a political party dedicated to articulating rural concerns, a distinctive rural political identity would have faded many decades ago, and been absorbed into the platforms of the two major parties. This was the fate of the agrarian parties which emerged in continental Europe in the early twentieth century (Urwin 1980). As long as the National Party remains in existence to politicise the urban-rural division, it is likely to exert a continuing influence on Australian politics.

Socio-economic Status

The traditional view of Australian politics is that class has determined electoral behaviour for most of the twentieth century. However, this conclusion began to be questioned in the 1970s. Aitkin, for example, argued that while there was a stable level of class voting, it was relatively weak; he concluded that 'Australian politics is the politics of parties, not of classes' (1977: 142). Similarly, Kemp (1978) claimed that the electoral importance of class had declined significantly in the 1960s and 70s. More specifically, he argued that changes in advanced industrial society — such as the decline in traditional blue collar occupations and the greater availability of higher education — were undermining the class cleavage.

The measurement of class and its consequent impact on political behaviour has generated considerable controversy (see, for example, Baxter, Emmison, Western and Western 1991; Graetz and McAllister 1988). For the purposes of this analysis, class is conceptualised into occupation and economic lifestyle. Political scientists have traditionally measured occupation by the manual/non-manual/farmer distinction, which formed the basis for early voting studies (Berelson, Lazarsfeld and McPhee 1954; Campbell, Gurin and Miller 1954). In recent years, however, conflict aspects of class have been viewed as important, reflected in self-employment, supervision, and public sector employment (Kelley and McAllister 1985).

The relationship between occupational class and vote in 1990 indicates that no single party gains overwhelming support from one occupational group, although Labor does attract support from a narrow majority of manual workers, and the Liberal-Nationals gain the support of 46 per cent of non-manual workers (Table 11.6). Almost three-quarters of all farmers support the Coalition, mostly in the form of the National Party. The Democrats attract disproportionate support from non-manual workers, and find least support among farmers.

There is strong support among the self-employed for the Liberal-Nationals, with no less than 64 per cent of the self-employed voting for the Coalition in the 1990 election, compared with one-quarter who voted Labor. This accords with the conservative political priorities of the self-employed, including reduced taxation, more economic incentives, and less government regulation of business. However, since the proportion of the self-employed in the workforce is relatively small — just over one in five — the net Liberal-National electoral advantage is limited. Those who exercise authority in the workplace through supervision are also more likely to support the Liberal-Nationals, although the advantage over Labor is much less, at 7 percentage points. Public sector employees are significantly more likely to

Table 11.6 Occupational Class and Vote, 1990*

	Labor	Liberal-National	Democrat	Total	(N)	(Column %)
Manual/Non-manual						
Non-manual	38	46	15	100	(915)	(54)
Manual	50	38	12	100	(684)	(40)
Farmer	21	72	7	100	(100)	(6)
Self-employment	26	64	10	100	(411)	(22)
Supervision	40	47	13	100	(977)	(52)
Public sector						
employment	51	34	15	100	(494)	(26)

*All estimates are for head of household
Source: 1990 Australian Election Study

support Labor, the party most likely to sustain a large government bureaucracy, and here the gap is a substantial 17 percentage points.

Placed in a longitudinal perspective, there has, as others have found, been a decline in the electoral importance of occupational class, judged by three of the four occupational measures (Figure 11.6). In 1967, the impact of the manual/non-manual distinction stood at a 28 points—indicating that manual workers were 28 per cent more likely to vote Labor than non-manual workers. This declined gradually during the 1970s and 1980s, falling to 12 per cent in 1990. Indeed, among those who have entered the electorate in the past decade, patterns of class voting are non-existent (McAllister 1992: 161). Similarly, the impact of supervision has declined, from 18 to 5 percentage points. The only exception to this pattern is public sector employment, which stands at about the same level in 1990 as it did in 1979, the first year for which data are available.

Occupational class has important consequences for the material conditions of people's lives — their 'economic lifestyle'. One aspect of economic lifestyle is class self-image, while another is trade union membership.[11] There have been a variety of studies examining class identity or class consciousness in Australia, and the extent to which citizens' perceptions of the class structure influence their behaviour (Graetz 1986; Chamberlain 1983). Most have concluded that class self-image is a major determinant of voting behaviour in its own right, in Australia as well as overseas (Kelley and McAllister 1985; Graetz and McAllister 1988: 290–91).

When asked about their place within the class structure, in

Figure 11.6 Four Measures of Occupational Class and the Vote, 1967–90

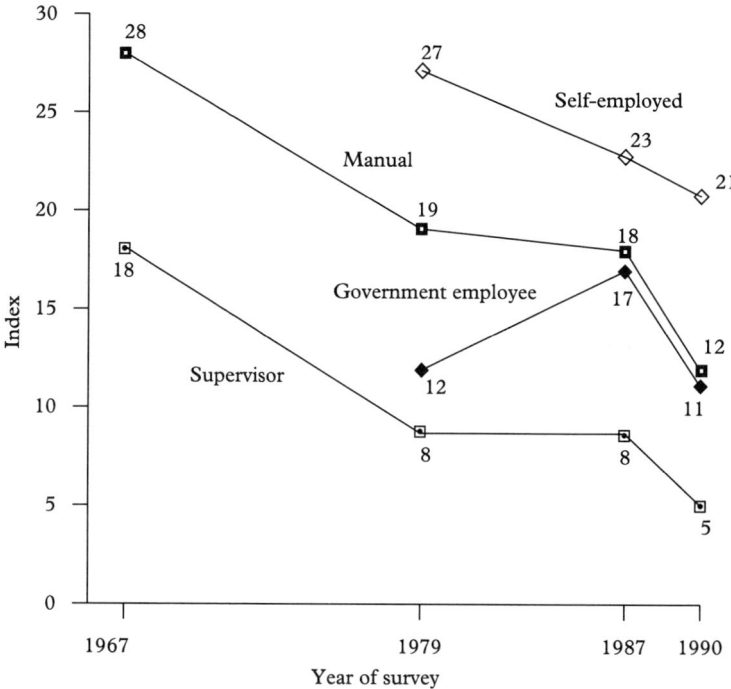

Note: The index is the percentage of manual workers, supervisors, government employees and the self-employed voting Labor, minus the percentage of non-manual workers, non-supervisors, private sector employees and employees voting Labor. Data on government and self-employment are not available for 1967. Estimates are for the head of the household, except for supervisors in 1967 and 1979, where only respondent data are available.

Source: As for Figure 11.2

practice most voters will readily volunteer a social class. As the final column in Table 11.7 demonstrates, in 1990 less than one in ten of those interviewed in the survey refused to name a social class to which they felt they belonged. Among the 92 per cent who mentioned a class, affiliation is divided almost equally between the middle and the working class.[12] By any standards, class image has a significant impact on vote. Among those who feel they belong to the middle class, support for the Liberal-Nationals exceeds Labor by 21 percentage points; similarly, among those who identify with the working class, Labor has an

Table 11.7 Economic Lifestyle and Vote, 1990

	Labor	Liberal-National	Democrat	Total	(N)	(Column %)
Class self-image						
Middle	32	54	14	100	(760)	(43)
Working	52	36	12	100	(807)	(46)
None	43	43	14	100	(186)	(11)
Trade union membership*						
Trade union member	53	34	13	100	(628)	(34)
Staff association	42	41	17	100	(169)	(9)
Non-member	37	51	12	100	(1,076)	(57)

*Estimates are for head of household.
Source: 1990 Australian Election Study

advantage of 18 percentage points. Support for the major parties is evenly balanced among those who refuse to volunteer a class affiliation.

In 1990, 34 per cent of voters belonged to a trade union or lived in a household where the head was a union member; a further 9 per cent were members of staff associations. Trade union membership has a significant impact on the vote, with 53 per cent of union members supporting Labor, compared with 37 per cent of non-members, reflecting Labor's origins in the trade union movement at the turn of the century. Members of staff associations occupy an intermediate position in their voting behaviour, and it is from this white collar group that the Democrats attract significant support.

Along with occupational class, economic lifestyle has declined significantly in electoral importance since 1967 (Figure 11.7). Trade union membership has declined from 26 percentage points to 16 points over the 23-year period, while class self-image has declined by 15 percentage points. Comparing the results with those in Table 11.6 shows that throughout the period, economic lifestyle is at least as important in determining the vote as objective class location. Popular sentiments about class and class consciousness have therefore remained more important electorally than the job that a person performs; the ideological context within which work is conducted is politically important, not just the job itself.

The evidence, then, is clear: there has been a gradual decline in the importance of class voting since the 1960s, using a range of measures. Explanations for this change include the increasing

Figure 11.7   Economic Lifestyle and the Vote, 1967–90

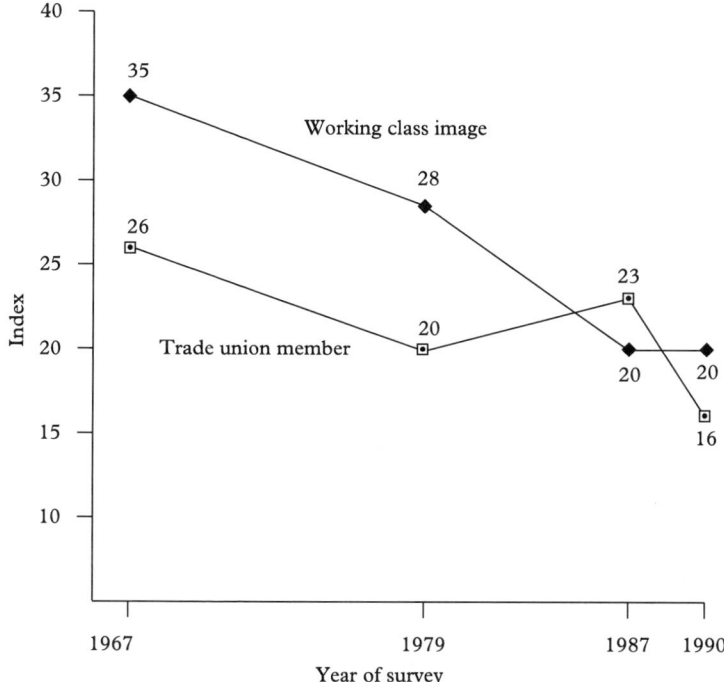

Note: The index is the percentage of working class and trade union members
         voting Labor, minus the percentage of middle class and non-union
         members voting Labor; the estimates are for the head of the household
Source: As for Figure 11.2

complexity of work, such as the increased skills required to carry
out particular tasks, which undermines the simple manual-non-
manual occupational division. Alternative dimensions of work,
such as the supervision of others in the workplace and location
within either the public or private sectors, now cross-cut the older
dimensions and make them less politically salient. Finally, the
increased importance of other economic aspects of work, such as
material lifestyle, have to some extent displaced occupational class
as major determinants of electoral behaviour.

Party Performance

The application of economic models to political behaviour, coupled with the decline in the influence of group loyalties on voting, has popularised the view that voters make rational, calculated decisions about how to cast their ballots. This view began to gain currency after the publication of Anthony Downs' *An Economic Theory of Democracy* (1957), which advanced a simple model of voting in which the actions of both candidates and voters were guided by rational calculation. Election candidates were seen as being motivated solely by a desire to maximise their vote, presenting goals to the electorate that were exclusively policy-oriented. For their part, voters were assumed to have fixed policy preferences and to possess complete information about the policy stances of the candidates. Downs' model has provided the theoretical foundation for a new approach to the study of political behaviour known as the 'rational voter' model.

This new approach has been used to analyse how far party performance, judged by the management of the economy, influences the vote. Competent economic management has long been viewed as an indispensable ingredient for electoral success; politicians expend most of their efforts trying to create the favourable economic circumstances that they believe will ensure their re-election. However, understanding how and why voters respond to economic changes has taken longer to unravel. At least three questions complicate any simple one-to-one relationship between economic performance and election outcomes.

First, there is the issue of what *measure of performance* voters use to evaluate economic conditions, and this may be their own personal economic circumstances or those of the country as a whole. Kinder and Kiewiet (1979, 1981) have shown that it is largely the latter: voters respond to their perceptions of the national economy, not to their own personal economic circumstances. The second question concerns the *time-span* over which voters make their economic judgements, which may be either past-oriented (that is, retrospective) or future-oriented (that is, prospective). Once again, research has shown that the major influence is retrospective (Fiorina 1981).[13] Finally, there is the issue of *attribution*: whom do voters hold responsible for economic performance, governments or wider economic forces within the society, such as business, trade unions or even global economic conditions? In Australia it would appear that voters blame wider economic forces. As Mughan (1987: 73) argues, 'the villain in the piece is not an effective national government, but powerful, self-interested forces outside Australia whose actions distort an otherwise robust national economy'.

Three out of four voters regarded Australia's economy as having got worse in the year prior to the 1990 federal election,

Table 11.8   Evaluations of the Economy and the Vote, 1990*

	Labor	Liberal-National	Democrat	Total	(N)	(Column %)
Retrospective evaluation of country's economy						
Better	86	8	6	100	(151)	(8)
Same	70	17	13	100	(331)	(17)
Worse	31	55	14	100	(1,436)	(75)
Government's responsibility						
Good effect	89	4	7	100	(166)	(9)
No difference	64	21	15	100	(738)	(39)
Bad effect	19	68	13	100	(1,014)	(53)

*The exact questions were: 'How do you think the general economic situation in the country now compares with what it was a year ago?'; 'And what effect do you think [the federal government] have had on the general economic situation in the country as a whole?'
Source: 1990 Australian Election Study

with less than 1 in 10 considering it had got better (Table 11.8). However, just over one-half of the voters thought that the government had made no difference to the economy, while a further 10 per cent thought that they had had a beneficial effect. As we would expect, the impact on the vote is considerable, with 89 per cent of those who considered that the government had exercised a good effect on the economy being Labor voters, and 68 per cent of those who thought that the government had had a bad effect being Liberal-National voters.

This is, then, suggestive evidence that attributing blame to the government for poor economic performance is more limited in Australia than it is in other countries, as Mughan (1987) and others have argued. Although the voting differences on attributing blame to the government are large, nearly 4 out of 10 voters see the government as having made no difference to the economy whatsoever. Unlike the United States, where changing economic conditions are rapidly translated into party political support, Australians appear reluctant to alter their voting habits because of personal or national economic circumstances. This may be a consequence of the fact that they tend to blame international forces. But it may also be a result of the comparatively high living standards Australians have enjoyed throughout most of the twentieth century.

The economy is, of course, only one of a range of election

issues that emerge during the course of a campaign. An additional aspect to the rational voter approach is the view that voters are guided by the election issues and by their interpretation of the candidates' positions on them. This interpretation has been further emphasised by the large proportion of voters who now wait until the election campaign is well underway before deciding on how to vote; in 1990, 44 per cent of voters fell into this category, a 17 per cent increase on 1987. The increasing hesitancy with which voters make up their minds has also been observed in Britain and other countries (Heath *et al.* 1991: 15).

In the 1990 federal election, voters rated interest rates as the most important issue, followed by inflation and taxation (Table 11.9). At the other end of the scale, unemployment was seen as being of least importance; just over one in three voters considered this to be 'extremely important' in determining how they voted. Although Labor was viewed by voters as lagging behind the Liberal-Nationals in formulating policies to cope with six of the nine issues, their disadvantage was not large. Labor gained most advantage from their policies on the environment, which 37 per cent more voters considered closest to their own views than Liberal-National environment policies. Despite the importance of economic issues to voters, and voters' preferences for the Coalition's

Table 11.9   Election Issues and Voting, 1990*

	Per cent say 'Extremely important'	Party closest to own view			
		Lab	Neither	Lib. Nat.	Total
1. Interest rates	60	24	34	42	100
2. Inflation	55	25	34	41	100
3. Taxation	55	25	30	45	100
4. Health	51	42	23	35	100
5. Environment	48	50	27	23	100
6. Education	46	31	39	30	100
7. Government spending	44	18	37	45	100
8. Wages	41	35	29	36	100
9. Unemployment	35	33	24	43	100

*The exact questions were: 'Here is a list of nine important issues that were discussed during the election campaign. Which of the party's views — the Labor Party or the Liberal-National Coalition — would you say comes closest to your own views on each of these issues?'; 'Still thinking about these same issues, when you were deciding how to vote, how important was each of these issues to you personally?'

Source: 1990 Australian Election Study

economic policies, it was clearly Labor's advantage on the environment which was a major component of their re-election in 1990 (McAllister and Bean 1990).

Australian voters, like those in other liberal democracies, are now more likely to make a decision on how to vote based on short-term factors, rather than on long-term loyalties to parties or social groups. More voters than ever before report that they delay their decision until the election campaign and are therefore likely to be influenced by last-minute events and issues — some random, some planned by the parties. Many voters base their decision on a party's economic performance while in government, as well as on an evaluation of party politics across a range of issues. This suggests that there will be greater volatility in voting patterns in the future, as voters are swayed by the many appeals that are conveyed to them through the mass media.

Conclusion

Compared with other advanced industrial societies, Australia has experienced substantial political stability during the twentieth century. In Britain, the weakening partisanship of a significant minority of voters has resulted in an accelerating process of partisan dealignment, exemplified by the votes for the Liberal-Social Democrat Party Alliance in 1983 and 1987, and the Liberal Democrats in 1992 (Rose and McAllister 1990). In the United States, substantial numbers of voters categorise themselves as political independents, weakening support for the major parties and leading to the rise of candidate, rather than party-centred, politics (Wattenberg 1991). The popular support for the independent Ross Perot during the 1992 presidential campaign is one practical example of this process of party dealignment.

The causes of popular disaffection from the established parties are many, but they would appear to have their roots in the declining role of parties in modern democratic politics and in parties' failure to meet the economic expectations of their supporters. Where once parties acted as the main channel of communication between the citizen and the government, this role has now been transferred to a myriad of interest groups, representing everything from business and the trade unions, to consumers and environmentalists (Dalton 1988: 191). Similarly, most major parties have been unable to cope with the periodic economic crises of the 1970s and 1980s while in government, undermining citizen confidence in their economic competence.

Why has Australia not followed these international trends, with greater questioning of the parties' abilities to invoke change and a political crisis of confidence? Three specific factors appear to be important. First, Australia's system of compulsory voting ensures that all voters—even those lacking any interest in the election—have to make a party choice in the polling booth. This, in turn, means that they maintain at least some level of conscious partisan attachment, which influences their long-term view of parties and politicians. Second, while the most recent economic crises have been at least as severe in Australia as elsewhere, parties are still viewed as economically competent, and there is some evidence that voters blame international economic conditions, not the government, for their economic ills.

Third, the major political parties have very effectively adapted to the changing social and economic conditions of the late twentieth century. While virtually all Western parties have become adept at this art, the Australian political parties have demonstrated this ability *par excellence* (McAllister 1991). The net effect of all of these factors on Australian political behaviour has been a highly stable political system. While these factors do not guarantee political stability in the future, they suggest a high probability that it will continue for some time.

Notes

1. Most of the analyses that follow in this chapter are adapted from McAllister (1992), which provides a more detailed examination of these and other issues in the study of Australian political behaviour.
2. An additional explanation is the stability and consensus found within Australian political élites. This is not considered here, though it is examined in detail in McAllister (1992) and in Higley, Deacon and Smart (1979).
3. Comparisons with levels of participation in other countries are difficult, as most international studies ask the frequency of these activities, while the survey used here asked about their occurrence during the course of the respondent's lifetime. This was because the survey was aimed primarily at immigrants, for whom levels of political participation are necessarily low. See McAllister and Makkai (1992).
4. Namely, 1943 (16.3 per cent), 1958 (10.6 per cent), 1977 (12.2 per cent) and 1990 (17.2 per cent).
5. In the 1990 federal election the Australian Democrats won 11.3 per cent of the first preference vote.
6. Voting was compulsory in the Netherlands until 1971, when it was abolished, and it was also used in Chile and Greece prior to the overthrow of their democratic systems by the military. Italy does not fine non-voters, but they have their identification papers stamped and as a result 'it is widely believed that [non-voters] are dis-

criminated against in employment and other benefits' (Powell 1982: 113).

7. Religion has three dimensions: affiliation, behaviour and belief. Affiliation and belief have been shown to be inherited from the family, while behaviour (such as church attendance) is shaped more by the socio-economic status of the individual than by family background.

8. The extension of the vote to women in the states was more uneven. South Australia and Western Australia were the first to grant women the vote, in 1894 and 1899 respectively, with the last state to give women the vote being Victoria, in 1908 (McAllister *et al.* 1990: 59).

9. Patterns over time in the influence of religion on politics cannot be analysed, since the relevant questions were asked in different ways in the four surveys.

10. This is, of course, partly a consequence of the fact that the Nationals have tended not to contest urban seats in many states.

11. Other aspects of economic lifestyle are income and housing. Income is notoriously difficult to measure in opinion surveys, and for that reason was not included in either the 1987 or 1990 Australian Election Studies. Housing, while electorally important in Britain, has few consequences for electoral behaviour in Australia (McAllister 1984).

12. One per cent of the respondents said that they belonged to the upper class; these responses have been included within the middle class category.

13. There is some evidence (see McAllister 1992: 196) that prospective evaluations may be at least as important as retrospective ones in determining how people vote. For consistency with overseas research, the present analyses are limited to retrospective judgements.

Appendix

The data are four opinions surveys: the 1967 and 1979 Australian National Political Attitudes Surveys (ns=2,054 and 2,016, respectively) and the 1987 and 1990 Australian Election Studies (ns=1,825 and 2,037, respectively). Full details of the first two surveys can be found in Aitkin (1982: Appendix), and the latter two surveys in Bean, McAllister and Warhurst (1990: Appendix B). All four surveys were random samples of the national electorate, aged 18 years and over (aged 21 years and over in 1967 only). An additional source of data used in the analysis of political participation is the Issues in Multicultural Australia Survey, which was designed by Roger Jones and Ian McAllister, collected by AGB-McNair and funded by the Office of Multicultural Affairs. Once again, the data are available publicly from the Social Science Data Archive at the Australian National University. The analyses using the data are based on the general population sample (n=1,552).

In measuring the vote, the analyses include only respondents who reported voting for the Labor, Liberal or National parties, the Australian Democrats (in 1979, 1987 and 1990) or the Democratic Labor Party (in 1967). Non-voters and supporters of minor parties and Independents are excluded. This has implications only in 1990, when there was a significant vote for Green candidates. For comparability in the over-time analyses, these groups are excluded in 1990.

References

Aitkin, Don A. (1982) *Stability and Change in Australian Politics*. Canberra: Australian National University Press.

Alford, Robert A. (1963) *Party and Society: The Anglo-American Democracies*. Chicago: Rand-McNally.

Barnes, Samuel H. and Kaase, Max *et al.* (1979) *Political Action: Mass Participation in Five Western Democracies*. Beverly Hills, Calif.: Sage.

Baxter, Janeen, Emmison, Mike, Western, John and Western, Mark (1991) *Class Analyses and Contemporary Australia*. Melbourne: Macmillan.

Bean, Clive (1991) 'Participation and Political Protest: A Causal Model with Australian Evidence', *Political Behaviour* 13: 253–83.

——Ian McAllister and John Warhurst (eds) (1990) *The Greening of Australian Politics*. Melbourne: Longman Cheshire.

Berelson, Bernard R., Lazarsfeld, Paul F. and McPhee, Willian N. (1954) *Voting*. Chicago: University of Chicago Press.

Bryce, James (1921) *Modern Democracies*. New York: Macmillan.

Campbell, Angus, Converse, Philip E. Miller, Warren E. and Stokes, Donald E. (1960) *The American Voter*. New York: Wiley.

——Gurin, Gerald and Miller Warren E. (1954) *The Voter Decides*. Evanston, Ill.: Row, Peterson.

Chamberlain, Chris (1983) *Class Consciousness in Australia*. Sydney: Allen and Unwin.

Dalton, Russell J. (1988) *Citizen Politics in Western Democracies*. Chatham, NJ: Chatham House.

De Vaus, David and McAllister, Ian (1989) 'The Changing Politics of Women: Gender and Political Alignment in Eleven Nations', *European Journal of Political Research* 17: 241–62.

Downs, Anthony (1957) *An Economic Theory of Democracy*. New York: Harper and Row.

Fiorina, Morris P. (1981) *Retrospective Voting in American National Elections*. New Haven, Conn: Yale University Press.

Goot, Murray and Reid, Elizabeth (1975) *Women and Voting Studies: Mindless Matrons or Sexist Scientism?* London: Sage Contemporary Political Sociology Series 06–008.

————and McAllister, Ian (1988) *Dimensions of Australian Society.* Melbourne: Macmillan.

Graetz, Brian (1986) 'Social Structure and Class Consciousness: Facts, Fictions and Fantasies', *Australian and New Zealand Journal of Sociology* 22: 46–64.

Heath, Anthony *et al.* (1991) *Understanding Political Change.* New York: Pergamon.

Higley, John, Deacon, Desley and Smart, Don (1979) *Elites in Australia.* London: Routledge and Kegan Paul.

Hogan, Michael (1979) 'Australian Secularists: The Disavowal of Denominational Allegiance', *Journal for the Scientific Study of Religion* 18: 390–404.

Hughes, Colin A. (1973) 'Political Culture', in Henry Mayer and Helen Nelson (eds), *Australian Politics: A Third Reader.* Melbourne: Cheshire.

Jones, F.L. and McAllister, Ian (1989) 'The Changing Structural Base of Australian Politics Since 1946', *Politics* 24: 7–17.

Kelley, Jonathan and McAllister, Ian (1985), 'Class and Party in Australia: Comparison with Britain and the USA', *British Journal of Sociology* 36: 383–420.

Kemp, David (1978) *Society and Electoral Behaviour in Australia.* Brisbane: University of Queensland Press.

Kinder, Donald R. and Kiewiet, D. Roderick (1979), 'Economic Discontent and Political Behaviour: The Role of Personal Grievances and Collective Economic Judgements in Congressional Voting', *American Journal of Political Science* 23: 495–527.

————(1981), 'Sociotropic Politics: The American Case', *British Journal of Political Science* 11: 129–61.

Lazarsfeld, Paul F., Berelson, Bernard R. and Gaudet, Helen (1948) *The People's Choice.* New York: Columbia University Press.

Leithner, Christian (1991) 'National Behaviour, Economic Conditions and the Australian Country Party, 1922–37', *Australian Journal of Political Science* 26: 240–59.

Lipset, Seymour Martin and Rokkan, Stein (1967) 'Introduction' in Seymour Martin Lipset and Stein Rokkan (eds), *Party Systems and Voter Alignments.* New York: Free Press.

Loveday, Peter (1977) 'Emergence, Realignment and Consolidation' in Peter Loveday, Alan W. Martin and Robert S. Parker (eds), *The Emergence of the Australian Party System.* Sydney: Hale and Iremonger.

Mair, Peter (1983) 'Adaptation and Control: Towards an Understanding of Party and Party System Change', in Hans Daalder and Peter Mair (eds), *Western European Party Systems.* London: Sage.

McAllister, Ian (1984) 'Housing Tenure and Party Choice in Australia, Britain and the United States', *British Journal of Political Science* 14: 387–400.

————(1988) 'Religious Change and Secularization: The Transmission of Religious Values in Australia', *Sociological Analysis 49*: 249–63.

————(1991) 'Party Adaptation and Factionalism within the Australian Party System', *American Journal of Political Science* 35: 206–27.

————(1992) 'Australia: Changing Social Structure, Stable Politics', in

Mark Franklin, Tom Mackie and Henry Valen (eds), *Electoral Change*. Cambridge: Cambridge University Press.

———and Bean, Clive (1990), 'Explaining Labor's Victory' in Clive Bean, Ian McAllister and John Warhurst (eds), *The Greening of Australian Politics*. Melbourne: Longman Cheshire.

———and Makkai, Toni (1992) 'Resource and Social Learning Theories of Political Participation: Ethnic Patterns in Australia', *Canadian Journal of Political Science*, forthcoming.

———Mackerras, Malcolm, Ascui, Alvaro and Moss, Sue (1990) *Australian Political Facts*. Melbourne: Longman Cheshire.

Mughan, Anthony (1987) 'The "Hip-Pocket Nerve" and Electoral Volatility in Australia and Great Britain', *Politics* 22: 66–75

Powell, G. Bingham (1982) *Contemporary Democracies: Participation, Stability, and Violence*. Cambridge, Mass.: Harvard University Press.

Rose, Richard and McAllister, Ian (1990) *The Loyalties of Voters: A Lifetime Learning Model*. London: Sage.

Urwin, Derek W. (1980) *From Ploughshare to Ballot Box*. Oslo: Universitetforlaget.

Verba, Sidney and Nie, Norman H. (1972) *Participation in America*. Chicago: University of Chicago Press.

———, ———and Kim, Jae-On (1971) *The Modes of Democratic Participation: A Cross-National Comparison*, Beverly Hills, Calif.: Sage Professional Paper in Comparative Politics No 01–013.

———, ———and ———(1978) *Participation and Political Equality*. Cambridge: Cambridge University Press.

Wattenberg, Martin P. (1991) *The Rise of Candidate-Centered Politics*. Cambridge, Mass: Harvard University Press.

Chapter Twelve

Crime in Australia

Kayleen M. Hazlehurst and John Braithwaite*

In this chapter we will briefly review some theoretical issues concerning the causes and consequences of crime. We will summarise what we know about levels of crime, and about what kinds of people are most likely to be offenders and victims of crime. Knowing these correlates of crime is the first step towards grasping the interests served by the criminal justice system and to understanding why police, court and prison systems are stable or expanding institutional domains in modern societies.

What Causes Crime?

The question of what causes crime is a complicated one. Criminology, as a formal area of research, is relatively recent. However, the thinking of eighteenth century philosophers such as Cesare Beccaria and Jeremy Bentham concerning 'free will', and 'let the punishment fit the crime' continue to influence contemporary criminal law.

During the nineteenth century, biological explanations grew in influence. Following the publication of his celebrated work *The*

* We would like to thank Matthew Cranitch, Professor Cameron Hazlehurst and Brett Mason for their assistance in reviewing this chapter, and John Walker and Dianne Dagger for their provision of statistical data.

Origin of Species in 1859, Darwin's theory of evolution led to vigorous debate. The positivist school of criminology, composed of several Italian thinkers, sought to develop a more individualised, scientific study of criminal behaviour. The positivists rejected the harsh legalism of the justice system of their time. Lombroso (1835–1909), often called the 'father of modern criminology', was most famous for his biological theories of crime. These held the attention of scholars for some time, but subsequently fell from favour.

Biological explanations of crime re-emerged with the refinement of scientific methods in the twentieth century. In the mid-1960s, for instance, Scottish researchers believed they had detected a chromosome abnormality when they found an extra Y chromosome in a significant proportion of the 197 male inmates they were studying. Females typically have XX and males XY chromosome sets. The prisoners in question had an extra Y chromosome: a 'supermale' XYY genetic makeup. Later studies of a similar kind, however, have shown that the genetic argument for violent behaviour is far from conclusive. In sum, over the last 150 years, criminal behaviour has been attributed to variations in body type, genetic make-up, the possible relationship between the nervous system, glandular system, and body chemistry, in a range of overlapping explanations advanced by psychologists, behaviouralists and sociologists.

Personality theory examines factors of emotional conflict and personality deviation in habitual offenders. Cognitive development theory explains criminal behaviour in relation to moral reasoning, and to the way people organise their thoughts about rules and law. Behaviouralists seek to understand how behaviour is learned, unlearned, or modified within particular settings. Social learning theorists emphasise the influence of family, subculture, and the media in this learning process.

Sutherland, who in the 1940s argued that criminal behaviour was learned through social interaction, believed that his theory of 'differential association' could be applied to widely divergent types of criminal behaviour, from the delinquency of slum youths to white collar crime. Sutherland recognised that in many occupations illegal practices were widely accepted as a way of doing business (Sutherland 1949; Sutherland and Cressey 1979). Drawing from his work, social learning theorists have demonstrated that excessive exposure to the motives, rationalisations, linguistic constructs, and vocabularies of alternative values can promote and reinforce criminal behaviour, thus overriding the values of wider society. Like deviant youth, employees of large corporations which regularly violated legal standards could also become 'habitual criminals'.

Other major explanatory frameworks for deviance and crime have arisen from sociological traditions. Control theory begins with an assumption that all individuals are subject to temptations and that human beings will seek advantages and rewards in life illegally unless they are held in check by fear of greater losses. People are coaxed into conformity through the threat of loss of reputation, loss of family, or loss of freedom.

Opportunity theory asserts that, given the opportunity for the achievement of cultural and group goals, individuals will internalise the legitimate means and processes of achievement. In the Western world, for instance, the goal of material success is ideally achieved through good education, a good job, and honest investments. If legitimate means for achievement are obstructed, however, individuals may come under pressure to resort to illegitimate means of achieving these goals. When whole neighbourhoods or communities experience poverty, unemployment or racism, the denial of life opportunities can feed into subcultures of crime.

Labelling theory suggests that a community's decision to bring sanctions against an individual activates rituals of transition, whereby a person is moved from a 'normal' position in society into the position of 'deviant'. The person becomes the label: 'untrustworthy', 'juvenile delinquent', 'criminal'. Subcultural theory also suggests that there is strong link between labelling and the formation of deviant personalities, criminal subcultures and lifestyles of crime. By creating outcasts society creates pockets of deviancy. Criminal subcultures give support to, and justification for, the continued rejection of the values and institutions of wider society (Braithwaite 1989: 16–43; Roach Anleu 1991: 1–49; Titus Reid 1991).

Levels of Crime Today and in Australian History

Most crimes can be defined as intentional acts, committed consciously and without legal justification, prohibited by the criminal law and punished by the state. There are exceptional domains where recklessness or negligent omission makes for criminality. But even here, culpability or guilt must be demonstrated. Thus, insanity is recognised as a defence within our legal system. Criminal acts have repercussions upon members of society, in addition to the victim of the offence. Criminal law is created to protect citizens from injury or loss of property, to safeguard the well-being of the young and disadvantaged, to punish offenders, and to maintain public order.

Comparisons of crime rates between countries are notoriously difficult because of different definitions of offences and different counting rules. Mass media exaggeration notwithstanding, Australia is not a society with an unusually large crime problem. When international comparisons of statistics on crimes reported to police are made, there is no suggestion of anything extraordinary about Australian crime rates (Clifford and Harding 1985: 47; Weatherburn and Devery 1991).

In recent years, sample survey techniques have been used to try to estimate relative levels of crime in different countries. In January 1989, victim surveys were conducted by telephone in Australia, Canada, the United States and eleven European countries. Results suggested that Australia fell just behind North America and ahead of several of the European countries in most crime categories tested. These included burglary, motor vehicle theft, robbery, and other theft, and both sexual incidents and assaults (Walker 1990; van Dijk *et al.* 1990).

But there are many problems with victim surveys and other forms of self-reported data collection. For a start, not everyone approached will co-operate with such a study. Telephone surveys relying on memory over the previous twelve months, as in the case above, generally lead to the disproportionate recall of trivial and minor offences occurring most recently. The highest incidence of crime occurs during the summer season in Australia. On the other hand, January is mid-winter in the Northern hemisphere, typically a time of low crime rates. This over-reporting of recent minor offences is confirmed by the fact that, in the serious offences categories, Australia's crime rates were more compatible with those of European countries. A more reliable approach would be to survey each national group in the same season, not in the same month (see New South Wales Bureau of Crime Statistics and Research 1992: 8, 13, 20–21).

Criminologists have generally relied upon homicide rates as providing the best comparative data on reported crime. While they do not measure the hidden homicide encompassed in missing persons data, it is here that problems of definitional differences and variable non-reporting of crime are at their least (Archer and Gartner 1984: 35–58; Weatherburn and Devery 1991: 28–33; Wallace 1986). International comparisons (Figure 12.1) show Australia to have a homicide rate comparable with, or slightly higher than, other OECD countries, but a very much lower rate than the United States and most Third World countries from which there are reliable data (National Committee on Violence 1990: 18; Mukherjee 1986; Mukherjee and Dagger 1990).

Are crime rates higher today than they were in earlier periods

Figure 12.1   Deaths by Homicide, Selected Nations Rate per 100,000 Population

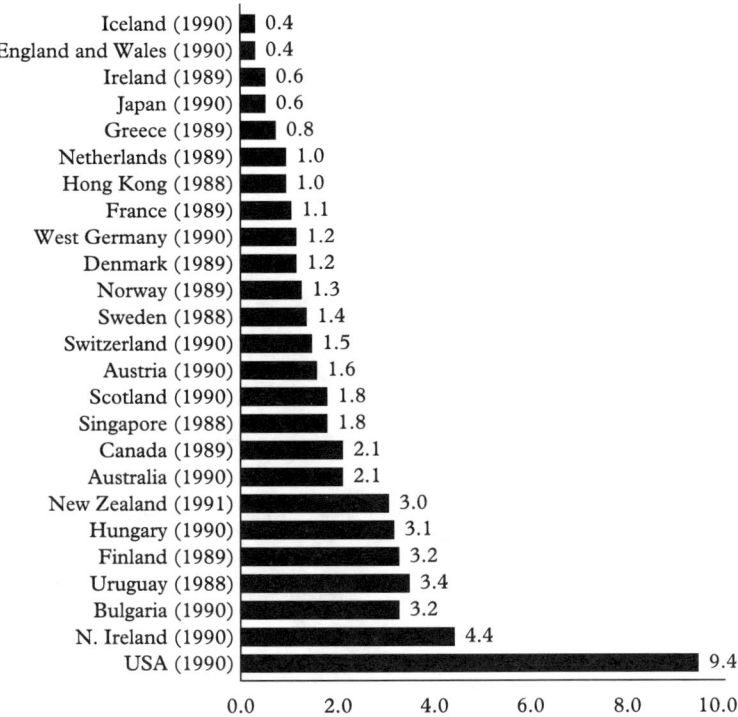

Sources: *World Health Statistics Annual* (1991) World Health Organization, Geneva (Compiled by Dianne Dagger, Australian Institute of Criminology)

of Australian history? Again the quality of the data is a real problem. Definitions of crime and rates of apprehension and reporting probably do not vary as much within one society across time as they do between societies. Even so, historical comparisons are best restricted to very general trends. Data from the nineteenth century are, not surprisingly, the least adequate.

From data drawn from New South Wales Supreme Court convictions, where serious crimes were tried (Grabosky 1977: 31–36; Mukherjee, Walker and Jacobsen 1986), and from daily average prisoner rate collections (Figure 12.2), we can safely conclude that crime rates in Australia increased from the establishment of the colony until just before the cessation of transportation of convicts in the mid-nineteenth century (1840 in New South Wales).

Figure 12.2   Daily Average Number of Prisoners per 100,000 Population, Australia 1860–1990

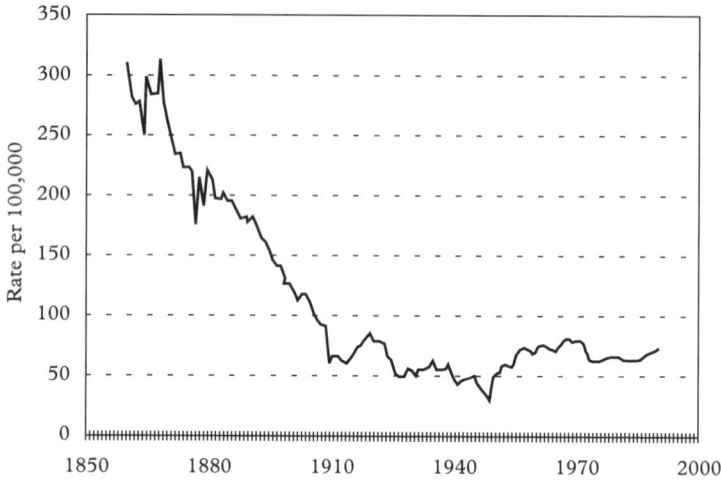

Sources: ABS *Official Year Book of the Commonwealth of Australia No. 2, 1901–1908*, (1988); Mukherjee, S.K. *et al. Source Book of Australian Criminal and Social Statistics, 1804–1988*, Bicentennial edition, Australian Institute of Criminology, 1976–90; Walker, J. *Australian Prison Trends*, Australian Institute of Criminology

During the next decades, until the early twentieth century, crime rates fell sharply. For the rest of Australian history, rates for serious crimes such as homicide, rape, robbery and serious theft, have remained more or less on a plateau, perhaps decreasing slightly for the first half of the century, and increasing gradually for the remainder (see Figure 12.2).

Much better data are available for the twentieth century, thanks to the statistical collections of Australian criminologists. Mukherjee concludes:

> Acts that are traditionally labelled as offences, that is, offences, against the person, against property and against good order, have remained remarkably constant during the entire century. The analyses indicate that increases in the total volume of crime have been primarily because of increases in petty offences
>
> (Mukherjee 1981: 61)

This perspective was confirmed ten years later, in 1990, by the National Committee on Violence. The recorded incidence of homicide in Australia had remained 'relatively low', the committee reported, 'by contemporary world standards, and in historical terms as well'. From available information 'one may conclude that the rate of homicide in the colonial period was much higher than the homicide rates which prevail today'. Homicide rates, which were high during the convict era, showed a decline throughout the nineteenth and early twentieth centuries until World War II. 'With the end of the war, homicide rates increased, fluctuating around an upward trend, and continued to do so until the late 1960s.' Since this time they have remained relatively stable (National Committee on Violence 1990:17).

In ascertaining how much crime there is today, it is important to recognise that official accounts only record the levels of *reported* crime. Crime victim surveys undertaken in Australia and overseas indicate that there is a 'dark figure of crime': a large proportion of offences are never reported to the police.

Offences categorised officially as 'serious crimes' include: homicide, rape/serious sexual assault, serious assault, robbery, burglary, larceny, motor vehicle theft, fraud and forgery. Serious assault is the most frequent form of violent crime. Robbery accounts for 33 per cent of all reported serious crime, and rape for 10 per cent. Homicide is the least frequently committed serious crime. Less grave offences are considerably more numerous. In a report produced by the Police Commissioners' Australian Crime Statistics Sub-Committee (1987), property crime was shown to outnumber violent crime by 21 to 1.

A study conducted between 1973 and 1987 of police department statistics throughout Australia revealed an increase in both per capita rates of crimes, and in the total number of crimes reported to police. 'Among the violent crimes, serious assaults increased by 236 per cent, rape by 132 per cent and robbery by 78 per cent. Property crimes, of which stealing accounts for half, increased by 89 per cent.' Changes in the law and public attitudes during this thirteen-year period, regarding the social acceptability of the offences of domestic violence and rape, appeared to have affected an increase of the number of serious assaults reported. Only murder showed little measurable change (Mukherjee, Neuhaus and Walker 1990: 3–7; Walker 1990).

Mukherjee *et al.* noted that, in the peak year 1986–87, rates of reported crime were highest in the Northern Territory and South Australia. These two jurisdictions showed the highest rates of violent crime throughout the study. Most reported crimes occurred in metropolitan and urban centres, particularly, but not surprisingly, robbery, serious assault and motor vehicle thefts.

Crime victims surveys support the findings that personal crime was much higher in urban areas. Victim studies also confirm that assault is the most common form of violent crime, and that men were likely to be the victims. Women were significantly affected by sexual assault and domestic violence.

People in their teens and twenties were the most likely to experience crimes of violence. The danger of being assaulted decreased with age, as did the likelihood of offending. Populations described as most vulnerable to crime had the highest rate of multiple victimisation. 'One in ten personal crime victims were the victim of more than one type of crime, and three in ten were multiple victims of the one offence' (Mukherjee, Neuhaus and Walker 1990: 7–13; Australian Bureau of Statistics 1979, 1986; Bonney 1988).

Mukherjee's work demonstrates the questionable association between 'real crime rates' and crime rates inferred from convictions in the courts. Mukherjee found that the crime rate was positively correlated with criminal justice resources. More police mean more arrests; indeed, he found that the number of offences charged per police officer has been fairly constant over the century. Yet the number of police officers per 100,000 population has varied considerably over that time, starting at a fairly high level, declining until 1930, then increasing steadily until the 1970s, when a sharp rise occurred (Mukherjee 1981: 35–39). He also found a very strong trade-off across the century between the number of arrests police make for minor offences ('good order' offences such as vagrancy, drunkenness, obscene language) and for serious offences: that is, when the police make more arrests for minor offences, serious offences appear to decline. Thus, it is highly problematic how much crime trends are the result of variations in real criminal activity versus changes in enforcement activity.

As with the international comparisons, criminologists have usually concentrated on the offence which provides the best comparative data in terms of high reportability and minimum changes in definition across time — namely, homicide. Homicide rates have varied within fairly narrow limits across this century. Data on homicide charges suggest a steady drop in rates to World War II, followed by a post-war increase which has taken rates back to where they were at the beginning of the century (Figure 12.3). However, the superior data on homicides reported, which are only available for the last three decades, show no upward trend. Homicide charges are higher than homicides reported partly because when different offenders are charged for the same homicide, they are counted separately. It is important to remember that medical and forensic advances are relevant to the changing reported incidence of homicide (for example infanticide or poisoning).

Figure 12.3   Number of Homicides per 100,000 Population, 1915–90

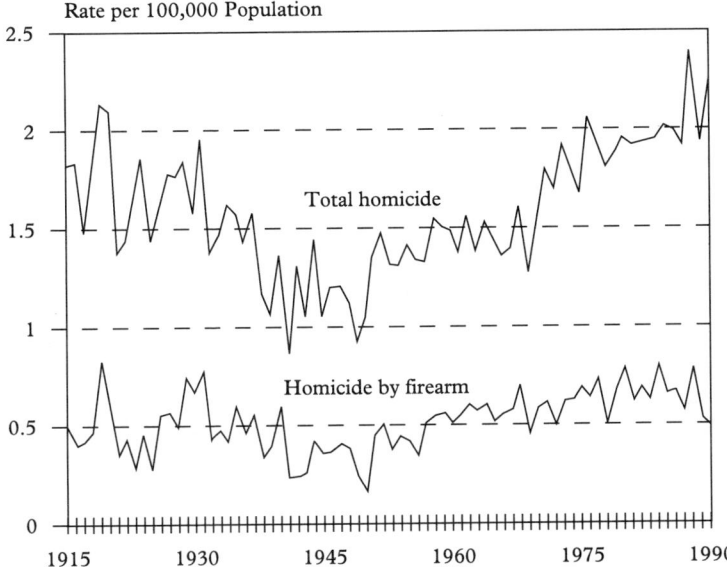

Sources: Mukherjee S.K. *et al.* (1989) *Source Book of Australian Criminal and Social Statistics, 1804–1988*, (updated), Australian Institute of Criminology

The mass media, of course, paint a very different picture of the modern era as one of unusual violence. This is in part a result of reporting of overseas as well as local crime. But, whatever the reality, each adult generation seems to be convinced that its younger generation constitutes a delinquent scourge such as has never been seen before. Thus, Australia has seen a succession of media-created folk devils (Cohen 1987), from the 'larrikins' of the 1890s (Grabosky 1977: 84–5), to the 'bodgies and widgies' of the 1950s (Braithwaite and Barker 1978), the 'hooligan menace' (Windschuttle 1978) and the 'hippies' of the late 1960s, to 'punks', 'boot-boys' and 'bikie gangs' (a recurring theme) from the 1970s to the 90s. The well-documented moral panics associated with these folk devils misrepresent the nature of juvenile delinquency. It has been shown systematically in data from the 1960s onwards that serious offending in Australia is an adult male problem, committed most-ly by men between the ages of 20 and 29 years (Mukherjee 1985; Walker, Hallinan and Dagger 1992a). Juveniles are far more likely to be apprehended for property crimes than for crimes against the person (Atkinson 1992). While juveniles were responsible for about 40 per cent of break, enter and steal offences in most jurisdictions, in 1990–91 relatively few serious assaults cleared by the police were carried out by juveniles — 9 per cent in Victoria; and 15 per cent in South Australia (Atkinson 1992: 1,3; O'Connor 1992; Mukherjee and Dagger 1990).

Self-report studies, in which adolescents are asked whether they have committed each of a variety of offences, indicate that most Australian adolescents are 'delinquents' in the sense that they have broken the law (Braithwaite 1977: 26; Braithwaite and Law 1978; Braithwaite and Braithwaite 1978; Warner 1982). Some caution, however, needs to be employed in the use of these studies. Young people are frequently tempted to exaggerate their offences as a display of bravado.

Most delinquency is of a minor nature, which children normally grow out of as they mature. Moral panics cause the minor delinquencies of a rather arbitrarily selected group of young people to be given a deeper social significance, as exemplifying the malaise of modern society. Substantial public resources may then be allocated to stigmatising these young people — apprehending, punishing, 'rehabilitating', conducting psychological and sociological studies of them — thus confirming them in a deviant identity which makes it more difficult to engage in the normal process of growing out of their delinquency (Schur 1973; West and Farrington 1977; Pearson 1983; Alder and Polk 1985; Braithwaite 1989; Bessant 1991). In fact, the street gangs to which so much contemporary media attention is devoted, attract a tiny proportion of Australian young people, and their behaviour bears little resemblance to the violent drug and turf wars of American 'colour' gangs.

The Political Economy of Punishment

It is not strictly correct to say that the selection of juveniles for criminal justice system processing is 'rather arbitrary'. It is arbitrary in the sense that their law breaking often is not much different from that of their peers, whose deviance goes undetected. But sometimes they are selected less because their offences threaten law and order than because their lifestyles are seen to threaten more fundamental social values such as the work ethic, deference to authority and, in unmarried girls, sexual restraint (Roach Anleu 1991; Gale, Bailey-Harris and Wundersitz 1990).

Many sociologists have sought to understand the social functions of punishment as distinct from its crime control functions.

Unfortunately, much Australian work has been influenced by American theorising which relates to historical trends in punishment which are exactly the opposite to ours. While in the United States imprisonment rates have substantially and fairly consistently increased between the mid-nineteenth century to the present (Calahan 1979; Clifford and Harding 1985: 50), the pattern in Australia has been one of steep decline from the second half of the nineteenth century up until 1920, followed by fairly constant rates from 1920 to the present.

One explanation employed to explain this trend has been Scull's (1977) contention that 'decarceration' is a result of the fiscal crisis faced by modern capitalist states. In considerable measure the fiscal crisis is seen as a result of welfare expenditures crowding out investment in wealth generating enterprises. At the same time the infrastructure of unemployment benefits and other welfare measures makes increasingly possible the maintenance of offenders in the community. In this analysis, the expanding welfare state both causes the fiscal crisis that makes decarceration necessary, and supplies the infrastructure of community support that makes decarceration possible.

In fact this theory has little appeal. With the exception of a sharp dip during World War II, the most dramatic decline in imprisonment rates had occurred prior to 1925, before the reforms of the welfare state and 'the fiscal crisis of the state' (Figure 12.2). O'Malley (1981: 158–60) tries to rescue the theory by suggesting that while decarceration has not occurred in 'absolute' terms, it has occurred in 'relative' terms. He suggests from Grabosky's (1977) data that 'most of the decline in imprisonment rates in the early period can be put down to massive declines in serious criminal offending' (O'Malley 1981: 158). This claim does not appear to be supported by the evidence. Grabosky's (1977) data suggest that while 'the massive decline in serious criminal offending' occurred between 1830 and 1860, imprisonment rates did not begin to decline in New South Wales until at least 1880 (compare Figures 2.2 and 2.13 in Grabosky 1977). Further, O'Malley (1981) suggests that while imprisonment rates may have been more or less on a plateau since the 1920s, 'rates for serious acquisitive crime trebled between 1920 and 1970'. Mukherjee's work lays to rest any suggestion of an explosion in serious crime during this period. While acquisitive crime increased substantially during the latter half of this century, total serious crime did not. The massive increase in post-war criminal prosecutions was largely a result of what Mukherjee (1981, 1989) called 'petty offences', a great number of which were traffic offences.

Australia has seen an explosion of minor crime, or rather an explosion of social control of minor crimes, which earlier in the century, when police were not so numerous, tended to be ignored. This expanded enforcement against minor crime has not inflated our prison populations. The extension of social control has occurred by increased use of fines, probation, community work and other non-custodial sanctions (Alder and Polk 1985). Though it is doubtful that a post welfare-state decarceration has occurred in either absolute or proportional terms, O'Malley's (1981: 161) ultimate conclusion that there has been 'a widening, refining and disguising of the entire control network' is correct.

While we must reject Scull's interpretation of Australian decarceration, it certainly did occur prior to the advent of the welfare state and remains to be explained. Additional research is required on what seems to be some tendency, within the framework of an overall trend towards decarceration, for severe economic crises to be associated with the heightened punitiveness of the criminal justice system (Grabosky 1984: 170; Braithwaite 1980: 195, 203–4; Jankovic 1977). Whether this suggests a greater need for the state to control crime when unemployment is high, a heightened demand for class domination during crises of capitalism, as Quinney (1977) would suggest, or simply a propensity to blame the victims of the crisis for the situation (the poor, Aborigines), is worthy of examination.

Who are the Criminals?

A variety of features have been identified by researchers as being common to observance of the law, on the one hand, and criminality on the other. More stable social environments are produced in settings where relationships between people are numerous, cross-linked, and characterised by qualities of mutual helpfulness and trust. Socially interdependent persons are more susceptible to shaming, and tend to be more committed to the institutions and processes of community life (Braithwaite 1989). Those people living in situations of interdependency share the characteristics of those people most likely to obey the law. Typically, they are those under the age of 15, or over the age of 25; married; female; employed and with high educational and employment aspirations, with opportunities to match.

The answer to the question of which types of people in Australia engage in most crime is not difficult. They are predominantly respectable business people who breach the enormous array of laws regulating business. White collar or corporate crime (crime involving the abuse of the power inherent in occupational roles) is often calculated and quite deliberate; however, many offences of this nature can arise from recklessness, negligence or inattention to detail. Braithwaite and Grabosky have argued that:

> A factory manager may not intend that a worker be injured, but production quotas, financial pressures or willingness to run risks with the health and safety of others may have harmful consequences.
>
> (Braithwaite and Grabosky 1985: 1)

White collar and corporate offenders often do great harm to large numbers of people (in occupational health and safety offences, for example); and they cause a greater loss of finances and property (e.g. company frauds) than traditional street or household offenders (Braithwaite 1982: 742–45; Grabosky and Braithwaite 1986). Murder and assault are responsible for fewer deaths and injuries than violations of industrial health and safety laws by employers and sale of hazardous consumer products by manufacturers. Many Australian tax and company frauds have netted more than all the money stolen during robberies of banks, service stations, shops and homes. The best way to rob a bank is to own it!

One can further establish that the number of offences and offenders against persons and property is greater with white collar than with blue-collar crime simply by taking one minor example of white collar crime, and showing the huge volume of offences involved. Surveys in New South Wales and Canberra have found 15 and 32 per cent of petrol pumps to be giving short measure petrol to motorists (*Sunday Telegraph*, 3 February, 1980; *Canberra Times*, 13 January 1981; Grabosky and Braithwaite 1986; Grabosky and Sutton 1989). Every one of the sales on these vast numbers of pumps involved weights and measures offences, or indeed fraud, should consumer affairs agencies choose to prosecute for this offence.

In 1982, the Victorian Department of Labour and Industry surveyed compliance with regulations concerning the guarding of power presses. Of 2,381 power presses, 51 per cent did not comply with the requirements of the law (Department of Labour and Industry 1983: 20). In 1983, the Queensland Mines Department surveyed compliance with statutory standards for stone dusting in coal mine roadways to prevent the spread of explosions. Thirty-five per cent of the 1,095 dust samples failed to comply with the standard prescribed by the Coal Mining Act (Queensland Department of Mines 1983: 19; Hopkins and Parnell 1984).

A study of odometer fraud in Queensland found that over one-third of vehicles randomly selected from used car lots had had their odometer turned back (Braithwaite 1978). The sample was not sufficient to assert with confidence that this kind of fraud occurred for one-third of used cars sold in Queensland, but using this as the best estimate available, would imply about 70,000 odometer frauds in Queensland in the year of the study, compared with 81,181 offences of all types (including victimless crimes, but excluding public order offences) reported to the Queensland police that year. Moreover, in most odometer frauds, as in most other kinds of white collar crime, there is a conspiracy involving more than one individual offender, plus a corporate offender.

Given the potential for corporate crime or wanton irresponsibility, the logistics of policing regulatory transgressions can be staggering. These range from radiation control in the mining of uranium, environmental pollution control from factories and industry, the maintenance of food standards, and the safety of workers, public transport, and investment schemes. Scandals can affect more than public health. They can have a major impact on the economy of the country. When horsemeat and kangaroo was found in a consignment of 'Australian beef', for instance, a highly competitive trade worth $600 million a year with the United States was placed in jeopardy (Grabosky and Sutton 1989: 60–75; Grabosky and Braithwaite 1986). Large-scale organised crime has been shown to be rife in the Australian meat, transport, construction and waterside industries.

Since the mid-1980s there have been increasing press reports of law enforcement agency investigations of Australian residents with connections with major criminal groups in the United States, Central America, Hong Kong, Japan, Italy, Thailand and other South-east Asian countries. Because Australia is the closest Western neighbour to the South-east Asian region, there has been some apprehension in this country that representatives of South-east Asia's 'Golden Triangle' triads will move their notorious operations into Australia. When Customs seizures of illegal drugs trebled between 1988 and 1989, concerns were raised that Australia was facing the same crisis of heroin importation through Asia as the United States faced with cocaine from Colombia.

In its 1990 Annual Report, the Australian Customs Service reported that 'approximately 1,156 kilograms of cannabis, 76 kilograms of cocaine and 42 kilograms of heroin were seized overall' at Australian ports of entry (Australian Customs Service 1990: 89–90). Compelling evidence of major criminal activity in Australia from the South-east Asian underworld has been uncovered by the National Crime Authority. Between 1983 and

1990, Asian syndicates were involved in 70–80 per cent of the heroin, cocaine and cannabis seizures in this country. More recently, the press has speculated that the drug barons of Central America are casting their eyes in the direction of Australia for new business. Federal government intelligence suggests that, having saturated North American and European markets, Colombian and Peruvian traffickers were seeking to join forces with traditional distributors of drugs in Australia, the Mafia, to run their Australian distribution networks.

Irrespective of how much substance there is in this evidence or these fears of organised crime, drug control is clearly an expensive business. It costs $300 million a year for Customs and the Australian Federal Police to run air, land, and sea surveillance, and to operate overseas liaison officer networks, in the fight against drug importation (Doyle 1988: 14; Mellor and Ricketson 1991; Barnao and Lipson 1991; *Age* 7 April 1989; *Weekend Australian,* 22–23 July 1989; *Sunday Telegraph,* 18 June 1989; *Canberra Times,* 7 June 1990, 1–2 September 1990; *Courier-Mail,* 17 February 1990, 15 October 1992).

Governments and the criminal justice system itself are not immune to corruption by well-resourced criminal interests. In Queensland, the Fitzgerald Commission of Inquiry was set up as a result of allegations in the media regarding the police and their association with organised prostitution, gambling, and drug trafficking. The terms of reference of the Inquiry were widened when it became clear that the corruption was widespread, not only through all levels of the police department, but also involving state government ministers, business people, and many organised crime figures. Money laundering, protection rackets, and some violent criminal activity was occurring (Dickie 1989: 174–266).

Following the 238 days of public sittings, 21,504 pages of transcripts, and the evidence of 339 witnesses, the Inquiry resulted in a series of prosecutions at enormous cost to the community, both in financial terms and in terms of public trust of police and authority in general (Fitzgerald 1989: 4; Swanton and Wilson 1992: 54; see also Grabosky and Braithwaite 1986; Polk and Alder 1986; Western Australia government 1992).

Apart from organised and white collar crime, who commits most of the other kinds of common crimes? Those who are more likely to offend, and who may become increasingly initiated into subcultures of crime, share similar characteristics with those most likely to fall victim to crime. Perhaps the most significant variable is that of gender. 'One of the most striking aspects of violence in Australia is that the vast majority of those who commit acts of violence are males,' noted the National Committee on Violence.

Men were charged with 80–95 per cent of all homicide, serious assault, robbery and sexual assault in this country (National Committee on Violence 1990: 33; Mukherjee, Neuhaus and Walker 1990: 27; Walker, Hallinan and Dagger 1992: 121,40).

Statistics show that both victims and perpetrators of crime are predominantly under the age of twenty-nine; are unmarried, male, and unemployed; have low employment and educational opportunities; live in highly urbanised areas and/or display a high level of residential mobility (Braithwaite 1989; Walker and Hallinan 1991; Australian Bureau of Statistics 1979, 1986; Mukherjee, Neuhaus and Walker 1990; National Committee on Violence 1990).

Disproportionate numbers of offenders are also likely to be drawn from the indigenous population. In the late 1980s, the Royal Commission into Aboriginal Deaths in Custody reported that Aborigines and Torres Strait Islanders were 10 times more likely than non-Aboriginal people to be imprisoned. While comprising just under 1.46 per cent of the total community, in 1987 they represented 10.11 per cent of the Australian prisoner population (Muirhead 1988: 98–99; see also Mukherjee, Neuhaus and Walker 1990, South Australian Office of Crime Statistics 1984: 79; Gorta and Huntley 1985; Duckworth *et al.* 1982; Eggleston 1976). In fact, an analysis of national prisoner Census data indicates that the Royal Commission calculation might have been an underestimation. Consistently, from 1982 until 1991, Aboriginal prisoner rates ranged from 13 to almost 15 per cent of the total Australian prisoner population (Walker 1991: 121).

In explaining Aboriginal over-representation in prison statistics, researchers have raised serious questions regarding racial and class bias within the criminal justice system itself — from the point where police discretion to arrest is exercised, to decisions taken throughout the sentencing process. Studies in South Australia indicate that Aboriginal youngsters are cumulatively disadvantaged as a result of determinations made at different points within the justice system (Sarri and Bradley 1989; Gale, Bailey-Harris and Wundersitz 1990; Wundersitz 1992; see also Hazlehurst 1987; Hanks and Keon-Cohen 1984; Eggleston 1976; Armstrong and Neumann 1976; Sanson-Fisher 1978).

In the 1980s, Wilson (1982, 1985: 51), pointed out extraordinarily high levels of interpersonal violence, accidents, and self-mutilation in some Northern Queensland Aboriginal communities. The homicide rate in some communities was ten times that of the rate for Australia as a whole. Police in remote areas, and Aboriginal community members themselves, assert that the majority of Aboriginal offending is alcohol-related. Aborigines are most likely to be in prison for minor offences, rather than for more serious, premeditated forms of crime (Walker 1992b: 69–70; Mukherjee, Neuhaus and Walker 1990: 28).

A striking characteristic of offenders in Australia is unemployment (Mukherjee, Neuhaus and Walker 1990; Institute of Criminology 1978; South Australian Office of Crime Statistics 1979, 1980a, 1984), and low socio-economic status generally (Barber 1973; New South Wales Bureau of Crime Statistics and Research 1974; Kraus 1975; Smith 1975; Dunstan and Roberts 1977; Braithwaite 1979, cf. Warner 1982). The annual prisoner Census indicates that only 21 per cent of male inmates and 8 per cent of female inmates were employed (or self-employed) at the time they were arrested or charged (Mukherjee, Neuhaus and Walker 1990: 28).

At yet another level of analysis, the ecological, there is consistent evidence that areas of cities with high levels of unemployment or high concentrations of lower socio-economic status inhabitants, experience higher crime rates (Braithwaite 1989; Dunstan and Roberts 1977; Vinson and Homel 1972; Kraus 1977). Braithwaite's (1979, 1989) work suggests that, in increasing delinquency, the combined effect of coming from a lower class family and living in a lower class area may be greater than the sum of their individual effects.

The strongest correlate of criminality in Australia, however, is gender (Biles 1977; Althuizen 1977; Challinger 1977). Only about 5 per cent of all prisoners are females (Mukherjee, Neuhaus and Walker 1990: 27), and 5 per cent of homicide offenders are females (Walker, Hallinan and Dagger 1992: 121, 40). If one takes self-report measures seriously as anything other than a doubtful measure of trivial offences, Australian self-report studies show by contrast fairly small sex differences in offending rates (Warner 1982; Braithwaite 1977: 26). Following up on this evidence, some have suggested that women benefit from a 'chivalry' factor in enforcement and criminal sentencing (Krohn *et al.* 1983), but this has been hotly disputed in the literature (Scutt 1979; Hancock 1980; Hancock and Chesney-Lind 1985). Any evidence of 'chivalry' in the criminal justice system is insufficient to explain the presence of nineteen times as many male homicide offenders as female ones in Australian prisons.

Exaggerated assertions have been made about growing feminist consciousness in recent decades, causing the 'rise of the new female criminal' (Alder 1975). While the proportion of property crime committed by females has increased since the mid-1960s, this is not true of crimes against the person (Mukherjee and Fitzgerald 1981; Mukherjee and Dagger 1990), and much of the rise in the proportion of property crime perpetrated by females may be in 'traditional' female areas such as shoplifting (Alder 1985: 57; Naffin 1986).

Another very clear correlate of crime is age. In the 1991 National Prison Census, 20–29 year-old males comprised 47.1 per cent of the prisoner population. Only 27.9 per cent of inmates in Australian prisons were 35 years of age and over and, of course, many of these were in prison for offences they committed in their 20s (Walker, Hallinan and Dagger 1992: 18).

With juveniles, a particularly strong association exists between poor school performance and delinquency (Braithwaite 1979: 271; Warner 1982; Coventry 1984). This association generated an influential reformist literature on reshaping education so that segregationist and other practices which label students as failures are rejected, and competition against other children is replaced by competition against the student's own past performance (Knight 1985; Conventry *et al.* 1984; Wilson and Braithwaite 1977, Marnier 1980). Crime rates are higher in the capital cities than in country areas (New South Wales Bureau of Crime Statistics and Research 1972, 1974; Kraus 1973; Braithwaite and Biles 1979), and offenders are more likely to be unmarried than married (Mukherjee, Neuhaus and Walker 1990: 28; South Australian Office of Crime Statistics 1980b). This exhausts what we can say with confidence about correlates of crime in Australia.

Who are the Victims of Crime?

Surprisingly, the answer to the question of who the victims are is very similar to who the offenders might be. The primary source of data for exploring the characteristics of victims is two National Crime Surveys conducted by the Australian Bureau of Statistics in 1975 and 1983 (Australian Bureau of Statistics 1979, 1986), and the Australian component of the international crime victim survey conducted by the Australian Institute of Criminology in 1989 (Walker, Dagger and Collins 1991). Results obtained from the Crime Survey of 1983 alerted us to the fact that there was a striking tendency for unemployed people to be more susceptible to victimisation. Such a person was twice as likely to be a victim of crime. The strongest association was with assault, where the unemployed were more than twice as likely to report being a victim of assault than those in full-time jobs, and six times as likely to have been assaulted over the previous year than respondents in the workforce or in part-time jobs. Unfortunately, there are no systematic data on the ethnicity of Australian victims of crime (Mukherjee, Neuhaus and Walker 1990: 12).

In Najman's (1980: 266) study of homicide, he found a strong tendency for its victims to be in the lowest socio-economic group. In fact, age-standardised homicide victimisation rates per 10,000 population were nine times as high for those in the lowest socio-economic group compared with those in the highest. Similarly, a study based on New South Wales' Police Homicide files found that just under 42 per cent of homicide victims were unskilled workers, as opposed to only 5.4 per cent of victims from professional or semi-professional backgrounds (Wallace 1986: 38).

In aggregate, women are less likely to be victims of crime than men (Mukherjee, Neuhaus and Walker 1990: 12; Braithwaite and Biles 1984: 4), though women are more likely to be victims of domestic violence, sexual assault, 'peeping', indecent exposure and nuisance telephone calls (Naffin 1986). They are also more at risk of being murdered by a relative than were men (23 per cent of all homicides occurring between husbands and wives). Men are disproportionately victims of other kinds of crime, including homicide (Scutt 1983; Wallace 1986; Bonney 1988; Najman 1980: 274; South Australia 1980b; Strang 1992), vehicle and other theft, fraud, forgery, false pretences, and assault (Mukherjee and Dagger 1990: 67–69; Braithwaite and Biles 1984: 4).

The National Crime Surveys show that males in their teens and early twenties are most at risk to crime, with the aged (over 60) having the lowest rates. They also show that residents in cities with populations of more than 10,000 (particularly state capital cities), are much more likely to be crime victims than people living in less populated areas. Unmarried people have higher rates of victimisation than those who are married. Extraordinarily high victimisation rates prevail for those who are separated or divorced (Walker, Dagger and Collins 1991; Mukherjee, Neuhaus and Walker 1990; Braithwaite and Biles 1979; Braithwaite and Biles 1984; Congalton and Najman 1974; Najman 1980; Australian Bureau of Statistics 1986).

In summary, it can be said that the characteristics of victims of crime in Australia are very similar to the characteristics of offenders, excluding white collar criminals: both groups are disproportionately unemployed, male, young, unmarried and residents of state capital cities. This mirrors almost exactly the situation found in the United Kingdom (Gottfredson 1984) and in the United States.

... offenders involved in the types of crimes of interest here are disproportionately male, young, urban residents, black, of lower socio-economic status, unemployed (and not in school), and unmarried. In our brief review of victim characteristics ... it was seen that victims disproportionately share these characteristics.

(Hindelang *et al.* 1978: 259; see also Muhkerjee, Neuhaus and Walker 1990)

The most credible explanation for this finding, in light of other evidence, is that people with victim/offender characteristics (young, male, unemployed, unmarried etc.) are more likely to spend their time in public space — in trains and buses rather than private cars; in streets and parks rather than offices and homes; and in public bars rather than in private clubs. Most crucially, they are more likely to spend time in public space in the evening, when crimes disproportionately occur. Sitting at home watching television, one is not likely to seize on an opportunity to commit a crime, have one's purse snatched, or be arrested for a crime one did not commit (Braithwaite and Biles 1984: 7).

The Costs and Consequences of Crime

Crime affects its victims, and society in general, in different ways. Physical injury and property loss affect the financial well-being of victims. They can be measured directly in terms of the cost of property replacement, the loss in work time, or the loss of a person's means of support. If items were insured, in many cases they were not insured for their replacement value. But whether the crime was a minor break-and-entry or a serious assault, the psychological consequences, inconvenience, and breach of personal security are far more difficult to ascertain.

Householder break-ins result in greater losses than most other crimes of theft. Based on selected data, annual losses to the community from break-ins to private and commercial premises have been estimated to be in the order of $270–280 million dollars (Mukherjee, Neuhaus and Walker 1990: 16–17). Car thefts in New South Wales alone (including the ACT) cost NRMA Insurance Ltd $256 million in 1991 (NRMA 1992: 6).

The 1983 Crime Victims Survey reported that at least 125,400 injuries resulted from violent crimes, not including homicide. Over one-quarter of these injuries resulted in hospitalisation. Reporting rates varied according to the type of crime committed and whether the offender was known or related to the victim. Robbery and motor vehicle theft are most likely to be reported to the police, while sexual assault was still considerably under-reported (Australian Bureau of Statistics 1986; Walker, Dagger and Collins 1991: 73–77).

The plight of the victim has been increasingly recognised. All Australian state and territory governments have established victim compensation schemes. These programs provide compensation for the financial losses, medical expenses and emotional trauma suffered by victims. In 1985–86, about $20 million dollars was paid to victims of crime. Only a small proportion of government compensation is recouped by way of offenders' contributions and by levies or fines (Mukherjee, Neuhaus and Walker 1990: 20). Refuge accommodation for victims of domestic violence was placed at $27.6 million for 1986–87 (Mugford 1989). For 1988–89, the cost of maintaining the criminal justice system was placed in the order of $3 billion (Walker, Dagger and Collins 1991: 17), but the total cost of crime would certainly exceed that figure. The director of the Australian Institute of Criminology, Professor Duncan Chappell, has estimated that crime costs the country at least $27 billion a year — 2.7 per cent of the Gross Domestic Product (*Australian*, 13 August 1992).

The largest proportion of justice administration spending goes to the police services, followed by courts and legal services, and corrective services. Almost two-thirds of state government justice expenditure is on policing. Imprisonment itself is very costly. Correctional statistics indicate that it costs about $45,000 to keep a person in prison for a year. Across all Australian states and territories, violent offenders dominate prison statistics, particularly in the Northern Territory (Figure 12.4). This is not surprising, of course. Society finds violent offenders the least acceptable candidates for alternative sentences such as fines, community service orders or community correction. Violent offenders also receive the longest sentences. In terms of processing offenders through the system, violence costs the country more.

There is also the social cost. Crime impacts differently upon different areas of social life. It affects our sense of safety in our own homes and how we secure our properties: with locks, window grilles or alarms. It affects decisions about social interaction: who do we trust, our neighbours, or those whom we mix with socially? Who do we let know when we are away on holidays? The quality of our life is affected: whether we will attend a concert in a particular part of the city; whether we will leave a picnic basket unattended on the beach; whether we will let our children play in the park or walk home after a movie at night. Certain sectors of the community, such as the very young, the handicapped, and the elderly, suffer greatly, and may never recover their confidence after a criminal incident. Some become virtual prisoners in their own homes, merely in fear of crime.

Decisions about the allocation of resources within the justice

Figure 12.4 Prisoners by Jurisdiction and Most Serious Offence/Charge (Rate per 100,000 Adult Population, 1991)

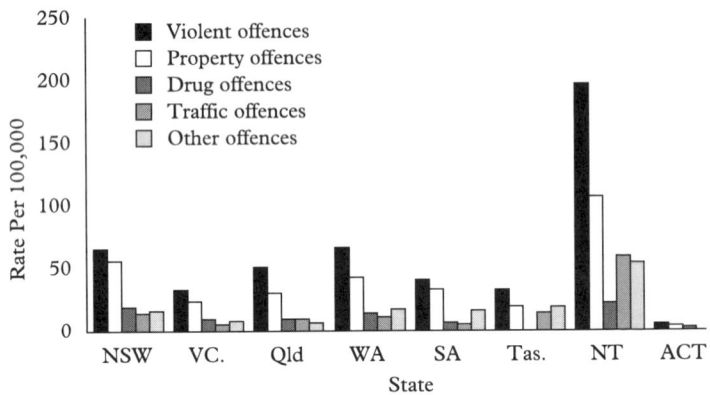

Violent offences: Homicide and assault, sex offences; other against person, robbery, extortion
Property offences: Break and enter, fraud and misappropriation, receiving, other theft, property damage
Drug offences: Possession, use, deal/traffic, manufacture/grow
Traffic offences: Driving offences, licence, registration, other traffic offences
Other offences: Environmental, goverment security, justice procedures, possession of weapon, other in custody, unknown, other offences
Sources: Walker, J., assisted by Hallinan, J. and Dagger, D. *Australian Prisoners 1991*, Australian Institute of Criminology

system will be influenced by perceptions of the community, and of politicians, as to the seriousness of 'the crime problem'. Fear of crime in the community can be greatly exacerbated by media coverage of real offending, and by high levels of media-portrayed violence. When crime is said to be 'out of control', it may become the centre of a political debate. An election may be run on the 'law and order' issue. Historical and social events will also affect justice spending. They include the increase of computer fraud following widespread technological change, or the burgeoning of drug importation with the increasing ease of international travel. The reactions of the community, the media and the government to reported spates of crime can, in turn, increase public reporting of similar incidents, raising crime statistics and later government spending.

In 1986, a study undertaken by the Australian Institute of Criminology demonstrated very clear public attitudes about the seriousness of particular offences. The public ranked stabbing to death and heroin trafficking as the most serious offences, followed by industrial pollution, or negligence resulting in death or injury. Armed robbery, and child and wife bashing were listed as the next most serious offences in the public mind. Offences such as social security fraud, income tax evasion, and Medicare fraud were placed before break and enter and shoplifting, reflecting a concern for the greater public loss involved in the former (Wilson, Walker and Mukherjee 1986).

Throughout Australia, the number of reported crimes has risen almost two-thirds, from 845,923 in 1980–81 to 1.41 million in 1988–89. However, when we consider rising crime statistics, Walker and Henderson (1991) caution that we must also consider some of the factors affecting the reporting of crime. Community groups may bring pressure on governments to take tougher measures against crime. An increase in uniformed officers on the streets enables police to attend to incidents which might earlier have been dismissed as trivial. Improved technology shortens police response time, but also heightens public expectations of them. Changing community attitudes, and an increase in their willingness to report crimes which might have once gone unreported, such as child abuse and domestic violence, must also account for increases in crime statistics.

Our lifestyles, it would appear, predispose us to much minor crime. The physical layout of our cities and neighbourhoods, our loose-knit social life, and our treatment of possessions, expose us to opportunist burglars and thieves. For long periods we leave our homes vacant. We leave our cars unattended during the day. The long summer evenings which tempt us to enjoy recreational activities, and our drinking habits in pubs and clubs, all make us vulnerable to injury and misfortune (Walker, Wilson, Chappell, and Weatherburn 1990).

Yet some simple forms of preventive action can have an impact on crime rates. Heightening public watchfulness and awareness, particularly in urban areas, can reduce opportunities for criminal activities. The most well-known are Neighbourhood Watch, Business Watch and Women's Safety programs. Some criminologists have argued that such schemes merely displace crime to less well protected areas. But this has not diminished the popularity of community crime prevention activities or police commitment to them (Mukherjee and Wilson 1987).

Lateral thinking in crime prevention, claims one criminologist (Walker 1992a: 13), can reduce crime. In England and Wales, and later in Victoria, when compulsory helmet legislation was introduced, a drop in the theft of motorcycle thefts was noticed. The reason was that opportunist thieves seldom 'prowl the streets with a bicycle helmet secreted on their person', stated Walker. 'The minute they steal a bicycle and attempt to make their get-away, their helmetless head will brand them as thieves!' (Walker 1992a: 13).

Of course, there are deeper features of our social fabric — unemployment, the plight of Aborigines, domination and exploit-ation of women, toleration of violence, alienation of youth, loss of community — that are the most fundamental sources of our crime problem. It is through attacking them that we might forge a genuinely safer society.

Whose Interests does the Criminal Justice System Serve?

Australia has a criminal justice system which is remarkably stable, which can survive major corruption scandals, rumours of police brutality, prison bashings, and riots, and even intermittent sus-pension of administrative neutrality so that the police can be used against striking unionists and 'political extremists'. It can retain a high degree of community compliance and has commanded support for an exponential increase in criminal justice system expenditure during the past thirty years, which cannot be justified by any appeal to evidence that increased criminal justice expen-diture actually reduces crime, or even that the crime problem is getting 'out of hand' (Mukherjee, Neuhaus and Walker 1990: 54–60; Mukherjee 1981: 31–38, 99–105; Chan and Zdenkowski 1985: 61–71).

Ironically, the criminal justice system, having secured the stability of the Australian social order in the late nineteenth century by ceasing to be a blatant tool of ruling class interests (O'Malley 1983), now provides this country with a proliferation of business regulatory statutes which criminalise the exploitative behaviour of capital. This situation could be expected to destabilise the criminal justice system, were it not for the fact that the multitude of laws criminalising aspects of corporate behaviour are rarely enforced. Responsibility for enforcing the regulatory statutes is not generally with the police, but with specialist agencies with an ideology of negotiation rather than enforcement. For example, consumer protection laws are the responsibility of state consumer affairs bureaux which predominantly resolve complaints by con-ciliation between consumers and traders, rather than enforce-ment. 'Over-zealous' enforcement of the Trade Practices Act destabilises the Trade Practices Commission, but not the criminal justice system.

The criminal justice system is stable and expanding in Australia precisely because it has something to offer all interests. Corporate Australia might be threatened by the letter of the law, but the law in action has in the past rarely threatened powerful economic groups — while it can impose enormous private security costs on them. Victim surveys clearly show that individual victimisations for offences such as burglary far exceed corporate victimisations. One remarkable study worthy of replication in Australia showed that in a police department near Toronto, Canada, nearly two-thirds of complaints dealt with by the police were from corporate victims, and only one-third from individual victims (Hagan 1982). Moreover, complaints from corporate victims were more likely to lead to convictions, and the corporate victims expressed greater satisfaction at the assistance they received from the criminal justice system compared with individual victims.

Even the post-Watergate explosion of public concern about white collar crime was captured by the corporate sector, so that enforcement resources were directed towards white collar crimes where corporations are victims rather than offenders (computer crime and embezzlement). By 1992, however, there was a new resolve at federal government level not only to pursue organised crime, but also to turn the resources of the Australian Securities Commission towards the investigation of white collar crime in general, as well as offences against corporation law (*Australian*, 7 October 1992).

We have also seen, on the other hand, that the criminal justice system potentially has much more to offer the working class, because they stand a greater risk than the ruling class of suffering the ultimate loss from crime, their lives, as a result of an occupational safety offence or murder. The fear of bodily harm is something which all members of the working class experience, while only a fraction of one per cent of them suffer the horrors of our prisons. With Aborigines, the balancing of sympathies may be different, however. The minority among them are those adults who have not at some stage been processed by the criminal justice system. Aborigines, then, may be the only group in Australian society, perhaps together with an assortment of radical youth subgroups, for whom destabilising the criminal justice system might have any collective appeal.

Beyond the ruling class and the working class, a third growing force is welfare recipients, who are mostly retired and, finally, women in the home are also slowly becoming a more potent political force. Women at home and the aged are curious cases. They do not exploit the criminal justice system to cut their security costs in the way that is characteristic of major business interests; they do not confront the level of risk of loss of life or serious injury from crime to which male workers and the unemployed are exposed; yet their commitment to the criminal justice system has a deeper emotional content, because they suffer understandable fears about their vulnerability, even in their homes.

Australian research confirms overseas findings that even though women and the aged have lower objective risks of criminal victimisation, their subjective fear of crime is higher than other groups in the society (Mugford 1984; Braithwaite, Biles and Whitrod 1982). With women, the explanation is undoubtedly that the crimes to which they are disproportionately exposed, notably rape, are unusually terrifying, in the way they compound prolonged sexual degradation upon protracted physical violence. Some sections of the women's movement have been amongst the most vocal advocates of repressive criminal justice solutions to social problems. On the other hand, Broadhurst and Indermaur (1982: 228) found women generally to be less punitive than men in their suggestions on what sentences different offences should attract. With the aged, the generally posited explanation for high fear of crime in the face of lower objective risk is that they are traumatised by the prospect of their physical incapacity to cope with crime: to stay on their feet, call for help, think quickly, flee, or fight back.

Conclusion

We have argued that there are more laws in Australia which criminalise exploitative behaviour of the powerful than there are laws which criminalise the behaviour of the poor. Moreover, the unemployed and working class are more likely to be victims of serious crime — from occupational safety offences to homicide. These two facts render simplistic any sweeping proposition that laws are enacted by Australian parliaments fundamentally to serve ruling class interests.

What we have in Australia is a criminal justice system which can, and has, endured a great deal of scandal — be it police corruption or prison riots — without destabilisation, because of the enormous support it has from most sectors of the community. So pervasive is this support that while there might be a fiscal crisis of the state, and while crime rates in Australia are rising comparatively slowly, the exponential growth in criminal justice expenditures endured by Australian taxpayers over the recent decades is likely to continue.

It can be argued that the law was once the servant of ruling class interests during the colonial era, and that today the Australian criminal justice system continues to have a hegemonic quality. But it also has a limited but valued capacity to deliver protection to many interests, from the captain of industry to the pensioner. This gives the system a robustness as part of our institutional landscape that may see it endure without radical change as many more fragile institutions come and go.

References

Alder, C. (1985) 'Theories of Female Delinquency', in A. Borowski and J.M. Murray (eds), *Juvenile Delinquency in Australia*. Sydney: Methuen.

———and Polk, K. (1985) 'Diversion Programmes', in Borowski and Murray.

———and Polk, Kenneth (1985) 'Diversion Programmes' in Borowski and Murray. (eds)

Alder, F. (1975) *Sisters in Crime: the Rise of the New Female Criminal*. New York: McGraw-Hill.

Althuizen, F. (1977) 'Juvenile Offenders in South Australia', in P.R. Wilson (ed.), *Delinquency in Australia: A Critical Appraisal*. Brisbane: University of Queensland Press.

Archer, D. and Gartner, R. (1984) *Violence and Crime in Cross-National Perspective*. New Haven: Yale University Press.

Armstrong, S. and Neumann, E. (1976) 'Bail in New South Wales', *University of New South Wales Law Journal* 1: 298–326.

Australian Bureau of Statistics (1979) *General Social Survey: Crime Victims* [1975 Survey]. Canberra: Australian Bureau of Statistics.

———(1986) *Victims of Crime Australia* [1983 Survey]. Canberra: Australian Bureau of Statistics.

Australian Customs Service (1990) Australian Customs Service Annual Report 1989–90. Canberra: Australian Government Publishing Service.

Barber, R. (1973) 'An Investigation into Rape and Attempted Rape Cases in Queensland', *Australian and New Zealand Journal of Criminology* 6: 214–30.

Barnao, Tony and Lipson, Norm (1991) 'The Asian Connection', *Bulletin*, 2 April.

Bessant, Judith (1991) 'Described, Measured and Labelled: Eugenics, Youth Policy and Moral Panic in Victoria in the 1950s', in R. White and B. Wilson (eds), *For Your Own Good: Young People and State Intervention in Australia*. Special Issue of the Journal of Australian Studies: 8–28.

Biles, D. (1977) 'Car Stealing in Australia', in P.R. Wilson (ed.), *Delinquency in Australia: A Critical Appraisal*. Brisbane: University of Queensland Press.

Bonney, Roseanne (1988) *Homicide II*. Sydney: NSW Bureau of Crime Statistics and Research.

Braithwaite, J. (1977) 'Australian Delinquency: Research and Practical Considerations' in P.R. Wilson (ed.), *Delinquency in Australia: A Critical Appraisal*. Brisbane: University of Queensland Press.

———(1978) 'An Exploratory Study of Used Car Fraud', in P.R. Wilson, and J. Braithwaite (eds), *Two Faces of Deviance: Crimes of the Powerless and Powerful*. Brisbane: University of Queensland Press.

———(1979) *Inequality, Crime, and Public Policy*. London: Routledge and Kegan Paul.

———(1980) 'Political Economy of Punishment', in E.L. Wheelwright and K. Buckley (eds), *Essays in the Political Economy of Australian Capitalism*, Vol. IV. Sydney: ANZ Books.

———(1982) 'Challenging Just Deserts: Punishing White-Collar Criminals', *Journal of Criminal Law and Criminology* 73: 723–63.

———(1989) *Crime, Shame and Reintegration*. Cambridge: Cambridge University Press.

———and Barker, M. (1978) 'Bodgies and Widgies: Folk Devils of the Fifties', in P.R. Wilson and J. Braithwaite (eds), *Two Faces of Deviance: Crimes of the Powerless and Powerful*. Brisbane: University of Queensland Press.

———and Biles, D. (1979) 'On Being Unemployed and Being a Victim of Crime', *Australian Journal of Social Issues* 14: 192–200.

———and Biles, D. (1984) 'Victims and Offenders: The Australian Experience' in R. Block (ed.), *Victimization and Fear of Crime: World Perspectives*. Washington, DC: US Department of Justice.

———and Braithwaite, V. (1978) 'An Exploratory Study of Delinquency and the Nature of Schooling', *Australian and New Zealand Journal of Sociology* 14: 25–332.

———and Grabosky, P. (1985) *Occupational Health and Safety Enforcement in Australia*. Canberra: Australian Institute of Criminology.

———and Law, H. (1978) 'The Structure of Self-Reported Delinquency', *Applied Psychological Measurement* 2: 221–37.

———Biles, D. and Whitrod, R. (1982) 'Fear of Crime in Australia', in H.J. Schneider (ed.), *The Victim in International Perspective*. Berlin and New York: Walter de Gruyter.

Broadhurst, R. and Indermaur, D. (1982) 'Crime Seriousness Ratings: The Relationship of Information Accuracy and General Attitudes in Western Australia', *Australian and New Zealand Journal of Criminology* 15: 219–34.

Calahan, M. (1979) 'Trends in Incarceration in the United States since 1880', *Crime and Delinquency* 25: 9–41.

Challinger, D. (1977) *Young Offenders*. Carlton: Victorian Association for the Care and Resettlement of Offenders.

Chan, J. and Zdenkowski, G. (1985) 'Just Alternatives: Trends and Issues in Deinstitutionalization of Punishment', Draft Working Paper, Australian Law Reform Commission.

Clifford, W. and Harding, R.W. (1985) 'Criminal Justice Processes and Perspectives in a Changing World', in *Australian Discussion Papers* for the Seventh United Nations Congress on the Prevention of Crime and Treatment of Offenders. Canberra: Australian Institute of Criminology.

Cohen, Stanley (1987) *Folk Devils and Moral Panics*. Oxford: Basil Blackwell.

Congalton, A.A. and Najman, J.M. (1974) *Who are the Victims?* Sydney: New South Wales Bureau of Crime Statistics and Research.

Coventry, G. (1984) *Skipping School: An Examination of Truancy in Victorian Secondary Schools*. Melbourne: Victorian Institute of Secondary Education.

———Cornish, G. and Cramer, B. (1984) *Student Perspectives on Truancy*. Melbourne: Victorian Institute of Secondary Education.

Department of Labour and Industry, Victoria (1983) *Annual Report 1982*. Melbourne: Government Printer.

Dickie, Phil (1989) *The Road to Fitzgerald and Beyond*. Brisbane: University of Queensland Press.

Doyle, Bernard John (Detective Inspector) (1988) 'Organised Crime in Australia', *The Police Chief* 55 (12), December: 12–15.

Duckworth, A.M.E., Foley-Jones, C.R., Lowe, P. and Maller, M. (1982) 'Imprisonment of Aborigines in North Western Australia', *Australian and New Zealand Journal of Criminology* 15: 26–46.

Dunstan, J.A.P. and Roberts, S.F. (1977) *Delinquency and Socioeconomic Status: An Ecological Analysis of Melbourne*. Melbourne: Caulfield Institute of Technology.

Eggleston, E. (1976) *Fear, Favour or Affection: Aborigines and the Criminal Law in Victoria, South Australia and Western Australia*. Canberra: Australian National University Press.

Fitzgerald, G.E. (Chairman) (1989) *Report of a Commission of Inquiry Pursuant to Orders in Council — Queensland. Commission of Inquiry into Possible Illegal Activities and Associated Police Misconduct*. Dated (i) 26 May 1987 (ii) 24 June 1987 (iii) 25 August 1988 (iv) 29 June 1989. Brisbane: Government Printer.

Gale, Fay, Bailey-Harris, Rebecca, and Wundersitz, Joy (1990) *Aboriginal Youth and the Criminal Justice System: The Injustice of Justice?*. Cambridge: Cambridge University Press.

Gorta, A. and Hunter, R. (1985) 'Aborigines in NSW Prisons', *Australian and New Zealand Journal of Criminology* 18: 25–40.

Gottfredson, M.R. (1984) *Victims of Crime: The Dimensions of Risk*. London: Home Office Research and Planning Unit.

Grabosky, P.N. (1977) *Sydney in Ferment: Crime, Dissent and Official Reaction*. Canberra: Australian National University Press.

———(1984) 'The Variability of Punishment', in D. Black (ed.), *Toward A General Theory of Social Control, Vol. I: Fundamentals*. Academic Press.

———and Braithwaite, J. (1986) *Of Manners Gentle: Enforcement Strategies of Australian Business Regulatory Agencies*. Melbourne: Oxford University Press.

———and Braithwaite, J. (1986) 'Corporate Crime and Government Response in Australia', in D. Chappell and P.R. Wilson (eds), *The Australian Criminal Justice System: the mid-1980s*. Sydney: Butterworths.

————and Braithwaite, J. (1987) 'Corporate Crime in Australia', in *Trends and Issues No. 5*. Canberra: Australian Institute of Criminology.

————and Sutton, A. (eds.) (1989) *Stains on a White Collar*. Annandale: Federation Press.

Gusfield, J. (1967) *Symbolic Crusade*. Urbana: University of Illinois Press.

Hagan, J. (1982) 'The Corporate Advances: A Study of the Involvement of Corporate and Individual Victims in a Criminal Justice System', *Social Forces* 60: 993–1,022.

Hancock, L. (1980) 'The Myth that Females are Treated More Leniently than Males in the Juvenile Justice System', *Australian and New Zealand Journal of Sociology* 16: 4–14.

————and Chesney-Lind, M. (1985) 'Juvenile Justice Legislation and Gender Discrimination' in A. Borowski and J.M. Murray, *Juvenile Delinquency in Australia*. Sydney: Methuen.

Hanks, P., and Keon-Cohen, B. (eds) (1984) *Aborigines and the Law*. Sydney: Allen and Unwin.

Hazlehurst, Kayleen M. (ed.) (1987) *Ivory Scales: Black Australia and the Law*. Sydney/Canberra: NSW University Press, in association with the Australian Institute of Criminology.

Hindelang, M.J., Gottfredson, M.R. and Garofalo, J. (1978) *Victims of Personal Crime: An Empirical Foundation for a Theory of Personal Victimization*. Cambridge, Mass.: Ballinger.

Hopkins, A. and Parnell, N. (1984) 'Why Coal Mine Safety Regulations in Australia are not Enforced', *International Journal of the Sociology of Law* 12: 179–84.

Institute of Criminology (1978) *Unemployment and Crime*. Sydney University Law School.

Jankovic, I. (1977) 'Labour Market and Imprisonment', *Crime and Social Justice* 8: 17–31.

Knight, T. (1985) 'Schools and Delinquency', in A. Borowski and J.M. Murray, *Juvenile Delinquency in Australia*. Sydney: Methuen.

Kraus, J. (1973) 'Urbanization Patterns of Juvenile Delinquency in New South Wales', *Australian Journal of Social Issues* 8: 277–33.

————(1975) 'Ecology of Juvenile Delinquency in Metropolitan Sydney', *Journal of Community Psychology* 3: 384–95.

————(1977) 'Some Aspects of Delinquency in Australia', in P.R. Wilson (ed.), *Delinquency in Australia: A Critical Appraisal*. Brisbane: University of Queensland Press.

Krohn, M., Curry, J.P. and Nelson-Kilger, S. (1983) 'Is Chivalry Dead?', *Criminology* 21: 417–37.

Marnier, L. (1980) *The Affective Education Project*. Adelaide: Education Department of South Australia.

Mellor, Bill and Ricketson, Matthew (1991) 'Suburbanasia!: Fifteen years after the Kein Giang, Indochinese join the nation's mainstream', *Time*, 8 April.

Mugford, Jane (1989) 'Domestic Violence', *Violence Today* 2. Canberra: Australian Institute of Criminology.

Mugford, Stephen (1984) 'Fear of Crime — Rational Or Not? A Discussion and Some Australian Data', *Australian and New Zealand Journal of Criminology* 17: 267–75.

Muirhead, J.H. (Commissioner) (1988) *Royal Commission into Aboriginal*

Deaths in Custody: Interim Report. Canberra: Australian Government Publishing Service.

Mukherjee, S.K. (1981) *Crime Trends in Twentieth-Century Australia.* Sydney: Allen and Unwin.

———(1985) 'Juvenile Delinquency: Dimensions of the Problem', in Borowski and Murray.

———(1986) 'The Nature of Crime Trends in Australia' in D. Chappell and P. Wilson (eds) *The Australian Criminal Justice System-The mid-1980s.* Sydney: Butterworths.

———(1989) *Source Book of Australian Criminal and Social Statistics.* Canberra: Australian Institute of Criminology.

———and Dagger, D. (1990) *The Size of the Crime Problem in Australia.* Canberra: Australian Institute of Criminology.

———and Fitzgerald, R.W. (1981) 'The Myth of Rising Female Crime', in S.K. Mukherjee and J.A. Scutt, *Women and Crime.* Sydney: Allen and Unwin.

———Neuhaus, D. and Walker, J. (1990) *Crime and Justice in Australia.* Canberra: Australian Institute of Criminology.

———Walker, J.R. and Jacobsen, E.N. (1986) *Crime and Punishment in the Colonies.* Sydney: University of New South Wales, History Project Inc.

———and Wilson, P.R. (1987) 'Neighbourhood Watch: Issues and Policy Implications', in *Trends and Issues* 8. Canberra: Australian Institute of Criminology.

Naffin, Ngaire (1986) 'Women and Crime', in Chappell and Wilson.

Najman, J.M. (1980) 'Victims of Homicide: An Epidemiological Approach to Social Policy', *Australian and New Zealand Journal of Criminology* 13: 272–80.

National Committee on Violence (1990) *Violence: Directions for Australia.* Canberra Australian Institute of Criminology.

New South Wales Bureau of Crime Statistics and Research (1972) *Crime in Our Cities: A Comparative Report,* Statistical Report 6. Sydney: NSW Bureau of Crime Statistics and Research.

———(1974) *A Thousand Prisoners,* Statistical Report 3. Sydney: NSW Bureau of Crime Statistics and Research.

———(1992) *New South Wales Recorded Crime Statistics 1991,* Statistical Report 80. Sydney: NSW Bureau of Crime Statistics and Research.

NRMA (1992) *Car Theft in New South Wales and ACT.* Sydney: NRMA Insurance Ltd.

O'Connor, Ian (1992) *Youth, Crime and Justice in Queensland.* Brisbane: Criminal Justice Commission.

O'Malley, P. (1981) 'Theories of Structural Versus Causal Determination: Accounting for Legislative Change in Capitalist Societies', in R. Tomasic (ed.), *Legislation and Society in Australia.* Sydney: Allen and Unwin.

———(1983) *Law, Capitalism and Democracy.* Sydney: Allen and Unwin.

Pearson, Geoffrey (1983) *Hooligan: A History of Respectable Fears.* New York: Schocken.

Police Commissioners' Australian Crime Statistics Sub-Committee (1987) *Selected Crime Statistics, Australia.*

Polk, K. and Alder, C. (1986) 'Criminal Justice Reform in Australia', in Chappell and Wilson.

Queensland Department of Mines (1983) *Annual Report 1983*. Brisbane: Government Printer.

Quinney, R. (1977) *Class, State and Crime: On the Theory and Practice of Criminal Justice*. New York: Longman.

Roach Anleu, Sharyn L. (1991) *Deviance, Conformity and Control*. Melbourne: Longman Cheshire.

Sanson-Fisher, R.W. (1978) 'Aborigines and Crime Statistics: An Interaction Between Poverty and Detectors', *Australian and New Zealand Journal of Criminology* 11: 71–78.

Sarri, R. and Bradley, P.W. (1980) 'Juvenile Aid Panels: An Alternative to Juvenile Court Processing in South Australia', *Crime and Delinquency* 20: 42–62.

Schur, E.M. (1973) *Radical Non-Intervention: Rethinking the Delinquency Problem*. Englewood Cliffs: Prentice-Hall.

Scull, A. (1977) *Decarceration: Community Treatment and the Deviant: A Radical View*. Englewood Cliffs: Prentice-Hall.

Scutt, J. (1979) 'The Myth of the 'Chivalry Factor' in Female Crime', *Australian Journal of Social Issues* 14: 3–20.

——(1983) *Even in the Best of Homes: Violence in the Family*. Ringwood: Penguin.

Smith, G. (1975) 'Leisure, Recreation and Delinquency', MA Thesis, Department of Anthropology and Sociology, University of Queensland.

South Australian Office of Crime Statistics (1979) *Crime and Justice in South Australia: Quarterly Report for the Period Ending 31 December, 1978*. Adelaide: Attorney-General's Department.

——(1980a) *Robbery in South Australia*. Adelaide: Attorney-General's Department.

——(1980b) *Statistics from Courts of Summary Jurisdiction* (4). Adelaide: Attorney-General's Department.

——(1984) *Crime and Justice in South Australia, 1 July–31 December 1982*. Adelaide: Attorney-General's Department.

Strang, Heather (1991) *Homicides in Australia 1990–91*. Canberra: Australian Institute of Criminology.

Sutherland, E.H. (1949) *White Collar Crime*. New York: Holt, Rinehart and Winston.

——and Cressey, D.R. (1970) *Criminology*. Philadelphia: Lippincott.

Swanton, B. and Wilson, P.R. (1992) 'Public Perspectives on Police', in P.R. Wilson (ed.), *Issues in Crime, Morality and Justice*. Canberra: Australian Institute of Criminology.

Titus Reid, Sue (1991) *Crime and Criminology*. Fort Worth/Chicago: Holt, Rinehart and Winston.

van Dijk, J.J.M., Mayhew, P. and Killias, M. (1990) *Experiences of Crime Across the World, Key Findings of the 1989 International Crime Survey*. The Netherlands: Deventer.

Vinson, T. and Homel, R. (1972) *The Coincidence of Medical and Social Problems Throughout a Region*. Sydney: NSW Bureau of Crime Statistics and Research.

Walker, J. (1990) 'A Comparison of Crime in Australia and other Countries', *Trends and Issues* 23. Canberra: Australian Institute of Criminology.

————(1992a) 'Lateral Thinking in Crime Prevention — Holmes and the Case of the Disappearing Bicycle Thieves', *Criminology Australia*, 3 (4), April–May:13.

————and Hallinan, J. (1991) *Australian Prisoners 1990: Results of the National Prison Census — 30 June*. Canberra: Australian Institute of Criminology.

————and Henderson, M. (1991) 'Understanding Crime Trends in Australia', *Trends and Issues Series* 28. Canberra: Australian Institute of Criminology.

————(1992b) 'Prison Sentences in Australia: Estimates of the Characteristics of Offenders Sentenced to Prison in 1987–88', in Wilson.

————Dagger, D. and Collins, Mark (1991) *Crime in Australia* [as measured by the Australian component of the International Crime Victim Survey 1989]. Canberra: Australian Institute of Criminology.

————Hallinan, J. and Dagger, D. (1992) *Australian Prisoners 1991: Results of the National Prison Census — 30 June*. Canberra: Australian Institute of Criminology.

————Wilson, P.R., Chappell, D. and Weatherburn, D. (1990) *A Comparison of Crime in Australia and Other Countries*. Canberra: Australian Institute of Criminology.

Wallace, Alison (1986) *Homicide: The Social Reality*. Sydney: New South Wales Bureau of Crime Statistics and Research.

Warner, C. (1982) 'A Study of Self-Reported Crime of a Group of Male and Female High School Students', *Australian and New Zealand Journal of Criminology* 15: 255–72.

Weatherburn, D. and Devery, C. (1991) 'How Violent is Australia?', in D. Chappell *et al.*, *Australian Violence: Contemporary Perspectives*. Canberra: Australian Institute of Criminology.

West, D.J. and Farrington, D.P. (1977) *The Delinquent Way of Life*. London: Heinemann..

Western Australia Government (1992) *Report of the Royal Commission into Commercial Activities of Government and Other Matters*. Perth: Government Printer.

Wilson, P. R. Walker, J. and Mukherjee, S. (1986) 'How the Public sees Crime: An Australian Survey', *Trends and Issues* 2. Canberra: Australian Institute of Criminology.

————(1982) *Black Death, White Hands*. Sydney: Allen and Unwin.

————(1985) 'Black Death White Hands Revisited: The Case of Palm Island', *Australian and New Zealand Journal of Criminology* 18: 49–57.

————and Braithwaite, J. (1977) 'School, Truancy and Delinquency', in P.R. Wilson (ed.), *Delinquency in Australia: A Critical Appraisal*. Brisbane: University of Queensland Press.

Windschuttle, K. (1978) 'Granny Versus the Hooligans', in P.R. Wilson and J. Braithwaite (eds), *Two Faces of Deviance: Crimes of the Powerless and Powerful*. Brisbane: University of Queensland Press.

Wundersitz, Joy (1992) 'The Net-widening Effect of the Aid Panels and Screening Panels in the South Australian Juvenile Justice System', *ANZ Journal of Criminology* 25 (2): 115–34.

Chapter Thirteen

Leisure: Freedom or Control?

David F. Ip

Leisure as Freedom

Leisure as a field of discourse and investigation within academic sociology has only a recent beginning. According to Parry and Coatler (in Rojek 1985: 2), it first emerged as a footnote to the narrowly focused 'plant' sociology of World War I and the inter-war years. For the most part, it was studied as an appendix to questions of workplace productivity and efficiency. It was only after World War II that sociologists began to pay more attention to questions of leisure, which was seen to result from the rise of Western leisure centred affluent societies.

The coming of the 'leisure society' has contributed much first to the establishment of the tradition of social formalism in the sociology of leisure. Essentially, leisure is recognised as a unique modern phenomenon, which did not exist in pre-industrial society: its emergence was the result of the changing organisation of the work process with the advent of the factory system, and the forced separation of workplace and home. Leisure is thus defined as *activities* in which people *choose* to participate during their *free* time. It is seen as to be distinct from all other aspects of life. It is non-instrumental, non-productive and emancipatory. It is conceived as release from work and as human self-expression. It is an end in itself, and it is intrinsically satisfying and demanding. As Kaplan (1975) states:

Leisure consists of relatively self-determined activity/experience that falls into one's free time roles, that is seen as leisure by participants, that is psychologically pleasant in anticipation and recollection, that potentially covers the whole range of commitment and intensity, that contains characteristic norms and constraints, that provides opportunities for recreation, personal growth and service to others.

Leisure is freedom. One important assumption of this perspective is that an individual is free to choose a particular leisure form and practice. The study of leisure is therefore the description of leisure and recreation in all their various forms, an inquiry into leisure and its 'associated variables' (Rojek 1985: 1). Yet its main concern is best exemplified by Wilensky's (1960) analysis that as society witnesses the growth of leisure, there is also the danger of the decline of the work ethic. Questions arise to whether or not concepts of work will be replaced by other values which 'integrate' people into society. Issues such as the changing basis of social solidarity, the 'pluralisation' of social structures, the relative decline of the collective conscience and the concomitant strengthening of the cult of the individual as a moral value, and the problems of the anomic potentiality of much of modern leisure have, according to Coatler and Parry (1982: 5), 'all formed the agenda of an admittedly non-cumulative and diffuse leisure sociology'. One effect of such 'recreational/leisure' studies has been a tendency towards a functionalist approach, in which leisure is understood in terms of its positive functions within society, either at the individual or the social level. This means that it is more concerned with how leisure is used, and the idea of viewing leisure as compensatory or as a safety valve. Implicitly, the concern is also whether freedom in leisure has been positively or negatively used.

Leisure as Control

The idea of leisure as individual freedom, however, has not been accepted by everyone. For the theorists of the Frankfurt school, freedom in leisure is illusory. In the main, they recognise that leisure has become one of the central dynamics of the modern capitalist economy. The leisure industry has emerged in the post-war years as a huge and expanding sector of the capitalist economy. It is also, according to this view, a key factor in explaining the persistence of capitalist society. Modern leisure resembles more a mechanism of social control than freedom.

This is because the major concern of such theorists is: if leisure is considered to be freedom, how does capitalism permit the private existence of such a sphere of autonomy and still reproduce a disciplined workforce? How does capitalism maintain the separation of work and play and simultaneously maintain a necessary link between the two? This is particularly important when not all forms of leisure are necessarily conducive to good order: drinking, for example. This emphasises the contradiction between the need to organise or control workers' leisure (so that it does not disrupt work time), and leisure's ideological importance as free time (the time when workers experience themselves as free labourers).

The theorists therefore argue that it is important to see that individuals' choices in leisure are not necessarily all free ones. Individuals are in fact trapped within the ideology of capitalism and consumerism. Human instincts and creativity are repressed into false needs and desires. What has been offered through the leisure market, it may be argued, is no choice at all, since leisure has become packaged, promoted and processed for mass markets like any other commodity (Haywood *et al.*, 1990: 280). Choices, if any, are constrained by existing institutional structures, and are constantly directed to the legitimate form of consumption. To Gorz, the directive to consume 'numbs a stunted, mass-produced humanity with satisfactions that leave the basic satisfaction untouched, but still distract the mind from it' (in Haralambos 1980: 236). Similarly, Marcuse (1972) claims that if work under capitalism is 'exhausting, stupefying, inhuman slavery', leisure simply involves 'modes of relaxation which soothe and prolong this stupefaction', because it is based on and directed by 'false needs'. In sum, there is no freedom nor pleasure in leisure.

Modern leisure, in this context, is viewed to have been used to mystify the working class so that the necessary counter-balance to the real subordination of workers in the labour process can be restored. In other words, the mass manipulation of leisure acts to reproduce class society (Held 1980; Rojek 1985: 107-20).

The theorists may have highlighted the important sociological fact that relations of leisure are relations of power, and that leisure practice continually functions to remake the power structure of capitalist society. Paradoxically, it also assumes that the consumer is passive, that the totally 'administered society' or 'one dimensional' leisure is accepted 'without opposition' (Dumazedier 1989: 151). Disappointingly, too, it displays 'the brand-mark of functionalist reasoning' (Rojek 1985: 121; Haywood *et al.* 1990: 281; Moorhouse 1989: 15).

The sociology of leisure is marooned in these two narrow and opposing perspectives. The first, the social formalist tradition 'is dogged by the major problems of superficial concepts and spurious distinctions ... a preoccupation with a desire to plan leisure ... and frequently stemming from a functionalist framework'. Neo-Marxist theorists are unable to transcend their own brand of self-referential and functionalist notions (Rojek 1985: 5). What, then, can we do about the state of the sociology of leisure? How else can we look at the phenomenon of modern leisure?

Stedman-Jones (1977) argues that leisure cannot be seen in isolation; but must be situated within the broader social structure, particularly that of capitalism. Rojek (1985, 1989) further suggests that when sociology is dominated by forms of theory which deal with the extensive critical literature on power, knowledge and the mode of production, leisure as well as recreation can be re-examined in the light of leisure relations and leisure forms, and how they are produced and reproduced in the context of an historically specific system of power, to reflect the principles, ideology and development of capitalist society. Dumazedier (1989: 154) also argues for a neo-dialectic theorisation of leisure, recognising both the constraint and freedom in mass leisure. Elias emphasises that the complex and changing inter-relationships between individuals in societies, the 'figurational' networks, must be understood in leisure activities (Horne and Jay 1987; Dunning 1989; Rojek 1985; Haywood *et al.* 1990: 284-88).

This introductory chapter intends to explore the sociological concept of leisure with a set of parameters similar to those suggested by the cited authors. We will re-examine the nature of leisure and its connection to production, particularly in the context of capitalism. However, in further delineating the practices and forms of leisure in society, it will be viewed not simply as freedom or control, but as freedom and constraint. I argue that leisure and recreation might be seen as social control — but they are not total control. It is important to clarify the validity of the concept of leisure to assess its relevance for some specific groups, such as women, in our society. By looking at Australian experiences of leisure and those overseas, we propose to gain an understanding of its role and varying manifestations in the context of the historical development of capitalist society.

The Freedom and Constraint of Leisure

The concept of leisure in its modern sense, according to many (Dumazedier 1974; Parker 1976; Burkart and Medlik 1981; Parker and Paddick 1990), simply did not exist until the advent of industrial capitalism. In other words, work was not considered as

instrumental; as a means-to-an-end obligation for economic subsistence, until industrial capitalism came of age. Burns, for example,
believes that work in pre-industrial society was basically 'part and
parcel of everyday life and leisure was not a separate section of the
day' (1974: 43). Quoting Varagnae, Dumazedier (1974: 14) also
describes work's rhythm as 'natural, interrupted by breaks, by
songs, by games and ceremonies. It tended to coincide with the
pattern of the day, from sunrise to sunset. There was no clear cut
division between work and rest.'

The change in concept, from an undistinguished conceptual-
isation of both work and rest, to a dichotomised distinction between
the two, came about only when wage labour was introduced to
workers entering economic subsistence. A recognition of free time
began to take shape. As Parker points out, 'it was only when work
came to be done in a special place, at a special time and under
special conditions that leisure came to be demanded as a right'
(1976: 24). This is echoed by others: 'only when the place of
earning one's living began to be separated from the place where
one reared one's family, could the modern separation of work and
leisure be valid' (Burkhart and Medlik 1981: 4).

Within the household, men and, increasingly, women and
children, were also being drawn into the labour force in order to
secure a minimum level of economic survival. Industrialisation
created not only an increasingly sharp separation between home
and work, but also of production and consumption. Leisure
became the time when commodities were purchased and consumed.
Frith observes that by the end of the nineteenth century, there
was a well-established market for consumer durables, of which
consumption was made possible by new, binding arrangements of
credit or hire-purchase. In his words, 'leisure meant certain
commitments' (1982: 250).

All this meant that when industrial production was organised
around the developing principles of rational work discipline, when
workers were subjected to the social organisation of the factory
and to the technical requirements of machinery, with work
becoming a matter of routine and repetition, inflexible in its use
of time and space, an equally rational leisure discipline also
emerged. By the end of the nineteenth century, leisure was no
longer an occasional event like a fair, a carnival or a harvest
festival, but more a routine, a daily experience of 'non-work'.

The ideology which accompanied the growth of such 'free
time' was that people worked in order to enjoy their leisure as
they wished, the money they made being spent on the commodities
they wanted to purchase. Marx argues that consumption and
'consumerism' are the major forms of domination and reification

(1970: 72). In other words, while the Malthusians worried that if the workers ever became affluent enough to enjoy 'idleness', they might never work again, we should note that in practice, work and the experience of work remained the only justifications for such idleness. During the Depression of the 1930s, mass unemployment did not mean mass leisure; but rather, it made more urgent the need for a job. 'Free' time without a job meant only shame and boredom. And as Frith further suggests, 'postwar affluence rested not on idleness but overtime, as people worked harder and harder to buy the leisure goods they didn't have time to enjoy' (1982: 250).

Despite the fact that leisure is generally defined as 'time free from work and other obligations, and it also encompasses activities which are characterised by a feeling of (comparative) freedom' (Parker 1976: 12), the 'freedom' involved in standard accounts of leisure like his and Dumazedier's is, in fact, deceptive. Leisure is a necessary component of industrial capitalism. It is the time when labour is replenished physically and culturally: re-creation time. It is also, however, the time when people consume, when surplus value is realised. 'Free' time is not only structured by ideas, but also by material forces, by the availability of goods and resources, by the effects of the labour process on people's capacities and desires. The size of their pay packet determines what resources people can have; work prospects and career possibilities limit the leisure risks they are prepared to take; work discipline and the organisation of workers mentally and physically on the job, limits their leisure capacities. This tension is the expression of the general relationship between production and consumption.

Leisure is, on the one hand, a source of fun and freedom and pleasure (Kaplan 1975: 26), a necessary counter to alienating labour. It must also be, on the other hand, constrained and controlled and made trivial, so as not to interfere with the labour process. Historians acknowledge the fact that the implementation of the British Factory Acts, providing a free Saturday afternoon, had as much to do with capitalist support as workers' campaigns (Walvin 1978: 5, 60). After all, happy workers were more efficient and amenable than those who were selling their labour power under the dull compulsion of necessity. The weekend is precisely what this tension between work and leisure is all about: Friday and Saturday nights are party times because there is no work to go to the next morning. Leisure, then, is not really free time at all, but an organisation of non-work that is determined by capitalist production. The needs of industrial capitalism for the regulation and synchronisation of production and consumption, and the continuance of necessary discipline, are achieved via the organisation of leisure. Far from being a private and free domain, leisure forms part of a 'universal sphere of consumption'.

The theorists may have made a very important point in suggesting that work itself, because it may be dull, routine and mindless, destroys workers' abilities to be free, and to enjoy themselves in other meaningful ways. Commercial leisure commodities can indeed be seen as instruments designed to confirm their cultural incapacities. The theorists' viewpoint, however, is also one which denies the concept of pleasure: that is, that workers have no cultural purpose of their own, and cannot experience anything else other than provided by powerful capitalists. Frith (1982: 264), quoting Marx (*Grundrisse*), suggests that the capitalist, needing consumers for his products, searches

> . . . for means to spur workers on to consumption, to give his wares new charms, to inspire them with new needs by constant chatter, etc. It is precisely this side of the relation of capital and labour which is an essential civilising moment, and on which the capital rests.

In short, he argues that leisure commodities may support the power of the capitalists, but also have their civilising moments. The argument that workers are totally passive and therefore can be controlled both at work and leisure is too glib and simplistic.

Basically, the 'control' of leisure is difficult. Both workers' ideological freedom as consumers, and the different interests of commodity producers have made such control problematic. Frith (1982: 254) is correct in pointing out that regulation has always been more important than repression (except in brief experiments like Prohibition), and capitalist leisure has developed within a framework of licences and licensing authorities. Malcolmson's (1973) history of popular recreation in England between 1780 to 1850 documents the fall of traditional popular recreations and increasing state intervention. He notes that 'the most direct (and the traditional) means to encourage labour discipline was through the application of state power, and this kind of control continued to be generally applauded' (Malcolmson 1973: 97).

The state's efforts were indeed significant. Storch (1976) argues that the police force in England was developed primarily to patrol leisure: to apply the licensing laws. In the English industrial cities of the nineteenth century, the working class was isolated in its own areas and confined to its own activities. It was the police who had to supervise the pubs, the crowds and the street corners, to enforce regulations on drink and prostitution, gambling and performance. The emphasis was on surveillance rather than prevention; the policeman's duty was to prevent workers' leisure from becoming public disorder, and public holidays from becoming political events. In Storch's view, the policeman was a 'domestic missionary', bringing middle class restraint and decency to working class lives. Class divisions were also a symbol of nineteenth century leisure. Employers and their workers did not meet in their free time in the ways that the landed gentry and their tenants and labourers met in rural feasts and sports. The aristocracy and *lumpenproletariat* met on the race track and around the boxing ring (Bailey 1978).

Fuller (1977) sees a similar picture in his study on class bias legislation relating to gambling in England, while Downes and others (1976) and Walvin (1978) also record that various attempts were made to regulate and prohibit alcohol consumption among the working class. Such regulations were based mainly on moral grounds. Labelling activities such as drinking and gambling as 'unsuitable' pastimes meant that leisure in the nineteenth century was seen from above as a means of self-improvement.

Coalter (1990: 5) sees popular pastimes as systematically suppressed by English public authorities. For example, magistrates banned wakes as threats to public order, and the Highway Act of 1835 introduced fines for playing 'at football or any other game or any other part of the said Highway to the annoyance of any passenger'. Various other factory Acts and bank holiday Acts served to organise leisure into specific and defined time periods, to undermine pre-industrial practices such as Saint Monday, extending the weekend by taking Monday as a holiday.

Coatler believes that such concerns of the state were twofold: public order and work discipline. He suggests that 'large public gatherings of rowdy crowds in urban areas raised the spectre of the French and American revolutions and the possibilities of assaults on the existing order. . . The rational and systematic ordering of work into specific places and times also required the reciprocal organisation of leisure' (Coatler 1990: 5). The resultant changes and the emergence of new forms of leisure, in his view, are not merely the result of structural changes due to industrialisation, but were the consequence of reinforcing legislation, as well as national and local government policies.

The 'rational recreation' of Victoria England is perhaps a good illustration. Legislation such as the Museum Act 1845 and the Libraries Act 1850 usually referred to as the 'rational recreational movement', were aimed at providing a cultural content for leisure time, as alternatives to the 'degeneracy' of working class social life (Coatler 1990: 6). The rationale for such a movement was the 'merit good' argument: intervention was necessary because the consumers were not the best judges of their own (or society's) welfare. Mellor (in Coatler 1990: 6) has noted that the majority of nineteenth century public facilities were provided not because they were in demand, but because they were regarded as socially desirable. Goldman and Wilson's (1977) study of the industrial recreation movement further shows how scientific rationality became applied not only to work, but to leisure. They point out that 'the industrial recreation movement was part of a general orientation to the phenomenon of leisure stimulated by three principal concerns: technical efficiency, control over the production process, and the maintenance of legitimacy. The industrial recreation programmes were designed to integrate structurally and ideologically the working man's leisure into the needs of corporate capital' (Goldman and Wilson 1977: 183).

Underlying such a movement is the Protestant work ethic: pleasure must be justified, and leisure, too, should mean effort and self-discipline. This applies not only to labourers, but to the middle class as well. The subordination of leisure to work has meant, at its simplest, the organisation of middle class social life around business needs, every activity being chosen for its career effects. There is also, however, an ideological distinction involved, between improving experiences, embodied in certain forms of arts and sports, and 'wasteful' hedonism. By the end of the nineteenth century, the distinction between rational and irrational leisure was institutionally enforced: rational leisure was promoted in schools, municipal parks and libraries; irrational leisure was patrolled and regulated by the police, and directly or indirectly by policies on housing, education, health and the family. There were systematic efforts by teachers and clergymen and journalists in England to apply to the working classes the moral principles embedded in public school games — discipline, effort, competition, team spirit and good manner — according to Frith (1982: 255).

From a reading of Foucault's work, one might tend to agree that leisure relations are not entirely relations of freedom. Instead they are relations of discipline, training, coding and control (Foucault 1977: 152-64). The municipalisation of recreation under Welfare Capitalism in the 1920s in America, in O'Connor's (1973) view, is another example of such promotion and regulation of leisure. O'Connor notes that in this process, the socialisation costs of production have been gradually handed over to the state, eventually cumulating in the contemporary fiscal crisis of the state.

'Rational' recreation was basically a contradictory concept: leisure is, by definition, a contrast to work, duty and routine. Leisure is also the setting for non-routine experiences of love and art and ecstasy. The nineteenth century problem had been how to combine the necessary discipline and relaxation, the necessary order and disorder, freedom and constraint. To be fair, as Coatler (1990: 5) points out, 'the concerns of public policy were not wholly repressive or prohibitive. Like much of social policy, that which concerned itself with work and work disciplines contained elements of both control and liberation. The Factory Act served also to limit over-exploitative employers and to serve as a formal recognition of the legitimacy of the idea of free and private time separate from work.' More importantly, Coatler also comments (p. 7) that 'to view these initiatives merely as efforts at "social control" is, however, to misrepresent the ambiguities in the "rational recreation" movement', since it ultimately largely failed to reach its target groups. Even those among the urban working class who did participate eventually did so on their own terms. The middle-class sponsorship of Working Men's Clubs, for instance, was accepted only until alternative forms of finance were established via profits from the sale of alcohol (Cunningham 1980; Bailey 1979).

As the religious or moral control of leisure waned, and the state became increasingly reluctant to become further involved in leisure provision despite political rhetoric, the development of leisure policy was left to the permissive powers of local government, voluntary effort and the commercial sector (Coatler 1990: 8); eventually, commercial entrepreneurs just took over. They churned out leisure goods to make profits and to bring leisure 'needs' into line with available leisure goods. Commercial entrepreneurs were also concerned about the problems of routine and order. 'Irrational' leisure, like spontaneity, drunkenness, disruption and the like, were likely to affect profits. As Frith (1982) points out, it is no surprise that the characteristics of the production of leisure commodities have been the premium emphasis on the organisation of leisure by notions of professionalism and predictability, the latter being especially significant because it is important to reduce commercial risk. Giving the paying customers what they want has always been the guiding principle of the commercial process, to secure an orderly mass audience.

The development of mass media and their bureaucratic control eventually further contributed much to the 'refinement' of leisure in the twentieth century. The rise of the cinema, radio and television meant not only the standardisation of popular entertainment, but also the regulation of its spontaneous, disruptive and anarchical elements. In Frith's words, this is the 'translation of working class pleasures into middlebrow formulas' (1982: 257). To put it in another way, the older leisure occupations finally had to give way

to more ordered and disciplined recreations which the new industrial society demanded, entertainments which were consonant with
the wider social and economic interests of contemporary society.

Leisure in Australia

Despite its different history, the development of leisure in Australia
falls into a similar pattern to that of England.

When the white settlers arrived in 1788, according to Parker
and Paddick (1990: 6), the way of life of the Aborigines was not
immediately challenged. Nevertheless, the contrast between the
work ethic of the new white dominant group and the 'undivided
life' of the indigenous group, soon became apparent. The division
between the two groups of white settlers, the military officers and
other high-ranking officials, and the 'other ranks', convicts and
'free' labourers, became most clear-cut during leisure or recreational
activities. The former sought to reproduce their leisure activities
from their country of origin: elegant dining and drinking, parties
and balls, cricket and other refined sports and pastimes were the
order of the day. The leisure of the 'lower classes' was, however,
characterised by indulgence in alcohol, gross sexual practices,
blood sports and the cruder manifestations of the theatre (Parker
and Paddick 1990: 6).

It was not until the late 1830s that Australia systematically
experienced the impacts the industrialisation on everyday life
(Connell and Irving 1978). One of the major consequences was
shorter working hours. In 1856, the Eight Hour Movement won
the building trade an eight-hour day (Murphy 1896). But such
practice remained uneven. Lack (1978: 50) suggests that 'at the
beginning of the 1880s only a minority of urban working men —
including most building craftsmen, quarrymen and a few groups
in the metal trades — had won the eight hours boon'. However,
because of the openness of Australian society, especially through
the influence of employers, who were formerly tradesmen, shorter
hours were less a threat than a goal aspired to by both workers
and small capitalists. Consequently the 8-hour day or the 48-hour
week gradually became a general feature in Australian working
life, from the early 1900s (Cannon 1973).

The move to such leisure coincided with the suburban development of the 1880s. When industrial production was combined
with a high commitment to suburban home ownership, not only
was an ideology of individualism, familism, private ownership and
privacy cemented, but a peculiar pattern of leisure centred around
the home also emerged.

This is particularly true for the middle class. In his study of middle class leisure in Victoria, Cannon (1973: 223) suggests that in the late nineteenth century, it seemed that both husbands and wives were spending more and more time in and around the home. Wives, for example, were engaged in often hectic and ritualistic rounds of social calls, patterned after the British example. A superior home life, education and surplus wealth seemed to be their ideal. Their leisure outside the home and family, on the other hand, were more display activities, to reinforce their middle class consciousness, rather than provide enjoyment. Balls, garden parties and organised picnics were often constrained activities, indicating hierarchical status.

The study of Footscray by Lack (1978), however, offers a different picture in the case of the working class. Lack sees the home as the centre of leisure for the working class as simply limited to games and reading. 'Home life must have been a round of never-ending chores for wives, and with the best will in the world, a large majority of working men would have had only two or three waking hours each weekday, to relax at home' (Lack 1978: 53). The typical pattern of working class leisure in Victoria, in his view, was largely located in entertainment outside the home, because of the size of the house, quality and location differences.

Parker and Paddick (1990: 7) further describe popular working class recreation as 'centred around drinking, informal street activities and irregular visits from commercial entertainers in the pubs, streets and circuses'. Bottomley (1980) suggests that the reason why in Melbourne there was such a frequent mention of high commitment to sport and spectatorship during leisure, was due to the fact that leisure for the working class *had* to take place outdoors.

Parallel to developments in England, towards the end of the nineteenth century, the dominant work values of establishing a new industrial society were gradually mediated by more cultural and 'serious leisure' values, fostered in the arts and sciences by professional clubs and societies. Parker and Paddick (1990) highlight various attempts made by local government as well as church groups and temperance reformers to actively 'improve' the leisure of the working class, and provide them with alternative established entertainments in pubs and music halls. For example, state libraries, galleries and museums were provided, and various Mechanics Institutes were set up to offer workers tuition in practical and cultural matters to guide and stimulate them to 'better' use of their free time. At the same time, such interventions were reinforced by the regulation of drinking, gambling and other social vices (Dunstan 1968; McMillen 1985; Pearson 1977; Pearson and O'Hara 1977; Lynch 1990).

Interestingly, the 'general way of life' in Australia, including that of the working class, has become home-centred leisure (Oeser and Hammond 1954; Cleland and Stimson 1972; Pearson 1977). Bottomley (1980) suggests that this may be the consequence of the expansion of the suburban ideal, possibly through the principle of stratified diffusion (Wilmott and Young 1975). In the 1940s, a survey in a New South Wales town found that the five most popular pastimes were reading, radio listening, going to the pictures, watching football, and gardening (Walker 1945). In 1956, a Gallup Poll carried out before the advent of television, revealed that listening to the radio and reading accounted for 64 per cent of weeknight time, and 43 per cent of weekend time. Olley (1962) confirmed that the average person (male) spent about three-quarters of his active leisure (non-working and non-sleeping) in and around the home. Scott and U'Ren (1962), in another study of a suburban housing estate, found a similar pattern for working class residents.

More recently, Lansbury (1970) found that the middle class leisure pattern was based on family, home, car and garden. Findings from Cleland and Stimson's (1972) study on leisure pursuits in Adelaide, emphasised a similar picture. Kalkett pointed out in 1975 (p. 7) that the backyard was 'far and away the most important venue for recreation, besides which pubs, clubs, the beaches and public parks pale into insignificance'. His estimate was that residents in Adelaide spent on average ten hours per week in the garden. Extrapolating from this figure, Kemeny (1978) estimates that about $300 million in labour cost is expended by homeowners on garden maintenance each year. Such patterns of leisure remain even in the 1980s: Bottomley (1980) researched the work-leisure relationship of outer suburban male workers in Melbourne.

It has been suggested that if one were to rank leisure activities in terms of visibility, gardening would probably win out. In terms of time allocation, however, the most significant leisure activity is undoubtedly watching television.

In 1963, according to a Gallup Poll, seven out of ten Australians watched television regularly; three in ten watched almost every night; four in ten watched three nights a week, and only three in ten hardly ever saw it (Smith 1983: 30). Mansutti (1981) cites more recent information from the Federation of Australian TV Stations: 'Ninety-eight percent of Australians live in TV homes. The TV set in those homes is on for an average of 30 hours and 21 minutes a week. Of those homes 79 percent have both a colour

TV set and a black and white one' (Goodluck 1981: 46). Television viewing time might constitute an even greater component of leisure time spent at home nowadays if we consider the statistics offered by the *Sydney Morning Herald* (29 March, 1986: 7). It was reported that 50 per cent of homes in Australia now have a VCR (videocassette recorder) compared with only 11 per cent in 1982, despite the fact that sales of VCRs have decreased from 768,000 units in 1983–84, to 658,000 units in 1984–85. The average number of movies rented by a VCR household is suggested to be 1.4 a week. It is argued that the typical 'user profile' today in Sydney is a married couple on lower incomes over the age of 35. The success of many video outlets in Sydney's western suburbs and in low-income areas tend to confirm this. It is therefore not surprising to find that the result of Australian Department of Sport, Recreation and Tourism's (DSRT) Recreation Participation Survey of April-May 1985 shows that top of the list of leisure activities in the age group 25-39 years (i.e., the child bearing years) is television watching (Wearing 1986: 7).

This picture has changed very little. In the national surveys of leisure activities carried out by DSRT in 1985–86 and 1986-87, watching television continued to be the most popular choice for spending one's leisure time. There was very little difference between men and women, age and income groups and figures for different seasons of the year (Tables 13.1 and 13.2).

Similarly, in the 1987 Time Use Pilot Survey conducted by the Australian Bureau of Statistics, it was shown that Australians spend almost two hours a day watching television and videos, and

Table 13.1 Australians' Participation in Leisure Activities, 1985–86

Activities	Men (%)	Women (%)	Total (%)
Watching TV at home	93	94	93
Visiting friends/relatives	62	69	65
Reading	59	70	65
Listening to music	61	65	63
Relaxing/doing nothing	41	40	41
Gardening for pleasure	35	40	37
Dining/eating out	31	33	32
Walking for pleasure	26	36	31
Informal sport	35	23	29
Entertaining at home	25	31	28

Source: Parker and Paddick 1990: 19

Table 13.2   Australians' Participation in Leisure Activities, 1987

Activities	Men (%)	Women (%)
Watching TV at home	94.2	–
Visiting friends	62.9	–
Listening to music	62.9	–
Reading	58.1	–
Relaxing/doing nothing	43.8	–
Gardening	43.1	–
Informal sports	37.9	24

Source: Sigrid Kirk and Cathy Johnson (1990) 'What Do We Really Do in Our Spare Time?', *Sydney Morning Herald*, 14 June

less than twenty minutes on sport, exercise and outdoor activities. On average, we devote substantially more of our day to socialising (54 minutes), reading (25 minutes) and talking, including telephone conversation (22 minutes). Bottom of the list are writing and reading letters, with the average person spending just two minutes a day on their penpals (Kirk and Johnson 1990). More interestingly, when George Patterson, a commercial agency specialising in media marketing switched in 1991 to using the 'people meter' to monitor audience television viewing patterns instead of the conventional diary recording method, it was found that Australians watched significantly more television, especially daytime and late night television, than previously thought. The meters showed that during February–March 1991 Sydneysiders (in homes using television) watched 26.3 per cent more television per week, at 39.26 hours, compared with the 31.08 hours recorded by diaries in 1990. In Melbourne, household viewing from 6 am to midnight was up 19.2 per cent, to 37.55 hours ((*Sydney Morning Herald*, 14 April 1991).

Outside the home environment, Caldwell (1972) claims that three of the most frequently cited Australian leisure activities are sport, gambling and drinking. We have to note, however, according to Cleland and Stimson's study (1972), that when respondents were asked an open-ended question on what their main spare time activity was, it was found that sport received a higher rating than would have been expected from participation rates. Hallows (1970) also points out that the image of Australia as a nation of sportsmen is substantially incorrect. It is the total availability of sport which is unmatched anywhere else, and which makes it safe to assume that Australians spend more of their leisure time in the open air than any other people. In a more recent study of Queensland Telecom workers, Williams (1983: 232) finds that sport is the most favoured leisure activity after hobbies as a whole, but only among single people. Among the married, gardening is the preferred activity. It is interesting to note that the least approved leisure activity, and the one which has the lowest priority, is 'political activity'.

Both drinking and gambling, however, possibly play a larger role in Australia than in other Western countries, according to Taft and Walker (1958: 181). McGregor claims that 'if one excludes sex and conversation, drinking is probably the most important social activity in Australia' (1966: 131). Smith (1983: 31) maintains that consumption of beer is also very high by world standards, and has become an integral part of the 'mateship sub-culture'. The significance of gambling is not to be underestimated, either. McGregor, in his study, found that the national estimate turnover for the year 1960–61 was twice as high as expenditure on social services, and three times as much as the defence bill (1966: 142). Caldwell (1972) indicates that Australians spend about $160 each year per head on legalised forms of gambling. This is certainly higher than England ($30), New Zealand ($52) or the United States ($90). More recently, it was reported that gambling in Australia in total had jumped from more than $400 million in 1973 to almost $2,000 million in 1983 (*Courier Mail*, 16 August 1986: 1). Australians gambled between $650 and $850 per head each year. This was twice the English level and four times the level at which Americans gambled legally. In terms of the amount of spare household cash gambled each year, figures have quadrupled between 1973 and 1983. In terms of percentage of personal consumption expenditure, Haig (1985: 74) agrees that Australia has the highest level of gambling expenditure per head of advanced Western countries. Arguably, the comparison is a little unfair because presumably much of this money is continually recycled. Nevertheless, 'Australians have always had a reputation as remarkable gamblers, and gambling has been, and still is an integral and romanticised part of Australian culture' (McMillen 1983).

In a more recent study on Australian gambling, Haig (1985: 72) further compares gross and net expenditure on gambling with expenditure on selected items of personal consumption. According to his calculations, on average, personal gambling accounts for about 15 per cent of expenditure on food. However, if only 75 per cent of people gamble (and they spend the same amount), then their expenditure on gambling is about 20 per cent of expenditure on food.

The important point though, according to McMillen (1985), is that both drinking and gambling have been part of the attempt by the state to regulate and provide the population, especially the working class, with organised leisure. The regulation of both drinking and gambling is, in fact, the provision of a dual structure dominated by private enterprises. The state supervises the public conditions of existence of such activities, which take place in institutionalised facilities such as pubs, clubs, race courses or casinos. While Bottomley (1980) argues that the government's policy on urban development shapes the distinctive pattern of Australian home-centred leisure, McMillen takes the argument further, to insist that the state's intervention in leisure activities such as drinking and gambling, which are central aspects of working class culture, is evidence of the imposition of bourgeois rationality to define class boundaries and institutionalise new forms of distinction. Privatised gambling, after all, simultaneously expresses and symbolises contradictions between the freedom and constraint inherent in capitalist leisure. If gambling is the source of self-indulged gratification and the expression of active dissatisfaction with, and alienation from, society, such activities have to be brought into an accepted moral framework, in which the visibility of working class gambling (read reckless spending, speculative and impulsive practices) will not be an affront to the 'respectable' morality of the bourgeoisie (personal commitment to thrift, hard work and self-denial).

Gough Whitlam's policy speech, delivered in November 1972, summarised the sentiment well: 'There is no greater social problem facing Australia than the *good use* of leisure... this may well be the problem of the 1980s' (in Goodluck 1981: 7). The fear of uncontrolled or 'wasted' leisure was also expressed in a 1981 seminar on the creative or destructive use of future leisure in Australia:

> We are beginning to awaken to the reality that the leisure crisis is not simply a problem of increased free time which people are not equipped to use, or a want of more recreational facilities. ...We are beginning to feel the vibrations of a social disaster, a breakdown of social cohesion throughout the industrialised world which has not been experienced before and is hard for us to imagine.
>
> (Goodluck 1981: 7)

Morals aside, the regulation and control of leisure activities such as drinking and gambling underline the broader macro-structural problem of the state: its legitimacy crisis and problem of hegemony (Habermas 1973).

As the 'hand of the state' is becoming more visible and more diversified, not only has the bureaucratic structure of its apparatus grown increasingly complicated, but it also requires an expanding state budget. The state has to finance itself through taxation and loans from capital markets, but it cannot do this in ways which interfere with the capital accumulation process, or jeopardise economic growth. Viewed in this context, rationalised gambling, and perhaps drinking, are necessarily profitable enterprises for government revenue, and also a means to overcome the fiscal crisis. In providing centralised facilities, extended opportunities for gambling through improved technologies and efficiency (McMillen 1990), contradictions between the dominant bourgeois ideology and that of the 'destructive' ideology of working class gambling might be resolved, and hegemony restored.

In the final analysis, there is little doubt that Australia in recent decades has seen strong growth in the economic significance of leisure. Parker and Paddick (1990: 13) summarise it well: 'This has taken place in two major linked respects: more people are spending more of their income on leisure goods and services, and more people are working to cater for the leisure needs of others'. Brown (1985, in Parker and Paddick 1990: 13) notes that in 1984 'recreation' constituted 11.5 per cent of total household expenditure, and was the fourth greatest expenditure after food, transport and housing costs. In the same year, statistics released by the Australian Bureau of Statistics confirmed that employment in 'recreation, personal and other services' was the eighth largest area of employment, with 430,900 workers. Other estimates indicate that such figures might be a bit too conservative. For example, the Sport and Recreation Ministers' Council reckons that in 1987, between 15 to 35 per cent of clothing expenditure, and 25 to 40 per cent of expenditure on motor vehicle usage, was for leisure (Parker and Paddick 1990: 13). Similarly, Sicari in 1985, noted that at least 20 per cent of food expenditure was for pleasure (Parker and Paddick 1990: 13). With these and other inclusions, Parker and Paddick (1990: 13) conclude that total leisure expenditure could have been as high as 32 to 38 per cent of total household expenditure in 1984.

Women and Leisure

The argument so far is that modern leisure is about both freedom and constraint. As Frith (1982) points out, leisure politics are more about situations than intentions. If there is any control of leisure, it is not of ideas but of cultural practice. If there have been attempts at intervention and control, they have not been able completely to determine the shape of working class leisure. We need to look more closely into workers' own use of leisure, and their experiences, as well as their responses to provisions.

According to McIntosh (1981), Deem (1987) and Wearing (1990), such a perspective tends to overlook the very significant issue of gender in leisure. They both point out that patriarchy as a critical dimension is often ignored. Griffin (1981: 122), for example, suggests that women are leisure for men, and vital to it:

> Firstly women service men's leisure, in that it is only because of women's unpaid work in the home, and the primary childcare responsibilities, that men can go out for drinks with the lads, and have as much leisure time as they do. Secondly, women are an integral part of men's leisure, as 'escorts', whether paid or unpaid, or in relation to the myriad ways in which women must present and construct themselves for men, both materially and psychologically.

Women are thus constructed *as leisure* by men, and men's activity in work, existence and leisure practically determine the activity of women.

Hobson's (1981) research supports this view. She finds that one of the most obvious changes in the lives of women after marriage is the lack of any 'leisure' or time they consider to be 'spare', when they could do what they wanted. Studies by Cole (1980), Cass (1979) and Bottomley (1980) in Australia reach a similar conclusion: strictly defined, in the home there is very little leisure, at least for married working mothers. As Wearing and Wearing (1990: 165) succintly state: 'for many women, 'leisure equals child care and housework'. Women's 'leisure', if any, thus appears to be home-centred and relatively passive (Wilson 1980). Much of it seems to be part of domestic labour, producing goods for use, to be consumed by the family.

If 'leisure' activities involve women outside the home, they are more likely to be the ones defined as acceptable by their husbands, such as bingo or socialising (gossiping) with friends, or take place in a family group context (parties, nights out or trips). It is not surprising to find that even social participation in voluntary organisations in Australia between men and women in their leisure time manifests a dividing line: men predominate in sporting, recreational and social groups, and women in religious, civic and service activities (Bryson and Thompson 1972: 175). McKay (1990) concludes that sport in Australia is male-dominated, and that there is little democratisation of leisure for women (see also Table 13.2).

Williams contends that current leisure concepts are masculine-biased, and are also closely related to the way we conceive paid work, being intimately linked to consumerism (1983: 233). As our society increasingly aligns consumption to leisure, consumerism is construed by women to be 'leisure' for them. To Wearing (1986: 13), it is thus understandable to find that many housewives considered shopping not only as a leisure activity, but as one of their most enjoyable activities.

When leisure values are based on consumption as well as paid income, it means that only those who have unimpeded access to open-ended incomes will be able to turn non-work time into leisure, since leisure derives its meaning from relationships of production, while contributing to the reproduction of those relationships.

Conclusion

The nature of leisure has conventionally been assumed to be identified with free time, choice, flexibility, spontaneity and self-determination (Parker 1981). It has also been recognised as social experience, in which institutional constraints and obligations are minimised (Neulinger 1981: 21). While there is often a discharge of spontaneous and intense emotion, and an outburst of excitement in leisure activities, we have argued that modern leisure is not synonymous with freedom, and our leisure activities are increasingly constrained in a 'civilised' way. This is because modern leisure obeys an historically specific economy of balances and restraints, so that intense emotions are unleashed in a controlled form, defined as legitimate. In other words, behind our leisure activities, there is always a socially produced effect, structural rules of pleasure and unpleasure. Few of these rules can be divorced from their immediate economic and class context. Yet one also has to keep in mind that such regulation of leisure need not imply conspiracy or manipulation (though it certainly is encouraged); nor is it complete.

Ultimately, the study of leisure and popular recreation in our society cannot be seen in isolation. It must be situated within the work/wage-relation context, where class expression and social control take place, as complementary dimensions of the same social process. Searbrook (1988: 4) has made a poignant point: leisure is full of paradox. If leisure is about freedom, choice, fun and consumption of commodities, it is also about constraint, regulation, power and production. If leisure is about struggle and needs, such struggle and needs are defined by capitalism and patriarchy. Critcher (1988: 55) is right. He says that 'leisure remains the leisure of capitalist society'. Frith (1982) summarieses it well: leisure does not challenge the system, but reflects and illuminates it. Nor is leisure about living outside the system: the final issue is how to live within it.

References

Bailey, P. (1978) *Leisure and Class in Victorian England*. London: Routledge and Kegan Paul.

Basini, A. (1975) 'Education for Leisure: A Sociological Analysis', in J.T. Howorth, and M.A. Smith (eds), *Work and Leisure*. London: Lepus Books.

Best, G. (1973) *Mid-Victorian Britain 1851-1875*. St Albans: Panther.

Bottomley, B. (1980), 'Work and Leisure in a Melbourne Suburb' Unpublished MA. Thesis, Monash University, Melbourne.

Bryson, L. and Thompson, F. (1972) *An Australian Newtown*. Malmsbury: Kibble Books.

Burkhart, A.J. and Medlik, S. (1981) *Tourism: Past, Present and Future*. London: Heinemann.

Burns, T. (1973) 'Leisure in Industrial Society', in M.A. Smith, *et al.* (eds), *Leisure and Society in Britain*. London: Allen Lane.

Caldwell, G.T. (1972) 'Leisure Cooperatives: The Institutionalisation of Gambling and the Growth of Large Leisure Organisations in New south Wales', Unpublished PhD Thesis, Australian National University, Canberra.

Cannon, M. (1973) *Life in the Cities*. Melbourne: Nelson.

Cass, B. (1978) 'Women's Place in the Class Structure', in E.L. Wheelwright, and K. Buckley (eds), *Essays in the Political Economy of Australian Capitalism*, Vol. 3. Sydney: ANZ Books.

Cleland and Stimson (1972) *A Survey of Entertainment Habits and Needs in Adelaide*. Adelaide: School of Social Sciences, Flinders University of South Australia.

Coalter, F. (1990) 'The "Mixed Economy" of Leisure: The Historical Background to the Development of the Commercial, Voluntary and Public Sectors of the Leisure Industries,' in I.P. Henry (ed.), *Management and Planning in the Leisure Industries*. London: Macmillan Education.

———and Parry, N. (1982) *Leisure Sociology or the Sociology of Leisure?* London: The Polytechnic of North London, Papers in Leisure Studies 4.

Coles, L. (1980) 'Women and Leisure: A Critical Perspective', in D. Mercer, and E. Hamilton-Smith (eds), *Recreational Planning and Social Change in Urban Australia*. Melbourne: Sorrett Publications.

Connell, R.W. and Irving, T. (1978) 'The Making of the Australian Industrial Bourgeoisie 1930-1975,' *Intervention* 10–11: 5–38.

Critcher, C. (1988) 'The Politics of Leisure: Social Control and Social Development', in F. Coatler (ed.), *Freedom and Constraint: The Paradoxes of Leisure: Ten Years of Leisure Studies Association*. London: Routledge.

Cunningham, H. (1980) *Leisure in the Industrial Revoultion*. London: Croom Helm.

Deem, Rosemary (1987) 'The Politics of Women's Leisure', in J. Horne, D. Jary, and A. Tomlinson (eds), *Sport, Leisure and Social Relations*. London: Routledge and Kegan Paul.

Dixon, D. (1981) 'Gambling and the Law: The Street Betting Act, 1906 as an Attack on Working Class Culture', in A. Tomlinson (ed.), *Leisure and Social Control*. Brighton: Brighton Polytechnic, Chelsea School of Human Movement.

Downes, D.M., Davies, B.P., David, M. and Stone, P. (1976) *Gambling, Work and Leisure. A Study Across Three Areas*. London: Routledge and Kegan Paul.

Dumazedier, J. (1974) *Sociology of Leisure*. New York: Elsevier.

———(1989) 'France: Leisure Sociology in the 1980s', in A. Olszewska and K. Roberts (eds), *Leisure and Lifestyle. A Comparative Analysis of Free Time*. London: Sage Publications.

Dunstan, K. (1968) *Wowsers*. Melbourne: Cassell.

Foucault, M. (1977) *Discipline and Punishment*. Harmondsworth: Penguin.

Frith, S. (1982) *Sound Effects. Youth, Leisure and the Politics of Rock 'n' Roll*. New York: Pantheon Books.

Fuller, P. (1977) 'Gambling: A Secular "Religion" for the Obsessional Neurotic?', in J. Halliday, and P. Fuller (eds), *The Psychology of Gambling*. Harmondsworth: Penguin.

Goldman, J. and Wilson, J. (1977) *The Rationalisation of Leisure, Politics and Society*, Vol. 7.

Goodluck, P. and Goodluck, J. (eds) (1981) *The Future of Leisure in Australia*. Glenelg, SA: J. and P. Goodluck, Van Cle Foundation.

Griffin, C. (1981) 'Young Women and Leisure', in A. Tomlinson (ed.), *Leisure and Social Control*. Brighton: Brighton Polytechnic, Chelsea School of Human Movement.

Haywood, Les *et al.* (1990) *Understanding Leisure*. Cheltenham: Stanley Thornes.

Held, D. (1980) *Introduction to Critical Theory*. London: Hutchinson.

Habermas, J. (1973) *Legitimation Crisis*. London: Heinemann Education.

Haig, B. (1985) 'Expenditure on Legal Gambling', in G. Caldwell *et al.* (eds), *Gambling in Australia*. Sydney: Croom Helm.

Hallows, J. (1970) *The Dreamtime Society*. Sydney: Collins.

Haralambos, M., with Heald, R.M. (1980) *Sociology: Themes and Perspectives*. Slough: University Tutorial Press.

Hobson, D. (1981) 'Young Women at Home and "Leisure",' in A. Tomlinson (ed.), *Leisure and Social Control*. Brighton: Brighton Polytechnic, Chelsea School of Human Movement.

Horne, J. and Jary, D. (1987) 'The Figurational Sociology of Sport and Leisure of Elias and Dunning: An Exposition and a Critique', in J. Horne, D. Jary, and A. Tomlinson (eds), *Sport, Leisure and Social Relations*. London: Routledge and Kegan Paul.

Kalkett, I. (1975) 'Private Gardens, Private Worlds. The Need for Greater Consideration of the Residential Garden as a Venue for Recreational Activities', *Communications* 2(1): 4-8.

Kaplan, M. (1975) *Leisure: Theory and Policy*. New York: Wiley and Sons.

Kemeny, J. (1978) 'Australia's Privatized Cities: Detached House Ownership and Urban Exploitation', Paper presented to Housing

Problems and Policy Seminar, Centre for Urban Studies, Swinburne Institute of Technology.

Kirk, S. and Johnson, C. (1990) 'What Do We Really Do in Our Spare Time?, *Sydney Morning Herald*, June 14: 13.

Lack, J. (1978) 'Working Class Leisure,' *Victorian Historical Journal* 1 (49): 49-65.

Lansbury, R. (1970) 'Leisure in New Suburbs', *Sociologiske Meddelelser* 14: 79-92.

Lynch, R. (1990) 'Working Class Luck and Vocabularies of Hope Among Regular Poker-machine Players,' in D. Rowe, and G. Lawrence (eds), *Sport and Leisure. Trends in Australian Popular Culture*. Sydney: Harcourt Brace Jovanovich.

Malcolmson, R.W. (1973) *Popular Recreation in English Society 1700-1850*. Cambridge: Cambridge University Press.

Mansutti, E. (1981) 'Mass Media in Creative or Destructive Use of Free Time', in P. Goodluck and J. Goodluck (eds), *The Future of Leisure in Australia*. Glenelg, SA: J. and P. Goodluck, Van Cle Foundation.

Marcuse, H. (1972) *One Dimensional Man*. London: Abacus.

Marx, K. (1970) *A Contribution to the Critique of Political Economy*. Moscow: Progress.

McGregor, C. (1966) *Profile of Australia*. Ringwood: Penguin.

McIntosh, S. (1981) 'Leisure Studies and Women', in A. Tomlinson (ed.), *Leisure and Social Control*. Brighton: Brighton Polytechnic, Chelsea School of Human Movement.

McKay, J. (1990) 'Sport, Leisure and Social Inequality in Australia,' in D. Rowe and G. Lawrence (eds), *Sport and Leisure. Trends in Australian Popular Culture*. Sydney: Harcourt Brace Jovanovich.

McMillen, J. (1983) 'Loaded Dice: The Transformation of Gambling in Queensland', Unpublished Honours' Thesis, Department of Sociology, University of Queensland.

———(1985) 'Gambling and the State: Queensland's Plunge on the Trifecta.' Paper presented to SAANZ 85 Conference, University of Queensland, 30 August – 2 September.

———(1990) 'The Politics of Queensland Tourism,' in P. Carroll *et al.* (eds), *Tourism in Australia*. Sydney: Harcourt Brace Jovanovich.

Mercer, D.C. (1985) 'Australia's Time Use and Preferences: Some Recent Findings', *Australian and New Zealand Journal of Sociology* 21 (3), November: 371-94.

Moorhouse, H.F. (1989) 'Models of Work, Models of Leisure', in C. Rojek (ed.), *Leisure for Leisure. Critical Essays*. London: Macmillan.

Murphy, W.E. (1986) *History of the Eight Hour Movement*. Melbourne: Spectator.

Neulinger, J. (1981) *To Leisure: An Introduction*. Boston: Allyn and Bacon.

Oeser, O.A. and Hammond, S.B. (eds) (1954) *Social Structure and Personality in a City*. London: Routledge and Kegan Paul.

O'Connor, J. (1973) *The Fiscal Crisis of the State*. New York: St Martin's Press.

Olley, A.K. (1964) Leisure in Australia. *Hemisphere*, January: 2-7.

Parker, S. (1975) The Sociology of Leisure: Progress and Problems. *British Journal of Sociology* 26(1): 91-101.

——(1976) *The Sociology of Leisure*. London: Allen and Unwin.

——(1981) 'Choice, Flexibility, Spontaneity and Self-determination in Leisure', *Social Forces* 60 (2): 323–31.

——and Paddick, R. (1990) *Leisure in Australia*. Melbourne: Longman Cheshire.

Pearson, K. (1977) 'Leisure in Australia,' in D. Mercer (ed.), *Leisure and Recreation in Australia*. Melbourne: Sorrett Publications.

Pearson, K. and O'Hara, J. (1977) 'The Flavour of Australian Sport' in D. Mercer (ed.), *Leisure and Recreation in Australia*. Melbourne: Sorrett Publications.

Powell, J. (1980) 'The Philistines and the Populace: Leisure and Recreation Before 1945', in D. Mercer and E. Hamilton-Smith (eds), *Recreation Planning and Social Change in Urban Australia*. Melbourne: Sorrett Publications.

Rojek, C. (1985) *Capitalism and Leisure Theory*. London: Tavistock Publications.

——(ed.) (1989) *Leisure for Leisure. Critical Essays*. London: Macmillan.

Scott, D. and U'Ren, R. (1962) *Leisure*. Melbourne: Cheshire.

——and —— (1966) 'Leisure in the Suburbs', *Architecture in Australia* 54: 59-60.

Searbrook, J. (1988) *The Leisure Society*. Oxford: Basil Blackwell.

Smith, J.E.M. (1983) 'Leisure Theory and Australian Public Policy', Unpublished MSPD Thesis, University of Queensland.

Stedman-Jones, G. (1977) 'Class Expression vs Social Control', *History Workshop — A Journal of Social Historian* 4, Autumn: 162–70.

Storch, R.D. (1976) 'The Policeman as Domestic Missionary', *Journal of Social History* 9.

Taft, R. and Walker, K. (1958) 'Australia', in A. Rose (ed.), *Institutions of Advanced Societies*. Minneapolis: University of Minnesota Press.

Walker, A. (1945) *Coaltown: A Social Survey of Cessnock, NSW*. Melbourne: Melbourne University Press.

Walvin, J. (1978) *Leisure and Society: 1830-1950*. London: Longman.

Wearing, B. (1986) 'All in a Day's Leisure: Gender and the Concept of Leisure', Paper presented at the Annual Conference of the Sociological Association of Australia and New Zealand, University of New England, Armidale, NSW, 9-12 July.

——and Wearing, S. (1990) 'Leisure for All? Gender and Policy', in D. Rowe and G. Lawrence (eds), *Sport and Leisure. Trends in Australian Popular Culture*. Sydney: Harcourt Brace Jovanovich.

Williams, C. (1983) 'The "Work Ethic", Non-work and Leisure in an Age of Automation', *Australian and New Zealand Journal of Sociology* 19(2): 216-37.

Wilensky, H.L. (1960) 'Work, Careers and Social Integration', *International Social Science Journal* 4: 543-60.

Wilmott, P. and Young, M. (1975) *The Symmetrical Family*. Harmondsworth: Penguin.

Wilson, J. (1980) Sociology of Leisure. *Annual Review of Sociology* 6: 21-40.

Part III

Current Issues and Concerns

Chapter Fourteen

The Nuclear Family and Its Future

Michael Bittman

Introduction

In the last few years there has been a lot of public clamour about the family. Sociologists have learnt to be suspicious when politicians start calling for 'a return to the traditional values of . . .' Generally such calls are made precisely at a time when traditional patterns are in historical decline. For example, politicians praise the values of small 'village' communities when most people have moved to live in sprawling, anonymous metropolises.

There are no other set of socially-patterned relationships which bear such a strong association with an individual's biography as those associated with the family. Consequently, many discussions of the family generate a great deal of heat but very little light! Very often, the family is the social setting in which our identities are formed and upon which many of our current hopes are concentrated. Sociologists often have to struggle against the very familiarity of the family in trying to pursue an analysis of this social institution.

In the following chapter, we will examine theories and evidence about the nuclear family, that is, a family composed of husband, wife and their offspring. Is the nuclear family universal or in decline? Is it a transitory historical form?

Is the Nuclear Family Universal?

1. Is the family a universal result of human biology?
The idea that family relationships are given to us by nature often seems initially plausible. Closer examination, however, proves it to be mistaken. It is worth considering the extent to which the facts of human reproduction[1] explain the form of the contemporary Australian family.

Pregnancy and the care of young infants, say some evolutionary theorists (Morris 1968; Tiger 1969; Tiger and Fox 1972), confined women to domestic work, while men were free to roam wide territories hunting game. Sometimes other differences, such as average ones in the quantity of muscle fibre, difference in the use of regions of the brain, or small hormonal differences between men and women, are used as additional support for this explanation of the original division of labour.

Anthropologists have found that all societies distinguish between 'women's work' and 'men's work'. However, only some writers have assumed the sexual division of labour to be the outcome of the evolutionary origins of the human species.

Morris (1968) extends this logic into an attempted explanation of marriage. With the confinement of women to 'home base' as a result of the demands of children, Morris argues that hunting parties, unlike 'pure carnivores' became all-male groups. This, he says, really goes against the 'primate grain', because it meant that a virile male would depart on 'feeding trips' leaving his 'female unprotected from the advances of other males that might happen to come by' (Morris 1968: 9). The answer to this dilemma, he claimed, was the development of 'pair bonding'. According to Morris, this solved three problems at one stroke: females remained faithful to a male while he was away on the hunt; rivalries between males were greatly reduced, with the consequence that the co-operation necessary for hunting was greatly facilitated; and finally, offspring benefited, because they received 'maximum care and attention' (Morris 1968: 10).

The great weakness of this analysis is its neglect of the variability of family arrangements in nature, and the difficulties in generalising from the behaviour of animals to that of humans. Just exactly what follows from the sexual nature of human reproduction? Many species found in nature, including plants, have a sexual mode of reproduction, but even if we restrict ourselves to mammals, there is a wide variety of solutions to the problem of how to care for dependent young. Evidence in the animal kingdom for division into hunters and nurturers according to the sex of the animal is relatively unconvincing. Females of many carnivorous species hunt, and the males of some species display what might be called 'maternal' behaviour.[2] In a pattern that is almost the exact reverse of those Morris claims to be 'natural' among humans, male emperor penguins endure months of freezing Antarctic conditions at 'home base' to keep eggs warm, while their mates journey to the ocean to hunt food for the young.

It is remarkable that, despite his emphasis on the beast within us all (the 'Naked Ape'), a theorist like Morris should draw his characterisation of 'pair bonding' from his observation of the behaviour of birds and fish. It would surely be more relevant to give an example of the behaviour of higher primates like gorillas (although resemblances between current human behaviour and that of primates is not sufficient to suggest that these have been inherited).[3] Presumably, this is because among the gorilla species, as among Eastern grey kangaroos, males compete with one another for access to fertile females: males establish a hierarchy based on ritualised combat, in which only the dominant males mate with females, and there is no evidence of 'pair bonding'. Morris' speculative 'evolutionary' history, disguised as explanation, is used to justify the kind of social arrangements approved by the author.

Oakley has described these speculative histories as self-servingly androcentric (male-centred), pointing out that these theories are a variation of 'man the mighty hunter' myth (1974: 161). Such myths put value on male activity and append female activity almost as an afterthought. Anthropologists' studies of hunting and gathering societies over the past 150 years show that while hunting is the high prestige activity, often it is women's activity as gatherers that feeds most members.

The evidence that hormones are decisive in determining the assignment of males and females to their places in the sexual division of labour also encounters some significant difficulties. Firstly, the argument moves from small differences in average blood concentrations of hormones to categorical differences between women and men. The levels of hormones vary among both men and women. A small difference in averages suggests a wide area of overlap between the distribution for women and men. That is, only a small portion of women have levels lower than men with the lowest levels, and only a tiny proportion of men have levels higher than women with the highest levels. There is also a large daily variation of hormone levels in both women and men. Accordingly, conventional psychologists who specialise in the measurement of aggression find a great deal of overlap between female and male distributions.

A further blow to those who wish to argue that biology (sexual differences in hormones) explains the aggression, assertiveness, and ultimately the domination of males, comes from experiments with monkeys. Rutter and Giller (1983) report that although aggression in both male and female monkeys appears to be altered by manipulating levels of the hormone testosterone, providing monkeys with opportunities to dominate actually increases the testosterone produced. This suggests that aggressive behaviour may be the *cause* of the production of the hormone, rather than the other way around.

There is no doubt that some sexual differences can be attributed to biological causes. The difficulties arise when it is assumed that human biology, in addition to establishing the ground for human possibility, actually determines particular human social forms such as the sexual division of labour and the nuclear family.

2. Is the family a result of universal social imperatives?
An alternative to the biological explanations of the universality of the family is an explanation based on requirements arising out of human social organisation. This style of reasoning is known by sociologists as 'functionalist'. The name most associated with this argument is Murdock, who argued in 1949, after examining data from 250 societies, that the nuclear family is found in all societies because no other institution can simultaneously fulfil vital requirements for the continuation of social life. Even extended families, according to Murdock, are composed of nuclear building blocks.

Murdock defined the family as 'a social group characterised by common residence, economic co-operation, and reproduction'. He concluded that the nuclear family serves four basic social functions: sexual, economic, reproductive and educational (1968: 37). Taken together, these make the family 'inevitable' (Murdock 1968: 39).

Like many other social theorists, including Freud, Murdock views the human sex drive as a socially disruptive impulse. Thus 'sex cannot safely be left without restraints' but 'regulation must not be carried to excess' because this produces psychologically maladjusted individuals and/or insufficient procreation to replace the population (Murdock 1968: 39). Marriage is a social device that permits sexual gratification between approved partners, but prevents its socially disruptive expression beyond these constraints.

The institution of marriage, argued Murdock, combines a socially sanctioned gratification of sexual needs with 'economic co-operation' in a single social form. Murdock, like classical economist Adam Smith, assumes that the economic benefits of co-operation and the division of labour outweigh the benefits of each individual labouring in isolation. Husband, wife and children, says Murdock, co-operate within the division of labour to achieve greater collective welfare.

While it is clear that without replacement of its population, a society would become extinct and its culture disappear, Murdock's logic leads him to argue that to avoid extinction, socially recognised lovers must become parents (Murdock 1968: 43). Social rearing of the young is no less important than their physical care, because what is at stake is the transmission of culture. During the process of socialisation, young humans must learn to temper their potentially anti-social drives and acquire an 'immense amount of traditional knowledge and skill' (Murdock 1968: 43).

Criticism of Functionalist Theories of the Family

The style of reasoning employed by Murdock, in explaining an individual social institution in terms of the contribution it fulfils for the whole society, is called functionalism. This kind of reasoning is very common in the biological sciences. The sweat glands, for instance, may be explained by their function, the promotion of cooling through evaporation, thereby maintaining the body at a constant temperature. However, in important respects, societies are not like biological organisms.

Among organisms it makes sense to talk about two states of being — life and death. It may very well be the case that whole societies perish instead of thrive, but generally what happens is that societies change. In other words, human society has a history. Later in this chapter, I will argue that marriage, the duties of parents towards their children, and the relationship of the family to the community, have been fundamentally transformed in the recent history of industrialised countries.

In order to demonstrate the universality of the family, Murdock must show that it alone can fulfil the sexual, economic and reproductive functions he lists. No other social institutions or group of social institutions could fulfil such functions.

In regard to the social management of sexual impulses, Murdock presumes that only heterosexual activity can satisfy the human sex drive. However, one could mention the socially sanctioned incorporation of homosexual activity, in adolescent 'boys' houses' in Southeast Asia and Melanesia, or in the social figure of the *berdache*[4] among the plains Indians of North America (Giddens 1989: 190; Forgey 1975). Murdock himself mentions the wide variety of attitudes to pre-marital and extra-marital sex (1968: 40). These examples imply that the family is only one of a number of institutions concerned with the channelling of sexual impulses.

In Australian and other societies, groups of people may regard themselves as a family without being a household (that is, without co-residing). One has only to think of the 'families' of sailors. Among the Ashanti, sibling households are the dominant form. Samoan children reside in the household of their choice and frequently change residence (Gittins 1985: 60).

Variations in the sexual division of labour (economic co-operation) are also profound, and are often based on factors that Murdock neglects. Women have ploughed fields and mined minerals and still do; men have gathered fruit, minded children and done the laundry. Importantly, as Gittins points out, 'the allocation of these tasks is also strongly based on age, ... so that it may be *young* men who hunt and *old* men or women who care for children; old women may be responsible for cooking, while both young men and women may work in the fields or mines' (Gittins 1985: 69, emphasis in original).

A similar case can be made for reproduction. In Tahiti 'young women often have one or two children before they are considered, or consider themselves to be, ready for an approved and stable relationship' (Edholm 1982: 170). Care of dependent infants is not always the responsibility of the biological mother. Bottle feeding of babies was practised in ancient Egypt, and the use of 'wet nurses' has been widespread in various societies. Often the biological father is unknown or culturally unimportant.

The greatest difficulty for Murdock's theory is posed by his (mis)understanding of the link between family and reproduction. Murdock assumes that kinship or family relationships is a biological category. A peculiarity of Western culture is that kinship is traced in terms of biological descent. Other societies classify these relations according to a quite different set of ideas.

Relatives are made, not born. As Edholm points out, kinship is 'primarily concerned with the ways in which mating is socially organised and regulated, the ways in which parentage is attributed and recognised, descent traced, relatives are classified, rights are transferred across generations and groups are formed' (Edholm 1982: 167). Trobriand Islanders think that the role of the father in procreation is to open the passage to the womb, allowing the spirit to enter. A child's 'blood' comes from the mother's side, from her mother and her mother's brother, not from the father. The Lakker of Burma, on the other hand, 'consider that the mother is only a container in which the child grows; she has no blood connection with her children, and children of the same mother and different fathers are not considered related to each other' (Edholm 1982: 169). Notions of what is considered incest are adjusted accordingly. Some societies (among some Australian Aboriginal groups) extend the category of mother or sister to include many females purportedly descended from the same 'grandfather', and 'great-grandfather', so that frequently this whole group is sexually unavailable, and young people are obliged to marry outside it (Hiatt 1965).

All the above point to Murdock's tendency to see families all over the world and at all times as clones of the mid-century American family. The claim that this set of family relationships results from social necessity and is unavoidable, has a powerful ideological effect. It endorses current family arrangements, and strikes discussion of social change from the political agenda. The very effort to prove the universality of the family, to stretch the boundaries of the concept means that significant and subtle changes are lost.

Is the Nuclear Family in Decline?

At the very time many people feel that the nuclear family is a 'natural' social unit, others are arguing it is in terminal decline. Partly, this is the result of the over-enthusiastic debunking of the myth of the universal nuclear family by sociologists and journalists.

Although there is some formal truth to the proposition that nuclear families are a minority of households, this is largely an illusion created by examining data collected only at one point in time, i.e. cross-sectional data. The June 1992 Labour Force Survey (Australian Bureau of Statistics 1992), for example, estimated that there were approximately four and half million families in Australia, of which 84 per cent were 'married couple families'; a clear majority of these married couple households (51 per cent) currently have dependent children. The remaining 'married couples families' fall into two broad groups: first, the larger group, those who no longer have dependent children at home; and second, a smaller group of those who have never had children. Among this second 'childless' group, it is estimated that 20 per cent will remain childless, and therefore that the remainder are transitional families on their way to becoming nuclear families (McDonald 1990: 17).

It has been common to attribute the fall in size of the average Australian family to the widespread adoption of the contraceptive pill in the 1960s, but in fact this is the continuation of a trend which began in the late nineteenth century (Carmichael 1988). It is estimated that Australian women of child bearing age during the 1850s averaged at least seven live births (Gilding 1991: 65). The average number of children born to married women aged between 45 and 49 fell from more than six in 1901 to three in 1942, reached its nadir in the 1970s, and in the 1986 Census had recovered slightly, to less than three (Gilding 1991: 76; Hugo 1992: 58). Painstaking historical research has shown that late marriage has been used to keep fertility levels well below the maximum since (at least) the seventeenth century; postponing marriage was a typical response to economic recession (Anderson 1979: 51–52). The current tendency to marry later, which became evident in the 1970s, conforms with this general trend (Carmichael 1988). Over the last two decades Australian women have, in contrast with their own mothers, delayed having children until middle and later child bearing years. Women delaying childbearing are not a random cross-section of the population but are disproportionately 'drawn from more highly educated, dual income, higher status, professional groups' (Hugo 1992: 23). This suggests that a woman's career influences the timing of births. According to McDonald, 'increased childlessness and the delay of the first birth . . . are not simply products of economic recession' and are 'unlikely to be reversed' (1989: 102).

The most spectacular growth, due chiefly to ageing and late marriage, is among lone adult households, which increased 56 per cent between 1976 and 1986, compared with an increase of 8 per cent for married couples with dependent children over the same period (Hugo 1992: 29). Household formation has continued 'to outstrip population growth' so that 'households became smaller' (Gilding 1991: 127–28). Projections show that lone adult households will become the dominant household next century (Ironmonger and Lloyd 1990). Greater life expectancy for both women and men, falling family size and the later timing of births, have also resulted in steadily increasing numbers of 'couple households' without dependent children.

There is no denying the growth of single-parent families, which have more than doubled between 1969 and 1992. At the time of the 1986 Census, 12.2 per cent of children aged 0–14 lived in single-parent families. Over one-quarter of Australian children will spend at least part of their childhood in a single-parent family (Hugo 1992: 30). However, this process works in other directions as well.

Concern with single-parent households arises from two sources: first, anxiety about the moral disintegration of contemporary society; and second, the rising cost of government benefits paid to this group. Worry about the cost of sole parents is related to the disproportionate numbers of sole-parent families living below the poverty line, and the consequent demand for welfare services (Saunders and Matheson 1991: 21). Anxiety about the family and moral disintegration is almost as old as sociology itself. Durkheim, in his 1905 discussion of suicide, suggested that family membership was a bulwark against the kind of suicide that results from normlessness. Subsequent research has questioned whether families are equally beneficial for women (Bernard 1976: 43), but many thinkers continue to view divorce as a threat to social order.

Rates of divorce in Australia have risen steadily, from a low base at the turn of the century until the introduction of the 1976 Family Law Act. In 1921–25, there were 2.7 divorces per 10,000 of the population. By 1960, the rate had risen to 6.9. Before the introduction of the new Act, in 1974, the rate had reached 13. After the new legislation, the divorce rate rocketed, to 45.5 in 1976 (when a backlog of people waiting for the new legislation was processed), and by 1991 had settled back to 26 per 10,000 (James 1979: 205; Joint Select Committee on the Family Law Act 1980: 45; Australian Bureau of Statistics 1991). If current rates of divorce apply over the next thirty years, it is estimated that one in three marriages will end in divorce (McDonald 1990: 16).

Interpreting this apparent epidemic of divorce is less than straightforward. First, before the law changed, and when official divorce rates were low, there was widespread reporting of men deserting their wives (Roe 1987). However, as Pixley points out, 'desertion figures are difficult to assess, partly because of enforced absences due to work or lack of work, and gold lust frequently extended for years' (1991: 300). The Western Australian Census of 1901 found that 28 per cent of men were living away from their wives (Burns 1983: 51). Secondly, few marriages at the turn of the century would have survived thirty years without enforced separation due to the death of a partner. This implies that much of the apparent rise in divorce is a by-product of longer life expectancy. Thirdly, high divorce rates, rather than symbolising modern decadence, may actually be the outcome of the increased value placed on marriage. Contemporary expectations of marriage are high. Mate selection on the basis of romantic love, as distinct from economically advantageous unions, places great emphasis on companionship, and is far less tolerant of physical cruelty, neglect and lack of financial support (O'Brien 1988). It could be argued that the expectation of such complete companionship promotes high levels of dissatisfaction with anything less: a search for the perfect partner (see, for example, McDonald 1989: 103–4). Support for this argument comes from the high rates of re-marriage after divorce. As Hugo points out, 'in 1982 some 30 percent of Australia's 117,275 marriages involved at least one divorced person, and in 10 per cent of cases both participants had been divorced' (1992: 44).

However, the moral panic surrounding divorce cannot alter the fact that the overwhelming majority of households with dependent children (82 per cent) are currently two-parent family households (Australian Bureau of Statistics 1992: 1). If one looks at people rather than households, then the preponderance of the nuclear family is even more marked. Figures from the 1986 Census show that nearly 90 per cent of Australians lived in 'family settings' (Graycar and Jamrozik 1989).

Growth of *de facto* marriages over the last decade (Brachter and Santow 1988: 9–10; Khoo and McDonald 1988) has been accompanied by official moves to assimilate this form to marriage, in legal terms, to occupational benefits, and official statistics. It has been noted that homosexual unions may follow a similar path, although this is by no means certain (Gilding 1991: 131).

Summarising these findings, what is often passed off as 'the decline of the nuclear family' by pointing to the growth of single-parents, and *de facto* and non-heterosexual units, actually rely for their numerical support on the consequences of entirely different processes: falling family size and the ageing of the population. Among other things, what these findings show is that most children are born to two-parent households, and that the overwhelming majority of the population has some direct experience of living in a nuclear family.

If you have a more specific nuclear family in mind, a 'traditional family' (where the father is a full-time breadwinner and the mother a full-time housewife), the case for its decline is far stronger. More than one-half of all families with dependent children are two-parent households where both partners are employed. Less than one-third of all families with dependent children conform to the 'traditional pattern' (Australian Bureau of Statistics 1992: 13, 27). A fifteen-year-old woman born in 1900 could expect to spend a total of 12 years in the labour force, whereas if she was born in 1960, she could expect to spend 27 years in the labour force (Young 1990: 4). A pattern of women leaving the labour force on marriage or the birth of a first child, never to return, has been superseded by a more continuous pattern of attachment to the labour force with time out for children (Young 1990: 17–18).

But even these figures can mislead. In 1985, over 50 per cent of women re-entering the labour force had been away for more than 5 years, and 20 per cent for more than 10 years (Young 1990: 25). The proportion of women with infant and pre-school children who are full-time carers, is much higher than this (66 per cent of two-parent households and 73 per cent of single-parent families). Only 24 per cent of mothers with dependent children are in full-time paid employment; 56 per cent of all employed women worked part-time (Australian Bureau of Statistics 1992: 15, 26). As Jallinoja points out, this pattern of predominantly part-time work is consistent with a set of community values which requires a full-time mother rather than a full-time housewife (1989: 107–9). Indicative of such attitudes is the fact that children whose mothers work part-time actually do less housework than those whose mothers are not in paid employment (Bittman 1991: 24). Data from the Class Structure of Australia Project showed that women's responsibilities towards children and husbands were significantly associated with disadvantage in the labour market, and with increases in part-time work (Baxter, Gibson and Lynch-Blosse 1990: 86–92).

Although women's part-time employment represents a distinct change from the 'traditional' family, it preserves many elements of this former pattern, notably that the husband's role is merely modified, to that of chief provider rather than sole provider, and women's aspirations are subordinated to those compatible with full-time motherhood. In other words, the form of increased female labour force participation is that most compatible with the demands of the traditional family. Moreover, while there is significant and growing support for the value of equality in domestic labour, there is little evidence of any reassignment of domestic tasks in practice. 'Non-traditional' men have not assumed responsibility for tasks which are not defined as traditionally masculine (Bittman 1990, 1991; Bittman and Lovejoy 1991).

What does seem to have changed are commentators' attitudes to the nuclear family. Whereas mid-century writers viewed it as *the* family, and consequently saw all other types as failed (or 'broken homes'), contemporary commentators assume a plurality of family forms, and happily speak of 'one-parent families' (Gilding 1991: 110, 131). Thus the nuclear family has lost its monopolistic position, while retaining a powerful cultural pre-eminence based on the personal experience of the majority.

Is the Nuclear Family a Distinctively Modern Form?

Structural-Functionalist Approaches to the Modern Family

The structuralist-functionalist tradition contrasts the contemporary family with the pre-modern or traditional one. The modern family is modern because it is the only family form compatible with a modern society, that is, the kind of society created by the Industrial Revolution. According to this group of theories, industrialisation required a particular set of institutional underpinnings. Parsons, who is perhaps the leading figure of this group, argued that societies could be understood by analogy to embryology (1966). Society evolves by movement from simple to complex, like the development of a foetus, passing through various stages resembling the organisation of more primitive organisms, with each stage marked by a progressive differentiation. Parsons believes that in simpler societies kinship provides the framework for all other social organisation. Complex modern society is characterised by impersonal processes of market allocation and bureaucratic organisation. Following Weber (1968: 86–109), Parsons argues for the incompatibility of modern enterprises with methods of organisation characteristic of patrimonial household forms: modern society requires the separation of home and work.

Unlike many others, he does not consider that this leaves the family in crisis, as an institution without significance or function. On the contrary, he believes that the differentiated modern family performs a crucial role in social reproduction. In modern society, the family is charged with responsibility for producing socialised newer members, and with the stabilisation of adult personalities. This is achieved by strictly limiting the relevance of kinship. Stem or extended families containing many generations give way to an irreducible nuclear family. Parsons calls this the conjugal family, in order to emphasise that the group is formed by marriage and contains only the marital partners and their immature offspring. Like others, Parsons believed this structure to be most compatible with demands for the geographical mobility originating in industrial organisation. More importantly, he thought a nuclear family organisation was modern because of its specialisation in the indispensable functions of socialisation and stabilisation. Only the modern form of the family can mediate between the impulse for anti-social gratification of infant needs, and the complex requirements for achievement and performance which will be demanded in later life. The modern family alone can secure and stabilise the personal identities of adults in the face of a world which judges them by abstract, universal, impersonal and affectionless standards.

What's Modern about the Modern Family?: Historians' Replies to Parsons

The failure to find a widespread pattern of stem or extended families in pre-industrial records led to a collapse of faith in the narrative of extended families, shrinking to a nuclear core under the influence of industrialisation (Anderson 1979; Pollock 1983; Poster 1978; Harris 1983). Consequently, the nuclear family could no longer be regarded as a creation of industrialisation. If any evidence exists for the shrinkage from extended to nuclear family, then it is among the higher ranks of society, not the geographically mobile propertyless (Stone 1979: 421). Hence, the newer set of theories have regarded the differences in household size as broadly disproven, and have concentrated instead on changes in the qualities of relations within the family (Shorter 1977; Stone 1979; Aries 1973), and on relationships between family households and the new institutions of industrial society (Anderson 1979; Davidoff and Hall 1987). According to these writers, similarities in form mask significant differences in the content of relations.

Major differences between the pre-industrial (or more strictly proto-industrial) family and the contemporary family consist of:

1. altered relations between husband and wife;
2. a new conception of children and of motherhood;
3. separation of home and work; and
4. privatisation of the family.

Collectively, these developments have been labelled 'affective individualism' (Stone 1979), and the 'surge of sentiment' (Shorter 1977). Despite slightly different emphases, the similarities between the two authors are more striking than their differences. Both agree that in the pre-modern family, mate selection is primarily an exchange between kin groups in which considerations of property and alliance are predominant. Once married, the pre-modern husband and wife are unequal partners: patriarchal authority is absolute. The novelty of the modern family lies in the fact that for the first time the figures of mistress and wife are combined. A wife becomes more than a helpmate, more than an economic resource. A wife becomes a lover and companion as well.

For such a dramatic change to take place, these authors argue, certain other developments necessarily have to occur. In the first place there must be some relaxation of control exercised by external groups (principally other kin and community), over courting, mate selection, and the details of marriage thereafter. This implies the construction of a 'wall of privacy' between the new conjugal unit and the outside world. Secondly, Shorter and Stone contend that obedient inferiors make poor companions. Marriage must therefore become more a relationship between equals. Wives must stop standing behind their husbands at mealtimes, obediently waiting to ladle out a second portion to the man of the house. They must begin to sit at the same dinner table, to banish the servants from sight, and even be bold enough 'to hold hands in front of the fire' (Shorter 1977).

Children, these authors argue, benefit from a similar process. From being born into original sin, they are now a symbol of innocence; from being considered a burden, they are a blessing, a source of amusement and pleasure. Apart from the interpretation of iconography (Aries 1973), the evidence for these changes is the cessation of the practice of swaddling,[5] the diminishing use of wet nurses, the reduction in the incidence of abandonment or infanticide, and the end of the practice of sending children away on apprenticeships (Pollock 1983: 23). Stone advances a theory of emotional capital to account for many of the changes. The prevalence of infant mortality is a cause of the neglect of children in pre-modern times. Parents invest in emotional bonds with an individual offspring only when there is some expectation of his or her survival (1979: 407). The emotional investment in them is, in modern times, seen as a further guarantee of their survival. According to Stone and Shorter, each advance is signalled by an alteration affecting women's activities. The narrative is, therefore, chiefly about motherhood, but, since there can be no mothers without children, it is the mother-child bond which is modern. The burden of emotional capital in children has been unequally borne. The reverse side of the coin of the elaboration of modern motherhood has been the sustained pattern of father absence.

Stone and Shorter present their material as a story of progressive emancipation of women and children from traditional forms of indifference, maltreatment and patriarchal domination. What they actually describe, however, is a series of changes in the sexual division of labour — not the end of patriarchy but a change in its form. In the households of former days there was a division of household labour by gender. Since household production was more or less identical with social production, this domestic division of labour was more or less identical with the sexual division of labour in society. The development of the market for human labour also comes to mean that there is a division between homemaking and breadwinning, where formerly the two had been combined in a single unit. The fact that men ultimately managed to have themselves defined and recognised as the breadwinners complicates the relation between the sexual division of labour and the domestic division. In other words, the separation of tasks in the household by gender is overlaid with a gendered division between public and private. Once such a division has been established, each follows a different trajectory. The curious history of attempts to mechanise and rationalise the home further bears out this pattern (Reiger 1985; MacKenzie and Wajcman 1985; Faulkner and Arnold 1985). A detailed consideration of what mechanisation implies for households will be undertaken in the section on the Future of Family Households.

One of the major consequences of the physical removal of much formerly male activity from the household, is that only a few insignificant tasks remain men's responsibility. This is accompanied by processes of the exclusion of women from the public world. Despite the claims of the growth of companionship and equality, the history of the division of household tasks by gender is striking because of the dissolution of the partnership evident in the pre-modern pattern.

Feminist Challenges

The prominent sociologist Giddens has remarked that once 'the study of the family used to seem to one of the dullest of endeavours' whereas 'now it appears as one of the most provocative and involving' (quoted in Cheal 1991: 1). The key force behind the revitalising of family studies has been the re-emergence of a powerful feminist social movement. Over the past two decades hardly an area of Australian social life has not been influenced by feminism. This is also true of Australian sociology. The family is to feminism what the labour market is to students of social class. Feminism propelled the family to the centre stage of a sociology which took as its new task the explanation of the subordination of women. So it is natural to begin a description of recent developments in family theory with a discussion of feminist approaches to the topic. Let us consider how the three main variants of feminist theory, liberal feminism, radical feminism and socialist feminism, analyse the family.

Liberal Feminism
Liberal feminism is the doctrine which lies behind our Commonwealth legislation on Equal Employment Opportunity, Affirmative Action and Anti-discrimination. For many commentators it is associated with the writings of Freidan (1965) exemplified by the character of Nora in Ibsen's play *A Doll's House*, and epitomised by the actions of the National Organisation for Women in the United States (Williams 1989: 45).

Liberal feminism broadly accepts the structural functionalist framework, and concurs with its description of contemporary society as meritocratic. It is committed to equality of opportunity, that is, to the idea that everyone should have an equal opportunity to become unequal. Liberal feminism argues that women, who as a group are not less talented and diligent than men, are denied these opportunities, simply because of their sex. Discrimination against women, claims liberal feminism, arises from stereotyped expectations.

According to liberal feminism, women must step out of the kitchen and compete with men for positions of power and prestige in the public world. Stereotypes inhibit women's progress in two ways. First, liberal feminists believe prejudices discourage employers from employing women in positions of authority (Curthoys 1986: 327). Second, women internalise these attitudes as characteristics of their selves, limiting their own aspirations and achievements.

Liberal feminism, therefore, places great emphasis on the 'agencies of socialisation', families, schools and the mass media, as the means by which such stereotypes are acquired. Like structural functionalism, liberal feminism sees the family as an institution which specialises in socialisation. Liberal feminism uses theories of learning to argue that children learn sex roles in the family, using role models available to them which are 'reinforced' or 'sanctioned' by the wider society. Accordingly, as Connell suggests, the inequitable influence of sex roles can be reversed, by simply giving girls 'better role models, bringing in anti-discrimination laws, establishing equal-opportunity in education and employment, and the like' (1986: 345–46).

Characteristically, liberal feminism sees changes in family patterns as the outcome of shifts in sex role expectations. Men become 'new fathers' (Russell 1983), women seek education and careers, and the domestic division of labour is rejigged because of a breakdown in conventional attitudes about what is appropriate for men and women. If women recognise that they are equal and have learnt the correct techniques of communication and assertiveness, they can re-negotiate relationships with their partners (Goodnow 1989).

Sex roles, it is claimed, change in response to alterations in external circumstances such as shifts in technology, economic conditions or changing community values. Change can also come from the tension between the 'real' self and the artificial constraints of role playing. Talking about what she called 'the problem that has no name', Freidan says that women felt dissatisfied, empty and guilty because they did not get that 'mysterious sense of fulfilment waxing the kitchen floor' (1965: 17)

We examine many of the claims of this liberal feminist position in greater detail in the next section, on The Future of Family Households. There, we shall consider the 'symmetrical family' thesis, which argues many of the changes promoted by liberal feminism are, in fact, going on.

Radical Feminism and Socialist Feminism

Liberal feminism argues the structural functionalist explanation for the allocation of roles by sex as mere prejudice. Other forms of feminism have been far more sweeping in their rejection of the structural functionalism of the family. Home may have been a comforting refuge from powerlessness, impersonality and alienation experienced at 'work' but, as radical and socialist feminists pointed out, for most women it was actually a site of work. In place of the separation of home and work, feminists substituted the distinction between paid and unpaid work, thereby raising the spectre of exploitation. Instead of the alleged warmth and personal freedom of family life, evidence of dependence, powerlessness, brutality (rape, incest, and domestic violence) began to mount. All this led both radical and socialist feminists to abandon the presupposition of harmony that characterised the structural functionalist approach to the nuclear family, and to see the family as an arena of relationships of domination and subordination. The family is therefore an arena of political struggle or, as the famous slogan says, 'the personal is political'.

Radical feminism argued that 'patriarchy', the subordination of women, was as old as society itself. The class of all women has everywhere up to this present point in history been subject to the subtle rule of the class of all men. Brownmiller's analysis of rape is a typical form of this argument. She argues that rape is 'a conscious process of intimidation by which all men keep all women in a state of fear' (Brownmiller 1975: 15). Delphy and Leonard (1992) see women's unpaid labour in the home as valuable work performed as a service to their husbands; by virtue of their membership of families, all men share in the expropriation of women's unpaid labour. More generally, the core of this social division between women and men, radical feminists argue, is women's capacity for procreative production. This not only marks women off from men, but is the material basis for women's exclusion from public life.

Child bearing and child rearing, moreover, are the basis of women's culture. As Eisenstein has pointed out, liberal feminism has argued, explicitly or implicitly, for 'the replacement of gender polarisation [in sex roles] with some form of androgyny' (1984: xi). Women are urged to adapt themselves to the existing ('patriarchal') structures rather than the other way around. By contrast, recent radical feminism builds the difference between women and men into a positive celebration of 'women values'.

Radical feminists argue that because women are responsible for procreation and nurturing, they have a special affinity with the values of sharing and caring, and are inherently closer to nature, opposed to the male values of competition, self-centredness, aggression and violence (see, for example, Rich 1979; Gilligan 1984).

Socialist feminism emerged among women with a background in the socialist Left. It is differentiated from radical feminism by its belief that the subordination of women is only one system of oppression within a contemporary world characterised by a variety of oppressions (Hartmann 1981). While radical feminists emphasise the universality of patriarchy, socialist feminists tend to point to its historically changing forms. According to socialist feminists, the fact that contemporary patriarchy is not identical to patriarchal rule in the Arabian desert during the rule of Caliph, implies that patriarchy changes in response to changing historical circumstances. Consequently, they believe, concentrating on unchanging aspects of women's biology, as radical feminists do, will not be of much use in understanding the politics of transforming patriarchy. Instead, socialist feminists have concentrated on the links between the dynamics of capitalism and the forms of patriarchy. Practically, this has meant an emphasis on the emergence of the modern domestic household (Reiger 1985; Wajcman 1991), the interplay between women's low-paid and domestic labour (Baxter, Gibson and Lynch-Blosse 1990; Williams 1981), and the relation between the capitalist welfare state and modern domestic forms (Cass and Baldock 1983).

Politically, socialist feminists, while maintaining autonomous forms of political organisation, have sought alliances with other groups on the Left in a joint struggle for expanded human possibilities. Characteristics of this are well illustrated in the approach to the issue of technological transformation of the household, discussed in the following section.

The Future of Family Households[6]

How is the contemporary household changing, and what can we expect in the future? We will consider each of the three scenarios which are often raised in discussions of the future of family households. They are: the symmetrical family, the technological conception of the future, and electronic cottages.

The Symmetrical Family

Although many of the ideas on this have been around since the

1930s (Lasch 1977: 22–61), this description of the emerging family form was first developed by Young and Wilmott (1973) in their book of the same name, and has been enthusiastically promoted in recent times. In particular, it embodies many of the assumptions of the liberal feminist approach. The symmetrical family is a culmination of processes which began with the dissolution of the pre-industrial family, which was the basic unit of production. Most individuals depended for their existence on membership in a household which was broadly self-sustaining. Most of what they ate was produced by themselves for this purpose, and the same applied to clothes, shelter and fuel.

There was a strict segregation of tasks by sex, and anything less than conformity with gender-appropriate behaviour brought a swift response from other villagers. Although there was an obvious connection between all tasks performed and the economic security and well-being of the household, men were considered more important than women. The patriarch expected and received the submission of wife and children and, where they could be afforded, servants. The brutal exercise of this power was tempered by a common recognition of the economic value of wives and children (Shorter 1977: 66, 74).

Gradually, the factory replaced the cottage as the centre of industry, and the family lost its productive function, or so the story goes. Men became breadwinners. This converted wives and children from economic assets (helpmeets) to economic dependants and, indeed, from the husbands' point of view, into liabilities. As Young and Wilmott say: 'The husband could exercise his power more despotically even than in the past because, if they had children, the wife needed him more than he needed her. The marriage was asymmetrical' (1973: 75–76). Husbands enforced obedience through beatings and control of the purse. Evidence of this asymmetrical relationship is provided by husbands choosing to spend the greater portion of their meagre wages on themselves, rather than upon their dependants, and having the pick of the paltry supply of protein at mealtimes. Home was a place where husbands slept and ate; they sought company and entertainment elsewhere, in the ale house or the betting shop.

The origins of the contemporary symmetrical family are said to lie in the middle classes of the late nineteenth century. They were affluent enough for wives to be an ornament to a man's property, as well as part of it. The comfortable private haven they established weakened what remained of dependence upon extended kin. 'The man's physical comfort, the general good order of the house and the sense of spiritual contentment gained from a consciousness of his own goodness depended upon the circumspection and the affection with which he treated his wife' (Young and Wilmott 1973: 84). This provided fertile soil for the first feminist movement which began altering the legal status of women, making them persons in their own right and not purely the property of their husbands.

According to this view, once a man's wife had become his companion, and he began to centre leisure upon his home, then it became a natural extension that he should 'help' his wife with her tasks. Thus the rigid segregation of domestic roles began to be undermined. When wives are also employed, they shed their former dependence on their husbands. The norm of this new form of domestic organisation is equality:

> All major decisions should be made together, and even in minor household matters they should help one another as much as possible. This norm is carried out in practice. In their division of labour, many tasks were shared or interchangeable. The husband often did the cooking and sometimes the washing and ironing. The wife did the gardening and often the household repairs as well. Much of their leisure time was spent together, and they shared similar interests in politics, music, literature, and in entertainment.
> (Bott in Young and Wilmott 1973: 30)

Once again there is some initial plausibility and appeal to this scenario. Certainly, as we have seen, women are steadily increasing their labour force participation. The time use data also show that men are indeed doing a proportion of tasks around the house that might formerly have been considered unmasculine. According to the 1983 Australian Values Study, 87 per cent of Australians agree with the statement: 'men and women should share household jobs' (Holmstrom 1985: 4).

There are three kinds of evidence which would be necessary to make this scenario a convincing description of the direction of change for future households. Firstly, evidence that men and women are increasingly competing in equal terms in the labour market. If the symmetrical family scenario is correct, then one would expect that women's labour force participation rates, the distribution of female employees across industry and occupation, and women's earnings, would increasingly resemble the pattern for men. Secondly, the scenario requires that women's increasing responsibilities for breadwinning translate into greater independence and equality within the household. On the basis of this vision of the future, one would expect too, that the distribution of assets and income within the home would be divided equitably. Thirdly, there would need to be evidence that there is a trend for men to begin to share the burdens of homemaking and child rearing.

There has been spectacular growth in the rates of women's participation in paid employment over the last few decades, most dramatically in the participation rates of married women, which in all the OECD countries has virtually doubled, rising from a quarter of such women to approximately half in the last three decades (Peattie and Rein 1983: 59–70). While participation has risen, a disproportionate amount of this growth has been in part-time employment (Affirmative Action Agency 1988).

It is now over a decade since the idea of fixing women's wages as a fraction of a 'family wage', sufficient to support a *male* wage earner and dependants was officially overturned by the Federal Arbitration Commission. Nevertheless, in 1990, women employees still earned about two-thirds of average male weekly earnings (National Women's Consultative Council 1990). Women are heavily concentrated in particular industries and occupations. This labour market segregation has proved to be remarkably durable.

Moreover, there is considerable evidence to suggest that women's lower rewards for paid work have their roots in the gender-specific burdens of the household division of labour. Women's work histories are more likely to be discontinuous (McDonald 1986: 76–77; Young 1990: 17–18). Time use studies have found significantly less time is devoted to paid employment by women with young children, while men's time in paid work usually increased (Bittman 1991: 25–27). This impression is reinforced by the ABS Labour Force Surveys, which showed that women made up the bulk of the people not working because of family reasons, whereas a negligible number of men gave this reason (Affirmative Action Agency 1988).

While any observer is forced to acknowledge the profound changes in women's labour force participation, it does not necessarily follow that the cash income translates into a greater power for wives *vis-à-vis* their husbands. Too often this is simply assumed by proponents of the symmetrical family view. An English study of dual earner households found that although women's earnings contributed very substantially towards the primary needs of the household and underpinned its achieved standards of living, a gendered division of responsibility also developed in expenditure patterns. This mimicked the traditional domestic division of labour, 'with men responsible for the roof over the family's head and women for the day-to-day shopping and childcare' (Brannen and Moss 1987: 84).

Edwards' study of the financial arrangements of fifty Australian families found that nine of the thirty wives contributing more than 30 per cent of family income had no control over family finances. Edwards found that wives tended to manage the family finances when it was a case of stretching to make ends met. Three wives as opposed to fourteen husbands received a set amount of personal spending money, and the husbands' expenditure on themselves was almost always greater than that on their wives (1984: 133–51).

The major stumbling block of the symmetrical family thesis has been in demonstrating that where wives do paid work, husbands do correspondingly more domestic work. There can be little doubt that comparisons between husbands whose partners are employed, with those of husbands whose partners are non-employed, reveal little by way of compensating domestic labour. Analysis of the 1987 pilot survey of time use showed that a wife who increases her paid employment from 0–60 hours per week could expect her husband to increase his contribution to unpaid labour by a bare hour per week (Bittman 1991: 22–23). In Japan, husbands reduced their contribution to the household labour from five to four minutes a day when their wives were employed. Three studies in the United States showed husbands' contribution remaining static. Scandinavian researchers report husbands of employed wives did an extra 3–6 minutes of housework per day (Michelson 1985: 63), hardly time to make a decisive difference!

The fall-back position has been to argue that the symmetrical division of labour is the result of a slow evolutionary change, and hence changes over time are more appropriate than straight comparison of sub-populations. Once again, the rare cases where movements are found are disappointingly small. Australian men have on average between 1974 and 1987 increased their contribution to 'housework and family care' by 2.4 hours per week. At this rate it will take 117 years before men's contribution to housework were to equal the present contribution of women (Bittman 1991:28)[7].

The Technological Conception of the Future

There is a tendency for people when they are asked to discuss the future to slip into discussions about machines. Before we realise it we have moved from the nature of social arrangements to the properties of micro-chips, artificial intelligence, the information revolution and superconductors. In this view, the domestic division of labour will ultimately disappear, because machines will first make domestic tasks significantly less burdensome, before abolishing them altogether through automation or robotisation.

At first glance this theory appears not only plausible but also well supported by solid evidence. For most of this century, households have been subject to intense technological change. Houses have been electrified, running water connected, toilets and bathrooms moved inside. Gas or electric ranges have replaced fuel stoves, and the washboard, mangle and copper have been displaced by washing machines. Irons no longer need to be warmed on the stove, and even produce their own steam. Some synthetic fabrics require no ironing at all. Carpets are vacuumed and not beaten. There are small electric motors to help us open cans, chop and blend food, sharpen knives, remove facial hair and even clean teeth.

Niemi, in a recent survey of changing patterns of time use, noted a tendency for time spent on housework to diminish in a series of industrialised countries (1988: 15). The time women devoted to housework in Australia has reduced by an average of 4 hours per week, representing a fall of 10 per cent over 13 years (Bittman 1991: 28).

So what is wrong with this vision? Obviously not its assumption of technological change in the home. However, despite this veritable 'industrial revolution in the home' (Cowan 1976: 1), the aggregate time spent by full-time housewives on housework has not significantly altered. Joann Vanek (1974) compared the findings of the American time use studies of housework from the 1920s to the late 60s. She argued that the aggregate time spent on housework by non-employed women had changed little (from 52–55 hours per week) since the 1920s. Vanek also found that employed women devoted about half as much time (26 hours per week) to housework. As women's participation in paid work has increased, time spent in housework has fallen. Since the households of non-employed housewives were, if anything, better equipped, these findings cannot be explained by the diffusion of technology.

There has been, according to Vanek, some redistribution of time between individual tasks. While time spent in food preparation and home care has diminished, time spent on shopping and managerial tasks, and time spent on 'family care' has increased despite the trend to smaller families. The introduction of domestic technology often had counter-intuitive effects. Time spent on laundry, for example, had increased, despite the introduction of running water, detergents, automatic appliances and wash and wear fabrics (Vanek 1974: 117).

But these difficulties highlight a deeper flaw in reasoning behind the technological conception of the future: its faulty understanding of the relationship between technology and the division of labour. It ascribes to technology unwarranted, if not mystical, abilities to change the course of history. The model for this mechanisation and automation of the household is the shift from cottage handicrafts to mechanised factories during the Industrial

Revolution. This shift, which first occurred in the textile industry, was thought to be a consequence of the impracticality of anything but a centralised power source. The difficulty is, however, that the first factories used more or less the same technology as the hand-weavers in their cottages (Clawson 1980; Marglin 1982). What was distinctive about the factory was the gathering together of craftworkers, and the new forms of co-operation and division of labour instituted between them. Far from being the result of some mechanical imperative, this detailed division of labour reduced the process of production to very simple elements. Given the factory owner's desire for control of output and profit (Bruland 1985), it was a short step to substitute machinery for the repetitive and highly simplified motions of the worker.

Precisely because it is blind to the significance of the social organisation of labour, the technological conception of the future also fails to see that the development of domestic technology has been fundamentally different. The contemporary housewife is the last of the unspecialised workers, the 'veritable jane-of-all-trades' at a time when the jacks-of-all-trades have disappeared (Cowan 1985: 198). The introduction of machinery into the household has, if anything, reduced the number of specialised workers since it has been associated with the demise of the domestic servant, the cook, the laundress, the nanny and chambermaid.

Furthermore, because the handicraft nature of housework has basically remained unaltered by machines, attempts to apply the logic of Taylorist 'scientific management' to the household have foundered on the nature of this form of organisation. Not only is production small–scale but, most importantly, in this sphere of work, 'the manager and the worker are the same person'. This has meant that the 'whole point of Taylor's management science — to concentrate planning and intellectual skills in management specialists — is necessarily lost in the one-woman kitchen' (Ehrenreich and English 1979: 147). Intensification of household labour takes the opposite path to industry, eschewing co-operative application of labour, specialisation, and increase in scale, and imposing instead a pattern of simultaneous time use (Bittman 1988). In this sense the automatic washing machine is the prototype modern domestic appliance because its 'set and forget' quality allows the operator to undertake another activity while the washing cycle is completed. Busy time-use diaries have many short activity episodes as a result of the pursuit of simultaneous tasks, all of which interrupt each other, so that eventually the whole day assumes the texture of a continuous interruption. It is interesting to note in this connection the close link between the contemporary concept of time and the commodification of human labour (Thompson 1967), with the absence of this concept in the domestic setting.[8]

There has been little division of labour between households: indeed, they may be even more homogeneous since World War II than they were before it (Cowan 1983: 196–201). While some tasks have been abandoned and mass-produced substitutes purchased in the marketplace — most notably canned and frozen goods substituting for home preserves — others have been handed back to the household. Housewives have paid for the time they saved in preserving, in the growth of time spent shopping, particularly in travelling to shopping. As Cowan aptly puts it:

> Several million American women cook supper each night in several million separate homes over several million separate stoves — a specter which should be sufficient to drive any rational technocrat into the loony bin ... Out there in the land of household work there are small industrial plants which sit idle for the better part of every working day; there are expensive pieces of highly mechanised equipment which only get used once or twice a month; there are consumption units which weekly trundle out to their markets to buy 8 ounces of this nonperishable product and 12 ounces of that one ...
>
> (Cowan 1979: 59)

It is ironic that such emphasis should be put on technology when the data clearly indicate that so much of the growth of housework this century derives from the care of children. This is true not only for cross-sectional comparisons, as we have seen, but also historically. In this area, the effect of technology has been peripheral and the effect of cultural changes profound (Reiger 1985; Ehrenreich and English 1979).

In summary, one could say that the evidence tends to support the idea that it is the form of social organisation of the family, particularly ideas about how women should relate to men and the cultural value placed on the care of children, that will determine the shape of the household technology of the future. Without the requisite changes in these forms it is unlikely that domestic technology will liberate women or men from housework.

Electronic Cottages

The stimulus for this scenario comes from anxiety about the future of industrial society. Put simply, this is provoked by the spectre of the demise of industrial society, understood as one centred firmly on the generation of wealth and employment through manufacturing. Rates of unemployment over the last decades, which exceeded the levels economic planners had thought desirable, tolerable, or even possible, have led to suggestions of 'de-industrialisation'. This has also been accompanied by intense speculation as to what social institution(s) will replace the factory as the pivot of social organisation. The most consistent answer to this question has been that the 'household' either will replace the factory (Gershuny 1983, 1985; Jones 1982; Toffler 1984), or should replace it (Gorz 1985; Bahro 1984; Frankel 1987), as the fulcrum of social and economic life.

Probably the clearest and most reasoned of the responses which imply that the household will succeed the factory, is the work of Gershuny (1978, 1983, 1985). In *After Industrial Society* and even more clearly in *Social Innovation and the Division of Labour*, Gershuny is critical of the conventional post-industrial scenario. In this scenario (cf. Bell, 1973) there is a progressive development from a rural pre-industrial society dominated by primary production, to industrialised society with its emphasis on secondary industries, which in turn gives way to a post-industrial society based on services. At first glance this idea is both attractive and reassuring because it implies that while automation increases the productivity of labour, and therefore reduces the demand for employment in manufacturing, surplus labourers will be smoothly absorbed into the burgeoning service sector where mechanisation cannot effect such massive increases in productivity.

Jones (1982) and much of the Australian labour movement argue that such smooth progress can only be achieved if the workforce has acquired a sufficient level of knowledge, and hence sufficiently high standards of formal education, to offer such services. Gershuny, however, raises a more fundamental objection. He argues that the demand for services will not take up the slack created by the decline of employment in manufacturing. He seeks to demonstrate that precisely because services are not susceptible to increases in productivity, the prices of 'final services' remain high relative to manufactured goods, where increases in productivity constantly reduce the costs of these items. This produces a tendency towards self-service, i.e. towards the self-provisioning of services within the household. According to this model, households purchase 'intermediate goods' instead of 'final services': the private car replaces the collective means of transport, commercial laundries give way to domestic washing machines; videos substitute for visits to the cinema and so on. Under this new self-provisioning regime the economic value of services produced by women in the home will once again be obvious. The household will become a post-industrial cottage but with two equal partners rather than a dominant patriarch.

Gershuny's argument for the shift in the mode of provision of services consists of a series of predictions about how households employ the economic resources available to them. On the basis of his model, we should expect a transfer of time away from paid employment and towards provision of services in the home.

A significant reduction in hours of paid work, however, can only be clearly demonstrated for males (Niemi 1988). During the thirteen years from 1974 to 1987, women of working age in Australia have increased the time they have devoted to paid work by an average of 25 per cent (4.4 hours per week). Over the same period, the difference of time men and women spent in paid employment was reduced by one-third (Bittman 1991: 28).

There appears to have been some redistribution of time spent in paid work from men to women. Although it may still be possible to argue for an overall reduction in the time households devoted to paid employment, there is just as convincing a case for total unpaid work time devoted by both sexes decreasing, due chiefly to women's increased employment. The problem of demonstrating men's transfer of time towards self-provisioning in the home is compounded by the static condition of their contribution to unpaid work in the home. Under these circumstances, it is difficult to avoid the conclusion that the chief beneficiaries of this supposedly symmetrical process have been men.

As was the case in the other scenarios, the electronic cottages model tends to ascribe too much power to machines. Like the other scenarios, it fails to acknowledge the persistence of the sexual division of labour and hence does not expect it to turn up in new forms. It is unable, therefore, to see how machines reflect the social relations in which they are created and applied. It is blind to the most obvious determinants of the household division of labour. It does not ask: Who is minding the children? If it did, it would have to acknowledge that women are struggling to escape imprisonment in the domestic sphere, and that the success of this struggle is dependent on the creation of alternative arrangements for child care. While male academics might dream about a return to the household of the future, women, it seems, are interested in a larger and freer labour market and in more collective provision of services.

Conclusion

The family, especially the nuclear family, is not an inevitable outcome of either human biology or human social organisation. Nor is the nuclear family the product of the Industrial Revolution. Certainly, important family changes are associated with the upheaval which accompanied industrialisation, but not the ones anticipated by structural functionalism. Not labour mobility, but intimacy, romance, and private, child-centred households or, in short, 'affective individualism' was the result.

At the same time, the nuclear family form is proving stubbornly durable. Its apparent decline is more an artefact of other changes, such as ageing, the result of divorce, cohabitation, childlessness and homosexuality. The nuclear family has merely lost some of the cultural hegemony it acquired in the middle of the twentieth century, when alternative forms were considered to be deformed or 'broken' families.

The challenge of feminism has produced a startling revitalisation of family theory. Feminism has made the issues of dependency, unequal exchange, physical coercion and ideological control central to family studies. However, it is also characterised by important theoretical and political divisions between liberal, radical and socialist variants.

Three widely-held ideas or scenarios about the future of family households are the growth of symmetrical families; the technological transformation of the role of housewife; and the 'return' to electronic cottages. The liberal feminist promise associated with the androgynous, egalitarian 'symmetrical family' appears to be contradicted by the persistence of male domination in the domestic sphere. The analysis of the 'industrial revolution in the home' shows that the social relations of household production actually shape the kind of technology applied to the household, rather than it being shaped by technology. 'De-industrialisation' and the movement of paid work from factory to electronic homes (through tele-commuting and the like), concentrates on the falling hours of men's work, and ignores the counter-tendency of growth in women's paid employment outside the home. Moreover, it relies on a variant of the 'symmetrical family' thesis for its prediction of the likely social effects of this change in work sites.

Each of these scenarios for the future family household fail because they do not acknowledge relations of gender and power either in the home, or between the home and other important social institutions. The future of Australian families is ultimately, in part, a political question about who has the power to change it.

Notes

1. Other biological forms reproduce asexually. A potato, for example, sprouts an embryo shoot from its 'eye'. The blue-green algae that threatens our waterways regenerates by cell division. Humans, on the other hand, reproduce sexually, as a result of the fusion of two cells, not by the fission of cells. Among humans, only females have ovaries and only males are capable of producing sperm. Human reproduction has, until recent interventions of medical science, required that females and males mate.

2. The male mallee fowl, for example, plays a significant part in the incubation of hatchlings by using his beak to test the heat of the nest and maintaining a constant temperature by adding warm composting materials or cooling nesting material as the necessity arises.

3. Stephen J. Gould has pointed out that evolutionary theorists distinguish between analogy and homology. Birds and insects both have wings (analogy) but morphologically birds' wings and human arms are homologous, and could be descended from a common ancestry, while the structure of insects' wings is entirely different and is derived from different ancestry (Gould 1977: 254).

4. The *berdache* is a male who dresses as a woman, is allowed to marry men, and under certain conditions, adopts children.

5. Binding the infant's limbs close to the body by winding them tightly in a cloth bandage.

6. Many of the ideas presented in this section were first developed in Bittman (1990) 'Division of Labour in the Household', Discussion Paper 11, Households Research Unit, Department of Economics, University of Melbourne. My thanks go to Duncan Ironmonger for his kind permission to reproduce excerpts from this monograph.

7. Gershuny and Robinson's (1988) study of six countries is numerically even less persuasive. There is solid evidence of a pattern of historical convergence between men and women in time spent on housework and child care, but the illusion of increase in men's participation is created by relative motion. The increase in men's relative share is not due to any reliable increase but to the shrinking quantities of time available to women.

8. Mandel, in describing the Industrial Revolution, notes that whereas in 1859 it took 1,437 hours manually to produce 100 hundred pairs of men's shoes, in 1895 it only took 153 hours to manufacture them using machines (Mandel 1968: 138).

References

Affirmative Action Agency (1988) *Women in the Workforce — A Statistical Summary*, July. Sydney: Affirmative Action Agency.

Anderson, M. (1979) 'The Relevance of Family History', in C. Harris *et al.* (eds), *The Sociology of the Family: New Directions for Britain*, Sociological Review Monograph 28. Keele: University of Keele.

Aries, P. (1973) *Centuries of Childhood*. Harmondsworth: Penguin.

Australian Bureau of Statistics (1991) *Divorces, Australia*, Catalogue No. 3307.0, Canberra.

———(1992) *Labour Force Status and Other Characteristics of Families, Australia*, Catalogue No. 6224.0, Canberra.

Bahro, R. (1984) *From Red to Green*. London: Verso.

Baxter, J., Gibson, D. and Lynch-Blosse, M. (1990) *Double Take: The Links Between Paid and Unpaid Work*. Canberra: Australian Government Publishing Service.

Bell, C. and Newby, H. (1976) 'Husbands and Wives: the Dynamics of

458   Current Issues and Concerns

the Deferential Dialectic' in D.L. Barker and S. Allen (eds), *Dependence and Exploitation in Work and Marriage*. London: Longman.

Bell, D. (1973) *The Coming of Post-Industrial Society: A Venture in Social Forecasting*. New York: Basic Books.

Bernard, J. (1976) *The Future of Marriage*. Harmondsworth: Penguin.

Bittman, M. (1988) 'Service Provision, Women and the Future of the Household: The Interpretation of Time Data in Child Care and Household Productive Activities', International Research Group on Time Budgets and Social Activities Conference, Budapest June 14–16.

———(1990) 'Division of Labour in the Household', Research Discussion Paper 11, University of Melbourne; Households Economic Unit, Department of Economics.

———(1991) *Juggling Time: How Australian Families Use Time*. Canberra: Office of the Status of Women.

Bittman, M. and Lovejoy, F. (1991) 'Domestic Power: Negotiating an Unequal Division of Labour within the Framework of Equality', Paper presented to TASA Conference, Murdoch University, December.

Brachter, M. and Santow, G. 'Changing Family Composition from Australian Life History Data', Working Paper 6, Australian Family Project, Australian National University, Research School of Social Sciences.

Brannen, J and Moss, P (1987) 'Dual Earner Households: Women's Financial Contributions After Birth of the First Child', in J. Brannen and G. Wilson (eds), *Give and Take in Families: Studies in Resource Distribution*. London: Allen and Unwin.

Brownmiller, S. (1975) *Against Our Will: Men, Women and Rape*. New York: Simon and Schuster.

Bruland, T. (1985) 'Industrial Conflict as a Source of Technical Innovation: The Development of the Automatic Spinning Mule', in D. MacKenzie and J. Wajcman (eds), *The Social Shaping of Technology*. Milton Keynes: Open University Press.

Burns, A. (1983) 'Population Structure and the Family', in A. Burns, G. Bottomley and P. Jools (eds), *The Family in the Modern World: Australian Perspectives*. Sydney: Allen and Unwin.

Carmichael, G. (1988) 'With This Ring: First Marriage Patterns, Trends and Prospects in Australia', Australian Family Formation Project Monograph 11. Canberra: Department of Demography, Australian National University and the Australian Institute of Family Studies.

Cass, B. and Baldock, C.V. (eds) (1983) *Women, Social Welfare and the State*. Sydney: Allen and Unwin.

Cheal, D. (1991) *Family and the State of Theory*. London: Harvester/Wheatsheaf.

Clawson, D. (1980) *Bureaucracy and the Labour Process*. New York: Monthly Review Press.

Connell, R.W. (1986) 'Theorizing Gender', in N. Grieve and A. Burns (eds), *Australian Women: New Feminist Perspectives*. Melbourne: Oxford University Press.

———(1987) *Gender and Power: Society, the Person and Sexual Politics*. Sydney: Allen and Unwin.

Cowan, R.S. (1976) 'The "Industrial Revolution" in the Home: Household Technology and Social Change in the Twentieth Century', *Technology and Culture* 17: 1–23.

———(1979) 'From Virginia Dare to Virginia Slims: Women and Technology in American Life', *Technology and Culture* 20: 51–63.

———(1983) *More Work for Mother: The Ironies of Household Technology from the Open Hearth to the Microwave*. New York: Basic Books.

———(1985) 'The Industrial Revolution in the Home' in D. MacKenzie, and J. Wajcman (eds), *The Social Shaping of Technology*. Milton Keynes: Open University Press.

Curthoys, A. (1986) 'The Sexual Division of Labour: Theoretical Arguments', in N. Grieve and A. Burns (eds), *Australian Women: New Feminist Perspectives*. Melbourne: Oxford University Press.

Davidoff, L. and Hall, C. (1987) *Family Fortunes: Men and Women of the English Middle Class 1780–1850*. London: Hutchinson.

Delphy, C. and Leonard, D. (1992) *Familiar Exploitation: A New Analysis of Marriage in Contemporary Western Societies*. Cambridge: Polity.

Edholm, F. (1982) 'The Unnatural Family', in Whitelegg *et al.*, *The Changing Experience of Women*. Oxford: Martin Robertson.

Edwards, M. (1984) *The Income Unit in the Australian Tax and Social Security System*. Melbourne: Institute of Family Studies.

Ehrenreich, B. and English, D. (1979) *For Her Own Good: 150 years of Experts' Advice to Women*. London: Pluto.

Eisenstein, H. (1984) *Contemporary Feminist Thought*. Sydney: Allen and Unwin.

Faulkner, W. and Arnold, E. (eds) (1985) *Smothered by Invention: Technology in Women's Lives*. London: Pluto.

Forgey, D.G. (1975) 'The Institution of *Berdache* Among the North American Plains Indians', *Journal of Sex Research* 11.

Frankel, B. (1987) *The Post-Industrial Utopians*. Cambridge: Polity Press.

Freidan, B. (1965) *The Feminine Mystique*. Harmondsworth: Penguin.

Gershuny, J. (1978) *After Industrial Society: The Emerging Self-Service Economy*. London: Macmillan.

———(1983) *Social Innovation and the Division of Labour*. Oxford: Oxford University Press.

———(1985) 'Economic Development and Change in the Mode of Provision of Services' in N. Redclift, and E. Minigione (eds), *Beyond Employment: Household, Gender and Subsistence*. Oxford: Basil Blackwell.

Gershuny, J. and Robinson, J. (1988) 'Historical Changes in the Household Division of Labour', *Demography* 25: 537–52.

Giddens, A. (1989) *Sociology*. Cambridge: Polity.

Gilding, M. (1991) *The Making and Breaking of the Australian Family*. Sydney: Allen and Unwin.

Gilligan, C. (1982) *In a Different Voice: Psychological Theory and Women's Development*. Cambridge, Mass.: Harvard University Press.

Gittins, D. (1985) *The Family in Question: Changing Households and Familiar Ideologies*. London: Macmillan.

Goodnow, J. (1989) 'Work in Households: An Overview and Three

Studies', in D. Ironmonger (ed.), *Household Work: Productive Activities, Women and Income in the Household*. Sydney: Allen and Unwin.

Gorz, A. (1985) *Paths to Paradise: On the Liberation From Work*. London: Pluto.

Gould, S.J. (1977) *Ever Since Darwin: Reflections in Natural History*. New York: W.W. Norton.

Graycar, A. and Jamrozik. A. (1989) *How Australians Live: Social Policy in Theory and Practice*. Melbourne: Macmillan.

Harris, C.C. (1983) *The Family and Industrial Society*. London: Allen and Unwin.

Hartmann, H. (1981) 'The Unhappy Marriage of Marxism and Feminism: Towards a More Progressive Union', in L. Sargent (ed.), *Women and Revolution*. London: Pluto.

Hiatt, L.R. (1965) *Kinship and Conflict*. Canberra: Australian National University Press.

Holmstrom, E. (1985) 'Women's Time, Men's Time: What We Say and What We Do', Paper presented to Australian and New Zealand Association for the Advancement of Science Conference, Monash University, 26–30 August.

Hugo, G. (1992) 'Australia's Contemporary and Future Fertility and Mortality: Trends, Differentials and Implications', in *Population Issues and Australia's Future: Environment, Economy and Society*, National Population Council, Canberra: Australian Government Publishing Service.

Ironmonger, D.S. and Lloyd, C.W. (1990) *Household Populations and Projections of Households*, University of Melbourne, Households Research Unit, Economics Department.

Jallinoja, R. (1989) 'Women between the Family and Employment', in K. Boh, M. Bak, C. Clason, M. Pankratova, J. Qvortrup, G.B. Sgritta and K. Waerness (eds), *Changing Patterns of European Family Life: A Comparative Analysis of 14 European Countries*. London: Routledge.

James, M. (1979) 'Double Standards in Divorce', in J. Mackinolty and H. Radi (eds), *In Pursuit of Justice: Australian Women and the Law 1788–1979*. Sydney: Hale and Iremonger.

Joint Select Committee on the *Family Law Act (1980) Family Law in Australia: A Report of the Joint Select Committee on the Family Law Act*, Vol. 2. Canberra: Australian Government Publishing Service.

Jones, B. (1982) *Sleepers Wake! Technology and the Future of Work*. Melbourne: Oxford University Press.

Khoo, S. and McDonald, P. (1988) 'Ex-nuptial Births and Unmarried Cohabitation in Australia', *Journal of the Australian Population Association* 5: 164–77.

Lasch, C. (1977) *Haven in a Heartless World*. New York: Basic Books.

Lewis, R.A. and Sussman, M.B. (eds) (1985) *Men's Changing Role in the Family*. New York: Haworth.

MacKenzie, D. and Wajcman, J. (eds) (1985) *The Social Shaping of Technology*. Milton Keynes: Open University Press.

Mandel, E. (1968) *Marxist Economic Theory*. London: Merlin.

Marglin, S. (1982) 'What Do the Bosses Do? The Origins and Functions of Hierarchy in Capitalist Production', in A. Giddens and D. Held (eds), *Classes, Power and Conflict*. London: Macmillan.

McDonald, P. (1989) 'Can the Family Survive?' in T. Jagtenberg and P. D'Alton, *Four Dimensional Social Space*. Sydney: Harper Educational.

———(1990) 'The 1980s: Social and Economic Change Affecting Families', *Family Matters* 26: 13–18.

McDonald, P. (ed.) (1986) *Settling Up: Property and Income Distribution on Divorce in Australia*. Sydney: Prentice-Hall.

Michelson, W. (1985) *From Sun to Sun: Daily Obligation and Community Structure in the Lives of Employed Women and Their Families*. Ottawa: Rowman and Allanheld.

Morris, D. (1968) *The Naked Ape*. London: Corgi.

Murdock, G.P. (1968) 'The Universality of the Nuclear Family' in N.W. Bell and E.F. Vogel (eds), *A Modern Introduction to The Family*. New York: Free Press.

National Women's Consultative Council (1990) *Pay Equity for Women in Australia*. National Labour Research Centre. Canberra: Australian Government Publishing Service.

Niemi, I. (1988) 'Main Trends in Time Use from the 1920s to the 1980s', Paper presented to Meeting of International Research on Time Budgets and Social Activities, Budapest, 14–16 June.

O'Brien, A. (1988) *Poverty's Prison: The Poor in NSW 1880–1918*. Melbourne: Melbourne University Press.

Oakley, A. (1974) *Housewife*. Harmondsworth: Penguin.

Parsons, T. (1966) *Societies: Evolutionary and Comparative Perspectives*. Englewood Cliffs, NJ: Prentice-Hall.

Peattie, L. and Rein, M. (1983) *Women's Claims: A Study in Political Economy*. Oxford: Oxford University Press.

Pixley, J. (1991) 'Wowser and Pro-Woman Politics: Temperance against Australian Patriarchy', *Australian and New Zealand Journal of Sociology* 27: 293–314.

Pollock, L. (1983) *Forgotten Children: Parent-Child Relations from 1500–1900*. Cambridge: Cambridge University Press.

Poster, M. (1978) *Critical Theory of the Family*. London: Pluto.

Reiger, K. (1985) *The Disenchantment of the Home: Modernizing the Australian Family 1880–1940*. Melbourne: Oxford University Press.

Rich, A. (1979) *Of Woman Born: Motherhood as Experience and Institution*. London: Virago.

Roe, J. (1987) 'Chivalry and Social Policy in the Antipodes', *Historical Studies* 22: 295–410.

Russell, G. (1983) *The Changing Role of Fathers?* St Lucia: University of Queensland Press.

Rutter, M. and Giller, H. (1983) *Juvenile Delinquency: Trends and Perspectives*. Harmondsworth: Penguin.

Saunders, P. and Matheson, G. (1991) 'An Ever Rising Tide? Poverty in Australia in the Eighties', SPRC Discussion Paper 30, University of New South Wales, Social Policy Research Centre.

Shorter, E. (1977) *The Making of the Modern Family*. Glasgow: Fontana.

Stone, L. (1979) *The Family, Sex and Marriage in England 1500–1800*. Harmondsworth: Penguin.

Thompson, E.P. (1967) 'Time, Work-Discipline and Industrial Capitalism', *Past and Present* 38: 51–96.

Tiger, L. (1969) *Men in Groups*. New York: Random House.

——and Fox, R. (1972) *The Imperial Animal*. London: Secker and Warburg.

Toffler, A. (1984) *Previews and Premises*. London: Pan.

Vanek, J. (1974) 'Time Spent in Housework', *Scientific American* 231: 116–20.

Wajcman, J. (1991) *Feminism Confronts Technology*. Sydney: Allen and Unwin.

Weber, M. (1968) *Economy and Society*. Berkeley: University of California Press.

Williams, C. (1981) *Open Cut: The Working Class in an Australian Mining Town*. Sydney: Allen and Unwin.

Williams, F. (1989) *Social Policy: A Critical Introduction*. Cambridge: Polity.

Young, C. (1990) *Balancing Families and Work: A Demographic Study of Women's Labour Force Participation*. Canberra: Australian Government Publishing Service.

Young, M. and Wilmott, P. (1973) *The Symmetrical Family*. London: Routledge and Kegan Paul.

Chapter Fifteen

Welfare Issues of the Nineties

Lois Bryson

Fundamental changes are taking place in the nature of welfare in Australia, in the way society's resources are distributed and redistributed. These changes are the focus of this chapter, and they are set in their historical context. To understand them, it is necessary to challenge what is conventionally understood by the term welfare, and its associated concepts. Such a challenge is not merely semantic. Definitions and conversations or discourses about any topic have the effect of shaping ideas and thus, ultimately, social policies. The chapter broadens conventional approaches to take account of the welfare or well-being of all citizens, not just the poor and relatively poor who are most often the target of discussions on welfare.

The chapter starts with concepts, definitions and discourses which relate to welfare and the welfare state. The history of the Australian welfare state is then broadly outlined, followed by a detailed discussion of the development of social welfare in Australia. This discussion brings us up to date with the significant changes which have been made over the past decade, and the important issues of the nineties. Finally fiscal and occupational welfare are considered as forms of welfare that are usually excluded from conventional discussions. This broadening of the debate allows us to draw conclusions about social welfare and social justice more generally.

Understanding Welfare

The way we talk about issues and the way we conceptualise them are fundamental to our understanding. As Yeatman (1990: 155) pointed out, 'discourse is the power to create reality by naming and giving it meaning'. This is an idea which Marx grappled with via the concept of ideology, and which later Gramsci highlighted through the concept of hegemony. Any consideration of the Australian welfare state must therefore start by unpacking conventional discourses, those general meanings that are implied when we raise the issue of welfare. These are usually limited not only by a failure to define the notion of welfare sufficiently broadly to include issues of economic equality more generally, but also by a failure to give a central place to issues connected with gender, race and other axes of disadvantage. As the discussion moves to the history of the development of the Australian welfare state and to its social, fiscal and occupational welfare provisions, the limitations of traditional discourses will become very obvious.

In its most general form, the word welfare simply means well-being. It is, however, systematically used also to refer to a very specific set of institutions of a society, those which have as their explicit aim the meeting of basic economic, physical and social needs. These institutions are meant to come into play when the provisions of the market fail. At the centre of welfare, or more precisely, social welfare, in this specific sense are the social security system and traditional charitable services. Public health and education services, public housing, and a range of personal services, particularly those targeted to people in dependent states, like children, those with disabilities, and the elderly, are also covered by conventional approaches. These social welfare provisions can be referred to as traditional or classic forms of welfare.

In this traditional sense the term social welfare in Australia, as in many other capitalist societies, tends not to be used in reference to the well-being of all the population. It is applied selectively to those who, for a variety of reasons, are seen as not able to provide for themselves. 'Welfare', then, is not so much about all citizens as about those who are poor or relatively poor. This is graphically illustrated by the notion of these services as a 'safety net'. There tends to be a negative cast to the idea of social welfare in Australia; it is not anchored in notions of universalism and citizenship. Many who are its recipients are stigmatised by being considered dependent and unable or unwilling to support themselves. History is rife with discussions about whether or not the poor are 'deserving' (Golding and Middleton 1982: Chapter 1), a debate which echoes down the centuries in the pejorative concepts of 'welfare cheat' and 'dole bludger'.

Discussions of welfare in this narrow mould imply that only the poor are in receipt of welfare, thus overlooking the extensive degree to which the better-off benefit from state activity, albeit differently from traditional social welfare means. The benefits that the better-off receive are quarantined from the negative overtones and the persistent scrutiny that is associated with welfare assistance to the poor, as traditionally defined.

Conventional discourses about welfare do not raise the issue of the well-being of those who are better-off, even though they clearly benefit substantially from state activities. When state and federal governments provide money for the Olympic Games, restructure the Wool Secretariat, or provide money to encourage manufacturing or scientific research, clearly someone benefits. Usually benefits are greatest for those who are already reasonably well-off. Such benefits also tend to be distributed along gender lines, with men benefiting more than women. They are distributed, too, in accord with other axes of inequality, including race, disability and age.

These forms of state benefit are dealt with quite separately from conventional social welfare, and largely divided from questioning about fair distribution and its benefits. Yet it is becoming increasingly important to ask such questions, since governments are spending more effort actively promoting the market and the private sector, areas that are the preserve of the better-off. At the same time, expenditure on social welfare, traditionally directed to the poor, has become doubly disapproved, under pressure from economic liberal discourses which reject collective forms of government spending as non-productive. If we focus only on stigmatised and threatened government welfare spending, we increase its visibility and inadvertently reinforce the notion that this is the only major area of government spending and activity in need of scrutiny.

Key Concepts: the Welfare State

When a nation is defined as a welfare state it tends to be so defined in terms of the provision of the classic forms of social welfare. However, regulation of the labour force and working conditions, general public health measures, and some active intervention to at least partially redress inequality, is usually implied as well. Mishra noted that the concept welfare state refers both to intention, that is 'the idea of state responsibility for welfare', and the state mechanisms, the 'institutions and practices', for delivering services and provisions (Mishra 1984: xi).

There is a great deal of cultural variation in the extent to which liberal democratic capitalist societies measure up in terms of conventional welfare state criteria. Some, such as the United States and Japan, have a weak form, which is referred to as residual. In contrast, the well-developed welfare states of the Scandinavian countries are referred to as institutional in form. As well as there being variations between countries in state provisions, there is variation within countries in the manner in which different groups have their welfare catered for. In particular those of non-dominant races and women are likely to receive fewer general societal benefits, even though they are often over-represented as recipients of direct social welfare, something which reflects their general disadvantaged status.

Esping-Andersen (1990) has recently categorised the Organisation for Economic Co-operation and Development (OECD) welfare states as being of three types, conservative, social democratic and liberal. He places Australia in the liberal category. According to Esping-Andersen, in conservative welfare state regimes (such as Austria, Germany and France), substantial welfare rights attach to membership of a class or status group, typically with distinctive occupational insurance schemes and generous pensions for civil servants. Such regimes attempt to build loyalty to a corporatist state and the traditional family. 'Day care, and similar family services, are conspicuously underdeveloped . . . the state will only interfere when the family's capacity to service its members is exhausted' (Esping-Andersen 1990: 27).

Social democratic states such as the Scandinavian states involve both egalitarianism and universalism. They offer benefits designed to guarantee to each citizen the highest possible standard of well-being, as of right, regardless of occupational or employment status. The regime's policy of emancipation addresses both the market and the family, the ideal being not to maximise dependence on the family, but to provide for independence. As well as making transfers to families, these welfare state regimes take direct responsibility for many services, such as for child care, the aged and the disabled (Esping-Andersen 1990: 28).

Esping-Andersen's third category is liberal welfare state regimes (including the United States, the United Kingdom, Canada and Australia). These he sees as characterised by a residual concept of welfare, with the state only assuming responsibility when the market and the family have failed. They feature 'means-tested assistance, modest universal transfers, or modest social insurance plans' (1990: 26–27). Essentially, reliance on private market mechanisms is encouraged.

Castles and Mitchell (1992) argue that a 'radical' subdivision of this liberal group of welfare states better characterises Australia (and New Zealand). Castles (1985) argues that what happened in Australia was that a 'wage earners' welfare state' developed. This was achieved by the labour movement securing reasonable levels of wages and working conditions, rather than focusing on citizenship rights and institutionalised social welfare measures. The result has been a low level of welfare state development, but at the same time (at least until recently), a comparatively high level of income equality. Essentially, the wage earners' welfare state was built on traditional notions of the family, through the concept of the family wage and lower official wage rates for women until 1972, when the principle of equal pay was adopted (Bryson 1989, 1992).

A Variety of Welfares and Welfare States

When we consider less conventional definitions of welfare, a popular place to start is a much-quoted paper published in 1958 by the British social theorist Richard Titmuss. He advocated the extension of our conception of welfare beyond the traditional elements, which he identified as 'social welfare'. He noted the relative arbitrariness with which the classification, 'social service' or 'social welfare' was applied, and suggested that these state interventions which are readily recognised as 'social' exist alongside a much broader area of intervention which, while not thought of in such terms, actually shares similar objectives (1974: 42).

He likened 'social welfare' to the visible tip of the iceberg, with two other forms of welfare, the equivalent of the part hidden below the water-line. Titmuss' submerged welfare is made up of two parts: benefits achieved through the taxation system, termed 'fiscal welfare', and benefits distributed through the employment system, termed 'occupational welfare'. As British examples of fiscal welfare, he included taxation allowances in respect of dependent children, and exemptions in respect of education. He suggested that even though fiscal benefits represent only another method of making transfers, they are perceived differently from social welfare benefits. Reactions to 'occupational welfare' are also different, and similarly positive. As examples of occupational welfare Titmuss cited a long list of benefits, including 'entertainment, dress and equipment; meal vouchers; cheap meals; motor cars and season tickets' (1974: 51). He noted that occupational benefits are significantly underpinned by the government through loss of taxation revenue.

Titmuss made a strong case for considering all three forms of welfare when assessing the equity effects of a nation's welfare state, a position that has been reiterated with monotonous regularity since (Sinfield 1978; Rose 1981; Keens and Cass 1982; Jamrozik *et al.* 1981; Jordan 1987). Yet despite the recognised merit of his argument and the fact that it has been widely accepted, most discussions or discourses on welfare still direct attention to those issues which are encompassed by Titmuss' 'social welfare'.

The focus in the Australian sociological literature on the welfare state (Jones 1990) is, like its overseas counterparts (Mishra 1984; Gough 1979; Thane 1982), largely confined to institutions such as social security, personal welfare services, health, public housing and education (Edwards 1988: 242). Even when the taxation system is recognised as a mechanism for the distribution of 'welfare', the analysis is likely not to deal with its full scope. Discussion tends to focus on categories of taxation that parallel traditional social welfare provisions, such as tax concessions in respect of superannuation (which in effect is a private form of age pension), or concessions in respect of dependent children, spouses or people with disabilities. Concessions that are paid in respect of the purchase of private housing, as are common in many European countries, may also receive attention. Yet all tax concessions and exemptions increase incomes and simultaneously reduce the government's purse, which in turns curtails its capacity to underwrite collective and other redistributive state activity.

Welfare and Accounting Systems

If the government fails to tax certain items, provides money at cheap interest rates to encourage the development of selected industries, fails to charge for the use of resources or picks up the tab for the pollution caused by a manufacturer, it is not currently easy to demonstrate precisely to whom the benefits accrue. Nonetheless, they do accrue and are of relevance to an analysis concerned with issues of state contributions to personal well-being and issues of equality. Krever has exposed benefits in the area of superannuation, where the benefits received by the better-off by way of tax concessions often far exceed a lifetime of direct benefits to the average age pensioner (Krever 1989).

Most analyses of welfare have not taken a broad approach to equality and the taxation (or more broadly, fiscal) system. They rarely raise, for example, the manner in which the better-off may be favoured by the very structures of the tax system. This is partly because we have not developed accounting systems which can effectively consider who benefits from these expenditures. The importance of systems of public accounting should thus not be underestimated. This is illustrated by considering one of the key international accounting systems, the United Nations System of National Accounts. Waring has demonstrated how, like most accounting systems, it ignores women's labour in the household, and informal economies. In Third World countries, women's role as agricultural producers is ignored as well, even when they are the major producers. The environment, too, is largely ignored, for essentially the same reason. Within the dominant discourse, where no economic value is explicitly assigned, such elements are largely treated as worthless (Waring 1988).

Nonetheless, Ironmonger (1989: 8) estimated that for 1975–76, the value of household production in Australia was about \$49 billion, compared with \$69 billion for Gross Domestic Product. About 75 per cent of the household labour that is ignored by the national and international statistics is undertaken by women (Ironmonger 1989: x). This bias towards that which is priced (and predominantly masculine) thus reinforces a lack of concern for issues of concern to women. Indeed, more fundamentally, it diverts attention away from issues of outcomes, in this case particularly the well-being of people, but also other unpriced outcomes such as effects on the environment. A similar separation of the 'economic' from the 'non-economic' is mirrored in the distinctions between social welfare (non-economic policy) and occupational and fiscal welfare (economic policy).

The Social Wage

The focus of accounting systems reinforces the point made earlier about the power of discourse. We have a useful conventional discourse focused on the 'social wage'. It is, nonetheless, far from being a comprehensive concept, since it ignores, among other things, the household economy, the environment and fiscal and occupational welfare. The social wage concept has traditionally been of special interest to trade unions and the labour movement. This largely explains why it is a discourse which has been heeded in official circles. Official accounting effort has been put into ways of measuring its distribution.

The social wage is conventionally defined as the sum of the collective benefits which are transferred to individuals or families in both cash and kind, via the state. It is distinguished from the 'private or personal wage which comes from employment' (Gough 1979: 108). The social wage, broadly encompasses benefits from classic social welfare provisions: that is, social security, health, education, public housing and the personal social services. The Australian Bureau of Statistics regularly undertakes Household Expenditure Surveys to provide the basis for computing the distribution of benefits from the social wage. Data from these surveys are drawn on later in the chapter. It would clearly be possible to develop a much broader concept, with appropriate accounting methods, to encompass distribution and redistribution more generally, and also encompassing the household economy and environmental costs and benefits. Such an index might be called a social justice index.

The Development of the Wage Earners' Welfare State

Around the turn of the twentieth century, Australia and New Zealand took something of an international lead in terms of progressive social policies. For example, in 1901, Australia became the first nation to give women both the right to vote and to stand for Parliament (Sawer and Simms 1984). The initial radical promise did not, however, continue, and Australia today must be counted among the world's welfare state laggards.

The strength of the trade union movement and the Australian Labor Party have left a distinctive and indelible stamp on Australia's welfare state. Social democratic efforts which elsewhere were devoted primarily to the development of the social wage were directed in Australia more at securing acceptable conditions of work and wage levels, though effectively only for white male workers. A great deal was actually achieved, hence Castles' (1985) aphorism 'wage earners' welfare state'. Labour or social democratic politics are traditionally associated with a strong state, and it was no different in Australia. Government action was employed to redress inequality. At its most optimistic, labour politics, in Australia as elsewhere, interpreted these state processes as leading down a parliamentary road to socialism. As Curtin, Prime Minister of Australia during the World War II, expressed it 'I believe predominantly that government should be the agency whereby the masses should be lifted up' (Wilenski 1986: 20).

Despite this tradition, the Australian Labor government of the 1990s clearly shows the hallmarks of economic liberalism, or economic rationalism as it is popularly termed in Australia. This is an international policy trend observable in most countries of the OECD, which is associated with a negative view of government intervention and a concentration on private markets and privatisation at the expense of the public sector. Another strand of economic liberal policy involves deregulation of the labour market, through weakening both the power of trade unions and central industrial relations processes in favour of bargaining at the workplace, or in the official jargon, 'enterprise level'. Changes to industrial relations in Australia, as in other OECD countries, are complemented by attempts to strengthen commitment to employment through ensuring 'that social security systems do not unduly weaken the incentives to work, to save and to change jobs' (Henderson 1989: 32–43).

A key early development in Australia was the establishment of a centralised system of industrial conciliation and arbitration. This was concerned with wage fixing, ruling on claims about other conditions of work, and with disputes. As Castles points out, the establishment of this system effectively meant that wages were no longer determined in terms of market forces, as is decreed by the pure logic of capitalism. The idea that the worker's freedom was merely confined to the freedom to enter into a contract or not, was rejected. The capacity of industry to pay was also ruled out as a basis for determining wage rates (Castles 1985: 14). Human need was injected into the system as a relevant consideration, and a minimum living wage, the basic wage, adopted.

A landmark decision was made with the Harvester Judgment of 1907. Here the President of the Commonwealth Court of Conciliation and Arbitration pronounced that wages for unskilled male workers should be paid at a level

> appropriate to the normal needs of the average employee regarded as a human being living in a civilised community.
>
> (Macarthy 1976: 41)

Importantly the 'basic' wage was to cover the needs not only of the worker, but also of a wife and three children, allowing them to live 'in frugal comfort'. This has had important ramifications for the relationship of women's wages to men's, since women's needs were assumed to be covered by the male rate. Women's minimum rate was for many years set at only half, and later three-quarters that of men. Equal pay was formally granted only in 1972, though it is yet to become a general reality.

A number of other policies successfully promoted by male workers also had the effect of excluding the competition of cheaper labour. The most notorious measure was the strict control of immigration through a White Australia Policy prohibiting all immigrants of colour. This infamous policy was built on the racist sentiments of workers, but it did have the effect of preventing employers undermining the white male wage through the employment of cheap labour from the South Pacific or Asia. While self-interest expressed through racism prompted unionists to support the policy, racism alone allowed Australia's indigenous people to have their labour exploited in a manner close to slavery. Australian Aborigines on pastoral properties, for example, worked without proper wages and often for meagre rations only. The union movement turned a blind eye to this until the 1960s (Sanders 1985).

The early strategy of the political Left of pursuing white males' interests largely through improved conditions of employment has left its stamp on the Australian welfare state. It has meant that the classic social welfare provisions remain underdeveloped. Even in the 1990s, Australian income security arrangements take a residualist and highly selective form. The only general provision based on insurance has been in the area of workers' compensation, where employers pay the total contribution. Thus moves to weaken the protection workers have within the industrial relations system are likely to result in their falling into a very flimsy safety net.

The Development of the Australian Welfare State: Social Welfare

Charities

In the early period of European colonisation, responsibility for welfare was taken by the governors, with some additional provision by public charitable societies. By the middle of the nineteenth century, charitable societies, often under religious auspices, dominated (Dickey 1980). It was not until early in the twentieth century that systematic government provisions were established, but even so charitable organisations have remained a feature of the delivery of welfare services in Australia. Some organisations like the St Vincent de Paul Society and the Salvation Army remain active today. Indeed, their role has been reinforced since the late 1980s. For example, responsibility for emergency relief, the dispensing of immediate assistance of cash and kind, ceased to be a state function and was handed over entirely to a number of these traditional agencies. The Home and Community Care Services (HACC), a new Commonwealth-funded program aimed at keeping people, particularly the elderly, out of institutions, also relies heavily on non-government agencies for services which the government partially funds. As well, the HACC program relies heavily on informal care provided largely by relatives (Fine 1992).

Figure 15.1 Social Security Portfolio Program Structure, 1990–91

Program	Sub-program	Component

1 Income security for the retired
- 1.1 Age pension
- 1.2 Wife pension
- 1.3 Carer pension

2 Income security for people with disabilities
- 2.1 Invalid pension
- 2.2 Wife pension
- 2.3 Carer pension
- 2.4 Other disability payments
  - 2.4.1 Sheltered employment allowance
  - 2.4.2 Rehabilitation allowance
  - 2.4.3 Mobility allowance

3 Income security for the unemployed and sick
- 3.1 Unemployment benefit
- 3.2 NEWSTART
- 3.3 Job search allowance
- 3.4 Sickness benefit

4 Income security for families with children
- 4.1 Family allowance
- 4.2 Family allowance supplement
- 4.3 Sole parent pension
- 4.4 Jobs, education and training
- 4.5 Child support scheme
- 4.6 Other child payments
  - 4.6.1 Child disability allowance
  - 4.6.2 Double orphan pension

5 Provisions for special circumstances
- 5.1 Special benefit and other payments
- 5.2 Class B widow pension
- 5.3 Widowed person allowance
- 5.4 Telephone rental and postal concessions

Source: DSS, *Annual Report 1990–1991*: 5

Age and Invalid Pensions

Age pensions were the first of the social security provisions to be legislated for at the national level, in 1908, although they had been in existence in some states from the turn of the century (Kewley 1977: Chapter 3). They provided a modest pension to men and women at the age of 65 years. When finances permitted, the age for women was to be lowered to 60, and this happened in 1910. Permanently incapacitated persons between the ages of 60 and 65 were made eligible in the same year for an invalid pension paid at the same rate. Pensions were subject to means testing on both income and property.

These pensions were largely for the deserving white poor (recipients had to be 'of good character'), who had resided in the country for more than twenty-five years. The vast majority of Australian Aborigines, all people of Asian origin (unless born in the country) and ex-prisoners, were excluded (Kewley 1977: 75–76). Racist exclusions were similarly made in relation to the next benefit to be struck, the maternity allowance. It was established in 1912 and provided a one-off payment of five pounds on the birth of a live (white) child. This payment was abolished in 1976, when it was absorbed into the family allowance payment.

Age pensions today remain similar in structure to their original form: they are flat rate, means-tested, and paid from consolidated revenue. Recent developments which extend the coverage of superannuation across the labour force do, however, insert new principles into the system. To move towards superannuation means ultimately the linking of retirement benefits to working life income. Eventually, age pensions will be provided only for those without occupational coverage. This will leave the age pension a provision for the very poor, and will undermine the equalising effect that a flat rate pension system has had. Income-related retirement benefits are not new, since throughout this century and the last, better-off workers have had access to superannuation benefits subsidised by employers and the government, through tax concession. The change that is occurring is that the government is now directly promoting this form of more privatised insurance scheme as a universal system.

Ex-service Welfare

The next major developments in social welfare in Australia took place after World War I, with the establishment of a range of provisions for ex-servicemen, their dependants and a few women nurses in their own right. These provisions have been a feature of the Australian welfare state, although they are often overlooked in traditional discussions of it (Wheeler 1989). This is an example of the way in which the more powerful are able to quarantine their advantages from the stigmatising effect of having them labelled welfare measures. Provisions for ex-servicemen and their dependants were also more generous than traditional social welfare benefits.

Child Endowment

It was not until the 1940s that the remaining framework of the Australian social security system was established. In 1941, child endowment, which in 1976 became family allowance, was introduced. It initially provided a flat rate of five shillings per week to families in respect of each child except the first. At its inception this provision was also denied to Asian and Aboriginal women, and women from Papua or the islands of the Pacific (Kewley 1977: 104). While this benefit has since become racially universal, it has been restricted according to income, as part of the Hawke Labor government's drive to cut government spending. In 1987, a means test for family allowance was instituted, and where family income reached $50,000 per annum, it became subject to a steep rate of taper, then quickly cut out altogether. From January 1991, partial payments ceased, but the allowable joint income was set at $62,057 for one child, increasing by $3,104 for each additional child.

Widows' Pensions

The next major element of the social security system to be put in place was widows' pensions, in 1942. These recognised both *de jure* and *de facto* widows, and covered three categories. Class A widows were those responsible for at least one child under sixteen years of age; class B were those over the age of fifty but without dependent children; class C widows were those under the age of fifty and without dependent children, who were eligible for support for twenty-six weeks after their spouse's death, to allow a period of rehabilitation. Widow was defined widely, to include women who were divorced, had been deserted for more than six months, and whose partners were in a mental hospital and, later, prison. In 1973 the supporting mother's benefit was introduced, and this did away with the waiting period of six months for support, and established the eligibility for support of single mothers who had had no permanent relationship. A minor but highly significant change occurred in 1977, when this provision became the supporting parent benefit, and thus also available to fathers. This was the first time that fathers' parental role was recognised in social security provisions, something recommended by the *Report of the Commission of Inquiry into Poverty* (Henderson 1975).

Since 1987, significant changes have been made to widows' and parental provisions, in line with ensuring that the social security system does 'not unduly weaken the incentives to work' (Henderson 1989: 34). Class A widows' pensions disappeared, and in 1989 were replaced by the sole parent pension. This is gender-neutral but remains dependent on having responsibility for a child under sixteen years. Class B widows' pensions can no longer be claimed, and are only available to see through the entitlements of earlier recipients. The Class C pension became the widowed person's allowance and equally available to men. The period of six months' rehabilitation was reduced to twelve weeks. These pensions are now associated with a special job training schemes, the Jobs, Education and Training (JET) scheme.

Unemployment, Sickness and Special Benefit

The 1944 introduction of unemployment, sickness and special benefits completed the main framework of Australia's social security provisions. These three provisions remain available today, but in a form modified in 1991. Sickness benefit has become the sickness allowance, and is linked to rehabilitation schemes. Unemployment benefit has been changed significantly over the past decade, as unemployment rates have risen and the government has attempted to direct recipients into the labour market through a variety of labour market programs such as Newstart, Jobtrain and JET. For those sixteen and seventeen years of age, a job search allowance, at a lower rate and means tested in terms of parental income for those living at home, has replaced unemployment benefit. For other unemployed people, there are entitlements which increase in complexity and conditions. In particular, training conditions are being placed on entitlements (DSS 1991: 106–7). The invalid pension, now the disability support pension, is also linked to active vocational training and labour market programs (DSS 1991).

During the 1980s, the stringency of administration of all benefits was increased, to minimise fraud and discourage the ready availability of social security support at a time when its costs were rising steeply. They were rising because of an increase in the aged population, an increase in the numbers of sole supporting parents, and increased unemployment. All categories of income security were affected by scarcity of employment, because people not able to find work are more likely to take up any entitlement for which they are eligible.

Unemployment has risen more or less continuously since the early 1970s. There have been frequent waverings, but the overall trend is unmistakeable. The unemployment rate in 1970 was 1.4

per cent of the labour force. This moved up to 5.9 per cent in 1980 and reached 9.9 per cent in 1983. The Hawke government's policies, focused as they were on job creation, had some success in reducing unemployment for a time, and between the election years of 1983 and 1989, the rate dropped to 6 per cent. However, the gains were short-lived, and by December 1991 the rate had reached an all-time high since the 1930s Depression of 10.6 per cent.

By June 1992, one-third of the jobless, more than 300,000 people, had been out of work for more that one year and more than one-third of the those between the ages of 15 and 19 years looking for full-time work were unemployed (Lagan 1992: 2). The Labor government's pursuit of economic liberal policies, with their emphasis on developing the market and cutting government spending, were clearly not successful, and by early 1992, some modification to involve pump priming of a type more typical of Keynesian than liberal economic strategies started to be canvassed. Job creation programs came back onto the agenda.

The issue of unemployment benefit, and policies related to employment, were a dominant theme of the 1980s, and promise to remain so throughout the 90s. Unprecedented low levels of unemployment, as enjoyed during the post-war era, have been left behind. The intractable nature of unemployment must be seen against the background of major restructuring of the labour market. This has been going on for more than a decade in many advanced capitalist societies. It involves, among other characteristics, a move away from full-time work and the development of flexible hours. The process has been described by Wajcman and Rosewarne as the 'feminisation of the workforce' (1986: 15). In Australia the trend is also away from full-time employment of young people. The trend is for longer education, and a recent government review of the future of training recommended that 'by the year 2001, 95 per cent of 19-year-olds should have completed year 12 or an initial post-school qualification, or be participating in education and training' (NBEET 1992: 1).

Family Allowance Supplement and Child Support

Two recent and significant additions to the social security program are the family allowance supplement and the child support scheme. The former was introduced in 1987, and represents a break with the past in so far as it is aimed at families with low incomes in which there is an employed person as well as, in more traditional vein, families in receipt of social security. Providing assistance to the working poor is a break with Australian tradition, and is in effect a subsidisation of low wages which has the effect of undermining the notion of a living wage. This has not escaped the notice of some employers, who hail it as an important step in the process of more closely linking wages and salaries to the productivity of an industry rather than, as was established in the Harvester Judgment, the needs of workers. The family allowance supplement is stringently means-tested, and paid in respect of children. A greater amount is paid for children of 13–15 years. A rent subsidy is also available, and a health benefits card.

The child support scheme is also new in its conception. It sheets home financial responsibility for support of children of separated parents to the non-custodial parent. The maintenance is collected along with Pay As You Earn taxation. Prior to the introduction of this scheme in 1989, individual custodial parents were responsible in the first instance for the collection of maintenance, even where this had been ordered by the courts.

The official aims of the program are:

- that non-custodial parents should share the cost of supporting their children according to their capacity to pay;
- that adequate support be available for all children of separated parents;
- that Commonwealth expenditure be limited to what is necessary to ensure that these needs are met;
- to ensure that neither parent is discouraged from participating in the workforce; and
- that overall arrangements should be simple, flexible, efficient and respect personal privacy. (Child Support Advisory Group 1992: 1)

The aims of the project clearly reveal the concerns of the government to reduce spending both directly and through reduction of demands on the social security system through the employment of potential recipients. Here we see a clear statement of intention to ensure that incentives to work are not weakened.

Housing

There have never been extensive public housing programs in Australia. The issue of housing has been dealt with mainly through private ownership. Only the poorest have ever been able to qualify for the small pool of publicly provided houses or flats. Despite some persistent attempts over recent decades to address the problem, Australian Aborigines, who make up about 2 per cent of the population, remain the worst off in housing, as they do in respect of so many indices of well-being. Many Aboriginal people have no housing, or remain housed in the sort of shelters associated with the worst shanties on the outskirts of the poorest Third World cities. Direct government expenditure on Aboriginal housing programs for 1986–87 represented 3.5 per cent of direct outlays on housing (Jones 1990: 197). As well, Aboriginal families are likely to be over-represented in public housing, again reflecting their generally impoverished circumstances. They have a rate of home ownership of about one-third of that of the population generally (Choo 1990: 42). The issue remains one of the country's most intractable social problems.

Health
Until the mid-1970s, health care was covered only by private insurance, together with a system of free medical treatment for the poor, located mainly in public hospitals. A national health scheme was established by the reforming Whitlam Labor government in 1975. It was then partially dismantled by the subsequent Liberal government, and then restored in somewhat different form by the Hawke Labor government in 1983. This type of to-ing and fro-ing has led Castles (1989: 30) to conclude that Australia has the world's 'most reversible' welfare state. He sees this occurring because of a lack of firm support for such a state by the middle classes.

Social Security Review
The latter part of the 1980s saw the most extensive review of social security ever undertaken. It was headed by Professor Bettina Cass, and its findings and recommendations have been influential in the extensive changes that have occurred since. A key, though largely implicit, debate revolved around whether targeted benefits, deliberately aimed at the poorest, are to be preferred over universal ones. This debate was implicit, because from the outset the apparent costliness of universal benefits ruled out any serious official discussion of this point of view. In a climate in which the dominant discourse was focused on the reduction of government spending and intervention, a universalist discourse was not politically acceptable (Cass 1986; Cass 1988).

Cass effectively took up a position supporting finely targeted benefits. This has proved effective in raising the income levels of the targeted group, largely through income directed at the working poor with families, and those receiving social security. The measures directed to these groups were, first, the family income supplement and later the family allowance supplement and the child support scheme.

For example, the income of sole parents, who had become the poorest group, increased by 12 per cent between 1982 and 1990, compared with an increase of only 3.3 per cent for two-parent non-farm families as a whole (Bradbury, Doyle and Whiteford 1990: 3). A similar effect was achieved through direct government policy in relation to the aged, following the discovery of their relative poverty by the Henderson Inquiry in the mid-1970s (Henderson 1975).

Nonetheless, critics of this approach point out that such gains are easily eroded, something which has happened to the aged while the government has been focusing on sole parent families and those with a number of children. Castles' criticism of the lack of support by the middle classes is germane here. Øyen (1986: 278) has also remarked on the vulnerability of the Australian social security system, suggesting that support for social welfare provisions actually arises from the degree to which they reflect established inequalities. If the better-off get more, as they are accustomed to in other arenas, they are likely to provide political support. Levels of inequality can then be reduced, at least to a degree. While flat rate and means-tested provisions do more effectively reduce in-equality (Mitchell 1991), in the process they produce dilemmas, because support from the middle classes remains tenuous for provisions from which they benefit little. The Swedish welfare state, which has been more successful than most in remaining intact through the political ascendency of economic liberalism in the 1980s, has deliberately provided universal benefits of high quality to maintain the commitment of the middle classes who benefit from these services. Redistribution in Sweden has been left to taxation policy (Bryson 1992: Chapter 3).

Fiscal Welfare

Taxation is a fundamental factor in any consideration of the general distribution of well-being in society: hence Titmuss' focus on fiscal welfare. Nonetheless, it is more common for fiscal policy to be seen entirely in economic terms, and for it to be divorced from considerations of welfare. What tends to happen is that welfare policies are seen as applying to the poor, while economic policies apply to the rest of the population. Keens and Cass, in a study of fiscal welfare in Australia, pointed out

> that fiscal welfare differs from social welfare not only in terms of the groups for whom it provides but also in terms of its generosity, stigma and the extent to which expenditure is made public.
>
> (Keens and Cass 1982: 33)

Fiscal affairs have two distinct dimensions: one is spending, the other is revenue raising, which provides the funds to spend. So far, in discussing social welfare, I have been dealing with spending. I will now consider more closely the equity effects of raising the money which pays for these and other state activities. Governments use a range of techniques for revenue raising, including taxation on income, sales, services or products, resource rent, royalties and bonds, to specify only a few examples of what, in advanced capitalist societies, is a complex operation. Because of the daunting task of considering fiscal policy in a comprehensive manner, the discussion here will focus mainly on taxation on income and wealth. However, in a comprehensive analysis of equity effects, all forms of revenue, and potential revenue raising should be subject to detailed analysis.

Taxation not only provides governments with money as a raw material. The process of taxation in itself offers the single most extensive tool for socio-political engineering available to the state. Taxation must be considered 'an instrument of social policy rather than merely as a source of finance' (Pond 1980: 47). Taxation can be used to redistribute money and other resources, and for the encouragement, or discouragement, of various activities and practices. Taxation relief may be given for investment in certain industries, farming being a time-honoured one. But there is a limitless range of possibilities. Attempts may be made to discourage certain behaviour patterns, as well. For example, taxes in many countries are high on tobacco and alcoholic beverages, not only to raise revenue, but at least partly in order to discourage the use of unhealthy products and cut the longer-term costs of their usage. The capacity of the taxation system to redistribute costs and benefits is extensive.

Ostensibly, fairness is built into a taxation system through the administrative device of progressivity. A tax system is progressive if, as income rises, the amount extracted as a tax liability rises as a proportion of the income (Prest and Barr 1985: 293). Progressivity of taxation can be supported on grounds other than fairness. The argument that users should pay can also be invoked because, on the whole, those who are better-off actually receive more benefits from the public coffers than do the less-well-off. They are also likely to have more to lose and therefore they benefit more from defence, the legal system, policing, and the general social infrastructure. Owners and shareholders of businesses are likely to reap most advantage from infrastructural services such as communications and financial systems. As well, the better-off are likely not only to reap the most direct benefits from the education system by becoming qualified themselves, but also make more use of other highly-qualified practitioners such as lawyers, architects, accountants, artists and the like. One could go on and on listing areas of greater benefit; a major problem, however, is how actually to value them. There seems to be no easy way of converting these advantages into money terms (Cope 1987: 42). Again, we are confronted with the inadequacies of conventional discourses and accounting systems, for effectively dealing with benefits received by the better-off.

The issue of what is a fair rate of progressivity with respect to income tax rates is contentious and clearly political. With the rise of economic liberalism, even the relatively low levels of redistribution that were being pursued have been reduced in many countries. In Australia, the top rate was dropped from 60 to 49 cents, and at the other end of the scale, taxation burdens were extended by, for example, including social security payments as income.

At the same time, however, some attempt has been made by the Australian government to do away with some shelters which have served the interests of the better-off. For example, fringe benefits taxes have been introduced which recognise as income for tax purposes, some occupational benefits, such as company cars, entertainment, meals and travel. Strictly speaking, such benefits had always been defined as income, but the taxation authorities had not pursued the matter with any diligence. A capital gains tax has also been introduced, and some taxation on lump sum payments of superannuation.

The taxation system in Australia draws proportionally more money from the better-off, as Graph 1 in Figure 15.2 shows. The graph sets out the amount of taxes paid by each of ten deciles of income, and also shows the distribution of the social wage. The figures are taken from the Australian Bureau of Statistics' 1988–89 Household Expenditures Survey (White and Posselt 1992: xii–xiii). The data show that lower income deciles pay lower taxes and receive more benefits, while higher deciles pay higher taxes and get fewer benefits, though only marginally fewer than all but the three lowest deciles.

Graph 2 provides a comparison of private and overall incomes after the deduction of tax and the added benefits. The change in dollar terms for the lowest and highest deciles are as follows: the lowest decile has a negative average private income per week of –$1.05, accounted for by net losses from business and property. This was increased to an average of $147 by the addition of benefits and subtraction of taxes. For the highest income group, an average of $1,665 becomes $1,228 after the distribution of taxes and services (White and Posselt 1992: xii). This still leaves a

Figure 15.2

Graph 1   All Households: Private and Final Income by Average
Weekly Gross Income Decile

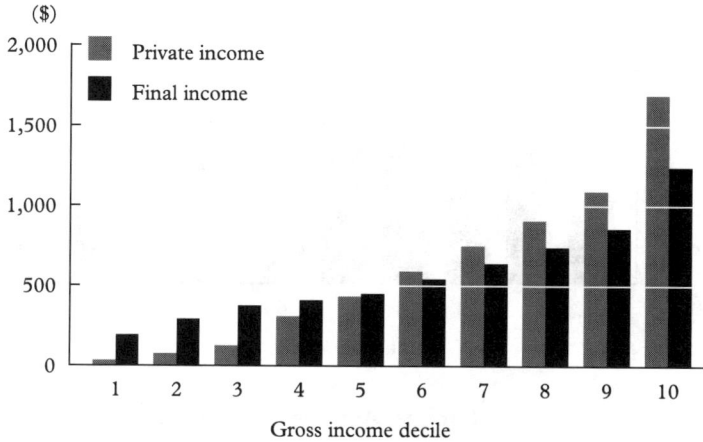

Graph 2   All Households: Taxes and Benefits by Average Weekly
Gross Income Decile

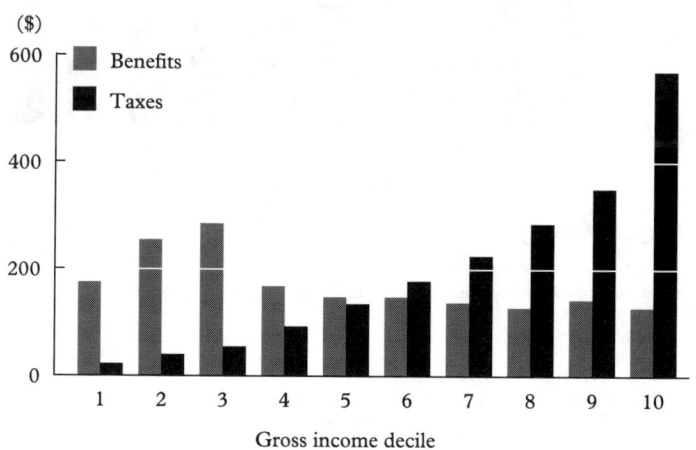

Graph 3   Life Cycle Groups: Average Weekly Private and Final Income

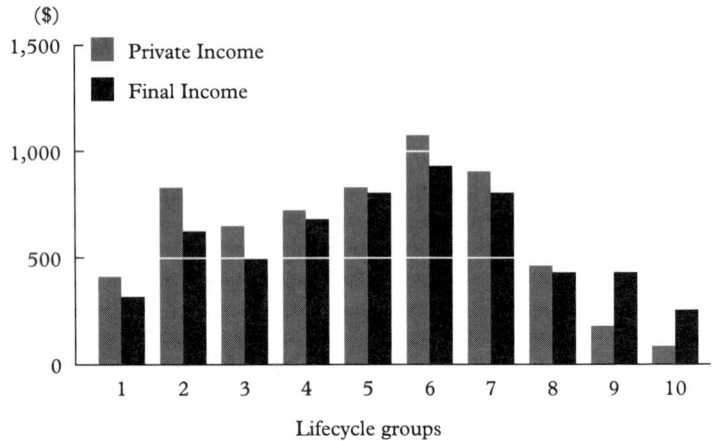

Graph 4   Life Cycle Groups: Average Weekly Benefits and Taxes

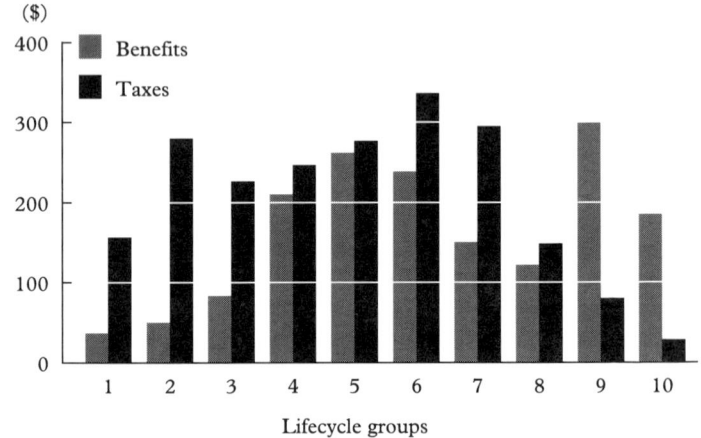

Lifecycle Groups

1	Single person only, under 35
2	Married couple — husband and wife only, reference person under 35
3	Eldest child under 5
4	Eldest child 5 to 14
5	Eldest child 15 to 20
6	Married couple with dependent and non-dependent children only
7	Married couple with non-dependent children only
	Married couple, husband and wife only
8	Reference person 55 to 64
9	Reference person 65 and over
10	Single person only, 65 and over

Source: White and Posselt 1992: xiii–xiv

wide gap between top and bottom income groups, and the assessment is made only in terms of the social wage, which currently excludes many fiscal and occupational benefits, which favour the better-off.

These data show an increase in what is referred to as vertical equity (that is, the relationship of the top to the bottom of the scale) through redistribution via benefits and taxes. We also can assess what is referred to as horizontal equity, that is, redistribution between those with fewer demands on their income to those with more demands. Horizontal equity can be approached through a consideration of lifecycle stages. Broadly, benefits are transferred to those in the child rearing phase and to the elderly, where needs are greater (see Graph 3, Figure 15.2), while taxes are lowest for the elderly (see Graph 4).

While Graph 1 does show an increase in equity through government intervention, the question remains as to whether this should be considered sufficient. The income of the highest decile averages eight times that of the lowest. On top of this, there is evidence to show that Australia is becoming a more unequal society. Overall, between 1983 and 1989, inequality of income has been calculated to have increased by around 21 per cent (Lombard 1991).

Perhaps the most important question in relation to fiscal welfare remains what is left out of calculations when income is taxed, and the differential opportunities people have to shelter their advantages. Currently, many increases in net worth are exempt from taxation. There has been much debate about a concept of 'a comprehensive income tax'. This involves the principle that tax is 'levied annually on all accretions to economic power', with these to be taxed at the same rate (Cope 1987: 78). There are inherent problems about what to include even using a comprehensive definition: what about increases in pension rights, the value of an increase in skill or education, profits retained by companies, or increased value of furniture or paintings not intended for sale? Then there are questions such as how to cope with inflation. What about the advantages of having a wife or husband at home full-time, versus the additional costs of employment? Fluctuations in benefits, too, would often be wide and such a scheme would be difficult to administer. However, the more computerised transactions become, the more feasible such accounting also becomes.

The importance of a broader concept of income can be illustrated by the issue of home ownership in Australia. Public expenditure on housing, like income security, has often been seen as providing direct benefits to lower income groups. This is through rent subsidies or the direct government provision of rental accommodation or homes for purchase at cheaper-than-market prices. It is true that government funds directly devoted to public housing advantage the poorest, since access to public housing, like pensions, is stringently means-tested. Traditionally in Australia, the largest proportion of public revenue devoted directly to housing has been spent on public housing and rental assistance, rather than assistance for private purchase (ABS 1987: 55; Harding 1984: 76), largely because there is no tax relief in respect of interest on mortgage payments, a common concession in many countries.

If we look to revenue foregone, however we find that it is home owners who are significantly advantaged, because the family home is privileged by being exempt from capital gains tax. Not only this, if the capital that the house represents were to be invested elsewhere, the income accruing would be taxable. Yet the taxation system ignores imputed income or imputed rent; this is not treated as income from capital for taxation purposes. Estimates are not even available of what this privileging of capital invested in family homes costs in foregone revenue, let alone any detailed statistics on how the benefits from this policy are distributed. Nonetheless, very clearly the benefits increase with the value of the home that is owned. It quickly becomes apparent that were the full picture to be taken into account in Australia, it would transpire that it is not the poor who benefit most from government housing policy, but home owners, and the owners of expensive homes more than the owners of cheaper homes (Kemeny 1983: 106).

The labour movement's strategy of establishing a living wage, together with various government schemes to assist home purchase, have been relatively effective in promoting a high rate of private home ownership for non-Aboriginal people. In its turn, this had something of a levelling effect on wealth distribution. The rate of home ownership peaked in the 1960s, at just on 72 per cent (Milligan 1983: 119). However, despite various incentives, including the introduction of a first home owners' scheme, which accounted for 6 per cent of direct Commonwealth outlays on housing in the 1986–87 financial year (Jones 1990: 195), the rate of home ownership has fallen over recent decades. In the mid-1980s, it was 69 per cent, due partly to a drop in disposable income coupled with rising house prices. However, the drop is partly a statistical effect caused by a widening of the base number of households. From the 1970s on, young people started moving out of the family home at a much earlier age, to establish their own households. Dwellings were almost always rented, and this has altered the balance between rented and owned accommodation. When the data are analysed in detail they show an increase in home ownership at each age level (Ironmonger 1989: 9).

In a formal sense, the Australian taxation system embodies the notion of equity through an apparently progressive structure and the principle that low incomes do not attract income tax. The effectiveness of the principles depend, however, on the rate to which they are actually put into effect. When we look at the total taxation system, it is clear that some groups of people are in a far better position than others to minimise the tax they pay. This is difficult for employees whose contributions are deducted as Pay As You Earn deductions, and much easier for those with their own businesses, or who are in those forms of employment with flexibility, allowing a complex system of deductions. We need a much more comprehensive understanding of the effects of fiscal policy, and whose welfare it actually underpins, before we can come close to an effective understanding of the distribution of benefits to all Australians.

Occupational Welfare

Occupation is a crucial determinant of well-being in all advanced industrial societies, as any contemplation of the effects of unemployment starkly demonstrates. Occupation remains the primary source of income for most people. The importance of an adequate income from occupation certainly did not escape the architects of the Australian wage earners' welfare state. However, occupations deliver far more than income. They also deliver status, interest, varying levels of comfort and amenity, and varying opportunities to increase one's resources both personal (e.g. skills) and economic. Occupational welfare is therefore a very broad concept. If a comprehensive approach to the topic were to be taken, it would include a vast range of benefits and disbenefits, which are unevenly distributed. Jamrozik (1984: 96) compares some of the advantages of professionals over manual workers, in terms of their implications for strengthening class interests:

> Unlike manual workers, the professionals and managers discuss work in paid time; the workers in their own time; the professionals have conferences; the workers have 'stop-work' meetings. The face-to face decision-making and conferences allow for exchange of ideas and identification of common views and interests, thus raising 'class consciousness'. Furthermore, such methods of work as conferences and conventions have a high component of social life, narrowing and blurring the distinction between production and consumption which in manual occupations are clearly separated.

In virtually all advanced capitalist countries, apart from New Zealand and Australia with their flat rate pension and benefit schemes, occupation is also a key determinant of the level of benefits available from the social security system. And even in Australia, retirement income has been very much affected by the availability of superannuation, which is really a private age pension. Working life earnings and retirement income will be linked for more and more Australians, as the government increasingly encourages private superannuation.

Superannuation represents a major form of occupational welfare and is disproportionately a benefit of the better-off. Contributions to superannuation funds attract very generous taxation concessions, and employers often pay contributions at twice the rate of employees. Tax concessions are related to the marginal tax rate. Higher income earners, therefore, receive more in concessions. For example, someone earning over $50,000 in 1992 was entitled to a concession of $490 for $1,000 invested in superannuation. Someone earning more than $21,000 but less than $50,000 was entitled to $390; someone earning around $10,000 was entitled to $200, and if one fell below the tax threshold and had a nil tax rate, then no concession was received. Krever has aptly called this an upside-down subsidy (1989).

Fewer Australian women than men are in private pension schemes. In 1988, the proportion of male workers covered was 61.2 per cent, while for women it was only 36.5 per cent, though this proportion has been systematically increasing over recent years. Overall, 58 per cent of full-time workers were covered, but only 19.3 per cent of part-time workers were (ABS 1989). The proportion covered increased steadily with income, from 3 per cent in 1987 in the lowest income category, to 72 per cent in the highest (Gunasekera and Powlay 1987: 15–20).

Because women live longer and receive the age pension at a younger age, they receive more from public pensions than men. However, not only are they less likely to have superannuation: if they do, it is likely to be of a modest kind. Because age pensions are means-tested, private superannuation often nullifies that entitlement, but the rate of private pension is likely to be far higher anyway. While superannuation has very much been a benefit for those who are better-off, the development of a national superannuation scheme, announced in 1991, aims to change this. Nonetheless, for the foreseeable future, lower paid workers will reap few benefits from this scheme and tax concessions to the wealthy remain substantial.

Part of the economic logic of encouraging private pensions in Australia was to promote savings, and for its potential to encourage investment and reduce inflation. The official position also suggests that private pensions would save the government money on age pensions, especially as the population ages during the coming decades. However, this is a contested point. It has been demonstrated that the government will not save money, especially where higher income earners are concerned, unless it does away with tax concessions. The tax subsidy to the private pension contributor is often greater than would be paid out to them through the social security system. This is partly accounted for by the fact that the rate of the basic pension remains low, at only around 26 per cent of average weekly earnings in 1992 (Toohey 1992: 3). Calculated in relation to the current rates, Toohey has estimated that it would not be until close to the end of the twenty-first century that budgetary savings on pensions would outweigh the tax concessions for superannuation (Toohey 1992: 3).

Australian private pension schemes provide a stark example of the manner in which government and employer policies can magnify inequality through the medium of the occupational system. A similar principle applies across many forms of occupational welfare. Benefits are almost always directly linked to occupational status and inversely linked to economic need. They are rarely related to principles of merit and efficiency.

The area remains analytically murky, with little systematic effort to unpack its distributional dimensions. The reasons for this are multiple, but it is often strategic for taxation and public relations reasons to keep such benefits away from publicity. This is facilitated by the fact that, because these advantages go to the better-off anyway, they can often be well hidden in the complex accounting systems used by those earning larger incomes. The process of exploiting taxation benefits is made easier when taxpayers are in command of the book keeping systems of private businesses, and where professional accountants can be employed. The art of 'creative' accounting was not, after all, developed to serve the interests of poorer people or those of the general public.

The introduction of the fringe benefit tax by the Hawke Labor government in 1987 did introduce a measure of equity as far as revenue raising was concerned. Nonetheless, there does not seem to have been any diminution of occupational welfare; indeed there is some evidence to suggest that this has become even more widespread. The introduction of the fringe benefit tax seems to have focused on the issue, and the enhancement of higher salaries has become a refined art. Employment packages, which consist of salaries and a range of benefits, are almost mandatory for higher status occupations.

Regular surveys of fringe benefits by the Australian Bureau of Statistics demonstrate that virtually all benefits are directly related to the income and status of occupations. The studies present information on roughly 14 categories of payment outside wages or salaries. These include: holiday costs, low interest finance, goods and services, housing, electricity, telephone, transport, medical expenses, union dues, club fees, entertainment allowances, shares, study leave and superannuation. The studies regularly demonstrate that those in the top earning category receive far more benefits than those in the lowest. In 1981, Jamrozik and his colleagues estimated that for top and middle management the benefits received added between 35 and 40 per cent to the value of their basic earnings. For low income earners, the estimated increase was less than 10 per cent (Jamrozik *et al.* 1981: 97). Benefits received by these low income earners typically consist of being able to purchase goods and services from their employer organisation at cost or discount prices (Graycar and Jamrozik 1989: 184).

In a recent survey of occupational welfare among immigrants, Jamrozik, Boland and Stewart (1991) demonstrate that the negative effects of the processes of restructuring the economy fall disproportionately on workers in the lower paid, lower skilled jobs. These employees are often immigrants from non-English-speaking backgrounds. This offers another example of the importance of occupational welfare as a fundamental contributor to well-being.

Conclusion

As the Australian welfare state changes, so too must our ways of analysing and understanding it. The past decade has seen fundamental changes, changes which have been focused more on the market and efficiency than on issues of equality and social justice. Government intervention generally has been under question, particularly in the areas encompassed by the social wage. This has brought about many changes to the social security system, for example, which has become intent on channelling dependent groups into the labour market. The pursuit of collective activities, such as education, health and social welfare services, as part of the social wage, have also become more and more subject to market principles. Fees for tertiary education are just one example. There is a strong commitment to expand the private, rather than the public, domain.

This state commitment to the market means that, more than ever, it is imperative that we cover the broadest canvas in our analysis of welfare, to answer the classic sociological question: who benefits? Historically, as we have seen, a broad approach to welfare delivered through the fiscal and occupational systems, has been lacking. This has resulted in a partial understanding of the beneficiaries of state interventions and non-interventions.

In the 1990s, with such an explicit concentration on, and commitment to, the private domain, which traditionally benefits the better-off, we can certainly no longer justify a narrow focus on social welfare. The challenge is to develop modes of analysis which adequately deal with the effects of all government interventions, not just the social wage, when assessing the 'welfare' effects of government policies for all citizens, not just the poor.

References

Australian Bureau of Statistics (ABS) (1987) *Effects of Government Benefits on Household Income: 1984 Household Expenditure Survey, Australia*, Catalogue No. 6537.0. Canberra: ABS.

Australian Bureau of Statistics (ABS) (1989) *Superannuation Australia, November 1988*, Catalogue No. 6319.0. Canberra: AGPS.

Bradbury, Bruce, J. Doyle and Peter Whiteford, (1990) *Trends in the Disposable Incomes of Australian Families, 1982–83 to 1989–90.* Sydney: Social Policy Research Centre.

Bryson, Lois (1989) 'The Proletarianisation of Women: Gender Justice in Australia', *Social Justice* 16 (3): 87–102.

————(1992) *Welfare and the State: Who Benefits?* London: Macmillan.

Cass, Bettina, (1986) 'The Case for A Review of Aspects of the Australian Social Security System', Background/Discussion Paper 1, Social Security Review. Canberra: Department of Social Security.

————(1988) 'Income Support for the Unemployed in Australia: Towards A More Active System', Background/Discussion Paper 1, Social Security Review. Canberra: Department of Social Security.

Castles, Frances (1985) *The Working Class and Welfare: Reflections on the Political Development of the Welfare State in Australia and New Zealand, 1890–1980.*Wellington: Allen and Unwin.

————(1989) 'Australia's Reversible Citizenship', *Australian Society*, September: 29–30.

————and Mitchell, Deborah 'Three Worlds of Welfare Capitalism or Four?', *Governance* 5(1).

Child Support Advisory Group (1992) *Child Support in Australia.* Canberra: Department of Social Security, Ref: 1552.

Choo, Christine (1990) *Aboriginal Child Poverty.* Melbourne: Brotherhood of St Laurence.

Cope, J. M. (1987) *Business Taxation: Policy and Practice.* Wokingham, Berkshire: Van Nostrand Reinhold.

Department of Social Security (DSS) (1991) *Annual Report 1990–91.* Canberra: AGPS.

Dickey, Brian (1980) *No Charity There*. Melbourne: Nelson.

Edwards, Anne (1989) 'Feminism and Social Welfare: Alternative Representations of Women and Gender in Social Policy Literature', in A. Jamrozik (ed.), *Social Policy in Australia: What Future for the Welfare State?* Sydney: Social Policy Research Centre.

Esping-Andersen, G. (1990) *The Three Worlds of Welfare Capitalism*. Oxford: Polity Press.

Fine, Michael, (1992) *Community Support Services and Their Users. The First Eighteen Months*, Social Policy Research Centre, Reports and Proceedings 100. Kensington: University of New South Wales.

Graycar, Adam and Jamrozik, Adam (1989) *How Australians Live: Social Policy in Theory and Practice*. Melbourne: Macmillan.

Golding P. and S. Middleton (1982) *Images of Welfare*. Oxford: Martin Robertson.

Gough, Ian (1979) *The Political Economy of the Welfare State*. London: Macmillan.

Gunasekera, M. and Powlay, J. (1987) 'Occupational Superannuation Arrangements in Australia', Background/Discussion Paper 21, Social Security Review. Canberra: Department of Social Security.

Harding, Ann (1984) *Who Benefits? The Australian Welfare State and Redistribution*. Sydney: Social Welfare Research Centre.

Henderson, David (1989) 'Perestroika in the West', in J. Nieuwenhuysen (ed.), *Towards Freer Trade Between Nations*. Melbourne: Oxford University Press.

Henderson, Ronald (1975) *Poverty in Australia*, Commission of Inquiry into Poverty, First Main Report. Canberra: AGPS.

Ironmonger, Duncan (ed.) (1989) *Households Work: Productive Activites, Women and Income in the Household Economy*. Sydney: Allen and Unwin.

Jamrozik, Adam, Marilyn Hoey and Marilyn Leeds (1981) *Employment Benefits: Private or Public?* Sydney: Social Welfare Research Centre.

———(1984) 'The Welfare State: An Instrument of Redistribution or of Inequality?', in Rosemary Hooke (ed.), 54th ANZAAS Congress: SWRC Papers SWRC Reports and Proceedings No. 47. Kensington: University of NSW.

———(1989) 'The Household Economy and Social Class' in D. Ironmonger (ed.), *Households Work: Productive Activities, Women and Income in the Household Economy*. Sydney: Allen and Unwin.

———(1991) Class *Inequality and the State*. Melbourne: Macmillan.

———Boland, Cathy and Stewart, Donald (1991) 'Immigrants and Occupational Welfare', Working Papers on Multiculturalism 10. University of Wollongong: Centre for Multicultural Studies.

Jones, Michael A. (1990) *The Australian Welfare State*. Sydney: Allen and Unwin.

Jordan, Bill (1987) *Rethinking Welfare*. Oxford: Basil Blackwell.

Keens, Carol and Cass, Bettina (1982) *Fiscal Welfare: Some Aspects of Australian Tax Policy. Class and Gender Considerations*. Sydney: Social Welfare Research Centre.

Kewley, T. H. (1977) *Social Security in Australia*. Sydney: Sydney University Press.

Krever, Rick (1989) 'The Plain Guide to the Super Saga', *Australian Society*, October.

Lagan, Bernard (1992) 'Jobless Rate Back to Record Level of 10.6%', *Sydney Morning Herald*, 12 June.

Lombard, Marc (1991) 'Income Distribution in Australia 1983–1989', *Economic Papers* 10(3), September: 52–63.

Macarthy, P. G. (1976) 'Justice Higgins and the Harvester Judgement', in J. Roe (ed.), *Social Policy in Australia*. Sydney: Cassell.

Milligan, Vivienne (1983) 'The State and Housing: Questions of Social Policy and Social Change', in A. Graycar (ed.) *Retreat from the Welfare State*. Sydney: Allen and Unwin.

Mishra, Ramish (1984) *The Welfare State in Crisis*. Brighton: Wheatsheaf.

Mitchell, Deborah (1991), 'Comparing Income Transfer Systems: Is Australia the Poor Relation?', in Francis Castles (ed.), *Australia Compared: People, Policies and Politics*. Sydney: Allen and Unwin.

National Board of Employment, Education and Training (NBEET) 'The Australian Vocational Certificate Training System', *NBEET Bulletin* 10, April.

OECD (1987), *OECD Economic Surveys 1986–87: Australia*. Paris: OECD, March.

Øyen, Else (1986) 'The Muffling Effect of Social Policy', *International Sociology* 1 (3): 271–82.

Pond, Chris (1980) 'Introduction' in C. Sandford, C. Pond and Robert Walker, *Taxation and Social Policy*. London, Heinemann.

Prest A. R.. and N. A. Barr (1985) *Public Finance in Theory and Practice*. London: Weidenfeld and Nicolson.

Rose, Hilary (1981) 'Re-reading Titmuss: The Sexual Division of Welfare', *Journal of Social Policy* 10 (4).

Sanders, Will (1985), 'The Politics of Unemployment Benefit for Aborigines', in D. Wade-Marshall and P. Loveday (eds), *Employment and Unemployment*. Darwin: North Australia Research Unit.

Saunders, Peter and Matheson, George (1992) *Perceptions of Poverty, Income Adequacy and Living Standards in Australia*, Social Policy Research Centre, Reports and Proceedings, No. 99. Kensington, University of New South Wales.

Sawer, Marian and Simms, Marian (1984), *A Woman's Place: Women and Politics in Australia*. Sydney: Allen and Unwin.

Sinfield, Adrian (1978) 'Analyses in the Division of Welfare', *Journal of Social Policy*, 7 April: 129–56.

Thane, Patricia (1982) *The Foundations of the Welfare State*. London: Longman.

Titmuss, Richard (1974) 'The Social Division of Welfare: Some Reflections on the Search for Equity', in *Essays on 'The Welfare State'*. London: Allen and Unwin.

Toohey, Brian (1992) 'Super's Billion-dollar Incentive', *Australian Society*, June.

Wajcman Judy and Rosewarne, Steve (1986) 'The "Feminisation" of Work', *Australian Society* 5 (9): 15–17.

Waring, Marilyn (1988) *Counting for Nothing: What Men Value and What Women are Worth*. Wellington: Allen and Unwin.

Wheeler, Lorraine (1989) 'War, Women and Welfare', in R. Kennedy (ed.), *Australian Welfare: Historical Sociology*. Melbourne: Macmillan.

White, Judith and Posselt, Horst (1992) 'Government Redistribution of Income', in Ian Castles (ed.), *Australian Economic Indicators: May 1992*, ABS Catalogue 1350.0. Queanbeyan: AGPS.

Wilenski, Peter (1986) *Public Power and Public Administration*. Sydney: Hale and Iremonger.

Yeatman, Anna (1990) *Bureaucrats, Technocrats, Femocrats: Essays on the Contemporary Australian State*. Sydney: Allen and Unwin.

Chapter Sixteen

The Attainment of Higher Education in Australian Society

Martin Hayden and Peter G. Carpenter

Introduction

Higher education in Australia has undergone extraordinary change during the past decade. There has been a complete restructuring of the system, so that there are now far fewer but much larger higher education institutions, and the binary system of universities and colleges of advanced education has been replaced by a 'unified national system' of universities and university colleges. Equally important has been the striking growth in the rates of attainment of higher education, particularly among young people, so that there are now far more students in higher education in Australian than at any time in our history as a nation. The higher education student population is probably more socially representative now than it has ever been in the past.

In this chapter we record changes in the rates of attainment of higher education in Australian society that have occurred during the past decade.We report government initiatives that have contributed to these changes, and we review the research literature concerning the determinants of the attainment of higher education in Australia, focusing particularly on the reasons why young people proceed from school to higher education. Our starting point for the chapter is a brief account of how sociologists tend to view the process of the attainment of higher education.

A Sociological Perspective on the Attainment of Higher Education

Saha (1990: 4–5) argues that the primary object of the sociology of education is

> the application of the sociological perspective to the study of educational structures and schooling processes. Its primary object is to investigate the manner in which societies through education both reproduce their structures, institutions, and culture, and at the same time initiate and introduce change. It also provides an important base for the development of educational policy.

This perspective is well illustrated by the way in which many sociologists have approached the topic of the attainment of higher education. In the usual form of these studies, entry to higher education has been regarded as representing the attainment of social status, and attempts have been made to identify how social origins affect this process, both directly and indirectly, by means of other social, educational and psychological factors. Path models are generally used to estimate the direct effects of social origins on the types of decisions taken about entry to higher education, together with their indirect effects by means of home, school, peer group, aspiration, ability and achievement variables. Important studies here are those of Blau and Duncan (1967), Sewell *et al.* (1975, 1976, 1980), Alexander *et al.* (1975, 1980, 1987), Jencks *et al.* (1983), and Halsey *et al.* (1980). In Australia, Broom *et al.* (1980) have investigated the general relationship between social origins and educational and social attainments, while Elsworth *et al.* (1982, 1983), Carpenter and Western (1984) and Williams (1987) have investigated the specific relationship between social origins and entry to higher education.

This approach differs from the one generally adopted by economists. In the most frequently adopted form of this approach, decisions about entry to higher education are said to be influenced by perceptions of the investment yield from having a higher education qualification. The basic proposition is: given the tastes and preferences of young people for higher education, demand for it will increase as the private rate of return (the income advantage of a higher education qualification less the cost, including income foregone, of obtaining it) increases relative to the return from other investment opportunities. Examples of this approach are numerous (see, for instance, Freeman 1971; Handa and Skolnik 1975; Leslie, Johnson and Carlson 1977, Jackson 1978; Wish and Hamilton 1980; Bowman 1981; Pissarides 1981; Manski and Wise 1983; and, from Australia, Nicholls 1984).

The sociological approach also differs from that adopted in some social psychological literature, where the main area of interest has been the ways in which the distinctive aspects of an individual's personality interact with key elements in the social situation to affect decision making on entry to higher education. Examples of this approach are provided by Beswick (1975), Ekehammar (1978), Rubenson (1976, 1983), Harnqvist (1978) and Carpenter and Fleishman (1987).

Each approach has contributed to an understanding of the influences on decision making of young people about going on to higher education. The economic approach, for example, has highlighted the role of financial expectations (Ferber and McMahon 1979; Williams and Gordon 1981; Psacharopoulos 1982), labour market opportunities for graduates (Freeman 1971, 1976, 1981) and the provision of student financial aid (Jackson 1981; Reuterberg and Svenson 1983). The sociological approach has highlighted the role of academic achievements in school, parent encouragement of further studies, educational and vocational aspirations, teacher encouragement of further studies and peer group influence (see, for example, Sewell and Hauser 1980; Carpenter and Western 1989). The social psychological approach has highlighted the role of individual differences in abilities and motivational attributes (Beswick 1975; Beswick, Hayden and Schofield 1983; Ekehammar 1978; Biggs 1982).

The relevant scientific literature on the attainment of higher education is extensive. For reviews from different countries, see Jackson and Weathersby (1975), Cohn and Morgan (1978), Gordon (1981), Jackson (1981), Hayden (1982), and Anderson and Vervoorn (1983).

The study of the attainment of higher education is of considerable significance to sociologists. Having a post-school educational qualification is known to affect later occupational and income attainments (Broom *et al.* 1980; Jones and Davis 1986). In 1986, for example, unemployment rates among people aged 25 years or more were 3.1 per cent for degree holders, but 8.3 per cent for those without a high school diploma (Department of Employment, Education and Training 1988). Furthermore, the holding of a higher education qualification is known to be distributed unequally among important social groupings in the population. In a recent (1986) Census in Australia, some 15 per cent of people aged 15 years or older held some form of tertiary education degree or diploma (Australian Bureau of Statistics 1988), yet this proportion was greater for males than for females, and young people were far more likely than older people to have attained a tertiary education qualification.

Since the early 1960s, there has been a strong tradition in social science research in Australia that has focused on the dimensions of inequality in the attainment of post-secondary educational qualifications among the population (see Western 1983 for a review). Recent empirical research (e.g. Graetz 1988) indicates a decline in the effects of social origins upon total years of education as the provision for schooling at both high school and university levels has expanded. But inequalities in both educational participation and outcome, associated with social class, gender, race, location and school sector, remain. Drawing on a variety of social science research orientations, Australian researchers have examined particular key stages in the educational attainment 'process' to try to uncover the sources of these observed inequalities. Examples of this kind of research have been collected in various readers in the sociology of education (for example, Katz and Browne 1970; Edgar 1974; Browne and Magin 1976; Browne and Foster 1983). Many of these studies, often using cross-tabular or correlational techniques, have sought to show the unequal representations of individuals from different social backgrounds in the educational system beyond the compulsory years (e.g. Radford 1962; Radford and Wilkes 1975; Lewis 1976; McGraw *et al.* 1977; Anderson *et al.* 1980; Sturman 1985; Power *et al.* 1986).

What has not been well understood in Australia until recent years is how the earlier influences of social and community origins and the 'intervening contingencies' (Broom *et al.* 1980: 8) of schooling and socialisation impact upon the likelihood of participation in higher education. Just as fundamentally, the question of why young people proceed from school to higher education in Australia, though it has attracted considerable attention over recent years, is not well understood. The policy implications of the question have no doubt contributed to a growth of interest in this area. The Commonwealth government has continued to express a desire for increases in the rates of participation by young people in higher education, especially among groups who are less well represented in higher education at present (the children of poorer families, members of certain ethnic minorities, rural dwellers and Aborigines). The search for more effective instruments for implementing this policy has inevitably directed attention back to the basic question of why young people go on to higher education.

The Changing Pattern of Higher Education Attainment in Australia

A feature of the past decade in Australian higher education has been the rapid growth both of enrolments in higher education and participation rates in higher education. The growth of enrolments has been spectacular, from 341,390 persons in 1982 to 534,538 in 1991, an increase of 56.6 per cent (Department of Employment, Education and Training 1991: Table 7). This reflected an increase in female enrolments (up 81.6 per cent between 1982 and 1991) much more than an increase in male enrolments (up only 35.3 per cent between 1982 and 1991). An effect of this pattern was that from 1987 onwards, and for the first time ever in Australia, there were more female than male enrolments in higher education. By 1991, 53.3 per cent of enrolments were female.

The growth in female enrolments was particularly pronounced in the area of study related to health. Such enrolments were considerably boosted by the progressive transfer of basic nurse education from hospitals to higher education institutions, beginning in 1985, but this development did not account for more than one-fifth of overall growth in female enrolments. Female enrolments increased in a wide range of health science disciplines, and also substantially in the business, arts, science and law fields (Department of Employment, Education and Training 1991a: Table 4). In addition, female enrolments in post-graduate studies increased substantially during the decade (Department of Employment, Education and Training 1990b: 2).

Further detail of the changes during the decade is provided by considering age participation rates in higher education at two points in time. Table 16.1 presents details of the participation rates in higher education of 17-to-24-year-olds, 25-to-29-year-olds and 30-to-64-year-olds in 1982 and then in 1990. The figures presented are offered according to gender.

Table 16.1 shows clearly that the age group experiencing the most rapid growth in higher education participation during the period from 1982 to 1990 was the 17-to-24-year-old age group. The growth in higher education participation for this group was strong overall (up from 9 per cent in 1982 to 13.2 per cent in 1990), and the growth was far more pronounced among females (up from 8.5 per cent in 1982 to 14.3 per cent in 1990) than among males (up from 9.5 per cent in 1982 to 12.2 per cent in 1990). The only growth in higher education participation over the period among the 25 to 29-year-old age group was among females (up from 3.4 per cent in 1982 to 4 per cent in 1990), and this was also the case among the 30 to 64-year-old age group (up for females from 1.5 per cent in 1982 to 2 per cent in 1990).

The rapid increase during the 1980s in the higher education participation rates of young people followed directly from a surge in their retention rates at school to Year 12. Rates of retention to Year 12 nearly doubled during the 1980s, from 34.8 per cent in

Table 16.1 Age Participation Rates in Higher Education in
Australia, 1982, 1990

Year and age groups	Participation rates in higher education (%)		
	Males	Females	Persons
	1982		
Aged 17–24	9.5	8.5	9.0
Aged 25–29	5.0	3.4	4.2
Aged 30–64	1.6	1.5	1.5
	1990		
Aged 17–24	12.2	14.3	13.2
Aged 25–29	4.3	4.0	4.2
Aged 30–64	1.6	2.0	1.8

Source: Department of Employment, Education and Training (1991) 'Education
Participation Rates', Higher Education Division, May: Table 3.3

1981 to 64 per cent in 1990. Figure 16.1, which presents details
of this growth, shows that the increase in retention rates to Year
12 was more pronounced among females. The reasons for the
growth in retention rates in school to Year 12, and subsequently
in the participation rates of young people in higher education,
have been the subject of widespread speculation in the relevant
literature. There can be no doubt that the Labor government's
policy, outlined below, of greatly expanding opportunities for young
people to proceed to higher education, enabled such growth to
take place. The conditions that precipitated the increased tendency for young people to stay on in the education system,
however, are not so well understood. High youth unemployment
rates during the period (see Figure 16.2) almost certainly reduced
the incentive for young people to leave school, and various
initiatives of the government during the period (outlined below)
were no doubt also effective in dissuading young people who
might have dropped out of the education system from doing so.
The reasons why they choose to remain in the system are complex, however, and, as will be reported later in this chapter,
involve not only externally-provided incentives and opportunities
for going on with school and higher education, but also a range of
individual psychological needs and judgements about what is of
value to their lives.

Government Initiatives During the 1980s

In marked contrast to the preceding conservative Liberal-National

Figure 16.1 Apparent Retention Rates to Year 12

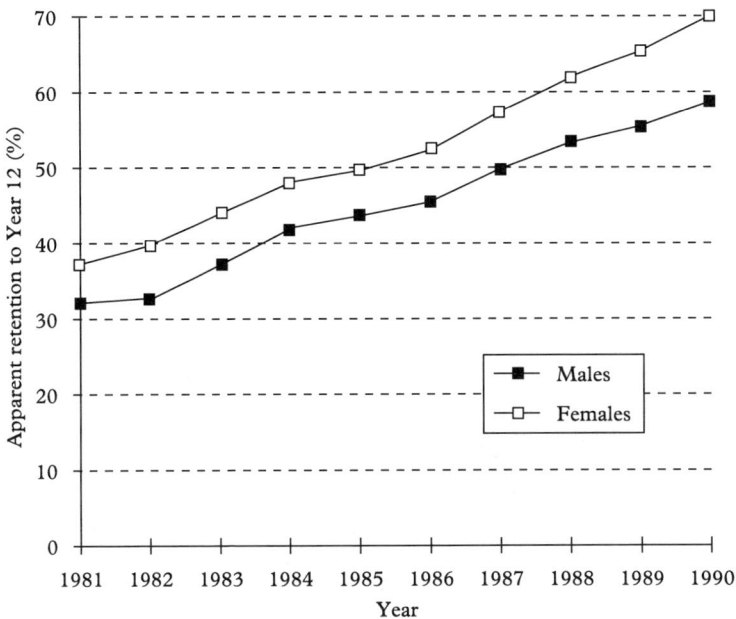

Sources: ABS (1991) *Schools Australia 1990*, Cat. No. 4221.0

Figure 16.2 Rates of Unemployment

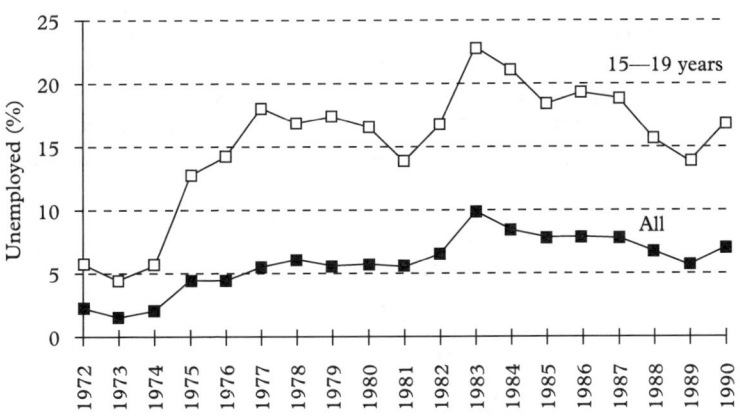

Sources: Personal Communication from Officers of ABS

government, which since the mid-1970s had exercised constraint on growth in higher education, and whose policies were not conspicuously driven by equity considerations, the Labor government elected to power in 1983, and re-elected in 1984, 1987 and 1990, embarked on a program of boosting participation rates in higher education, and directing these additional places as much as possible to young people from backgrounds regarded by the government as disadvantaged.

Labor's achievement in providing more places was spectacular. Soon after its election in 1983, the government gave notice that it would fund 3,000 new places in higher education for school leavers in 1984. This promise was fulfilled, and the initiative was followed up by an expansion of the funded student load for each of the remaining years of the 1980s: 1,300 new places in 1985, 2,000 new places in 1986, 3,000 new places in 1987, 3,890 new places in 1988, and 6,500 new places in 1989 (from figures supplied by the Department of Employment, Education and Training). The cumulative effect of this progressive expansion in the enrolment capacity of higher education, together with the increase in enrolments as a result of the retention of students into subsequent years (the so-called 'pipeline' effect), was substantial. The initiative is estimated to have contributed to an additional 80,000 enrolments in higher education between 1983 and 1990 (from figures supplied by the Department of Employment, Education and Training).

Associated with the expansion of capacity were initiatives intended to encourage young people from disadvantaged backgrounds to take up increased opportunities for participation in higher education. The Participation and Equity Program, involving direct financial grants to schools, was introduced in 1984 to improve retention rates to Year 12 among young people from socially and economically disadvantaged backgrounds. This initiative was supplemented by the decision that priority in funding for higher education for the 1985–87 triennium should be given to increasing the rates of participation in higher education of Aborigines, migrants, lower income families, women, the handicapped and people living in outer metropolitan areas with limited access to higher education. Most of the extra places subsequently made available to higher education during the triennium were allocated to institutions more likely to be attended by students from these backgrounds (Commonwealth Tertiary Education Commission 1987: 97). A further initiative was the establishment in 1985 of a Higher Education Equity Program to provide funding for innovative pilot projects aimed at increasing the higher education participation rates of specific disadvantaged groups (Commonwealth Tertiary Education Commission 1986).

During the period from 1985 to 1987, the government turned its attention to the removal of financial disincentives for young people staying on in the education system. The eligibility requirements for unemployment benefits were progressively restructured so that the financial incentive for a young person from a disadvantaged background to receive unemployment benefits became less than that of remaining in full-time education with support from alternative government sources (Maas 1990). In 1987, financial assistance for unemployed young people was made harder to get, and assistance to disadvantaged groups was more narrowly targeted: for example, unemployment benefits for 16 and 17-year-olds were abolished and replaced by a family means-tested Job Search Allowance, not payable for thirteen weeks after leaving school.

Student allowances also underwent major change. In 1987, AUSTUDY was introduced as the main scheme for the provision of financial assistance for students aged sixteen years and over in secondary and higher education in Australia. AUSTUDY replaced three other schemes, the Secondary Allowances Scheme, the Adult Secondary Education Assistance Scheme and the Tertiary Education Assistance Scheme, and in so doing simplified the provision of means-tested financial support to those from less-well-off backgrounds who remained in education. The real value of student allowances was generally maintained from 1983 onwards, and a guarantee of the importance attached by the government to this was given by its decision that from 1987 onwards AUSTUDY allowances were to be adjusted to keep pace with inflation.

In 1988, the government issued a policy statement on higher education in which it renewed its commitment to improving access to higher education for young people from low income families, rural areas, certain immigrant backgrounds, Aborigines and the disabled (Dawkins 1988: 20). In a subsequent document, entitled *A Fair Chance for All* (Department of Employment, Education and Training 1990c), specific objectives and targets for national and institutional planning for equity in access to higher education were stated. The government proposed implementing these by means of direct negotiations about funding with higher education institutions.

There were other important Labor government initiatives in relation to higher education during the 1980s. While not motivated primarily by equity considerations, these initiatives affected opportunities for participation in higher education by particular groups of young people regarded by the government as disadvantaged. The progressive transfer from 1985 of all nursing education, from hospitals to the higher education sector, has already been mentioned. The implications of this initiative in terms of the opportunities it provided for increased female participation in higher education were significant. Whereas in 1984 there were only 1,300 basic nursing students in courses within higher education institutions, by 1988 there were almost 13,000, the large majority of whom were female (Department of Employment, Education and Training 1991a).

In 1988, the government initiated reforms to the structure of higher education in Australia that reduced the number (but not the size) of institutions by about one-third, and abolished the binary system of universities and colleges. The effects of this were far-reaching: in 1987 there were 19 universities and 45 Colleges of Advanced Education in Australia, and by 1990 there were less than 40 institutions, mostly universities. The exact equity implications of these changes are difficult to isolate, but there is no doubt that young people from less well-off backgrounds, who were more likely to have been enrolled in the college system, benefited most from the additional prestige of obtaining a degree from a university.

One other important initiative was in relation to tuition fees. In 1987, the government introduced a higher education administration charge ($250 in 1987 and $263 in 1988) for all full-time and part-time higher education students. This was the first direct charge on higher education students since the abolition of tuition fees in 1974. Its potential as a disincentive for young people from less-well-off backgrounds to participate in higher education was limited, however, because various categories of students classified as needy were exempt from the charge. It is estimated that about 35 per cent of higher education students were thus exempt. In 1989, the government replaced the administrative charge with the Higher Education Contribution Scheme (HECS), which required a contribution of $1,800 (in 1989) for a year of equivalent full-time study, with charges on a proportional basis for part-time study. Two payment options were provided: an 'up-front' option, which reduced the contribution to 85 per cent of the normal rate, and a 'deferred-payment' option, under which students did not begin paying off the charge until their income reached a minimum threshold level. The impact of this initiative on the participation rates of young people in higher education appears to have been slight, regardless of their social and economic backgrounds (Robertson, Sloan and Bardsley 1990; National Board of Employment, Education and Training 1992: 20–21).

It should be recorded at this point that the various initiatives of the Labor government since 1983 in relation to higher education took place against a background of significant economic and social change in Australia. There was a serious economic recession in 1982–83, after which rates of unemployment, particularly among young people, remained relatively high (see Figure 16.2). Australia's standing as a wealthy country also declined sharply during the decade in response to, amongst other things, a deterioration in Australia's foreign trade position (Aitken 1988; Matthews 1988). This, in turn, prompted the government to place great emphasis on the importance of higher education to Australia's future prosperity as an exporter of goods and services, with a higher valued-added component based on international educational superiority.

Determinants of Higher Education Attainment in Australia

Before examining in some detail a recent extensive investigation of higher education participation in Australia, it is useful to review bivariate relationships between particular characteristics of individuals' backgrounds and achievements and their participation in higher education, and to clarify why such backgrounds and achievements might affect higher education participation in the first place. We commence with social class.

Social Class
Despite rising levels of educational participation in general in Australia (see Graetz 1987, 1988), the links between social class and educational attainment remain striking. As Beswick (1987) comments, however, the relationship between parental occupation, the common index of social class position (Western and Western 1988) and participation in higher education is exceptionally complex, and the widespread view that higher education participation in Australia continues to be the exclusive preserve of those from upper middle class homes needs careful examination.

Researchers have advanced a number of theories to explain observed social inequalities in educational participation in capitalist societies. Some suggest that secondary schools actually select and allocate students according to their social origins into a social class structure, thereby ensuring the continuity of élite groups from one generation to the next (Bowles and Gintis 1976; Lindsay 1981; Connell *et al.* 1982), a view strongly disputed by Williams 1976; Featherman 1980; Olneck and Bills 1980; and Bills 1983. Other researchers argue that schools and universities certify the cultural advantages of children from better-educated families by adopting teaching methods, styles, curricula and language appreciated only by such students (Bernstein 1977; Bourdieu 1973; Bourdieu and Boltanski 1978; Carpenter 1985). Another group argues that individuals' educational attainments are affected by their ability to employ particular enabling conditions within their social environments (Cuttance 1980; Marjoribanks 1980). Families from dominant social class groups can, for example, decide what is valued in the educational system and take whatever means are necessary to pass on to their children the skills and attitudes related to the achievement of the valued goals of schooling.

What seems to occur is that the social class milieu in which an individual is reared imposes major constraints upon educational aspirations and achievements. Studies in the United States, England, and Australia have shown that social class funnels young people towards particular types of school, as well as amounts and types of education (Featherman and Hauser 1978; Halsey, Heath and Ridge 1980; Poole 1983; Western 1983). One cogent explanation of this is that the plans or intentions of young people for the years after the completion of school may actually reflect the kinds of educational and employment experiences they have been exposed to in their homes. Parents may be able to pass on to children knowledge of the educational system using job or educational contacts (Roberts 1968, 1984), and may directly assist them to cope with its demands (Halsey *et al.* 1980). In times when the market for higher education graduates tightens, upper middle class families in particular have been found to allocate as large an amount of resources as necessary to ensure that their children gain access to higher education and are sponsored into economically rewarding careers (Gross and Western 1981).

Gender
Gender, like the socio-economic origins of individuals, may affect both aspirations for higher education and actual participation therein (Carpenter and Fleishman 1987). In this sense gender can be seen as reflecting opportunities provided by the social structure. In the past decade reports in Australia (Commonwealth Schools Commission 1975, 1984; Powles 1986) have highlighted problems associated with the way schools influence the education of women. Gender-based expectations within schools, restricted access to subject choices, gender stereotypes in career counselling, and teacher-student relationships all may function to lower women's self-esteem, competence and aspirations (Kessler, Ashenden, Connell and Dowsett 1985; Sampson 1984; Vickers 1984).

Type of School

One of the ways parents may attempt to assist their children in the struggle for scarce and valued jobs and places in higher education is to be prepared to buy what they perceive as the 'best' education. Australian secondary schools fall into three categories: government, Catholic, and independent; the latter two charge tuition fees. Currently 69 per cent of Australia's secondary school students attend government schools, 20 per cent attend Catholic schools, and 12 per cent attend independent schools (Australian Bureau of Statistics 1991).

Whether attendance at different types of school affects young people's educational attainments, independently of their social origins, is a matter of controversy both in Britain (Halsey, Heath and Ridge 1980; Edwards, Fitz and Whitty 1985) and Australia (Rosier 1978; Anderson and Vervoorn 1983; Graetz 1990; Williams and Carpenter 1991). Two main explanations have been advanced to account for school differences in educational attainments (Williams and Carpenter 1990). The first points to the quality of education at different types of school. It suggests that people who attend non-state schools generally have higher attainments because they receive a better education. In this view, the schools themselves are responsible for generating differences in attainment. The second explanation points to selective recruitment. It suggests that private schools are able to recruit students from privileged social backgrounds, with greater levels of ability and other advantages conducive to higher educational attainments. Here school-sector differences are due not to the schools themselves but to the students who attend those schools.

The question of school-system effects on participation in higher education has been addressed in the usual manner. Elsworth and others (Elsworth and Day 1983; Elsworth, Day, Hurworth and Andrews 1982), after controlling for social background, Year 12 academic results, school curriculum, and student perceptions of the benefits of higher education, reported that students from private schools were more likely to enter higher education. Almost all the apparent advantage was due to superior performance in Year 12 examinations. Beswick, Hayden and Schofield (1983), Power, Robertson and Baker (1986) and Williams (1987) establish similar patterns of effect. Carpenter and Western (1984) indicate that the patterns may be more complex, involving gender by school sector interactions.

British research (Halsey, Heath and Ridge 1980) offers some support for this picture. Similar patterns emerge in the United States. Falsey and Heyns (1984) used the 'High School and Beyond' data to show that private school students were more likely to enter higher education even when high school curriculum stream, aspirations, social origins and performance on tests of academic achievement were held constant. Much of the relevant literature presumes that non-government schools serve to perpetuate advantage by means of unique socialisation experiences and social contacts not available in other types of school. Falsey and Heyns suggest that private school advantage was due to the organisational context of private schools, their provision of counselling for university-bound students, and the orientation of staff to assist such students. Persell and Cookson (1985) took the matter further by identifying additional influences, including the ability of parents to meet high tuition costs, the pursuit of advanced courses during the final year of secondary school, and the use of personal contacts to smooth out the admissions process for entry to more selective universities.

Interpersonal Support

In addition to parents and teachers, peers also influence subjective norms about entering university. If one's classmates generally plan to pursue their education, this creates a perception that such behaviour is proper and expected. A substantial body of research documents peers' influence on educational aspirations (Spenner and Featherman 1978). Whereas parents and teachers are seen as normative referents, their expectations taking the form of social norms which encourage conformity, peers are seen as comparative referents, their educational plans or intentions forming a standard against which a person's own aspirations are reflected. Canadian studies (Gilbert 1977; Williams 1972) and Australian studies (Hayden 1982; Saha 1982) have emphasised the importance of gender as a moderator of perceived parental encouragement. Parental encouragement had greater impact on young men's behavioural intentions and early attainments than on those of young women. The available evidence generally suggests that the facilitative impact of encouragement for higher education is affected by gender.

Academic Self-concept and Academic Achievement

Academic self-concept, a reflection of an individual's assessments of personal academic abilities or accomplishments (Maruyama, Finch and Mortimer 1985) has been found to correlate with the educational attainments of young adults. Looker and Pineo (1983) report a correlation of 0.53 between academic self-concept measured at 17-18 years of age and educational attainment four years later. McKinnon and Anisef (1979) found a correlation of 0.49 between similar variables among a sample of Canadian youth, while Williams (1987) reported 0.40 as the correlation between academic self-concept and higher education participation among Australian youth.

An important issue of academic self-concept concerns its possible mediation of the effects of actual school academic achievements upon educational decision making. Academic achievement measured at school affects the likelihood of entrance to higher education, which in turn affects occupational attainment.

Ethnicity
Australia is a nation with a sizeable proportion of its population born in overseas countries. Since Australia has an active immigration program and a declared policy of multiculturalism, ethnicity takes on some importance as an aspect of social origins. Arguments about ethnic disadvantage flow easily from the notion that new arrivals must cope with beginning in a new culture and, for some, in a new language. Programs of compensation have grown up around this idea.

Where Australian adolescents are concerned, students from non-English-speaking immigrant backgrounds have high aspirations (Sturman 1985), and are less likely to drop out of high school than their Australian-born counterparts (Miller and Volker 1987; Williams 1987). Furthermore, data from the ACER (Williams 1987) show that people from non-English-born backgrounds have the highest rates of participation in higher education. Immigrant groups emphasise education for their children.

Rurality
The issue of the impact of geographic location upon educational participation generally, and higher education in particular, is one of long standing. The Commonwealth Schools Commission (1985) held to the position that specific educational responses were needed to address the special needs of students arising from the effects of geographic isolation. More recently, the National Board of Employment, Education and Training took up this argument again in its statement *A Fair Chance for All* (DEET 1990).

Geographical location seems to exercise its main effect in Australia on retention rates to Year 12 (Williams 1987), though there is evidence (Williams *et al.* 1980) that coming from a rural family or attending a rural school does not affect to any large extent these students' learning of basic skills. Research also shows that geographic location affects higher education participation via the intervening contingencies of the impact of perceived encouragement of parents and teachers for higher education and the models of peers, one's academic self-concept, career aspirations and orientations and, ultimately, academic achievement (Elsworth, Day, Hurworth, and Andrews 1982; Carpenter and Western 1989; Williams 1987).

The Process of Higher Education Attainment

Why do young people in Australia go on from school to higher education? Hayden and Carpenter (1990) propose that it is simply because young people find higher education to be both attractive and attainable.

The Attractiveness of Higher Education

An expectancy-valence theory of motivation provides a useful insight into the nature of the influences upon the attractiveness of higher education to a young person. Within such a theory, motivation, 'the strength of a tendency to act in a certain way' (Atkinson and Birch 1978: 348), is said to be a function of both perceptions of the value of an activity and expectations that certain valued outcomes of the activity will result from its adoption. The attractiveness of higher education to a young person may be said to be influenced, therefore, by whatever affects the young person's perceptions of the value of higher education, or shapes expectations about attaining valued outcomes from participation in it.

Perceptions of the value of an activity are a function of the way in which incentives from an individual's immediate situation combine with his or her psychological needs. There are many incentives for going on to higher education that are typically brought to the attention of a Year 12 student. Some of these are intrinsic to higher education (for example, the incentive of undertaking a new area of study that will be conceptually complex and challenging), and some are extrinsic to higher education (for example, the incentive of better financial rewards as a graduate). The extent to which these influence a young person's attraction to higher education depends on how they combine with psychological needs or motive structures. Thus, the incentive of undertaking a new area of study that will be conceptually complex will have greatest impact upon a young person with a tendency to be curious about the world; and the incentive of better financial rewards as a graduate will have the greatest impact on a young person with a tendency to be attracted to the material pay-offs of a course of action.

Expectations that certain valued outcomes will result from undertaking a course of action are affected by the cognitive structures of the individual in relation to the activity. Cognitive structures refer here to knowledge, beliefs and conceptions about a particular activity (Feather 1975: 13). As a result of interaction with family, teachers and friends, as well as through exposure to the media and through personal experiences of the education system, a young person in Year 12 can reasonably be anticipated to have developed a relatively stable set of cognitive structures, and thus expectations, in relation to higher education. These expectations can be changed, however, by any late change in circumstances, such as the offer of a valuable scholarship that markedly widens expectations about being able to enjoy the benefits of higher education, free of the worry of running out of money.

In summary, then, higher education will be attractive to a young person to the extent that motive forces relevant to higher education are aroused by incentives for going on to it, and to the extent that the young person's knowledge, beliefs and conceptions about higher education predispose him or her to expect that certain valued outcomes of participation in such education can be obtained. Both individual attributes (motive structures and cognitive structures) and characteristics of the individual's immediate situation (the availability of incentives, and any change in opportunities for obtaining desired outcomes from the pursuit of higher education) act in combination to affect the attractiveness of such education for the young person.

The Attainability of Higher Education
Such attainability is also affected by the way in which individual attributes act in combination with characteristics of a young person's situation. Relevant attributes concern abilities and achievements, and situational characteristics include the admission and selection policies of higher education institutions and the availability of financial support for studies.

In Australia selection into higher education is determined by individual institutions of higher education, within a context in which government policies and labour market requirements are important influences. Higher education in Australia is financed predominantly by government, the policies of which affect the aggregate number of places available in particular types of professional courses. Higher education institutions are also responsive to the demands of the labour market in deciding how many places should be provided in particular fields. The typical way of allocating the scarce number of places available to young people within higher education is by first offering a place to those applicants with the best Year 12 examination results. The attainability of a course in higher education is affected, therefore, by the interplay between a young person's achievements in Year 12 examinations and the selection policies of higher education institutions (which, in turn, reflect other situational characteristics, such as government policies and labour market conditions). Because prerequisite study requirements for entry to certain higher education courses (particularly within the sciences) are also applied, students wishing to enter these courses must have undertaken secondary school studies in certain groups of subject areas, that is, they must have particular types of Year 12 achievements.

Another characteristic of a young person's situation that can affect the attainability of higher education concerns financial support. In Australia, support from the government or from prospective employers is generally contingent upon having at least passed Year 12 examinations, and being offered a place in higher education. Its availability is linked, therefore, with Year 12 achievements. Support from parents may be similarly linked, in that parents may be more or less willing to make offers of financial support for full-time study, depending on Year 12 academic achievements and their estimate of the likelihood of subsequent academic success.

In summary, the attainability of higher education is affected by the way in which individual attributes (in this case, abilities and achievements) interact with opportunities provided. The two main types of opportunity for going on to higher education referred to here are the availability of places in higher education and the availability of financial support for studies.

Sources of Incentives and Opportunities

Six institutional sources of incentives and opportunities for a young person to proceed to higher education may be identified. These are: the home, the peer group, the school, the higher education system, the government and the labour market.

Members of the home (parents in particular) have been widely found (in the relevant literature cited above) to have a substantial influence upon decision making by young people on entry to higher education. The reason advanced here for this influence is the extensive nature of the incentives and opportunities parents can provide for going on higher education. They can provide both extrinsic incentives (for example, by making their approval or their financial support contingent upon participation in higher education), and intrinsic incentives (for example, by providing prompts that highlight the internal satisfaction to be obtained from further studies). They can also provide opportunities for going on to higher education by making available financial support, accommodation, assistance with travel, and so on. The extent to which parents provide these incentives and opportunities is likely to be related to their perceptions of the value of higher education, and these seem likely to be related to certain socio-cultural characteristics of the home. In general, parents who have themselves experienced the rewards provided by additional years of education are more likely to be willing and able to provide incentives and opportunities for a young person to go on to higher education.

Members of the peer group can also exert influence, for example, by making the incentive of continued membership of the group contingent on going on to higher education, by sharing knowledge and opinions about higher education that affect expectations of its likelihood of providing valued outcomes, or by making certain opportunities available (such as shared accommodation or travel) that affect the attainability of higher education. In general, the more members of the peer group aspire to proceed to higher education, the greater will be the incentives and opportunities provided by them for a young person to proceed.

The encouragement of teachers and the type of school attended can affect entry to higher education in various ways. Teachers can play an important role in making students aware of what further study at a university or college involves and, to that extent, can draw the attention of young people to possible incentives for going on to higher education, and to possible resultant outcomes. In some types of school, teachers may make a greater effort to do this than in others.

The influence of government on the probability of transition by young people to higher education in Australia occurs principally by means of the control exercised over both the provision of the capital and recurrent costs of higher education, and the provision of financial assistance to students. In the main this influence is directed mainly at affecting opportunities for going on to higher education, rather than at providing incentives.

The labour market is one of the most important sources of extrinsic incentives for participation in higher education. It is the case in Australia, as in many other countries, that a young person who goes on to qualify for a university or college qualification is more likely to obtain a well-paid occupation with high social standing.

A Model

The model of entry to higher education advanced by Hayden and Carpenter (1990) posits that the probability of a young person going on from school to higher education is a function of the combination of certain attributes of the young person, and certain characteristics of his or her immediate situation. The model does not give expression to all of the variables introduced in the theory from which it derives, but the main ones are included (and the linear model proposed is assumed to approximate the monotonic relationships implied by the theory).

Two attributes of individual young persons are included in the model. These are: a young person's motivation to proceed to higher education, and his or her achievement attributes. It is proposed that the stronger the attraction to certain readily identifiable features of higher education, the greater is the likelihood of the young person being influenced by incentives to proceed. It is also proposed that the better the Year 12 academic achievements of the young person, especially in science subjects (because of their widespread use as prerequisites for entry to various fields of study within higher education in Australia), the greater is the likelihood of being able to take advantage of opportunities to proceed from Year 12 to higher education.

Five characteristics of a young person's immediate situation are also included. These are: home location; parents' socio-economic status; parents' encouragement of further studies; teachers' encouragement of further studies; friends' plans for further study; and type of school attended. It is proposed that the young people who are more likely to go on to higher education are those:

1. whose homes are in the city rather than the country, because the opportunities (mainly in the form of lower costs) for young people from the city to go on to higher education are greater;

2. whose parents are better-off and better-educated, because such parents are considered likely to be more willing and able to provide both incentives and opportunities for going on to higher education on account of their personal experience of its rewards, their personal knowledge of what it involves, and their likely ability to be able to afford to support their children financially through higher education;

3. whose parents encourage participation in higher education, because such parents are more likely to provide incentives and opportunities for going on to it;

4. whose teachers encourage participation in higher education, because they are more likely to provide incentives

for going on to higher education and to point out the likely beneficial outcomes of proceeding;

5. whose friends are likely to go on higher education, because they may provide incentives for going on to higher education, and may also create opportunities for doing so (through shared travel and accommodation, for example); and

6. who attend private schools (particularly, non-Catholic independent schools) rather than government schools, because in private schools (in Australia, certainly) there tends to be an expectation that most Year 12 students will proceed to higher education, which provides social reinforcement for this kind of behaviour and shapes expectations about what the appropriate course of action is upon completing Year 12.

Hayden and Carpenter propose that the individual and situational factors introduced above combine both additively and interactively to affect the probability of entry by a young person from Year 12 to higher education. Interaction effects on decisions taken on entry to higher education have not been widely investigated in the relevant literature (but see Gasson, Haller and Sewell 1972; Elsworth *et al.* 1982: 73–78; and Alexander *et al.* 1987), and this contributes to some difficulty in predicting their exact nature.

Hayden and Carpenter (1990) have tested this model of higher education participation using data collected on direct entry from school to higher education from separate studies in Victoria and Queensland.

Their analyses indicated that, among both sample groups, Year 12 academic achievements and parent encouragement of further studies were significant independent predictors of direct entry to higher education, and that, among Victorian respondents, having done mainly science subjects in Year 12 was an additional significant independent predictor. Among Queensland respondents, the career value attached to higher education was an additional significant independent predictor. Analyses of certain interaction effects indicated that, among Victorian respondents, the combination of high teacher encouragement of further studies and a strong attraction to the extrinsic rewards of higher education significantly enhanced the likelihood of proceeding to it, while among Queensland respondents, the combination of low parent encouragement of further studies and low value attached to higher education significantly diminished the likelihood of going on.

These results add to the existing body of knowledge in several respects. First, they confirm and give additional precision to a developing pattern in Australian findings whereby factors such as Year 12 academic achievements (including the type of Year 12 subjects studied) and the encouragement of significant others such as parents, teachers and friends, have been found to have an important bearing upon the likelihood of direct entry from school to higher education. The importance of these factors has been found to be much greater than that of social background and home location variables (though such background variables certainly affect rates of retention in school to Year 12) (Hayden 1982). Second, the interaction effects identified in the results are interesting in themselves, in that they show how a certain combination of an individual motivational attribute and a circumstance of the immediate situation can have a significant impact upon direct entry to higher education. The interaction effects are also relatively new to the relevant empirical literature because, as indicated above, the effects of variables on entry to higher education have generally not been investigated in previous Australian studies.

What is most important about the results, however, is their meaning within the context of the theory developed. The importance of Year 12 academic achievements to the likelihood of direct entry to higher education is a clear indication that the availability of a place in higher education does matter in terms of who goes on from school to higher education. Higher education institutions in Australia are generally selective in their admission practices, and Year 12 examination results are the 'currency' used to gain admission to preferred courses. Year 12 students with good examination results have greater access to preferred courses within higher education, and students with good examination results in science subjects have an added advantage (particularly in Victoria) because of their even wider range of access to such courses (that is, not only to courses with science prerequisites but also to those without them).

The attractiveness of higher education is clearly also an important consideration affecting who goes on from school to higher education. Particularly among Queenslanders, but also among the Victorian respondents, those young people who showed a tendency to be attracted to higher education were more likely to have proceeded directly to it. Parent and teacher encouragement are especially important in this context. The results of the interactions provide supportive evidence of this. Among Victorian respondents, the combination of being attracted to the extrinsic benefits of higher education and having teachers point out the benefits of going on, significantly affected the likelihood of doing so. Among the Queensland respondents the negative effects on the likelihood of proceeding by placing a lower value on higher education, were significantly contained where parent encouragement of such education was strong.

The policy implications of the results, and of the theoretical context within which they have been derived, are extensive. Two broad sets of implications are identified here. First, the results suggest that measures designed to increase the availability of places in higher education will positively affect the likelihood of direct entry. Such measures might include greater provision of places at higher education institutions, a reduction in the use of prerequisite study requirements that restrict access by students to certain courses, an increase in the ability of parents to support their children in higher education (such as by the greater availability of student aid or by the use of taxation incentives). Second, the results suggest that measures that have a favourable impact upon the attractiveness of higher education will positively affect the likelihood of direct entry. In particular, if parents and teachers are well informed about the benefits of higher education for young people and are encouraged to exercise positive support for their going on to higher education, then the young people concerned are more likely to proceed. The best sources of this information would seem to be higher education institutions themselves, plus the government.

References

Aitken, D. (1988) 'The Background to the Green Paper', in W. Toombs and G. Harman (eds), *Higher Education and Social Goals in Australia and New Zealand*. Armidale: Department of Administration and Higher Education Studies, University of New Zealand.

Alexander, Karl L. and Eckland, Bruce K. (1975) 'Basic Attainment Processes: A Replication and Extension', *Sociology of Education* 48: 457–95.

———Eckland, Bruce K. and Griffin, Larry J. (1975) 'The Wisconsin Model of Socioeconomic Achievement: A Replication', *American Journal of Sociology* 81: 324–42.

———and ——— (1980) 'The "Explorations in Equality of Opportunity" Survey of 1955 High School Sophomores', *Research in Sociology of Education and Socialisation* 1: 31–58.

———, Pallas, Aaron M., and Holupka, Scott (1987) 'Consistency and Change in Educational Stratification: Recent Trends regarding Social Background and College Access', *Research in Social Stratification and Mobility* 6: 161–85.

Anderson, D.S., Boven, R., Fensham, P.J. and Powell, J.P. (1980)

Students in Australian Higher Education: A Study of their Social Composition since the Abolition of Fees, ERDC Report 23. Canberra: AGPS.

———and Vervoorn, A. (1983) *Access to Privilege*. Canberra: Australian National University Press.

Atkinson, John W. and Birch, David (1978) *An Introduction to Motivation*. New York: Van Nostrand.

Australian Bureau of Statistics (1988) *Census 1986 — Australia in Profile*, Catalogue No. 2502.0. Canberra: Australian Bureau of Statistics.

———(1991) *Schools Australia 1990*, Catalogue No. 4221.0.

Bernstein, B. (1977) *Class, Codes and Controls*, Vol. 3. London: Routledge and Kegan Paul.

Beswick D.G. (1975) 'Students', in D.S. Anderson, K.J. Batt, D.G. Beswick, G.S. Harman, and C. Selby Smith, *Regional Colleges: A Study of Non-Metropolitan Colleges of Advanced Education in Australia* 1 (3). Canberra: Australian National University.

———(1983) 'The Changing Student Population in Australia from the Seventies to the Eighties', *Journal of Tertiary Education Administration* 5: 5–19.

———Hayden, Martin, and Schofield, Hilary (1983) *Evaluation of the Tertiary Education Assistance Scheme: An Investigation and Review of Policy on Student Financial Assistance in Australia*, Vol. 4 of Studies of Tertiary Student Finances. Canberra: Australian Goverment Publishing Service.

Biggs, John (1982) 'Student Motivation and Study Strategies in University and College of Advanced Education Populations', *Higher Education Research and Development* 1: 33–55.

Bills, D.B. (1983) 'Social Reproduction and the Bowles-Gintis Thesis of a Correspondence Between School and Work Settings', in A.C. Kerckhoff (ed.), *Research in Sociology of Education and Socialisation*, Vol. 4. Greenwick, CT: JAI Press.

Blau, Peter M. and Duncan, Otis Dudley (1967) *The American Occupational Structure*. New York: Free Press.

Bourdieu, P. (1973) 'Cultural Reproduction and Social Reproduction', in R. Brown (ed.), *Knowledge, Education and Cultural Change*. London: Tavistock.

———and Boltanski, L. (1978) 'Changes in Social Structure and Changes in the Demand for Education', in S. Giner and M.S. Archer (eds), *Contemporary Europe: Structural Change and Cultural Patterns*.

Bowles, S. and Gintis, H. (1976) *Schooling in Capitalist America: Educational Reform and Economic Life*. New York: Basic Books.

Bowman, Mary Jean. (1981) *Educational Choice and Labour Markets in Japan*. Chicago: University of Chicago Press.

Broom, L., Duncan-Jones, P., Jones, F.L. and McDonnell, P. (1977) *Investigating Social Mobility*. Canberra: Australian National University Press.

———Jones, F.L., McDonnell, P. and Williams, T.H. (1980) *The Inheritance of Inequality*. London: Routledge and Kegan Paul.

Browne, R.K. and Magin, D.J. (eds) (1976) *Sociology of Education*. Melbourne: Macmillan.

————and Foster, L.E. (eds) (1983) *Sociology of Education*. Melbourne: Macmillan.

Carpenter, Peter G. and Western, John S. (1984) 'Transition to Higher Education', *Australian Journal of Education* 28: 249–73.

————and Fleishman, John A. (1987) 'Linking Intentions and Behaviour: Australian Students' College Plans and College Attendance', *American Educational Research Journal* 24: 79–105.

————, Fleishman, John A. and Western, John S. (1989) 'Job Intentions and Job Attainment: Young People's Career Beginnings', *Australian Journal of Education* 33(3): 299–319.

————and Western, John S. (1989) *Starting a Career*. Hawthorn, Victoria: ACER.

Cohn, Elchanan and Morgan, J. Michael (1978) 'The Demand for Higher Education: Survey of Recent Studies', *Higher Education Review* 1: 19–30.

Commonwealth Schools Commission (1975) *Girls, Schools and Society*. Canberra: Australian Government Publishing Service.

————(1984) *Girls and Tomorrow: The Challenge for Schools*. Canberra: Australian Government Publishing Service.

Commonwealth Tertiary Education Commission (1986) 'Initiatives in Advanced Education to Increase Participation and Equity', Discussion Paper prepared by the Advanced Education Council Working Party on Course-related Matters. Canberra: Advanced Education Council.

————(1987) *Report for the 1988–90 Triennium* 1 (2), Appendices, Canberra: AGPS.

Connell, R.W., Ashenden, D.J., Kessler, S. and Dowsett, G.W. (1982) *Making the Difference*. Sydney: Allen and Unwin.

Cuttance, P.F. (1980) 'Social Background, Aspirations and Academic Achievement: An Analysis Based on Longitudinal Data for Australia', *Alberta Journal of Educational Review* 26: 85–95.

Department of Employment, Education and Training (1988) *School Leavers*. Canberra: DEET.

————(1990a) *Aboriginal and Torres Strait Islander Students*, Higher Education Series. Canberra: AGPS.

————(1990b) *Mature Age Students*, Higher Education Series. Canberra: AGPS.

————(1990c) *A Fair Chance for All*. Canberra: AGPS.

————(1991a) *Retention and Participation in Australian Schools*. Canberra: AGPS.

————(1991b) *Female Students Update No. 1*, Higher Education Series. Canberra: AGPS.

Edgar, D.E. (ed.) (1974) *Sociology of Australian Education*. Sydney: McGraw-Hill.

Edwards, A., Fitz, J. and Whitty, G. (1985) 'Private Schools and Public Funding: A Comparison of Recent Policies in England and Australia', *Comparative Education* 21: 29–45.

Ekehammer, Bo (1978) 'Toward a Psychological Cost-Benefit Model for Educational and Vocational Choice', *Scandinavian Journal of Psychology* 19: 19–27.

Elsworth, G.R., Day, N.A., Hurworth, R. and Andrews, J. (1982) *From*

School to Tertiary Study: Transition to College and University in Victoria, Research Monograph No. 14. Hawthorn, Victoria: ACER.

————(1983) 'Eligibility and Self-selection: Discontinuities in Transition to Tertiary Education in Victoria', *Australian Journal of Education* 27: 62–77.

Falsey, B. and Heyns, B. (1984) 'The College Channel: Private and Public Schools Reconsidered', *Sociology of Education* 57: 111–22.

Feather, Norman T. (1975) *Values in Education and Society*. New York: The Free Press.

Featherman, D.L. (1980) 'Schooling and Occupational Careers: Constancy and Change in Worldly Success', in D.G. Brim and J. Kagan, *Constancy and Change in Human Development*. Cambridge, MA: Harvard University Press.

————and Hauser, R.M. (1978) *Opportunity and Change*. New York: Academic Press.

Ferber, Marianne A. and McMahon, Walter W. (1979) 'Women's Expected Earnings and Their Investment in Higher Education', *The Journal of Human Resources* 14: 405–20.

Foster, L. J. (1987) *Australian Education: A Sociological Perspective*. Sydney: Prentice-Hall.

Freeman, Richard B. (1971) *The Market for College-Trained Manpower: A Study in the Economics of Career Choice*, Cambridge, Massachusetts: Harvard University Press.

————(1976) *The Overeducated American*. New York: Academic Press.

————(1981) 'Response to Change in the United States', in Robert Lindley (ed.), *Higher Education and the Labour Market*, Chapter 4. Guildford, Surrey: Society for Research into Higher Education.

Gasson, R.M. Haller, A.O. and Sewell, W.H. (1972) *Attitudes and Facilitation in the Attainment of Status*. Washington, DC: American Sociological Association.

Gilbert, S. (1977) 'The Selection of Educational Aspirations', in R.A. Carlton, L.A. Colley and N.J. MacKinnon (eds), *Education, Change and Society: A Sociology of Canadian Education*. Toronto: Gage Educational Publishers, pp. 281–310.

Glass, D.V. (1954) *Social Mobility*. London: Routledge and Kegan Paul.

Gordon, Alan. (1981) 'The Educational Choices of Young People', in Oliver Fulton (ed.), *Access to Higher Education*, Chapter 4 Guilford, Surrey: Society for Research into Higher Education.

Graetz, B. (1987) 'Cohort Changes in Educational Inequality', *Social Science Research* 16: 329–44.

————(1988) 'The Reproduction of Privilege in Australian Education', *British Journal of Sociology* XXXIX (3): 358–76.

————(1990) 'Private Schools and Educational Attainment: Cohort and Generational Effects', *Australian Journal of Education* 34: 174–91.

Gross, E. and Western, J.S. (eds) (1981) *The End of a Golden Age: Higher Education in A Steady State*. St Lucia: University of Queensland Press.

Halsey, A.H., Health, A.F. and Ridge, J.M. (1980) *Origins and Destinations*, Oxford: Clarendon Press.

Handa, M.L. and Skolnik, M.L. (1975) 'Unemployment, Expected

Returns, and the Demand for University Education in Ontario: Some Empirical Results', *Higher Education* 4: 27–43.

Harnqvist, Kjell (1978) *Individual Demand for Education: Analytical Report.* Paris: Organisation for Economic Co-operation and Development.

Hayden, Martin. (1982) 'Factors Affecting Participation by Young People in Tertiary Education', in *Learning and Earning: A Study of Education and Employment Opportunities for Young People*, Vol. 2, Appendix B. Canberra: Australian Government Publishing Service.

——and Carpenter, Peter G. (1990) 'From School to Higher Education in Australia', *Higher Education* 20: 175–96.

Jackson, Gregory A. (1978) 'Financial Aid and Student Enrolment', *Journal of Higher Education* 49: 548–74.

——(1981) 'Sociological Economic and Policy Influences on College-going Decisions', Program Report 81–89, Institute for Research on Educational Finance and Governance, School of Education, Stanford University.

——and Weathersby, George B. (1975) 'Individual Demand for Higher Education. A Review and Analysis of Recent Empirical Studies', *Journal of Higher Education* XLVI: 623–52.

Jones, F.L. and Davis, P. (1986) *Models of Society*. Sydney: Croom Helm.

Katz, F.M. and Browne, R.K. (eds) (1970) *Sociology of Education*. Melbourne: Macmillan.

Kessler, S., Ashenden, D.J., Connell, R.W. and Dowsett, G.W. (1985) 'Gender Relations in Secondary Schooling', *Sociology of Education* 58: 34–48.

Leslie, Larry L., Johnson, Gary P. and Carlson, James (1977) 'The Impact of Need-based Student Aid upon the College Attendance Decision', *Journal of Education Finance* 2: 269–85.

Lewis, R. (1976) *Transition from School to Post Secondary Education in Australia*. Hawthorn, Victoria: Australian Council for Educational Research.

Looker, D.E. and Pineo, P.C. (1983) 'Social Psychological Variables and their Relevance to the Status Attainment of Teenagers', *American Journal of Sociology* 88: 1,195–219.

Maas, F. (1990). 'Shifting Responsibility — A Decade of Youth Policy', *Family Matters* 26: 19–24.

Marjoribanks, K. (1980) 'Schools, Families and Children's Achievements', *Studies in Educational Evaluation* 6: 253–64.

Manski, Charles, F. and Wise, David A. (1983) *College Choice in America*. Cambridge, Massachusetts: Harvard University Press.

Maruyama, G., Finch, M.D. and Mortimer, J.T. (1985) 'Processes of Achievement in the Transition to Adulthood', *Current Perspectives on Ageing and the Life Cycle* 1: 61–87.

Matthews, R. (1988) 'A Graduate Tax to Finance Higher Education?', *Australian Universities' Review* 1: 26–28.

McGaw, B., Warry, R.S., Varley, P.J. and Alcorn, J. (1977) 'Prospects for School Leavers', in Australia, *Commission of Inquiry into Poverty, School Leavers: Choice and Opportunity*. Canberra: Australian Government Publishing Service.

McKinnon, J.J. and Anisef P. (1979). 'Self-assessment in the Early Educational Attainment Process', *Canadian Review of Sociology and Anthropology* 16 (3): 305–19.

Miller, P.W. and Volker, P.A. (1987) 'The Youth Labour Market in Australia', Discussion Paper 171. Canberra: Centre for Economic Policy Research, Australian National University.

National Board of Employment, Education and Training (1992) Sixth Report to the NBEET on the Operation of Section 14 of the Higher Education Funding Act 1988, and the Higher Education Contribution Scheme. Canberra: NBEET.

Nicholls, Miles G. (1984) 'The Demand for Tertiary Education — An Australian Study', *Higher Education* 13: 369–77.

Olneck, M.R. and Bills, D.B. (1980) 'What makes Sammy Run? An Empirical Assessment of the Bowles-Gintis Correspondence Theory', *American Journal of Education* 89: 27–61.

Persell, C.H. and Cookson, P.W. (1985) *Preparing for Power*. New York: Basic Books.

Pissarides, Christopher A. (1981) 'From School to University: The Demand for Post-compulsory Education in Britain', Discussion Paper 70. Centre for Labour Economics, London School of Economics.

Poole, M.E. (1983) *Youth: Expectations and Transitions*. London: Routledge and Kegan Paul.

Power, C., Robertson, F. and Baker, M. (1986) *Access to Higher Education: Participation, Equity and Policy*. Canberra: Commonwealth Tertiary Education Commission.

Powles, M. (1986) *Women's Participation in Tertiary Education*. Canberra: Australian Government Publishing Service.

Psacharopoulos, George (1982) 'An Analysis of the Determinants of the Demand for Upper Secondary Education in Portugal', *Economics of Education Review* 2: 233–51.

Radford, W.C. (1962) *School Leavers in Australia 1959–1960*. Hawthorn, Victoria: Australian Council for Educational Research.

———and Wilkes, R.E. (1975) *School Leavers in Australia 1971–1972*. Hawthorn, Victoria: Australian Council for Educational Research.

Reuterberg, Sven-Eric and Svensson, Allan (1983) 'The Importance of Financial Aid: The Case of Higher Education in Sweden', *Higher Education* 12: 89–100.

Roberts, K. (1968) 'The Entry into Employment: An Approach towards a General Theory, *Sociological Review* 16: 165–84.

———(1984) *School Leavers and their Prospects*. Milton Keynes, Bucks: Open University Press.

Robertson, F., Sloan, J. and Bardsley, N. (1990) *The Impact of the Higher Education Contribution Scheme (HECS)*. Canberra: AGPS.

Rosier, M. (1978) *Early School Leavers in Australia*. Stockholm: Almquisk Wicksell.

Rubenson, Kjell (1976) *Recruitment in Adult Education: A Research Strategy*, Stockholm: Department of Educational Research, Stockholm University.

———(1983) 'Barriers to Participation in Adult Education', Background paper 4, prepared for the Task Force on Skill Development Leave of the Department of Employment and Immigration, Canada.

Saha, L.J. (1982) 'Gender, School Attainment and Occupational Plans: Determinants of Aspirations and Expectations among Australian Urban School Leavers', *Australian Journal of Education* 26: 247–65.

———(1990) 'Towards an Australian Sociology of Education', in L.J. Saha and J.P. Keeves (eds), *Schooling and Society in Australia: Sociological Perspectives*. Canberra: ANU Press.

Samson, S.N. (1984) 'Are Girls Youth?', *Youth Studies Bulletin* 3: 30–33.

Sewell, William H. and Hauser, Robert M. (1975) *Education, Occupation and Earnings*. New York: Academic Press.

———and Hauser, Robert M. (1976) 'Causes and Consequences of Higher Education: Models of the Status Attainment Process', in William H. Sewell, Robert M. Hauser, and David L. Featherman (eds), *Schooling and Achievement in American Society*, Chapter 1. New York: Academic Press.

———and ——— (1980) 'The Wisconsin Longitudinal Study of Social and Psychological Factors in Aspirations and Achievements', *Research in Sociology of Education and Socialisation* 1: 59–99.

Spenner, K.I. and Featherman, D.L. (1978). 'Achievement Ambitions', in R.H. Turner, J. Coleman and R.C. Fox (eds), *Annual Review of Sociology* 4: 373–420.

Sturman, A. (1985) 'Immigrant Australians and Education', *Australian Education Review* 22. Hawthorn, Victoria: ACER.

Vickers, M. (1984) 'The Culture of Our High Schools and its Impact on Girls', *Youth Studies Bulletin* 3: 34–41.

Western, J.S. (1983) *Social Inequalities in Australian Society*. Melbourne: Macmillan.

Western, Mark C. and Western, John S. (1988) 'Class and Inequality: Theory and Research', in J.M. Najman and J.S. Western (eds), *A Sociology of Australian Society*. Melbourne: Macmillan.

Williams, Gareth and Gordon, Alan (1981) 'Perceived Earnings Functions and Ex Ante Rates of Return to Post-compulsory Education in England', *Higher Education* 10: 199–227.

Williams, T. (1972) 'Educational Aspirations: Longitudinal Evidence of their Development in Canadian Youth', *Sociology of Education* 45: 107–33.

———(1976). 'Teacher Prophecies and the Inheritance of Inequality,' *Sociology of Education* 49: 223–36.

———Clancy, J., Batten, M., and Girling-Butcher, S. (1980) *School, Work and Career: 17-year-olds in Australia*. Hawthorn, Vic.: ACER.

———(1987) *Participation in Education*. Hawthorn, Victoria: Australian Council for Educational Research.

———and Carpenter, Peter G. (1990) 'Private Schooling and Public Achievement', *Australian Journal of Education* 34: 3–24.

———and Carpenter, Peter G. (1991) 'Private Schooling and Public Achievement in Australia', *International Journal of Education Research* 15 (5): 411–31.

Wish, John R. and Hamilton, William D. (1980) 'Replicating Freeman's Recursive Adjustment Model of Demand for Higher Education', *Research in Higher Education* 12: 83–95.

Chapter Seventeen

Decline of the Old, Rise of the New: Late Twentieth Century Australian Urbanisation

Patrick Mullins

At a time when Australian urbanisation is undergoing its most profound change in perhaps 100 years, Australian sociologists are
showing a surprising disinterest in what is happening. Other social
scientists, notably geographers (e.g. Badcock 1989a), political
economists (see Stilwell 1991), and urban and regional planners
(e.g. see Berry and Huxley 1992) are taking responsibility for this
work and, in doing so, are not only advancing their own disciplines,
but are arriving at sociological insights as well.

This chapter provides a brief sociological account of Australian
urbanisation — the Australian urban and regional development —
of the last two decades, but also sketches the urbanisation of the
preceding period, because to understand what is going on now,
the past must be comprehended. In targeting these goals, the chapter
provides an introduction to contemporary urban sociology, the
subfield of sociology responsible for studying urbanisation.

The urban sociology used and discussed here is historical and
comparative in focus, and locates urban and regional development within broader social processes. Many of these are global in
origin, but are influencing urban and regional, as well as international and national, developments. Having their beginnings in
catalytic events of the early 1970s, like the 1973 oil crisis, the
effects of current processes can be seen, for example, in the recent
collapse of several nation-states, like the Soviet Union, and in the
creation of new international alignments, like the united states of

Europe (see Harvey 1989; Lash and Urry 1989; Sassen 1991; Webber 1991).

The new urban and regional developments arising out of these global processes are stimulating a new internationally-oriented urban sociology, one which is extending the 'new urban sociology', an approach formulated in the 1970s by Europeans who were trying to make sense of 1940s-70s European urbanisation (see Castells 1977; Lebas 1981; Pickvance 1976). This 'new urban sociology' is, however, too limited to clarify the events of the last twenty years, and so this has led to a revised approach which will be used here to help make sense of contemporary Australian urbanisation. It contrasts sharply with traditional urban sociology, an American-initiated viewpoint frequently called 'human ecology and demography', dominating the sub-discipline for decades, and still holding sway in the United States. Formulated in the 1920s from observations made in the American city of Chicago, this traditional version used descriptive analyses of peoples living in different parts of cities, and of economic, political, and other social processes located there. By the 1960s, human ecology and demography was recognised as clearly limited and although it continues today to dominate a declining school of American urban sociology, it is slowly being replaced in the United States by the emergent internationally-oriented version (e.g. see Gottdiener and Feagin 1988; Smith and Feagin 1987; Gilderbloom 1988; Logan and Molotch 1987); for a comment on recent British urban sociology, see Mellor 1989).

It is important to note that both the 'new urban sociology' and its reformed version are strictly not 'sociology', but interdisciplinary in approach. They were formulated from contributions made by people working in a number of social science disciplines, particularly geography, and political economy, sociology itself, and the applied fields of urban and regional planning, social administration, and social and public policy. They draw upon a common pool of concepts, theories and methodologies which they have formulated, and which, along with other researchers, they are now adding to and modifying. This work can be seen in papers published in the *International Journal of Urban and Regional Research* and *Environment and Planning D: Society and Space*, as well as in the activities of Research Committee 21 of the International Sociological Association, the research committee on the sociology of urban and regional development.

Within sociology, this emergent international urban sociology is closely tied to world-systems analysis (e.g. see Timberlake 1985); and the historical social science of the sociologist Wallerstein (1979) and his colleagues (e.g. Chase-Dunn 1989). Their work is holistic in approach, focusing on global social relations (e.g. class relations) and global social structures (e.g. groups of societies), rather than on bits and pieces of social life (e.g. the family), as is typical of mainstream sociology. Links are observed between various parts of social life as these fit into broader social arrangements. Disciplinary distinctions, between sociology, economics, geography, etc. are rejected, and the innovative results (e.g. see Taylor 1986) contrast with the narrow and highly fragmented nature of contemporary sociology (see Turner 1989).

Before examining Australian urbanisation, definitions must first be given of urban sociology and of the central concepts used in this paper.

Urban Sociology

Urban sociology, or the sociology of urban and regional development, as it is now more frequently called, is the field of sociology which examines the way people shape and reshape their physical environments. From their actions, towns, cities, and regions emerge, and this process is called *urbanisation,* or *urban and regional development.*

Sociological studies of such development focus primarily on the city. This is understandable because it is the principal socio-spatial component of contemporary societies, where the population, productive capacity (e.g. factories), wealth, power, and social life more generally, are concentrated. Inevitably, such sociology is called *urban sociology.* However, over the last decade or two, a number of urban sociologists have looked beyond the city in order to understand broader socio-spatial arrangements. They are also now studying regions: that limited number of very large areas which together form a society's geography. Each region contains cities, towns, farming districts and natural environments, each distinguished by a distinctive set of economic, political and other social characteristics. This modified approach, then, has led to the term the *sociology of urban and regional development* being used, rather than 'urban sociology'. Accompanying this shift is a more sociological approach, one describing *and* explaining, rather than simply providing demographic descriptions, as is typical of traditional urban sociology (human ecology and demography).

In Australia, urban sociology has been a minor subfield, although there was an upsurge of interest in it in the 1970s. Practical concerns shared with other people about the direction in which Australian cities and regions were developing, along with the intellectual stimulus provided by the 'new urban sociology', led to this upsurge. It was reflected in a special issue of the *Australian and New Zealand Journal of Sociology* (17 (1): 1977), and in Kilmartin and Thorns (1978). However, by the 1980s, this effort had largely dissipated.

Central Concepts

Concepts provide the tools for studying and understanding social life, because they identify and define, it is hoped in a clear and unambiguous way, the different spheres and processes of life. Concepts are critical to empirical research, and the data produced, with the concepts themselves, make it possible to formulate theory and so explain the observations made. Since concepts are frequently confused with theory, it is necessary to distinguish between the two. Where concepts identify and *define* the spheres and processes of social life (e.g. the meaning of deviance) theory *explains* social life (e.g. why deviance persists).

Two major concepts are used in this chapter: 'urbanisation' (or 'urban and regional development') and 'social forces'. The former is important because it is the focus of the chapter, while the latter is defined because it identifies how urbanisation is a process: how cities, towns, and regions constantly change, and how this is brought about from the actions people take, from 'social forces'.

Urbanisation

Along with other social scientists, sociologists invariably define urbanisation in demographic, rather than sociological, terms. They see it as 'the proportion of the total population concentrated in urban settlements, or else to a rise in this proportion' (Davis 1974: 162). While this approach is important, it does not identify the *social* meaning of urbanisation. A sociological definition would say that 'urbanisation is the spatial patterning of that mode of production called capitalism' (Mullins 1988: 518).

'Spatial patterning' refers to the way people transform nature and so produce different landscapes: different spatial patternings. It comes about from the application of various tools and processes, with each mode of production exploiting nature differently and so producing different landscapes. Urbanisation is capitalism's spatial form and is distinguished by the concentration of life into a limited geographic area; into cities and towns and, in turn, into various regions. This is not, of course, to deny the presence of cities and towns before the rise of capitalism, but urbanisation was limited until then.

'Mode of production' refers to the way people organise themselves to use nature and so ensure their survival. Historically, there have been many different modes of production — slave, feudal, socialist, etc. — with capitalism being the mode of production dominating the world today. With its origins in European trade of 1500–1800, capitalism was established by the mid-nineteenth century. Socialism, the other major twentieth century mode of production, was unable firmly to establish itself, and its current demise is reflected in the collapse of the Soviet Union and the countries of Eastern Europe.

Capitalism is a mode of production based on the production and sale of goods and services for profit, and thus the accumulation of more and more wealth: the accumulation of 'capital'. Critical to this is the way different collections of peoples (different 'social classes') have different positions in this process, and the way dominant classes exploit subordinate ones, resulting in the unequal distribution of resources.

Social Forces[1]

Social forces refer to those actions people take which subsequently lead to change. Since urbanisation is a process involving the development and redevelopment of towns, cities and regions, it is necessary to understand what it is that people do to shape and reshape these socio-spatial structures. What happens emanates from a diverse and complex set of actions called social forces.

Before proceeding, a word of caution. 'Social forces' is a concept rarely used in sociology, mainly, it seems, because social change ('development') is of little empirical interest to sociologists. What attention is given to change comes mainly from those working in three minor subfields: the sociology of development, historical macrosociology, and the sociology of urban and regional development. Generally, however, rather than studying change, sociologists freeze time. They use, for example, survey research to collect information from people over a short period (e.g. two weeks) and then use these frozen moments to make generalisations about aspects of social life. This snapshot approach results in few concepts being available to help make empirical sense of change, and for this reason the term 'social forces' is introduced. Yet, to fully understand this concept, three related concepts must also be understood. These are social structure, social relations, and social change.

Social structures are enduring systems of social relations, and these take many forms, from individual societies (e.g. Australia) to groups of societies (e.g. 'Western society'), and from large bureaucracies (e.g. BHP) to cities (e.g. Townsville).

Social relations, as the elements forming social structures, are fundamental and persistent associations between people over basic issues (e.g. over the production of goods and services: class relations). In this way, social relations are dynamic and thus involve conflict, this being a basic element of change. Finally, social change refers to the transformations of social structures.

This conceptual framework, this way of trying to understand the social world, is complex, and for this reason only five social relations/social forces are considered here. These are class relations, political relations, consumption relations, gender relations, and race/ethnic relations (see Figure 17.1). These are probably the most important for shaping and reshaping urbanisation, as well as other social structures, and of the five, class relations tend to be considered the most influential, followed by political relations.

Class relations (the social relations of production) refer to exploitative associations between people over production, and are considered the most powerful social force, because they revolve around basic necessities. They appear as positions (classes) in production, specifically in terms of who owns and/or controls the means of production (e.g. the factories), who has particular skills, and who merely sells labour (see Wright 1985). Class relations, then, form class structures (see Figure 17.1), with the principal classes being capitalists (who own and control), the *petit bourgeoisie*, the various middle classes, and the working class (who are the most subordinate) (for details see Chapter 3). From their class position, people receive most of their resources, with their unequal distribution creating conflict: class conflict is the most overt expression of class relations. The antagonistic nature of class relations makes it a force for change: a social force.

'Political relations' refer to associations between people over

Figure 17.1 Social Relations as Social Forces

Type of social relationship	The structure forming the relationship	Overt action expressing the relationship (the social force)
Class relations ('social relations of production')	Class structure	Class conflict
Consumption relations ('special relations of consumption')	Household and residential organisation	Urban movements
Gender relations	Patriarchy	Gender conflicts
Political relations	The state	Political conflicts
Race/ethnic relations	Racial/ethnic groups	Cultural/racial conflicts

political control — over power — and involve varying degrees of domination and subordination. They are also antagonistic, and resulting conflicts can lead to change. In contemporary societies, power is largely institutionalised within the state and organised through political parties (see Figure 17.1). However, over the last two decades, social movements like the environmental movement have challenged the power of the state and political parties, and this is likely to bring fundamental changes in the nature of political relations.

Consumption relations (the social relations of consumption) are associations between people over quality of life, over goods and services consumed, primarily housing and related facilities (like the water supply) (e.g. see Pahl 1989; Warde 1990). Since necessary consumption is largely concentrated within households and residential areas, social relations of consumption can be said to be relations between different 'household and residential organisations' (see Figure 17.1) (and also Mullins 1987, 1988). Urban movements represent actions people take over the quality of urban life, and represent the clearest expression of consumption relations.

Gender relations are relations between men and women which, initially, were primarily linked to biological reproduction and subsistence, but in the contemporary context are intricately tied to all spheres of life (class, politics, race/ethnicity, consumption, etc.). They exist as an exploitative relationship of men over women (commonly called patriarchy) and are therefore also antagonistic relations, with the resulting conflict also bringing about change (see Figure 17.1 and Walby 1986).

Race/ethnic relations identify cultural associations: relations between people over values, customs, rules, attitudes, etc. Since racial/ethnic groups are the major holders of culture, cultural conflicts are mainly expressed in the form of racial or ethnic conflicts. These indicate domination and subordination in these relations, and can also contribute to change (see Figure 17.1).

Two critical qualifying points need to be made. First, although the five social relations/social forces are conceptually separate, in practice they are intricately inter-related, and so this makes it difficult to identify the independent influence of one force over another. Second, and more seriously, we lack the empirical evidence to confirm or reject the view that social relations are indeed social forces. Much is assumed, but little is *empirically* known (see Pahl 1989; Mullins 1991a). Such ignorance is an inevitable outcome of the very limited interest sociologists show in measuring social change, including the social forces involved. This explains why analyses of class, power, gender, etc. merely describe structures (e.g. the class structure) and the inequalities present (e.g. gender inequalities), rather than showing whether social relations contribute to change. It is impossible at this stage, then, to make confident claims about how (or even whether) the five social forces identified have shaped and reshaped Australian urbanisation. All that can be done here is to use this framework, in conjunction with available data, to raise a number of important questions about social forces and Australian urbanisation.

Australian Urbanisation, 1860–1970

To understand contemporary Australian urbanisation, its earlier form needs first to be known, since this will help identify the nature and magnitude of change. The year 1860 is taken as the starting point of the earlier era, because modern Australia had its beginnings in the 1860–90 economic boom. The end of the period is 1970, marking the end of the second economic boom (1945–70). The contemporary era began about 1970.

The urbanisation of 1860–1970 appeared in two main stages, each based on a different form of capitalism. There was mercantile urbanisation (1860–1945), and corporate urbanisation (1945–70), and they contrasted with the urbanisation of dominant ('core') capitalist countries, like the United Kingdom and the United States, where industrial urbanisation was present from the mid-nineteenth century to about 1945, when corporate urbanisation took hold (for details see Mullins 1981a, 1981b, 1988; see also Berry 1984; Frost 1991). Australian urbanisation, however, is historically similar to the urbanisation of countries with parallel patterns of development, like Canada and New Zealand. Marking the difference or similarity is a difference/similarity in social relations/social forces, since countries with similar social relations and social forces have similar patterns of urbanisation, and vice versa. The way the five social forces shaped Australian urbanisation of 1860–1970 can now briefly be considered, with discussion largely drawing upon Mullins (1981a, 1981b, 1988).

Class Relations

As the name implies, Australia's mercantile urbanisation was based on commercial capitalism: on the export of primary produce and the importation of manufactured goods (cf. Johns 1992). This meant, then, that relations between commercial capitalists and the working class essentially shaped this urbanisation, with capitalists' power having the greatest impact. Cities and towns developed as transport centres, specifically ports, and this helps explain why they, and Australia's population generally, were and are located on the coast (e.g. Butlin 1976). Other economic activities were also present, like manufacturing; but this was limited compared with the cities of the core.

Spatially, mercantile urbanisation developed around wharves and railway terminals, with other economic (and social) activities spreading out as low density development. Remnants of this urbanisation can be seen today, showing how spatial forms come to outlive the social processes leading to their formation.

The urban class relations of this period contrasted, for example, with those of Britain. There, class relations revolved mainly around manufacturing, specifically in the form of industrial capitalists and the industrial working class, with the former having the greatest impact in the shaping of British industrial urbanisation (see Buckley and Wheelwright 1988; Mullins 1988; see also Butlin 1976; Butlin *et al.* 1982).

Australia's corporate urbanisation emerged in response to the crisis years of the 1930's Depression and World War II, and involved the expansion of administration and planning, these operating within corporations (notably transnational corporations) and the state. Import substitution manufacturing also developed, emerging from foreign companies establishing factories in Australia under tariff protection to produce goods for the Australian market, with tariffs making foreign goods more expensive than locally produced ones. Indeed, this was the period when Australia industrialised, with factories being disproportionately concentrated in Sydney, Newcastle, Wollongong, Melbourne, Geelong and Adelaide (see Rich 1986).

These new developments transformed Australian urbanisation. State and corporate activities physically and socially changed the commercial core of large cities, with the construction of office towers, while manufacturing industry markedly expanded industrial precincts.

In class terms, planning and administration led to the expansion of the middle classes, while import substitution manufacturing brought a rapid growth in the industrial working class and small local industrial capitalists. Australian urban class relations therefore became more complex and fashioned a more economically diverse urban form: cities were now places of commerce, manufacturing, and state and corporate services.

Finally, the pervasive impact of foreign capitalists must be stressed. During the mercantile era, British capitalists were directly involved in the construction of Australian cities, as well as indirectly involved through commercial, financial, and primary industry investments. During the corporate era, American and Japanese capitalists were largely responsible for import substitution manufacturing, as well as for new mining developments. In this way, Australian urbanisation was shaped not only by indigenous class relations, but by foreign class relations as well.

Political Relations

The major impacts of the urban political relations of this time can be seen in four types of state action. First, there was colonial socialism (1860–1910), state action which laid the foundation of Australian capitalism and urbanisation. This came about from state control over land, its building of necessary infrastructure (notably railways), its success at attracting capital and labour, and its introduction of the conciliation and arbitration system to restrict class conflict, and provide conditions whereby the working class could achieve reasonable wages and living conditions. Colonial socialism contrasted starkly with the very limited role played by other Western states between 1860 and 1910 (see Butlin *et al.* 1982).

Second, unlike many European states, the Australian state provided little direct welfare assistance over the years 1945–70. In other words, the country failed to develop a welfare state, and thus provided few items of collective consumption: state provisioning of necessary goods and services, like housing. This lack of involvement is most apparent when compared with the way many European states developed extensive tracts of urban public housing over these years.

Third, as political and economic centres, Australian capital cities have dominated the rest of their colonies/states. Such is their size and importance that, historically, they have become primate cities: cities dominating their hinterlands. Interestingly, primate cities represent an urban form common to developing, rather than developed, countries (see Clark 1985; Lyman 1992; Chase-Dunn 1985; Rose 1966; Smith 1985).

Finally, federal political relations led to the establishment of one major city and the expansion of another. Canberra was created in the 1920s as the federal capital, while Darwin, the capital city of the Northern Territory, was developed largely from federal government activity.

Consumption Relations

The quality of Australian urban life of this time has been characterised by the term 'private wealth and public squalor', an assessment largely holding true today. This judgement is made comparatively with household and residential life in other developed societies, particularly European ones. 'Private wealth' refers to the way residents obtain relatively good housing, mainly in the form of home-ownership, as well as other necessary consumption items, through reasonably good incomes, incomes made possible by high labour demand, policies of full employment, and low taxes (see Castles 1988, 1989). This helps explain why Australian home-ownership rates have always been high, comparatively, expanding markedly after 1945 to peak in the 1960s, and now being around 70 per cent of all dwellings.

'Public squalor' refers to the limited provisioning of necessary consumption items (e.g. housing, transport) by the Australian state; relative to the state's role in other developed countries, particularly European ones (see Badcock 1984). Instead of directly providing collective consumption, the Australian state tried to ensure people's ability to buy necessary items, and so introduced policies attempting to ensure full employment, good wages and low taxes (see Castles 1988, 1989). The result is a quality of urban life which, historically, has been comparable with the best in the world (see Szelenyi 1981).

There is a dearth of information on the urban movements of this period, actions people took to protect and improve the quality of their urban life. However, it seems that progress associations (residents' organisations) were widespread at this time and appeared to play a role for Australian residential life paralleling that played by trade unions in the workplace (Mullins 1992a; Noakes n.d.). However, until detailed historical data are available on progress associations, their place in the consumption relations of the period will remain unknown.

Two other features of household and residential life of 1860–1970 are worth noting. The first is the presence of an elaborate domestic (or informal) economy, the urban peasantry, existing from 1860–1945 (see Mullins 1981a, 1981b, 1987, 1988). This was essentially run by women, with a great range of goods and services being produced — from poultry to the construction of houses — for the household, as well as for exchange with neighbours, family and friends (for a New Zealand discussion, see Fairbairn 1989). Second, the urban peasantry gave way after 1945 to a household and residential organisation focusing on the mass consumption of consumer durables, goods produced by Australia's import substitution manufacturing (e.g. cars).

Gender Relations

Although there is little comparative data available on gender relations, Australia seems to have been more strongly patriarchal than most other Western countries over these years, and this seems to have had a marked impact upon Australian urbanisation. Historically, Australian women have been more clearly excluded from the public worlds of government and the capitalist economy, an exclusion partly institutionalised at the turn of the century by the state, which defined wage labour in terms of *male* wage labour (see Castles 1985). With the exception of some increase in labour force participation (from a low base) in World Wars I and II, women were largely confined to household and residential life. They thus took primary responsibility for the informal economy (the urban peasantry), and it was not until the 1960s that a marked shift in gender relations occurred, following the impact of the women's movement.

Race/ethnic Relations
These relations have primarily been between dominant Anglo Australians and minority groups. At a regional level, British settlement forced Aboriginal societies off the rich coastal lands and into the hinterland (see Keen 1988: Chapter 7). In terms of urban development, race/ethnic relations have not had the impact on Australian cities and towns that they have had on American ones (see Wilson 1989). However, conflicts between the Irish Catholic minority and the Anglo Protestant majority were apparent until the 1940s; to some extent, these groups were spatially segregated within cities. From the 1940s to the 1960s, race/ethnic relations involved non-English-speaking Europeans and the Anglo-Celtic settlers and their descendants, leading to some ethnic segregation within major cities (see Jupp 1983, 1988).

Post-1970 Australian Urbanisation: The Decline of the Old and the Rise of the New

Against this background, contemporary Australian urbanisation can now be considered. What is emerging is an urbanisation partly replacing and partly extending the corporate urbanisation of 1945–70. The easiest way of demonstrating the magnitude of this change is to sketch the major demographic changes of the last twenty years. These provide a backdrop against which to examine the social forces involved.

The Demography of Australian Urbanisation, 1971–91
Two major demographic changes of the last twenty years are worth noting. The first is a marked regional shift in population,

and the second is the very rapid growth of a limited number of large cities.

Historically, Australia can be divided into three main regions: the core, the semi-periphery, and the periphery (for details, see Head 1986; Higgins and Zagorski 1989; Mullins 1986). The core comprises the economically and politically dominant states of New South Wales and Victoria, as well as the Australian Capital Territory. The periphery comprises the historically weak states of Queensland, Tasmania, and Western Australia, as well as the Northern Territory. South Australia forms the semi-periphery, as the in-between state.

From 1971 to 1991 there was a significant regional shift in the Australian population: from the core and the semi-periphery to the periphery. This involved the largest internal migration in Australia's history, a migration which is continuing (see Rowland 1979; Bell 1992). In 1971, Australia's core contained 64.9 per cent of the country's population, with 9.2 per cent at the semi-periphery, and 25.9 per cent at the periphery (see Table 17.1). Twenty years later, the core's share dropped to 60.9 per cent, the semi-periphery's to 8.3 per cent, and the periphery's increased to 30.8 per cent. Major migration streams involved were from New South Wales and Victoria to Queensland and Western Australia, with Queensland receiving the largest number of migrants (see Rowland 1979; Bell 1992). Tasmania is the only part of the periphery not benefiting from this redistribution and it continues to have a declining share of the Australian population, a decline which began last century.

Prior to this redistribution, the Australian population was reasonably stable geographically. Table 17.1 shows about two-thirds of the population lived in the core between 1901–71, about one-quarter at the periphery, and about one-tenth in the semi-periphery. Only between 1861–1901 was there a redistribution comparable to that of 1971–91, and this came about from the European settlement of Queensland and Western Australia.

The last twenty years has also seen the rapid growth of a number of large cities (see Table 17.2). In 1991, an extraordinary 70.6 per cent of Australians lived in the 13 cities of 100,000 and more people, with 38.9 per cent living in Sydney and Melbourne alone. Between 1971–91, 6 of these 13 had rates of population growth of 50 per cent or more, and all except Canberra were located on the periphery (see Table 17.2). The 2 fastest growing cities, by far, were the tourist centres of the Gold Coast and the Sunshine Coast, and such were their rates of growth that this suggests tourism is having a profound impact upon contemporary Australia, including its system of urban and regional development

Table 17.1 Population Distribution over the Three Main Australian Regions, 1861–1991 (%)

	Core				Semi-periphery		Periphery			T	Total
	NSW	Vic.	ACT	T	SA	Qld	WA	Tas.	NT	T	Total
1861	30.4	46.8	—	77.2	11.0	2.6	1.4	7.8	—	11.8	100.0
1881	33.3	38.3	—	71.6	12.3	9.5	1.3	5.1	0.2	16.1	100.0
1891	35.5	35.9	—	71.4	9.9	12.4	1.5	4.6	0.2	18.7	100.0
1901	35.9	31.8	—	67.7	9.5	13.2	4.9	4.6	0.1	22.8	100.0
1911	37.0	29.5	0.1	66.5	9.2	13.6	6.3	4.3	0.1	24.3	100.0
1921	38.6	28.2	0.1	66.9	9.1	13.9	6.1	3.9	0.1	24.0	100.0
1933	39.2	27.5	0.1	66.8	8.8	14.3	6.6	3.4	0.1	24.4	100.0
1947	39.4	27.1	0.2	66.7	8.5	14.6	6.6	3.4	0.2	24.8	100.0
1954	38.1	27.3	0.3	65.7	8.9	14.7	7.1	3.4	0.2	25.4	100.0
1961	37.1	27.8	0.6	65.5	9.2	14.5	7.1	3.3	0.4	25.3	100.0
1966	36.5	27.8	0.8	65.1	9.4	14.4	7.3	3.2	0.5	25.4	100.0
1971	36.2	27.6	1.1	64.9	9.2	14.2	8.1	3.0	0.6	25.9	100.0
1976	35.3	27.2	1.5	64.0	9.1	14.9	8.4	2.9	0.7	26.9	100.0
1981	35.1	26.5	1.5	63.1	8.8	15.7	8.7	2.9	0.8	28.1	100.0
1986	34.5	26.0	1.6	62.1	8.6	16.4	9.1	2.8	1.0	29.3	100.0
1991	34.0	25.2	1.7	60.9	8.3	17.7	9.4	2.7	1.0	30.8	100.0

Source: Year Book, Australia 1992

Table 17.2 Australian Cities of 100,000+: Population, 1991 and Population Change, 1971–91

Ranked urban areas of 100,000+ at 1991 Census	1991 Census populations ('000)	Distribution of 1991 population (%)	Population change				
			1971–76	1976–81	1981–86	1986–91	1971–91
1. Sydney (NSW)	3.54	21.0	7.6	6.0	5.0	5.2	26.0
2. Melbourne (Vic.)	3.02	17.9	4.0	4.6	4.0	5.4	20.7
3. Brisbane (Qld/NSW)	1.33	7.9	10.4	7.4	11.8	13.4	53.8
4. Perth (WA)	1.14	6.8	14.6	11.6	10.6	15.0	62.6
5. Adelaide (SA)	1.02	6.1	6.9	3.5	4.9	4.7	21.5
6. Newcastle (NSW)	0.43	2.6	3.3	7.2	4.1	5.6	21.7
7. Canberra (ACT/NSW)	0.30	2.5	35.6	11.3	13.1	12.1	91.2
8. Gold Coast (Qld/NSW)	0.29	1.7	34.3[1]	52.6	27.3	29.2	237.2
9. Wollongong (NSW)	0.24	1.4	6.0	5.4	1.2	4.8	18.6
10. Hobart (Tas.)	0.18	1.1	5.8	3.9	4.0	3.9	18.7
11. Geelong (Vic.)	0.15	0.9	7.8	4.2	1.9	4.0	19.1
12. Sunshine Coast (Qld)	0.13	0.8	49.2[a]	77.2[1]	21.7	40.0	350.5[a]
13. Townsville (Qld)	0.12	0.7	19.6	7.0	10.3	10.5	57.6
Total urban areas 100,000+	11.89	70.6	8.1	7.0	6.5	8.5	33.6
Rest of Australia	4.96	29.4	5.8	5.0	9.2	-2.1	18.9
Total Australia	16.85	100.0	7.4	6.3	7.3	5.2	28.9

Note:
[a] Estimate only
[1] Statistical Divisions and Statistical Districts. For Gold Coast, both Queensland and New South Wales parts. For Canberra, both Australian Capital Territory and New South Wales parts
Source: Australian Census, 1971–91

(see later). By contrast, the city with the slowest rate of growth was the industrial centre of Wollongong, a city which has been de-industrialising for the last two decades.

These demographic data, then, suggest that the epicentre of Australian urbanisation is shifting. Where historically it has been located in the conurbations of Sydney (Newcastle-Sydney-Wollongong) and Melbourne (Melbourne-Geelong), and later including Canberra, it seems to have shifted a little northwards as the Brisbane conurbation (Sunshine Coast-Brisbane-Gold Coast) has rapidly expanded over the last two decades, and as a number of smaller centres scattered along the coast from Sydney to Cairns have also expanded (Paris 1992). Cairns, for example, grew by an extraordinary 24.8 per cent between 1986–91, and now has a population of almost 100,000 people.

The five social forces involved in this transformation can now be considered.

Class Relations

Six major economic developments have so far been involved in the new urbanisation, and these have developed in association with new urban class relations. What is happening in Australia is also happening, to a greater or lesser extent, in other developed societies.

The first of the contemporary processes is de-industrialisation, the systematic withdrawal of capital from traditional manufacturing industry, notably from iron and steel, and from industries reliant upon them. This has occurred in all developed societies, but is most marked in Europe and North America, where manufacturing has been concentrated. It resulted from competition between industrial capitalists, which led to over-production, and from conflicts between industrial capitalists and the industrial working class, which encouraged capitalists to restructure their industries and relocate some of them to cities in newly industrialising countries like South Korea. Nevertheless, it is important to realise that traditional manufacturing persists and continues to have the most significant industrial impact upon urbanisation (see Gertler 1988).

De-industrialisation has had a devastating effect upon old industrial cities and towns. Major social consequences include a marked rise in unemployment and social decline. In Australia, the effects have been less severe, partly because there is not the same reliance on manufacturing, and partly because the few manufacturing-dependent centres (like Wollongong) have industries receiving tariff protection; this has cushioned the impact (see Haughton 1990).

Although de-industrialisation brought a sharp rise in unemployment, it is important to realise that the highest rates of Australian urban unemployment today are in the tourist cities of the Gold Coast and the Sunshine Coast, not in industrial centres like Wollongong (Mullins 1992b). It is perhaps odd that these accompany the rise of a new industry (mass tourism) and its principal spatial form (tourism urbanisation), rather than the decline of traditional manufacturing and the centres forming its principal spatial structure.

Inevitably, de-industrialisation led to marked changes in urban class relations. There is a decline of the industrial working class and of small Australian industrial capitalists, meaning that industrial class relations now have a decreasing urban influence in Australia, as well as elsewhere.

A second economic outcome, but one insignificant in Australia compared with the United States and many European countries, is the emergence of new manufacturing industries and thus new industrial spaces (see Henry 1992; Storper 1992). Involved are 'clean', capital-intensive industries which contrast with the pollution-producing labour-intensive industries of the past, those which are now affected by de-industrialisation.

The new industries are dependent upon a flexible labour force, particularly the expert middle classes who provide the research and development (scientists, engineers) and the management skills (planners and administrators). Silicon Valley in the southern San Francisco Bay area of California in the United States is the clearest example of these new industrial spaces, this particular space being based on the computer industry (e.g. see Saxenian 1989). Although nothing comparable exists in Australia, the multi-function polis (MFP) planned for Adelaide is one attempt to establish new industries in a new industrial space. The MFP was initiated by Japanese capitalists and the Japanese state, in association with the Australian state and a few Australian capitalists; it also involves a new residential space, to house up to 100,000 people, mainly the expert middle classes who will operate and formulate the new industries located there (see Inkster 1991; Stilwell 1991).

The third post-1970 change is the rapid expansion of administration and planning services, particularly business, legal and media services. In urban terms, this represents an extension of corporate urbanisation and is based on a growing global demand for these services. In Australia, they are disproportionately concentrated in Sydney and Melbourne, the cities most closely integrated with the growing network of global cities (e.g. see Fagan and Bryan 1991; Sassen 1991). In class terms, finance

Table 17.3 Four Cities and their Class Structures, 1986 (%)

	Gold Coast (n=73,224)	Canberra (n=124,732)	Wollongong (n=86,972)	Sydney (n=1,459,609)	Australia (n=6,504,147)
			Classes of owners		
Employers	10.0	3.7	4.3	5.2	6.2
Self-employed	13.3	4.7	5.9	7.4	10.0
Unpaid helpers	1.1	0.4	0.5	0.5	0.9
Total owners	24.4	8.8	10.7	13.2	17.1
			Classes of non-owners		
Experts:					
managers	5.3	10.1	3.6	6.4	5.6
professionals	6.4	18.1	10.7	11.5	10.2
others	4.8	10.3	6.4	7.4	7.0
Semi-credentialed workers	14.5	9.7	16.9	13.5	7.6
Other credentialed workers	7.6	8.7	10.5	9.7	12.9
Total middle classes	38.6	56.9	48.1	48.5	43.3
Working class	32.3	29.4	35.6	33.0	33.7
Non-definable	4.7	4.9	5.6	5.3	5.9
Total non-owners	75.6	91.2	89.3	86.8	82.9
Total	100.0	100.0	100.0	100.0	100.0

Source: Unpublished 1986 Australian Census data

capitalists (e.g. bankers) form the cog in this development and are the most powerful capitalists today. The middle classes, specifically the expert middle classes, are also expanding rapidly, with Table 17.3 showing their place in the Sydney class structure (Sydney being the largest Australian city and the one most integrated into the global urban system), and in Canberra (the centre of federal government activity). By contrast, the middle classes play a more limited role in Wollongong, a de-industrialising city, and in the Gold Coast, a booming tourist city (see Table 17.3). It is also worth noting the way the working class now forms only about one-third of the class structures of each of the four cities shown in the table, and in Australia as a whole.

Fourth, and closely tied to the rapid expansion of administration and planning is the redevelopment of the central business districts (CBDs) of the five largest cities, Sydney, Melbourne, Brisbane, Perth, and Adelaide, but particularly Sydney and Melbourne (see Daly 1982; Low and Moser 1991). The CBD office towers built over the last twenty years have largely been a response to predicted demands for planning and administrative services, and this has led to property booms in the early 1970s and mid-1980s. However, the increasing oversupply of office space brought the property crashes of the mid 1970s and the late 1980s, crashes particularly affecting Melbourne and Sydney (see McLoughlin 1992).

The classes involved in these speculative ventures, specifically capitalists (notably developers), the *petit bourgeoisie* (e.g. self-employed architects and builders), the expert middle classes (e.g. salaried architects and engineers), and the working class (e.g. building labourers) (see Ball 1986), have always played an important role in Australian urban development. Indeed, property speculation is a major component of such development, and goes back at least to the 1860-90 economic boom (e.g. see Davison, 1978). Moreover, much of the speculative CBD development of the 1970s and 80s drew upon capital withdrawn from manufacturing which, in turn, was associated with de-industrialisation (see Berry and Huxley 1992; Low and Wu 1987).

Fifth, of all the new developments in Australian urbanisation, tourism urbanisation is perhaps the most dramatic. There are entire cities and towns specially built, as were the Gold Coast and the Sunshine Coast, or being transformed, as is Cairns, to attract large numbers of short-term residents (tourists). They move into these centres to buy and consume some of the many pleasurable goods and services on sale (see Mullins 1984, 1990, 1991b, 1992c). In other words, tourism urbanisation is based on the sale and consumption of fun. Having its roots in the 1945–70 economic boom, it represents the most rapidly-expanding of the contemporary Australian urban forms, with the Gold Coast and the Sunshine Coast being by far the fastest-growing of the large cities. In fact, the Gold Coast recently displaced Wollongong as the eighth largest city in Australia (see Table 17.2), and is likely to displace Canberra to become the seventh largest city within the next few years (see Mullins 1992c).

The rapid construction of these pleasure-dispensing centres is also tied to the property speculations of the 1970s and 80s, the same speculative ventures which promoted CBD redevelopment. Capital switched from the crisis-ridden manufacturing sector to land, real estate, and the construction of new buildings in tourist centres like the Gold Coast (see Mullins 1984, 1992c; Rimmer 1988).

In class terms, tourism urbanisation is significantly affected by the *petit bourgeoisie* and by small capitalists. On the Gold Coast and the Sunshine Coast, they directed the construction of these cities, and are now largely responsible for the dispensing of tourism services (see Mullins 1984, 1991b, 1992c). This can be seen in Table 17.3, where one-quarter of the Gold Coast's social classes are classes of owners, capitalists and the *petit bourgeoisie*, a much larger share than in the other three cities. Moreover, if the size of the Gold Coast's middle classes is any indication, then these classes played a relatively minor role in tourism urbanisation compared with the role played by the middle classes in other cities (see Table 17.3).

Sixth, post-1970 Australian urbanisation has also been shaped by changes to primary production. The expansion of mining in the 1960s and 70s brought marked regional changes, specifically to the outland states of Queensland (coal) and Western Australia (iron ore). This was made possible by an alliance of foreign mining capitalists, some local capitalists, and some local *petit bourgeoisie* (see Mullins 1986). Moreover, crises in agriculture and pastoralism in the 1980s and 90s disproportionately hit the peripheral states, those more reliant upon rural industries (see Chapter 18). Apart from an increase in rural poverty, there has been a decline in the *petit bourgeoisie* (like farmers and small town shopkeepers). (For a discussion of contemporary regional change, see Taylor 1991.)

In sum, post-1970 Australian urbanisation has six major economic characteristics which are based on new forms of class relations. Where de-industrialisation and new manufacturing industries had a more limited impact upon Australian urbanisation, compared with the urbanisation of core capitalist countries, the growth of services and the accompanying redevelopment of CBDs paralleled what happened in the other countries. But the one other feature clearly distinguishing contemporary Australian urbanisation is tourism urbanisation, the construction of cities and towns for fun.

Political Relations
The 1970s saw a marked increase in interest in urban and regional planning (see Neutze 1978). This was led by the federal Labor government of 1972–75, which created the Department of Urban and Regional Development (DURD) to (among other things) decentralise population and economic activity away from the large cities, specifically Melbourne and Sydney, to growth centres within their states (see Lloyd and Troy 1981). In addition to responding to basic economic needs, these programs contained strong elements of social justice (see Troy 1981). However, they were prematurely halted following Labor's defeat in 1975, with DURD subsequently being dismantled.

It is ironic, however, that the decentralisation of the Australian population over the 1970s and 80s did not result from DURD initiatives, but from other (particularly economic) influences. These encouraged people to move to the outland states, specifically Queensland and Western Australia, and not out of Melbourne and Sydney to other parts of Victoria and New South Wales, as DURD intended.

In the late 1980s, the federal Labor government renewed its interest, with state and local governments, in planning urban and regional development. Particular attention was given to the largest cities, with programs of change largely being packaged in the form of the inter-governmental Building Better Cities Program. This initiative emphasises economic growth; improvements in the quality of residential life; social justice to the disadvantaged; removing environmental problems and creating ecologically sustainable development; improving physical infrastructure; and attempting to reduce the costs of urban development.

Urban consolidation — the attempt to attract people to the depopulated inner and middle suburbs of large cities in order to reduce the costs of urban development, particularly costs at the urban outskirts — represents one of the more forcefully advocated schemes. However, as McLoughlin (1991) argues, urban consolidation would not only be extremely expensive to implement, but is unlikely to curtail current urban development. The urban fringe is likely to continue to expand at about the same pace.

In conclusion, and as indicated above, the MFP is another state planning initiative. Through the federal and South Australian governments, a new industrial space, and an adjunct, new residential space, is planned for Adelaide. However, this has yet to be implemented, and there are doubts about whether it will ever be as significant as originally intended.

Consumption Relations

The most marked change in Australian urban consumption relations over recent years is the increasing number of people whose quality of life has deteriorated, a deterioration resulting from declining economic fortunes and other social upheavals of the last two decades. Many people are experiencing difficulties in obtaining adequate housing and good residential facilities, including access to home-ownership, the principal housing tenure in Australia (see Stilwell 1987). Aggravating the problem is the limited availability of government rentals and good secure private ones. These difficulties partly explain the increasing numbers of people who have moved to the outlying areas of the five largest cities where housing, in the form of home-ownership, is cheaper. Yet, these locations are disadvantaged in having a shortage of adequate residential facilities, like public transport.

The most marked indication of the decline in the quality of urban life is the sharp rise in urban poverty, and the most striking is the emergence of an urban underclass, people in chronic poverty (see Wilson 1989). This situation is more characteristic of American cities, particularly those experiencing de-industrialisation, while in Australia, the urban underclass is evident among some young adults and families headed by women (see James and Vipond 1985; Trethewey 1989).

Where urban poverty represents a severe underconsumption of necessities, the other striking change in consumption relations over the last two decades is over-consumption. This involves people with bigger and better (and maybe even more) housing, more health care, more education, etc., but who also have greater opportunities to consume more and more goods and services providing pleasure. The term the post-modern city is used to identify the urban form accompanying this consumption (see Mullins 1991b). Tourism urbanisation is the most dramatic representation of the post-modern city because here are entire cities and towns built specially for the sale and consumption of pleasure. That such large cities are devoted to this purpose indicates the importance of this form of consumption for Australia and Australian urbanisation.

The growth in the consumption of pleasure is also apparent in gentrification and the rise of consumption compounds. Gentrification usually occurs in the inner cities of large metropolitan areas, and involves the redevelopment of working class dwellings for affluent consumers (e.g. see Hamnett 1991). Involved is both the consumption of necessities, like housing, and the consumption of goods and services providing pleasure, like visiting local art galleries (for Australian examples, see Badcock 1989b; Jager 1986; Mullins 1982).

Consumption compounds refer to the way parts of cities have been redeveloped for spectacles and festivals, and they aim to attract residents, as well as tourists, to buy and consume pleasures that are for sale (e.g. see Ley and Olds 1988). Examples range from Sydney's Darling Harbour to Brisbane's South Bank, including the Cultural Centre.

Urban movements, as the most overt expression of consumption relations, are residents' actions over the quality of urban life, and they were very evident in the 1970s. In Australia, many were defensive actions attempting to protect inner city housing, actions ranging from the opposition to freeways (see Mullins 1979) to actions taken by gentrifiers to protect inner city housing (e.g. see Nittim 1980). Where many 1970s actions were over large-scale developments like freeways, the 1980s saw a decline in these types of developments, and opposing actions. Contemporary urban movements seem to revolve around a large number of smaller issues concerned with the quality of urban life (for a discussion of international issues, see Castells 1983; Pickvance 1985).

Gender Relations

The last two decades have seen the increasing power of the women's movement as an expression of gender relations, and this has contributed to the reshaping of cities and towns. Much of the literature in Australia and elsewhere focuses on gendered divisions of urban space, on the social and physical segregation of males and females, and various social activities and processes (e.g. see England 1991; Fincher 1990; Harman 1988; Pratt 1990). Most particularly, there is the division between household and residential organisation, which has traditionally been a major female domain, and places of employment, which traditionally have been major male domains.

Over the last twenty years these divisions have been broken down, as women have become a major part of the workforce and as household and residential organisation was changed (e.g. with fewer nuclear families, more solo parents, more people living by themselves). Nevertheless, there remains a sex-segregated workforce, with women disproportionately occupying low paid jobs, and being more reliant upon part-time work. Differences in social and geographic access to jobs between men and women have also been noted.

In some of the new urban developments mentioned above, women seem to be having a distinct impact. They appear to be playing a major role in gentrification (e.g. see Bondi 1991) and there is some suggestion that they may also be having an important effect upon tourism urbanisation (see Mullins 1992d).

Race/ethnic Relations

The two most notable features of race/ethnic relations and urbanisation over the last two decades is the Aboriginal land rights question, and multiculturalism. The former is tied to the impact of the Aboriginal land rights movement and the way the land question has been renegotiated in Australia over the last few decades (see Keen 1988). This renegotiation seems partly tied to the shift in land use over the years since the 1960s, notably with the expansion of mining, the restructuring of agriculture and pastoralism (including the rural crisis itself), the decline of manufacturing industry, the rise of environmental concerns, and the increasing use of land for tourism. The vacuum created by this move from an old way of using land to a new one, seems to have provided Aboriginal societies with an opportunity to influence the new meaning given to Australian land and its use.

At an urban level, multiculturalism has led to cultural diversity in cities and towns, and this is tempering the dominant Anglo culture. This is partly shown in a degree of ethnic segregation, but is also expressed more broadly throughout urban Australia (see Jupp 1988). Finally, it is also important to note the very significant impact race/ethnic relations have had on the cities of other societies (e.g. see Rex 1973; Rex *et al.* 1979; Wilson 1987).

Conclusion

This chapter has identified the way Australian urbanisation has changed over the last century, but particularly over the last two decades, a time of very marked change. The argument given revolves around understanding the social forces involved in this transformation, with social forces being actions people take which bring change.

In conclusion, there are two issues worth raising for purposes of discussion. The first is the way Australian urbanisation has, historically, failed to neatly fit the model used to describe the urbanisation of developed countries, the societies of which Australia is said to be part. Australia certainly has fundamental similarities with what can be called 'Western urbanisation', but also has parallels with the urbanisation of the 'periphery' (i.e. underdeveloped nations). Indeed, Australian urbanisation seems located somewhere between the core and the periphery, though closer to the former than to the latter. It can thus be said that Australia has a form of semi-peripheral urbanisation. At least five historic similarities can be identified between Australian and peripheral urbanisations. These are the presence of: (1) primate cities; (2) cities and towns based significantly on commercial rather than manufacturing activity; (3) high levels of home ownership; (4) poorly provided public infrastructure; and (5) widespread informal economies. It seems, as Chase-Dunn (1989, 1990) argues, that there is value in studying semi-peripheral urbanisation as a way of extending our understanding of capitalist urbanisation. For too long, a simple distinction has been made between the core and the periphery, and this has led to a failure to note the complexities of capitalist development and capitalist urbanisation (e.g. see Sanders 1992). Therefore, exploring the nature of semi-peripheral urbanisation, like that of Australia's, comes to be a useful way of exploring diversity in urbanisation. This exploration would include understanding the nature of the social relations and social forces involved.

The second issue is the land question: the way Australian development and Australian urbanisation has been based on the use and exploitation of land. This pattern differs from the way manufacturing industry was the basis of European, Japanese, and United States development. Land has been important in Australia in two main ways. The first is for productive capitalist exploitation in the form of pastoralism, agriculture (including horticulture), and mining. The second is in urban land development, particularly of a speculative kind, which today is seen in tourism urbanisation, and which in recent years was seen in CBD property development. The character of Australian urbanisation, therefore, is also shaped by the distinctive way social relations like gender relations have revolved around the land question.

Note

1. It should be noted that the social forces identified in this chapter are modified versions of those initially identified in Mullins 1988.

References

Badcock, B. (1984) *Unfairly Structured Cities*. Oxford: Basil Blackwell.
———(1989a) 'Homeownership and the Accumulation of Capital', *Environment and Planning D: Society and Space* 7 (1): 69–91.
———(1989b) 'An Australian View of the Rent Gap Hypothesis', *Annals of the Association of American Geographers* 79: 125–45.
Ball, M. (1986) 'The Built Environment and the Urban Question', *Environment and Planning D: Society and Space* 4 (4): 447–64.
Bell, M. (1992) *Internal Migration in Australia, 1981–86*. Canberra: Australian Government Publishing Service.
Berry, M. (1984) 'The Political Economy of Australian Urbanisation', *Progress in Planning* 22 (1): 1–83.
———and Huxley, M. (1992) 'Big Build: Property Capital, The State and Urban Change in Australia', *International Journal of Urban and Regional Research* 16 (1): 35–59.
Bondi, L. (1991) 'Gender Divisions and Gentrification: A Critique', *Transactions of the Institute of British Geographers (NS)* 16: 190–98.
Buckley, K. and Wheelwright, T. (1988) *No Paradise for Workers*. Oxford: Oxford University Press.
Butlin, N. (1976) *Investment in Australian Economic Development 1861–1900*. Canberra: Australian National University.
———Barnard, A. and Pincus, J. (1982) *Government and Capitalism*. Sydney: Allen and Unwin.

Castells, M. (1977) *The Urban Question*. London: Edward Arnold.
———(1983) *The City and the Grassroots*. London: Edward Arnold.
Castles, F. (1985) *The Working Class and Welfare*. Wellington: Allen and Unwin.
———(1988) *Australian Public Policy and Economic Vulnerability*. Sydney: Allen and Unwin.
———(1989) 'Social Protection by Other Means', in F. Castles (ed.), *The Comparative History of Public Policy*. Cambridge: Polity.
Chase-Dunn, C. (1985) 'The Coming of Urban Primacy in Latin America', *Comparative Urban Research* XI (1–2): 14–31.
———(1989) *Global Formation*. Oxford: Basil Blackwell.
———(1990) 'Resistance to Imperialism: Semiperipheral Actors', *Review (Fernand Braudel Center)* XIII (1): 1–31.
Clark, R. (1985) 'Urban Primacy and Incorporation into the World-Economy: The Case of Australia, 1850–1900', in M. Timberlake (ed.), *Urbanization in the World-Economy*. Orlando: Academic Press.
Davis, K. (1974) 'The Urbanisation of the Human Population', in C. Tilly (ed.), *An Urban World*. Boston: Little, Brown.
Davison, G. (1978) *Marvellous Melbourne*. Melbourne: Melbourne University Press.
Daly, M. (1982) *Sydney Boom, Sydney Bust*. Sydney: Allen and Unwin.
England, K. (1991) 'Gender Relations and the Spatial Structure of the City', *Geoforum* 22 (2): 135–47.
Fagan, B. and Bryan, D. (1991) 'Australia and the Changing Global Economy: Background to Social Inequality of the 1990s', in J. O'Leary and R. Sharp (eds), *Inequality in Australia*. Melbourne: William Heinemann Australia.
Fairbairn, M. (1989) *The Ideal Society and Its Enemies*. Auckland: Auckland University Press.
Fincher, R. (1990) 'Women in the City: Feminist Analyses of Urban Geography', *Australian Geographical Studies* 28 (1): 29–37.
Frost, L. (1991) *The New Urban Frontier*. Kensington: New South Wales University Press.
Gertler, M. (1988) 'The Limits of Flexibility', *Transactions of the Institute of British Geographers (NS)* 13: 419–32.
Gilderbloom, J. (1988) 'Is Urban Sociology Dying?, *Teaching Sociology* 16: 443–47.
Gottdiener, M. and Feagin, J. (1988) 'The Paradigm Shift in Urban Sociology', *Urban Affairs Quarterly* 24 (2): 163–87.
Hamnett, C. (1991) 'The Blind Men and the Elephant: The Explanation of Gentrification', *Transactions of the Institute of British Geographers (NS)* 16: 173–89.
Harman, E. (1988) 'Capitalism, Patriarchy, and the City', in C. Baldock and B. Cass (eds), *Women, Social Welfare, and the State*. Sydney: Allen and Unwin.
Harvey, D. (1989) *The Condition of Postmodernity*. Oxford: Basil Blackwell.
Haughton, G. (1990) 'Manufacturing Recession? BHP and the Recession in Wollongong', *International Journal of Urban and Regional Research* 14 (1): 70–88.

Head, B. (1986) 'Economic Development in State and Federal Politics', in B. Head (ed.), *The Politics of Development in Australia*. Sydney: Allen and Unwin.

Henry, N. (1992) 'The New Industrial Spaces: Locational Logic of a New Production Era?', *International Journal of Urban and Regional Research* 16 (1): 375–96.

Higgins, B. and Zagorski, K. (eds) (1989) *Australian Regional Developments*. Canberra: Australian Government Publishing Service.

Inkster, I. (1991) *The Clever City*. Sydney: Sydney University Press.

Jager, M. (1986) 'Class Definition and the Esthetics of Gentrification', in N. Smith and P. Williams (eds), *Gentrification and the City*. Boston: Allen and Unwin.

James, J. and Vipond, J. (1987) 'Changes in Poverty in Australian Mainland Capital Cities', *Urban Policy and Research* 5 (2): 51–60.

Johns, M. (1992) 'The Urbanization of Peripheral Capitalism: Buenos Aires, 1880–1920', *International Journal of Urban and Regional Research* 16 (3): 352–74.

Jupp, J. (1983) 'The Politics of "Ethnic" Areas of Melbourne, Sydney and Adelaide', in J. Halligan and C. Paris (eds), *Australian Urban Politics*. Melbourne: Longman Cheshire.

———(ed.) (1988) *The Australian People*. North Ryde: Angus and Robertson.

Keen, I. (1988) 'Aborigines and Islanders in Australia', in J. Najman and J. Western (eds), *A Sociology of Australian Society*. Melbourne: Macmillan.

Kilmartin, L. and Thorns, D. (1978) *Cities Unlimited*. Sydney: Allen and Unwin.

Lash, S. and Urry, J. (1987) *The End of Organised Capitalism*. Cambridge: Polity Press.

Lebas, E. (1982) 'Urban and Regional Sociology in Advanced Industrial Societies'. *Current Sociology* 30 (1): 1–271.

Ley, D. amd Olds, K. (1988) 'Landscape as Spectacle: World's Fairs and the Culture of Heroic Consumption', *Environment and Planning D: Society and Space* 6 (2): 191–92.

Logan, J. and Molotch, H. (1987) *Urban Fortunes*. Berkeley: University of California Press.

Lloyd, C. and Troy, P. (1981) *Innovation and Reaction*. Sydney: Allen and Unwin.

Low, N. and Wu, S. (1987) 'Movements of Capital and the Built Environment', *Urban Policy and Research* 5 (2): 80–85.

———and Moser, S. (1991) 'The Causes and Consequences of Melbourne's Central City Property Boom', *Urban Policy and Research* 9 (1): 5–27.

Lyman, B. (1992) 'Urban Primacy and World-system Position', *Urban Affairs Quarterly* 28 (1): 22–37.

McLoughlin, B. (1991) 'Urban Consolidation and Urban Sprawl', *Urban Policy and Research* 9 (3): 148–56.

———(1992) *Shaping Melbourne's Future*. Cambridge: Cambridge University Press.

Mellor, R. (1989) 'Urban Sociology: A Trend Report', *Sociology* 23 (3): 241–60.

Mullins, P. (1979) 'The Struggle Against Brisbane's Freeways, 1966–74', *International Journal of Urban and Regional Research* 3 (4): 542–52.

——(1981a) 'Theoretical Perspectives on Australian Urbanisation: I: Material Components in the Reproduction of Labour Power', *Australian and New Zealand Journal of Sociology* 17 (1): 65–76.

——(1981b) 'Theoretical Perspectives on Australian Urbanisation II: Social Components in the Reproduction of Labour Power', *Australian and New Zealand Journal of Sociology* 17 (3): 35–43.

——(1982) 'The "Middle Class" and the Inner City', *Journal of Australian Political Economy* 11: 44–58.

——(1984) 'Hedonism and Real Estate', in P. Williams (ed.), *Conflict and Development*. Sydney: Allen and Unwin.

——(1986) 'Queensland: Populist Politics and Development', in B. Head (ed.), *The Politics of Development in Australia*. Sydney: Allen and Unwin.

——(1987) 'Community and Urban Movements', *Sociological Review* 35 (2).

——(1988) 'Is Australian Urbanisation Different?', in J.M. Najman and J.S. Western, *A Sociology of Australian Society*. Melbourne: Macmillan.

——(1990) 'Tourist Cities as New Cities', *Australian Planner* 28: 37–41.

——(1991a) 'The Identification of Social Forces in Development as a General Problem in Sociology', *International Journal of Urban and Regional Research* 15 (1): 119–26.

——(1991b) 'Tourism Urbanization', *International Journal of Urban and Regional Research* 15 (3): 326–42.

——(1992a) 'Residents' Organisations as the Institutional Mechanism for Mobilising Urban Movements', Unpublished paper, Department of Anthropology and Sociology, University of Queensland.

——(1992b) 'Do Industrial Cities Have the Highest Rates of Urban Unemployment?', *Urban Policy and Research* 10 (1): 24–32.

——(1992c) 'Cities for Pleasure', *Built Environment* 18(3): 187–98.

——(1992d) 'The Social Forces Shaping Tourism Urbanisation', Paper given at the New Urban and Regional Hierarchy Conference, University of California, Los Angeles, April 23–25.

Neutze, M. (1978) *Australian Urban Policy*. Sydney: Allen and Unwin.

Nittim, Z. (1980) 'The Coalition of Resident Action Groups', In J. Roe (ed.), *Twentieth Century Sydney*. Sydney: Hale and Ironmonger.

Noakes, A. J. (n.d.) *The Work of a Progress Association*. South Brisbane: Rallings and Rallings.

Pickvance, C.G. (ed.) (1976) *Urban Sociology*. London: Tavistock.

——(1985) 'The Rise and Fall of Urban Movements and the Role of Comparative Analysis', *Environment and Planning D: Society and Space* 3 (1): 31–53.

Pahl, R. (1989) 'Is the Emperor Naked? Some Questions on the Adequacy of Theory in Urban and Regional Research', *International Journal of Urban and Regional Research* 13 (4): 709–20.

Paris, C. (1992) 'The Local Context of International Tourism: Economic and Demographic Restructuring and Urban/Regional Change', Paper given at the New Urban and Regional Hierarchy Conference, University of California, Los Angeles, April 23–25.

Pratt, G. (1990) 'Feminist Analyses of the Restructuring of Urban Life', *Urban Geography* 11 (6): 594–605.

Rex, J. (1973) 'Urban and Other Elements in Race Relations Theory', in J. Rex, *Race, Colonialism and the City*. London: Routledge.

——and Tomlinson, S., with Hearnden, D. and Ratcliffe, P. (1979) *Colonial Immigrants in a British City*. London, Routledge.

Rich, D. (1986) *The Industrial Geography of Australia*. Sydney: Methuen.

Rimmer, P. (1988) 'Japanese Construction Contractors and the Australian States: Another Round of Interstate Rivalry', *International Journal of Urban and Regional Research* 3: 404– 24.

Rose, A.J. (1966) 'Dissent from Down Under: Metropolitan Primacy as the Normal State', *Pacific Viewpoint* 7 (1): 1–27.

Rowland, D. (1979) *Internal Migration in Australia*. Canberra: Australian Bureau of Statistics.

Sanders, R. (1992) 'Eurocentric Bias in the Study of African Urbanization: A Provocation to Debate', *Antipode* 24 (3): 203–13.

Sassen, S. (1991) *The Global City*. Princeton: Princeton University Press.

Saxenian, A. (1989) 'In Search of Power: The Organization of Business in Silicon Valley and Route 8', *Economy and Society* 18 (1): 25–70.

Stilwell, F. (1987) 'The Housing Crisis, Squatters, and the State', *Urban Policy and Research* 5 (2): 73–79.

——(1991) 'An International New Town Down Under', *International Journal of Urban and Regional Research* 15 (4): 611–18.

Smith, C. (1985) 'Theories and Measures of Urban Primacy: A Critique', in M. Timberlake (ed.), *Urbanization in the World-Economy*. Orlando: Academic Press.

Smith, M.P. and Feagin (eds) (1987) *The Capitalist City*. Oxford: Basil Blackwell.

Storper, M. (1992) 'The Limits of Globalization: Technology Districts and International Trade', *Economic Geography* 68 (1): 60–93.

Szelenyi, I (1981) 'The Relative Autonomy of the State or State Mode of Production', in M. Dear and A. Scott (eds), *Urbanization and Urban Planning in Capitalist Society*. London: Methuen.

Taylor, M. J. (1991) 'Economic Restructuring and Regional Change in Australia,' *Australian Geographical Studies* 29 (2): 255–67.

Taylor, P.J. (1986) 'The World-systems Project', in R.J. Johnston and P.J. Taylor (eds), *A World in Crisis*. Oxford: Basil Blackwell.

Timberlake, M. (1985) 'The World-system Perspective and Urbanization', in M. Timberlake (ed.), *Urbanization in the World-Economy*. Orlando: Academic Press.

Trehewey, J. (1989) *Aussie Battlers*. Melbourne: Collins Dove.

Troy. P. (ed.) (1981) *Equity in the City*. Sydney: Allen and Unwin.

Turner, J. (1989) 'The Disintegration of American Sociology, *Sociological Perspectives* 32: 419–33.

Walby, S. (1986) *Patriarchy at Work*. Cambridge: Polity.

Wallerstein, I. (1979) *The Modern World-System.* New York: Academic Press.

Warde, A. (1990) 'Production, Consumption and Social Change: Reservations concerning Peter Saunders' Sociology of Consumption', *International Journal of Urban and Regional Research* 14 (2): 228–48.

Webber, M. (1991) 'The Contemporary Transition', *Environment and Planning D: Society and Space* 9 (2): 165–82.

Wilson, W.J. (1987) *The Truly Disadvantaged.* Chicago: University of Chicago Press.

Wright, E.O. (1985) *Classes.* London: Verso.

Chapter Eighteen

Rural Australia

Perry Share, Geoffrey Lawrence and Ian Gray

What is 'Rural'?

Before addressing a sociology of rural Australia, it is necessary to locate the object of study which, on the face of it, should be

> as easy to define as getting cow dung on your boots, tractor diesel on your hands or a hot scone at a CWA function.
>
> (Dunn 1989)

Commonsense tells us that there is such a thing as 'the rural': conceptually (we know what it is) and empirically (we know it when we see it). Often we contrast the rural with other sorts of space or society, particularly the (sub)urban. The former is related to cows and windmills, shearers and open spaces, the latter to trams and opera houses, office workers and busy streets. This approach is perfectly adequate most of the time, but there may also be occasion to look more critically at the concept of 'rural'. Commonsense ideas may not be precise enough for the analysis of particular spatial, economic or social differences.

Sociologists have also begun to focus on ways in which the concept of 'rural' itself has developed. Like many terms used in sociology, it has an interesting history of changing meanings and connotations, which have varied across social contexts and intellectual paradigms.

It is not surprising that rural sociologists have long argued about the best way to define and categorise their field of study. There are two opposing views, with a broad range of positions between them. For some the rural is most importantly a *place* where:

> land use, landscape and settlements are patently different from their urban equivalents by dint of scale, density, remoteness and predominant forms of economic production, especially agriculture.
>
> (Cloke 1988: 3)

Those who adopt this *spatial* approach argue that rural areas and people have their own particular social features and problems. This was certainly the view of classical sociologists such as Durkheim and Weber.

Other sociologists, particularly within the Marxist tradition, reject the theoretical or empirical importance of spatial difference. Rather than focus on the supposed differences between rural and urban areas, they argue that in most developed nations (including Australia) *all* people, wherever they live, are 'culturally urbanised', have similar sorts of social and economic problems, are governed by the same political and administrative bodies, and are shaped by common media, education and family structures (Cloke 1988: 3).

There is currently insufficient sociological research in Australia to resolve the debate. In this chapter we examine some of the structures and processes that help to shape rural people's lives. We also show the effects of economic and social restructuring on aspects of Australian rural society and how some existing definitions and categories are increasingly difficult to sustain. We suggest that the rural *is* different, but also that it can only be understood in a broader, structural context.

A History of 'The Rural'

The Belgian rural sociologist Mormont (1990) has traced the emergence of the rural within sociological discourse. In the 1920s and 30s, sociologists responded to the problems of rural social change by examining the cultural values of rural dwellers rather than their conflicting economic interests. The rural was defined in moral terms, rather than as a space supporting particular productive activities, like agriculture or mining. This interpretation was given further impetus by the widespread adoption of the concept of the rural-urban continuum, developed by German sociologist Ferdinand Tönnies, which posited ideal-typical rural and urban societies with a range of possibilities between them. Within this paradigm sociologists sought out the distinctive norms, values and beliefs of rural dwellers, but in so doing often ignored or played down the dramatic structural changes shaping twentieth century rural life. Australian sociologists, when they took the trouble to examine rural areas (which was seldom) tended to follow a similar approach.

A significant shift took place in rural sociological thinking during the 1970s and 80s. Many American and European scholars began to examine the important structural changes that were taking place in rural life and industries. There was renewed concern with what people did or could do within social structures, rather than what they thought or felt. A sociology of agricultural production developed, with a particular focus on transnational agribusiness. The sociological spotlight moved from the individual farmer and his (it had always been 'his') family, towards the regional, national and global social structures within which agricultural producers operated. Some rural sociologists in Australia were strongly influenced by this new approach (Lawrence 1987), and began to analyse Australian agriculture and rural society in similar terms. Feminist scholarship also had a strong influence, and women in rural areas were identified as the 'forgotten farmers' (Sachs 1983).

More recently, sociologists' understanding of the rural world has begun to reflect the concepts and arguments of post-industrialism and post-modernism (Harvey 1989). Rural areas are now recognised as much more than just places for farming or mining. Powerful new forces such as environmentalism and the burgeoning tourist industry have given rise to new 'meanings' for rural areas, where the issue is not whether an area is used for agriculture or not, but how value attaches to a particular space. An area of land (say the old-growth forest areas of South-eastern New South Wales) may be subject to competing claims from farmers, timber workers, logging companies, conservationists, politicians, planners, retired people or tourist bodies. Each seeks to define and control the space in their own terms. In this way we can understand the often passionate conflicts over land use and rural living, where there is a struggle between particular interested groups over ways of enhancing and maintaining the value of space. Space is also central to the social and personal identity of particular groups in Australian society. Aboriginal people often define their identity in relation to space. The land has powerful meanings. Farmers and even homeowners may have similar cocncerns. When we recognise the potential for conflict over the *meaning* of land, we can better understand struggles over Aboriginal Land Rights, toxic waste incinerators and 'wilderness' areas.

The concept of rural is a complex and dynamic one, and to understand it we must analyse the meaning of the term for specific social groups and be aware of the ways in which they can mobilise economic and political resources in support of their own definition. We need, then, to be clear what is meant by rural when used as a sociological concept or variable. Some recent works on rural welfare and policy (e.g. Australian Housing Research Council 1989) clearly outline the particular way in which rural is being used, rather than assuming that it is self-evident. This is a positive development, because there will always be disagreement about what rural means.

Everyday Life in Rural Areas

Recent sociology has returned to the study of 'everyday life', the routinised and taken-for-granted texture of everyday experience (Smith 1988). Much of this impetus has come from feminist sociology, which has sought to erase the division between public (male) and private (female) worlds. This dichotomy has long been central to sociological thought and has also divided rural sociology: the masculine world of farm and public affairs has been firmly separated from the feminine arena of kitchen, home paddock and Country Women's Association. Recent community studies and works on rural women have confirmed the indivisibility of the two spheres and have raised issues of space, ideology and identity in particularly interesting ways.

Rural people generally fail to figure in mainstream Australian sociology, where they are consigned to residual categories, subsumed into urban groups, or ignored altogether. The everyday lives of rural people have been overlooked, and there have been few studies of rural work, family life or consciousness. Urban models of social life have been imported and urban patterns assumed, or else rural people have been dismissed as a different and somehow mysterious 'Other' (Share and Lawrence 1990). Often sociologists share a general rather romantic view of country life that owes as much to *The Man from Snowy River* or *A Country Practice* as to sociological research.

If rural is essentially a spatial category, then territory, residence, population density, distance, space and movement must help to shape social structure and relationships (Suttles 1972). In cities people are fairly free to associate with those of their own choosing, and clearly graded neighbourhoods permit social groups and relationships that are relatively homogenous in class and status terms. In small rural settlements, even where substantial material inequalities and social exclusiveness exist, people of different classes may be linked by personal ties of work, kinship or friendship, and interact as neighbours, or have much informal and friendly contact in hotels, shops or at sporting events (Dempsey 1990). Regular interaction in a variety of institutional contexts leads to a strong social and psychological interest in ignoring or denying social inequalities. The geographic isolation and small size of rural settlements may increase social mobility, which in turn may affect people's social consciousness and lead to a more permeable set of distinctions, though it appears that gender-exclusive groups are common in even the smallest rural communities.

Work and Livelihood

While the physical communities in which rural people live are important, sociological analysis must also encompass the broader structures of society. Rural Australia has been shaped by its relationship with the metropolis and 'sprang, fully armed as it were, from the industrial world of the nineteenth century' (Kapferer 1990: 92). Rural labour markets are shaped by movements of population and capital within regional, national and global markets. Distinguishing features of the rural labour force include the high proportion of employers and self-employed, and the flexible and diverse workforce which includes many casual, seasonal and part-time employees (Powell 1987). These are dispersed across small workplaces and are often non-unionised or in 'compliant' unions (Kapferer 1990). Unemployment is higher in country areas, with considerable under-employment and hidden unemployment, especially among women (Powell 1987). There has been a long-term decline in farm employment, with many of the jobs that used to be done on farms transferred to country towns or regional centres, in the shape of specialist financial, technical and management services. While full-time male labour on farms has declined most sharply, there has been an increase in female, part-time and specialist labour. The employment situation of farmers and rural workers is often complex: farm owners may not be fully employed on their farm but also take off-farm work, while agricultural employees may be employed by a range of people (Powell 1987).

In country towns small-to-medium businesses have held an important position, servicing the needs of the hinterland and linking rural areas to regional and metropolitan centres. Many of their functions, such as the sales and maintenance of agricultural machinery, are now being relocated to regional or metropolitan centres. Transnational firms are also increasing their involvement in rural production, as described later in this chapter. Many country towns are now dominated by a single industry or company. This narrows the economic base and despite considerable labour migration between rural areas, severely limits occupational mobility. Good contacts and a knowledge of the local labour market remain the key to securing a job (Powell 1987).

Despite the narrowing of the occupational field, significant inequalities persist and help to shape the everyday lives and possibilities of rural town residents. Divisions within the working class are expressed in the concept of 'rough townspeople' (Poiner 1990) or 'no-hopers' (Wild 1978; Dempsey 1990), who have fewer formal skills and qualifications and are labelled 'different', largely in terms of lifestyle, and lack of both adherence to the work ethic and 'respectability'. Aboriginal workers are particularly marginalised and discriminated against, and are seldom employed in the retail or service type jobs that constitute the only growth sector in many country towns. Changes in the labour market, involving the destruction of many manual and casual jobs, have had a strong and direct impact in rural areas and have led to an intensification of black/white division (Cowlishaw 1988).

Though rural people routinely oppose government intervention, up to one-half the employment in country towns is in the public sector (Cowlishaw 1988). About one-third of such jobs involve special training or qualifications which are not available locally, and are generally taken up by 'outsiders'. These people may become part of the community if they accept the dominant ideology, commit their futures to the community, and form local ties. If their children remain in the area they will almost inevitably move down the class structure. Sons of professional or administrative families may work as drivers or equipment operators, and daughters as shop assistants or typists (Dempsey 1990).

Within such constraints, workers appear to adopt an accommodating attitude towards employers, shaped by the belief that country life is superior to that of the city. They tend to be supportive of business and development which are seen as the only means of providing local employment for themselves and their children: militant collective action may frighten away existing employers or discourage new investment. Such a stance is justified by the decline of employment opportunities. Kapferer (1990) has argued that Australian country towns are, by virtue of centralised governing structures and the nature of economic development, particularly attuned to their links with the metropolis and the global context.

Rural workers tend to see more similarity than difference between themselves and their employers. A key to this process is the influence of the Australian Workers' Union (AWU) which has acted as a stabilising force in agricultural and other rural industries. The industrial actions of shearers and other rural workers remain 'frozen at the perception of the need for collective action in pursuit of limited industrial ends' (Gill 1981: 146). Indeed, many rural workers do not express even this level of class consciousness or solidarity. Despite the claims of rural employers, the activity (and inactivity) of rural unions has consistently maintained inferior working conditions and rewards for rural workers, but this disparity is more commonly reflected in the image of the rapacious urban unionist, rather than the industrial weakness of rural workers and their unions. As we shall see, this leaves rural workers in a poor bargaining position in relation to national and transnational capital.

Gender

> Things are changing. A woman has as much chance as a man. All the women who go out to work here wouldn't if their husbands didn't believe in it. It's not a male-dominated society — was it ever? Women see themselves as having equal standing; they accept their place and seem quite happy with what's coming home.
>
> (Marulan woman, quoted in Poiner 1990: 130)

> Men and women are equal — the men go to the pub and the women go to their parties.
>
> (Marulan woman, quoted in Poiner 1990: 135)

Gender relations in the country, as in the cities, are fraught with ambiguity and contradiction. Sociological analyses of rural society have tended to be highly male-centred (Bryson and Wearing 1985), and the relationship between class, status and gender is still highly problematic. Sociologists, particularly feminists, have begun to penetrate the 'general climate of invisibility surrounding rural women', exposing their 'powerlessness, the lack of recognition for their contributions to rural life and the ideology of male dominance and female subservience' (Alston 1990a). Deeply structured gender inequality has been revealed in rural work (Gibson *et al.* 1990) and leisure (Dempsey 1989; James 1989), as well as in 'hidden' practices such as domestic violence (Coorey 1990). Immigrant and Aboriginal women in rural areas have been shown to be particularly marginalised (Andreoni 1989; Thorpe *et al.* 1989; Andreoni *et al.* 1990). Many so-called 'women's issues' are really central to rural life. Voluntary work, for example, while largely seen to be the domain of women, is crucial to the economic survival and quality of life of many communities.

Gender relations in rural areas intersect in complex ways with structures of class and ethnicity. It is not merely a question of aggregating these categories, for they 'do not sit together as descriptions of social realities which are comparable or even of the same order' (Kalantzis 1990: 46). Rural society is complex, and there is great variety in the way in which structures of inequality inter-relate. Based on his analysis of 'Smalltown', Dempsey (1990) argues that while gender divisions cut across class, they fail to unite rural women as a group: class has greater structural influence. Poiner (1990) suggests that in the New South Wales town of Marulan, women create and sustain 'public images' of class, but her use of a generalised concept of patriarchy tends to dilute class categories. There is still much debate on the relationship between class and gender in rural areas and more research is required before definitive statements can be made.

Public decision making, for example in local government, tends to be dominated by men (Rew 1989; Gray 1991). Women may defer to public displays of social power, 'falling into step three paces behind' (Poiner 1990: 129). It has been suggested that some rural women have been hostile towards feminism or concepts of gender equality, helping to transmit and maintain rural ideology, bourgeois hegemony and male domination (Alston 1990b; Poiner 1990). When women do emerge as more powerful or influential in some sphere, for example in social affairs, the situation may be redefined in such a way as to reaffirm male superiority. While it is mistaken to draw a solid line between 'public' and 'private' spheres, it may be that rural women do exert their own power through domestic and some public practices, and may also achieve status through various types of work and skill (James 1989; Redclift and Whatmore 1990). Domestic power relationships and decision making processes are elusive and notoriously difficult to measure (James 1990), but female researchers may, as Poiner argues, be able to gain information on networks of power that are invisible or inaccessible to male sociologists.

Rural women also face inequality in the area of employment (East 1989). The limited jobs are often unskilled, casual, part-time, poorly remunerated and without long-term security or prospects. A small number of professional or semi-professional positions (generally in the education, welfare and medical fields) are available to the suitably qualified, but appropriate qualifications must generally be obtained outside rural areas. Even in large regional centres, employment opportunities are scarce in 'female' occupations like computing, media and certain paramedical areas (Clarke 1989). Many rural women are very over-qualified for their jobs. Nurses, for example, may be found working as hospital cleaners (Gibson *et al.* 1990). This makes it difficult for sociologists to make generalisations about class based on education or credentials. Many rural women are also involved in economic activities like party selling and voluntary work which, though often trivialised by men and women alike, have important economic and social functions.

Patriarchal property relations also contribute markedly to gender inequality in rural areas. Inheritance practices favour sons over daughters and restrict access to land and property. Male-borne family names are often strongly linked to land and it is principally men who inherit and subsequently develop holdings. Women may often be incorporated into partnerships for taxation reasons, but have a minor role in land transactions (Poiner 1990) and a woman's legal equality in an enterprise will not prevent its public perception as the male's, with the woman at best a junior partner. Farm women usually take up residence near their husband's family and have little opportunity to make direct use of land in their own right, unless they remain single and/or farm on their own account. Those who do so may encounter the considerable hostility experienced by women entering 'non-traditional' areas of employment (Gibson *et al.* 1990). Furthermore, rural women's separation from the principal source of wealth and income makes them vulnerable in cases of marital breakdown or domestic violence (Coorey 1990).

The comparative lack of educational and employment opportunities may lead rural women into early marriage and childbirth. Domestic responsibilities may also weigh more heavily on women in rural areas, because of larger families, less acceptance of working mothers, inadequate child care provision and greater ideological commitment to 'the family' (Poiner 1990). This tendency is reinforced by the segregation of many social activities: men tend to exclude women from their activities, and when women are admitted, it is as subordinates and supporters rather than equals, for example in the area of leisure (Dempsey 1989). On the other hand, family and the material setting of the home may provide a basis for rural women's common experience. James (1989: 77) found that one-third of the women she studied 'did not care one way or another about any . . . activities beyond their home and circle of family and friends'. This intense domestic focus may be sustained by newcomers who, finding it hard to become fully accepted into the rural community, turn away from social activity and become increasingly centred on home and family, though such responses have also been found in suburban areas (Baxter and Gibson 1990; Richards 1990). Many farm women lead isolated lives, with social horizons restricted to near kin and neighbours. This situation may be exacerbated by lack of access to transport and the telephone may come to play a very important role in maintaining social contact (Office for the Status of Women 1988; Moyal 1989).

Class and Status

The material interests of farmers and small business people have tended to be neglected in analyses of rural class, but despite being a minority in rural populations, their position as owners and controllers of *property* makes them of key importance. Australian research into class and social inequality has focused on urban people and on measures of occupation and income, but a study of rural class shows how the transmission of property is crucial to the reproduction of social structure and relations:

> we generally think of property as defining our relationship to things ... It is, however, more accurate to think of property as defining sets of power relationships between people ... Encoded and enforced through law, it specifies rights and duties governing the behaviour of those with title and those without and these rights and duties both enable and constrain our actions in respect of one another.
>
> (Saunders and Harris 1990: 66)

The meaning of agricultural production lies not only in the production of commodities, but also in the production, reproduction and transmission of rights in property and the creation and maintenance of links between people. Land ownership may offer economic security and the ideal of self-employment, but is also a major determinant of social position (Gray 1991), contributing to worth and standing in the community. The interests of land holders are aligned, and differences between them concealed, with ownership and control of property a basis of social, political and ideological identity and solidarity. Property owning has:

> always drawn out the conservative element in the psyche and [is] the reason why the rural sector aligns with other 'country' forces whether they be pastoralists, squatters or wealthy landowners.
>
> (Duplain 1987: 2)

Discussions of rural social inequality have tended to focus more strongly on status relationships than those of *class*, if the latter is defined as the relationship to property or the means of production. The notion of rural class has been poorly theorised and unsystematically applied (McAllister 1978; Lawrence 1986), and related sociological issues of power, control, domination, exploitation, the labour process and politics have received scant attention. Some critical sociologists (McMichael 1984; Lawrence 1987; Cowlishaw 1988; Wells 1989) have linked local class processes to

the development of the global capitalist economic system, but
have still tended to neglect issues of everyday life and consciousness.

Baxter *et al.* (1991) have shown that class is an important
determinant of life chances and is related to macro-sociological
change, but that in everyday life and discourse it has little salience
for the majority of Australians. These findings have to a large
extent been borne out by recent community studies (Dempsey
1990; Poiner 1990), which have sought to disentangle the web of
relationships in rural areas through the concepts of class and
status — though the picture is still far from clear. Based on
extensive research in a Victorian country town, Dempsey suggests
(1990: 145) that class is perhaps too subtle and intricate to be
'capture[d] in the linear and fairly straightforward way that
sociologists so often believe they can [do]' but concludes that,
though relatively insignificant in discursive terms, class does have
distributive importance. The rural community offers least to
working class women but 'works well' for most, particularly
'upper middle class' men, who may achieve public prestige and
influence, satisfaction in their work, and a comfortable and secure
living.

Sociologists concerned with rural areas have had difficulty in
using class as an analytical tool and have tended instead to use
measures of social status. Weber saw class and status as analytically distinct, but overlapping in modern capitalist societies to
create particular social patterns in specific historical cases (Giddens
1971). Wild (1978) adopts this position and, in his study of
Bradstow (a country town in New South Wales), argues that class
and status overlap in complex ways and reinforce one another. On
the other hand, Lawrence (1986) has argued that rural status
systems may convey the 'appearances' of social inequality but not
address 'deeper class conflict'. Basically, sociologists who have
studied rural Australia cannot agree on the extent to which
dominant or common status systems are recognised or salient, or
even whether they exist. Though identified by Wild (1978) and
Poiner (1991), Dempsey (1990) could not locate such a system
within his population. No Australian sociologist has yet written
convincingly about rural social inequality in a way which links
local social interaction to the broader structures of social inequality and change.

Social Identity and Consciousness

Some rural residents argue that class is important in country towns. Others simply deny its existence. Dempsey (1990) has argued strongly that this denial is real, and is suspicious of earlier writers (e.g. Wild 1978) who have identified prevailing class discourses in country towns. Poiner (1990: 55–80) suggests that Marulan district residents 'share a broad understanding of the local system of social class', but does not show this in her study: class distinctions are not clearly perceived in the township or surrounding rural district,but are 'smudged'. These findings broadly reflect other recent Australian research into urban class and class consciousness (Baxter *et al.* 1991).

Rural people may actively resist seeing their community in class terms, stressing the homogeneity of a district and township, saying 'Oh! we're just all workers here' or 'We're just all country people' (Poiner 1990: 78; Gray 1991). While the existence of inequality in general terms is recognised, its local salience is denied. An egalitarian ideology and belief in a shared fate in the face of the common external enemy (the city, the government) work against the development of a class consciousness, as do the realities of living in a small and constrained community:

> the network of marriage and occupational ties esablished by farming, working- and business-class families must subject each of them to considerable cross pressures that reduce the likelihood of the members of any of these collectivities developing a strong sense of class identity.
>
> (Dempsey 1990: 265)

People focus on the types of difference that are salient to them: gender, age, occupation, religion, local or non-local, 'respectability' and contribution to the community. There are likely to be few outward markers of class such as speech, dress or conspicuous consumption, and to make claims on the basis of one's class is seen as snobbery. The influx, occuring in many rural settlements, of 'outsiders' who may range from extremely wealthy 'celebrities' to alternative lifestylers, may have the potential to change the nature of class relationships and ideologies in many country towns.

Community and other studies focus on the people who remain in rural areas, and it is important to recognise the long-standing pattern of out-migration to regional centres and metropolitan areas. The depopulation of rural areas is systematically patterned by gender, class, age and level of education (James 1989; Robinson 1990; Dempsey 1990). It is often suggested that the 'best' people leave, and that those who remain tend to be conservative and fatalistic. The implications of such migration for the class and gender structures of rural areas have been largely left unexplored.

Local Politics in Rural Areas

Studies of local politics in rural communities have been found broadly to reflect what has been said of gender, class and status relations. Local politics are usually defined by the arena of local government, which is particularly significant to rural communities as a planning power and provider of such essential services as roads, sewerage and water. Local government also acts as an advocate for local people in their relationships with central bodies, an important role in times of declining local economies and diminishing government services (Wild 1978; Gray 1991).

Local government bodies have tended to be élitist. Studies have usually shown them to be dominated by small groups of middle aged male employers, professionals and property owners of high status (Atkins 1979; Power *et al.* 1981; Bowman 1983; Chapman and Wood 1984; Sinclair 1987). Wild (1983) showed how the Victorian town of Heathcote had an unrepresentative council dominated, like many other rural councils, by a clique of employers. Oxley (1978) and Dempsey (1990) have each argued against the élitist position, suggesting that in the communities they studied, power was more dispersed.

It may be that the latter studies misperceived the operation of power in those communities: it is not just women's power networks that may be hidden from the sociological view. Power need not be wielded in an obvious or public way, particularly when contentious issues do not even get on to the political agenda. The Bradstow business élite sought to determine the direction of local politics (Wild 1978), but was thwarted by a higher status group which could call on higher ideals and better social connections. McIntyre and McIntyre (1944) found that while many country towns had leadership élites, people showed little concern about this and fatalistically believed that bad leadership was inevitable, which Oeser and Emery (1957) argued maintained the élitist structure. Gray's (1991) study of politics in Cowra (New South Wales) found that only certain issues came up for debate in the political arena. This process of agenda setting, though not necessarily deliberate or conscious, excluded some interests from decision making.

These political processes are reinforced by aspects of rural culture, particularly images of community and 'belonging' (Gray 1991). Political demands which are seen to be 'in the community's interest' make élitist politics acceptable to local people. Even those whose own particular interests are not being expressed may reasonably feel they are being served well as long as their community and its ideals are maintained. Local political structures based on local culture can thus outlive ruling cliques. Wild (1983) showed how a well-organised group of local people mobilised popular feeling to defeat the unrepresentative Heathcote council which had supported a state government decision to locate a toxic waste dump near the town. It was not hard for opponents of the dump to show that the broader community interest was being threatened.

Not all groups in the rural community can expect the same degree of success. Women, working class and Aboriginal people have little access to local politics, not necessarily in terms of getting a hearing, but certainly in terms of raising and winning issues. In rural areas where people have long had a farming identity and an opposition to urban interests, property owners and their organisations have substantial ideological and political resources, and while they do not necessarily attempt to deny these to others, their definitions of local interests often prevail. Local government has several institutional features which foster conservative and stereotyped decision making. Regressive rating systems favour conservative fiscal policies which are biased towards property services, and which limit progressive councillors and council staff alike. Rural local politics are beginning to change in some areas, however, as new populations move into many country towns and regions, raising new issues and forming new coalitions of power (Carson 1992).

We have attempted to show some of the complexity of everyday life and social structures in rural areas. Though the 1980s and 90s saw considerable sociological research on rural issues, there are still major gaps in our knowledge and understanding. We would suggest that spatial difference *is* of significance, and that patterns of inequality and interaction are qualitatively different in rural communities. But the nature of rural life cannot be understood apart from a consideration of the broader national and global structures that help shape it. The next section of this chapter addresses some of the changes that are taking place in this broader environment.

Agricultural Change and Rural Society

In 1950, agriculture contributed about one-quarter of Australian Gross Domestic Product (GDP) and about 90 per cent of export income. The growth of other industries, particularly mining and tourism, means that today rural production contributes about 4 per cent of GDP and less than one-third of our export dollars. While 7 out of 10 Australian workers are employed in the service sector, agriculture makes use of less than 5 per cent of the labour force (ABARE 1992). These dramatic changes, with falling commodity prices, have contributed to talk of a 'farm crisis'.

The origins of the 'crisis' are complex but it is possible to draw out some of the crucial global and local factors involved. The world economy has seen dramatic change since the 1970s. At the same time, the European Community (EC) started its program of expansion with three new members, Ireland, Denmark and Britain. The accession of Britain was particularly significant for Australian farmers, since they had long had guaranteed access to, and preferential treatment within, the large British market. Around the same time, the Bretton Woods Agreement, which had stabilised world currencies since World War II, collapsed, there was a sharp rise in oil prices, and wild fluctuations in world commodity prices (Marsden and Murdoch 1990; Buttel and Gillespie 1991; Goe and Kenney 1991).

The deterioration in commodity prices was accentuated by the EC's Common Agricultural Policy (CAP), which was designed to ensure European food security, to support rural populations, and to increase the efficiency of agricultural production (Commins 1990). In many ways, these were contradictory aims. The outcome has been a major embarrassment to EC policymakers: the CAP now consumes much of the EC budget, and has resulted in the notorious wine and milk 'lakes' and beef and butter 'mountains'. Much of this produce has been sold very cheaply (dumped) in countries of the former Soviet Union, and into other markets, some of which had long been supplied by Australia. The United States, which has its own long history of agricultural subsidisation (Vogeler 1981), has countered Europeans in the global market. Australian farmers, caught in the middle, have found it very difficult to challenge the two giant trading blocs.

Australian farmers have responded by attempting to improve their competitive position. One strategy has been to expand farms through the purchase of additional land. As the supply of land is virtually constant, this has led to a decline in the number of commercial farm units of the order of 4 per cent a year (ABARE 1988). It has been predicted that farm numbers (135,000 in 1992) will drop to about 70,000 by the year 2000 (Summons 1984). (The increase in 'hobby farms' is another process but contributes little to agricultural output.) Another strategy has been to replace labour (workers) with capital (technology). The result has been an expansion of rural debt and a changing farm workforce, with a sharp decline in full-time male labour and, as in other economic sectors, increased labour force participation by women, especially on a part-time or casual basis.

It is thought that farm poverty, while very difficult to measure, is nevertheless becoming prevalent in industries such as cereals, sugar and dairying. Many farmers have substantial assets but may, in times of continued low prices, be 'income poor'. In 1990–91, the average farmer had a net farm income of around $2,000, a figure expected to grow to no more than $10,300 by 1995 (*Bulletin*, 16 July 1990). Though it would seem likely that many farmers would leave agriculture, most seek to remain. Some are unable to sell their farms on a depressed market; others are convinced that prices will eventually improve. Many have neither the skills, education nor opportunity to move into alternative occupations.

Rural Decline

Changes in the agricultural sector are contributing to growing inequalities between rural and urban regions. Of the 37 poorest electorates in Australia, 33 are located in rural regions where average family income levels are less than half those recorded in the more affluent suburbs of Sydney, Melbourne and Canberra (Commonwealth Electoral Division 1988). Rural areas exhibit higher poverty and unemployment rates and a much narrower range of opportunities for work, education and retraining or welfare services. The federal Auditor-General (1988) has reported that in relation to wealth distribution and the availability of social services, those living in communities of under 10,000 face *considerable* disadvantage, while those in towns with populations below 5,000 face *extreme* disadvantage.

Contrary to popular perception, rural living does not contribute to better health. The rural downturn has damaged people's health and contributed to an increase in rates of domestic violence and suicide (Coorey 1990; Kellehear 1990; Lawrence and Williams 1990; Lohse 1992). Rural populations experience above-average rates of premature mortality and of death through ischaemic heart disease, cancer, suicide, tuberculosis and malnutrition (Humphreys 1990; Cullen *et al.* 1990). Aboriginal people in rural areas lack appropriate health services and experience significantly poorer health, including a mortality rate over four times that for whites, and a life expectancy up to 21 years lower (Thomson 1991).

The rural areas of Australia have experienced mixed patterns of demographic change. The most rapidly growing areas are the coastal regions, particularly of New South Wales and Queensland, which have experienced an influx of tourists and retirees. Other areas which have expanded dramatically have been those on the fringes of cities such as Berwick (Victoria), Picton (New South Wales) and Redlands (Queensland). In inland regions the picture is complex, with some centres such as Cowra and Tumut (New South Wales) and Emerald (Queensland) experiencing considerable growth, while many others are in decline. The trends are still unclear, yet there are many settlements in inland regions where agriculture continues to provide the basis for the generation of wealth and where long-term population decline is being experienced (Planning Research Centre 1989). This uneven pattern has led to a suggestion (Stayner and Reeve 1990) that rural towns are 'uncoupling' from their agricultural hinterlands and developing other sources of income, like government employment, tourism and transport services.

Many rural settlements have begun to experience the 'dynamic of decline' which stems from reduced economic activity, population loss and the withdrawal of state infrastructure. The impetus may be a commodity price crash, failure of a large company like a meatworks, or pulpmill or the closure of a government employer, like a gaol or a psychiatric hospital. As incomes decline, household expenditure is reduced, businesses close, people lose their jobs and school leavers must migrate to seek work or further education. Financially constrained governments declare that the town, which may now have limited political strength, no longer has the 'critical mass' to support particular services and may close down post and Telecom offices, pathology centres or branch libraries (Lawrence and Williams 1990). The town may be bypassed for recreation and shopping. Those who can may quit the area, while the unemployed and aged may remain trapped by their circumstances. Unable to sell their devalued homes or obtain work or appropriate services, they become candidates for rural poverty. The full extent of rural social deprivation has yet to be evaluated, but it appears that the economic decline of agriculture and the withdrawal of state provision from rural towns has resulted in a marked economic and social decline throughout some parts of rural Australia.

In addition to the social impact of agricultural change, there are important environmental implications arising from the use of non-sustainable agricultural practices over the last two centuries. Australia is the world's driest continent and seven-tenths of its area comprises arid or semi-arid lands. Though only one-tenth of Australian land is classed as arable, six times this amount is farmed or grazed (Woods 1983). Soils are of low fertility and highly susceptible to erosion, with soil formation virtually non-existent (Heathcote and Mabbutt 1988). Production of a tonne of grain contributes to the loss of about 13 tonnes of topsoil (O'Reilly 1988: 85) and an estimated $144 million worth of soil nutrients are lost from the soil each year (Fray 1991: 6).

The Murray-Darling Basin (MDB), which stretches from Charleville in Queensland to Adelaide, is Australia's most productive agricultural region, yet existing agricultural practices, salinity and soil degradation have led to declining yields, fewer crop varieties and the death of soil micro-organisms, reducing farm income by up to $220 million a year (MDB Ministerial Council 1990: 4). The works needed to address the problems have been costed at $1.6 billion (Crabb 1988). There are also severe problems with the Basin's water. In dry seasons, the salinity levels in bores exceed those recommended by the World Health Organization (Beale and Fray 1990). It is estimated that the Murray River carries over 1.3 million tonnes of salt to Adelaide each year and there has been concern about the safety and quality of the city's water supply. The Basin's rivers and creeks are affected by turbidity, industrial waste and sewage, agrochemicals and weeds (Crabb 1988), as well as toxic blue-green algal blooms. Much of this degradation is a result of intensive irrigation and poor farming.

In the 1990s Australian agriculture is as concentrated on the export of such commodities as it was in 1900, yet the world economic system has since changed dramatically. World product demand has altered substantially, due partly to technological development and the growing influence of transnational corporations (TNCs) (Dunkley and Kulkarni 1990). Concern for the environment and other 'externalities' of growth has increased, while governments have sought to reduce inflation and trade deficits through tight monetary policies.

At least half of Australian exports still consist of simply transformed manufactures (products remaining in raw or semi-processed form), a declining sector of world trade vulnerable to periodic price slumps. This represents a major structural problem in the economy. The Australian government and National Farmers' Federation (1993) have argued that 'value adding' — processing raw commodities here rather than leaving this to overseas companies — is the solution to the problems of agriculture, but success is difficult to achieve. Australia's Pacific Basin and Middle East trading partners generally have lower costs and local companies or TNCs can process there more profitably. It is in the interests of TNCs to maximise profits through using the best combination of low cost inputs and labour to assemble their products. The 'global sourcing' strategies of transnational trading companies in Australia has contributed to the fact that half of the

$15 billion worth of agricultural exports leaves the country in unprocessed form (*Australian Financial Review*, 15 March 1988).

The Structure of Agricultural Production

Federal government policies (Department of Trade 1987; DPIE 1989; ABARE 1991) have strongly supported the agribusiness model of farming (Juchau and Newman 1987; Lawrence 1987). Farm companies with higher levels of capital, often linked to TNCs, will strengthen their position in relation to more 'traditional' family farms, especially as the 'cost/price squeeze' increases. While it is unlikely that corporations will take over family properties on a significant scale (90 per cent of farms are still owner-operated), they are moving rapidly into the more dynamic and innovative branches of rural production such as feedlotting, horticulture and aquaculture. As the focus on value added and niche marketing grows, farmers trapped in traditional sectors may be disadvantaged. Those who depend on family labour and small-scale capital will increasingly be forced to merge with, or be displaced by, larger-than-family-farm units. Sophisticated management regimes and the application of agribusiness inputs has already allowed just one-fifth of farmers to produce about four-fifths of Australian agricultural output *(Australian Farm Journal*, February 1992).

Rural Australia may come to reflect the American experience of the 'disappearing middle' (Buttel and LaRamee 1991). Small farmers with off-farm income may be able to survive, though their contribution to overall agricultural production will be negligble. Middle sized farmers relying solely on income from agricultural commodities will decline in number, while large, corporate-linked, technically sophisticated farms which employ labour will increase in size and importance. Some smaller units will continue to be run as 'hobby farms' (Schwarzweller 1988). While urban-educated professionals often choose this lifestyle for taxation reasons, they are often highly conscious of environmental and pollution issues and have the knowledge and training to mobilise support for ecological causes. There is potential for considerable conflict between 'hobby' farmers and large-scale farmers who employ agribusiness technology to maximise production.

Such technologies increase farm incomes, but their cost leads to further specialisation and increased output. The absence of new markets contributes to falling prices, which stimulates productivity, setting up a vicious circle of over-production and low incomes. When family-farm agriculture was protected by a mantle of subsidies and price supports, the effects of such cycles could be mitigated. In this era of free market agriculture, family farmers are far more vulnerable. The federal government has thus sought to integrate Australian agriculture into the rapidly developing Pacific Basin. Foreign investment is being encouraged into sectors, such as cotton and grain-fed beef, that will appeal to Pacific Basin customers.

The feedlot beef industry, supplying grain-fed beef to Asian markets, especially Japan, is a good example of the shift towards the corporate-linked, vertically-integrated production that may result in new and potentially negative social relationships in Australian agriculture and rural society. It is predicted that by 1996 feedlots will be 'turning off' up to one-quarter of all cattle slaughtered in Australia (Alcorn 1991). The environmental impact could be significant: a 40,000 head feedlot produces as much effluent as a city the size of Canberra. It costs up to $100 million to establish treatment of such quantities of urban waste, but naturally feedlot developers are unprepared to make such investments. Their solution is to sun-dry animal manure for sale as fertiliser. This fails to solve problems of odour, seepage and run-off which are already causing complaints in the environs of feedlot developments (*Land*, 15 January 1989).

Agricultural Policies

Since the early 1980s, fiscal pressures and anti-intervention policies have led to a withdrawal of most of the substantial state support once enjoyed by rural producers. Such assistance as remains is targeted towards increasing agricultural efficiency and maximising the technological development of agriculture. For example, the federal government's Rural Adjustment Scheme serves two purposes: it allows farmers to borrow for expansion to take advantage of new technological developments in later years; it also helps to remove 'unviable' farmers from the industry. Other government policies such as changes to the regulation of banking, the removal of regulatory barriers to trade, and the abolition of statutory marketing authorities are all consistent with the government's desire to reduce levels of support for agriculture, and foster links between farmers and transnational agribusiness (Lawrence *et al.* 1992).

The publicly-funded laboratories of the CSIRO and the state agricultural research institutes once produced new seeds, animal breeds and technologies for the general benefit of the farming community. These organisations are now far more market-driven, and often collaborate with commercial firms. In such cases the knowledge generated can become private property through the application of patents or via plant variety rights (PVR) legislation. The Australian government has actively supported the development and application of new biotechnologies, which are seen as a key to improving Australia's agricultural competitiveness. Genetically-engineered products are expected to boost output while reducing input use, which should lead to less environmental damage. Plants may be developed which have a built-in resistance to insects or bacteria, and require fewer pesticide applications. Transgenic animals, new 'friendly' bacteria which improve rumen efficiency, new vaccines, the use of the cow as a chemical 'factory', embryo splitting and other developments are being encouraged in the hope of improving Australian agriculture's chances in the global marketplace (Begg and Peacock 1990; House of Representatives 1992).

Opponents of biotechnology point to possible consequences: herbicide-tolerant plants which actually *encourage* the increased use of chemicals; the possibility of 'rogue' genetically modified organisms escaping into the environment, mutating and then leading to displacement of existing organisms and environmental destruction; and increasing costs for farmers due to monopoly rights over patented genes (Hindmarsh 1992). Only recently has there been any attempt to evaluate the likely social impact of biotechnologies in agriculture (Lawrence and Vanclay 1993). While particular groups of farmers may benefit, agriculture may become increasingly vertically integrated as agribusiness corporations gain control of most aspects of input-provision and output-processing.

Agricultural Practices and Degradation of the Agricultural Environment

As in previous decades, farmers facing cost-price pressures turn to new methods, techniques and management practices. Those who are able use output boosting technologies such as expensive machinery. To maximise efficiency, land is cropped more intensively, and the most remunerative crops or livestock raised for as long as a profit can be returned. There is a tendency towards monoculture: continual production of a single crop. Soil nutrients must be maintained through repeated applications of fertiliser, while the build-up of pests requires increased pesticide use. Farmers overcrop, overgraze and overuse chemicals not out of greed, but for economic preservation in times of stagnant or falling commodity prices. The damage caused to farmlands and river systems is a symptom of a non-sustainable system of agriculture. Though farmers might be aware of ways they can alter production to reduce land degradation and water pollution, many put the short-term objective of staying in farming ahead of wider considerations of long-term sustainability of resources (Cameron and Elix 1991; Watson 1992).

Socio-economic Practices and Degradation of the Social Environment

Faced with an uncertain future, farm families are adopting a number of survival strategies. These include the replacement of hired labour with family members; keeping children home from school and college; becoming self-sufficient in food; reducing household expenditure; and, where possible, obtaining credit or applying for unemployment benefits (see Gray *et al.* 1993). While constructive in the short term for individual farm families, such strategies may have high social costs. Those who increase their on-farm work maybe unable to participate in community activities crucial to both the social and environmental well-being of rural communities. Removing children from school or college in order to save money on boarding fees or secure a cheap labour source may also have a similarly negative effect. Australian farmers of the future are not well educated: in 1987 only 7 per cent of rural boys and 10 per cent of rural girls who leave school after Year 12 went on to tertiary education, compared with 27 per cent for both urban girls and boys (CTEC 1987). Despite a general rise in retention and tertiary participation rates, there is no indication that this ratio has since changed. The problems of agriculture are contributing to the emergence of a poorly-educated group of farm operators who may be unable to make their way in the modern world of farming.

About one-third of Australian farm households gain income through off-farm work (Lawrence 1989). This is an important option for many farm families, but may become a problem when time and energy spent on wage labour leads to neglect of farm maintenance or machinery overhaul. Off-farm work may provide the necessary cash flow for survival without doing anything to help alter the farm production mix to achieve better results in the future. It may also limit the time farm members can give to voluntary activities such as Landcare or community development. 'Belt tightening' is also a viable short-term option for farmers. However, where reductions in household expenditure lead to restrictions on travel, telephone calls or social outings, the basis of family farm and rural community life is further eroded. Obtaining credit is a useful strategy only if debts can be repaid. The very impossibility of this in a period of recession has been one of the main factors responsible for the economic stress experienced by family-farm operators (see Bryant 1992). It has created major tensions between farmers and bankers.

Farmers may, as a final option, elect to leave agriculture. In a period of economic decline it may not be in the farmer's best interest to sell: indeed the price obtained for the farm may not even cover outstanding loans. The farmer may have few skills outside agriculture, and his or her removal from agriculture may simply add to the rural unemployment problem. The accumulated farming knowledge is lost to society while there may also be substantial welfare costs (Lawrence 1993). Bryant (1991) found that male former-farmers in the Eyre Peninsula of South Australia believed they were responsible for their own failure. They complained of deteriorating family life after they had left the farm, and had difficulty adapting to a new lifestyle. For such economic, social and personal reasons, economically marginal producers often attempt to stay on under any circumstances (Kidman 1991), but the social costs may be high (Gray *et al.* 1993).

There *is*, however, a positive side to restructuring. Those who survive are likely to have developed successful coping strategies which will help ensure longer-term survival. Some will have developed new products or discovered new markets. Others will have become 'pluriactive', combining agriculture with farm tourism or other income generating activities, in a permanent fashion. Urban professionals attracted to rural areas for lifestyle opportunities may begin to infuse capital into farming systems hoping to exploit opportunities for niche marketing in areas such as organic products. The growth of tourism, recreation and retirement in particular areas may assist farmers to develop new sources of income. The presence of a more educated and agriculturally-interested group, while potentially alienating more orthodox farmers, may help to disseminate information about alternative systems of rural production. Such a knowledge base may help contribute to future improvements in agriculture and rural society.

Conclusions

To understand the nature of contemporary rural Australia, people's values and beliefs, kinship structures and rural social institutions must be located within the context of the global capitalist economic system. Economic restructuring has exposed farmers to world markets in ways previously circumscribed by state intervention and producers' political influence. The removal of subsidies and the reduction of support for agriculture have been consistent with a strategy of encouraging transnational agribusiness. Changes to the regulation of financial institutions have provided international capital with incentives to 'globalise' food sourcing operations, while encouraging Australia's further integration into the Pacific Basin. The evidence suggests that these changes, in the context of a world agrofood system characterised by over-supply and unfair trading, place considerable pressure on small-scale capital in agriculture. At the same time there are developing opportunities for domestic and transnational capital to take advantage of the changing rural labour market. Increased 'flexibility' within the rural labour force, including a decline in the power of rural unions, has made some rural areas attractive sites for investment. In addition, new opportunities have emerged in tourism and other service industries, and a pool of cheap, relatively unorganised labour is available (Lawrence *et al.* 1992).

An examination of the everyday life of rural Australians reveals that there are many similarities between rural and urban societies. But there are also marked differences. Rural labour markets do not offer the same opportunities as those of the metropolis, and the dominance of self-employment and small and medium businesses influences local politics. Patriarchal attitudes, based on a desire to pass the family business or farm down the male line underpin the gender inequalities which permeate much of rural life. Widespread incorporation within the ethos (if not the reality) of property ownership supports the conservative attitudes and political interests which are widely espoused by country people.

Australian agriculture continues to play an important part in generating foreign exchange earnings and is, by world standards, one of the most labour-efficient and least protected. This does not imply a secure future for individual farm families or rural communities. As agricultural output and efficiency are increasing, farmers are leaving agriculture and many rural communities, particularly those inland, are contracting. At the same time, governments are rationalising their services, increasing the social and environmental problems of smaller rural communities. Australian people face the challenge of creating a rural society that is sustainable in both social and environmental terms. It may be that this means a declining role for agricultural and extractive production as we now know it, and a reshaping of rural Australia. The issues facing rural people and communities will continue to hold the attention of sociologists and many others, for their resolution will impinge on the lives of all Australians.

References

Alcorn, G. (1991) 'Feeding on Success', *Australian Farm Journal*, April.

Alston, M. (1990a) 'Introduction', to M. Alston (ed.), *Rural Women*. Wagga Wagga: Centre for Rural Social Research, Charles Sturt University.

———(1990b) 'Farm Women and Work' in Alston (1990a).

Andreoni, H. (1989) 'Immigrant Women in an Isolated Rural Community', in K. James (ed.), *Women in Rural Australia*. St Lucia: University of Queensland Press.

———, Wilton J. and Weinand, H. (1990) 'Non-english-speaking Women in Rural Australia: New England for Non-English Speakers' in Alston (1990a).

Atkins, R. (1979) *Albany to Zeehan: A New Look at Local Governments*. Sydney: Law Book Company.

Auditor General (1988) *Efficiency Audit Report: Department of Community Services and Health, Home and Community Care Program*. Canberra: AGPS.

ABARE (Australian Bureau of Agricultural and Resource Economics) (1988) *Quarterly Review of the Rural Economy* 10 (4).

———(1991) *Agriculture and Resources Quarterly* 3 (2).

———(1992) *Agriculture and Resources Quarterly* 4 (1).

Australian Housing Research Council (1989) *Rural Centres Housing Study*. Canberra: AGPS

Baxter, J. and Gibson, D. with Lynch-Blosse, M. (1990) *Double Take: the Links Between Paid and Unpaid Work*. Canberra: AGPS

———, Emmison, M., Western, J. and Western, M. (eds) (1991) *Class Analysis and Contemporary Australia*. Melbourne: Macmillan.

Beale, B. and Fray, P. (1990) *The Vanishing Continent*. Sydney: Hodder and Stoughton.

Begg, J. and J. Peacock (1990) 'Modern Genetic and Management Technologies in Australian Agriculture', in D. Williams (ed.), *Agriculture in the Australian Economy*. Sydney: Sydney University Press.

Bowman, M. (1983) 'Local Government in Australia', in M. Bowman and W. Hampton (eds), *Local Democracies: A Study in Comparative Local Government*. Melbourne: Longman Cheshire.

Bryant, L. (1991) 'Farm Family Displacement' in Alston, *Family Farming: Australia and New Zealand*. Wagga Wagga: Centre for Rural Social Research, Charles Sturt University.

———(1992) 'Social Aspects of the Farm Financial Crisis', in G. Lawrence, F. Vanday and B. Furze (eds), *Agriculture, Environment and Society*. Melbourne: Macmillan.

Bryson, L. and Wearing, B. (1985) 'Australian Community Studies — a Feminist Critique', *ANZJS* 21 (3).

Buttel, F. and Gertler, M. (1982) 'Agricultural Structure, Agricultural Policy and Environmental Quality: Some Observations on the Context of Agricultural Research in North America', *Agriculture and Environment*.

———and G. Gillespie (1991) 'Rural Policy in Perspective: The Rise,

Fall and Uncertain Future of the American Welfare State' in K. Pigg (ed.), *The Future of Rural America*. Boulder: Westview.

———and La Ramee, P. (1991) 'The "Disappearing Middle": A Sociological Perspective' in W. Friedland, L. Busch, F. Buttel and A. Rudy (eds), *Towards a New Political Economy of Agriculture*. Boulder: Westview

Cameron, J. and Elix, J. (1991) *Recovering Ground: A Case Study Approach to Ecologically Sustainable Rural Land Management*. Melbourne: Australian Conservation Foundation.

Carson, L. (1992) 'Lismore: Where the Men Manage Preschools and the Women Build Bridges', *Refractory Girl* 42.

Chapman, R. and Wood, M. (1984) *Australian Local Government: the Federal Dimension*. Sydney: Allen and Unwin.

Clarke, E. (1989) 'Community Organisations and Women's Work', in K. James (ed.), *Women in Rural Australia*. St Lucia: University of Queensland Press.

Cloke, P. (ed) (1988) *Policies and Plans for Rural People — An International Perspective*. London: Unwin Hyman.

Commins, P. (1990) 'Restructuring Agriculture in Advanced Societies: Transformation, Crisis and Responses', in T. Marsden, P. Lowe and S. Whatmore (eds), *Rural Restructuring: Global Processes and their Responses*. London: David Fulton.

Commonwealth Electoral Division (1988) 'Comparison of 1986 Census Characteristics', Current Issues Paper 11, Legislation Research Service. Canberra: Commonwealth Electoral Division.

Coorey, L. (1990) 'Domestic Violence in Rural Areas', in Alston (1990a).

Cowlishaw, G. (1988) *Black, White or Brindle — Race in Rural Australia*. Melbourne: Cambridge University Press.

Crabb, P. (1988) *Managing Water and Land Use in Interstate River Basins*. Sydney: School of Earth Science, Macquarie University.

CTEC (Commonwealth Tertiary Education Commission) (1987) *Report of the Working Party on Post-Secondary Rural Education*. Canberra: AGPS.

Cullen, T., P. Dunn and G. Lawrence (eds) *Rural Health and Welfare in Australia*. Melbourne: Arena.

Dempsey, K. (1990) *Smalltown, A Study of Social Inequality, Cohesion and Belonging*. Sydney: Sydney University Press.

———(1989) 'Maintaining the Boundaries in a Victorian Rural Community', in K. James (ed.), *Women in Rural Australia*. St Lucia: University of Queensland Press.

Denoon, D. (1983) *Settler Capitalism — the Dynamics of Dependent Development in the Southern Hemisphere*. Oxford University Press.

Department of Community Services and Health (1986) *The Home and Community Care Program: Commonwealth Priorities for Service Development*. Canberra: AGPS.

DPIE (Department of Primary Industries and Energy) (1989) *International Agribusiness Trends and their Implications for Australia*. Canberra: AGPS.

Department of Trade (1987) *Agribusiness: Structural Developments in Agriculture and the Implications for Australian Trade*. Canberra: AGPS.

Dunkley, G. and A. Kulkarni (1990) 'Structural Change and Industry Policy in Australia', *Regional Journal of Social Issues* 24.

Dunn, P. (1989) 'Rural Australia: Are you Standing in it?', *Rural Welfare Research Bulletin* 2.

Duplain, R. (1987) 'Agrarian Myths and Realities: Labor Victories in the Wheat/Sheep Belt of New South Wales, 1894–1916', Paper to Australian Historical Association Conference, Armidale College of Advanced Education, Armidale.

East, C. (1989) 'Some Observations on the Experiences of Women in Geographical Isolation', in R. Thorpe, R. Putt and J. Thomson (eds), *Women in Isolation*, Collected Papers, Women's Studies Section, ANZAAS Congress. Townsville: James Cook University.

Fray, P. (1991) 'On Fertile Ground?', *Habitat Australia* 19 (2).

Gibson, D., Baxter, J. and Kingston C. (1990) 'Beyond the Dichotomy: The Paid and Unpaid Work of Rural Women', in Alston (1990a).

Giddens, A. (1971) *Capitalism and Modern Social Theory*. Cambridge: Cambridge University Press.

Gill, H. (1981) 'Land, Labour and Capital, Industrial Relations in the Australasian Primary Sector', *Journal of Industrial Relations*, June.

Goe, W. and Kenney, M. (1991) 'The Restructuring of the Global Economy and the Future of US Agriculture' in K. Pigg (ed.), *The Future of Rural America*, Boulder: Westview.

Gray, I. (1991) *Politics in Place — a Study of Power Relationships in an Australian Country Town*. Sydney: Cambridge University Press.

———, Lawrence, G. and Dunn, T. (1993) *Coping Strategies among Farmers facing Structural Adjustment*, Report to the Rural Industries Research and Development Corporation. Wagga Wagga: Centre for Rural Social Research.

Harvey, D. (1989) *The Condition of Postmodernity*. Oxford: Blackwell.

Heathcote, R. and J. Mabbutt (eds) (1988) *Land, Water and People*. Sydney: Allen and Unwin.

Hindmarsh, R. (1992) 'Agricultural Biotechnologies: Ecosocial Concerns About Genetic Engineering for a Sustainable Agriculture', in G. Lawrence, F. Vanclay and B. Furze (eds), *Agriculture, Environment and Society*. Melbourne: Macmillan.

House of Representatives Standing Committee on Industry Science and Technology (1992) *Genetic Manipulation: The Threat or the Glory?* Canberra: AGPS.

Humphreys, J. (1990) 'Health Care in Rural Australia: Geographical Implications', in T. Cullen, P. Dunn and G. Lawrence (eds), *Rural Health and Welfare in Australia*. Melbourne: Arena.

James, K. (1989) 'Work, Leisure and Choice' in K. James (ed.), *Women in Rural Australia*. St Lucia: University of Queensland Press.

———(1990) 'Women's Decision Making in Extended Family Farm Businesses', in Alston (1990a).

Kalantzis, M. (1990) 'Ethnicity Meets Gender Meets Class in Australia', in S. Watson (ed.), *Playing the State: Australian Feminist Interventions*. Sydney: Allen and Unwin.

Kapferer, J. (1990) 'Rural Myths and Urban Ideologies', *ANZJS* 26 (1).

Kellehear, A. (1990) 'A Critique of National Health Policies for Country People', in T. Cullen, P. Dunn and G. Lawrence (eds), *Rural Health and Welfare in Australia*. Melbourne: Arena.

Kidman, M. (1991) 'New Town: Belonging, Believing and Bearing Down' in M. Alston (ed.), *Family Farming: Australia and New Zealand*, Wagga Wagga: Centre for Rural Social Research, Charles Sturt University.

Lawrence, G. (1986) 'Class in Australian Rural Society', Community Studies Occasional Paper. Coburg: Phillip Institute of Technology.

———(1987) *Capitalism and the Countryside: The Rural Crisis in Australia*. Sydney: Pluto.

———(1989) 'The Rural Crisis Downunder: Australia's Declining Fortunes in the Global Farm Economy', in D. Goodman and M. Redclift (eds), *The International Farm Crisis*. London: Macmillan.

———(1992) 'A Sociological Understanding of Agricultural Biotechnologies', *Australasian Biotechnology* 2 (1).

———(1993) 'Community Ownership and Change', in J. Kerby (ed.), *Proceedings* of a Workshop on Socioeconomic Issues and Research Needs in the Murray-Darling Basin. Adelaide: South Australian Department of Primary Industries.

———and Vanclay, F. (1992) 'Agricultural Production and Environmental Degradation in the Murray-Darling Basin' in G. Lawrence, F. Vanclay and B. Furze (eds), *Agriculture, Environment and Society: Contemporary Issues for Australia*. Melbourne: Macmillan.

———and ——— (1993) 'Biotechnology and Globalisation', Paper to XVth European Congress of Rural Sociology, Wageningen, The Netherlands, 2–6 August.

———and Williams, C. (1990) 'The Dynamics of Decline: Implications for Social Welfare Delivery in Rural Australia', in T. Cullen, P. Dunn and G. Lawrence (eds), *Rural Health and Welfare in Australia*. Melbourne: Arena.

———, Share, P. and Campbell, H. (1992) 'The Global Restructuring of Agriculture and its Implications for Australia and New Zealand', *Journal of Australian Political Economy* 30.

Lohse, H. (1992) 'Actual and Attempted Suicides in Broken Hill', *Youth Studies Australia* 11 (1).

Marsden, T. and Murdoch, J. (1990) 'Restructuring Rurality: Key Areas for Development in Assessing Rural Change', Countryside Change Working Papers, Series 4. Newcastle (UK): University of Newcastle.

McAllister, J. (1978) 'Social Barriers to the Diffusion of Innovations', MAgricSc Thesis, University of New England.

McIntyre, A. and J. McIntyre (1944) *Country Towns of Victoria*. Melbourne: Melbourne University Press.

McMichael, P. (1984) *Settlers and the Agrarian Question*. New York: Cambridge University Press.

Mormont, M. (1990) 'Who is Rural? or, How to be Rural: Towards a Sociology of the Rural', in T. Marsden, P. Lowe and S. Whatmore (eds), *Rural Restructuring: Global Processes and their Responses*. London: Fulton.

Moyal, A. (1989) *Women and the Telephone in Australia*, a study prepared for Telecom Australia.

MDB (Murray-Darling Basin) Ministerial Council (1989) *Draft Murray-Darling Basin Natural Resources Management Strategy: Getting in Together*. Canberra: MDB Ministerial Council.

——(1990) *Natural Resources Management Strategy: Towards a Sustainable Future*. Canberra: MDB Ministerial Council.

National Farmers' Federation (1993) *New Horizons — A Strategy for Australia's Agrifood Industries*. Canberra: National Farmers' Federation.

O'Reilly, D. (1988) 'Save Our Land!', *Bulletin*, 2 August.

Oeser, O. and F. Emery (1957) *Social Structure and Personality in a Rural Community*. London: Routledge and Kegan Paul.

Office of the Status of Women, Department of Prime Minister and Cabinet and the Country Women's Association (1988) *Life has Never Been Easy: Report of the Survey of Women in Rural Australia*. Canberra: AGPS.

Oxley, H. (1978) *Mateship in Local Organisation*. St Lucia: University of Queensland Press.

Planning Research Centre (1989) *Rural Settlements Project: Volume 1, Overview and Summary*. Sydney: Planning Research Centre, University of Sydney.

Poiner, G. (1990) *The Good Old Rule, Gender and Power Relationships in a Rural Community*. Sydney: Sydney University Press.

Powell, R. (1986) 'Forgotten Workers', *Inside Australia* 2 (1).

——(1987) 'Rural Employment' in J. Byrnes (ed.), *Rural Australia Symposium 1987*. Armidale: University of New England, Rural Development Centre.

Redclift, M. and Whatmore, S. (1990) 'Household Consumption and Livelihood' in T. Marsden, P. Lowe and S,. Whatmore (eds), *Rural Restructuring: Global Processes and their Responses*. London: Fulton

Rew, N. (1989) 'Rural Women in Local Government' in K. James (ed.), *Women in Rural Australia*. St Lucia: University of Queensland Press.

Richards. L. (1990) *Nobody's Home — Dreams and Reality in a New Suburb*. Melbourne: Oxford University Press.

Robinson, G. (1990) *Conflict and Change in the Countryside*. London: Belhaven.

Sachs, C. (1983) *The Invisible Farmers — Women in Agricultural Production*. Totowa, NJ: Rowman and Allenheld.

Saunders, P. and Harris, C. (1990) 'Privatism and the Consumer', *Sociology* 24 (1).

Schwarzweller, H. (1988) 'Agricultural Structure and Change in the Lower Hunter Valley of New South Wales — A Sociological Study of Farm Families and Their Work', Sociology Research Monograph 5. Armidale: University of New England.

Share, P. and G. Lawrence (1990) 'Fear and Loathing in Wagga Wagga: Cultural Representations of the Rural and Possible Policy Implications', *Culture and Policy* 1 (2).

Sinclair, A. (1987) *Getting the Numbers: Women in Local Government*. Melbourne: Hargreen.

Smith, D. (1988) *The Everyday World as Problematic: a Feminist Sociology.* Milton Keynes: Open University Press.

Stayner, R. and I. Reeve (1990) ' "Uncoupling": Relationships Between Agriculture and the Local Economics of Areas in New South Wales'. Armidale: The Rural Development Centre, University of New England.

Summons, M. (1984) 'The Big Battalions Will Dominate', *Australian*, 6 February.

Suttles, G. (1972) *The Social Construction of Communities.* Chicago: University of Chicago Press.

Thomson, N. (1991) 'A Review of Aboriginal Health Status', in J. Reid and P. Trompf (eds), *The Health of Aboriginal Australia.* Sydney: Harcourt Brace Jovanovich.

Thorpe, R., Putt, R. and Thomson, J. (eds) (1989) *Women in Isolation: Collected Papers.* Women's Studies Section, ANZAAS Congress, Townsville, James Cook University.

Vanclay, F. and Lawrence, G. (1992) 'A Blue-Green Politics?', *Arena* 98.

Vogeler, I. (1981) *The Myth of the Family Farm.* Boulder: Westview.

Watson, C. (1992) 'An Ecologically Unsustainable Agriculture', in G. Lawrence, F. Vanclay and B. Furze (eds), *Agriculture, Environment and Society.* Melbourne: Macmillan.

Wells, A. (1989) *Constructing Capitalism — an Economic History of Eastern Australia 1788–1901.* Sydney: Allen and Unwin.

Wild, R. (1978) *Bradstow — a Study of Status, Class and Power in a Small Australian Town.* Sydney: Angus and Robertson.

———(1983) *Heathcote.* Sydney: Allen and Unwin.

Woods, (1983) *Land Degradation in Australia.* Canberra: AGPS.

Chapter Nineteen

Queens of the Screen or Princes of Print: The Media and Concentration of Ownership

Julianne Schultz

The media is arguably the most pervasive and influential institution in our society. But as a major industry, it is also fraught with many contradictions. Its reach is enormous, its ability to set agendas is beyond dispute, and the political power it is thought to exercise as a consequence is considerable.

The media has changed dramatically during the twentieth century, driven by rapidly changing technologies and the development of mass, and then niche markets. The fundamentals of its role in providing news, information and entertainment have, however, remained unchanged.

Despite this increase in influence, the expansion of services, and the increasing professionalism of the product produced, the public is sceptical about the credibility, veracity and accuracy of the media. Two-thirds of those asked in a 1991 poll said that they thought the media in Australia was doing a poor job. The only other major institution which fared worse was the parliamentary process (Saulwick Poll, *Sydney Morning Herald*, 8 July 1991).

Other polls also point to a profound public dissatisfaction with the media: accuracy, and journalists ethics are regularly found to be wanting.[1]

The reason for this low public esteem can only be pondered, but it does raise serious questions. Is the public sceptical because of the perception that owners of media companies are excessively powerful individuals; because media policy is seen to be made on

the run by politicians, who are nervous of these powerful organisations; because the industry's attempts at self-regulation and
accountability are seen to be wanting; because the media concentrates on trivia and sensationalism; or because the reality of the
world, which to a greater or lesser degree the media attempts to
report, is itself unpleasant?

Fourth Estate or Just Another Business?

It has often been said that a free and independent media is
essential for the effective functioning of a democratic society such
as Australia (Keane 1991). Indeed the premiss that the media is
one of the major formative institutions in our society is one which
is well accepted. Its claim to independence is, however, something
that has been challenged by the changing political and,
particularly, economic realities since 1852, when John Delane,
editor of *The Times*, outlined the application of the principle of the
Fourth Estate to the role and conduct of the press in relation to
the political process:

> We cannot admit that a newspaper's purpose is to share the
> labours of statesmanship or that it is bound by the same limi-
> tations, the same duties and the same liabilities as the Ministers of
> the Crown. The purpose and duties of the two powers are con-
> stantly separate, generally independent, sometimes diametrically
> opposite. The freedom and dignity of the press are trammelled
> from the moment that it accepts an ancillary position. To perform
> its duties with entire independence, and consequently to the
> utmost public advantage, the press can enter into no close or
> binding alliances with the statesmen of the day.

Delane's formulation grew out of the particular circumstances of
his time. The social, political and (most importantly) economic
environment which gave rise to this view bear little similarity to
the situation today. Nonetheless this view has been remarkably
resilient and still informs the self-definition of the media in
Australia, and in most non-authoritarian nations. It informs the
attitudes of owners, editors and journalists. It could be argued
that the limitations of the doctrine may be reflected in the low
public esteem for the media, in this country and many others. As
Rupert Murdoch said in 1961: 'Unless we can return to the
principles of public service we will lose our claim to be the Fourth
Estate. What right have we to speak in the public interest when,
too often, we are motivated by personal gain?' (Mayer 1964: 51)

   The tension between the media as a marketable commodity

and an institution which provides a 'feedback mechanism for democratic system management' (Kunczik 1989) lies at the heart of the policy debate about how best to encourage competition and diversity. Less than thirty years ago, it was not uncommon to hear editors declare, as did an associate editor of the *West Australian*:

> When those engaged in journalism are compelled to acknowledge to themselves that the principal object of a newspaper is to get itself sold, then the press will have forfeited its right to be regarded as one of the great institutions of the country. A newspaper should be much more than an ordinary marketable commodity. If the ideal of service were to be entirely subordinated to the idea of profit, I should much rather be associated with the production of soap or sugar than with the production of a newspaper. Then at least one would not be a party to an organised hypocrisy.
>
> (in Mayer 1964: 51)

The notion that the press is the watchdog of government, and should not therefore not be subjected to regulation by the state has been a remarkably resilient concept: 'free speech given a corporate face' (Carlyon 1982). This is despite the dramatically changed commercial nature of the media in recent years, whereby media companies have become much larger, more diversified corporations, with extensive non-media interests. There is a conflict between the liberal theory of the role of the press and the economic circumstances under which it is produced, so that in the words of Garnham:

> The problem with liberal free press theory is not just that the market has produced conditions of oligopoly which undercut the liberal ideal, nor yet that private ownership leads to direct mani-pulation of political communications, although it does, but that there is a fundamental contradiction between the economic and political at the level of their value systems and of the social relations which these value systems require and support.
>
> In the political realm the individual is defined as a citizen exercising public rights of debate, voting etc. within a communally agreed structure of rules and towards communally defined ends. The value system is essentially social and the legitimate end of social action is the public good.
>
> But within the economic realm the individual is defined as a producer and consumer exercising private rights through purchasing power in pursuit of private interests, his or her actions being co-ordinated by the invisible hand of the market.
>
> (Garnham 1986: 31)

As a result the independence of the media in this country, and throughout much of the developed world, is today less under challenge from state intervention than from commercial imperatives. As the Report of the 1991 Parliamentary Committee inquiring into the print media noted: 'Separation of the legitimate business interests of the proprietor from the editorial process (by means of a charter) may not be possible' (Report: xxvii).

The experience of Eastern Europe and the Soviet Union since 1989 has profoundly demonstrated that the significance of access to information, ideas and different perspectives cannot be underestimated. In these newly-democratising societies, among the first statutes to be enacted were constitutional and legislative changes guaranteeing freedom of speech and expression (Schultz 1990b).

Moves to establish constitutional guarantees of freedom of speech and expression and the opening up of the national media systems throughout these countries was closely followed by the entrance of the major international media corporations. Shortly after the collapse of the Communist regimes, the major international media companies were offering to buy existing publications, open new ones, provide modern technology and establish advertising markets.

The inter-related issues of the fundamental human right to information and the commercial nature of the media were thrown together as the new governments attempted for the first time to draft democratic press statutes, broadcasting legislation, and defamation laws. As the eminent Irish jurist MacBride pointed out in his 1980 Report:

> The freedom of a citizen or social group to have access to communication, both as recipients and contributors, cannot be compared to the freedom of an investor to derive profit from the media. One protects a fundamental human right, the other permits the commercialisation of a social need.
>
> (MacBride 1980: 18)

Throughout the developed world the issue of concentration of media ownership has in the last decade become more pressing . In this time the major media corporations have become much larger, more diversified organisations, owning a greater share of total media output. The pattern of concentration is not confined to Australia. Throughout the world there has been a tremendous consolidation of media properties into a handful of major corporations. In the United States alone, 25,000 media companies, ranging from newspapers and magazines to books, television, radio, satellites, electronic databases and movie studios were owned by 23 companies in 1990. Only ten years earlier these outlets had been owned by 40 different corporations (Bagdikian 1990: 4).

The growth in size and scale of these companies makes the media companies even more powerful than they would otherwise be, as a result of the uniqueness of their business. At the end of the century this power and its potential abuse raise serious questions about the sources of power and influence in the society. Bagdikian wrote of the United States:

> Any surprise (about the pace and extent of concentration) of a few years ago is replaced by the demonstration that media giants have become so powerful that government no longer has the will to restrain them. Corporate news media and business orientated governments have made common cause. The public, dependent on the media giants for its basic information, is not told of the dangers. Governments can be voted out of office. But when corporations gain this level of centralised control over what the general public learns, the dominant corporations can, through their control of news and other public information postpone public awareness for dangerously long periods.
>
> (Bagdikian 1990: iv–x)

Over the last decade the Australian media, too, has undergone profound changes, largely as a result of changes in government policies and the economic environment that these policies created. Nonetheless, at the beginning of the 1980s, the Australian media was regarded as being the second most concentrated in the developed world, after Ireland. Ten years later, despite major policy changes which have forced media companies to choose between being 'queens of the screen or princes of print' (Schultz 1989: 69), the concentration had arguably intensified, with each sector dominated by one company.

In Australia the media has at least the potential to exercise the power Bagdikian described. Former Liberal Prime Minister Fraser addressed the question of the power of the media when he gave evidence in 1991 before the Parliamentary Select Committee Inquiry into the Print Media (Lee Committee). He said:

> The Parliament cannot ignore the environment it has to operate in; therefore it cannot ignore the media. If there are only a few [companies] the power of the media is enormous. But if there are only one or two, the power is sufficient, I think to rival the power of the Parliament itself.
>
> (Transcript, 22 October 1991: 911)

Changing the Rules

The most tumultuous period in Australian media history began on 27 November 1986, when the then-Minister for Communications, Michael Duffy, announced that the government would change its media ownership rules. This announcement was triggered by the consideration of the issues raised by the launch of the domestic satellite which had facilitated the establishment of full-scale television networks in Australia, and made the previous limit of two television stations per owner unworkable. The cross-media ownership rule change was seen as a clever way of killing two birds with one stone: making metropolitan commercial television available to almost all Australians and breaking up the power of existing media companies.[2]

Over several months, this most divisive issue of the first five years of the Labor government preoccupied members of the Cabinet and the Caucus, who argued about acceptable audience reach for a television network. The Minister regarded 43 per cent as an appropriate audience figure, while the Prime Minister and Treasurer favored 100 per cent, but were prepared to settle for 75 per cent. Chairman of the Caucus Economics Committee, Bob Brown, was among those who argued against the proposed 75 per cent figure, saying that the decision was not only about the media, but about the exercise of power. In the past, he said, those who had controlled the industry had exercised power in Australia but 'true power in future will be exercised by those who control the means of information', making this the most important decision the government would make (Chadwick 1989: 25).

When Caucus settled on 75 per cent, the Labor government, which was familiar with arguments about the dangers of concentration of media ownership, sought to ensure that the companies which would run the television networks would not also control Australia's print and radio media. Despite the Labor Party's agonising over the 75 per cent figure, the government's recommendation was rejected in the Senate, and in a compromise between the parties, a 60 per cent audience reach figure was finally passed in Parliament in mid-1987.

At this time the ownership of the media was divided between the Melbourne-based Herald and Weekly Times group, which had newspapers in every state, plus television interests; John Fairfax Ltd which published most of the nation's 'quality' newspapers, and had interests in television and radio; News Limited which owned newspapers, Channel 10, magazines and radio;

Table 19.1 Major Print Media Groups with Prescribed Interests[a] in Broadcasting (30 June 1986)

Group	Print	Radio	Television
News Ltd	*Australian* (national) *Daily Telegraph* (Sydney) *Daily Mirror* (Sydney) *Sunday Telegraph* (Sydney) *Daily Sun* (Brisbane) *Sunday Sun* (Brisbane) *News* (Adelaide) *Sunday Times* (Perth) *Northern Territory News* (Darwin) *Townsville Bulletin* Country/suburban newspaper interests Major magazine interests	3FOX (Melbourne) 4AM (Atherton)	Ten (Sydney) ATV (Melbourne)
HWT	*Herald* (Melbourne) *Sun News-Pictorial* (Melbourne) *Sunday Press*[e] (Melbourne) *Courier-Mail* (Brisbane) *Telegraph* (Brisbane) *Sunday Mail* (Brisbane) *Advertiser* (Adelaide) *West Australian* (Perth) *Mercury* (Hobart) *Sunday Tasmanian* (Hobart) *Geelong Advertiser* *Bendigo Advertiser* *Kalgoorlie Miner* *Lithgow Mercury* *Manly Daily* *Mercury* (Maitland) Country/suburban newspaper interests Magazine interests	3DB (Melbourne) 3GL (Geelong) 4AK (Oakey)[b] 4BK (Brisbane)[b] 5AD (Adelaide)[c] 5PI (Crystal Brook)[c] 5SE (Mount Gambier)[c]	HSV (Melbourne) ADS (Adelaide)

Table 19.1 (cont'd)

Group	Print	Radio	Television
Fairfax	*Australian Financial Review* (national) *National Times* (national) *Sydney Morning Herald* *Sun* (Sydney) *Sun-Herald* (Sydney) *Age* (Melbourne) *Sunday Press* (Melbourne)[c] *Canberra Times* *Newcastle Herald* *Illawarra Mercury* (Wollongong) *Warrnambool Standard* Country/suburban newspaper interests Magazine interests	2CA (Canberra) 2GB (Sydney) 2WL (Wollongong) 3AW (Melbourne) 4AY (Ayre) 4BH (Brisbane) 5DN (Adelaide) 4MMM (Brisbane) 2AD (Armidale)[b]	ATN (Sydney) BTQ (Brisbane)
ACP/CPH	Country/suburban newspaper interests[f] Major magazine interests	2UE (Sydney) 3AK (Melbourne) 6AM (Northern) 6PM (Perth) 6KG (Kalgoorlie) 6GE (Geraldton)	TCN (Sydney) GTV (Melbourne)

Notes: [a] Prescribed interest defined as a shareholding of at least 15 per cent for radio and 5 per cent for television
  [b] Interest through Queensland Press in which HWT held 41.5 per cent of issued shares
  [c] Interest through Advertiser Newspapers Ltd in which HWT held 36.57 per cent of the issued shares
  [d] Interest through Rural Press Ltd in which Fairfax held 47.17 per cent of the issued shares
  [e] Jointly owned by HWT and Fairfax
  [f] Prescribed interests defined as an interest exceeding 15 per cent of shareholdings for radio and 5 per cent for television

Source: AGPS (1992) *News and Fair Facts: The Australian Print Media Industry*, pp. 300–01

and Consolidated Press, which owned Channel 9 and most of the major magazines. The rivalry between these four groups was legendary, and their ability to cross-promote their activities was dramatically enhanced by their ownership of print, radio and television. They were able 'to feed off their strength', according to one media executive.

Two months after the government's policy change, the Federal Court ruled that despite legal moves to distance the ownership of News Ltd from Rupert Murdoch, as an American citizen Murdoch was no longer entitled to own the Sydney, Melbourne and Brisbane Channel 10s. This decision was in the wind in late 1986, when News Ltd launched one of the most audacious takeovers in Australian corporate history. For the second time in less than a decade, it bid for the Herald and Weekly Times group. The first time the company sought to acquire the Melbourne-based group, in 1979, it had been stymied by an expensive defence by John Fairfax Ltd, and the other companies affiliated with the Herald and Weekly Times group. Seven years later, the group was lumbering under a burden of over-bureaucratic management and falling newspaper circulation. It was ready to be taken over.

The boldness of the News Ltd bid, which was to cost $2.3 billion, much of it later recouped through asset sales (Chadwick 1989: 87) was astounding, and the timing, early in December 1986, threw the media, politicians, public servants and merchant bankers, who were preparing for the annual summer slowdown, into a tizz. The sentimental explanation was that Murdoch was intent on acquiring the company his father had created to avenge the family name, and give a son's ultimate thank-you to his mother, Dame Elisabeth. Although sentiment may have played a part in Murdoch's targeting the Herald and Weekly Times for a second joust, at the time News Ltd was busily acquiring media properties all over the world. As its chief executive, Ken Cowley, said: 'We [News Ltd's Australian operations] just felt we were becoming a bit of a backwater. Australia [by the purchase of the HWT] could once again play a major role in News Corporation' (*Sydney Morning Herald*, 25 April 1987).

It was the mid-1980s, and banks all around the world were engaging in a lending binge, the likes of which had not been seen for decades. Even before it was excluded from television, News Ltd was the first Australian media group to make the choice between print and television. During the months of negotiation about the new media ownership rules, senior government figures were consulting and discussing the proposals with two of the major media groups: not just News Ltd, but also Kerry Packer's

Consolidated Press group (Chadwick: 1989: 20–21). With the benefit of hindsight it is strikingly obvious that these two companies made the best of the policy change and the opportunities it presented. Eight years later, these companies are not only still intact, but have prospered.

News Ltd's acquisition of the Herald and Weekly Times was not unproblematic. There were numerous legal challenges and counter-bids by other would-be owners of the group. The bid faced little political opposition, although the Liberal Party's Shadow Minister for Communications, Ian McPhee, was a high profile critic of the takeover. The Labor government was muted in any opposition it may have felt, even though it would lead to one company controlling 62 per cent of the daily newspapers produced in the country. The only senior politician to publicly voice any disquiet over the proposal was Bill Hayden, the then-Minister for Foreign Affairs. He said:

'It is undesirable to have an excessive degree of concentration of ownership and control of the media in any country, in pluralistic societies like ours, democracies where minds can be influenced, opinions bent by the way which news is presented and Mr Murdoch has a solid record of doing that behind him. I think that's bad.' All proprietors engaged in distortion, Hayden said, but Murdoch 'had lifted it to a very rough art form'.

(Chadwick: 1989: 49)

In December 1986 the Trade Practices Commission considered the takeover and gave its preliminary go-ahead on the condition that News Ltd sell papers in Brisbane and Adelaide, to ensure that monopolies were not created in those cities. As an American citizen, Murdoch needed Foreign Investment Review Board approval for the takeover, and this was granted on 13 January, despite objections from unions, churches, public interest groups and some politicians. The reasoning which informed the FIRB's crucial decision has never been made public, despite repeated freedom of information requests.

The Trade Practices Commission examined the takeover, but the test it had to satisfy was whether it would lead to a dominance of the industry by one company. During the years of the Fraser government, the key test was changed from one prohibiting any takeover or merger which would lead to a 'substantial lessening of competition', to one which would only prohibit mergers which would enable one company to 'dominate' the market. As a result, during the 1980s an unprecedented aggregation of business occurred in the media and a range of other industries, and by 1992, following the recommendations of three parliamentary committees, the Labor government reverted to the earlier test.

Fraser, who had been Prime Minister in 1977, at the time of the change to the Trade Practices Act, described it fourteen years later as 'a total and absolute disaster'. He said: 'Without that legislation the takeover of the Herald and Weekly Times could not have taken place and a great move forward in terms of media dominance was undertaken ... As a result of those changes the media is now more concentrated in fewer hands than ever before' (Transcript of Evidence given to Parliamentary Inquiry into the Print Media, 20 October 1991: 906).

The Trade Practices Commission examined whether as a result of the News Ltd acquisition one company would dominate the market for advertising in each city market, and found that this would not be the case, since there was competition from other media for the advertising dollar. As a result, the TPC did not allow the fact that News Ltd would publish more than 60 per cent, by circulation, of the papers produced in Australia, to prevent the takeover.

At that time, and following the sale of News Ltd's Brisbane *Sun* and Adelaide *News* to former executives of the company, no new monopolies were created. But over the following six years, eleven daily newspapers and six Sunday papers folded. By early 1992, only Sydney and Melbourne had more than one daily newspaper; in every other capital city, there was a monopoly newspaper.

The News Ltd bid for the Herald and Weekly Times group and the buying and selling spree that it triggered was unprecedented in Australian corporate history. Within twelve months, the ownership of the media industry in Australia had completely changed, in a frantic jockeying for position in what was thought to be one of the most lucrative industries in the country. Those who did the buying were described as entrepreneurs of a new era; they included, most notably, Alan Bond and Christopher Skase. Rather than ushering in a new era of media diversity, within five years these men would lose hundreds of millions of dollars, before being declared bankrupt and facing criminal charges.

Protecting the Mates

The formation and development of media policy has always been a highly emotive activity in Australia, and never more so than during the fundamental change of policy that occurred in the mid-1980s. The Labor Party has had a history of being particularly suspicious of 'media barons', and in government was reluctant to be seen to be doing anything that might advantage its historical political enemies.

The animosity between the ALP and the press was deeply rooted in history. As evidence presented before the Parliamentary Select Committee Inquiry into the Print Media showed, between 1955 and 1984, of the 231 election editorials published in 17 daily newspapers, in relation to 15 federal elections, only 38 advised readers to vote for the Labor Party (see Table 19.2). This changed dramatically in 1984, when almost all the papers indicated they believed it was time for a Labor government.

There was no love lost between the Labor government and the Fairfax or Herald and Weekly Times media companies, and the 1986 change of policy had the effect of 'unleashing the force of money on to those groups it dislikes most' (Chadwick 1989: 20). Peter Bowers, a leading political commentator of the time, wrote in the *Sydney Morning Herald*:

> The Labor leadership view is that if they cannot reach an accommodation with Murdoch and Packer they can at least learn to live with them. Hawke, Keating and [NSW Premier] Wran's attitude to Packer and Murdoch is as relaxed as it is uneasy about Fairfax and HWT. The perception involves more than personalities and passing prejudice; its origin is entrenched in Labor's psyche, a hoary shibboleth with a lively contemporary quality. The Labor Party distinguishes between new money and old money; old money is Tory establishment; new money personifies wheeler dealers. Labor leaders can wheel and deal with the best of them.
>
> (quoted in Chadwick 1989)

Although the relationship between News Ltd and the ALP had been difficult — particularly when in 1975 the Murdoch papers turned against the Labor government that they had supported in 1972 — there was a sense that the Herald and Weekly Times was a part of the Melbourne establishment, and would never be reached by the ALP. Politicians frequently find it easier to deal with a high profile individual owner than with a more bureaucratic corporation. This relationship was thought by some to have influenced the muted reaction of the Cabinet to the Herald and Weekly Times takeover bid. As the former Fairfax Editor-in-Chief, David Bowman wrote:

> Recent Australian history shows that media groups that get close to governments prosper, while to oppose or even to maintain an independent position is to invite attack. Our Prime Minister and Treasurer are politicians with absurdly tender egos, and the

Table 19.2   Political Content of Pre-election Editorials in Daily Newspapers, Election Day, 1955–90

Election Date	Australian	Australian Financial Review	Sydney Morning Herald	Sun (Sydney)	Daily Telegraph	Daily Mirror	Age	Herald	Sun	Courier Mail	Telegraph	Advertiser	News	West Australian	Mercury	Canberra Times	Northern Territory News
10 Dec 55	○	○		○							○		⊕				○
22 Nov 58	○	⊕		○							○		⊕			⊕	○
9 Dec 61	○	⊕	■			■					○					⊕	⊕
30 Nov 63	○	⊕				■					○		⊕	⊕			⊕
26 Nov 66		⊕							○		○						
25 Oct 69		⊕		○					○		○					⊕	
2 Dec 72		⊕		⊕	■		■						■			⊕	⊕
18 May 74	■					⊕							⊕			⊕	⊕
13 Dec 75											○					⊕	
10 Dec 77											○			⊕		⊕	
18 Oct 80		⊕		⊕												⊕	
5 Mar 83		⊕									■					⊕	⊕
1 Dec 84	■	■	■	■	■	■	⊕	⊕	■		⊕		◉	■		⊕	■
11 July 87											○	⊕			⊕	⊕	
24 Mar 90				○						■					⊕	⊕	⊕

Liberal/Coalition ■   ALP ⊕   Neutral ○

No editorial published ☐

No paper, or paper not available

Source: From AGPS (1992) *News and Fair Facts: The Australian Print Media Industry*: 258–59

intensity of their efforts to square or squash the press is decidedly unhealthy. It's anti-democratic. The tragedy is . . . that they are winning.

(Bowman 1987)

In 1976, Paul Keating, then a 33-year-old Opposition backbencher, spelt out the widely-held disquiet within the Labor Party about the concentration of media ownership, and the urgency of the need to do something about it:

The present provisions of the Broadcasting and Television Act allow three companies to dominate the Australia media to an extent that would not be tolerated in countries comparable with Australia . . . What also makes the situation frightening is that most of the proprietors who operate these groups share a common social background and in political terms, share a common point of view. Divestment must occur. In future, newspaper groupings should not be permitted to take over other groupings with holdings in radio and television.

(*Hansard*, House of Representatives: 3,016)

Ten years later, as the strongest personality in the federal Cabinet, Keating was in a position to influence the shape of the next decade of media policy. By June 1992, when he was Prime Minister, he spectacularly determined the rules for pay television. They govern the operators eligible to bid for new pay television services. In doing this, he simultaneously criticised the old media establishment and opened the way for both Murdoch and Packer to acquire an interest in pay television.

Many of the 1986 arguments about the percentage of the population that the television networks should be able to reach were tinged with what has been described as 'concerns' about Prime Minister Hawke's 'mates'. Senator John Button, the Minister for Industry, indicated that he felt the decision to settle on a high audience reach was influenced by the friendship between Packer and the Prime Minister. During a tense moment in Cabinet's consideration of the question, Button turned to Hawke and asked: 'Why don't you tell us precisely how you want us to help your mates?' Hawke replied: 'Remember they're the only mates we've got' (Chadwick 1989:16).

The decision to grant the networks access to so much of the Australian population made the top-rating Nine network considerably more valuable. The extent of this revaluation became obvious in January 1987, when Packer sold it to Alan Bond for the astonishing figure of $1 billion.

Money to Burn

The change of policy on cross-media ownership and the News Ltd takeover of the Herald and Weekly Times may have been the two major triggers for the shakeout in media ownership in Australia. The other major influence was the willingness of the banks during the 1980s to lend vast sums of money, and the impact of the share market crash in October 1987.

Just prior to the crash, in Spring 1987, Warwick Fairfax, the 26-year-old scion of the Fairfax family newspaper dynasty, announced an audacious bid to privatise the 160-year-old family company. By borrowing $1 billion Warwick Fairfax proposed to buy out other members of the family and other shares in the listed company. His intention was then to refloat parts of the company on the stock exchange. His aim was to protect the company from hostile takeovers and to ensure the continuance of the dynasty. Instead, he precipitated its collapse.[3]

His ambitious plan was sorely mistimed. The stock market crash dramatically devalued the company, and made an immediate refloat of sections of it an impossibility. The other members of the Fairfax family opted to take the money he offered and sold their shares to 'young Warwick'. Within months, the extent of the folly was becoming obvious, and in late 1990 a receiver manager was appointed to the company. It had debts of $1.5 billion, and although the major daily newspapers were still produced by the company, its range of properties was no longer as great as it had been when Warwick had set out on his course three years earlier.

At the end of 1991, after a year of corporate and political wrangling and full-scale public campaigns, the Fairfax group was sold to a consortium called Tourang, which had as its leading member Conrad Black, the Canadian publisher who owned the London *Daily Telegraph* and the *Jerusalem Post*, among other interests.

The Australian television networks all changed owners during 1987, and by 1991 were again under new management. The new operators had little media experience, but all recognised the profit and potential of the medium. With entrepreneurial track records in other industries, they were reluctant to see the media as being any different to these. As Frank Lowy, who purchased the Channel 10 network from Murdoch, told a journalist in 1987: 'Media people say it's a different business. They're wrong. They think there is something unique about it. It is a unique business, but the business decisions are the same. They are preoccupied with themselves. Because they are media they think they are something special' (*Sydney Morning Herald*, 22 September 1987).

Alan Bond was the first of the entrepreneurs to buy a television network, when he acquired the Nine network from Packer in January 1987. Property developer and former journalist Christopher Skase bought the Seven network from Fairfax for $670 million, and property developer Frank Lowy paid $800 million for the Ten network. Lowy was the first to bail out, two years later, when his company Westfield Capital Corp sold the network for $575 million to Broadcom and Capitol Television. Broadcom, a small media production company, ran the network's Sydney, Melbourne and Brisbane stations for twelve months, before it too was placed in receivership. In 1989, Qintex, Christopher Skase's company also went into receivership, leaving the Seven network without its high profile owner. The receivers discovered that new owners for Seven and Ten were difficult to find. Television was no longer regarded as the goose that would lay the golden egg on demand, and the banks were left to carry the debt. By 1992, industry observers valued each of the networks at around $250 million, and late that year Channel 10 was sold for $230 million to a consortium led by the Canadian broadcaster Canwest Global Communications, with $145 million in debt still outstanding.

Bond's ownership of the Nine network was short-lived, but like much of his career, it was spectacular. Bond, unlike the other new television tycoons, had had some experience in running media businesses, but he soon discovered the extent of the uniqueness of the television. The beginning of his television demise came when he appeared on his own network's top-rating program, *A Current Affair*. During an interview with the high profile host, Jana Wendt, Bond said that he had settled a defamation case brought by former Queensland Premier Joh Bjelke-Petersen, as the price of doing future business in the state:

> Commercially the decision to pay up made sense: $400,000 was nothing to Bond Corporation alongside its billion dollar business interests in the state, and Sir Joh ruled Queensland as if it were his personal fiefdom. But TV licence holders were supposed to operate fearlessly in the pursuit of truth. Bribing premiers to keep them sweet, which was conceivably what Bond had done, was not meant to be on the agenda.
>
> (Barry 1991: 314)

Bond's admission highlighted the difference between running a media business and other kinds. The Australian Broadcasting Tribunal, which regulated the television and radio industries until 1992, when the Australian Broadcasting Authority was established, following the demise of the Australian Broadcasting Control Board in 1975, began to examine whether Bond was a 'fit and proper person' to hold a television licence. The resultant Inquiry, began in 1988, after numerous appeals eventually reaching the High Court. The Tribunal brought down findings of fact against Bond, indicating that it believed he had lied to the Tribunal, had attempted to conceal the $400,000 payment to Sir Joh, and had threatened AMP's investment manager Leigh Hall.

Before the subsequent Inquiry into Alan Bond's fitness to hold a television licence could begin, Bond Corporation failed to make a final payment to Packer. The television network then reverted to effective Packer ownership. Having sold the stations for $1 billion, he acquired them two years later for $250 million. Packer later said: 'You only get one Alan Bond in a lifetime.'

The Rush Out of Print

The turbulence of these years was not felt only in the television industry. In the print media there were extraordinary developments, as papers changed hands, merged, moved from morning to afternoon publication and began 24-hour editions. The recession of the late 1980s forced seventeen newspaper closures, more than at any time in Australia since the 1920s (see Table 19.3).[4]

During this time, more than one thousand journalists lost their jobs, jobs which were unlikely to be restored because the papers on which they worked had folded. The federal government's policy initiative, prohibiting companies from having control of media outlets in more than one medium, had succeeded in breaking down the concentration of ownership across the media. But the trade-off was much greater concentration within sectors. As the journalists' union, the AJA's submission to the Parliamentary Print Media Inquiry (Lee Committee) noted (p. 759):

> Now ... virtually every phase and facet is dominated by one company — the News group — with most other publications grouped into about four minor groups largely dependent on the News group and incapable of challenging its national dominance.

At the end of 1991, measured in terms of national circulation, News Ltd produced 62 per cent of daily newspapers, 50 per cent of suburban newspapers, 17 per cent of regional dailies and 36 per cent of magazines; Fairfax owned about 20 per cent of the capital city newspaper market, and about 15 per cent of suburban newspapers; Australian Consolidated Press produced nearly 50 per cent of magazines and Channel 9 is consistently the highest rating television network.

Table 19.3 Newspaper Closures 1982–92

1982	Herald and Weekly Times purchases 12 per cent of Queensland Newspapers
	Fairfax purchases David Syme and Co's shares in the *Age*
	News Ltd launches Brisbane *Daily Sun*
1986	Herald and Weekly Times purchases Australian Consolidated Press's suburban and regional papers
	Herald and Weekly Times purchases suburban newspaper group, Leader Associated Newspapers
	National Times closes
	Saurday edition *Herald* (Melbourne) closes
	Attorney-General Michael Duffy announces new restrictions on cross-media ownership
1987	News Ltd acquires Herald and Weekly Times
	Buiness Daily closes
	Western Mail closes
1988	*Telegraph* (Brisbane) closes
	Times on Sunday closes
	Sun (Sydney) closes
1989	*Observer* (Melbourne) closes
	Sunday Press (Melbourne) closes
1990	*Daily Telegraph* closes*
	Daily Mirror closes*
	Sun (Melbourne) closes**
	Herald (Melbourne) closes**
	Daily News (Perth) closes
	Fairfax Group in receivership
	Mathews Inquiry, Victoria
1991	*Sunday Herald* (Melbourne) closes***
	West Australian in receivership
	Print Media Inquiry
	Daily Sun (Brisbane) closes
	Fairfax Group acquired by Tourang
1992	*News* (Adelaide) closes
	Sunday Sun (Brisbane) closes

* Combined 24-hour paper, *Daily Telegraph Mirror*, launched
** Combined 24-hour paper, *Herald Sun*, launched
*** Merges with the *Sunday Sun* to become the *Herald Sun*

Sources: Communications Law Centre; *Age*, 5 August 1991; *Media Information Australia*, August 1992

This pattern of ownership, plus the economies of scale and group economies implicit in it, has produced a range of 'formidable barriers' which according to *News and Fair Facts* would make it almost impossible for another company to begin to produce a new daily newspaper in an Australian capital city (Report: xix).

Despite this dominance of the print media industry, News Ltd's newspapers were the ones which continued to be hit by declining circulation figures. The per capita circulation of newspapers had been falling since 1950, but by the beginning of the 1990s the quality papers were noticeably holding readers and profitability, whereas mass market ones continued to suffer a declining audience. Anthony Smith, in *Goodbye Gutenberg*[5] has predicted that by the mid-1990s there could be a resurgence in 'quality' media (*Australian*, 19 June 1992: 7), and signs of this are emerging.

Print Media Inquiry

Continued growth in circulation, and dominance of the classified advertising market in Australia's two largest cities had helped to make the Fairfax newspapers particularly profitable. When these papers were offered for sale in 1991, there was widely-held concern that all available avenues needed to be examined to ensure they remained strong and vibrant, and in predominantly Australian hands. The putative Fairfax sale also led to the first national inquiry into the print media in Australia, although two inquiries had previously been held in Victoria.

The federal government reluctantly agreed to establish a House of Representatives select committee, with wide terms of reference to inquire into the print media, following a motion at the ALP Conference in June 1991. Not surprisingly, this focused public and political activity around the Fairfax issue, although the committee, which was chaired by Right-wing Labor backbencher and Member for Dobell, Michael Lee, was ill-placed to influence the outcome of the commercial decision. Two of the consortia bidding for Fairfax raised questions about the desirable limits of foreign ownership of the press, a question that was settled politically when the Federal Labor parliamentary Caucus decided that foreign ownership should be restricted to 20 per cent.

The twin issues of foreign ownership and media concentration, and the associated possibility that the cross-media laws might be circumvented, forced some unlikely alliances. On 16 October 1991, a letter to the *Age* from two former Prime Ministers, Gough Whitlam and Malcolm Fraser, and six other emeritus politicians, claimed: 'the Fairfax newspaper sale is the last chance to arrest the growing concentration of Australian media ownership'. The letter also expressed concern about market dominance in the media, the danger of media power being used to influence policies, and opposed foreign control of the media (Report: 372).

Former Prime Ministers Fraser and Whitlam, who in 1975 had headed opposing sides in the greatest modern rift in national politics, became the new political odd couple. They appeared on platforms together, warning of the greater evil of further media concentration. Fraser subsequently appeared before the Lee Committee to reiterate underlying Liberal principles, and urge it to be bold and recommend divestment without compensation.

In a further unusual display of bipartisanship, the Liberals' David Connelly (MHR Bradfield) and Labor's John Langmore (MHR Fraser) drafted a petition which was signed by 137 of the 224 Members of Parliament and Senators. It asked the Prime Minister to 'oppose the sale of the Fairfax Group to any individual or consortium that would result in a greater concentration of media ownership, and thus a diminution of competition in and diversity of information sources in Australia.' (Report: 373)

The Lee Committee was expected to report on its wide-ranging terms of reference before Christmas, but the majority report, *News and Fair Facts*, and two dissenting versions were tabled on 26 February 1992, two months late. By then, Tourang's takeover of Fairfax was well under way, and one more capital city newspaper, the Brisbane *Sun*, had closed. Within days of the Report being tabled, the Adelaide *News* also folded, and several weeks later the Brisbane *Sunday Sun* produced its last edition. News Ltd then had a monopoly in four capital cities: only Sydney and Melbourne retained competing papers.

News and Fair Facts convincingly established the virtual inevitability of monopolies developing in metropolitan newspaper markets, because of the industry's economics. This was not a matter of dispute. Its key recommendation was that the Trade Practices Commission test should revert to the pre-1977 'substantial lessening of competition' approach; that there should be mandatory pre-notification of mergers involving papers with a circulation of more than 30,000; and that the TPC should consider the unique characteristics of the press, particularly the possible impact on freedom of expression, fairness and accuracy of news, and economic viability, when considering any future takeovers or mergers. As most Australian cities already had monopoly newspapers, by then the immediate impact of the recommendations would inevitably be limited.[6]

Power and Influence

Many of those who study the media do so because they are curious about its role in society. There are several different approaches to its study. Key amongst them is a positivist, effects-based approach, which attempts to quantify the impact the media has on individuals and the society as a whole. The cultural studies approach, which adopts more qualitative measures[7], seeks to examine the media within its social, political and economic framework. The study of the impact of the media has evolved, as Western observed, and ranged 'all the way from convictions that effects are major through convictions about nil or mediated effects, to convictions of grand conspiracies and hidden agendas. . . .'

The media is clearly an institution which warrants such attention. Studies have consistently shown that after sleep and work, consuming the media absorbs most of people's time. Australians are particularly enthusiastic purchasers of new media and communications technologies; well over 90 per cent of homes have television, almost all have radios, 75 per cent have video players and two-thirds regularly buy newspapers. In television households, 93 per cent of people watch commercial television at least once a week; 86 per cent of the population listens to some commercial radio every week, and reads a daily newspaper on an average day. The ABC claims that 86 per cent of the population listens to its radio or watches its television programs in an average week, and the Special Broadcasting Service claims that 3.5 million Australians watch its television programs at least once a week. By the time young people turn sixteen they will have spent at least as much time watching television as they will have spent at school (Western 1973: 81; McCann and Sheehan 1985). This knowledge has led to attempts by the Australian Broadcasting Tribunal to regulate the programs broadcast for children.[8] The importance of the media in explaining us to ourselves, and in informing national cultural identity[9] has also lead to regulations stipulating the minimum amounts of Australian content broadcast on television,[10] and consideration of ways of ensuring that the broadcast media more adequately represent the cultural diversity of the country.

The effect that the content of the media has on the public has been an area of considerable academic and community interest: no area has been more studied than television violence. As Cunningham noted in his re-examination of television and violence:

> The debate over television and violence has certainly been one of the hardiest perennials in the thicket of media research and policy . . . Media violence is a perennial issue because it is of enduring, if regularly changing, public concern.
>
> (Cunningham 1992: 137)

The impact of exposure to television (and video) violence has been dramatically and tragically highlighted with several mass shootings in Melbourne and Sydney. In the popular imagination, attacks on citizens by psychologically disturbed individuals, following their repeated viewing of violent videos, mean they may have played some part. There is a widely-held belief that a positive relationship exists between 'televised violence and aggressive behaviour' (McCann and Sheehan 1985: 40), and there have been numerous attempts to measure the link. It has been estimated that up until 1978, 80 per cent of the research on media effects was concerned with the issue of violence.

> Despite massive effort in both academic and policy arenas, no unequivocal connection between levels and types of violent content, audiences' consumption of television and measurable increases in societal violence has been established.
>
> (Cunningham 1992: 139)

In 1990, a special Australian Broadcasting Tribunal panel, partly set up in response to massacres in Melbourne, headed by Professor Peter Sheehan, reported to the Minister for Transport and Communications on the impact of television violence, and noted that 'new approaches are necessary to make progress on violence research'. The Tribunal was satisfied that the answer to 'the problem of television violence' was not censorship, but self-regulation and public education. As a result, the industry implemented new codes regulating the televising of violent material.

Despite the undoubted impact of the media on individuals and the society as a whole, the public is increasingly sceptical about its veracity and reliability. Western has noted:

> These data are important because they suggest that media audiences do not simply soak up the coverage to which they are exposed. They can critically evaluate press, radio and television, and while these media may be passive bearers of the dominant culture, the audience is inclined to somewhat more active participation in any media event.
>
> (Najman and Western 1988: 561)

Intervention to Foster Diversity

The Lee Committee agreed that concentration of media ownership was potentially harmful to plurality of opinion, increasing the risk that news could be distorted. Some members concluded that there was a connection between high concentration of media ownership and lack of diversity of information and ideas in the press, but most did not think this led to bias. The Committee failed to acknowledge what many saw as the problem of media concentration. It did not find the next step of recommending intervention to foster greater diversity and competition in the print media compelling. Although there are international precedents for a wide range of direct and indirect subsidies being made available to ensure the maintenance of a diverse media, these suggestions were treated dismissively by the Report, on what was acknowledged as a base of incomplete information (Report: 39ff).

The argument about whether there is a legitimate role for governments to intervene to ensure greater diversity in the media is one which is now attracting high level political debate throughout the world. Although there is a well-established history of government funding of public service broadcasting in many countries, including Australia, the application of similar principles to the print media raises fears of government control of content. The debate on the legitimate role of government has been triggered by the move towards greater concentration and monopoly across all sectors of the media in many parts of the developed world. As a consequence, bodies such as the United Nation's Commission on Human Rights, the European Parliament, and the European Court, have acknowledged that there may be a need for intervention to ensure that diversity can be encouraged to flourish.

The United Nation's Economic and Social Council, Commission on Human Rights, noted that as media pluralism is an indispensable attribute of a democracy, there are questions of 'positive obligations of the state to avoid concentrations of the press':

> In other words, the state must assure the exercise of the right to freedom of expression, notably by guaranteeing the existence of media that can make this right effective. It must also ensure that freedom of expression is not threatened by third parties; since the individual is entitled to pluralist information, the state is bound to take all measures to assure diversity of the media.
>
> (UN Commission on Human Rights, 18 July 1990: 37)

In Australia the notion of government intervention by direct and indirect subsidies to ensure diversity in the media is frequently dismissed as a 'Pravda solution'. As Ken Cowley told the Lee Committee: 'I would be mortified if I thought that the thinnest thread of government would find its way to print. I think the editors of our newspapers in this country are a very important part of our democracy and freedom. I would not see why and I have heard no argument or reasons why the quality of our readers and the calibre of our journalists will be improved by answering to governments' (Transcript, 4 October 1991: 457). This argument under-estimates the editorial independence which the Australian Broadcasting Corporation and Special Broadcasting Service have won from governments. As Bagdikian concluded: 'The object of reform is not to silence voices, but to multiply them, not to foreclose ideas, but to awaken them' (Bagdikian 1990: 237).

Assistance to ensure the diversity and plurality of the media may take many forms, from subsidies of telecommunications, post, freight and printing costs, accelerated depreciation allowances, tax concessions for new starts, exemption from sales taxes and the like. The Australian newspaper industry has received subsidies valued at between $4 million and $8 million a year, according to Brown (1986: 37).

The possibility of launching new publications without some assistance in a market such as that which exists in Australia today is extremely limited, as *News and Fair Facts* conclusively demonstrates. However, the possibility of what Bowman described as a subsidy for readers (ACIJ: 48) was treated derisively by the Committee's report.

In the end, the Committee opted for the 'hand of fate', and the inevitability of new technologies to foster greater diversity and competition within the print industry:

> The history of newspaper groups dominated by strong personalities . . . suggests that a group such as News Limited will eventually be broken up . . . In that eventuality, the Committee's proposals should ensure that subsequent ownership groupings will not reach the current level of concentration.
>
> In the longer term therefore the Committee's proposals for the print media industry are likely to achieve increased competition without divestiture. Eventually the proposals should also have a substantial impact on the ownership structure of the Australian print media.
>
> (Report: 236)

The history of newspaper dynasties is replete with families who have managed to hold on to 'their' papers for more than one generation. The three major Australian groups fall into this category. Furthermore, the aggregation of media properties in a handful of transnational companies has proceeded at an un-precedented pace over the last decade. These companies have not simply acquired newspapers and magazines, but the full range of print, broadcast and electronic media properties, acquisition patterns designed to ensure that the largest companies continue to exert their influence into the next generation of the media market.

The Committee, however, was optimistic that a likely collapse of empires, coupled with anticipated technological changes, would 'result in an array of new services as well as a significant expansion of traditional services':

> The barriers to entry in the provision of value added communi-cation services are likely to be lowered. The future market is likely to be characterised by stronger competition for audiences and a greater diversity of services ... the creation of smaller (niche) markets could mean that the power of major media groups to influence public opinion may be diminished.
>
> (Report: 342–43)

It is undoubtedly true that there will be a proliferation of new technologies in the communications industry over the next decade, and highly likely that niche markets will be established. It is, however, also probable that the same transnational media companies which have grown exponentially over the past decade, aggregating an enormous range of media products and organ-isations, will also dominate the new electronic markets.

It is the paradox of the Information Age that at a time when we have access to more information than has ever been known before, what is available is controlled by a decreasing number of corporations. This has the potential to lead to feelings of public exclusion, denial and powerlessness. Consumers and citizens may suspect that media corporations and their employees are more inclined to look after their own interests than act as watchdogs.

Notes

1. For a more detailed discussion of the lack of public confidence in the news media, see Julianne Schultz (1990) *Accuracy in Australian Newspapers*, Working Paper No 1. Sydney: Australian Centre for Independent Journalism, University of Technology.

2. For a more detailed discussion of the processes leading up to, and the consequences of, the change of media cross-ownership laws in Australia in 1986, see Paul Chadwick (1989) *Media Mates*, Macmillan, and David Bowman (1988) *A Captive Press*, Penguin.

3. The decline and fall of the Fairfax family in its ownership of the

newspaper group has been documented in several books, including Trevor Sykes (1989) *Operation Dynasty*, Greenhouse, Vic Carroll (1991) *The Man Who Would Be King*, Heinemann; Gavin Souter (1991) *Heralds and Angels*, Melbourne University Press; James Fairfax, *My Regards to Broadway*, HarperCollins; Colleen Ryan and Glenn Burge (1992) *Corporate Cannibals*, Heinemann. The earlier history of the Fairfax company is comprehensively documented in Gavin Souter (1981) *A Company of Heralds*, Melbourne University Press.

4. The early history of the Australian media is recorded in Henry Mayer (1964) *The Press in Australia*, Lansdowne; and Ken Inglis (1982) *This is the ABC*, Melbourne University Press.

5. Anthony Smith's books include *Goodbye Gutenberg: The Newspaper Revolution of the 1980s* (Oxford University Press, 1980), about the changing technologies of the media, *The Politics of Information* (Macmillan, 1978) about the development of policy and practice; *The Newspaper: An International History* (Thames and Hudson, 1979).

6. The process, findings, and recommendations of the Print Media Inquiry are covered extensively in *Media Information Australia* 65, August 1992, Sydney: AFTRS.

7. For a comprehensive overview of the use of qualitative methods in communications research, see K.B. Jensen, and N.W. Jankowski (eds) (1991) *A Handbook of Qualitative Methodologies for Mass Communication Research*, London: Routledge.

8. For a discussion of the debate about the policy changes in children's television regulation, see *Media Information Australia* 65, August 1992.

9. For a discussion of role the media in the development of cultural identity see Stuart Cunningham (1992) *Framing Culture*, Allen and Unwin, Sydney.

10. See Terry, Flew 'Foreign Ownership and Australian Content: Do they matter?' *Media Information Australia* 62, November 1991.

References

Article 19 (1991) *Information Freedom and Censorship, World Report*. London: Library Association Publishing.

Bagdikian, Ben (1990) *The Media Monopoly*. Boston: Beacon Press.

Barry, Paul (1991) *The Rise and Fall of Alan Bond*. Sydney: Bantam/ABC Books.

Beecher, Eric (1990) 'Print Power and Democracy', *Age*, 7 October.

Bowman, David (1983) 'The Owner's Boot is Mightier than the Editor's Pen', *Australian Society*, December.

———(1988) *The Captive Press*. Ringwood: Penguin.

———(1987) article in *Australian Society*, June.

Brown, Alan (1986) *Commercial Media in Australia*. St Lucia: UQP.

Candussi, Dores and Winter, James (1986) 'Monopoly and Content in

Winnipeg', in Picard *et al.* (eds) *Press Concentration and Monopoly,* Norwood, New Jersey: Ablex.

Carlyon, Les (1982) *Paperchase.* Melbourne: Herald and Weekly Times.

Carroll, Vic (1991) *The Man Who Couldn't Wait.* Melbourne: Heinemann.

Chadwick, Paul (1989) *Media Mates.* Melbourne: Macmillan.

———(1991) *Charters of Editorial Independence.* Communications Law Centre, UNSW.

Cunningham, Stuart (1992) *Framing Culture.* Sydney: Allen and Unwin.

———and Turner, Graham (eds) (1993) *The Media in Australia.* Sydney: Allen and Unwin.

Fairfax, James (1991) *My Regards to Broadway.* Sydney: HarperCollins.

Garnham, Nicholas (1986) 'The Media and the Public Sphere', *Intermedia* 14 (1): 28–33.

———(1990) *Capitalism and Communication.* London: Sage.

Grabosky, Peter and Wilson, Paul (1989) *Journalism and Justice, How Crime is Reported.* Sydney: Pluto Press.

Henningham, John (1988) *Looking at Television News.* Melbourne: Longman.

Hester, A (1989) 'Guarding Against the Abuse of Power: The Alternative Press in the USA', in *The Vigilant Press,* UNESCO.

Inglis, Ken (1981) *This is the ABC.* Melbourne: Melbourne University Press.

Jensen, Klaus Bruhn and Jankowski, Nicholas W. (eds) (1991) *A Handbook of Qualitative Methods for Mass Communication Research.* London: Routledge.

Journalists, Academics and Public Intellectual Life in Australia (1991) Ideas for Australia, National Centre for Australian Studies, Monash University, Clayton.

Keane, John (1991) *The Media and Democracy.* Cambridge: Polity Press.

Kofler, Brigit (1991) *Database on Broadcasting Laws in Western Europe and North America,* UNESCO Communication Division.

Kunczik, Michael (1989) *Concepts of Journalism.* Bonn: FES.

Loffler, M. and Ricker, R. (1978) *Handbuch des Presserechts.* Munich.

MacBride, Sean (1980) *Many Voices One World,* London: UNESCO, Kogan Page.

Mathews Committee (1990) *Report to the Victorian Attorney-General of the Working Party into Print Media Ownership,* 24 December.

Mathews, John (1988) *The Promotion of Press Diversity, Options Available to the Australian Government,* Griffith University, Qld: Institute for Cultural Policy Studies.

Mayer, Henry (1964) *The Press in Australia.* Melbourne: Lansdowne Press.

Mayer, Henry (1987) 'Public Opinion and Media Concentration', *Media Information Australia* 44: 18–19.

McCann, T.E. and Sheechan, P.W. (1985) 'Violence Content in Australian Television', *Australian Psychologist* 20: 30–42.

McCombs, Maxwell (1986) 'Concentration, Monopoly and Content', in Picard *et al.* (ed.) (1987) *Press Concentration and Monopoly.* Norwood, New Jersey: Ablex.

News and Fair Facts: The Australian Print Media Industry (1992) Report from the House of Representatives Select Committee on the Print Media, March 1992. Canberra: AGPS.

Norris, John (1981) *Report of the Inquiry into the Ownership and Control of Newspapers in Victoria*, 15 September.

Picard *et al.* (eds) (1988) *Press Concentration and Monopoly.* Norwood, New Jersey: Ablex.

Print Competition and Diversity (1991) Seminar Papers 2, September. Australian Centre for Independent Journalism (ACIJ), University of Technology, Sydney.

Putnis, Peter (1987) 'Newspaper Databases', *Australian Journalism Review* 9 (1–2): 128–36.

Queensland Watchdog Committee (1991) Submission to the Electoral and Administrative Review Commission, Protection of Whistleblowers, March.

Raum, Odd (1989) 'The Press Council in Norway: A Buffer between the Press and Society', in *The Vigilant Press*, UNESCO.

Robertson, Geoffrey (1983) *People Against the Press.* London: Quartet.

Saulwick Poll (1991) 'The Sad Truth About Politics', *Sydney Morning Herald*, 8 July.

Schultz, Julianne (1989) 'Failing the Public: The Media Marketplace', in A. Wilson (ed.), *Australian Communications and the Public Sphere.* Melbourne: Macmillan.

———(1990a) *Accuracy and Australian Newspapers.* Australian Centre for Independent Journalism, University of Technology, Sydney.

———(1990b) 'Media Giants Move Into Eastern Europe', *Australian Society*, October.

———(1992) How to Encourage Competition and Diversity without Offending the Monopolists', *Media Information Australia* 65, August.

Schulz, Winifred and Hofmann, Josef (1989) 'Control Functions of the Media in the Federal Republic of Germany', in *The Vigilant Press.* UNESCO.

Smith, Anthony (1979) *The Newspaper: An international history.* London: Thames and Hudson.

———(1980a) *Goodbye Gutenberg.* Oxford: Oxford University Press.

———(1980b) *The Politics of Information.* London: Macmillan.

Souter, Gavin (1981) *A Company of Heralds.* Melbourne: MUP.

———(1991) *Heralds and Angels.* Melbourne: MUP.

Submissions presented to the House of Representatives Select Committee on the Print Media (referred to in text as Submissions)

Sykes , Trevor (1990) *Operation Dynasty.* Sydney: Greenhouse.

The Vigilant Press: A Collection of Case Studies (1989) UNESCO, 1989.

Tiffen, Rodney (1989) *News and Power.* Sydney: Allen and Unwin.

Toohey, Brian (1987) 'Fairfax and the New Establishment', *The Eye*, October.

Transcript of evidence presented before the House of Representatives Select Committee on the Print Media.

TV Violence in Australia, Report to the Minister for Transport and

Communications, Vols 1–4 (1990) Australian Broadcasting Tribunal.

United Nations, Economic and Social Council, Commission on Human Rights (1990) *Sub Commission on Prevention of Discrimination and Protection of Minorities*, 41st Session, 18 July.

Walsh, Max (1987) 'Dries think media are just business', *Sydney Morning Herald*, 23 April.

Western, John (1988) 'The Mass Media', in first edition of *A Sociology of Australian Society*. Melbourne: Macmillan.

Wilson, Helen (ed.) (1989) *Australian Communications and the Public Sphere*. Melbourne: Macmillan.

Windshuttle, Keith (1985) *The Media*. Ringwood: Penguin.

Chapter Twenty

Whither Sociology?

John S. Western and Jake M. Najman

Introduction

This has been a book about sociology and about Australian society. Its readings reflect both the state of sociology and of our knowledge of Australian society at the present time. In Chapter 1 we described how by 'doing sociology' we can develop an understanding of our society that is different from what would have emerged had we been 'doing history' or 'doing psychology'. We have argued that there is something distinctly 'sociological' about sociology. What do we understand this to be?

Sociology, we have argued, takes a structural perspective in interpreting human behaviour. Such a perspective is a common theme in many of the readings. Boreham and Hall (Chapter 9), for example, describe changes in the Australian workforce. As a result of technological developments, there has been an increase in part-time and female workers, and a steady decline in the proportion of the population working in manufacturing industry. Ip (Chapter 13) describes changes in patterns of leisure and recreation, occasioned in large part by changes in work and increases in the availability of 'free' time. Mullins (Chapter 17) goes so far as to write of the emergence of 'pleasure dispensing centres' as a new form of urbanisation, reflecting the extent to which leisure is sold as a commodity in our capitalist economic system. Bittman (Chapter 14) discusses changes in marriage and the family, and the division of labour within families. Not only have the nature of work, leisure and the family changed, but laws which influence human behaviour have also been modified. These legislative changes, which both reflect and initiate social change, have increased in number in recent times (Tomasic, Chapter 5). Some of these changes have been directed at reducing social class inequalities (analysed by Mark Western, Chapter 3) and have been specifically directed to improving the circumstances of the socio-economically disadvantaged (Bryson, Chapter 15), and providing child care for working parents.

Other important structural changes have included our education system (higher high school retention rates: see Anderson, Chapter 8), and increased access to higher prestige tertiary courses (Hayden and Carpenter, Chapter 16). In addition, other technological and economic developments have steadily reduced the proportion of the population 'living off the land' (Share, Lawrence and Gray, Chapter 18).

When technological innovation and other structural changes lead to different and sometimes new employment, social and recreational activities, family relationships, and to increases in the level of knowledge and information possessed by a population (to select only a few examples), we may think of human behaviour as being structurally determined. Of course, the individual who becomes unemployed, or moves to a new job (from, say, being a farmer to becoming a computer operator), will not necessarily consciously report on the structural basis of the change to which he or she has been exposed. When his or her marriage breaks up, then it may seem more relevant to focus on the characteristics of the circumstances rather than the structural forces which produce these changes. It is the recognition that individual experiences and behaviours frequently reflect more general social processes that provides the basis for a sociological understanding of society.

In Chapter 1 we also identified four structural bases of society that are important in understanding human behaviour. These were social class, gender, ethnicity and Aboriginality. We saw them as the basis of social location. While other sectors or characteristics could also be identified (see Mullins, Chapter 17), these four provide for some of the most important distinctions observed in society. Many of the chapters in the book have discussed these distinctions and their behavioural components.

Najman (Chapter 10) points out that there are class differences in lifestyle, life expectancy and health in Australian society. McAllister (Chapter 11) notes class-related patterns of voting behaviour. Hazlehurst and Braithwaite (Chapter 12) identify the preponderance of both victims and offenders of crime in socio-economically disadvantaged (e.g. unemployed) groups. Ip (Chapter 13) points to class differences in patterns of recreation and leisure. Three of our contributors provide a salutary note when they reveal increases in socio-economic inequality in recent times (Bryson, Chapter 15, Mullins, Chapter 17) and specifically the fact that, of the 37 poorest electorates in Australia, 33 are in rural areas (Share, Lawrence and Gray Chapter 18). Schultz (Chapter 19) is concerned with the concentration of media ownership in Australia, particularly in light of the historical support of the newspaper media for conservative political (economic) parties. Curiously, since 1984 most newspaper election editorials have changed their support to the Labor Party — though the cynic may argue that this may still reflect a preference for conservative social and economic policies.

Gender differences in Australian society provide one of the most fundamental of all social distinctions. Williams (Chapter 4) is correct in observing that women have been exploited by men and historically used as a basis of cheap labour. Ip (Chapter 13) emphasises that women have been perceived as leisure for men. Women's leisure activities have been restricted (as Ip points out) in two important respects. Firstly, much of women's 'free' time is taken up with child rearing and housekeeping activities, leaving them little time for real leisure and recreation. Secondly, women's leisure activities have been subordinated to those of their partner, providing few opportunities for their own preferences.

Women differ from men in a wide variety of behaviours, and most of these differences appear to be learned. Women have higher morbidity rates than men (i.e. they are sicker), but men have higher mortality rates. Men are more often overweight, smoke more often and more often drink alcohol to excess (see Najman, Chapter 10). Men are also much more likely to commit crimes, with only 5 per cent of Australia's prison population being women (Hazlehurst and Braithwaite, Chapter 12).

Government policies have, with some success, sought to redress the gender differences which are observed in society, particularly those to do with employment opportunities. Thus there has been a growth of women in the workforce generally (Boreham and Hall, Chapter 9) in more senior administrative and executive positions, and in higher education (Hayden and Carpenter, Chapter 16).

While there can be no doubt that many gender inequalities persist, some changes have occurred, and some processes are in place to facilitate further changes. Gender differences appear to reflect a series of constraints, the bulk of which have little to do with biology, and a great deal to do with social and cultural expectations. We have yet to learn the extent to which change in gender, employment, recreation and lifestyle patterns is possible.

With some 25 per cent of Australia's population being foreign born, ethnic differences in behaviour, values and lifestyles are clearly important. Immigrants provide a natural laboratory for the study of structurally determined social and cultural differences in society. In most instances, immigrants have the same biological make-up as members of the host population, and observed behavioural differences can be unambiguously ascribed to social and structural forces. Much has been written about this, and it is easy to observe ethnic and cultural differences in action. Despite this, the thrust of the readings suggests that relatively little is known about ethnicity as a basis for behaviour in Australian society. Makkai and McAllister (Chapter 6) observe the concentration of particular ethnic groups in particular industries. Australia's migrants have been disproportionately employed in manufacturing industry, that area of the economy most subject to the current economic recession. It is thus not surprising that unemployment rates for some ethnic minorities (e.g. Vietnamese) have been particularly high. In general, immigrant groups emphasise the value of education for their children (Hayden and Carpenter, Chapter 16).

Australian Aborigines comprise only 1.5 per cent of the population, and they manifest a variation in lifestyles which makes a consideration of them as a single group an exercise of limited validity (Keen, Chapter 7). To understand the cultural and social circumstances of Aborigines it is necessary to comprehend the history of racial oppression which has been characteristic of Australian society. Aborigines have appalling health profiles and, relative to other indigenous peoples in comparable countries (New Zealand, Canada, the United States), they have a much lower life expectancy (Najman, Chapter 10). Aborigines are greatly over-represented in Australia's prison population (Hazlehurst and Braithwaite, Chapter 12), and are much more likely to be unemployed than other Australians (Boreham and Hall, Chapter 9).

It is possible to debate the reasons for these disadvantages, and many differences of opinion exist. Whatever the direction of the debate, two points are clear: injustice has characterised dealings with the Aboriginal population, and social and cultural forces maintain these injustices. Certainly some government policies have addressed the needs of Australia's Aboriginal population, but with very limited success.

We suggest that the chapters included in this volume all reflect in one way or another basic facets of the sociological orientation. However, lest it be felt that all is well, and that sociologists everywhere are pursuing similar goals in similar ways, it should be noted that some turbulence characterises the sociological enterprise. Sociologists are wont to differ on a number of matters.

Varieties of Sociology

First, and perhaps most fundamentally, there are differences in views as to the nature of the discipline. At the centre of such differences is a debate about the extent to which sociology is, or ought to be, a cumulative discipline. Have sociologists built up a body of knowledge about society and how it functions so that our understanding today is better, more adequate or more comprehensive than it was fifty or a hundred years ago? Moreover, given that we continue in the same way, will our understanding be better fifty years from now?

The obvious and immediate response to this question would seem to be that of course we now have a better understanding. Certainly there is a greater diversity of theories, and an increase in the amount of sociological research. It is less clear, however, that these changes have improved our understanding of society. We need to have some criteria for judging what a 'better' understanding means. Let us start with some very simple examples.

Sociologists by and large would probably reject fundamentalist religious beliefs about the nature of society, and the emergence of the world in seven days. Few would accept creationism, the view that the earth is flat, or the centre of the universe, or that some divine being is the motivator of all behaviour. On what grounds are these beliefs, at one time near-universal, rejected? Very probably because the social reality that the sociologist confronts in his or her pursuit of an understanding of the social world suggests that explanations and actions based on such principles would founder — action taken on the basis of such understandings, that is, would be unlikely to lead to the attainment of intended goals. Ignoring brick walls does not allow one to walk through them; instead they must be circumnavigated. Putting it a little less colloquially, theorising and practice go hand in hand. One develops one's ideas and theories and tests them against the real world, modifying them as a consequence; then one continues the process of theorising, testing, re-theorising. If our theories are wrong, if we act as if the earth is flat or a divine being is at work, then we are likely to come to grief, necessitating a modification of the theory before further action occurs. Of course, some may act on false premises and occasionally be successful (for example, those who seek faith healing cures for cancer), but these are generally rare exceptions. The majority of people will fail to reach intended goals if they act on inaccurate knowledge.

This has been a rather lengthy way of getting to an understanding of the criterion we can use to determine whether one explanation is 'better' than another. Our criterion is testing our understanding against the social world to see if it fits. As one of us said some time ago, 'the weakest link in the theoretical chain is the recalcitrant fact' (Western 1983). Implicit in this argument is the judgement that sociology should be a cumulative discipline.

Not all our colleagues would accept this position. Some would argue strongly that developments in sociology provide basically alternative views of the world. They would argue that there is very little that is, or ought to be, cumulative about sociological knowledge. Perspectives and interpretations change, but levels of knowledge do not. Alexander, in his four-volume work on theories of society, arguably has not advanced the knowledge or understanding we have of the social world, although he has provided us with a particular way of looking at it. Giddens, with his myriad volumes, similarly has not provided us with a better understanding of, or basis for making predictions about, the society in which we live. Rather he has invited us to view the world as he does. To what end?

There is very clearly a tension in sociology between those who see the sociological task as one of providing alternative and at times imaginative syntheses of existing understandings, and those who see the sociological task as extending the boundaries of knowledge so that more is known and understood about the social structures in which we live.

Sociology: Profession or Pastime

An equally persistent matter which we believe underlies much of sociological controversy concerns the lack of an underlying paradigm. It has sometimes been said that, unlike many other disciplines (often economics has been chosen as the example), sociology lacks an underlying and unifying paradigm. The sociological orientation, we have suggested, is characterised by a number of loosely connected factors; we hold to that position. But it is not as strong a position as exists in a field such as economics, where there is an underlying paradigm which in a sense unites the discipline. Whether this paradigm revolves around the notion of scarcity or a related concept, or whether or not there is disagreement as to how the concept operates or what its significance is, it is in a sense still the core of the discipline.

The notions of 'economics' and 'being an economist' therefore carry a shared meaning which is perhaps lacking in talking about 'sociology' and 'being a sociologist'. There is less consensus among practitioners as to what sociology is, and what 'doing sociology' means. It is seriously advanced in some quarters that no special skills or knowledge are necessary to practice sociology. Every person can be their own sociologist, providing their frame of mind is right, and they are convinced of the righteousness of their cause. It is perhaps not an accident that this view appears to be most enthusiastically expressed by those unaffected by the travails of the labour market. Those for whom the case for job stability and security still has to be made may be a little less sanguine about this perspective some of their better paid and more secure colleagues assume.

While it is admittedly something of an over-simplification, this issue can be seen as importantly connected to the question of professionalisation. Where does the future of sociology lie? As a pastime for the intelligent layperson, or as a discipline characterised by a body of knowledge and set of skills which can best be transmitted through a formalised educational experience? This is an issue which has confronted sociology not only in Australia, but elsewhere, over many years. It is not one for which any easy resolution appears possible. Both ends of the continuum are defended with equal vehemence.

Why should sociologists, unlike practitioners of other disciplines, be anxious to deny their own expertise, and the importance of acquiring both a formally prescribed body of knowledge and a set of skills for the practice of sociology? Not all sociologists would deny the existence of a body of sociological knowledge and of skills acquired through a formalised educational experience. However, that debate on the sociological agenda in our view sets sociology apart from a number of related disciplines, and indeed does the discipline some disservice. Put simply, if sociologists are reluctant to argue for their integrity and the credibility of their discipline — or indeed that the discipline exists — who will?

The basis for concern at the perceived dangers of professionalism (for this is what the argument is fundamentally about), is not hard to find. Much has been written by sociologists over the years about the power acquired by professionals because of their control over, and exclusive access to, particular bodies of knowledge, in particular about the illegitimate use of such power. Those who see professionalisation in this light are often reluctant to assign professional status to themselves. Nevertheless, one position can surely be that while an illegitimate use of power may follow from prolonged training in, and exclusive access to, a particular body of knowledge, there is no inevitable causal link between the two. The fact that some professionals use their power to advance their interests against those of their clients does not deny that there are others who use their power for the public good. It is also not difficult to find committed, 'right thinking' individuals who have done harm, despite their lack of professional status. Denying the reality of an existent knowledge base and its acquisition through a formalised educational process is unlikely to control the excesses that access to such a knowledge base is sometimes seen as providing.

Every person is not their own sociologist. In these difficult times, total anarchy is a luxury, we believe, we can ill afford. We may be living in a structureless post-modern world, but that does not require the discipline, chameleon-like, to respond in kind.

Sociology: Society's Conscience or Social Scientist?

Unlike many disciplines, sociology, or at least sociologists, experience a tension between their academic/intellectual contribution and their capacity to engage in social engineering. Are sociologists primarily social scientists, or can it be argued that their primary responsibility is to contribute to the creation of a more just and/or happier society?

For Comte, whom some call the father of sociology, there was such no problem. The new high priests of society, the sociologists, were going to lead us to the promised land. Marx in his more enthusiastic moments championed the vanguard of the proletariat, who were going to participate in securing the millennium. Booth, whom some might not regard as a sociologist, was concerned not only with documenting the extent of poverty in England at the turn of the century, but also with advocating Fabian solutions to the inequality he saw around him. Sidney and Beatrice Webb championed the same cause. These early sociologists pursued what were for them clearly identified ends or goals. They knew what a good society would look like, and sought its attainment with some vigour.

In the United States, the early members of the Chicago school mixed their scholarly activities directed to an analysis of the outer reaches of society — street-corner society, the jackroller, the gold coast and the slum — with strong concerns about the improvement of the social conditions of the powerless and socially disadvantaged.

One of the first systematic attempts to address the issue of the goals of sociology was Lynd's *Knowledge for What?*, which appeared in 1939. He squarely confronted the question of sociology's task, and made the point that 'it is precisely the role of the social sciences to be troublesome, to discount the traditional arrangements by which we manage to live and to demonstrate the possibility of change *in a more adequate direction* [our emphasis]' (Lynd 1939: 18). He goes on to say, 'but how are we to determine what ought to be?', and then suggests that, if we lack an answer to this question, 'there is no firm basis for doing more than following the determinisms of the moment' (Lynd 1939: 201).

In rejecting this position and suggesting that the task of the social sciences is to identify the basic needs of humankind, and what sort of social arrangements will be most effective in ensuring these needs are satisfied, he then suggests working towards their establishment. To those familiar with his famous empirical study *Middletown*, it will come as no surprise that he saw both understanding the nature of the social system and the power relations that characterise it as fundamental to the social sciences. He argued that it was important to use this understanding to produce change towards a more equitable system. *Knowledge for What* had an enormous impact at the time it was written, although significantly perhaps it did little to change the nature of activity in sociology.

C. Wright Mills followed in Lynd's footsteps. He was perhaps the first of a group of sociologists, some from decades ago, who were described as the 'new sociologists'. For ten years or so, in American sociology at least, Mills was almost a lone protagonist, arguing strongly for a radical sociology directed towards the production of social change.

Mainstream American sociology of the period, alternatively, took empirical science as its major paradigm. Structural functionalism and quantitative research methodology pointed the way ahead. The task of sociology was to understand in a systematic way the nature of the patterning of social behaviour. This meant identifying relationships between independent and dependent variables, and the establishment of a body of knowledge based on the systematic examination of social reality.

The Civil Rights movement in the United States, the Vietnam War and the move within universities for greater participation by staff and students in decision making, plus the seeming reluctance of sociology to engage with the major problems of the day, led to a re-emergence in the mid-to-late 1960s of a concern with the contribution sociology should make to a 'better' society.

Probably the most significant book to come out of this period addressing these issues, was Gouldner's *The Coming Crisis of Western Sociology*. It appeared in 1970 and was based on a number of years of work. Gouldner argued for an aware and critical sociology that addressed the important issues of the day. His criticism of the discipline was that it had abrogated this role.

In the late 1960s, 70s and early 80s there was a resurgence of interest in sociology seen as a commitment to social change, versus sociology as a science. The so-called 'new sociology' or 'critical sociology' clearly had a significant impact. The emergence, or perhaps more correctly, the increasing awareness by sociologists, of a variety of neo-Marxist writers, some within a clear sociological tradition, also had a major impact on what sociologists said and did. Sociologists were visible at the forefront of many key 'social change' movements of the period. Horowitz, for instance, received great support in rejecting the ethical propriety of social research intended to undermine governments unsympathetic to the United States. Others pointed to the capacity of the wealthy and powerful to manipulate not only the legislative process, but public perceptions of reality. As a discipline within universities, sociology flourished. Students flocked to the discipline, departments were established, new PhD programs arose, and the number of applicants for PhDs, particularly in North America, grew markedly.

These halcyon days were not to last. In North America, the United Kingdom and Australia, the curtailment of funds, not only to sociology departments but to universities in general, and to the social sciences in particular, plus questioning of the credibility of the social sciences in general and sociology in particular, presented the discipline with formidable problems, and led to some reappraisal of its objectives and methods.

Sociology: Its Methodological Underpinnings and Theoretical Base

A British response to this situation can be found in the *British Journal of Sociology*, September 1989. An entire issue was devoted to the current state of British sociology. It was edited by A.H. Halsey, and contained papers by a number of prominent British sociologists.

The thrust of the papers is that sociology is a discipline that needs to be taken seriously as such. It is not a part-time occupation and its skills are not acquired through bed-time reading. This is not to say that for many the desire for a just society will dominate their sociological activities; it is to stress, however, that this desire alone is not sufficient or even necessary for the practice of sociology. Sociology is no better equipped than is, for example, nuclear physics, to provide an answer to the normative question: 'What is the good society?'

In his Introduction to this issue of the *British Journal of Sociology*, Halsey argues, not entirely uncontroversially:

> But above all I would suggest progress within the discipline is owed to positivism. I mean of course not the positivism of Auguste Comte, but the positivism which is best expressed in the method-ological views of Karl Popper. Paradoxically, it is this steady drive towards explanation, patiently sought through the rigorous, empirical testing of theories — a painstaking and often pedestrian enterprise so decried and despised by the active spirits of 1968 — that has gradually secured for sociology the foundations of its claims to autonomy. (1989: 61)

He continues in the following vein:

> A further related healing influence is less often remarked. Popper's teaching was rooted just as deeply in morals as in methods. *The Open Society* argued for freedom and justice just as passionately as the *Poverty of Historicism* made the case for the logic of discovery most likely to realise such a society. A concept of the good life, civic and cognitive, informs the work as a whole. If utopian vision can be stripped of its associations with either impractical dreaming or tyrannical government, then the open society is a utopia that describes the aspirations of many of the founding fathers of sociology and their contemporary descendants. (1989: 361)

Americans, too, in recent times have addressed similar issues. In the April 1988 issue of the *American Sociological Review*, Gerhard Lenski's article 'Rethinking Macro-sociological Theory' appeared. Then, in February 1989, in the same journal, Herbert Gans wrote about 'Sociology in America: The Discipline and the Public'. In the following June, Blalock contributed 'The Real and Unrealised Contributions of Quantitative Sociology'. In the June issue of the *Journal of Health and Social Behavior* (1989), David Mechanic, writing more generally than just about medical socio-logy, reported on 'Medical Sociology: Some Tensions among Theory, Method and Substance'.

In all these five reviews we see a similar view of the discipline of sociology. There is clearly an identifiable body of knowledge; there are clearly sets of skills to be acquired by neophyte socio-logists; and there are clearly sociological approaches to generating information, and to the testing of that information for its veracity.

There is a degree of consensus about how such information should be tested. This is not to say that there are no debates. These are, however, debates within identifiable parameters. They are, for example, about the appropriateness of particular data gathering techniques, given particular problems, or about the fruitfulness of particular theoretical positions with respect to the manner in which they inform particular empirical questions. While there is now more agreement than there has been in the past, there is still a great deal of 'talking past' one another.

Macro-sociological theory has recently been subjected to critical scrutiny. Macro-sociological theories tend to be presented at a high level of abstraction (for example, theories which argue that all human behaviour reflects economic forces), and tend to be supported by illustrations and examples. In his 1988 article 'Rethinking Macro-sociological Theory', Lenski argues that the ultimate aim of sociology, like that of other codified disciplines, should be the development of a body of verified general theory. However, he believes that macro-sociological theories fall short when judged by at least two important criteria. First, he says, most macro-sociological theories are not capable of falsification. Empirical tests which would enable the rejection of a proposition within the theory are typically not available. Second, macro-sociological theories lack substantive conceptual links to establish-ed theories in other disciplines. For example, one cannot move from an abstract theory at the level of social structure to a theory at the level of individual intentions. He suggests that, in the social sciences, theory has not advanced nearly so much as it has proliferated. It would be difficult to find evidence to support the view that theory has been continuously refined and improved. Theories in other disciplines, on the other hand, stimulate research, and research leads to theoretical advances. While it is true that there are some instances of this in macro-sociology, this kind of fruitful interaction has not been common. The issue of the cumulative nature of sociology is clearly relevant to Lenski's discussion.

On discussing the teaching of theory, Lenski suggests that the content of theory courses is usually a sample of the writings of the holy trinity, Marx, Weber and Durkheim, plus more limited attention to the work of others such as Simmel, Mead, Parsons, Giddens, Habermas, Goffman and, of course, to others who happen to be in favour at any time. Emphasis in theory courses usually seems to be on exegesis and/or critique of texts rather than on the relevance of theory for research. In this respect, he says, the teaching of sociological theory has more in common with seminary instruction in theology and Biblical studies than with instruction in the sciences. By teaching theory for its own sake, rather than in conjunction with a distinctive research tradition, we tend to raise up new generations of theorists who too often emulate the old masters in ways that hinder, rather than advance, the cause of macro-sociology.

Much the same view is espoused by Turner in his introduction to the edited book of readings *Theory Building in Sociology* (Turner 1989). Turner asserts that far too much theorising in sociology is talk *about* theory, philosophising *about* theory, and history *about* the rise of sociology:

> While all of this discourse . . . is interesting and scholarly, it is not theory and it does not advance sociology as a science . . . and does not ask nor answer the following questions: what are the critical and invariant properties of the social universe and what are their operative dynamics?
>
> (Turner 1989: 8)

Clearly the Lenski-Turner position does not sit easily with all sociologists.

Conclusion

In this book we have investigated research and theories which represent the state of the sociological art in Australia. Despite the doubts of some of our colleagues, there can be no doubt in our minds that, over the last two to three decades, our knowledge of society has improved, as indeed have some of our research methods. There remain, however, some fundamental problems. In our judgement we, as sociologists 'at large' have too great a fascination with the theoretical exegesis or critique that Lenski, Turner and others have identified. We would want to argue that sociology, like other empirical sciences (or, to put it perhaps more comfortably, other empirical fields of inquiry) should start with a problem to be investigated. How stable is behavioural change following an intervention program concerned with changing food habits? How salient is social class to the life chances of members of Australian society? What impact does professional training have on the future practice of professionals? What factors condition the transition from school to work? What impact have AIDS education programs had on target groups? Others may, of course, wish to address problems which are perhaps more theoretically derivative. The problem should be couched in conceptual terms, translated into a research program, and investigated. The results should allow for modification of the conceptual framework, and suggest a further program of research.

Unfortunately, this is not the way that a great deal of sociology has been practised in the past, and is still being done. It is not empirical questions derived either from a problem in the real world, or a concern to examine a particular theoretical proposition that has provided the main thrust for a great deal of sociological work in recent times. A great deal of sociology in fact involves disputation over concepts, and higher and higher orders of synthesisation of existing work.

Has Goldthorpe got it right and Erik Wright got it wrong? How significant is Carchedi's critique of Wright's most recent class model? Is post-structuralism the wave of the future? Whatever happened to Foucault? The fact that these questions are asked and occupy significant space in sociological writings indicates that those asking the questions suffer a major misapprehension.

You cannot have 'better' or 'worse' concepts or definitions when the definitions which specify concepts are dealing with different aspects of empirical reality. It makes little sense to say that Goldthorpe's definition of class is 'better' than Wright's, or that Wright's is 'better' than Goldthorpe's. They are admittedly concerned with the one phenomenon, mechanisms of production and distribution — but with significantly different aspects of it. To put it simply, there cannot be 'better' or 'worse' definitions of social class without reference to some empirical criterion. There are *different* definitions of *different* things, and one needs to be clear as to the thing with which one is concerned. To put it more concretely, in understanding the patterning of social behaviour, the process of production may be more relevant than the process of distribution: that is to say, Wright may be more relevant than Goldthorpe, or of course the reverse. The critical question is not which definition is 'better' but which aspect of social reality, production or distribution, is more important as a causal mechanism in understanding social regularities. This critical distinction we lament as lost to many of our colleagues.

Parkin once said a number of years ago that, while a great deal of discussion in sociology may be functional for the career mobility of sociologists, it does little to advance the development of the discipline, because it is fundamentally misplaced. How, then, should we proceed? We should move forward with the recognition that there is a body of knowledge which characterises the discipline of sociology, which is perhaps blurred at the outer reaches, but which is unambiguous towards its core. It is a body of knowledge which can ultimately be couched in the form of testable propositions, subject to refutation. From this would follow an acceptance of generally agreed-upon ways in which this body of knowledge can be addressed.

There is obviously no unitary way of proceeding. Rather there are a number of ways — and for certain problems some ways are more appropriate than others. These ways or methods need to have one fundamental characteristic in common. They need to provide results which, in the words of the logician of science Ernest Hempel (1952), are 'intersubjectively ascertainable': i.e. they need to produce results which, under similar circumstances, can be reproduced. The same investigator carrying out the same procedures will be likely to come up with much the same results. Alternatively, a different investigator carrying out the same procedures is also likely to come up with much the same results. These proposals do not have a great deal of novelty about them, but they are increasingly coming to the attention of sociologists (Smith 1991). They are important matters and, particularly if we cannot look forward to some 'intersubjective ascertainability' of results, then sociology becomes a private game rather than a public enterprise which has some justification for public support.

References

Berger, P.L. (1966) *Invitation to Sociology*. Harmondsworth: Penguin.

Gans, H.J. (1989) 'Sociology in America: The Discipline and the Public', *American Sociological Review* 54: 447–60.

Gouldner, A.W. (1970) *The Coming Crisis of Western Sociology*. New York: Basic Books.

Halsey, A.H. (1989) 'A Turning to the Tide? The Prospects for Sociology in Britain', *British Journal of Sociology* 40: 353–73.

Hempel, C. (1952) 'Fundamentals of Concept Formation in Empirical Science', *International Encyclopedia of Empirical Science* II (7). Chicago: University of Chicago Press.

Lenski, G. (1988) 'Rethinking Macro Sociological Theory', *American Sociological Theory* 53: 163–71.

Lynd, R.S. (1939) *Knowledge for What?* Princeton: Princeton University Press.

Lynd, R.S. and Lynd, H.M. (1929) *Middletown*. New York: Harcourt Brace.

Mechanic, D. (1989) 'Medical Sociology: Some Tensions among Theory, Method and Substance', *Journal of Health and Social Behavior* 30: 147–60.

Merton, R.K. (1957) *Social Theory and Social Structure*. Glencoe, Ill.: The Free Press.

Smith, J. (1991) 'A Methodology for Twenty-first Century Sociology', *Social Forces* 70: 1–17.

Szelenyi, I. (1992) 'Why Socialism Did Not Work: Toward a Theory of System Breakdown', Paper presented at the Annual Meeting of the American Sociology Association, Pittsburgh, August. Newbury Park: Sage.

Turner, J.H. (ed.) (1989) 'Can Sociology be a Cumulative Science?', in J.H. Turner (ed.), *Theory Building in Sociology*. Sage.

Western, J.S. (1983) *Social Inequality in Australian Society*. Melbourne: Macmillan.

Index

Page numbers followed by the letter *t* refer to tables.
Page numbers followed by the letter *n* refer to notes.